JOSEF HOFFMANN
1870–1956

Progress Through Beauty

The Guide to His Oeuvre

JOSEF HOFFMANN

1870–1956

Progress Through Beauty

The Guide to His Oeuvre

Edited by
Christoph Thun-Hohenstein
Matthias Boeckl
Rainald Franz
Christian Witt-Dörring

MAK

Birkhäuser
Basel

Emil Orlik, portrait of
Josef Hoffmann, 1903
Color woodcut
MAK, KI 13740-2-1

Contents

Contents

Christoph Thun-Hohenstein
General Director, MAK

Hoffmann's Dream of a High-Quality Society

Yoichi R. Okamoto,
Josef Hoffmann, 1954
MAK, KI 13740-5

This handbook on Josef Hoffmann's oeuvre shines a spotlight on the various facets of the multidisciplinary designer's creative output over the six decades of his career. In this text I would like to take the opposite approach and reduce this design genius, intuitive teacher, and skilled networker to his essence: besides his outstanding buildings like Sanatorium Westend and Stoclet House, what is Josef Hoffmann's most important cultural legacy?

The answer can be found in the book's subtitle *Progress Through Beauty*: Hoffmann's enduring achievement—and hence an important building block of Viennese Modernity—is his belief in the life-improving, even healing power of beauty. A joint artistic founder of the Wiener Werkstätte (WW) together with Koloman Moser in 1903, Hoffmann was its *spiritus rector* until its liquidation in 1932. The cooperative's program was the distillation of Hoffmann's artistic and cultural philosophy. What he created before the WW's founding was at its core an anticipation of his basic ideas for the Wiener Werkstätte; what he brought into the world after the WW's closure remained—and would remain throughout his life—indebted to its ideals. Is Hoffmann's oeuvre therefore one-dimensional? Does is lack genuine artistic development? The answer to both is negative if for no other reason than the Wiener Werkstätte comprised not only Josef Hoffmann but also many other creatives and his designs were closely intertwined with the work of or were the product of fruitful discussions with other male designers at the WW, like Moser and later Dagobert Peche, and women artists at the WW. Moreover, both questions disregard Hoffmann's unique qualities: the unbridled enthusiasm for design that is tangible throughout Hoffmann's oeuvre, combined with an unwavering desire for reform in order to have a positive impact on people's lives by means of applied beauty. To achieve this end, he had an almost infinite range of artistic means of expression at his disposal, which he had acquired the fine knack of exploiting to the full without ever falling into a dull routine. Consequently, numerous designs by Hoffmann are inspired—to take an obvious example—by fauna and above all flora and succeed in communicating with us in an entirely unsentimental way through artistically designed beauty.

Of course, the fact is that Hoffmann's work has not always been considered equally relevant; in the last decades of his life in particular, it was instead deemed outdated and unworldly. How ironic of human civilization that today, in the third decade of the 21st century, it is regarded as more modern than ever before! Doubly ironic, in fact, because Hoffmann was struggling against the flaws of industrial mass production at a time when the gravely destructive ecological repercussions of fossil fuel-driven industrialization and the resulting global heating were not deemed a big issue. Rather, the main concern was the social impact of inhuman labor in the giant factories, to which Hoffmann counterposed the ideal of artisanal production.

Today the world is different: As soon as we have Covid under control once and for all—hopefully later in 2021—the outlines of the new Climate Modernity will become perfectly clear. We have already been living in a new modernity for the past two decades, which I have called Digital Modernity because its driving force was digitalization. The advent of a new modernity means that we are challenged to reset the fundamental course for the future. All the digital innovations in the world will not help humanity if we do not tackle climate change and the accompanying general ecological crisis. For that reason, we must develop our Digital Modernity into an ecologically and socially sustainable Climate Modernity. The transition from Digital Modernity to Climate Modernity implies a clear change of focus. In future, digital innovations can no longer be implemented at any cost, but only in order to secure long-term quality of life for humankind and other species in this age of rapid climate change and dramatic loss of ecosystems and biodiversity. Barely anyone still doubts the necessity for a radical rejection of fossil fuel-based industrialization-as-usual. The crucial questions now are: how will we realize the Great Transformation and how do we want to shape Climate Modernity?

It seems to me that we can learn all sorts of things in this regard from the work of Josef Hoffmann and his much-loved (despite its manifold financial troubles) Wiener Werkstätte, whose archive is preserved at the MAK. As the essence of Hoffmann's artistic and creative philosophy, the WW championed the sustainability, artisanal quality, and longevity of its wares, local production, and social responsibility—values that *mutatis mutandis* are also extremely important in Climate Modernity. Just as the Wiener Werkstätte's program of reform was intended to bring beauty into people's everyday lives through artistically designed, high-quality practical objects, Climate Modernity has a program of reform whose aim is to attain progress through climate beauty[1]. Climate beauty, a term I have coined, means a society's aspiration to create a lasting balance with the Earth by means of an ecologically and socially sustainable economy and lifestyle and in appreciation of other species and ecosystems, thereby limiting global heating in line with the Paris Agreement. Both Hoffmann's idea of progress through beauty, as perfected at the Wiener Werkstätte, and today's goal of progress through climate beauty share the vision of a high-quality society, which relies not on the mass consumption of disposable items but on high-quality and long-lasting products. Both programs of reform aim to convince people to adopt a fundamentally new attitude toward civilization.

Whether we can and will ever learn from history, we can never know. But from our cultural legacy we can learn countless lessons that will help us to shape the future. Like the major MAK exhibition of the same name that it accompanies, this handbook is an attempt to demonstrate the impact of a reform-minded aesthete and design genius and inspire new approaches to our lives.

To make the dream of a sustainable, high-quality society a reality, we need another avant-garde of designers, architects, and artists who are capable of helping art achieve enduring sociopolitical relevance. Josef Hoffmann was one of the exceptional personalities of Vienna's avant-garde around 1900. He stands out for having never stopped dreaming. And perhaps the time for realizing his dream of a sustainable, high-quality society has finally come. For him and for us, we can but hope. ∎

1 See the essay I published in June 2020 entitled *CLIMATE BEAUTY: The Art of Reimagining Progress*, available at https://www.mak.at/jart/prj3/mak-resp/images/img-db/1591494770589.pdf

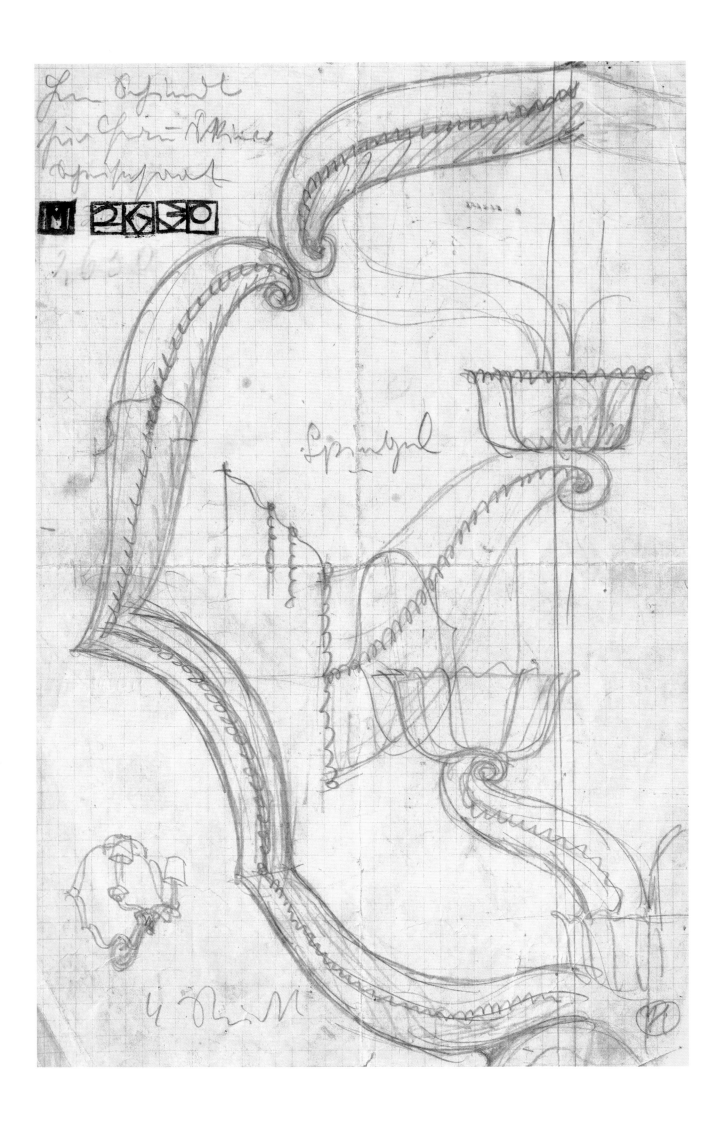

Christian Witt-Dörring, Matthias Boeckl, Rainald Franz

150 Years of Josef Hoffmann

A Retrospect of His Oeuvre

No other 20th-century Austrian architect and designer divided contemporary and subsequent opinion as much as Josef Hoffmann. Even during his lifetime, in 1945, Fritz Wotruba critically assessed him—alongside Adolf Loos and Oskar Kokoschka—to be one of the three incisive and influential luminaries of Austrian art around 1900:

> "[…] Hoffmann, in equal measure a spoiled and often misunderstood architect, had a not insignificant impact on the world of fashion and taste. He quickly became famous and was just as quickly challenged. His dangerous dual gift, which fluctuated back and forth between solemnity and playfulness, brought this graceful artist into—partly undeserved—disrepute; yet the seed that he spread is still flourishing today, even though he has almost been forgotten."[1]

In over 40 articles, this book traces the marks left by this 60-year creative career. The appreciation and interpretation of Hoffmann's work changed over the years. From the outset his creations—from the largest to the smallest dimension—have been examined and evaluated in the context of the search for a modern style or rather a modern society.[2] Their formal interpretation remained the main focus of the Western art world until well into the second half of the 20th century. Only in the late 1970s, with the reinterpretation of the concept of function during the emergence of Postmodernism, does a new appreciation develop for Hoffmann's oeuvre as a result of the departure from the art historical dogma of purely linear stylistic development and restrictive definition of Modernism that excludes alternative approaches.

There is an ideological constant running through Josef Hoffmann's entire oeuvre. Based on the belief in beauty's capacity to heal society and the economy, which he adopted from the English Arts & Crafts movement, his work is shaped by the primacy of individual artistic expression. Hoffmann did not differentiate between high and low art, between fine and applied art and hence assumed the task of converting people's everyday lives through his work. In the context of the Vienna Secession, this meant creating a modern Austrian and bourgeois style. Hoffmann remained true to this conviction for half a century, for the rest of his life. Its formal artistic realization remained unaffected by social, economic, or political developments. Therefore, he would later pay no heed to an international modern style emanating from the Bauhaus—an attitude that Hoffmann, if for different motives, curiously enough shares with his opponents Adolf Loos and Josef Frank.

Hoffmann's immunity to social and economic realities and changes is the defining theme identified by Dagobert Peche in his 1922 manuscript on reforming the Wiener Werkstätte (WW), "Der brennende Dornbusch":

> "For now, let it simply be said as the most important point, which will immediately make everything plain for a perceptive person, that this kind of foundation for or rather leadership of the Wiener Werkstätte is absolutely rooted in the nature of Hoffmann's art, which I call egotistical. Once one has recognized it as such, which is possible by looking at the products of this art at its peak […], once one therefore arrives at the result of egotistical art by viewing Hoffmann's art, this realization naturally includes all the necessities

<

Design for the sconces and mirror in the dining room of the Skywa-Primavesi villa, 1914/15

MAK, KI 12112-30

and possibilities of making and promoting this art. […] In order to arrive at this clear realization that Josef Hoffmann's works are egotistical art, that the supporter themselves hence avows an egotistical worldview (something that is at base not a worldview at all because it rests only on oneself, is made for the self-centered purpose 'I,' and thus plays no part in the world) […]."[3]

Hoffmann's adherence to the unity of art and function in the form of the Gesamtkunstwerk—or total work of art—polarized as much as his abandonment of the simple, unornamented form, which had been hard won in the early stages, in favor of developing a specific, modern Viennese ornament. His talent for not pitting construction against individual artistic expression, but rather for leading the way to a new aesthetic defined by unusual proportions, had a similar impact. He also divided opinion with his preference for luxury artisanal creation over industrial mass production. Nevertheless, his work has the potential to become the point of departure for a further synthesis of contrasting ideas for the next generation. As a testament to this, we can return to Peche:

> "I myself venerate the idea and the realization of this idea [of the WW as a 20th-century cultural department store; authors' note]; I owe that to the spirit of Josef Hoffmann. If I owe anything at all in this world to anyone, then I am indebted to the spirit of this artistic titan. Because he was the first to break ground; he was the first to throw the lightning bolt. I am indebted to him and his spirit—after all, where would I be, had he not gone before me? For that reason, but also because I am steeped in all this, I want to protect the fire within me."[4]

It is beyond question that Hoffmann, after Otto Wagner, helped the modern form achieve its breakthrough in Vienna. For him, it was not merely an end in itself, but rather the starting point for the free workings of the individual artistic imagination. He replaced the anonymity of the appropriate stylistic form with the subjective quality of beauty.

Josef Hoffmann, who at the suggestion of his academic teacher Otto Wagner became the head of an architecture class at the Vienna School of Arts and Crafts in 1899, was able to spend almost four decades imparting this message to several generations of students at the country's leading design school. Together with Koloman Moser, Alfred Roller, Felician von Myrbach, and other artists of the Vienna Secession, he transformed the school of decorative arts—originally conceived to meet the interior design needs of the city's late 19th-century building boom—into a laboratory of Modernism where individual creativity superseded compulsory stylistic norms and specializations for the first time. From now on this revolutionary liberation of "Eigenart" (uniqueness), as Hoffmann called individual artistic identity, was able to develop without constraint in an unbounded cosmos of free forms with every task of a comprehensive, identity-building environmental design, from furniture and houses to gardens and urban planning. In turn, some of his students went on to teach at the University of Applied Arts— as the School of Arts and Crafts came to be known—for decades, handing down Modernist ideals to students of each generation, regardless of regime changes, well into the 1960s.

Exhibiting Hoffmann?

This catalog is being published on the occasion of the first comprehensive museum retrospective of Hoffmann's oeuvre, presented at the MAK in Vienna in 2021. The exhibition as a medium raises questions: Hoffmann himself was the inventor of the cross-genre modern art exhibition on the basis of a consistent aesthetic ideal. From 1900 it was successfully presented time and again in the form of the novel *Raumkunst* (or "room art," i.e. interior design as a work of art) as an example of a comprehensive artistic life reform. Consequently, it is vital that a documentary show on Josef Hoffmann not be staged as an aesthetic event or even as a competing parallel artwork—especially considering that our modern-day customs of exhibition reception in the media age and our limited resources would forbid it. Whereas all Secession exhibitions and the Kunstschau were designed as curated sales exhibitions, in other words as commercial enterprises, today a Josef Hoffmann retrospective in a museum accomplishes a public education mission.

The display includes on the one hand a chronology of his works and on the other an introduction to the artist's unique, at that time revolutionary methods as a nuclear reactor for his inventions and impact to the present day. The MAK's large exhibition hall in Vienna was constructed in 1906–1909 not by a Secessionist, but by Ludwig Baumann, whose mellow Neobaroque style was favored by the regime of the time. Its ample space of 1 600 m² on the ground floor and 1 100 m² on the upper floor, as well as the ideal proportions of around 40 x 40 m, henceforth served the presentation of 1:1 interiors, such as in the museum's famous spring and fall exhibitions. Yet these rooms were also host to the Kunstschau in 1920 and the Werkbund exhibition in 1930; both were designed by Hoffmann. The MAK was also the venue for two anniversary exhibitions on Hoffmann's oeuvre, namely for his 60th birthday in 1930 and for his 70th birthday in 1940/41. In reference to this MAK tradition, the retrospective in 2021 also includes the large-format photo panels of which the frugal anniversary shows constituted. Valuable contemporary documents like this give us a clue how Hoffmann himself wanted his work to be perceived.

They are integrated in our exhibition concept in a concentric system within which visitors can navigate the show freely, whether tangentially or radially (design: Gregor Eichinger). The outer layer comprises a textile covering of the space with essential information about his biography and oeuvre in chronological order. It accompanies the circular peripheral zone of the exhibition hall, which traces the six decades of Hoffmann's artistic output with principal works from numerous national and international collections, featuring his wide range of decorative-art objects, photographs and plans, drawings and models. In certain places, visitors can move from here into the central space, where fundamental methods of Modernist architecture and design are identified in several core aspects of Hoffmann's design work and in an exemplary 1:1 reconstruction of his famous *Boudoir d'une grande vedette* [Boudoir for a Big Star] from 1937. These core aspects include the ideal combination of an individual creative design with its equally individual execution by a skilled artisan. And Hoffmann's very extensive attempt to realize the Gesamtkunstwerk ideal in Sanatorium Westend in Purkersdorf and in the legendary Stoclet House in Brussels. As well as the serial design strategy as an artistic reaction to industrialization and the dissemination of all these utterly modern artistic innovations through new decorative-arts organizations and many *Raumkunst* exhibitions.

It is consistent with Hoffmann's artistic thinking in endless creative variations and alternatives that there is not just one but several ideal paths through this exhibition. Visitors can immerse themselves in a creative cosmos and navigate through it freely, from the structuring timeline to the exemplary design laboratory and back again. The deep inner connection between Hoffmann's forms and works, which reveals countless anticipations and recourses, parallels and repetitions, can only be demonstrated in such a matrix and not in a linear sequence. It also epitomizes the intensely humane and emancipatory dimension of Josef Hoffmann's oeuvre: We are permitted to define who we are, and we are permitted to use everything that is beautiful to portray our individuality—regardless whether it was invented yesterday or today. And regardless of its dimension between architecture and cigarette case.

Hoffmann Research: Yesterday, Today, Tomorrow

"Art history will speak especially highly of him." It was with this closing sentence that the architect and cultural journalist Armand Weiser (1877–1933), editor of *Österreichs Bau und Werkkunst*, the journal of the Zentralvereinigung der Architekten (Central Association of Architects), paid tribute to Josef Hoffmann in his monograph, which was published in 1930 as part of the series "Meister der Baukunst." This was already the second, now multilingual monograph after the book released as early as 1927 by Hoffmann's assistant Leopold Kleiner.[5] At 60, Hoffmann was at the peak of his fame in 1930, an internationally renowned architect who had been honored with a solo show at the Triennale in Monza alongside Frank Lloyd Wright, Ludwig Mies van der Rohe, and Le Corbusier, and who had sat on the international jury of architects for the construction of the Palais des Nations in Geneva. Hoffmann's oeuvre, having faded into obscurity soon after World War II, was rediscovered in the course of the reappraisal of art in Vienna around 1900, which began in the 1960s.[6] A year before Josef Hoffmann's death, the then Austrian Museum of Applied Arts (today's MAK) had acquired the Wiener Werkstätte's estate and with it an assortment of several thousand drawings by the architect. The Viennese avant-garde mentor and author Günther Feuerstein wrote about Josef Hoffmann and the Wiener Werkstätte in 1964[7]—a clear sign of young Viennese architects' reemerging interest in his oeuvre. That paved the way for the first comprehensive accounts in book form: the design-oriented publication by Daniele Baroni and Antonio d'Auria *Josef Hoffmann e la Wiener Werkstätte* from 1981 and the monograph devoted to his architectural work by Eduard F. Sekler from 1982 (published in English in 1985), which is still recognized as a standard reference work to this day. The major exhibition *Traum und Wirklichkeit* [Dream and Reality] at Vienna's Künstlerhaus (1985) and the show organized at the MAK called *Josef Hoffmann. Ornament zwischen Hoffnung und Verbrechen* [Josef Hoffmann: Ornament between Hope and Crime] (1987) made Hoffmann's work accessible once again to the general public.[8] Symposia like *Ornament und Askese* (1985), and here primarily the contribution by Peter Gorsen, provided the research basis for an analysis of Josef Hoffmann's significance for his productive period and for new Postmodernist approaches.[9] It is as a result of this revaluation of Josef Hoffmann that the engagement of the MAK Vienna and the Moravian Gallery in Brno should be understood, which have developed a packed exhibition program for the Josef Hoffmann Museum in the house where he was born in Brtnice (CZ), which has been open since 2005. This engagement has led to new publications like the reedition of Josef Hoffmann's *Selbstbiographie/ Autobiography* (2009). In the 2000s it was the traveling exhibition on the Wiener Werkstätte *Yearning for Beauty* (MAK, Vienna, 2003, and BOZAR, Brussels, 2006), which subjected Josef Hoffmann's creative work to an in-depth analysis, while in his volume *Junge Meister* Jindřich Vybíral expressly focused on the discord between or rather the synthesis of Domestic Revival and urban mundanity in Hoffmann's oeuvre and centered his observations on the architect's Moravian "foothill architectures."[10] The exhibition *Josef Hoffmann: Interiors 1902–1913* (Neue Galerie, New York, 2006) concentrated on the *Raumkunst* of this period. It questioned: "Space as a framework of action that is defined by human beings and serves them, or as an aesthetic Gesamtkunstwerk that conditions them?"[11] The exhibitions/publications *Ways to Modernism: Josef Hoffmann, Adolf Loos, and Their Impact* (MAK, Vienna, 2014/15) and *Wiener Werkstätte 1903–1932: The Luxury of Beauty* (Neue Galerie, New York, 2017/18) made a start at establishing a new view of Josef Hoffmann side by side with his contemporaries.

This catalog fills many gaps in the existing research into Hoffmann. It spotlights his as yet less well-known late work with equal intensity as his revolutionary early work. In new research, it evaluates much more archive material than was previously known. For the first time, it documents in detail Hoffmann's activities in the shadow of the dictatorships of the 1930s. And it contextualizes his creative work within its period, circumstances, and the international avant-garde by means of articles written from a wide range of perspectives. A desideratum for future investigations of Hoffmann's oeuvre would include—also in light of these new findings—a revised and augmented edition of the catalogue raisonné by Eduard F. Sekler from 1982.[12] Given the enormous number of previously unknown texts, manuscripts, and newspaper articles written by Hoffmann, which were discovered during the research for this catalog, there is a strong argument for publishing a volume of "collected writings" with editorial classification. The preconception that Josef Hoffmann was adverse to theory must be challenged, as must the notion that he had left little to compete with the vociferous invectives of the likes of Adolf Loos or the fundamental writings of his teacher Otto Wagner. Hoffmann's theorizing often took place in concert with trusted authors like Berta Zuckerkandl-Szeps, which would warrant research dedicated to these creative relationships. Josef Hoffmann's statement from a RAVAG interview on this is well known: "There are two types of artist: those who construct something rationally and develop it systematically, and those who dream something up—I prefer the dreamers." Hence an aesthetic theory should be developed that explains Hoffmann's work better than the currently dominant theories of ornament. It should analyze the social functions of the beauty produced through individual creativity in which Hoffmann believed and which was not intended to benefit the upper classes alone. Hoffmann's works deserve further, in-depth study in all areas of arts-and-crafts design, where his achievements were groundbreaking—for example, in ceramics and in glass design for the School of Arts and Crafts, but also in furniture in collaboration with Koloman Moser. Moreover, the international impact of Josef Hoffmann's work on architecture and design into Postmodernism, in all its diverse incarnations, could also be explored more systematically than in existing research. As a first step along this path, this publication offers ample material for a new insight into the life and work of Josef Hoffmann. ∎

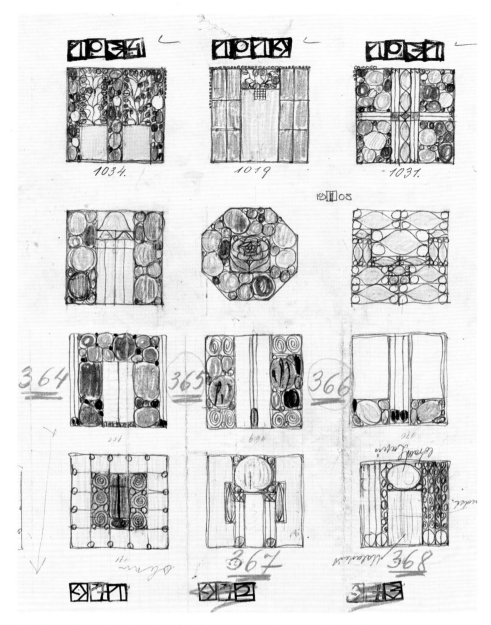

JH, design for twelve brooches for the Wiener Werkstätte, 1905–1908
MAK, KI 12144-45

1   Wotruba, Fritz, *Überlegungen. Gedanken zur Kunst*, Zurich 1945, 49.

2   Thun-Hohenstein, Christoph/Boeckl, Matthias/Witt-Dörring, Christian (eds.), *Ways to Modernism: Josef Hoffmann, Adolf Loos, and Their Impact*, Basel 2015.

3   Peche, Dagobert, "Der brennende Dornbusch" (1922), in: Noever, Peter (ed.), *Die Überwindung der Utilität. Dagobert Peche und die Wiener Werkstätte*, Ostfildern 1998, 169–191: 180 f.

4   Ibid., 187.

5   Weiser, Armand, *Josef Hoffmann*, "Meister der Baukunst" series, Geneva 1930; Kleiner, Leopold, "Einleitung," in: *Josef Hoffmann*, "Neue Werkkunst" series, Berlin 1927.

6   The then Austrian Museum of Applied Arts (now the MAK) played a crucial role in this rediscovery. After inventorying the Wiener Werkstätte Archive that had been acquired by the museum in 1955, its director Wilhelm Mrazek jointly organized with the Federal Ministry of Education the exhibition *Die Wiener Werkstätte: modernes Kunsthandwerk von 1903–1932* [The Wiener Werkstätte: Modern Arts and Crafts from 1903 to 1932] in 1967, which showed objects after Josef Hoffmann's design at the museum again for the first time.

7   Feuerstein, Günther, "Josef Hoffmann und die Wiener Werkstätte," in: *Der Aufbau. Fachschrift der Stadtbaudirektion* 19 1964, 177 ff.

8   The MAK exhibition, one of the first under Peter Noever's direction, was only able to present the holdings of the museum and the University of Applied Arts on Josef Hoffmann and drew attention to the necessity of comprehensive research into his oeuvre.

9   Gorsen, Peter, "Josef Hoffmann. Zur Modernität eines konservativen Baumeisters," in: Pfabigan, Alfred (ed.), *Ornament und Askese im Zeitgeist des Wien der Jahrhundertwende*, Vienna 1985, 57–68.

10 Vybíral, Jindřich, "Labyrinth der Großstadt und Paradies der Heimat: Josef Hoffmann," in: id., *Junge Meister. Architekten aus der Schule Otto Wagners in Mähren und Schlesien*, Vienna 2007, 225–261.

11 Witt-Dörring, Christian (ed.), *Josef Hoffmann: Interiors 1902–1913*, Munich 2006, 12.

12 Witt-Dörring has been working on the revised edition of Eduard F. Sekler's publication for over a decade and was doing so in collaboration with Sekler until the latter's death in 2017.

1870
1900

Students at the State Technical School in Brünn/Brno, 1889
Josef Hoffmann is standing on the far right
Josef Hoffmann Museum, Brtnice

Fig. 1 JH, cover sheet for *Ver Sacrum*, 1899, issue 7

Fig. 2 JH, designs for interiors, 1899
DI (1) 1899, plate 32

Fig. 3 JH, design for a study, 1898
DI (1) 1899, plate 2

Fig. 4 JH, desk for Paul
Wittgenstein's Bergerhöhe
country house, 1899
Oak, stained green,
brass, copper
Private collection
© MAK/Georg Mayer

Fig. 5 JH, armchair for the Bergerhöhe country house, 1899
Oak, buckskin
Private collection
© MAK/Georg Mayer

Fig. 6 JH, armchair for the Bergerhöhe country house, 1899
Oak, stained brown
Private collection
© MAK/Georg Mayer

Fig. 7 JH, cabinet for the *Ver Sacrum* room, 3rd Secession exhibition, 1898
Alderwood, stained black (originally green), copper

MAK, H 2062
© MAK/Georg Mayer

Fig. 8 JH, competition project for an exhibition pavilion for
the City of Vienna for the jubilee exhibition in 1898, 1897
DK (2) 1898, 208

Fig. 9 JH, Hoffmann's letter paper, 1899
Belvedere, Vienna, Hans Ankwicz-Kleehoven's estate
© Christian Witt-Dörring

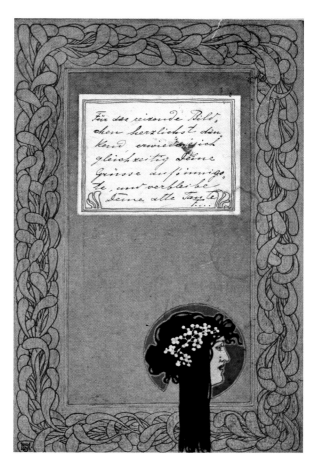

Fig. 10 JH, Viennese art postcard *Stilistisches
XXXIII/10* [Stylish XXXIII/10], 1898
MAK, WWPK 268-1

Fig. 11 JH, Bergerhöhe country house,
Hohenberg, sleeping alcove, 1899
VS (3) 5 1900, 81

Fig. 12 JH, Apollo shop, Vienna, 1899
Der Architekt 1899, 44

Fig. 13 JH, fishbowl, executed by Meyr's Neffe,
Adolf bei Winterberg/Adolfov ve Vimperk for
E. Bakalowits & Söhne, Vienna, 1899
Wood, brass, optically blown glass
Dr. E. Ploil Collection, LHG-1984-22
© Wolfgang Woessner/MAK

Fig. 14 JH, salon cabinet, executed by Portois & Fix, Vienna, 8th Secession exhibition, 1900
Zerigotti and cedar pyramid, Synaigunde treated in the xylektypom way (etched to emphasize the grain)
bel etage Kunsthandel GmbH

Fig. 15 JH, small cabinet for
a dining room, executed by
Anton Pospischil, winter exhibition
at the AMAI, 1899
Walnut, copper, mirror, glass
bel etage Kunsthandel GmbH

Fig. 16 JH, forestry office and house for the forestry workers of
the Wittgenstein Forestry Administration, Hohenberg, 1900
Der Architekt (7) 1901, plate 47

Fig. 17 JH, design for the hall of a country house, 1899
MAK, KI 10439-6

Fig. 18 JH, design for a Moravian country house, 1899
MAK, KI 10439-4

Fig. 19 JH, design of the School of Arts and Crafts room,
Grand Palais, World's Fair, Paris, 1900
MAK, KI 7401-4

Josef Hoffmann
1870
1900

Josef Hoffmann's birthplace in Pirnitz/Brtnice
Photo before 1930
Josef Hoffmann Museum, Brtnice

1870
Josef Franz Maria Hoffmann is born on 15 December as the third of six children in the small Moravian town of Pirnitz/Brtnice. His father, Josef Franz Karl, is coproprietor of cotton manufacturing in the textile factory of the Princes of Collalto, who also own the town's castle, and mayor of the town. The vibrant tradition of Moravian folk art, the fertile landscape, and a family life that can almost be classed as Biedermeier, are the strongest impressions from his childhood that would go on to have a formative influence on his later life—as he testifies in his autobiography.

1879
Attends the grammar school in Iglau/Jihlava, where Adolf Loos (from Brünn/Brno) is a fellow student. According to his father's wishes, Hoffmann is supposed to aspire to a legal career in the civil service. Traumatized by the authoritarian school system, he develops an interest in art and architecture, visiting nearby construction sites with the son of the town's master builder in order to help with the work. Finally, after arguments within the family, he is allowed to attend the architecture department at the Höhere Staatsgewerbeschule (State Technical School) in Brno in 1887, where he once again meets Adolf Loos in 1888/89. Having passed the Matura (school leaving examination), he works as an architecture intern at the military surveyor's office in Würzburg in 1891 and after completing his year of practical experience, he applies to the academy in Vienna.

1892
Starts his degree at the Academy of Fine Arts Vienna in the specialized architecture school of Baron Carl von Hasenauer, the Ringstraße architect who was at the zenith of his career at the time. When he dies in 1894, Otto Wagner takes over the class and revolutionizes the syllabus with progressive programs and problems faced by the emerging metropolis. In his third year Hoffmann chooses as his final-year project the topic *Insel des Friedens/Forum orbis, insula pacis* [Island of Peace], an international congressional palace of vast proportions, which earns him an award and the so-called Rome Prize. Again and again, Hoffmann acknowledges the enormous influence of Otto Wagner on his work and remains an ardent admirer of his teacher throughout his life. Even after his studies, he re-

mains in close contact with his colleagues from the Wagner school and Otto Wagner's architecture firm, including Joseph Maria Olbrich, Franz Krásný, Jan Kotěra, Franz and Hubert Gessner, Max Fabiani, and Rudolph Michael Schindler.

1895–1896
The Siebener-Club of young artists in Vienna is established. The group of friends around Josef Hoffmann, which includes artists and architects like Olbrich, Koloman Moser, Maximilian Kurzweil, and Fabiani, discusses contemporary issues in the private rooms of Viennese cafés and can be considered the avant-garde forum of the intense debates that were raging about art and architecture in Vienna around 1900. Otto Wagner's private studio be-

Students at the State Technical School in Brünn/Brno, 1889,
Josef Hoffmann (standing) on the far right, Adolf Loos on the far left
Josef Hoffmann Museum, Brtnice

Josef Hoffmann drawing
during his travels in Italy, 1896
Josef Hoffmann Museum, Brtnice

comes the group's mecca. After Joseph Maria Olbrich—like Hoffmann born in Moravia and Otto Wagner's favorite student—Hoffmann also tours Italy with the grant he received from the academy with the Rome Prize. The route—which can be reconstructed with the aid of his surviving travel sketches—took him via Venice and Rome to Naples and finally Capri. He describes the anonymous architecture of the island, the visual qualities of the simple, white peasants' houses, and sees them as a source of inspiration for expressing well-balanced social conditions and as characteristic of the landscape and its inhabitants.

1897

Back in Vienna Hoffmann starts working in the studio of Otto Wagner, who is busy designing and building Vienna's Stadtbahn (light urban railway). Furthermore, Hoffmann produces designs for the City of Vienna's exhibition pavilion for the *Kaiser-Jubiläumsausstellung* [Imperial Jubilee Exhibition] of 1898; with Franz Krásný he develops competition designs for the new construction of the Bohemian People's Theater in Pilsen and the trades bank in Prague, projects that—like his essay "Architektonisches von der Insel Capri – Ein Beitrag für malerische Architekturempfindungen"—are published in the journal *Der Architekt*. This year also

sees the founding of the Union of Austrian Artists Secession, which assembles the city's avant-garde forces in a single society and will have a formative influence on the modern artistic topography of Vienna. Josef Hoffmann is a founding member and designs one of the first exhibition halls for the Secession. Olbrich's programmatic design for the union's exhibition building gives Hoffmann architectural scope for the interior, for which he assumes partial responsibility as the designer of the rooms related to the Gesamtkunstwerk—or total work of art—concept of the *Ver Sacrum* (sacred spring).

JH, "Architektonisches aus der
österreichischen Riviera"
Der Architekt (I) 1895, 37

Josef Hoffmann in Koloman Moser's studio
on the seat he designed, Vienna, 1898
Private collection, Vienna

1898

The English Arts & Crafts movement and the Belgian/French Art Nouveau style influence Hoffmann's furnishings for the *Ver Sacrum* room in the Secession building, for the union's "Viribus Unitis" room at the *Kaiser-Jubiläums-ausstellung*, and for the studios of Koloman Moser and the painter Ernst Stöhr, which were produced at the same time. Stylized ornaments, above all the characteristic palmette forms, shape the furniture's appearance, as do fundamental considerations of truth to the material, which for example prevent wood from being stained so as to imitate the natural color of another wood, making it nothing more than a copy. Truth calls for gray, blue, or green and by no means shades of brown, writes Hoffmann in his programmatic text "Moderne Möbel." Hoffmann designs the 3rd exhibition of the Secession, which is dedicated to Max Klinger, and establishes himself as an impactful presenter of art. Marries Anna Hladik.

1899

Hoffmann continues to be instrumental in designing the Secession exhibitions that are so vital to Viennese cultural life and makes contact with potential customers. Among his first commissions are the furnishings and portal of the Vienna shop of the Apollo soap and candle factory and the conversion of the Bergerhöhe country house in Hohenberg, Lower Austria, for the industrialist Paul Wittgenstein, who remains loyal to Hoffmann throughout his life as a construction client, patron, and friend. The 29-year-old Hoffmann and Koloman Moser are both appointed professors at the Vienna School of Arts and Crafts on Otto Wagner's suggestion. Until his retirement in 1936, Hoffmann teaches an architecture class, and from the 1920s also a class in metal- and enamelwork, as well as the decorative arts. The engagement of the Secessionists Hoffmann and Moser at the renowned school, which in Baron Felician von Myrbach also acquired a new director from within the union, is rapturously celebrated as the victory of the "modern artists" over the "old guard" (Ludwig Hevesi in *Ver Sacrum*, April 1899).

1900

For the World's Fair in Paris, Hoffmann furnishes the rooms of the Vienna School of Arts and Crafts and the Secession in the Grand Palais, and he exhibits a dining room of his own design. In the room of the School of Arts and Crafts, which is realized in the curvilinear style, works by the first students from Hoffmann's specialized class are presented. Further exhibitions of his students' works take place in Prague in 1901, at Vienna's Austrian Museum of Art and Industry (AMAI, today's MAK) in 1903, at the World's Fair in St. Louis in 1904, and in the context of numerous other national and international art exhibitions until Hoffmann's retirement. Study trip to England to learn about the workshop principle of the Guild of Handicraft in London. Hoffmann is interested in the furniture by Charles Robert Ashbee and via his future business partner Fritz Waerndorfer invites the Scottish arts-and-crafts artists Charles Rennie Mackintosh and his wife Margaret Macdonald, Frances Macdonald, and James Herbert MacNair (the "Glasgow Four") to furnish a Scottish room at the 8th Secession exhibition, whose austerity and strong individual statement arouse the enthusiasm of the Viennese artists and is considered a confirmation of the Secessionist ideals. At the same time as the preparations for the 8th exhibition, Hoffmann is occupied by the idea of a villa or artists' colony on the Hohe Warte and, after Joseph Maria Olbrich's departure for Darmstadt, he is commissioned with planning houses for the painters Carl Moll and Koloman Moser, the photographer Hugo Henneberg, and the art collector Victor Spitzer. Hoffmann's son Wolfgang is born. ■

Koloman Moser, Alfred Roller, and Josef Hoffmann in front of Café Museum, Vienna, 1900
Josef Hoffmann Museum, Brtnice

Caricature, Josef Hoffmann and Koloman Moser
VS (4) 3 1901, 61

Fig. 1 JH, travel sketch from Amalfi, group of houses by the town wall, 1895
Graphic Collection, Academy of Fine Arts Vienna, HZ 26297

Rainald Franz

"It Was No Simple Matter to [...] Reach an Understanding of the Real Sense of Building"

Josef Hoffmann: Studies at the Vienna Academy

At the age of 22 Josef Hoffmann, graduate of the architecture department at the Höhere Staatsgewerbeschule (State Technical School) in Brno and architecture intern at the military surveyor's office in Würzburg, moved from the Moravian province to Vienna, the capital city and seat of the royal family, to start his architecture degree at the Academy of Fine Arts. In 1892 a total of 24 new students were admitted to the academy's two architecture schools. Josef Hoffmann's surviving academy ID identifies him as a student of Carl von Hasenauer (1833–1894), the head of the specialized school and the rector of the academy. At that time the architect of the Ringstraße was at the zenith of his career, supervising the completion of the central buildings of the Imperial Forum, which he had started together with Gottfried Semper: the Hofburgtheater (from 1874 to 1888, now Burgtheater) and the Neue Burg section of the Hofburg Palace (1880–1923).[1] Josef Hoffmann himself describes his early days at the academy as follows:

> "I was admitted to the class of Baron Hasenauer and, after a brief welcoming, was left to my own devices. Hasenauer was in the process of building the Burgtheater and the Hofburg; he had so much work at hand with these monumental buildings that we seldom got to see him. His assistant, an elderly gentleman, did what he could to maintain the interest of the students in the prescribed tasks, but a number of us felt the urge to get to the root of things. It was no simple matter to make our way through the confusion of countless motifs, not least those of the High Renaissance, and so reach an understanding of the real sense of building."[2]

In the late 19th-century architecture curriculum, stylistic imitation was viewed as the basis for all further design. Studying historical architectural styles down to the details of the orders was intended to lay the foundation for understanding architecture; this was taught by Hasenauer's assistant Bruno Gruber, whom Hoffmann mentions in the quotation above, though the students did not seem particularly impressed: "Instinctively, we wished to move away from the copying of old styles, firmly determined to develop a form of purpose and beauty."[3]

So typical of the late Historicist period, this experience of disparity between taught content and the students' own search for new design solutions connected Josef Hoffmann with like-minded students: As early as 1894 he had joined forces with Koloman Moser and the painters Adolf Karpellus, Leo Kainradl, and Maximilian Kurzweil in the Siebener-Club. A casual grouping of students from the academy and the School of Arts and Crafts, they met regularly at the Blaues Freihaus or Café Sperl on Vienna's Gumpendorferstraße. Other members were Joseph Maria Olbrich and Friedrich Pilz, while Jan Kotěra, Max Fabiani, and Joseph Urban only took part sporadically. For Maximilian Kurzweil Hoffmann designed studio furnishings and with Koloman Moser he developed a close friendship and partnered on future projects. Alongside the "Hagengesellschaft," the Siebener-Club was the second precursor organization that would, via the Künstlerhaus, merge to form the "Vereinigung bildender Künstler Österreichs Secession" (Union of Austrian Artists Secession).[4]

Despite his frustration with stylistic imitation, Josef Hoffmann evidently completed his studies in Hasenauer's class conscientiously. A report from 22 July 1894 attests to the student's "laudable diligence, especially rich aptitude" and design of the required student projects: a villa, a castle, an apartment building, and a palace. Hoffmann is awarded every prize at the academy: the Gundel prize in 1893, the prize of the specialized school, the Goldene Füger-Medaille ("Golden Joiner Medal"), and the Rosenbaum prize in 1894.[5]

Carl von Hasenauer's death in January 1894 necessitated the appointment of a new head of the specialized school. For Hasenauer's successor a replacement was sought who was rooted in antiquity and championed the classical Renaissance, who had talent, ability, and a teaching qualification. What spoke in favor of Otto Wagner was that he understood how to "reconcile the needs of contemporary life and the use of modern building materials and constructions with artistic requirements."[6] Otto Wagner was made a tenured professor as early as 16 July 1894. At first his takeover of the specialized architecture school did not seem like a revolutionary change. The established architect and *Oberbaurat* (chief building officer) Otto Wagner had a large studio and was financially successful; in his youth a keen champion of Historicism, he was now starting to leave his mark on Vienna: that same year he had been appointed *Künstlerischer Beirat* (artistic adviser) to undertake the uniform architectural design

Fig. 2 JH, postcard to Koloman Moser
with architectural study, 5 Jun 1897
Kunsthandel Widder, Vienna

of the Stadtbahn (light urban railway). In his inaugural lecture at the Academy of Fine Arts in October 1894, Wagner declared the school concept of the École des Beaux Arts in Paris to be his model, in line with Semper's motto "Artis sola domina necessitatis." He encouraged on the one hand his students' imagination by assigning them fantasy projects of their own choice as final projects and on the other their practical experience by allowing them to work on his construction projects in his private studio. Otto Wagner's training raised his students' awareness of the conscious integration of interior decoration—from wall to furniture design—that was inherent in all his projects. Damjan Prelovšek points out that it was teaching at the academy that made Wagner a theorist: it was only when he was obliged to explain his own conception of architectural art in his role as a professor that Wagner started to occupy himself with theory. What was crucial in this regard was the inspiration he found in Semper's cladding theory, with the aid of which he aimed to keep pace with his progressive contemporaries in Western Europe.[7] Both Eduard F. Sekler and Josef Hoffmann himself emphatically expressed the "wake-up call" that Wagner's arrival must have meant for Hoffmann. In Hoffmann's autobiography, he writes:

"At last, we had among us a strong personality, and this personality was full of ideas, went its own way, and was able to rouse our enthusiasm for all that was new and necessary. We admired Wagner's palatial domestic architecture, which was exemplary not only in terms of its construction and the soundness of its building methods but also in its free use of old forms to surprising effect. Among the buildings conventional for the time, Wagner's stood out by their quality and singularity. We were especially impressed by his charming residential house and studio on Rennweg and the two apartment houses by which this was flanked, and we were fired with enthusiasm for our new teacher and master. It became his custom to direct our work on a daily basis and, drawing on his vast technical knowledge, to make us aware over and again of the most important elements of building. He was

Figs. 3, 4 JH, *Forum Orbis
Insula Pacis* project, 1895
Side view, main façade
Der Architekt (I) 1895

Fig. 5 JH, travel sketches in
watercolor from Anacapri, 1895
National Gallery Prague, K 17672-74

never less than stimulating and, with his Viennese manner of speaking, had a fascinating natural charm. Before long our small circle had grouped itself around him; out of school, too, albeit only over our daily afternoon coffee in the Heinrichshof, we remained in regular contact with him. Thus we had the opportunity to inform ourselves on all kinds of artistic questions."[8]

It was under Wagner that Hoffmann completed his degree in the summer of 1895 with a design for the utopian structure *Forum orbis, insula pacis*, one of the first final-year projects under Wagner's supervision. Hoffmann imagined a precursor to today's United Nations headquarters, a massive, domed building that would stand on an artificial island over a kilometer long.[9] Sekler remarks that this design had met with approval at the École des Beaux Arts in Paris, while also drawing attention to its reliance on Wagner's early projects: the *Artibus* ideal museum district or the competition design for the Hungarian parliament, both from the early 1880s.[10] The design, structure, and rhythmic arrangement of the building's sections in Josef Hoffmann's project *Forum orbis, insula pacis* became a lodestar in the early Wagner school—for example, for the diploma project produced two years later by his fellow student and colleague in the Siebener-Club Jan Kotěra (1871–1923)[11] and for the planning of a new Academy of Fine Arts Vienna in Otto Wagner's atelier (1897–1898). The architectural forms chosen by Josef Hoffmann for his diploma project are still entirely indebted to the historical canon. Wagner's enthusiasm for Hoffmann's solution and the state travel grant, the so-called Rome Prize, which Wagner ensured that Hoffmann would receive, prove what the teacher admired most about his student Josef Hoffmann: excellent drawing skills and a mastery of the repertoire of classical forms.

In November 1895 Josef Hoffmann traveled to Italy via Verona, Venice, and Florence to Rome, Naples, Capri, and Palermo, for "a whole year [of studies] at the famed sites of centuries-old architecture."[12]

"From the first I, a disciple of architecture in the first flush of youth, was overcome by the onrush of impressions, with the remains of the classical monuments having a practically shattering effect on me. Nevertheless, as the school of Otto Wagner intended to keep us from falling sacrifice to the blind style copyism […] [p]erhaps my appreciation of the simple yet peculiar Italian building style most prevalent in the country […] came of its own accord. In any case, it had far more to impart for our endeavours to give shape to purpose and material."[13]

The young architect was impressed not only by the classical architecture and art, but also by the vernacular buildings of Campagna and Capri. He dedicated two essays to this "people's architecture," which were published in the Wagner school's magazine *Der Architekt* in 1895 and 1897 complete with sketches from Hoffmann's hand. They are travel sketches from Istria and Italy, as well as the first design for a *Mediterrane Villa* [Mediterranean Villa]. They contain programmatic observations that Hoffmann would only be able to realize years later. In "Architektonisches von der Insel Capri" from 1897, Hoffmann calls for a genuinely practicable type of modern country house, an abiding theme throughout Hoffmann's career. His constant interest in popular culture is also manifest in this article, and the statement "here, too, the day will come when one will not order one's wallpaper, one's ceiling paintings from a retailer like furniture and practical objects, but from an artist,"[14] hints at the zeitgeist that would soon find expression in the Secession and later in the Wiener Werkstätte. Nevertheless, antiquity also proved inspiring and his exploration of classical architectural vocabulary gained significant momentum here that would have an impact on his future work:

6 p. 29

"Yet my first encounter with an ancient temple was an experience of greater import still. The short, strong columns with the overhanging capitals so wide that they almost touched, thus supporting the architrave, the natural triangle of the tympanum, the vocabulary of whose forms came from a construction originally made in wood but immortalized in stone: all these thing served to challenge and inspire me.
At last I recognized intuitively that monumental architecture has its own laws, that in special circumstances it is appropriate to employ a special morphology."[15]

Josef Hoffmann summarizes the impressions from his travels through Italy as follows: "I spent some very happy days; indeed they were feast days of a sort. In Capri and Anacapri, too, the unpretentious, natural style of the architecture left a host of impressions on me."[16] ■

1   Kurdiovsky, R., *Carl von Hasenauer (1833–1894)*, dissertation at the University of Vienna, 2008.
2   Noever, Peter/Pokorný, Marek (eds.), *Josef Hoffmann. Selbstbiographie/Autobiography*, Ostfildern 2009, 89. Trans. Bernd Magar and Andrew Oakland.
3   Ibid.
4   Pausch, Oskar, *Gründung und Baugeschichte der Wiener Secession: Mit Erstedition des Protokollbuchs von Alfred Roller*, Vienna 2006; Sekler, Eduard F., *Josef Hoffmann: The Architectural Work*, Princeton, NJ 1985, 17. Trans. Eduard F. Sekler and John Maass.
5   Sekler 1985 (see note 4), 12.

6   Wagner, Walter, *Die Geschichte der Akademie der bildenden Künste in Wien*, Vienna 1967, 252.
7   Prelovšek, Damjan, *Josef Hoffmann und die Wagner Schule, Sammelband der Beiträge aus der Konferenz vom 29. Juni 2002, die in Zusammenarbeit mit der Stadt Pirnitz zum 10. Gründungsjubiläum der Josef Hoffmann-Gesellschaft veranstaltet wurde*, Brtnice 2002, 10. See Semper, Gottfried, *Der Stil in den technischen und tektonischen Künsten, oder praktische Ästhetik*, vol. 1: *Textile Kunst*, Frankfurt 1860, vol. 2: *Tektonik, Stereometrie, Metallotechnik*, Munich 1863; see also: Prelovšek, Damjan, *Josef Plečnik 1872–1957*, Salzburg/Vienna 1992, 12–16.

8   Noever/Pokorný 2009 (see note 2), 90.
9   Printed in: *Der Architekt* (I) 1895, 53, 55, plates 93–94.
10   Sekler 1985 (see note 4), 13–15.
11   "Aus der Wagner Schule," in: *Der Architekt*, Supplement 2, 1898, 18–19.
12   Noever/Pokorný 2009 (see note 2), 90.
13   Ibid.
14   Hoffmann, Josef, "Architektonisches von der Insel Capri," in: *Der Architekt* (III) 1897, 13.
15   Noever/Pokorný 2009 (see note 2), 90–91.
16   Ibid., 91.

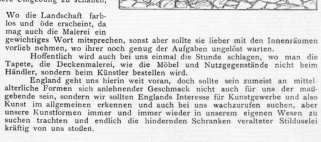

ARCHITEKTONISCHES VON DER INSEL CAPRI.

Ein Beitrag für malerische Architekturempfindungen.
Vom Architekten Josef Hoffmann.

Die Insel Capri ist allen Italienreisenden ans Herz gewachsen. Ihre herrliche, meerumspielte Lage gegenüber dem Golfe von Neapel, ihre abgeschlossene Naturschönheit in Bergen und Grotten, die merkwürdige Freundlichkeit und zufriedene Heiterkeit seiner Bewohner und, was mich besonders reizte, die fast durchwegs noch reine, volksthümliche Bauweise macht sie jedem lieb und unvergesslich.

Dort stimmt der malerisch bewegte Baugedanke in seiner glatten Einfachheit, frei von künstlicher Überhäufung mit schlechten Decorationen, noch herzerfrischend in die glühende Landschaft und spricht für jedermann eine offene, verständige Sprache. Die blendend weißen Wände mit, des übermäßigen Lichtes wegen, kleinen, tiefen Fenstern umschließen den Raum (fast immer nur einen). Diesen deckt die gemauerte flache Kuppel oder Tonne.

Eine geräumige Freitreppe mit Vorplatz und Weinpergola führt zu demselben durch den Hof, und rings in malerischer, vielen Schatten bietender Gruppierung setzen die größeren und kleineren Nutzräume an und bilden immer ein ganzes, abgeschlossenes, einheitliches Bild, welches sich in seiner lichten Farbe und einfachen Silhouette klar und deutlich vom blauen Himmel oder dunkeln Hintergrunde der Berge abhebt.

Hier ist noch Gott sei Dank die Bauspeculation nicht eingedrungen, und Villen neueren Ursprungs, wie z. B. die des Malers Allers, behalten jene vortrefflichen Eigenheiten bei und gliedern sich dankbar in die reizende Gesammtheit.

Das Beispiel von Volkskunst, wie solche thatsächlich hier in diesen einfachen Landhäusern besteht, ist auf jedes unbefangene Gemüth von großer Wirkung und lässt uns immer mehr fühlen, wie sehr wir bei uns zu Hause daran Mangel leiden.

So ist es nach meiner Meinung bis jetzt gewiss noch nicht gelungen, auch nur einen wirklich brauchbaren Typus eines modernen Landhauses für unsere Verhältnisse, unser Klima, unsere Umgebung zu schaffen, trotz der übergroßen Anzahl neuerer Villenanlagen.

Das Beispiel Capris und einiger anderer Orte, die ich noch später zu beschreiben mir vorbehalte, soll aber nicht zur Nachahmung dieser Bauweise führen, sondern es soll nur den Zweck haben, in uns einen anheimelnden Wohngedanken zu wecken, der nicht in Verdecorierung des schlechten Baugerippes mit lächerlichen, fabriksmäßig hergestellten Cementgussornamenten, oder in aufoctroirten Schweizer- und Giebelhausarchitectur besteht, sondern in einer einfachen, dem Individuum angepassten, verständnis- und stimmungsvollen Gruppierung, gleichmäßiger, natürlicher Farbe und, wo es der Reichthum gestattet, in lieber weniger, aber dafür von wirklicher Künstlerhand stammender Plastik.

Die Natur, namentlich unsere, ist ohnehin reich an Gestaltung, Mannigfaltigkeit in den Baumgattungen, an Farbe und Formen, so dass die einfachen geraden oder decent gekrümmten Linien unserer Bauten mit derselben glücklich contrastieren werden. Nie aber kann man jene vielspitzigen, vielgiebeligen Schwindelarchitekturen als zu unserer Landschaft passend bezeichnen.

Die Silhouettierung möge man lieber in richtiger Terrain- und Platzausnützung und in stilvoller Umgebung der Gärten und Villenstraßen zu suchen trachten.

Wo die Landschaft farblos und öde erscheint, da mag auch die Malerei ein gewichtiges Wort mitsprechen, sonst aber sollte sie lieber mit den Innenräumen vorlieb nehmen, wo ihrer noch genug der Aufgaben ungelöst warten.

Hoffentlich wird auch bei uns einmal die Stunde schlagen, wo man die Tapete, die Deckenmalerei, wie die Möbel und Nutzgegenstände nicht beim Händler, sondern beim Künstler bestellen wird.

England geht uns hierin weit voran, doch sollte sein zumeist an mittelalterliche Formen sich anlehnender Geschmack nicht auch für uns der maßgebende sein, sondern wir sollten Englands Interesse für Kunstgewerbe und also Kunst im allgemeinen erkennen und auch bei uns wachzurufen suchen, aber unsere Kunstformen immer und immer wieder in unserem eigenen Wesen zu suchen trachten und endlich die hindernden Schranken veralteter Stilduselei kräftig von uns stoßen.

Die Tempelhalle am Teich zu Madura in Süd-Indien.
(Tafel 32.)
Vom Architekten M. Heider.

Die Baukunst der Bewohner von Hindostan hat zwei Quellen, die zugleich die Anknüpfungspunkte an die Baukunst des europäischen Orients bilden. Während aber die Baukunst des Islam mit der Religion Mohammeds möglichst unverändert übernommen wurde und sich in Indien ihrer ursprünglichen Reinheit, und damit den alten Bauwerken Persiens und Cairos sich näherte, hat sich die alexandrinisch-hellenistische Architektur mit altpersischen Elementen versetzt und ist nur in den alten Denkmalen von Kaschmir noch klar zu erkennen, wo dorische und korinthische Capitäle gefunden wurden.

Je mehr man aber gegen Süden wandert, desto blasser und undeutlicher wird die Erinnerung an das alte classische Schema und desto mehr treten die localen Einflüsse in den Bauwerken zutage. Überall aber ist an den nicht mohammedanischen Bauten das tektonische Princip rein erhalten, welches die Tempelhallen aus dem Unterbau, Säulen, horizontalen Gesimsen und der ganz nach griechischer Art gebildeten Tempeldecke zusammensetzt. Und so wunderlich und phantastisch auch diese reich geschmückten Elemente aussehen mögen, so erzeugt die einfache Composition des Ganzen doch immerhin Effecte, die uns manchmal, vielleicht ketzerischer Weise, bedauern lässt, dass das alte Griechenthum nicht mit einem kleinen Bruchtheil indischer Phantasie bereichert war. Wer die Mannigfaltigkeit indischer Säulen kennt und damit die ungeheure Anzahl von möglichen geschmackvollen Ausbildungen der verticalen Stütze ahnt, der wird sicher auch bedauern, dass unsere Baukunst noch immer auf die fünf alten Ordnungen von der »Ordine dorica bis zur Ordine composita« der italienischen Unterweisungen beschränkt, man möchte beinahe sagen borniert ist.

Die alte Bevölkerung der Südspitze von Indien ist dravidischen Ursprunges, verschieden den Ariern des Nordens und den Malagen des Ostens. Es ist ein fast schwarzes Volk von guter künstlerischer Anlage, allerdings ohne den großen Sinn der Mongolen, aber voll der träumerischen Phantasie des Orients und einer Liebe zur Durchführung zeitraubender und schwieriger Arbeiten, die weniger den künstlerischen Effect als das Prunken mit der aufgewendeten Mühe zum Ziele hat.

Fig. 6   JH, "Architektonisches von der Insel Capri"
Der Architekt (III) 1897, 13

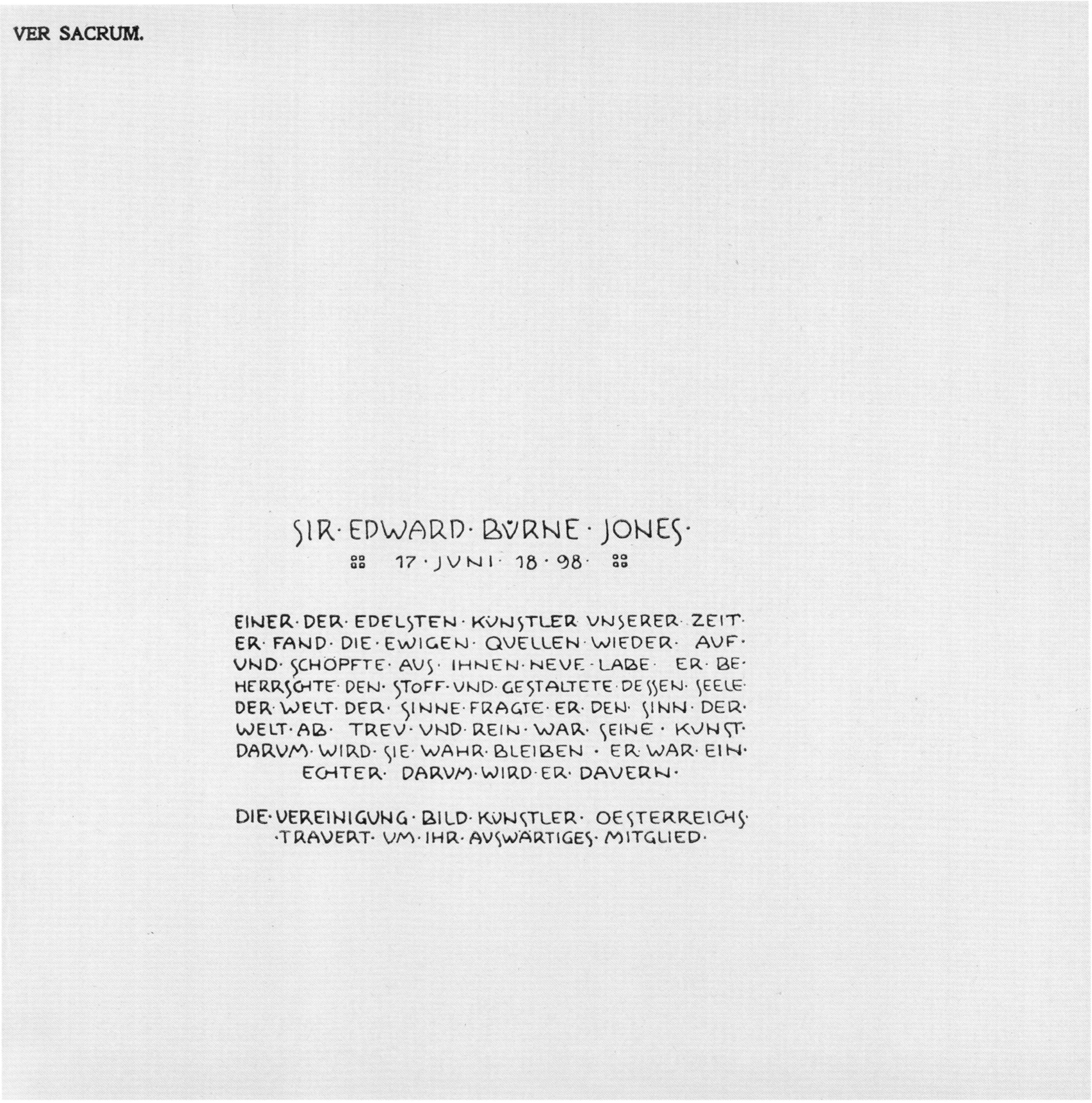

VER SACRUM.

SIR·EDWARD·BVRNE·JONES·
17·JVNI·18·98·

EINER·DER·EDELSTEN·KVNSTLER·VNSERER·ZEIT·
ER·FAND·DIE·EWIGEN·QVELLEN·WIEDER·AVF·
VND·SCHOPFTE·AVS·IHNEN·NEVE·LABE·ER·BE·
HERRSCHTE·DEN·STOFF·VND·GESTALTETE·DESSEN·SEELE·
DER·WELT·DER·SINNE·FRAGTE·ER·DEN·SINN·DER·
WELT·AB·TREV·VND·REIN·WAR·SEINE·KVNST·
DARVM·WIRD·SIE·WAHR·BLEIBEN·ER·WAR·EIN·
ECHTER·DARVM·WIRD·ER·DAVERN·

DIE·VEREINIGVNG·BILD·KVNSTLER·OESTERREICHS·
·TRAVERT·VM·IHR·AVSWÄRTIGES·MITGLIED·

Fig. 1 Obituary of the corresponding member of the Secession Sir Edward Burne-Jones.
Text by Ludwig Hevesi and typeface by Joseph M. Olbrich
VS (1) 8 1898, 1

Christian Witt-Dörring

Protestant Materialism Meets Catholic Emotions

The English Exemplar

In a manuscript written in November 1928—quite probably prompted by the 25th anniversary of the Wiener Werkstätte's founding—Hoffmann elucidates the beginnings of Vienna's art spring around 1900.

[1] "The modern movement in Austria has now been ongoing for thirty years. Inspired by the English society the Art Workers [sic] Guild, a group of young artists centering around Otto Wagner wanted to break with the customary use of past styles and attempted to find for all necessary objects new forms that would be in keeping with the times."[1]

Here Hoffmann names one of the most important sources of inspiration behind the development of an independent Austrian Modernism. Hermann Bahr, one of the young Secessionists' literary allies, also views the exemplary English Arts & Crafts movement as being on the front line in the battle against an anachronistic, purely commercially driven artistic landscape that stifles individual artistic expression. In his enthusiastic appraisal of the 1st Secession exhibition, which was intended to familiarize the Viennese public for the first time with, among other things, the Western European Modernism that the young artists considered an exemplar, he focuses in particular on Hoffmann's *Ver Sacrum* room. In it he sees a successful if lurid first step on the path to modern domestic culture in Vienna. Long since translated into action in the Western world, the ideologies of Modernism have now clearly been internalized in Vienna; consequently, Bahr calls for the next step to be taken: a local interpretation of these ideologies to "create our Austrian style for inside the home."[2]

Bahr recommends the adoption of three considerations that were developed in different cultural contexts. Foremost for him is Morris's idea, which he summarizes with the appeal for all of our surroundings to be beautiful. From this he concludes that the craftsperson should become an artist. His second consideration pertains to the correct use of materials, which he attributes to the Americans, and which must necessarily lead to the artist becoming a craftsperson. The third and final consideration connects Bahr with the Parisian gallery owner and interior decorator Siegfried Bing and the Belgian architect Henry van de Velde. They call for all of the individual components of a room to be in harmony with one another. This gives rise to the concept of the Gesamtkunstwerk—or total work of art. In this context Bahr employs the metaphor of the orchestra by comparing the role of the interior designer to that of the conductor.

At almost the same time as the Secession was founded, the Imperial Royal Austrian Museum of Art and Industry (today's MAK) welcomes a new director. He is the Anglophile former director of the trade museum Arthur von Scala. With his first Christmas exhibition, which opens on 16 November 1897, he leaves no doubt as to his understanding of a late 19th-century decorative-art museum's role as an arbiter of quality and taste. Stylistic imitation has served its purpose and the exemplars now come predominantly from the Anglo-Saxon art world. Hence his show features contemporary objects from England and America, as well as seats after designs by Chippendale and Sheraton. As a result, [2] [3] Scala triggers a heated debate about the "English style" not only in his own museum in the institution of the Kunstgewerbeverein (Arts-and-Crafts Association), but also among the contemporary artists of the Secession. This discussion symbolizes the search for modern solutions that was necessitated by the widespread social and artistic thirst for change in the capital. In this debate we can already identify the future camps into which Viennese Modernism will divide after Otto Wagner has laid the path to an Austrian Modernism around 1900—namely the Secessionists on the one hand and Adolf Loos and his supporters on the other.

The "English style" is thus instantaneously addressed both by the Secessionists and by Loos, though with a different emphasis. In the very first issue of *Ver Sacrum*, Franz Servaes reports on the Christmas exhibition and sees it as a first positive indication of the future under the new directorship. It is deemed encouraging that the English and American products bear witness to an independently developed national style and taste. At the same time, however, he warns: "imitate no longer; be the inventor, be the maker—that is the lesson we learn from this inspiration."[3] Hermann Bahr is on the same page, but he adds to the argument the fundamental question of a prescribed taste's validity by means of an imaginary conversation between opposing parties.[4] It is not difficult to identify Adolf Loos's position in this fictionalized discussion, who vehemently

Fig. 2 Revolving bookcase, London, Christmas exhibition at the AMAI, 1897
MAK, KI 7268-2

Fig. 3 Armchair by the Collinson & Lock company, London, Christmas exhibition at the AMAI, 1897
MAK, KI 7268-4

resisted the invention of a modern style from the outset. Loos gives his own view of the Christmas exhibition as early as 18 December 1897. He summarizes his fellow citizens' opinion of Scala's new exhibition policy by naming his introduction of the modern style, his presentation of Anglicism, and his emphasis on the practical in everyday objects. Though he accepts all this, he holds another dimension to be far more important: For him Scala had "discovered bourgeois household effects."[5] The exhibited reproductions of Chippendale, Sheraton, and Hepplewhite furniture are for Loos the expression of a tradition that had existed in England since the 18th century, namely that of an independent bourgeois consumer culture, which does not and did not exist in Austria. The evidence he provides for this is the Austrian practice of reusing old styles developed in the context of courtly, aristocratic society. This is dramatically at odds with the modern, democratically oriented self-image of the middle class around the turn of the century, whom both the Secessionists and Loos himself wanted to offer or provide a fitting formal expression.

The third winter exhibition (which opened on 21 November 1899) of the Imperial Royal Austrian Museum of Art and Industry under Scala already shows the impact of the Western European models on the domestic production of decorative arts in terms of a departure from the forms of Historicism. In his report on the exhibition, which he entitles "Der englische Stil" ("The English Style"), Bahr praises the progress made by the domestic producers with regard to the objects' tasteful and fine execution.[6] In the same breath, however, he criticizes the fact that the exhibited works— with the exception of the two rooms designed by Hoffmann and Joseph Maria Olbrich—copied the foreign products instead of being inspired by them. For him there is no difference between copying styles and cultures. Achieving the ideal of reviving domestic art by means of a contemporary artistic individualism—as called for by the Secessionists— is not supported by Scala's exhibition policy. The museum still sees itself in the role of a provider of exemplars for domestic trade. Coinciding with the administrative disaffiliation of the School of Arts and Crafts under its new director Baron Felician von Myrbach and its majority Secessionist new teaching staff including Hoffmann, Koloman Moser,

and Alfred Roller, the two institutes find their approaches in conflict. Only with the end of the Scala era in 1909 do the Secessionists once again find a home in the Austrian Museum under its new director Eduard Leisching. Hoffmann can now realize a series of his best exhibition designs and the museum acquires its first objects by the Wiener Werkstätte for its collection.

A chronological analysis of the acquisitions of the most important theoretical writings by John Ruskin, William Morris, and Walter Crane by the library of the Austrian Museum, the control room of the Austrian decorative-art reform of the 1860s, sheds light on the Viennese reception of the values specific to the English Arts & Crafts movement. This includes in particular the aspect of "pleasure in labor" touched on by Ruskin and Morris; despite making only a rudimentary appearance in the context of the Austrian decorative-art reform, this concept is crucial to the ideology of the Arts & Crafts movement. Ruskin's early works like *The Seven Lamps of Architecture* (1849) and *The Stones of Venice* (1851–1853) are only purchased in 1890 and 1887 respectively.[7] Their acquisition is undoubtedly directly related to the appointment of Jacob von Falke as the director (1885–1895) of the museum. After all, he is the first to take theoretical steps out of the formal dead end of Historicism and to call for the unity of design and execution processes— which had been expressed in England since Augustus Pugin—as an imperative necessity for the high-quality production of decorative arts.[8] Books illustrated by Walter Crane had already been purchased from 1879;[9] Ruskin's and William Morris's[10] theoretical writings are also incorporated into the museum's library from 1895. It cannot be a coincidence that this increased acknowledgment of English Arts & Crafts literature occurred at the same time as the founding of the Siebenerclub artists' association (1895) and the Vienna Secession (1897). From 1898 the first German translations of books by the aforementioned authors are published and in most cases are acquired by the museum immediately after their publication.[11] Simultaneously there is also an active interest in Vienna in the American Arts & Crafts movement. Hence the museum purchases the works *The King of the Golden River* by Ruskin and *Maud* by Lord Tennyson, both printed by Roycroft Press, a reformist community of

4 6 p. 49

Fig. 4 Joseph Maria Olbrich, interior, executed by August Ungethüm, winter exhibition at the AMAI, 1899
MAK, KI 7391-5

craftspeople and artists in East Aurora, N.Y. Alongside the theoretical texts on Arts & Crafts ideology, the English art magazine *The Studio* is not only named as an exemplary source of information in the official organ of the Vienna Secession, *Ver Sacrum*,[12] but can also be read in some Viennese coffeehouses. ▪

1 Manuscript "Österreichisches Kunstgewerbe Oktober 1928," MAK, KI 23506-7-1.
2 Bahr, Hermann, "Kunstgewerbe," in: id., *Secession*, Vienna 1900, 35 f.
3 Servaes, Franz, "Lieber spät als nie!," in: *Ver Sacrum* (1) 1 1898, 25.
4 Bahr, Hermann, "Der englische Stil," in: *Ver Sacrum* (1) 7 1898, 3 f.
5 Loos, Adolf, "Christmas Exhibition in the Austrian Museum (1897)," in: id., *Ornament and Crime: Thoughts on Design and Materials*, London 2019, 11–24: 14. Trans. Shaun Whiteside.
6 Bahr 1900 (see note 2), 182–187.
7 The following books by John Ruskin were also acquired by the library (publication date in brackets): *Examples etc. Illustrative of the Stones Of Venice* (1851)—acquired in 1878; *Giotto and his Works in Padua* (1854)—acquired in 1887; *The Elements of Perspective* (1859)—acquired in 1864; *St. Mark's Rest* (1877–1879)—acquired in 1885; *The Laws of Fésole* (1882)—acquired in 1883; *Val d'Arno* (1890)—acquired in 1890; *The King of the Golden River* (1900)—acquired in 1900; *Ausgewählte Werke* (1900)—acquired in 1900; *Grundlagen des Zeichnens* (1901)—acquired in 1901; *Das Adlernest* (1901)—acquired in 1901.
8 Von Falke, Jacob, *Ästhetik des Kunstgewerbes*, Stuttgart 1883, 61 f.: "Hence it is the purpose that first creates the form, the general form of the genre. However, there are moments, even beyond the artist's will, that contribute to the creation, or rather the design, of form, i.e., to its specialization, though without yet necessarily contributing to its individualization. That is the material from which the object is created and the technique by which it emerges. But the material is confronted with the purpose only in the second instance and with the technique in the third, because the choice of material depends on its fitness for purpose, and the choice of technique on the material. The artist is dependent on the purpose; he is bound by the general form, which is prescribed by the object's use. […] In the end, therefore, the decorative-art object is the result of all three factors—the purpose, the material, and the technique—to which is added as a fourth factor, antithetical to all three together: the artist's idea, intention."
9 Walter Crane: *The Baby's Opera* (1877)—acquired in 1879; *The Baby's Bouquet* (1878)—acquired in 1879 and 1895; *Columbia's Courtship* (n.d.)—acquired in 1895; *The Quiver of Love* (1876)—acquired in 1895; *A Romance of the Three Rs* (1886)—acquired in 1895; *Baby's Own Aesop* (1887)—acquired in 1895; *Legends of for Lionel* (1887)—acquired in 1895; *Flora's Feast* (1892)—acquired in 1895; *Household Stories from the Collection of the Bros. Grimm* (1893)—acquired in 1895; *Spenser's Faerie Queene* (1894–97)—acquired in 1897; *A Floral Fantasy in an Old English Garden* (1898)—acquired in 1899; *The Claims of Decorative Art* (1892)—acquired in 1895; *Of the Decorative Illustration of Books Old and New* (1896)—acquired in 1896; *The Bases of Design* (1898)—acquired in 1899. W. G. Paulson Townsend (preface by W. Crane): *Embroidery or the Craft of the Needle* (1899)—acquired in 1899. W. Crane: *Line and Form* (1900)—acquired in 1900. P. G. Konody: *The Art of Walter Crane* (1902)—acquired in 1902. W. Crane: *Ideals in Art* (1905)—acquired in 1905; *An Artist's Reminiscences* (1907)—acquired in 1907.
10 Interestingly the writings of Morris are only acquired when the German edition is published.
11 John Ruskin (see note 7). William Morris: *Die Kunst und die Schönheit der Erde* (1901), *Kunstgewerbliches Sendschreiben* (1901), *Kunsthoffnungen und Kunstsorgen* (1901), *Ein Paar Winke über das Kunstzeichnen* (1902).
12 *Ver Sacrum* (1) 2 1898, 24; (1) 4 1898, 24.

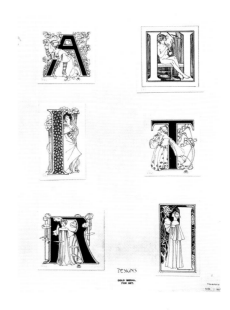

Fig. 5 Margaret Thompson, designs for initials, *Ausstellung von Arbeiten englischer Kunstgewerbe- u. Fachschulen* [Exhibition of Works by English Arts-and-Crafts & Specialist Schools] at the AMAI, 1898
MAK, KI 7332-45

Fig. 1 JH, design for the Secession pavilion, May 1897
Theatermuseum, Vienna, Alfred Roller's estate, TM 1598
© KHM-Museumsverband

Rainald Franz

"Deeply Honored to Have Been Nominated…"

Josef Hoffmann and the Founding of the Union of Austrian Artists Secession

"Deeply honored to have been nominated, I hereby venture to announce my accession to the Union of Austrian Artists. Respectfully yours, Josef Hoffmann." With this letter from 27 January 1897, Josef Hoffmann joined the Vereinigung bildender Künstler Österreichs (Union of Austrian Artists), which had been constituted in Vienna's Künstlerhaus, at the suggestion of the working committee.[1] Having recently returned from his state-funded travels through Italy,[2] been employed at Otto Wagner's private studio, and become a member of the Künstlerhaus (Vienna Artists' Society), the young architect thereby made a decision that would prove pivotal in his entire subsequent career: he had committed himself to rejuvenation and internationalization in all areas of art, architecture, and the decorative arts. At this point in time, the Secessionists still believed that they could reform the Künstlerhaus—strongly influenced by the art of Vienna's Ringstraße and its protagonists—from within.[3] Recent research into and publications on the background to this *ver sacrum* (or sacred spring, as this era came to be known) also clarify the role played by Josef Hoffmann in this period of change.[4] In 1897 he himself described this time as follows:

> "Much had happened […]. Wagner had some great commissions to accomplish for the city. The urban railway was in the process of being built, and straight away and for a short time I found work in Otto Wagner's epoch-making studio. Meetings with painters, architects and sculptors, whom I was friends with, indicated new directions; a dissatisfaction with the artistic life of Vienna, which seemed to us increasingly shallow, soon brought us into contact with revolutionary forces which were striving for change and spurred on by developments worldwide, which we had meanwhile learnt about. Klimt, Moll, Engelhart, Krämer, Wagner and Olbrich wanted to have nothing more to do with the manner of exhibition customary in the Künstlerhaus […]."[5]

The discussions in which he partook in the Siebener-Club, with fellow students and his teacher Otto Wagner at the academy, and later in Wagner's studio, transformed Josef Hoffmann into an important protagonist of this fresh start and into a networker in the artists' union.[6] The Secession gave the 27-year-old the opportunity to try his hand at every area of applied art and architecture, and it would also pave the way for his professorship at the School of Arts and Crafts.[7] The group of 40 Secessionists who finally left the Künstlerhaus on 24 May 1897 due to insurmountable differences of

opinion—all of them established male artists in their thirties to fifties, sculptors, painters, and architects from all over the monarchy—was united by their endeavor to liberate themselves from provincialism, to reevaluate the relationship to art, and to encourage an exchange of ideas and opinions with the most progressive artists in Europe. Important figures from within the Künstlerhaus joined forces with them: Despite only becoming a member of the Secession in October 1899, Otto Wagner—as a member of the architects' club at the Künstlerhaus—was already intensively involved in the "boys'" theorization in the fields of architecture and the decorative arts and he both directly and indirectly influenced the development of the Secession building's architecture through his students Josef Hoffmann and Joseph Maria Olbrich.[8] Gustav Klimt joined the future Secessionists in fall 1896 during the initial discussions about founding the union and would go on to be elected president of the Union of Austrian Artists on 3 April 1897. From the outset he and Josef Hoffmann were united by their shared interest in surface and spatial design, with whose impact they were able to experiment in the graphic and spatial art of the Secession.[9]

Hoffmann's Architectural Plans during the Secession's Founding

The "boys" at the Künstlerhaus had first considered constructing their own exhibition building as early as the fall of 1896.[10] On 10 January 1897 the preparatory committee of the Union of Austrian Artists applied to the interior ministry for building permission.[11] In their application they request a parcel of land for the construction of a "pavilion for exhibition purposes realized with artistic elegance" on the former parade ground of the Franz Joseph barracks near the Wollzeile.[12] Alfred Roller, the secretary from Brno and later one of Josef Hoffmann's teaching colleagues at the School of Arts and Crafts, and Joseph Maria Olbrich, Hoffmann's friend from the academy, supplied initial sketches that prove their involvement in planning this precursor to the future Secession building. Furthermore, the student of Wagner and later president of the Secession Otto Schönthal emphasized the important role played by Wagner's studio in planning the Secession building. He wrote of the "founding of the Secession, which was set on course by the Wagner studio. All preparations were carried out in strict confidence

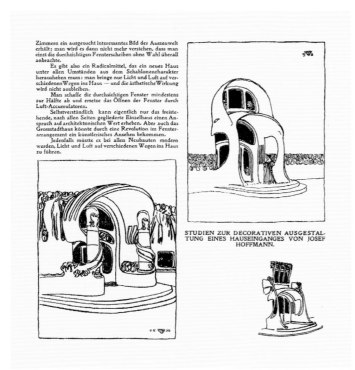

Fig. 2 JH, study on the decorative
design of a house entrance
VS (I) 7 1898, 16

Fig. 3 JH, architectural study
VS (I) 7 1898, 23

down to the smallest detail and only when everything was ascertained did one come forward."[13] Furloughed from his work in Wagner's studio, it was Schönthal who drew the submission plans for the Secession building for Olbrich; they were then corrected by Olbrich and the builder Anton Krasny, "whom Hoffmann had so interested in constructing the building that he too was considered a co-conspirator. And Wagner took part in all preparations with advice and perhaps the most enthusiasm."[14] Josef Hoffmann was already involved in planning the new Secession building at this point. In 1896 he had responded to the call for tenders for the new construction of a theater in Pilsen with a project created together with his colleague from the Wagner school Franz Krásný (1865–1947). Their design received one of the two highest awards. Together with Krásný Hoffmann then also took part in the competition to construct the trades bank in Prague in 1897.[15] The original exhibition pavilion on the Wollzeile, with a design from Olbrich's hand, was discussed by Vienna City Council on 23 March 1897.[16] It is known that Josef Hoffmann produced façade designs and floor plans for the building on the back of a sheet of text in late May 1897.[17] All these sketches stemmed from an internal call for tenders for pavilion plans from within the Secession, in which Josef Hoffmann was invited to participate even before he had become a full member of the union.[18] In his design the front section of the pavilion manages without lateral pylons; in their place there stand two trees. The basic ideas of the plan—an arch with vegetal edging—would be reused by Josef Hoffmann in 1900 in his plans for the Apollo candle factory's shop in Vienna and for the room of the School of Arts and Crafts in the Austrian pavilion at the Paris World's Fair.[19]

1

12 p. 23

19 p. 27

Josef Hoffmann's Graphics for the Early Days of the Secession

In a meeting on 21 July 1897 the founding members of the Union of Austrian Artists Secession adopted the resolution to publish their own magazine under the title *Ver Sacrum*. As the first modern art magazine in Austria, *Ver Sacrum* became a testing ground for the ideas of the Secession's artists—including Josef Hoffmann who officially joined the union during that same session—often before these ideas could physically take shape in exhibitions. As an extremely active member of the working committee, he was crucial to the success of the new concept, namely as the designer of the *Ver Sacrum* magazine, the "leading and model organ of modern art,"[20] work on which had started in 1897, even before the construction of the union's own exhibition building. In all six volumes of the publication produced between the first issue in January 1898 and 1903, the same weight was attached to the graphic and artistic content as to the art theoretical articles and literary texts; *Ver Sacrum* had not only an artistic editorial team but also a literary one. Until the magazine was discontinued in 1903, its graphic design corresponded to that of the Secession's exhibition catalogs.

Even in the very first issue of *Ver Sacrum* (January 1898), the talents that would leave their mark on the Secession's style with their abstracting surface art—with Josef Hoffmann, Joseph Maria Olbrich, and Koloman Moser at the forefront—stand out from the more naturalistic artists. For the first issues of *Ver Sacrum* and the catalog for the 1st Secession exhibition in the Gartenbaugebäude (home to the Viennese horticultural society), Hoffmann created vignettes and architectural studies entirely in line with the strict architectural style of the Wagner school, which resemble the stations of

3

8 p. 22

Fig. 4 JH, woven fabric
Ver Sacrum Hügl [Ver
Sacrum Hills], executed by
J. Backhausen & Söhne
(design no. 4347), 1902
Backhausen Archive, BA05663

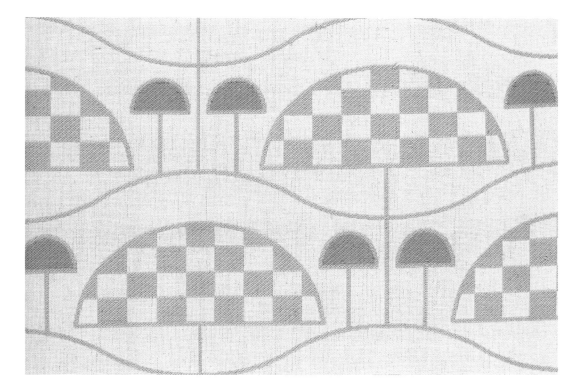

the Stadtbahn (urban light railway) under construction at the time and prove the influence on Hoffmann of details from antiquity, such as the herm and decorative border (*Ver Sacrum* (I) 7 1898, 26), and in the case of the *Studien zur decorativen Ausgestaltung eines Hauseinganges* [Studies on the Decorative Design of a House Entrance] (*VS* (I) 7 1898, 16) point the way to an architectural approach informed by

French Art Nouveau and aligned with forms from nature. The graphic line would henceforth become a leitmotif in Hoffmann's spatial designs, too, transferring the interplay between surface and space into and onto the Secession building. For Josef Hoffmann the founding of the Secession launched the "multimedia" design work that would go on to define his entire subsequent career.

1   The enrollment declaration can be found in Alfred Roller's estate, which is held at the Theatermuseum in Vienna. Published in: Pausch, Oskar, *Gründung und Baugeschichte der Wiener Secession. Mit Erstedition des Protokollbuchs von Alfred Roller*, Vienna 2006, 151 f.

2   Hoffmann had been awarded the state grant known as the Rome Prize, see the article "'It Was No Simple Matter to […] Reach an Understanding of the Real Sense of Building.' Josef Hoffmann: Studies at the Vienna Academy" by Rainald Franz in this catalog.

3   Bisanz-Prakken, Marian, "Der 'Heilige Frühling' der Wiener Secession, Secession und Ver Sacrum – Anfänge und Programmatik," in: id., *Heiliger Frühling, Gustav Klimt und die Anfänge der Wiener Secession 1895–1905*, exh. cat. Graphische Sammlung Albertina Vienna, Vienna 1998, 13: "The very first discussions about the founding of a new union within the Künstlerhaus Society took place in fall 1896 between representatives of the Hagengesellschaft and the Siebener-Club, as well as with other members of the Künstlerhaus." According to Pausch 2006 (see note 1), 26, "in fact only a fraction of those in favor of reform wanted the split, while moderates like Klimt, [Edmund] Hellmer, and Otto Wagner advised a separate union under the umbrella of the Künstlerhaus." On this see also: Ankwicz-Kleehoven, Hans, "Die Anfänge der Secession," in: *Alte und Moderne Kunst* (5) 6/7 1960, 6 ff.

4   Pausch 2006 (see note 1); Bisanz-Prakken 1998 (see note 3); Husslein-Arco, Agnes/Weidinger,

Alfred (eds.), *Gustav Klimt/Josef Hoffmann: Pioneers of Modernism*, exh. cat. Belvedere Vienna, Munich 2011.

5   Noever, Peter/Pokorný, Marek (eds.), *Josef Hoffmann. Selbstbiographie/Autobiography*, Ostfildern 2009, 91. Trans. Bernd Magar and Andrew Oakland.

6   Pichler, Gerd, "Der Siebener-Club," in: Leopold, Rudolf/Pichler, Gerd (eds.), *Koloman Moser 1868–1918*, exh. cat. Leopold Museum Vienna, Munich 2007, 38–47. See also the article "'It Was No Simple Matter to […] Reach an Understanding of the Real Sense of Building.' Josef Hoffmann: Studies at the Vienna Academy" by Rainald Franz in this catalog.

7   Franz, Rainald, "Muster für die Metropole," in: Pokorný, Marek/Ambroz, Miroslav (eds.), *Die Wiener Secession und die Moderne 1900–1925, Kunstgewerbe und Fotografien in den Böhmischen Ländern*, Brno 2005, 32.

8   Pausch 2006 (see note 1), 36.

9   Franz, Rainald, "Gustav Klimt and Josef Hoffmann as Reformers of the Graphic Arts and Interior Design in the Founding Phase of the Vienna Secession and the Wiener Werkstätte," in: Husslein-Arco/Weidinger 2011 (see note 4), 36–48.

10 *Katalog der II. Kunstausstellung der Vereinigung bildender Künstler Österreichs*, Vienna 1898, 3.

11 Printed in Pausch 2006 (see note 1), appendix A, 168.

12 Constructed after 1848, the defense barracks was only razed during the completion of the Ringstraße around the turn of the century. It was

located to the north of the Ringstraße in what is now the Stubenviertel.

13 Kapfinger, Otto/Krischanitz, Adolf, *Die Wiener Secession. Das Haus: Entstehung, Geschichte, Erneuerung*, Vienna/Graz/Cologne 1986, 137n17.

14 Ibid.

15 Sekler, Eduard F., *Josef Hoffmann: The Architectural Work*, Princeton, NJ 1985, 27. Trans. Eduard F. Sekler and John Maass. Hoffmann's designs for the Pecuniis Potestas (trade bank) can be seen in: *Der Architekt* (III) 1897, 21, plate 42; for Ars Arti (Bohemian people's theater), see: ibid., 9, 10, plates 17, 18.

16 Municipal and Provincial Archives of Vienna, Q 12-143908/1897; Pausch 2006 (see note 1), 14.

17 Illustrated in Pausch 2006 (see note 1), 132.

18 On Josef Hoffmann's spatial art at the Secession, cf. the article "Interior Design as a Work of Art: From 'Brettlstil' to Viennese Style" by Christian Witt-Dörring in this catalog, and Pausch 2006 (see note 1), 16, 64. On the constructed Secession building, see: Pötschner, Angelina, "The Secession Building. A Viennese Modernist Manifesto," in: *Coup de Fouet* 28 2016, 16–23.

19 The corresponding drawings, including *Artibus*, can be seen in: *Ver Sacrum* (1) 7 1898. On the Apollo candle shop, see Sekler 1985 (see note 15), CR 31, 258; on the Paris World's Fair, see ibid., CR 38, 260 f.

20 Hevesi, Ludwig, "Ver Sacrum," in: id., *Acht Jahre Secession (März 1897–Juni 1905)*, Vienna 1906, 36.

Fig. 1 JH, bed with nightstand and trunk from furnishings for Ernst Stöhr's
studio building in St. Johann am Wocheneinersee/Lake Bohinj, ca. 1898
Spruce, formerly stained green
MAK, H 2708

Christian Witt-Dörring

Interior Design as a Work of Art

From "Brettlstil" to Viennese Style 1898–1900

At the opening of the 1st exhibition of the Secession in the rooms of the Gartenbaugesellschaft (Viennese horticultural society) on 25 March 1898, Josef Hoffmann makes his first public appearance as a freelance architect. Together with Joseph Maria Olbrich, he is responsible for the architectural and decorative design of the exhibition. It is the Secessionists' first step on the path toward an independent, Austrian, modern artistic expression. Initially they are still dependent on exemplars developed in Western Europe, especially England and Belgium. These models are not only theoretical but also formal. On the one hand, the faithful copying of old styles—as criticized by Otto Wagner since the 1880s—is deemed an anachronistic form of expression for contemporary social and technological developments. On the other hand, mechanical labor is considered the chief culprit behind the aesthetic and social brutalization of the time; individual artistic expression in artisanal production is seen as an antidote with the ability to cure these social ills. Consequently, every aspect of everyday life must be reassessed in terms of both content and form. A claim to *Gesamtgestaltung*—or total design—thus arises, the aim of which is the creation of a Gesamtkunstwerk—or total work of art—in tandem with artistically designed objects. The prerequisite for this construct is the unity of the arts, as called for by William Morris, which rejects any hierarchical difference between the so-called high and low arts. The fine and applied or decorative arts are therefore equal partners in the realization of a Gesamtkunstwerk, which in the field of interior design finds its specifically Viennese incarnation in *Raumkunst* ("room art," i.e., interior design as a work of art).

Not a private living space but the ephemeral world of exhibition design is the testing ground on which Hoffmann is able to realize his new ideas. Alongside the central room, Hoffmann designs the exhibition office, the so-called *Ver Sacrum* room. It offers, as Ludwig Hevesi so aptly remarks, "an overall impression of modern room furnishings."[1] Both the furniture itself and wall and ceiling divisions are worked from the simplest of softwood planks, which are then stained blue and adorned with copper fittings. This is what gives the works from the first two years of Vienna's art spring their contemporary stylistic label: "Brettlstil" (plank style).[2] The main formal accents of this style are—in addition to modest

materials, such as planks of spruce or alderwood—a decidedly high-contrast and strong color scheme and above all the meandering, curved line, which unlike its French and Belgian creators is never applied three-dimensionally but rather only ever in its flat variety. It is an aesthetic that clamors for the viewers' attention, exacting their subjective reaction. It demands the individuality that is abhorred by the good taste of established society. In order to reach a public that yearns for harmony and is distrustful of the new, this provocation is part of a customary marketing strategy. It is used as such by the young generation of artists around 1900 and even Adolf Loos understood that this was the purpose behind the *Ver Sacrum* room's furnishings: "Although I cannot in any way declare myself in agreement with the furniture, it should nevertheless be considered that in our stagnant circumstances an awakening of the spirits could only be achieved if one made a really loud and really strident hullabaloo."[3]

Somewhat over six months after the 1st exhibition of the Secession, the jubilee exhibition to celebrate the 50th anniversary of Emperor Franz Josef I's coronation opens on the grounds of the Prater park on 18 October 1898. Quite probably at the recommendation of his teacher Otto Wagner, who is himself represented in the exhibition by his fixtures for the bedroom and bathroom of his apartment on Köstlergasse, Hoffmann is commissioned with designing a room in which to present the treasure binding of *Viribus Unitis. Das Buch vom Kaiser*. While the design for the book's cover, as well as its endpapers and some vignettes, are from Hoffmann's hand, his fellow artist Koloman Moser contributes whole-page allegorical illustrations. However, with the aid of bolts of fabric stretched vertically over the walls and in combination with display stands against the walls, Hoffmann manages to create a holistic spatial impression, this time in white and green.

Today it is difficult to imagine the bold chromaticity of early Secessionist interiors. Compared to the brown and black or white and gold rooms that dominated until that point, the Secessionist palette amounted to a revolution. Otto Wagner's colorfully tiled façade on the apartment building at Linke Wienzeile 40 must have had a similar impact on the contemporary Viennese public as a billboard for

≡VER SACRUM-ZIMMER.≡
ENTWORFEN VON JOSEF
HOFFMANN. O. M.

Fig. 3 JH, book cover for *Viribus Unitis. Das Buch vom Kaiser*, 1898
MAK, BI 31441

Fig. 2 JH, *Ver Sacrum* room, 1st Secession exhibition in the rooms of the Viennese horticultural society, 1898
VS (1) 5/6 1898, 7

nascent Modernism.[4] The interior designs painted in water-color are able to give us some indication of this once brightly colored world: Over the years light exposure has faded the formerly colorful stains applied to the large-pored surface of coniferous woods. For example, the original green stain of fixtures designed by Hoffmann in 1898 for the painter Ernst Stöhr can only be appreciated on the parts that are concealed from sunlight. This unaccustomed vibrancy for furniture in no way contradicts the repeated demand for truth to the material, which inevitably results from criticisms of the unlimited use of ersatz techniques and ersatz materials in the course of mass production. Indeed, Hoffmann writes in his programmatic article on the tastes of his time: "Only such and many other aspects—such as painting and staining, the latter exclusively in shades that do not imitate any other wood, the former where another color application technique is impossible, e.g., pure white."[5]

These initial experiences and reactions to his works are followed in 1899 by a pivotal year for Hoffmann's future career and development. On 1 May, at the age of just 28, he is installed as professor of architecture at the School of Arts and Crafts.[6] His appointment is part of a fundamental reform and restructuring process at the School of Arts and Crafts, which also involves the engagement of Koloman Moser as professor of painting. One of the driving forces behind the verbalization and implementation of this reform is Otto Wagner, who considers the practice of stylistic imitation followed and promoted until that time and the scientification of art to be divorced from reality and in opposition to contemporary artistic developments. He holds individual artistic expression alone—as championed by Modernism—capable

of paving the way to the future. Consequently, his recommendations include the appointment of four new professors, without actually naming names. From the description of their artistic profiles, however, it is not hard to deduce that he is quite probably implying two colleagues from his studio, the architects Joseph Maria Olbrich and Josef Hoffmann. Wagner refers to their artistic achievements in the context of the Secession and to the fact that both of them have "a distinct 'individuality,' a trait that I value all the more because through it their works take on a local character, so do not stray into foreign territory. All are quite aware of the mistake made by foreigners (lack of the structural)."[7] With this criticism Wagner is alluding to the curvilinear, French-Belgian variety of Art Nouveau, which invokes the national roots of the French Régence style of the Louis XV period.

His new role as a professor at the School of Arts and Crafts, as well as his regular activities in the context of Secession exhibitions, enables Hoffmann to attain a public presence that has an impact on his first private commissions and to move into an apartment—furnished according to his own designs—only a short walk away from the Secession at Magdalenenstraße 12 in Vienna's 6th district. Stylistically, these interior decoration jobs[8] can still be classed as "Brettl-stil." The curved line is now found mostly only in decorative elements, while the straight line is preferred for furniture, where it is combined to create simple geometric shapes. Carcass furniture is mostly interpreted by Hoffmann as part of the wall design and as a string of components belonging to a single whole. As individual pieces of furniture and as space-defining and -dividing elements, they possess a structurally and tectonically clear vocabulary. The only interior

Fig. 4 JH, central hall of the
5th Secession exhibition, 1899
DI (1) 1900, 25

decoration jobs from this creative period to still survive in
their entirety are part of the Bergerhöhe farmhouse that

9 was adapted into a country house for Paul Wittgenstein,

4 5 6 p. 20 the brother of Karl Wittgenstein and director of the iron-
works in St. Ägyd, Lower Austria. It is the last commission
that Hoffmann realizes in the "Brettlstil" and its associated
bright color scheme. For example, the living room is made
of coniferous wood stained green and the entrance hall and
staircase is red. In late 1899 Hoffmann signs the living room's

10 wainscoting "JH 99"—like a painting. Here Hoffmann is
making a programmatic statement, which elevates interior
design to an equal partner alongside the other arts: it has
now become *Raumkunst*. That same year, when Adolf Loos
publishes in *Ver Sacrum* and suggests that he furnish the
Secession's meeting room but is refused by Hoffmann,[9] Loos
also signs pieces of furniture—the dining room furnishings
for Eugen Stössler—with his initials "AL." Loos's signature
on the buffet strikes me as symptomatic of the potential at
this point in time for the two protagonists of Viennese Modernism's second generation to coexist peacefully if alter-
natively. Henceforth, however, Loos's maxim stands in
marked contrast to Hoffmann: "But above all, modern man
perceives the amalgamation of art with the practical object
as the greatest abasement to which it could be subjected."[10]

Designed by Josef Hoffmann and executed by the Vien-

6 nese carpenter Anton Pospischil, the dining room for the

15 p. 25 winter exhibition, which opened at the Imperial Royal
Austrian Museum of Art and Industry (today's MAK) on 21
November 1899, marks a clear stylistic turning point in Hoffmann's oeuvre that is symptomatic of his formal aesthetic
development. The curved line has served its purpose. The

Fig. 5 JH, *Viribus Unitis* room, *Kaiser-Jubiläumsausstellung*
[Imperial Jubilee Exhibition] in the grounds of the Prater park,
1898. Wall and ceiling white with green stripes, fields
of patterned cretonne, furniture and wood paneling made
of alder stained green
DK (2) 1898, 206

Fig. 6 JH, dining room,
executed by Anton Pospischil,
winter exhibition at the
AMAI, 1899
MAK, KI 7391-4

plank no longer appears as an independent aesthetic construction element in carcass furniture; it is nothing more than a means to an end to facilitate a cohesive stereometric entity. In other words, even the materiality of the softwood plank no longer has any aesthetic value; instead it serves merely as the bearer of an expensive veneer or is colorfully painted. As such Hoffmann and the Secessionists have emancipated themselves from their stylistic models abroad after only two years and successfully arrived at an autonomous modern Austrian style. Just one year later, on 3 November 1900, the Secessionists will enter into competition with international artists at the opening of their 8th exhibition, which is dedicated exclusively to modern decorative arts. ■

Figs. 7, 8 JH, Hoffmann's own
living room, Magdalenenstraße 12,
Vienna's 6th district, ca. 1900
DK (7) 1901, 113

Fig. 9 JH, living area in the Bergerhöhe country house, 1899
Courtesy of the Michael Huey and Christian Witt-Dörring Photo Archive

Fig. 10 JH's signature on the wainscoting of the living area in the Bergerhöhe country house, 1899
© Paul Salzer

1   Hevesi, Ludwig, *Acht Jahre Secession*, Vienna 1906, 14.
2   Ibid.
3   Loos, Adolf, "Ein Wiener Architekt," in: *Dekorative Kunst* (2) 1898, 227.
4   Bahr, Hermann, "Kunstgewerbe," in: id., *Secession*, Vienna 1900, 35.
5   Hoffmann, Josef, "Einfache Möbel," in: *Das Interieur* (2) 1901, 203.
6   Personnel card in the archive of the University of Applied Arts Vienna.
7   Printed minutes of the meeting from 30 Jan 1899; MAK, Zl. 259/1899, 6.
8   Studio for Max Kurzweil, Dr. Walter Brix's law firm, Gustav Pollak's villavilla and apartment.
9   Sekler, Eduard F., *Josef Hoffmann: The Architectural Work*, Princeton, NJ 1985, 30. Trans. Eduard F. Sekler and John Maass.
10 Loos, Adolf, "Kulturentartung [1908]," in: Glück, Franz (ed.), *Adolf Loos. Sämtliche Schriften 1*, Vienna/Munich 1962, 271–275: 274.

Fig. 1 JH, house for Ing. Alexander Brauner on the
Hohe Warte, Vienna, 1905–1906, attic floor
MAK, WWF 102-106-1

Matthias Boeckl

From Life Reform to Bourgeois Daily Life

The Villa Colony on the Hohe Warte

Originally planned as an *artists'* colony, the cluster of houses on the Hohe Warte that was later euphemistically called a "*villa* colony"[1] tested out practical strategies for realizing the Gesamtkunstwerk—or total work of art—ideal. Its basic conception was thus also a contribution to the international life reform movement. The site lies on a hilltop in the residential and garden district of Döbling in the west of Vienna. Comprising a duplex and six neighboring detached single-family houses, it was constructed between 1900 and 1911.[2] They were the first residential buildings that the 30-year-old Josef Hoffmann was able to plan in Vienna. With their completion and subsequent detailed publication in extensive photo stories in the new architecture and interior magazines,[3] Hoffmann laid a solid foundation for his career as the favorite planner of houses and apartments among a wealthy, art-loving generation whose parents were successful mid-19th-century *Gründerzeit* entrepreneurs. Eduard F. Sekler aptly characterized this milieu as follows:

> "The financial independence of the *haute bourgeoisie* enabled this group to devote themselves entirely to an ideal of self-realization through cultural refinement. The arts were indispensable for achieving that avant-gardist exclusivity which could engender spiritual superiority—whether toward the Philistine *petite bourgeoisie* or toward the traditionalist old nobility."[4]

This self-realization could be acted out perfectly in the detached suburban single-family house with its own garden. This new building type had arisen with industrialization, rapid urbanization, and the growth of the middle class in the 19th century as an affordable miniature of the lordly villa with park positioned in the middle of the landscape. The art revolution around 1900 used it as a means to demonstrate the movement's notion of an individualistic, artistic, and meaningful lifestyle. Hoffman's houses on the Hohe Warte fulfilled this model function particularly effectively: the "discovery" of these buildings and gardens by Adolphe Stoclet and Suzanne Stoclet-Stevens, the young Belgian magnates who lived in Vienna at the time, while walking around the Hohe Warte in 1904 was followed immediately by them commissioning Hoffmann with what would become his architectural magnum opus, Stoclet House in Brussels.

Vision of an Artists' Town

The enterprise's beginnings were described by Ludwig Hevesi in 1899 as the conspiring group of rebels' artistic fantasy:

> "No wonder that the brotherhood wants to well-nigh enforce on itself a kind of form […]. Rent an old abbey and live in it together. Or settle down 'in the caves of the Bisamberg mountain'—which would obviously first have to be dug out."[5]

This vision of a monastic community of artists is consistent with the pseudo religious rhetoric of the Secession, which had been founded two years previously and used expressions like its slogan "sacred spring," as well as sacralizing arrangements for exhibitions and buildings. Together with its own exhibition building and in-house media like the magazine *Ver Sacrum*, its intention was to gradually give rise to a complete ideal counterworld in line with artistic criteria. It was believed that the humane nature of the aesthetic would automatically ensure equal social conditions. This aesthetic social vision of the Secessionists is prefigured in William Morris's utopian futuristic novel *News from Nowhere (or An Epoch of Rest)*, published in 1890, and is also quoted in the Wiener Werkstätte's *Arbeitsprogramm*:

> "The [Wiener Werkstätte] shall create a caesura for us on domestic soil amid the cheerful clamor of handicraft and be welcomed by those who affirm their allegiance to Ruskin and Morris. We appeal to all those who consider culture in this sense to be valuable."[6]

The ideal of a monastic community of innovative artists seeking alternative means of living and producing is rooted not only in the English Arts & Crafts movement but also in Romanticism. As early as 1810 a Viennese group of painters called the Brotherhood of St. Luke moved into the monastery of Sant'Isidoro in Rome to work together and study medieval Italian art; they would later be known as the Nazarenes. Numerous other artists' colonies would emerge prior to 1900 in which the theism of the Nazarenes was replaced by an (equally religious) experience of nature: they include the artists' colonies of Barbizon, Szolnok, Worpswede, and Dachau. The ideal lifestyle model of such origin seekers who were critical of civilization was thus common knowledge in Vienna

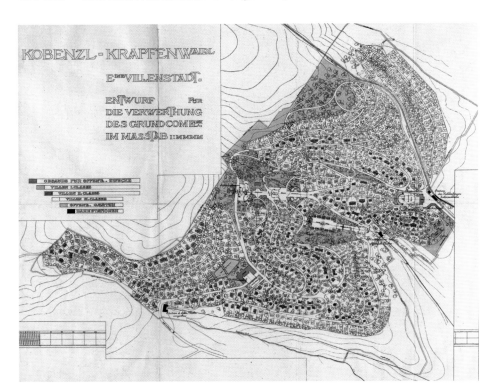

Fig. 2 Joseph Maria Olbrich, design for a villa town on the Cobenzl-Krapfenwaldl site near Vienna, 1896
Vienna City Library, Printed Works Collection

around 1900. It would therefore have been surprising if the latest revolutionary group of artists had not also striven for their own exclusive community upon departing from the established institution of the Künstlerhaus (Vienna Artists' Society) and erecting their own exhibition building. After the Secession's 1st exhibition had opened on 26 March 1898, Olbrich called for

> "a wide and empty and open field where we can create our world, with a temple of work in a copse for art and arts and crafts, and around it the cabins in which we live, in which our spirit would dominate the entire site, even every chair and pot."[7]

In fact, the main reason why this project—originally envisaged for Vienna's villa district of Hietzing—was not realized was the resounding success of the Secession's first appearances. At the instigation of Otto Wagner and the progressive head of department and education minister Wilhelm von Hartel (1896–1905), Vienna's art revolution was immediately institutionalized in the form of the appointment of Josef Hoffmann and Koloman Moser in 1899 as professors at the state School of Arts and Crafts.

From Utopia to Market Reality

Due to their teaching commitments and the studios at the School of Arts and Crafts,[8] the desired "temple of work" had become superfluous for the movement's most important protagonists even before they had actually started planning it. Furthermore, Joseph Maria Olbrich's appointment in Darmstadt—again in 1899—had robbed the artists' colony project of its main driver right at the outset. As no initiative by the city administration and no entrepreneurial interest by a commercial or nonprofit backer was on the horizon—as had been the case in 1892 with the founding of the "Familienhäuser-Colonie Nymphenburg-Gern" in Munich by the builder Jakob Heilmann, who offered the houses specifically to artists from the Dachau painters' colony and the academy—the scheme soon fragmented into a handful of houses that were constructed and paid for independently by the

artists themselves. Moreover, there was hardly any precedent in Vienna for suburban *Siedlungen* (housing developments) or garden cities being planned uniformly by private construction companies or for respective zoning by the city administration—in contrast to Berlin, for example, where the resourceful entrepreneur Johann Anton Wilhelm von Carstenn had erected the Lichterfelde villa colony after his own plans from 1865. In Vienna this town planning model was only practiced by the Wiener Cottage Verein (Vienna Cottage Society) around the Ringstraße architect Heinrich von Ferstel and his fellow architect Carl von Borkowski, which had constructed a suburban "villa" neighborhood (the buildings are actually single- and multifamily houses) from 1872 at the foot of the Türkenschanze (old Turkish fortifications) in line with strict community rules. It was intended that the buildings would give "in their entirety a pleasant, utterly unique, and yet uniform impression that conveys the character of the city and countryside most splendidly."[9] Commercial activities were strictly prohibited in this exclusively residential area.

Despite the loss of the original urban planning and social dimension, on the Hohe Warte a reference project nevertheless emerged that was a paragon of the Modernist movement's aims and was no longer tailored exclusively to the needs of artists: At its heart was daily life in an aesthetic environment of ornately designed interiors and gardens, which would create a sense of identity and whose suburban location immediately signalized a distancing from conventions. Working together in a studio building, such as that built by Olbrich in Darmstadt, was no longer an issue as the needs of the first artist-builders (painting, decorative arts, and photography studios) were too technically diverse, required no community center, and could be easily accommodated in the individual houses.[10] On the other hand, the later homeowners were not artists, meaning that they had no need for shared facilities and hence this central characteristic of collective lifestyles in other *Siedlungen* or colonies did not apply. Consequently, the neighborhood that arose on the Hohe Warte was in essence a "bourgeois bohemian" hybrid.

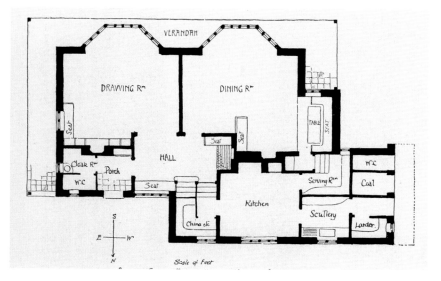

Figs. 3, 4 M. H. Baillie Scott, *An Artist's House*, 1897,
attic studio and ground floor plan
The Studio 1897, 28–35

Change of Planner from Olbrich to Hoffmann

Even the people for whom the very first houses on the Hohe Warte were built were not exclusively professional artists. The Secessionist friendship group was joined by two personalities who on the one hand were pioneers in the most progressive artistic medium—photography—and on the other followed a bourgeois career path and had ample means at their disposal: Dr. Friedrich Victor Spitzer (1854–1922) was an heir to sugar refineries and Dr. Hugo Henneberg (1863–1918) similarly had a solid middle-class lifestyle.[11] Also involved at the start was the enthusiastic collector of Modernism and Styrian industrialist Carl von Reininghaus, though he soon left. Among the Secessionists' own ranks only Carl Moll and Koloman Moser decided to participate in the project that now comprised just a handful of exemplary modern single-family houses. At this point Moll already owned a house with a garden in a prominent inner-city location: it had been built in 1895, the year he married Anna Schindler-Bergen, the widow of his teacher Emil Jakob Schindler, by the innovative Viennese developer Julius Mayreder at Theresianumgasse 6 in the vicinity of the two Rothschild palaces.[12] Koloman Moser, on the other hand, obviously had enough creditworthiness to build a small house thanks to his position as a professor at the School of Arts and Crafts.[13] Yet the future planner Josef Hoffmann, likewise a professor, would remain in his rental apartment on Magdalenenstraße in Vienna's Mariahilf district,[14] which he had furnished in 1899. Perhaps he preferred for personal reasons to lead a less public life than would have been possible at the heart of the planned artists' colony. Unlike most other prominent students of Otto Wagner,[15] Hoffmann refrained from flaunting his artistic approach in a single-family home of his own design, choosing instead to stay in an inner-city rental apartment for the rest of his life.[16]

Joseph Maria Olbrich had constructed the Secession's exhibition building in 1897/98 and demonstrated his great enthusiasm for the task of constructing an artist's home with the house for the poet and Young Vienna-supporter Hermann Bahr in Vienna's Hietzing district in 1899. Moreover, he had planned the interior of a city apartment for Friedrich Victor Spitzer, who would later become a homeowner in the villa colony, and converted the villa of the wine merchant Alfred Stifft as a reference project on the Hohe Warte. He had already gained experience in planning such a garden city-like *Siedlung* in 1896 with the project for the Cobenzl-Krapfenwaldl "Villenstadt" (villa town).[17] If he had not been appointed to Darmstadt in July 1899 by the enthusiastic art reformer the Grand Duke of Hesse and by Rhine, Ernest Louis—who was the same age as Olbrich and had been reigning since 1892—to realize precisely the same construction task of building an artists' colony as that which Olbrich had long been seeking, though on a much larger scale, then he would probably have moved to the Hohe Warte himself, much as he settled in a house of his own design on the Mathildenhöhe in Darmstadt in 1900. By his own admission he had already produced studies for the "Freundort" (friends' place), as he called the Viennese artists' colony project, in 1899. Yet Moll speaks only of a "beautiful portfolio with the overprint 'Freundort' and empty pages" being presented by Olbrich during his visit to Vienna (probably in the fall of 1899), which was—alongside Olbrich's now definitive relocation to Darmstadt—part of the reason for the planner being changed to Hoffmann.[18]

Moser-Moll Duplex, 1900/01

The failure of the artists' colony project led to what was now a villa colony not following any overarching plan but becoming established in several phases over a period of ten years. These were the defining years in Josef Hoffmann's early oeuvre in which a turbulent development can be traced in his work from the curvilinear style to the English model and what Eduard F. Sekler referred to as the "puristic" phase to the beginning of the classicizing stage in the Ast house, the final building on the Hohe Warte. As such the colony comprises an impressive concentration of Hoffmann's notions of the modern lifestyle in house and garden. Few other such programmatic suburban housing ensembles of early Modernism could be realized in this density and quality; they in-

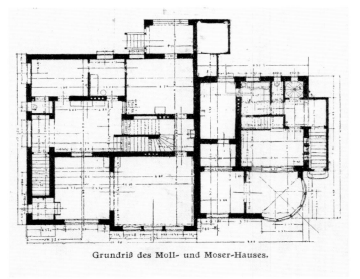

Grundriß des Moll- und Moser-Hauses.

Figs. 5, 6 JH, duplex for Koloman Moser and
Carl Moll on the Hohe Warte, Vienna, 1900/01,
garden view and ground floor plan
Der Architekt 1908, plate 85 and 1903, plate 91

Arts & Crafts movement it was used rather to symbolize artists harking back to old craft traditions, as evidenced for example by Mackay Hugh Baillie Scott's design for the *Artist's House*, which was described and illustrated in detail in *The Studio* in 1897, a widely read magazine in Vienna.[20] Baillie Scott's house has half-timbered façades and a high-ceilinged studio on the upper floor, similar to that found in Moser's half of the house on the Hohe Warte. For Moll's half Hoffmann also planned the furnishings for two rooms (in the other rooms Moll used his own old furniture), while Koloman Moser designed his interiors himself.

The Moser-Moll duplex for which Hoffmann also designed the gardens,[21] remained probably the only house on the Hohe Warte around which the everyday life of an artists' colony was able to develop, with mutual daily visits and art debates. Moll reports:

> "My neighbor Kolo Moser and I were wall to wall, and I thank not just this convenience but also the meeting of our minds for the stimulating conversation that lasted years. Moser lived with his mother and siblings; when the old lady went to bed at nine in the evening, he jumped over the fence, and over schnapps and cigarettes we chatted until almost eleven every day. Only his marriage estranged him from us and himself."[22]

On the Hohe Warte such spontaneous visits and countless mutual invitations, networking with the Secessionist milieu, and hosting foreign artists who had been invited by the Secession,[23] replaced the teamwork in a studio building that would have been the ideal in a genuine artists' colony.

Henneberg and Spitzer Houses, 1901–1903

The next two houses were already able to benefit from the experience gained with the Moser-Moll duplex, though as detached single-family houses they constituted slightly different building types and were constructed for clients who did not pursue exclusively artistic careers.[24] The lot on which the imaginative Henneberg house stands does not abut that of the Moser-Moll house, whereas that of the Spitzer house is the immediate neighbor of Moser's half of the duplex. In these projects Hoffmann went several steps further along his path to ever more radical formal reductions, which sim-

clude Olbrich's artists' colony on the Mathildenhöhe in Darmstadt (1900–1908), the buildings by Frank Lloyd Wright in Oak Park near Chicago (1889–1909), and the garden city artists' colony of Hohenhagen by the patron Karl-Ernst Osthaus (from 1909).

Hoffmann was most guided by the original ideal of an artists' colony in the first construction phase on Hohe Warte (1900–1902): his customers were two artists from the Secession and two bourgeois photographers who regularly exhibited at the Secession. In its building type and details, the first project—the Moser-Moll duplex—reveals a strong connection to the English model: the floor plans are loosely based on functional requirements, Moser's half of the house containing a drawing-room-like corner salon with polygonal bay windows, and purely ornamental half-timbering has been applied to the façades of the upper floors to create "atmosphere." Hoffmann had first experimented with half-timbering shortly beforehand in the staff residence of the Wittgenstein Forestry Administration in Hohenberg, though it was also used at this time by Olbrich and Max Fabiani.[19] Timber framing motifs had been part of the repertoire of country villas built by educated urbanites in Austria since the 1870s and—as there was no such architectural tradition in the eastern part of the country—were clearly to be understood as a cosmopolitan allusion to the English country house. Due to the medieval provenance of this motif, however, in the English

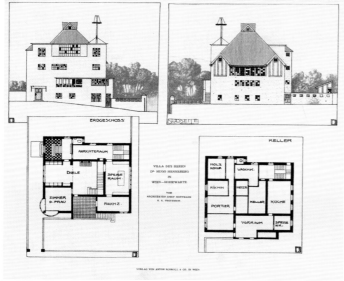

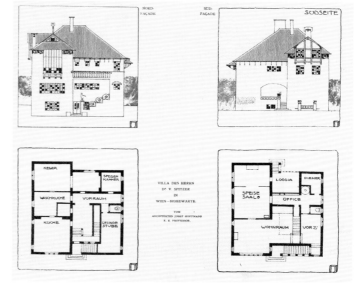

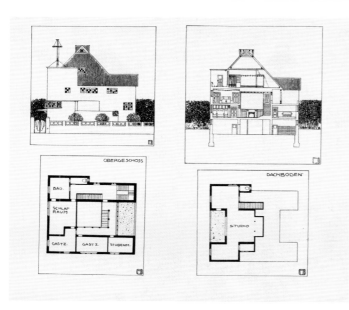

Figs. 7–12 JH, Dr. Hugo Henneberg's and Dr. Friedrich Victor
Spitzer's houses on the Hohe Warte, Vienna, 1900–1902,
elevations and floor plans

Der Architekt 1903, plate 90 (photos), 1901, plates 50–51 (plans)

Fig. 13 JH, Dr. Hugo Henneberg's house,
1900/01, attic studio
DI (4) 1903, 148

ultaneously started to penetrate ever more areas of environmental design and ultimately culminated—in terms of the
consistent application of the "nullform" that is the square—
in Sanatorium Westend in Purkersdorf, which was built three
years later. On this Eduard F. Sekler quotes Hoffmann himself:
"In retrospect, he said of this attitude that he had been particularly interested 'in the square as such and in the use of
black and white … because these clear elements never appeared in earlier styles.'"[25] Certainly in need of a footnote,[26]
this art historical argument is a definite understatement.
Above all it seems to stem more from the avant-garde's rhetoric of dissociating itself from Historicism than from the cultural
impact of discovering the elementary abstract world that ex-
ceeds internal debates in art. Indeed, with these infinitely
variable means infinite new cultural "identities" can theoreti-
cally (in an unintended analogy to the industrial production
they criticized) be constructed—a potential that Charles Rennie Mackintosh, Joseph M. Olbrich, Koloman Moser, and
Josef Hoffmann all discovered intuitively in 1900/01. The corresponding "theories" were only written later.[27]

In the Henneberg house, however, Hoffmann still uses a
broader palette of "atmospheric production" that employs
both classical elements, like the partially symmetrical structure of the "Tuscan villa" with a cornice in the Otto Wagner
style, and "English" aspects, like the purely decorative half-
timbering, the round bay window, open fireplaces, an up-
stairs studio, and for the first time a double-height hall as
the center of the house. Striven for as the achievement of
the Modernist movement, the unity of inside and out—"a
house the exterior of which would … have to reveal its interior"[28]—emerges particularly clearly in this project: the
contemporary publications of the interiors of the Henneberg
and Spitzer houses extend over 60 pages and present floor
plans on which the furniture and floor tiles are already
marked.[29]

In the Spitzer house—whose lot abuts the Moser-Moll
duplex—Hoffmann reduces the decorative media:

> "While the total impression made by the exterior of the Henne-
> berg house suffers from the architect's being carried away with
> joining different motifs, the general disposition of the house for
> Dr. Spitzer, approximately half a year later, was much more tranquil
> and unified. In this building the compositional elements of all

the facades belong to the same family and are applied more
sparingly, though not less effectively, as at the Henneberg
house."[30]

The Four Later Houses

The other houses in the villa colony were only erected some-
time later; their inner cohesion is less obvious than in the
three initial houses and already represents new stages in the
turbulent evolution of Hoffmann's early work and rapid succession of ever new forms of expression. Furthermore, the
building for Alexander Brauner (1905/06), the house for
Helene Hochstetter (1906/07), the second Moll house (1906/
07), and the villa for Eduard Ast (1909–1911) must be considered in connection with the Wiener Werkstätte, which
since its founding in 1903 had made significant contributions
to these projects. The three houses designed in 1905/06
translate the square motif that Hoffmann had "discovered"
five years previously into three dimensions (the building
shapes increasingly resemble a cube) and are crowned with
pavilion roofs typical of the era. The result is an elementary
geometry comprising cube and pyramid, which segued from
the purism of the years 1903–1905 with its climax in Sanatorium Westend into a new, playful phase. Four more years
later Hoffmann designed a home for his professional partner
of many years, the master builder and reinforced concrete
pioneer Eduard Ast. With its deeply sculptural decorative
elements and classicizing motifs, this house belongs to yet
another stage of Hoffmann's oeuvre, in which he vigorously
enriched his repertoire of motifs and combined classical and
vernacular traditions.[31] Examples are the Primavesi country
house, the Skywa-Primavesi villa, and the Austrian House at
the Werkbund exhibition in Cologne in 1914.

In this way the cluster of houses that originally started
out as an idealistic artists' project increasingly evolved into
a loose arrangement of solid middle-class modern residential
buildings whose individuality and privacy did not aspire to
promote any formally institutionalized communal artistic life.
The lack of community facilities, dedicated development
areas, and any master plan differentiates these buildings
from actual artists' colonies (such as the Mathildenhöhe in
Darmstadt) and from large reform *Siedlungen* like Hellerau

14 15 16 17
18 19 20 21

19 20 21

Fig. 14 JH, Ing. Brauner's house, 1905/06
MAK, WWF-102-103-1

Figs. 15–18 JH, Helene Hochstetter's house (top)
and Carl Moll's second house (below), 1906/07
MAK, MAK, WWF-104-202-1, 104-203-1, 104-215-1-1, and 104-214-1

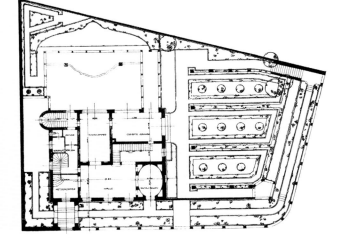

Figs. 19, 20 JH, Eduard Ast's villa, Vienna, 1909–1911,
street side and ground plan
Der Architekt 1911, plates 47, 56

in Dresden (constructed from 1909), which were strongly in-fluenced both formally and ideologically by the English garden-city movement.[32] In Austria this artistically inspired and socially critical construction of reform developments could not gain a foothold before World War I because the conditions were simultaneously too conservative and too progressive: too conservative because few wealthy entre-preneurs—among the exceptions are Max Todesco, Heinrich Liebig, Josef Werndl, Arthur Krupp, and Hugo Bunzl—were interested in genuine social reforms,[33] and too progressive

because those artists and architects who would have been able to plan such reform colonies had been permanently "absorbed" by the existing system—in the form of profes-sorships and official advisory roles—immediately after their first public appearances. Life reform on the scale of social *Siedlung* projects and large garden cities for thousands of inhabitants only began in Vienna after 1918 with the students of Heinrich Tessenow, who taught at the Vienna School of Arts and Crafts from 1913 to 1919 on the initiative of Josef Hoffmann and Alfred Roller.[34]   ■

1   Strictly speaking they are not villas but single-family houses, and due to the lack of a master plan not a colony but a loose cluster of houses.
2   Pichler, Gerd, "Die Künstlerkolonie auf der Hohen Warte in Wien," in: Philipsen, Christian/Bauer-Friedrich, Thomas/Büche, Wolfgang (eds.), *Gustav Klimt & Hugo Henneberg*, exh. cat. Kunstmuseum Moritzburg Halle/Saale, Cologne 2018, 137–146; Kristan, Markus, *Josef Hoffmann. Villenkolonie Hohe Warte*, Vienna 2004. For architectural his-torical analyses of the seven houses, see: Sekler, Eduard F., *Josef Hoffmann: The Architectural Work*, Princeton, NJ 1985, 44–56, as well as CR 52 and 53 (Moser-Moll house), 54 (Henneberg house), 63 (Spitzer house), 101 (Brauner house), 111 (Hochstetter house), 112 (second Moll house), and 134 (Ast house). Trans. Eduard F. Sekler and John Maass.
3   Long articles about the houses are published, among other places, in the magazine *Der Archi-tekt*, the key mouthpiece for the Modernist move-ment in Vienna that had been edited by Theophil Hansen's student Ferdinand Fellner von Feldegg since 1895; in *Innendekoration*, published in Darmstadt by Alexander Koch since 1890; in the influential *The Studio: An Illustrated Magazine of Fine and Applied Art*, published in London since 1893; and in the *Wiener Monatshefte für ange-wandte Kunst – Das Interieur*, founded in 1900 by Ludwig Abels and edited by the future biog-rapher of Otto Wagner and Joseph M. Olbrich, Joseph August Lux. In 1904 Lux founded the magazine *Hohe Warte. Illustrierte Halbmonatss-*

chrift für die künstlerischen, geistigen und wirts-chaftlichen Interessen der städtischen Kultur in a nod to the ideals of the villa colony.
4   Sekler 1985 (see note 2), 41.
5   Hevesi, Ludwig, *Acht Jahre Secession*, Vienna 1906, 54.
6   *Arbeitsprogramm der Wiener Werkstätte*, Vienna 1905.
7   Hermann Bahr about the Secession in 1900 and 1901, quoted in Kristan 2004 (see note 2), 13.
8   Josef Hoffmann ran his private architecture firm in offices at the School of Arts and Crafts while also managing the Wiener Werkstätte's construc-tion drawing office on Neustiftgasse from 1903. Furthermore, as early as 1900/01 he planned a large extension to Heinrich von Ferstel's School of Arts and Crafts for studios and workshops; cf. the article "In the Modernist Laboratory: Josef Hoffmann's Architecture Class at the Vienna School of Arts and Crafts" by Matthias Boeckl in this catalog.
9   From the statutes of the Wiener Cottage Verein from 1873; see www.cottageverein.at [4 Aug 2020].
10   Such as Hugo Henneberg's top-floor photography studio with a darkroom, cf. Mahler, Astrid, *Lieb-haberei der Millionäre. Der Wiener Camera-Club um 1900*, exh. cat. Photoinstitut Bonartes Vienna, Salzburg 2019, 40–41.
11   Friedrich Victor Spitzer and Hugo Henneberg were members of the Camera-Club, cf. ibid.
12   Kristan 2004 (see note 2), 11.
13   Witt-Dörring, Christian, "Koloman Moser: A multi-

talented Viennese Modernist," in: Thun-Hohen-stein, Christoph/Witt-Dörring, Christian/Schmut-termeier, Elisabeth (eds.), *Koloman Moser: Uni-versal Artist between Gustav Klimt and Josef Hoffmann*, exh. cat. MAK, Vienna/Basel 2019, 18–80. Trans. Maria Slater.
14   Sekler 1985 (see note 2), CR 28, 257.
15   Jan Kotěra, the Gessner brothers, Leopold Bauer, and many other Wagner students built their own villas even before the First World War broke out.
16   On Hoffmann's private apartments, cf. Huey, Michael, "Art Itself," in: Witt-Dörring, Christian (ed.), *Josef Hoffmann. Interiors 1902–1913*, exh. cat. Neue Galerie New York, Munich 2006, 74–97.
17   Kristan, Markus/Ottillinger, Eva, "'Kapriziös und praktisch zugleich.' Die Wohn- und Geschäft-shäuser der Wiener Zeit," in: Beil, Ralf/Stephan, Regina (eds.): *Joseph Maria Olbrich 1867–1908. Architekt und Gestalter der frühen Moderne*, Ost-fildern 2010, 116–135; and Wagner-Conzelmann, Sandra, "'Eine Stadt müssen wir erbauen, eine ganze Stadt!' Siedlungsplanung im Werk von J. M. Olbrich," in: ibid., 204–223.
18   Letter to Moll from 26 May 1900; Moll's autobiog-raphy, quoted in Kristan 2004 (see note 2), 18–19.
19   Sekler 1985 (see note 2), 44; M. Fabiani, Baumann villa, Anton-Langer-Gasse 3, Hietzing, Vienna, 1898.
20   M. H. Baillie Scott, *An Artist's House*, in: *The Studio* (IX) 43 1897, 28–37. Sekler (1985, 44) also names the Rowantreehill house by J. Salmon & Son, which was illustrated in the magazine *Deko-*

Fig. 21 JH, garden views of the Ast villa, 1909–1911,
and the Spitzer house (right), 1900–1902
MBF (12) 1913, 3

rative Kunst in 1900, as a possible source of inspiration for Hoffmann.

21 Hoffmann's garden furniture can be seen in Carl Moll's picture *Das Haus des Künstlers auf der Hohen Warte* [The Artist's House on the Hohe Warte], 1904, which can be found in the National Gallery Prague, and fig. 11 on p. 67 of this catalog. Cf. also the article "Plant and Square: The Gardens of Josef Hoffmann" by Anette Freytag in this catalog.

22 Quoted in Kristan 2004 (see note 2), 19.

23 My thanks to Monika Faber for this information, 18 Jun 2020.

24 Faber, Monika, "Hugo Henneberg – Meister des fotografischen Stimmungsbildes," in: Philipsen/Bauer-Friedrich/Büche (eds.) 2018 (see note 2), 177–194.

25 Sekler 1985 (see note 2), 54.

26 Square and black-and-white patterns were used frequently in the early Italian Renaissance, which Josef Frank analyzed in his dissertation on Alberti in 1910; see Frank, Josef, "On the Original Form of the Religious Buildings of Leone Battista Alberti: Dissertation to obtain the degree of Doctor of Technical Science, submitted to Professor Carl König, Technical University Vienna, 1910," trans. Mark Gilbert, in: Bojankin, Tano/Long, Christopher/Meder, Iris (eds.), *Josef Frank. Writings, Volume 1: Published Writings 1910–1930*, Vienna 2012, 47–115.

27 In 1911 Kandinsky describes the "constructive ambitions in painting," as well as the difficulty of forming a theory out of the current practical creative work: "From the characteristics of our present-day harmony, it automatically follows that in our age it is less possible than ever to develop an entirely complete theory […]." Kandinsky, Wassily, *Über das Geistige in der Kunst. Insbesondere in der Malerei*, Munich 1912[3], 96.

28 Hoffmann, Josef, quoted in Sekler 1985 (see note 2), 45.

29 Cf. the article "The Viennese Style: Interiors 1900–1918" by Christian Witt-Dörring in this catalog.

30 Sekler 1985 (see note 2), 49.

31 About the latter Otto Kapfinger, whom I thank for this analysis, adds: "The external appearance of the Ast villa shows the way Hoffmann toys with the autonomous surface, with the shell of the wall, in the next dimension. He transforms formerly tectonic elements—column cannelure, cornice profile—into relief-like cladding of the structure. We see external walls clad in seamlessly applied layers of concrete, the cannelure rolled out into a flat, relief-like dress, crowned in an effervescent 'cornice' knitted over it from openwork stone lace—a [Louis] Sullivan-esque ornament not *on* but *out of* the material, and as a third point: sumptuously corporeal woven concrete borders, which garland, outline, the windows at the same height as the story. Wagner's 'pomp and paneling,' transformed from ephemeral festival decoration into permanent everyday life—in Purkersdorf still applied with the lightest of touches—in the next sleight of hand by Hoffmann here becomes an enigmatic art-stone-work: decoration becomes substance, comment the thing itself."

32 A contemporary overview is provided by Hans Kampffmeyer's article "Gartenstadt und Baukunst," in: *Moderne Bauformen* (VII) 3 1908, 89–112, with numerous example realizations (Ludwig Bopp, Gronauerwald in Bergisch Gladbach; Robert Friedrich Schmohl, Krupp workers' housing, Altenhof near Essen; Barry Parker and Raymond Unwin, Robert Bennett and Wilson Bidwell, as well as Geoffry Lucas, Letchworth Garden City near London; Parker and Unwin, workers' houses in New Earswick near York; an "American industrial village" by the National Cash Register Company; William Alexander Harvey, Bournville, Birmingham; William Owen, Port Sunlight, Wirral).

33 These industrialists constructed large housing developments for their workers near their factories complete with central social services: Todesco from 1846 in Marienthal, Liebig from 1868 in Reichenberg/Liberec, Werndl from 1875 in Steyr, Krupp from 1880 in Berndorf, and Bunzl from 1919 in Pernitz/Ortmann.

34 Boeckl, Matthias, "Von der Kunstrevolution zur Lebensreform. Heinrich Tessenow und die Integrationsstrategien der Wiener Moderne," in: Reinhold, Bernadette/Kernbauer, Eva (eds.), *zwischenräume zwischentöne. Wiener Moderne, Gegenwartskunst, Sammlungspraxis. Festschrift für Patrick Werkner*, Berlin/Boston 2018, 142–149.

1901
1906

Friedrich V. Spitzer, Josef Hoffmann, 1903
MAK, WWF 137-1-2

Fig. 1 JH, small cabinet for photographs from the salon of Dr. Hugo Koller's apartment, executed by W. Müller, 1900/01
Rosewood and maple, nickel silver
The Art Institute of Chicago, 1992.93
© bpk/The Art Institute of Chicago/Art Resource, NY

Fig. 2 JH, fauteuil for Dr. Johannes and Johanna Salzer's apartment, 1902
Mahogany, renewed upholstery
Private collection
© MAK/Georg Mayer

Fig. 3 JH, fauteuil for Gustav Pollak's study, executed by Portois & Fix, 1901/02
Rosewood with Zerigotti marquetry, brass, renewed upholstery
Oscar Graf Gallery, London
© Jacques Pépion, Paris

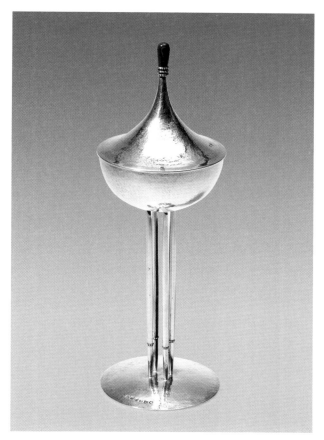

Fig. 4 JH, sports trophy, executed
by Würbel & Czokally, Vienna, 1902
Silver, malachite
Private collection
© MAK/Georg Mayer

Fig. 5 JH, centerpiece for Dr. Hermann Wittgenstein,
executed by the Wiener Werkstätte, 1905
Silver, agate
MAK, GO 2011
© MAK/Katrin Wißkirchen

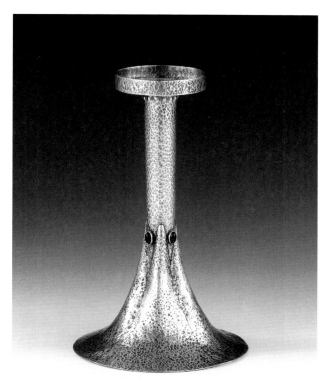

Fig. 6 JH, candlestick, 1902
Nickel silver, semiprecious stones
GALERIE BEI DER ALBERTINA · ZETTER

Fig. 7 JH, vase, executed by the
Wiener Werkstätte, 1905
Silver
GALERIE BEI DER ALBERTINA · ZETTER

<
Fig. 8 JH, union hotel for
the Poldihütte steel plant,
Kladen/Kladno, 1903
Die Kunst (10) 1904, 23

>
Fig. 10 Carl Moll, *My Living
Room (Anna Moll at the
Desk)*, 1903
Wien Museum, 77880

>
Fig. 11 Carl Moll, *Das Haus
des Künstlers auf der Hohen
Warte* [The Artist's House on
the Hohe Warte], ca. 1905
National Gallery Prague, 11263

<
Fig. 9 JH, Dr. Richard
Beer-Hofmann's house,
Vienna, 1905/06
MAK, WWF 104-184-1

Fig. 12 JH, tea and
coffee set, executed by
Alexander Sturm, 1902
Silver, ebony
Private collection
© MAK/Georg Mayer

Fig. 13 JH, tea set, executed by
the Wiener Werkstätte, 1903
Silver, coral, and ebony
MAK, GO 2005
© MAK/Katrin Wißkirchen

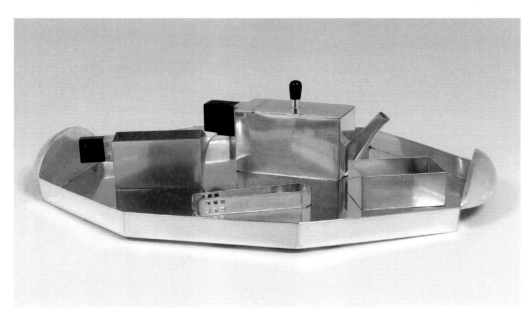

Fig. 14 JH, espresso set, executed
by the Wiener Werkstätte, 1904
Nickel silver, silver-plated,
and ebony
Private collection

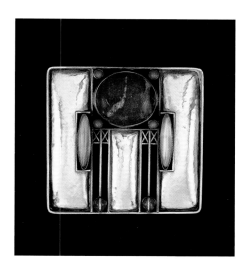
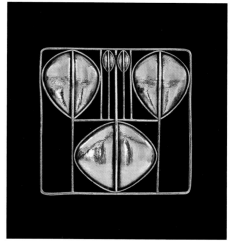
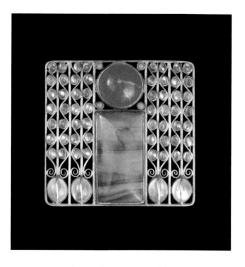

Fig. 15 JH, brooch, executed by
the Wiener Werkstätte, 1905
Silver, gold-plated, coral, lapis
lazuli, moonstone
GALERIE BEI DER ALBERTINA · ZETTER

Fig. 16 Brooch owned by Emilie and
Gertrude Flöge, executed by the
Wiener Werkstätte, 1905
Silver and gold
Private collection, courtesy of the Klimt Foundation, Vienna

Fig. 17 JH, brooch, executed by
the Wiener Werkstätte, 1905
Silver, coral, lapis lazuli, malachite,
and moonstone
GALERIE BEI DER ALBERTINA · ZETTER

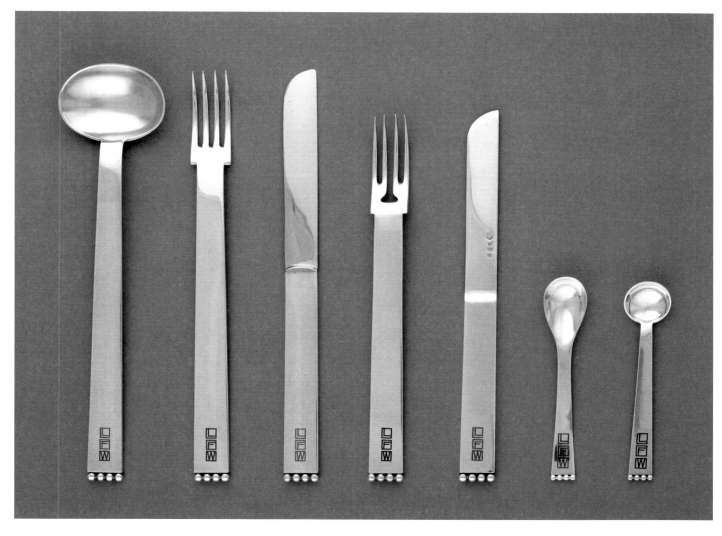

Fig. 18 JH, pieces from a flatware set for Fritz and Lili Waerndorfer,
executed by the Wiener Werkstätte, 1903
Silver, niello
MAK, GO 2009
© MAK/Aslan Kudrnofsky

Fig. 19 JH, cabinet for the office of the
Schwestern Flöge fashion salon, executed
by the Wiener Werkstätte, 1904
Spruce, painted white and black
Galerie Yves Macaux, Brussels
© Luk Vander Plaetse

Fig. 20 JH, wardrobe for the nursery of Jerome and
Margaret Stonborough-Wittgenstein's Berlin apartment,
executed by the Wiener Werkstätte, 1905
Wood, painted white, paktong
Galerie Yves Macaux, Brussels
© Photo Studio Philippe de Formanoir/Paso Doble

Fig. 21 JH, buffet for
Dr. Hermann and Lyda
Wittgenstein's apartment,
executed by the Wiener
Werkstätte, 1905/06
Spruce, painted white
and blue, marble
GALERIE BEI DER ALBERTINA · ZETTER

Fig. 23 JH, plant stand,
executed by the Wiener
Werkstätte, ca. 1905
Iron, painted white
Dr. E. Ploil Collection

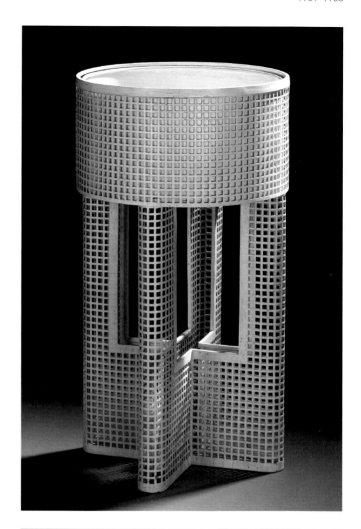

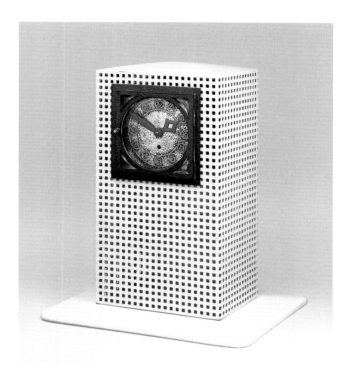

Fig. 22 JH, clock, executed by the Wiener
Werkstätte, 1904
Sheet zinc, painted white
Dr. E. Ploil Collection

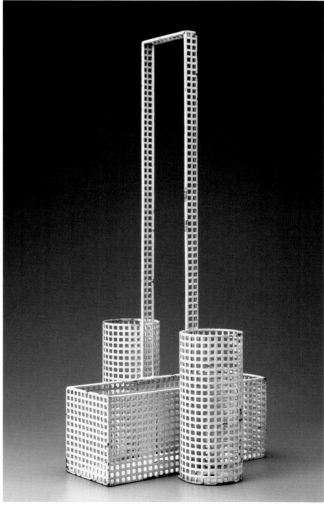

Fig. 24 JH, flower basket,
executed by the Wiener
Werkstätte, 1906
Sheet zinc, painted white
Dr. E. Ploil Collection

Fig. 25 JH, Sanatorium Westend,
Purkersdorf, 1904, east façade with
entrance to the park
MAK, WWF 102-83-1

Fig. 26 JH, west façade
with vehicle access
MAK, WWF 102-99-3

Fig. 27 JH, Sanatorium Westend, Purkersdorf, 1904, entrance hall
DKuD (18) 1906, 427

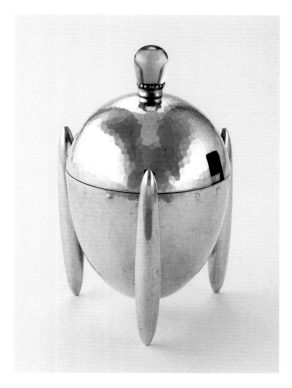

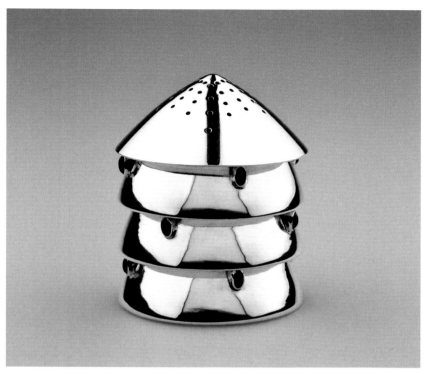

Fig. 31 JH, mustard pot, executed
by Alexander Sturm, 1902
Silver, citrine
Private collection
© MAK/Georg Mayer

Fig. 32 JH, pepper/paprika pot, executed
by the Wiener Werkstätte, 1903
Silver, carnelian
MAK, GO 2108
© MAK/Katrin Wißkirchen

\>
Fig. 33 JH, eggcup, executed
by the Wiener Werkstätte, 1904
Silver
MAK, GO 2057
© MAK/Katrin Wißkirchen

<
Fig. 28 JH, desk for Magda Mautner v. Markhof's studio,
executed by the Wiener Werkstätte, 1905/06
Walnut stained to look like mahogany, rrenewed leather desk pad
GALERIE BEI DER ALBERTINA · ZETTER
© MAK/Georg Mayer

<
Figs. 29, 30 JH, armchair for Magda Mautner v. Markhof's living room, 1902
Walnut stained to look like mahogany, renewed leather upholstery
GALERIE BEI DER ALBERTINA · ZETTER
© MAK/Georg Mayer

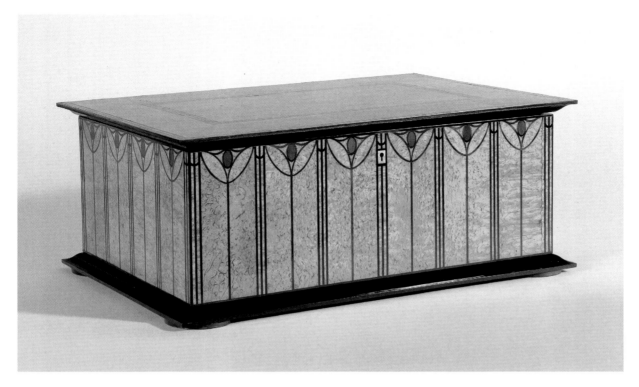

Fig. 34 JH, jewelry box, executed by the Wiener Werkstätte, 1904
Silver birch, mahogany, ebony
MAK, H 1182
© MAK/Georg Mayer

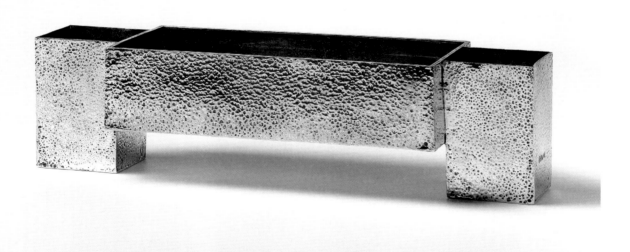

Fig. 35 JH, jardiniere, executed by the Wiener Werkstätte, 1904
Nickel silver, silver-plated
Leopold Museum – Private Foundation, Vienna, 4604
© MAK/Georg Mayer

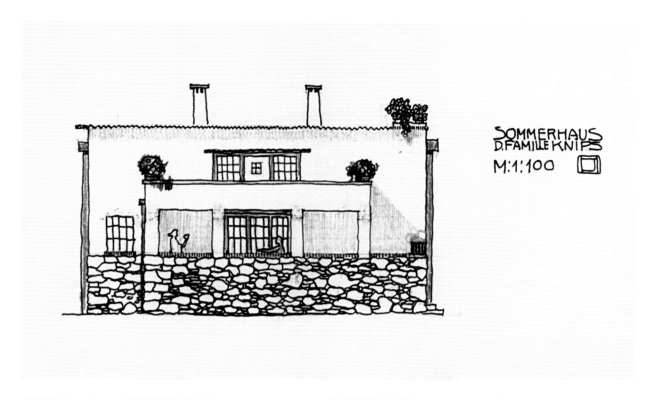

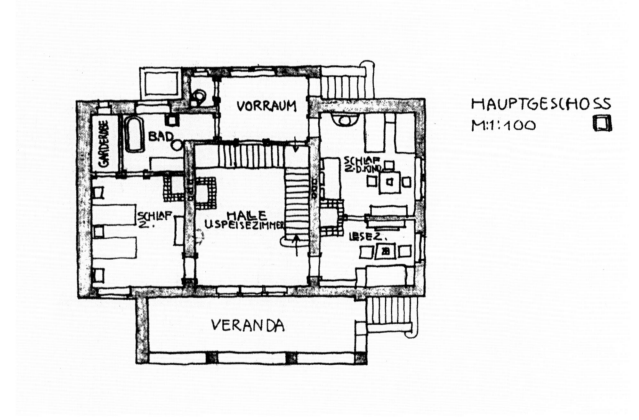

Fig. 36 JH, Knips country house in Seeboden on Lake Millstättersee, 1905
Design for the garden façade and floor plan for the main story
E. F. Sekler, *Josef Hoffmann*, 56, 283

Fig. 37 JH, table for the living room of
Dr. Hermann and Lyda Wittgenstein's
apartment, executed by the Wiener
Werkstätte, 1905
Oak, stained black, with pores
filled white, marble
MAK, H 2082
© MAK/Georg Mayer

Fig. 38 JH, table for the living room of Dr. Salzer's apartment, 1902
Maple, stained brown, marble
MAK, H 2079
© Wolfgang Woessner/MAK

Fig. 39 JH, table, executed by the
Wiener Werkstätte, 1905
Oak, stained black, with pores
filled white, maple
Galerie Yves Macaux, Brussels
© Photo Studio Philippe de Formanoir/Paso Doble

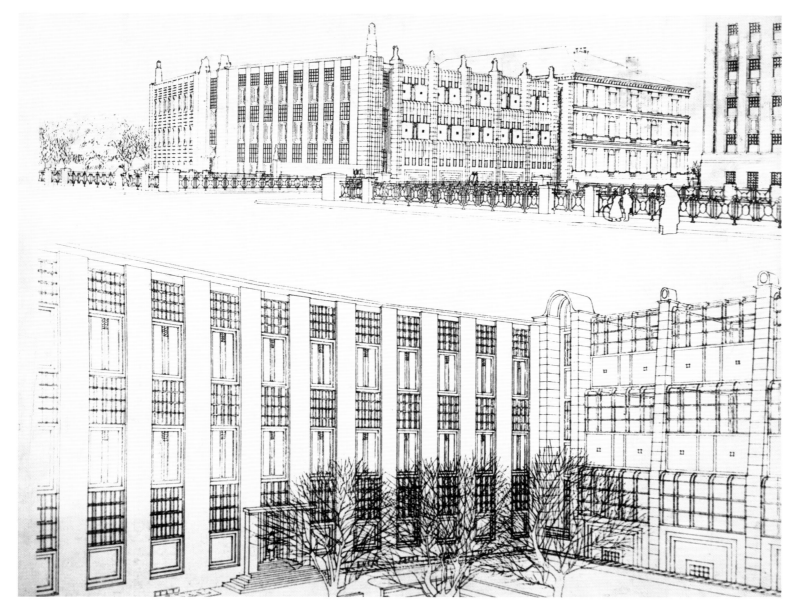

Fig. 40 JH, project for the extension of the School
of Arts and Crafts, Vienna, 1905/06
Street and courtyard views
MAK, KI 8951-39

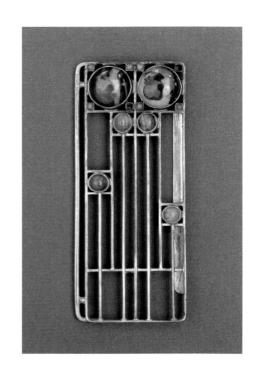

Fig. 41 JH, clasp, executed
by the Wiener Werkstätte
(Karl Ponocny), 1904/05
Silver, opal, malachite, and coral
MAK, BJ 1302
© MAK/Georg Mayer

Josef Hoffmann

1901
1906

Josef Hoffmann and Fritz Waerndorfer with the first silver object produced by the WW, 1903
MAK KI 13740-1-1

Carl König, caricature of Josef Hoffmann fighting with Pallas Athena against the ruler and compass, from the portfolio given to the architect J. M. Olbrich by his friends as a memento of the construction of the Secession building
VS (4) 3 1901, 50

1901

Design and construction of the office building for the Wittgenstein Forestry Administration (for Karl Wittgenstein) and the residential building for the forestry workers in Hohenberg. The first houses on the Hohe Warte, the duplex for Moll and Moser and the Henneberg house, are completed and document for the first time Josef Hoffmann's life reform-inspired desire to achieve a comprehensive unity between house, furnishings, and garden as the ideal way to build and live. He carries out numerous interior decoration commissions, including for Helene Hochstetter, Magda Mautner-Markhof, Hugo Koller, and Gustav Pollak. They are jointly planned with his student Franz Messner and other young architects from his studio at the School of Arts and Crafts.

1902

14th Secession exhibition: Josef Hoffmann is in charge of the overall artistic direction and the interior design. At the heart of the show is the polychrome Beethoven statue by Max Klinger, around which other Secession artists, including Gustav Klimt with his famous *Beethoven Frieze*, impeccably realize the ideal of a Gesamtkunstwerk for the purpose of heroizing an artistic personality. So eminently important for the development of an abstract, constructive direction within Austrian art, Josef Hoffmann's overdoor reliefs in this ensemble mark his departure from the organic and curvilinear in favor of elementary geometric forms in his designs for architecture and the decorative arts. 1902 also gives rise to his dining room for Fritz Waerndorfer and furnishings for the apartment of Dr. Johannes Salzer, Karl Wittgenstein's son-in-law.

1903

This is the year that the Wiener Werkstätte is founded. Josef Hoffmann and Koloman Moser assume its artistic direction; as financier, the industrialist Fritz Waerndorfer is the commercial director. Originally only planned as a metal workshop, the cooperative moves into a small apartment at Heumühlgasse 6 in Vienna with three trained craftsmen. Hoffmann furnishes an apartment on the Gumpendorferstraße for Sonja Knips in the WW's strict early style. That same year, a summer- and boathouse is realized for the Knips family on Lake Millstättersee in Seeboden, Carinthia. As another large construction project, Hoffmann realizes the Poldihütte steel plant's union hotel in

Kladen/Kladno, Bohemia, which had been the property of Karl Wittgenstein until 1898. For the Wittgenstein family, Hoffmann completes the Protestant forest church and parsonage in St. Aegyd in Lower Austria.

1904

In a factory building at Neustiftgasse 32–34, workshops for metal-, enamel-, and leatherwork, bookbinding, carpentry, and painting, as well as offices and salesrooms, are all furnished by Hoffmann. At first a construction drawing office is also affiliated with the workshop business. Alongside the production of one-off objects of the highest quality in its endeavor to develop a time-appropriate design vocabulary, the Wiener Werkstätte's other main objective is the production of complete interiors, in which everything from furniture to pastry forks is subject to the founders' creative will. The company exists until 1932. Construction of the Sanatorium Westend in Purkersdorf near Vienna, one of the programmatic highlights in Hoffmann's architectural oeuvre. The luxury health spa for Victor Zuckerkandl, the brother-in-law of the art critic and patron of the Secession Berta Zuckerkandl-Szeps, is a milestone in modern Austrian architecture thanks to the clarity of its formal disposition, the revolutionary simplicity of its cubic layout, and its innovative reinforced concrete construction. In addition to the building itself, Hoffmann and Koloman Moser jointly design the entire interior and all technical and decorative elements, which are executed by the Wiener Werkstätte. Another joint proj-

Gustav Klimt, Fritz Waerndorfer, Josef Hoffmann, and Koloman Moser in the garden of the Waerndorfer villa, 1903
MAK, KI 13740-1-3

Visible from left: Josef Hoffmann, Max Reinhardt, Anna Moll, and Gustav Klimt in the garden of the Moll villa, Hohe Warte, 1905
Photograph by Moritz Nähr
MAK, KI 13740-1-2

ect with Moser is the furnishing of the Schwestern Flöge fashion salon in Vienna, which is opened by Gustav Klimt's common-law wife and her sisters Helene (widow of Gustav Klimt's brother Ernst) and Pauline, at Maria-hilfer Straße 1a. For Gustav Klimt, Hoffmann furnishes his studio at Josef-städter Straße 21.

1905

Hoffmann works mostly in Vienna on constructing more villas, which feature design ideas from the English Arts & Crafts movement, an elementary geo-metric form of expression, and new interpretations of the classical design vocabulary: the house and interior design for Alexander Brauner on the Hohe Warte and the house for the poet Richard Beer-Hofmann on Hasenauer-straße. Josef Hoffmann travels to Belgium and concludes the contract with Adolphe Stoclet, whom he had met during the latter's stay in Vienna, for the construction of a city palace on the outskirts of Brussels. Meets with Constantin Meunier and George Minne. Departure of the Klimt Group, including Josef Hoffmann, from the Secession due to insurmountable differences regarding the ideological implementation of the unity of the arts and hence the Gesamtkunstwerk ideal.

1905–1911

Construction of Stoclet House in Brus-sels. Hoffmann designs the house, the complete interior, gardens, and all an-nexes. The façade of the three-story building with its characteristic tower is clad in a homogeneous skin of marble plates whose edges are framed in tex-tured metal profiles. The interiors are conceived as a carefully arranged sequence of impressions and culminate in the central, open, double-height hall. Artists like Gustav Klimt (mosaic frieze in the dining room), George Minne (marble fountain), Carl Otto Czeschka (glass windows), Michael

Powolny (ceramics), Leopold Forstner (mosaics), and Franz Metzner (sculp-tures) all contribute to the elaborate decoration of this town house in line with the Gesamtkunstwerk idea. The building remains almost unchanged to this day. The major commission finances the expansion of production at the Wiener Werkstätte. Hoffmann converts and furnishes the Hochreith hunting lodge near Hohenberg in Lower Austria for Karl Wittgenstein and dec-orates an apartment for Hermann Wittgenstein in Vienna; both works are realized in 1905/06. ∎

Anteroom of Gustav Klimt's studio at Josefstädter Straße 21
with furnishings by Josef Hoffmann, 1904
MAK, KI 13740-14

Fig. 1 Wilhelm Schmidt (design), display case, section of the Vienna School
of Arts and Crafts at the Paris World's Fair, 1900
MAK, KI 7401-3

Matthias Boeckl

In the Modernist Laboratory

Josef Hoffmann's Architecture Class at the Vienna School of Arts and Crafts 1899–1918

Criticism of the lacking practical relevance and historical language of form—learned on the basis of models in museum collections—at the Vienna School of Arts and Crafts started as early as the 1880s and intensified continuously in the years thereafter.[1] It was with the appointment of Otto Wagner to the Academy of Fine Arts Vienna in 1894 and to the advisory board of the Imperial Royal Austrian Museum of Art and Industry (today's MAK) in 1898 that the modernization of these institutions began. On the advisory board Wagner saw to it in 1899 that the wave of retirements among the founding professors of the School of Arts and Crafts, who had been in office since the 1860s, was used for its transition to Modernism, proposing four of his students as candidates to succeed the architecture professor Josef von Storck.[2] The subsequent appointment of the 28-year-old Josef Hoffmann, who had graduated from the state trade school in Brünn/Brno in addition to Carl von Hasenauer's and Otto Wagner's masterclasses in Vienna, as the head of one of the three architecture classes accelerated the modernization of design and architecture training. Shortly beforehand and afterward other young Secessionists in the form of Felician von Myrbach, Alfred Roller, and Koloman Moser were also engaged at the School of Arts and Crafts, meaning that Vienna's art revolution—the "sacred spring"—had been institutionalized by the state immediately after it had first transpired. The replacement of the mid-19th-century *Gründerzeit* generation with the fin-de-siècle Modernist generation in the architecture department of the Vienna School of Arts and Crafts was completed with the appointment of Heinrich Tessenow in 1913 and Oskar Strnad in 1914.

Artists' Idiosyncrasies and Unity of the Arts

In the architecture class of Hoffmann's predecessor Josef von Storck, the exact reproduction of historical forms and their application in cabinetry had taken center stage for decades. However, in 1899 the class actually only existed on paper because the ornamental draftsman Storck had withdrawn to teach in the special studio for lacework drawing. Prior to Hoffmann assuming office in 1899, there were only two students in Storck's old architecture class.[3] The next academic year, 1900/01, this number had grown to 14 students,

though Hoffmann had been obliged to take them over from other departments and had not yet selected the applicants himself. Eight of them graduated that same year and left the class.[4] Although they had only studied under Hoffmann for one year, he nevertheless had an influence on them—for example on Gustav Siegel, who had been at the school since 1897, graduated under Hoffmann in 1901, and at his recommendation was employed as the head designer of the innovative bentwood furniture manufacturer Jacob & Josef Kohn.[5] Of the remaining six students from this first year, only Max Benirschke and Johann Scharfen continued their degree with Hoffmann.[6] Together with the students whom Hoffmann himself had admitted in the fall—Karl Bräuer, Fritz Dietl, Mauritius Herrgesell, Adolf Holub, Julius von Kalmar, Johann Stubner, Carl Witzmann, and nine others—the academic year of 1901/02 produced the first compact group of young artists who could be trained entirely in the spirit of Modernism by one of Otto Wagner's students and as he had envisaged.[7] Even during their degree these students played a part in numerous of the movement's events as "junior staff." After only a few years the Secessionists were able to guarantee the future of this modern revolution in art education at the School of Arts and Crafts by hiring their own graduates, especially Hoffmann's former students: For example, Otto Prutscher taught at the school for over three decades (1909–1939 and 1944–1946); Carl Witzmann (1908–1915, a hiatus for the war, then 1918–1945), Eduard Josef Wimmer-Wisgrill (1912–1923 and 1925–1955), and Otto Niedermoser (as an assistant from 1923 and then as a professor from 1936 to 1973) worked on Stubenring for some 40 years.[8]

Immediately upon taking office, Hoffmann radically changed Storck's syllabus and teaching methods. Everything was aimed at liberating and revealing individual "idiosyncrasies": studying historical forms was dropped without replacement (it continued in the general classes and in courses parallel to the teaching in specialized classes) and the students were able to choose the topics of their work—which was now by no means limited to furniture alone—relatively freely within a set group of options. With his renunciation of any "division of labor" between specialists in "applied" and "fine" art—in architecture between building design and interior design—Hoffmann actualized a fundamental demand

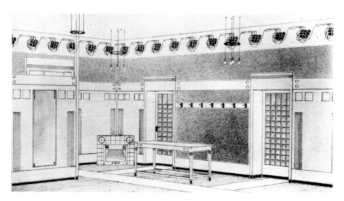

Figs. 2, 3, 4 Exhibition by Josef Hoffmann's specialized class in Prague, 1901, fireplace (designed by Gisela von Falke, executed by L. & C. Hardtmuth, Franz Messner), salon cabinet (designed by Emil Holzinger, executed by G. Gilgen), tailor shop (design drawing by Carl Witzmann)
MAK, KI 7425-84, -32, -28

of Modernism in an instant: the unity of the arts in the spirit of the age was already the Secession's agenda and was now also applied to art education with long-term effects. One future academic repercussion of this revolution was the final victory over the *Gründerzeit* hierarchy of the arts when the School of Arts and Crafts was upgraded to a university in 1941, i.e., from the secondary to the tertiary education sector, putting it on an equal footing with the Academy of Fine Arts and the Technical University.[9] This solved an old problem faced by former students of the architecture class at the School of Arts and Crafts: as they were "only" graduates of secondary education and hence had not acquired an academic (or from 1937 a professional) qualification as architects, prior to 1941 many of them had completed their studies in a masterclass at the Academy of Fine Arts.[10]

Surrounded by Life

Just how different and vibrant Hoffmann's teaching was in comparison with that of his two architect colleagues from the school's founding generation,[11] is clearly demonstrated by a juxtaposition of their reports about the academic year 1906/07. Hermann Herdtle's students developed

"designs for simple furniture of a secular and ecclesiastical nature, for arrangements of entire interiors (homes and business premises), and for simple architectural objects. In addition most students produced sketches after objects in the collection and perspectival scale drawings from the Austrian Museum and churches."

There are no such traditional scale drawings of historical objects from the neighboring museum in Hoffmann's report. His architecture class is surrounded by urban everyday life and visibly helps to shape it:

"Designs were produced for endpapers, fabric patterns, printed patterns, wallpapers, posters, furniture, interiors, smaller and larger buildings. Many designs were also purchased for execution, partly by companies, partly by private citizens. In the *Kunst und Dekoration* competitions held by the publisher Koch, the school came away with almost all the awards. Further, the decorative and costume designs for some plays for the people's theater were produced in the school; similarly, by supplying the complete stage set to the fetes in the Dreherpark and in Pechlarn, the school had the opportunity, for which we were very grateful, to practice its skill and harness all its strength for a specific purpose. This applies in the main to the stage set and costumes for the pantomime *Tänzerin und Marionette* and the comedy *Balder*, the latter being completed in conjunction with Professor Ceschka's school. A small exhibition of students' works, which was hosted by the Berlin society of decorative arts late last summer, attracted universal attention to the school's achievements, which were also published and discussed in many art magazines. In agreement with the railroad ministry, the attempt was recently made for the school to study the issue of workers' settlements in order to facilitate the proposal of potential beautifications and improvements in this all too important area."[12]

With this impressive breadth of student activities in all areas of modern life and all product stages from design to manufacture to use, an egalitarian basic ideal of Modernism was also realized. In his Modernist laboratory Hoffmann worked on some significant sites of change: Even in this early phase his work on social housing projects for railroad workers manages to invalidate the accusation of elitism directed at

the Secessionists by many of their opponents and proves the relevance of aesthetics even in the everyday lives of the working class. The active collaboration of the School of Arts and Crafts on an urban open-air theater project in Vienna, for which the students not only designed the costumes and stage scenery but also made and used them themselves as actors,[13] is a testament to the Modernist team spirit and is a vivid example of Modernism's unity ideal: its notion of designing every aspect of one's surroundings knows neither genre nor functional boundaries. Finally, the acquisition of students' designs, as well as their presentation in many exhibitions and publications, proves the great market demand for modern design strategies and the modernity of these concepts.

Figs. 5, 6, 7 Exhibitions by Josef Hoffmann's specialized class at the AMAI, views of the exhibition (1903) and house design by Fritz Zeymer (1906)
MAK, KI 7557-7, -9, 7652-30

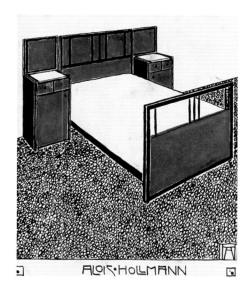

Figs. 8, 9 Exhibition by Josef Hoffmann's specialized class at the St. Louis World's Fair, 1904, designs for a bedroom (Alois Hollmann) and a living room (Max Benirschke)
MAK, KI 14171-12-2 and -1-4

PERSONEN-VERZEICHNIS

DER JUNGE KÖNIG	HR. STROHOFER
DIE TÄNZERIN	FRL. GRETE WIESENTHAL
DER KANZLER	HR. FELIX TIETZE
DER HOFMARSCHALL	HR. LEON AMAAR
DER HANSWURST	HR. MORITZ JUNG
	HR. EMANUEL MARGOLD
	HR. ANTON HAFERL
DIE SECHS WÜRDENTRÄGER	HR. REINHOLD THIEDE
	HR. RUDOLF BÖTTGER
	HR. RUDOLF HÜBER
	HR. VICTOR WASCHNITIUS
	FRL. MARIE BERNATZIK
	FRL. NELLY ATLAS
DIE SECHS HOFDAMEN	BARONESSE ENGERTH
	FRL. LISL V. WOLTER
	FRL. ELLA KENDE
	BARONESSE MAR. WIESER
	HR. FRANZ DELAVILLA
DIE VIER EDELKNABEN	HR. FELIX HEUBERGER
	HR. HANS BOLEK
	BARON FRITZ WIESER
	HR. ALFRED GERSTENBRAND
	HR. ADOLF HOLUB
SECHS BAUERN	HR. ALFRED BISCHOF
	HR. FRITZ ZEYMER
	HR. RUDOLF GUSSENBAUER
	HR. ANTON KLING
	FRL. HELENE BERNATZIK
	FRL. LILITH LANG
SECHS BÄUERINNEN	BARONESSE BEATR. WIESER
	FRL. BERTHA WIESENTHAL
	FRL. HILDA WIESENTHAL
	FRL. WIESENTHAL
DER HIRT	HR. ERWIN LANG
ZWEI SCHARFRICHTER	BARON WOLFGANG WIESER
	HR. DR. FRANZ EXNER
DIE BAUERNKINDER	

☐ DER JUNGE KÖNIG und die TÄNZERIN treten, Arm in Arm, auf. Er streichelt und küßt ihre Hände, dann ihre Arme, dann will er sie küssen. Sie wirft den Kopf zurück und sieht ihn strafend an. Er ist gekränkt und erzürnt und beruft sich auf seine Königswürde. In diesem Augenblick ertönt von Ferne eine Hirtenflöte. Die Tänzerin läßt ihn los und lauscht, ergriffen und wie verloren. Die Flöte verstummt, die Tänzerin steht eine Weile sinnend da, dann erwacht sie wie aus einem Traum und küßt den König leidenschaftlich: Er nickt befriedigt, klatscht in die Hände, und es zieht der HOFSTAAT auf, voran Pagen, dann der Kanzler, ein kleines dürres Männchen, der Hofmarschall, groß und stark, die Würdenträger und Hofdamen. Zwei Lakaien tragen den Thronsessel herbei, auf den sich der König niederläßt. Er erklärt der Versammlung, daß er der Tänzerin seine Huld geschenkt hat, und winkt den Lakaien, einen zweiten Thronsessel herzutragen. Das geschieht und die Tänzerin will sich hocherfreut, kindisch in die Hände klatschend, darauf setzen, nimmt dem König schon das Szepter aus der Hand, als dieser etwas erstaunt mit dem Ausdruck "Wie kann Dir so was einfallen!" es ihr wieder wegnimmt, sie vom Thronsessel weist und ihr erklärt, daß er leer bleiben wird; sie dürfte zu seinen Füßen sich niederlassen, was sie dann auch tut, die herabhängende Hand des Königs zärtlich küssend. Die Hofleute zeigen darüber Beruhigung und Befriedigung.
☐ Der König wird aufmerksam darauf, daß an der anderen Seite des Planes Leute aus dem Volke aufgetreten sind, bunt und lustig gekleidet, noch mit den Zeichen ihrer Beschäftigung in der Hand: mit Gras in der aufgebundenen Schürze und Sichel die Frauen, die Männer mit aufgestreiften Hemdärmeln, alle aber in froher Erwartung von etwas Kommendem, wobei sie dem Hofstaat nur flüchtige Blicke zuwerfen, die Mädchen knixen und wenden sich rasch ab. Der König befiehlt dem Hofmarschall nachzufragen, was das Volk hat; der Hof-

Fig. 10 *Die Tänzerin und die Marionette*, garden party at Weigls Dreherpark, 6–7 Jun 1907, program to accompany the pantomime, cast list with students of Hoffmann
Theatermuseum Wien
© KHM-Museumsverband

International Presence

From the outset Hoffmann and his class actively participated in large official exhibition projects. Furthermore, the class's own exhibitions were presented almost every year both in Austria and abroad. As the cofounder of the "modern media strategy" of presenting 1:1 models[14] and their intensive appraisal in the numerous newly founded illustrated specialist and consumer magazines, Hoffmann set new standards. This began as early as 1900 with his design of the room for the School of Arts and Crafts at the World's Fair in Paris, which led to a kind of epiphany for Hoffmann's student Carl Witzmann:

"His works were revolutions; it was a *Sturm und Drang* age for high and applied art. One of his first works especially, the design of the applied art room for the World's Fair in Paris in 1900, gave the entire formal creative output of the time a sharp jolt, setting the sense of form on an entirely new track."[15]

The first works by students from Hoffmann's own class were on display in this exhibition, including a showcase by Wilhelm Schmidt. [1]

In the years until 1914 this spectacular international first appearance was followed by numerous other exhibitions—as a rule designed by Hoffmann himself—by the School of Arts and Crafts and presentations solely by his architecture class. Some of the class's most successful solo shows and exhibition participations prior to World War I are well documented. The first show in Prague was organized by Hoffmann in 1901 together with Jan Kotěra, a colleague from the Wagner school who had also been appointed professor in 1899, though in his case at the School of Decorative Arts in Prague. The interim result of these two influential Wagner students after just one and a half years of teaching already showed unmistakable signs of Hoffmann's impact on his students: The floral decoration on the tiles of a fireplace by Gisela von Falke is already clearly abstracted and no longer historicizing or realistic; a salon cabinet by Emil Holzinger bears the cornice typical of Wagner; with its curvilinear floral decoration a lady's bedroom by Wilhelm Schmidt is reminiscent of the Parisian presentation from the previous year; and the design for a tailor shop by Carl Witzmann already uses the square motif extensively that Hoffmann had just discovered for design and architecture. [2 3 4]

Other presentations by Hoffmann's class took place in 1903 at the neighboring Austrian Museum of Art and Industry, in 1904 at the World's Fair in St. Louis, in 1906 again at the Austrian Museum, in 1907 at the decorative arts society in Berlin,[16] in 1908 in London, and in 1912 back in Vienna. These exhibitions demonstrate the school's remarkable national and international presence. [5 6 7]

The school's 1903 exhibition shows quite clearly that Hoffmann's class had long transcended the former limitation to interior design and was already able to present fully formulated models of single-family houses complete with landscaped gardens (such as that by Fritz Zeymer). In St. Louis the specialized class displayed a large series of spectacular

Fig. 11 Fritz Zeymer, country house design, prob. shown at a school exhibition in London in 1908
Kunsthandel Widder, Vienna

Fig. 12 Maria Strauss-Likarz, fashion plate,
Wiener Werkstätte postcard no. 769, 1912
MAK, KI 8873-149

>
Fig. 13 Otto Prutscher,
vitrine cabinet in the
"Room for an Art
Enthusiast," Kunstschau,
Vienna, 1908
MAK, H 3985

color perspectives of interiors in which the square motif
dominated floors, ceilings, and walls.[17] At the school's "home
game" in 1906 at the Austrian Museum of Art and Industry
in Vienna, Hoffmann's class could already show fully executed
interiors, for example a bedroom by Fritz Zeymer whose
clear surfaces seem to be a direct realization of his designs
from St. Louis. Some designs were also presented at the
school exhibition in London in 1908.[18] At the famous Viennese Kunstschau by the Klimt Group that same year, whose
buildings Hoffmann had of course designed, the School of
Arts and Crafts—in contrast to the Wiener Werkstätte—did
not have its own display. However, Hoffmann was able to
show works by his first graduates who had meanwhile become self-employed, including the now famous *Vitrinen-*
13 *schrank für eine Glassammlung* [Vitrine Cabinet for a Glass
Collection] by Otto Prutscher. Finally, the 1912 spring exhibition of Austrian decorative arts—complete with a display
by the School of Arts and Crafts—which was held in the large
14 halls of the extension to the Austrian Museum built in 1909
by Ludwig Baumann, presented works by both current Hoffmann students and his graduates. They included a country
house model by Carl Witzmann and complete interiors by
Adolf Holub, Otto Prutscher, and Eduard Josef Wimmer-
Wisgrill, furniture by Josef Zotti, and a drawing room by
Hoffmann himself.

Women Architects and Designers[19]

In Austria women were only allowed full access to the architectural profession from 1919, when all universities started
to admit female students. Nevertheless, there were unofficial
opportunities for women to learn the profession before this—
though not at a university but at a vocational post-secondary
school. Prior to the second civil engineering act of March
1937, "architect" was not a protected title, meaning in effect
that anyone could call themselves an architect, produce
building designs, and have them submitted to the planning
authorities by licensed builders. This enabled women archi-

Fig. 14 Spring exhibition of Austrian decorative arts and
exhibition by the School of Arts and Crafts at the AMAI,
room XX, Vienna, 1912
MAK, KI 7835-17

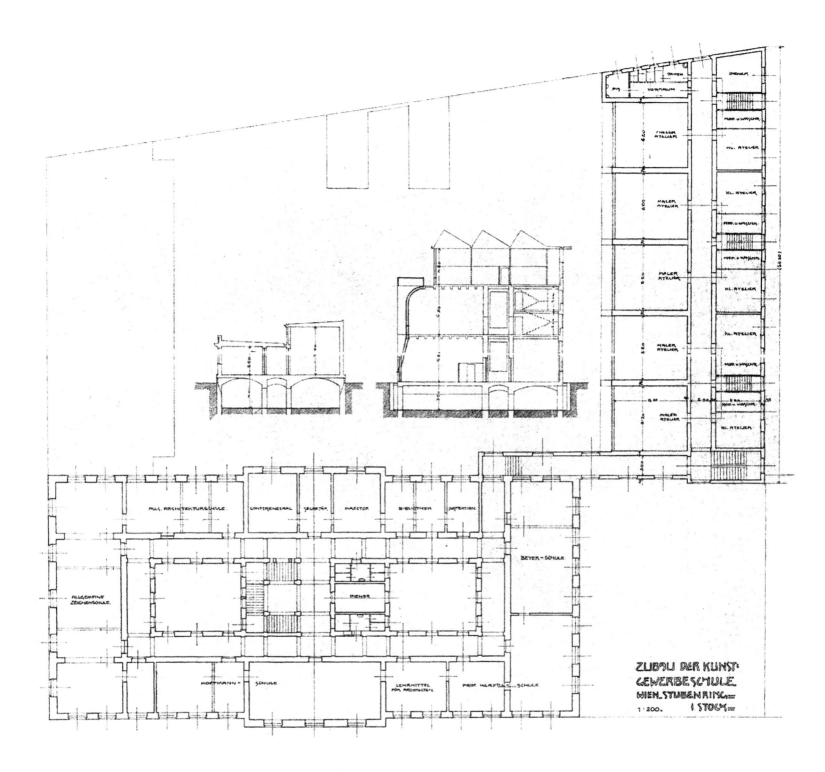

Fig. 15 JH, design for an extension to the
School of Arts and Crafts, Vienna, 1901,
floor plan of the 1st floor, sections
© ASA, AVA, Unterricht 29.550, 1901

Fig. 16 "Professor Josef Hoffmann hurries to
submit his project for the new School of Arts
and Crafts so that no one beats him to it,"
caricature in *Figaro*, 27 Jul 1907, 431
ANL

Figs. 17, 18 Designs for surface decorations from Hoffmann's specialized class by Johann Stubner, Jutta Sika, and Franz Burian
Die Fläche 1 1903, 82, 6

tects who had studied at the Vienna School of Arts and Crafts, like Margarete Lihotzky, to practice the profession by focusing on interior design. The school had in fact admitted women to the architecture classes—where they generally learned furniture and decorative design—long before 1900. In Josef Hoffmann's class, with an average of between 15 and 20 students, the proportion of women grew continuously between 1899 and 1918: While there were only two women during Hoffmann's first year, in the academic year 1917/18—in part due to the war—no less than 17 female students were in his architecture class. Before the war had broken out, the proportion of women students had been between five and 36 percent. Conscriptions caused this number to surge during the war to between 40 and 85 percent. Under Hoffmann the female students worked on the same design program as the male students from the outset and were in no way limited to interior design; their works were exhibited and published as equals. Despite this, many of them subsequently specialized in decorative-art techniques, which they later practiced in the context of the Wiener Werkstätte or as freelance artists.[20]

A Hothouse for Artists

A central vision of the Modernist movement was to work collectively on joint projects in the workshop and studio.

The workshop was the symbol of a grassroots democracy among artists and craftspeople *in nucleo*. Here the avant-gardists wanted to achieve ultimate craft quality and "honest" truth to the material while working selflessly side by side with simple but equal workers. As soon as the Secessionists Roller, Myrbach, Moser, and Hoffmann were installed at the Vienna School of Arts and Crafts, it was possible to start planning the spatial prerequisites for the realization of this ideal in the form of new studios and workshops. The school building constructed in 1873/74 by the Ringstraße architect Heinrich von Ferstel had long run out of space for such an endeavor; indeed, it had in essence been too small from the outset. Consequently, between 1901 and 1909 Josef Hoffmann designed several advanced extension projects for the lot that had been created behind the school by the regulation of the river Wien; just like the alternative plans prior to 1918 by Ludwig Baumann, Oskar Beyer, Ernst Pliwa/Richard Greiffenhagen, Eduard Zotter, and Heinrich Tessenow, every single one of them was rejected as a result of dogged resistance from the ministry.[21]

Of Hoffmann's extension projects, the first dating from 1901 presents the most innovative, sincere, and uncompromising solution for the Secessionists' idealistic objectives. Without any ostentatious gesture, Hoffmann proposes two ascetic workshop wings, which abut the back of Ferstel's exposed brick building at a right angle. With its two-story studios covered on the north side in large curved-glass panels, the south wing in particular is in keeping with state-of-the-art avant-garde buildings for art—when compared, for example, to Charles Rennie Mackintosh's Glasgow School of Art (1897–1909), Joseph Maria Olbrich's Ernst Ludwig House in Darmstadt (1899–1901), and Henry van de Velde's Grand-Ducal Vocational Arts School in Weimar (1904–1911). Yet even the extension projects he developed in 1905 and 1908 did not make it past the design stage.[22]

World War I

Hoffmann's class showed a final spirited sign of life before the end of the monarchy with their designs for construction projects necessitated by the war. As it was already foreseeable in the fall of 1914 that private construction work and related themed exhibitions would come to an almost absolute standstill, the School of Arts and Crafts was on the lookout for other opportunities to draw public attention to their achievements. The publication *Einfacher Hausrat* by the Austrian Museum of Art and Industry[23] was well suited to this endeavor, with Karl Hagenauer and Richard Diller, among others from Hoffmann's class, contributing some concise furniture designs. Moreover, there was a cooperation with the Imperial Royal Trade Advancement Bureau under Adolf Vetter, who would later be the first manager to run the Austrian federal theaters,[24] "with the intention of contributing to the memory of the Great War and of the men who fell in it being preserved and handed down to posterity in a dignified manner."[25] Oskar Strnad coordinated this design program for the School of Arts and Crafts in which—in addition to his own class—the departments of Franz Barwig, Josef Breitner, Anton Hanak, Josef Hoffmann, Rudolf von Larisch, Robert Obsieger, Michael Powolny, Marie Schmid, and Heinrich Tessenow took part. Of the 130 published designs,[26] no less than 36 came from Hoffmann's class, while the two other architecture classes under Strnad and Tessenow contributed 13 and 10 respectively. Strnad himself supplied 22 projects. The works from Hoffmann's class were designed by Artur Berger, Moritz Blumann, Mathilde Flögl, Wilhelm Foltin, Franz Hudec, Rudolf Jirasko, Josef Mata, Maria Strauss-Likarz, and Gustav Tejcka. Many of Hoffmann's students from the period before 1918 helped advance architecture and design in the new First Austrian Republic; by becoming teachers at the School of Arts and Crafts themselves, some of them were able to continue passing down his aesthetic strategies to new generations of students throughout dramatic historical watersheds and until well into the 1960s.   ■

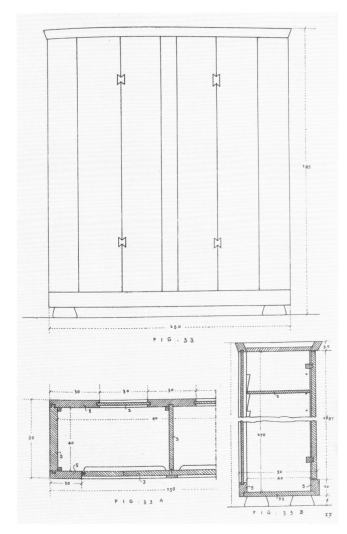

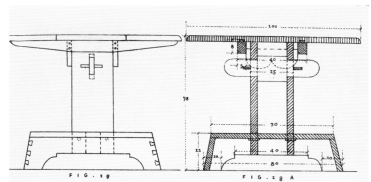

Figs. 19, 20 Karl Hagenauer (Hoffmann's specialized class), designs for a clothes closet and a table, 1916
Einfacher Hausrat, 1916

DENKMAL
(106).

Eine Parkanlage als Denkmal, mit gezogenen und geſtutzten Hecken,
mit einem Waſſerbecken und einer Springbrunnenfigur. Größe 40 × 40,
mittlere Säule 2 m im Durchmeſſer, Höhe 15 m.

Entwurf:

Schule Hoffmann: WILHELM FOLTIN, aus Innsbruck.

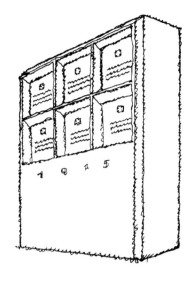

Fig. 21 Wilhelm Foltin (Hoffmann's specialized class), monument, 1915
Soldatengräber und Kriegsdenkmale, Vienna 1915, 280, plate 106

Fig. 22 JH, design for a war memorial, 1915
Soldatengräber und Kriegsdenkmale, Vienna 1915

1   "It is as if the pupil's own soul were being drawn, corrected, built, modelled and taught out of his body and replaced by a rigid dogma. […] But the dogma that will inevitably destroy this school is the view that our arts and crafts should be reformed from the top down, from the studio. But revolutions always come from below. And that 'below' is the workshop.
"The view still prevails here that the design of a chair should only be entrusted to someone who knows the five orders of columns off by heart. Such a man, I think, would primarily be bound to know something about sitting." Loos, Adolf, "Our School of Applied Art (1897)," in: id., *Ornament and Crime: Thoughts on Design and Materials*, London 2019, 1–9: 6 f. Trans. Shaun Whiteside.

2   Boeckl, Matthias, "Baukunst aus Reformgeist. Die Architekturschule der Angewandten," in: Bast, Gerald/Seipenbusch-Hufschmied, Anja/Werkner, Patrick (eds.), *150 Jahre Universität für angewandte Kunst in Wien. Ästhetik der Veränderung*, Berlin 2017, 44–65: 48.

3   "Ausweis über die Frequenz der Kunstgewerbeschule […] des Schuljahres 1899/1900," UAA, Collection and Archive, Zl. 285/1899 and 1175/1900.

4   Hoffmann's student list in 1900/01, UAA, Collection and Archive.

5   J. & J. Kohn supplied some of the most famous modern furniture types and worked with the most renowned designers of Viennese Modernism, such as with Otto Wagner on the *Die Zeit* dispatch office and with Adolf Loos on the chairs for Café Museum.

6   Hoffmann's student list from 1901/02, UAA, Collection and Archive.

7   Hoffmann appears not to have admitted any women in the first year when he alone decided who would be enrolled in his class.

8   Prutscher ran the public design drawing room for craftspeople; Witzmann taught the general theory of form course in the general department, another design drawing room for craftspeople (1918–1923), and the workshop for carpentry and cabinetry (1923–1949); Niedermoser's last class was a masterclass for interior design, industry, and craft design; and Wimmer-Wisgrill taught the fashion class.

9   The School of Arts and Crafts would ultimately be renamed the University of Applied Arts Vienna.

10 For example Ernst Anton Plischke, who studied under Oskar Strnad from 1919 to 1923 and then graduated with a diploma from Peter Behrens's masterclass at the Academy of Fine Arts in 1926.

11 Oskar Beyer, at times substituted for by Hans Schlechta, worked until 1909, Hermann Herdtle even until 1913.

12 Herdtle's and Hoffmann's annual reports from 1906/07, UAA, Collection and Archive.

13 The cast list reveals for example that Hoffmann's students Emanuel Margold, Fritz Zeymer, Hans Bolek, and Adolf Holub, as well as Czeschka's students Franz Karl Delavilla and Moritz Jung, performed in various roles as actors: *Die Tänzerin und die Marionette. Pantomime*, garden party in Weigls Dreherpark (Meidling), 6 and 7 Jun 1907, program, Vienna 1907. Some of the rehearsals for the theater in Weigls Dreherpark were reused by Hoffmann and his students for the Kunstschau stage in 1908.

14 For example, for the Kunstschau in 1908 Hoffmann designed an entire country house, complete with interior. Cf. Forsthuber, Sabine, *Moderne Raumkunst. Wiener Ausstellungsbauten von 1898 bis 1914*, Vienna 1991.

15 "Oberbaurat Prof. Dr. Josef Hoffmann ein Siebziger. Geburtstagsbesuch bei dem Gründer der Wiener Werkstätte," in: *Neues Wiener Tagblatt* 13 Dec 1940, 7. My thanks to Markus Kristan for this and many other reference sources.

16 Quoted in Hoffmann's annual report from 1906/07, UAA, Collection and Archive.

17 The designs came from Petru Balan, Max Benirschke, Alois Hollmann, Adolf Holub, and Carl Witzmann, among others.

18 Such as the hitherto anonymous *Projekt eines Landhauses* [Country House Project] from the MAK collection, KI 7696-49-1.

19 Doser, Barbara, "Das Frauenkunststudium in Österreich 1870–1935," dissertation at the University of Innsbruck 1988, 111–167, and Plakolm, Sabine, "Beruf: 'Frau Architekt.' Zur Ausbildung der ersten Architektinnen in Wien," in: Bois, Marcel/Reinhold, Bernadette (eds.), *Margarete Schütte-Lihotzky. Architektur. Politik. Geschlecht. Neue Perspektiven auf Leben und Werk*, Vienna/Basel 2019, 38–51.

20 The 40 female students in Hoffmann's specialized class between 1899 and 1918 were Martha Alber, Elisabeth Birnbacher, Ida Burian, Charlotte Calm, Anna Ehrenfest, Gisela von Falke, Beatrix Foltin, Mathilde Flögl, Charlotte Fochler, Olga Freund, Olga Fricke, Helene Geiringer, Paula Greischer, Valerie Klier, Ernestine Kopriva, Valentine Kovacic, Rosa Krenn, Hedwig Landesmann-Hirsch, Friederike Lazar-Löw, Editha Mautner-Markhof, Margarete von Noé, Camilla Peyrer, Angela Piotrowska-Wittmann, Felice Rix, Stephanie Robitschek, Juliana Rysavy, Irene Schaschl-Schuster, Elisabeth Schmeja, Hilde Schmid-Jesser, Ulrike Schreiber, Erika Schuller-Paulas, Maria Strauss-Likarz, Maria Trinkl, Else Unger-Holzinger, Marie Vogl, Gertrud Weinberger, Regine Weinfeld, Hedwig Marie Weinstein, Anna Wirth, and Dr. Friederike Wurmfeld; see student lists, UAA, Collection and Archive.

21 Kapfinger, Otto/Boeckl, Matthias, *Abgelehnt: Nicht ausgeführt. Die Bau- und Projektgeschichte der Hochschule für angewandte Kunst in Wien 1873–1993*, Vienna 1993.

22 Only in 1960 could a sober seven-story extension to the now University of Applied Arts, complete with sculpture studio, be realized by the architects Max Fellerer, Eugen Wörle, and Karl Schwanzer. It was renovated in 2018 by the Riepl-Kaufmann-Bammer team of architects together with a former administrative building constructed around 1900 on the other side of the river Wien. In 2020 the University of Applied Arts completed its expansion program, which had by now been ongoing for over a century, by renting sizable spaces e.g., in the nearby Postal Savings Bank, which had been built by Josef Hoffmann's teacher Otto Wagner in 1903–1912.

23 *Einfacher Hausrat*, exh. cat. AMAI, Vienna 1916.

24 Adolf Vetter's son Hans Adolf Vetter studied under Strnad and Tessenow at the School of Arts and Crafts, was Strnad's assistant, briefly acted as Hoffmann's successor in 1936/37, and edited the progressive architecture magazine *profil* for the Zentralvereinigung der Architekten (Central Organization of Architects) in 1933–1936.

25 Vetter, Adolf, "Vorwort," in: *Soldatengräber und Kriegsdenkmale*, ed. by k.k. Gewerbeförderungs-Amte (Imperial Royal Trade Advancement Bureau), Vienna 1915, 5.

26 Ibid., 34–335.

Fig. 1 JH, chair from the dining hall of Sanatorium Westend,
Purkersdorf (model no. 322 by J. & J. Kohn), Vienna, 1904

MAK, H 2189-1/1969, donation from Bundeskammer der gewerblichen Wirtschaft
© MAK/Georg Mayer

Sebastian Hackenschmidt, Wolfgang Thillmann

System Designs

Josef Hoffmann's Cooperation with J. & J. Kohn

Rather than first with Viennese Modernism at the turn of the 20th century, the renowned bentwood furniture manufacturer J. & J. Kohn began decisively expanding its range of products already in the mid-1870s. In addition to simple chairs for coffeehouses, which as "common factory goods" made up the majority of their sales volume,[1] they developed furniture types with which they could set themselves apart from the driving force in the area of restaurant and coffeehouse seating from the Thonet company. With so-called "salon furniture" to suit a more distinguished taste, Kohn followed

[2]

> "a new direction, meant to end the exclusive rule of the round rod and bring the manufacture of period furniture of angular bent rods decorated with millings, engravings, and sculptural works into the circle of factory production."[2]

The firm turned increasingly to elaborately designed luxury bentwood furniture in various styles—"Baroque, Renaissance, and Gothic"[3]—in the last quarter of the 19th century, leading us to assume that there was a market for such furniture, which even Thonet could not entirely ignore. Starting in 1883, there, too, salon furniture was in the program, albeit only sporadically, as they were aware that the elaborately decorated furniture ran counter to the concept of a serial production appropriate to the material. Furthermore, such furniture was not nearly as profitable as traditional bentwood products, as it could be sold in only limited numbers. While Thonet mainly satisfied mass demand for simple and affordable seating models, Kohn further expanded its luxury furniture segment for the Ringstraße salons of the upper class. Already at the 1885 Antwerp World's Fair, the company

[3]

also presented, for the first time, a space designed entirely by an architect. The smoking room by Nikolaus Hofmann, lecturer for technical drawing at the Technologisches Gewerbemuseum (Industrial Technology Museum) in Vienna, demonstrated "in a very artistically successful way, that the technique of bending wood could also be made serviceable for artistic demands."[4]

Based on this early change of direction toward luxury furniture and artistically designed furnishings, the Kohn enterprise was predestined to take on production of the demanding furniture required by the turn-of-the-century Secessionist spatial artists. Yet here, too, like with the salon

furniture, they could not count on any large distribution: furniture items and entire furnishings were often produced simply for short-lived exhibitions or one single contract. Additionally, the bentwood avant-garde's use of the technically demanding process developed by J. & J. Kohn of applying rectangular wooden cross sections with the possibility of nearly right-angled bends, made production even more expensive.

[7]

The furniture historian and architect Karl Mang, in his day, was privy to the information from the Hoffmann student Gustav Siegel (1880–1970)—who joined J. & J. Kohn's design office just before the turn of the century—that at this time, "the company routinely sought consultation from Josef Hoffmann."[5] Siegel himself was employed to design the Kohn enterprise's stand at the Paris World's Fair in 1900, and he also designed the company's stands for various exhibitions in the following years. Four drawings published in the magazine *Innendekoration* in 1901—one signed with the monogram GS—give a good impression of the new formal language to which the firm had obliged itself by employing Siegel.

[5]

Art historian Christian Witt-Dörring has meanwhile directed attention to a J. & J. Kohn advertisement in the magazine *Hohe Warte* in 1905 offering a "system design [by] Professor Josef Hoffmann." In the foreground of the illustration, a piece of furniture can be seen that had previously been published as a design by Koloman Moser and was shown at the winter exhibition of the Austrian Museum of Art and Industry (today's MAK) in 1901/02:

[6]

> "The question thus arises as to whether this 'new system,' comprised of chairs and case pieces of enclosed bent-wood frames, with the runners so typical of Hoffmann, was in fact designed by Hoffmann and simply used by Moser as a convenient framework for one of his own designs. The system might also represent a collaboration between the two designers; it has been confirmed that both worked together closely in designing the storefront of the J. & J. Kohn showroom in Berlin."[6]

Several issues to be considered in the ascription of bentwood furniture to Josef Hoffmann therewith appear together. Not only concerning the close collaboration with Moser, but

Fig. 2 Salon suite no. 405 (late 19th c.) from the catalog
of the J. & J. Kohn company from 1906
Thillmann Archive

Fig. 3 Nikolaus Hofmann, smoking lounge for J. & J. Kohn
at the World's Fair in Antwerp, 1885
*Mittheilungen des Technologischen Gewerbe-Museums,
Section für Holz-Industrie, Wien* (VI) 71, 15 Nov 1885, 165

also the meager and often contradictory information in the
then-current publications, on which we are reliant today due
to the lack of explicit information in the producers' and ex-
hibiters' catalogs or designers' own records. In the mean-
time, it has become customary to draw conclusions from
the first images published at the time of interior furnishings
and exhibition berths and ascribe all of the furniture seen
in the space to the architect when he is the only creator
named or known. But also conceivable is that Hoffmann—
to refer to him again—took recourse to existing models from
the J. & J. Kohn firm, with whom he regularly collaborated,
to furnish an interior that he had designed. For the Cabaret
Fledermaus, opened in Vienna in October 1907, for
example, black-and-white painted bentwood chairs manufactured by J. & J. Kohn were used as seating. In a contemporary critique Ludwig Hevesi describes them as "comfortable chairs of a new form; genuine Hoffmann."[7]

However, the form was not actually "new"; the chair Hoffmann used had been published in the Kohn catalog in 1906
as part of suite no. 728—and the variant belonging to it,
had already served in spring 1906 in a hall of the *Esposizione
internazionale del Sempione* in Milan as chairs for visitors.[8]
That is not meant to say that Hoffmann did not design this
furniture, but no clear evidence can be provided. The bentwood furniture that Hoffmann presented in his *Kleines Landhaus* [Small Country House] at the Kunstschau in Vienna in
1908, on the contrary, can be reliably attributed to him. In
a detailed discussion of the Kunstschau, Joseph August Lux
wrote: "The Jakob und Joseph Kohn firm, namely, brings
ideas from Joseph [sic] Hoffmann."[9] Suite no. 729, very similar to suite no. 728, was also among this furniture: is it now
possible, from the close formal relationship of the two sets,
to draw the conclusion that he is the creator of the Fledermaus set—relying first and foremost on the shape of the
base, so characteristic of Hoffmann's furniture?

In the secondary literature, the attempt has also been
made to ascribe the *Fledermaus Suite* to Gustav Siegel.[10]
In doing so, the authors invoke information from Karl
Mang—and thereby tread on thin ice. In a publication Mang
compiled in 1969, he commented with reference to armchair
no. 728/F, which Thonet later also adopted in their program,
that it is "probably from the architect Siegel."[11] However,

in his book *Thonet Bugholzmöbel* from 1982, he appraised
armchair no. 728 again as a design by Hoffmann.[12] Of
course, it seems appealing to speculate on Siegel's role in
J. & J. Kohn's design office: As a technical manager of sorts,
was he meant to look after mainly practical or coordinative
tasks? Did it rest upon him to implement the ideas of his
teacher Josef Hoffmann, and adapt them to the interests of
the firm? Or as "the man of bent wood"—as he was called
by Hevesi in his day[13]—was he, instead, personally responsible for a majority of the bentwood furniture designs with
a "Secessionist element," which Hoffmann merely needed
to use in his own interiors? The answer must remain open.
Nonetheless, it seems quite safe to assume that as a very
busy architect, Hoffmann had little interest in personally
finetuning his aesthetic notions for bentwood furniture to
the manufacturer's technical and commercial requirements:
this may well have been the job of the drafting office, even
more so since his student was employed there.

The so-called *Purkersdorf Suite* can serve as an example
of this. The chair used to furnish the dining hall and the
glazed veranda of Sanatorium Westend in Purkersdorf,
opened in 1904, is, with great certainty, a design by Hoffmann. But whether this also applies to the rest of the suite
is doubtful, since the chair has remarkable technical details
not found on the armchair or sofa. The back legs of the chair
are rectangular, but in the area of the backrest, the cross
section is round whereby it tapers through to the curve of
the upper backrest. On the contrary, with the armchair and
sofa that were not used in Purkersdorf, the legs, stiles, and
crest rail have a continuously round cross section. In addition,
to yield a consistent suite, all three seats had to have the
same height—which led the wider and deeper armchair to
seem heavy and stocky, an effect intensified by the broad,
double-row perforated plywood panel in the backrest and
the upholstered armrests. The same applies to the sofa. Like
in many other cases, it stands to reason that the firm's design
office—not the actual designer himself—took a single piece
of designed furniture and developed it to a complete suite.
For stabilizing his chair, Hoffmann introduced ball-shaped
reinforcements bolted onto the seat frame and the legs.
This aesthetic solution was adopted not only for the entire
Purkersdorf Suite, but also later for further models. However,

Fig. 4 Trumeau mirror and console table no. 1145 from the supplement to the catalog of the J. & J. Kohn company from 1902
Thillmann Archive

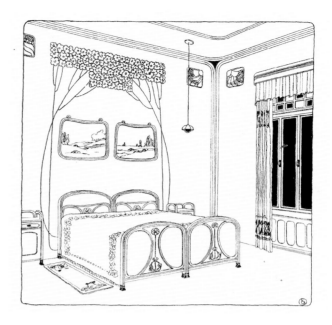

Fig. 5 Gustav Siegel, design for bedroom furnishings by the J. & J. Kohn company
ID (12) 1901, 102

also these balls present no guarantee in the attribution of authorship.

Even when it is not possible in the context of this article to discuss all models that come into question in terms of their authorship, the close connection between Josef Hoffmann and J. & J. Kohn nonetheless remains beyond doubt. But what could have inspired the architect to work as a designer for this industrial enterprise and to develop in addition to "system designs" and "furnishing concepts" also individual items of bentwood furniture? When large amounts of identical seating were required for the dining hall of the Sanatorium, and it seemed advantageous for economic reasons to include also industrially produced serial furniture in the Gesamtkunstwerk—or total work of art—it must have seemed obvious to cooperate with Kohn to supplement the furniture produced by hand in the joinery of the Wiener Werkstätte as Hoffmann had already had good experiences with them in the realization of his system designs made of closed bentwood frames. However, based on the armchairs designed by Koloman Moser and produced by the wicker-work factory Prag-Rudniker, of which only relatively low quantities were needed for the hall, it is conceivable that more than economic reasons were at play in Purkers-dorf. For Hoffmann and Moser, the collaborations with Kohn and Prag-Rudniker were most likely largely about accepting the challenge of serial production of contemporary furniture.

The two designers remarked in the *Arbeitsprogramm der Wiener Werkstätte* (work program of the Wiener Werk-stätte) published in 1904, as a diagnosis of the times: Replacing the hand, for the most part, is the machine; and replacing the artisan, is the businessman. They nonetheless founded a workshop for the creation of items of decorative arts in "intimate contact between public, designer, and artisan."[14] Even when the "Productivgenossenschaft von Kunsthandwerkern in Wien" (Productive Cooperative of Craftspeople in Vienna) envisioned by the founders of the Wiener Werkstätte, primarily had the "production of objects of all types of arts and crafts based on artistic designs by members of the cooperative"[15] in mind, at the end of their work program, Hoffmann and Moser conceded the

SALONECKE

Installation und Möbel aus gebogenem Holze, scharf-kantige Biegungen nach dem neuen System-Entwurf

Professor JOSEPH HOFFMANNS

Erste österreichische Aktiengesellschaft zur Erzeugung von Möbeln aus gebogenem Holze

JAKOB & JOSEF KOHN
Wien, I. Elisabethstrasse Nr. 24.

Fig. 6 Advertisement for the J. & J. Kohn company
Hohe Warte, supplement to (2) 19/20 1905/06, 2

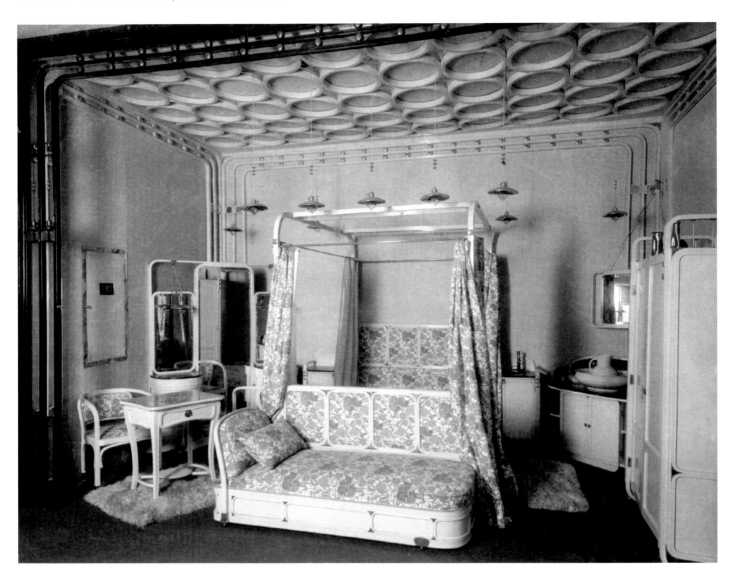

Fig. 7 Bedroom furnishings by the J. & J. Kohn company
in the winter exhibition at the AMAI, Vienna, 1901/02
MAK, KI 7480

possibility of designing appropriate articles also for industrial
production:

> "It is still permissible to draw attention to the fact that we, too,
> are aware that in certain conditions, a reasonable mass-produced
> article can be created with the help of machines: the same, must,
> though, unconditionally bear the imprint of fabrication."[16]

Although they were convinced that mainly high-quality
handcrafted work should be promoted, in their manifesto,
Hoffmann and Moser also accounted for the idea of high-
grade mass production—whose vanishing point can be
found in today's industrial design.[17] And in the cooperation
with furniture manufacturers such as J. & J. Kohn and Prag-
Rudniker, the artists in the circles of the Wiener Werkstätte
attempted to approach this nearly utopian ideal of distinguished industrial production also in practice.

In a lecture held about his work in 1911, Hoffmann voiced
the opinion that nothing has "been more damaging for the
modern movement"[18] than industry's assumption that it can
simply replicate modern forms. However, he went on to
explain that there is a difference between styles that have
already been scientifically studied and can therefore be
reconstructed, and forms that are still "just developing."
Hoffmann therewith alluded to the difficulty of convincing

established firms to devote themselves in full to the development of a new formal language in cooperation with designing artists: "Fortunately, we now have in Vienna four or
five such enterprises, and we can therefore claim that our
efforts seem to advance and develop."[19]

Whether Hoffmann considered J. & J. Kohn—which parallel to its "Secessionist" work, still produced anachronistic
furniture for contemporary tastes—among these enterprises,
remains undecided. Meanwhile indisputable is that his artistic
designs for Kohn possessed the previously quoted "imprint
of fabrication." The bentwood technology offered Hoffmann
a material technology process with the help of which high-
quality products could be manufactured on an industrial
scale. And the characteristic forms could achieve large quantities only in a major concern with the corresponding mechanical facilities.

In any case, Hoffmann's and Moser's endeavors at an
affordable and nonetheless high-quality manufacture of
bentwood and wicker furniture in serial production were
recognized. The critic Joseph August Lux, in his previously
mentioned review of the Kunstschau, thus wrote:

> "The artists should also think with the machine. In furniture
> manufacture, which is entirely industrial, it is most clearly the case.

Fig. 8 JH, dining hall at Sanatorium Westend, Purkersdorf, 1904
MAK, WWF-102-97-2

J. & J. Kohn offer ideas by Joseph [sic] Hoffmann to the market, which do justice to the highest demands of good taste and elegance. Also the Prag-Rudnikger [sic] wickerwork factory does the utmost to keep their products at the height of good taste."[20]

A further critique of the Kunstschau on the contrary, took lengthy stock of the artistic development of the bentwood furniture industry under Hoffmann's supervision:

"It is a known fact that J. & J. Kohn was the one who brought the bentwood furniture technique, hitherto known only in not very beautiful mass-produced articles, to unexpected heights […]. The way that the artistic designs (Professor Josef Hoffmann) were implemented, can serve as evidence that the modern industry, by virtue of the fact that it speaks its own language, can also seem artistic in its essence."[21]

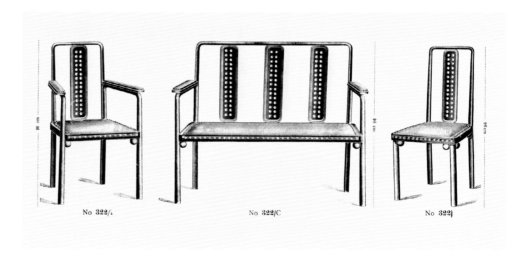

No 322/ₐ   No 322/C   No 322J

Fig. 9 Salon suite no. 322 "Purkersdorf" in the catalog of the J. & J. Kohn company from 1906
Thillmann Archive

Fig. 10 Fauteuil from the so-called "Fledermaus" suite (model no. 728/F by J. & J. Kohn) as a visitor's chair
in the Sala del Tirolo in the Austrian pavilion at the *Esposizione internazionale del Sempione*, Milan, 1906
Thillmann Archive

Fig. 11 The so-called "Fledermaus" chair (model no. 738
by J. & J. Kohn) in the auditorium of Josef Hoffmann's
Cabaret Fledermaus, Vienna, 1907
DKuD (22) 1908, 158

The attempt to elevate the quality of mass production
in an interplay of art and industry, was in fact among the
most urgent creative tasks of the time around 1900 and led
to the founding of the German Werkbund in 1907. For
several more years, as a founding member of the German
Werkbund—and in 1912, also the Austrian Werkbund—
Hoffmann would follow the path described in the critique.
At the Werkbund exhibition in Cologne in 1914, with a
specially designed exhibition space and a great number of   14
individual, imaginative chair models, he was able to celebrate a final artistic highlight in the cooperation with the
industrial enterprise J. & J. Kohn.   ▪

Fig. 12 JH (attributed), the so-called
"Fledermaus" chair (model no. 728 by
J. & J. Kohn), Vienna, 1905/06
Donation from Stefan and Paul Asenbaum
MAK, H 2870
© MAK/Georg Mayer

Fig. 13 JH, salon with suite 729 by J. & J. Kohn on the upper floor of the
Kleines Landhaus [Small Country House] at the Kunstschau, Vienna, 1908
MBF (VII) 1908, 374

Fig. 14 JH, exhibition space by J. & J. Kohn
at the German Werkbund exhibition in
Cologne, 1914
Österreichische Werkkultur, Vienna 1916, 30

1   See *Denkschrift der Firma Jacob & Josef Kohn
    zur Weltausstellung zu Philadelphia 1876*, German/
    English/French, 25, https://digital.hagley.org
    (Hagley ID: AVD_2003_255_05_025) [Feb 2021].
2   See "Jacob & Josef Kohn. Fabriken für gebogene
    Möbel. Wien," in: *Die Gross-Industrie Österreichs,
    Jubiläumsbuch der Industrie anlässlich des fünfzig-
    jährigen Regierungsjubiläums Kaiser Franz Josefs*,
    Vienna 1898, vol. 3, 320–322: 321.
3   Ibid.
4   "Die Holz-Industrie auf der internationalen Aus-
    stellung in Antwerpen," in: *Mittheilungen des
    Technologischen Gewerbe-Museums, Section für
    Holz-Industrie* (VI) 71, 15 Nov 1885, 161–164: 163.
5   Mang, Karl, *Thonet Bugholzmöbel. Von der hand-
    werklichen Produktion zur industriellen Fertigung*,
    Vienna 1982, 104.
6   Witt-Dörring, Christian, "Bent-wood production
    and the Viennese avant-garde: The Thonet and
    Kohn firms 1899–1914," in: Ostergard, Derek E.,

Bent Wood and Metal Furniture 1850–1946, New
York 1987, 95–120: 110. For the ascription of the
cabinet to Koloman Moser, see *Kunst und Kunsthandwerk* (5) 1 1902, 4.
7   Ibid.; Hevesi, Ludwig, *Altkunst – Neukunst, Wien
    1894–1908*, Vienna 1909, 243.
8   See Renzi, Giovanni, *Il mobile moderno*, Milan
    2008, 164 ff.
9   See Lux, Joseph August, "Kunstschau – Wien
    1908," quoted in: Kristan, Markus (ed.), *Kunst-
    schau Wien 1908*, Weitra 2016, 185–200: 196.
10 See Renzi 2008 (see note 8) and Dry, Graham,
    "The development of the bent-wood furniture
    industry 1869–1914," in: Ostergard 1987 (see
    note 6), 53–93: 89n41, 42.
11 See *Das Haus Thonet*, Frankenberg 1969, n. p.
12 See Mang 1982 (see note 5), 107.
13 Hevesi, Ludwig, *Acht Jahre Secession*, Vienna
    1906, 336.

14 "Arbeitsprogramm der Wiener Werkstätte," in:
    Hohe Warte 1904/5, 268.
15 See Handelsregister Wien, Reg. der Genossen-
    schaft, vol. VIII, 124.
16 Arbeitsprogramm 1904/05 (see note 14).
17 See Posener, Julius, "Zwischen Kunst und Indus-
    trie: Der Deutsche Werkbund," in: Burckhardt,
    Lucius (ed.), *Der Werkbund in Deutschland, Öster-
    reich und der Schweiz. Form ohne Ornament*,
    Stuttgart 1978, 7–15: 7.
18 "Industry had to realize that it had to let the
    apples ripen first." Hoffmann, Josef, "My Work"
    (lecture, 1911), quoted in: Sekler, Eduard F., *Josef
    Hoffmann: The Architectural Work*, Princeton, NJ
    1985, 486–492: 488. Trans. Eduard F. Sekler and
    John Maass.
19 Ibid., 489.
20 Lux 1908/2016 (see note 9), 196.
21 "Die Bilanz der Kunstschau," quoted in: Kristan
    2016 (see note 9), 201–203: 203.

Fig. 1 JH, library stepladder for Karl Wittgenstein, executed by the Wiener Werkstätte, 1905
Oak, stained black, with pores chalked yellow, brass
Private collection
© MAK/Georg Mayer

Christian Witt-Dörring

From Art Object to Standard Product

The Wiener Werkstätte 1903–1918

"Hoff is the only one who can bring off a new blouse as easily as a new public building."[1]

The Wiener Werkstätte (WW) emerges at a time when the Secession's early years of rebellion have already passed and it has become a formidable force for innovation in the Austrian creative economy. Simultaneously it finds its values being embraced by a self-confident upper middle class that is starting to break with the aristocratic lifestyle model and now requires its own representative style. The aesthetic concept of the Wiener Werkstätte makes it possible for this upper middle class to be recognized by the public as an independent social stratum that patronizes the arts, much like the court society of the 17th and 18th centuries. It is a small, committed group of artists and predominantly wealthy Jewish families who are linked by family ties, friendships, or business interests and whose commissions support the project of Vienna's art spring. Bearing in mind that the Jewish population of Austria-Hungary was only granted full civil rights in 1867, the members of these families are mostly just the second generation to be assimilated into the Christian culture of Vienna. Their desire for integration is accommodated among other things by the Secession's programmatic search for a modern Austrian style. This Austrian style should not be interpreted as an expression of nationalistic or rather German nationalist tendencies, such as those extremes that are dotted across the multilingual Austro-Hungarian Empire at this time. Rather, it means an emphasis on the unique individual artistic statement: the Secessionists categorically reject the approach and aesthetics of Historicism. For the assimilated Jewish population this Austrian style, which will come to be known internationally as the "Viennese style," has the potential to provide a sense of belonging that is not defined by nationality.

The Wiener Werkstätte is virtually synonymous with Josef Hoffmann—and vice versa. Hoffmann fights almost his entire life for the values and the survival of the Wiener Werkstätte. It is a battle against bad taste and inferior production, against the dominance of mechanical production, and against trade dictating which product range is available. The WW represents a sustainable, artisanally produced, identity-forming, local product with individual artistic expression—values that had been invoked by the Arts & Crafts movement in England from the 1850s to counter the negative effects of the Industrial Revolution. These values

are based on John Ruskin's and William Morris's social criticism and aspirations for aesthetic reform. Calling for a return to preindustrial artisanal production methods, they anticipate that this reversal will cure the brutalization of tastes and society of their age. The former is the result of an anything-is-possible mentality promoted by low-cost substitute materials and technologies that flood the market with cheap mechanical mass production, which demands fast fashions to incentivize increased sales. The latter addresses the inhumane and joyless living conditions of the industrial proletariat. In the course of the division of labor for industrial manufacturing, the craftsperson mutated into a laborer. The intention behind a return to artisanal production is to restore these people's pleasure in their work—and with it their dignity. This requires the reestablishment of the preindustrial unity of design and execution processes, whereby the craftsperson realizes an object from its concept to its completion. The logical consequence of this construct is the demand for the unity of the arts, a notion that was taken for granted in the Middle Ages. The hierarchical division of fine and decorative art established in the course of the Industrial Revolution is thus repealed. In general, the English Arts & Crafts movement also draws on the design vocabulary of the Middle Ages until the late 19th century.

The great achievement of the Secession—whose founding members include the protagonists of the Wiener Werkstätte, Josef Hoffmann and Koloman Moser—is that it gives the Arts & Crafts ideology a modern, contemporary, Viennese incarnation some half a century after the movement's inception. The members of the Secession call for the development of an independent, modern, Austrian, and bourgeois style. They see unique artistic expression as a modern alternative to the anachronistic forms of Historicism, which are deemed internationally indistinguishable, and consider it to have the potential to enable modern citizens to emerge as individuals. Inspired by the Arts & Crafts movement, the Secessionists adopt the credo of the unity of the arts, which draws on the belief in humankind's salvation through art and the directly related consequence of tearing down the barrier between art and everyday life. Hence the artist now takes on the responsibility for designing everyday objects. Among other things, this is intended to guarantee that

Fig. 3 JH, buffet in white maple with copper fittings, and Koloman Moser, corner cabinet *Die verwunschenen Prinzessinnen* [The Enchanted Princesses], 8th Secession exhibition, 1900
ID (12) 1901, 32

Fig. 2 JH, design of room V at the 8th Secession exhibition, 1900
Künstlerhaus Archive

beauty reappears in people's everyday lives via artistic design, thereby making life worth living again. This becomes manifest in the ideal of the Gesamtkunstwerk—or total work of art.

From the outset the Secessionists present applied art (decorative arts) and fine art as equal in their exhibitions. Together with the painter Koloman Moser, the architects Joseph Maria Olbrich and Josef Hoffmann provide designs for modern Viennese decorative arts, organize their realization by local producers, and set in motion an educational program for consumers and producers alike in the framework of exhibitions. Presenting decorative arts in the context of an art exhibition in contrast to a trade fair is an absolute novelty at that time. The Secessionists' decision to dedicate their 8th exhibition exclusively to international and domestic decorative arts must accordingly be understood as programmatic. The who's who of the international decorative-art avant-garde is invited to the opening on 3 November 1900: from Julius Meier-Graefe's Parisian gallery La Maison Moderne to the Copenhagen-based porcelain manufactory Bing & Grøndahl, from the French ceramicists Pierre Adrien Dalpayrat, Ernest Chaplet, and Auguste Delaherche to the decorative artist Maurice Dufrène and the Belgian Henry van de Velde, from Charles R. Ashbee's London Guild of Handicraft and the Scots Frances and Herbert MacNair to Charles Rennie Mackintosh and his wife Margaret Macdonald Mackintosh. The exhibition can be considered a kind of status report by the Secessionists as to how close they had come to achieving their goal, namely the development of an independent modern Austrian style. Even during the preparations for the exhibition, Meier-Graefe and Hoffmann come to verbal blows over the formal aesthetics of Van de Velde's curvilinear design for the presentation of the gallery La Maison Moderne. This argument makes clear the extent of Vienna's emancipation from its sources of inspiration abroad:

"The design strikes me as amiss and unworkable in every respect […]. I will not allow a transgression of the wood grains. Disregarding the outrageously festive lines—kindly consider how the curves of the flat surfaces are canceled out—the gentleman who produced the design hasn't a clue about construction. This is what we here fear like poison as the false Secession. The aforementioned design could only be executed correctly in bentwood […]. Moreover, consider the showcases, what bent glass is desired for them. One can but marvel that one could invent such a thing […]. Having your design sawn out of ordinary wood like fretwork is something I would not even dream of doing […]. Here, the age of false curves has passed, thank goodness, and we have utter respect for the material above all."[2]

The exhibition architecture for the works from La Maison Moderne is ultimately designed by Koloman Moser, while Hoffmann takes over the majority of the remaining exhibition design. It is also Hoffmann who invites Charles Rennie Mackintosh and Margaret Macdonald to participate in the exhibition when Fritz Waerndorfer visits Glasgow.[3] Their room, which the art critic and champion of the Secessionists Ludwig Hevesi describes as "off the charts,"[4] plays an important part in Hoffmann's further development—not so much in terms of formal aesthetic details as with respect to a fundamental approach to space and coloration. Here Hoffmann is confronted with an entirely new sensuality. It will inspire his early interiors from the years 1901/02, which he creates for the villas on the Hohe Warte and the dining room in the Waerndorfer villa, and ultimately to ask Mackintosh's opinion on possibly founding a Viennese workshop.

His disagreement with Meier-Graefe about fundamental modern stylistic notions may have induced Hoffmann to argue his or rather the Viennese viewpoint even more clearly in his article "Einfache Möbel" ("Simple Furniture").[5] The link between the two cannot be denied, as right at the outset Hoffmann remarks that the initial outline of the article

Fig. 5 Works by Charles Rennie Mackintosh
and Margaret Macdonald Mackintosh,
8th Secession exhibition, 1900
ID (12), 1901, 36

Fig. 4 JH, fireplace,
8th Secession exhibition, 1900
ID (12), 1901, 33

had been written a year beforehand and he is reusing the vignettes he had drawn for the catalog of the 8th Secession exhibition to decorate his article. Long sections of the text read like a new gospel to convert the heathen masses. The unequal struggle to be fought arises from the "obligation to make happy those few who are devoted to us. They must not be deluded at any cost. They must feel that we have sacrificed ourselves to please them; they must intuit our priesthood and believe in our earnest enthusiasm."[6] The credo of the Arts & Crafts movement emanates from these words. By sacrificing himself for the suffering of humankind, the artist becomes the savior of the world. A symbolic monument will be erected in honor of this artist, who is symbolized by Ludwig van Beethoven, in the form of a Gesamtkunstwerk exhibition concept by the Secession's members: the 14th exhibition in 1902, the so-called Beethoven exhibition. Hoff-

mann is in charge of the interior design for this show and among other contributions, Gustav Klimt designs his *Beethoven Frieze* for the left side room, the subject of which is likewise the salvation of the suffering by the arts.

Through his designs for the interior of the Secession's exhibitions and for the decorative-art objects displayed there, Hoffmann reaches a public from which his most important and most affluent patrons and customers would hail. However, in the context of the Secession the most portentous encounter for Hoffmann and Viennese decorative arts as a whole is that with the wealthy textile industrialist Fritz Waerndorfer.

In a letter to Josef Hoffmann dated 23 December 1902, Fritz Waerndorfer expresses his complete admiration and gratitude for the world of art opened up to him by Moser and Hoffmann:

Fig. 6 JH, designs for cloakroom and lady's
dressing room. Illustration for Hoffmann's
article "Einfache Möbel"
DI (2) 1901, plate 87

Fig. 7 JH, main room of the 14th Secession exhibition
with Max Klinger's Beethoven sculpture, 1902
DKuD (10) 1902, 483

"You know, sometimes when I look at my things, it seems as though the whole Secession had been founded just for me. I found my two friends or rather Viennese buddies [Hoffmann and Moser] via the Secession. You sent me to Glasgow; I wouldn't have had a clue about Minne without you. In short, I feel like a pig fattened on your fat. But it doesn't matter."[7]

18 19 20
p. 160

It must have been on his visit to the 8th Secession exhibition in the year 1900 that Waerndorfer was bitten by the bug of Viennese Modernism once and for all. Two years later he starts to commission Hoffmann, Moser, and Mackintosh with decorating rooms in his house. In the course of this project, he finds the effusive words "You splendid man and paragon of taste and decency"[8] for Hoffmann and the idea voiced by Hoffmann and Moser blossoms: to found a company that would produce decorative-art objects of the highest artisanal quality, after artistic designs, and independent of middlemen. Waerndorfer presents this proposal to Mackintosh and asks for his opinion. The latter responds enthusiastically, as Waerndorfer writes to Hoffmann:

"I sympathize wholeheartedly with your 'latest' idea and consider it simply magnificent, and I want to tell you everything in detail. If Hoffmann and Moser and the rest have a large enough circle of admirers, who more than merely admire but actively want to help—through their support and their influence—then the sooner you found the workshops, the sooner you will attain a glorious ideal. Moser is entirely right in his intention provisionally to realize only ordered items. If one wants to achieve artistic success with your scheme (and artistic success must be your foremost intention), then every object that you hand over must bear a distinct mark of individuality, beauty, and the most meticulous execution.

Right from the outset your aim must be for every object that you produce to be made for a specific purpose and place. Later, when your hand and your position are strengthened by the high quality of your product and by financial success, you can confidently venture out into the world's spotlight, attack the factory trade on its own turf, and you can accomplish the greatest achievement that can be accomplished this century: namely the production of all practical objects in a delightful form and at such a price that they are within the purchasing power of the poorest, and in such quantities that the average man on the street is forced to buy them because he cannot acquire anything else and because soon he will not want to buy anything else."[9]

In May 1903 Moser, Hoffmann, and Waerndorfer finally found the "Wiener Werkstätte Productivgenossenschaft von Kunsthandwerkern in Wien" (Viennese Workshop Productive Cooperative of Craftspeople in Vienna). Their artistic aim is based on the ideal of the Gesamtkunstwerk as developed by the Vienna Secession. Its realization until that point had only been possible under extremely difficult working conditions; the fundamental irreconcilability of tradespeople and artists had precluded it. Until well into the 1930s Hoffmann misses no opportunity to caution against middlemen.[10] With direct contact between artist and artisan, it is now feasible to bring to fruition artistically designed everyday objects without any compromises and in compelling artisanal quality; these objects of daily life range from architecture to every aspect of interior decoration, fashion, and even postcards. With the realization of individual artistic expression ever the priority, the result is a kaleidoscope of a unique product culture that is constantly being reinvented until the

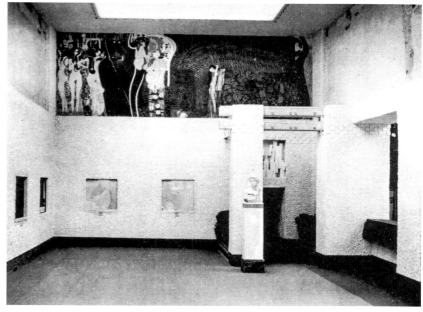

Fig. 8 JH, portal with geometric composition as an overdoor; right side room of the 14th Secession exhibition, 1902
DKuD (10) 1902, 490

Fig. 9 JH, left side room of the 14th Secession exhibition with Gustav Klimt's *Beethoven Frieze*, 1902
DKuD (10) 1902, 479

WW's liquidation in 1932. At the same time, however, the dictate of artistic authority hinders the actualization of parity between artisan and artist, an ideal of the Arts & Crafts movement that was modeled on the medieval reality.

The WW begins with its own metal workshop, for which a small apartment is rented at Heumühlgasse 6 in Vienna's fourth district. In all likelihood the reason why metal is the first material to be worked when the WW launches its general operations is because from 1902 Hoffmann turns his attention to designing silver objects for the first time, which he has realized by the companies Würbel & Czokally and Alexander Sturm. One year later, in May 1904, the Wiener Werkstätte is granted trade licenses for bookbinding, painting, varnishing, and carpentry and moves into its own, much larger workshop building at Neustiftgasse 32–34 in Vienna's seventh district, which also affords the opportunity for salesrooms and offices. The WW's raison d'être, namely respect for the individual artistic design and its high-quality artisanal execution, is expressed on every object: it is signed by both its designer and its craftsperson and is branded with the WW's trademark. For this purpose Moser designs hallmarks with corresponding monograms. They are published in 1905 together with the WW's work program, which was written by Hoffmann. The latter is based in part on Hoffmann's aforementioned text on "Einfache Möbel" that had been published back in 1901, in which among other things he refers to the vital necessity of signing works.[11]

It is significant that Hoffmann and Moser, neither of whom could speak English, approach—via Waerndorfer—Mackintosh and not Ashbee with their idea. Though Ashbee was the founder of the Guild of Handicraft and had participated in the 8th exhibition of the Secession, in Mackintosh they see a kindred artistic spirit who gives precedence to the persuasive power of the artistic design over the moral values of a social utopia. Even financial considerations are subordinated to this conviction to the point of self-destruction.[12] In this sense Waerndorfer's role as the facilitator of the Wiener Werkstätte's idealistic project has been entirely underestimated until now. He is not only the financier but above all the manager, ambassador, and champion of the movement or rather canvasser of commissions to guarantee the WW's continued operation. Waerndorfer's boundless faith in Hoffmann's genius constantly oscillates between two extremes: "… can I afford it, or do I owe it to the world to make myself afford it?" As early as 1906, just three years after the Wiener Werkstätte was founded, this develops into an arduous struggle for survival that makes patently clear that a business entity entirely dependent on patronage simply cannot survive. The WW's catastrophic financial situation is primarily the fault of the commission to build and decorate Stoclet House in Brussels, which Waerndorfer accepted for the lump sum of 500,000 kronen (equivalent to approx. €3.5 million today),[13] as well as from 1907 Waerndorfer's acquisition of Cabaret Fledermaus and its decoration by the WW. The drastically deteriorating financial situation induces Waerndorfer to appeal in early 1907 to Moser's wife Editha for financial support without her husband's knowledge, a move that would ultimately lead to Moser's departure from the WW.[14] Moser makes reference to the workshop's untenable financial management and the constant uncertainty surrounding its continued existence shortly thereafter in a letter to Hoffmann dated 20 February 1907, in which he writes:

> "I have and will never reproach Fritz [Waerndorfer]—but I am absolutely convinced that it [the Wiener Werkstätte] can never achieve a healthy basis, as it has failed to do so to date. How [it should do so], I am not enough of a businessman [to say]—and as colossally as I esteem you, I must also tell you that you understand nothing of business. So there are artist designers who understand nothing and an enthusiastic art lover who is also far removed from being a businessman—I find that hopeless. The W.W. has well-nigh become an albatross to me. Always the thought that Fritz will simply close it down and that people are bound to blame the wrong, incorrect actions of the designers, that not even the standing we had before starting the W.W. will be possible anymore … How one should give advice in that situation, I just don't know."[15]

Although from 1910 Waerndorfer accepts that the time-consuming execution of unique artistic designs is no longer

Fig. 10 JH, overdoor, left and right side rooms
of the 14th Secession exhibition, 1902
DKuD (10) 1902, 486

financially tenable and the workshop consequently focuses increasingly on designs (postcards, clothing and decorative fabrics) that can be produced in great number, the WW's financial situation continues to deteriorate dramatically. In 1911, in the seventh year of Stoclet House's construction, there is still no end in sight and the building's owner refuses to increase the budget. Waerndorfer and Hoffmann realize that the end of the WW is nigh and start looking for solutions. As is revealed in a letter from Waerndorfer to Carl Otto Czeschka from 11 May 1911, their sentiments are diametrically opposed:

"My stance today is that the difficulty can best be overcome through the cheapness of the products. For this reason I advocate mass-produced items that we do not manufacture ourselves, that are only better than other mass-produced items in their design that but do not cost more. However, this means considerably if not completely forsaking the WW's original quality principles. What speaks against this is the difficulty of mass-producing anything half decent or better than is already being manufactured; what speaks for this is that with cheap mass-produced items one can reach the broad consumer class. Hoffmann says: from now on only make the most expensive things. What speaks against this is that rich people are actually the most ignorant and nowadays only buy securities. They buy old pictures, secure in the knowledge that they will make money out of them, and precious stones for jewelry, likewise as assets."[16]

For his part, Hoffmann sends a supplicatory begging letter to Stoclet, in which he closes with the following sentences:

"I ask you, dear Mister Stoklet [sic], to be assured that nothing is more embarrassing to me than this letter and that I am nevertheless tremendously grateful to you for artistic reasons. I can think of nothing more wonderful than completing such a work, so please do help me and find a possibility, a solution. Must everything in life end with discord? Can we not trust and believe one another as humans? I implore you to do everything possible, which I also intend to do for the completion of your house."[17]

Stoclet communicates to Waerndorfer his complete incomprehension of Hoffmann's letter. He does not react to

Hoffmann's emotional attempts at justification but instead refers to facts and demands an explanation of the obvious inconsistencies in Hoffmann's calculation, which amounts to a sum total of 1,254,366.90 kronen (equivalent to over €7 million today).[18]

Hoffmann and Waerndorfer have another difference of opinion regarding a house project for Paul Poiret, in the course of which the architectural drawing office at the WW—under Hoffmann's management until that point—is closed in 1912.[19] Hoffmann relocates it to the School of Arts and Crafts; in light of the Wiener Werkstätte's increasingly grave financial situation, this prompts Moser to make the following remark:

"WW has been in agony for years. Hoffmann has—finally—moved his construction drawing office to the school and hence is no longer so dependent on the WW. If it had continued for a while longer, he would have been able to make a little bird house for the Naschmarkt at most."[20]

By now Waerndorfer has lost the majority of his personal fortune through his involvement in the workshop and is forced in late March 1914 to withdraw from the WW. He is replaced by new financiers who in the main consist of Hoffmann's clientele.[21] Waerndorfer's departure as the main financier necessitates the liquidation of the Wiener Werkstätte; its immediate refounding in 1914 leads to a new contract being drawn up between the Wiener Werkstätte and Hoffmann that is limited to ten years. Among other things, it specifies that Hoffmann cannot claim any remuneration if his architecture studio awards commissions to the WW.[22] The new management reacts to the signs of the times and is permitted a trade license in September 1914 for the factory-like manufacture of decorative metalwork and wares made of bronze and electroplated nickel silver, as well as metal fashion accessories, in addition to the factory-like operation of the trades of gold- and silversmithing, jewel-working, and millinery.[23]

Shortly before the outbreak of the First World War, the Werkbund exhibition in Cologne opens on 16 May 1914. Hoffmann designs the Austrian House and the Wiener Werkstätte's products are present in the drawing room—likewise designed by Hoffmann—and elsewhere. During the ex-

18 p. 192

33 p. 195

Fig. 11 JH, three sports trophies, executed by Würbel & Czokally, Vienna
VS (5) 1902, 328

hibition the *Typisierung* (standardization) debate flares up between Henry van de Velde and Hermann Muthesius. It questions the sociopolitical right to exist of handmade individual artistic luxury products versus standardized mass-produced goods. In 1915 the industrialist and banker Otto Primavesi, for whom Hoffmann had constructed and furnished a country house in Winkelsdorf/Kouty nad Desnou, Moravia, in 1913/14, takes over the management of the WW. By now the growing scarcity of materials and workforce due to the First World War is naturally having a negative impact on the WW's output. Since the majority of the craftsmen are called up for military service, the management decides in 1916 to establish an Artists' Workshop in which artists would be able to realize their own designs, mostly in clay, paper, and wood.

In these years of scarcity unexpected help comes from the Imperial Royal Ministries of the Exterior and of Trade, as well as from the Imperial Royal War Press Bureau. In order to support their propaganda efforts to present the country as a cultural nation on neutral ground, in 1917 they urge the WW to found a branch in Zurich and to organize art exhibitions in Copenhagen, Stockholm, and Amsterdam. Along with focusing increasingly on mass-produced goods of adequate quality, the WW takes part in the Leipzig sample fair for the first time during the last year of the war. The company has now reached a turning point: although trade fairs do not replace art exhibitions as the WW's presentation medium, they are now held to be of equal value. ▪

1   Letter from Fritz Waerndorfer to Carl Otto Czeschka from 27 Oct 1910, in: Spielmann, Heinz, *Carl Otto Czeschka. Ein Wiener Künstler in Hamburg*, Göttingen 2019, 180.
2   Draft letter from Josef Hoffmann to Julius Meier-Graefe in the archive of the Secession. Cited in Forsthuber, Sabine, *Moderne Raumkunst*, Vienna 1991, 52.
3   Sekler, Eduard F., *Josef Hoffmann: The Architectural Work*, Princeton, NJ 1985, 39. Trans. Eduard F. Sekler and John Maass.
4   Hevesi, Ludwig, "Aus der Sezession 15.11.1900," in: id., *Acht Jahre Secession*, Vienna 1906, 292.
5   Hoffmann, Josef, "Einfache Möbel," in: *Das Interieur* (2) 1901, 193–208, plates 83–91.
6   Ibid., 199 f.
7   UAA, Collection and Archive, 3996.
8   Ibid.
9   Letter from Waerndorfer to Hoffmann from 17 Mar 1903; UAA, Collection and Archive, 3999.
10 "As the middleman today has the main influence on production and in only a few exceptions accepts the quality principle in any form whatsoever,

instead proposing the most unbelievable things in pursuit of his own perverse taste, demanding the most worthless and ugliest objects in glass, porcelain, bronze, leather, and wood, ivory in embroideries, weavings, and in thousands of other materials, then either he or the consumer must be educated. The consumer today is completely perverse and mostly falls for such shoddy articles to his certain detriment." Hoffmann, Josef, "Maschine gegen Handarbeit," undat. manuscript, MAK, KI 23506.
11 Hoffmann 1901 (see note 5), 204.
12 Waerndorfer leaves Vienna in 1914 after having lost almost his entire fortune to his investment in the Wiener Werkstätte and emigrates to the USA. See also Witt-Dörring, Christian, "Palais Stoclet," in: id./Staggs, Janis (eds.), *Wiener Werkstätte 1903–1932: The Luxury of Beauty*, Munich/London/New York 2017, 368–409.
13 Calculated using the Austrian National Bank's currency converter at https://www.eurologisch.at/docroot/waehrungsrechner/#/ [8 Jun 2020].
14 Schmuttermeier, Elisabeth, "The Wiener Werk-

stätte," in: Witt-Dörring, Christian (ed.), *Koloman Moser. Designing Modern Vienna 1897–1907*, Munich 2013, 344.
15 Foundation Collection Kamm, Zug.
16 Spielmann 2019 (see note 1), 190.
17 Undated letter from Hoffmann to Stoclet written shortly before 28 Jul 1911.
18 Letter from A. Stoclet to Waerndorfer from 28 Jul 1911. For currency conversion, see note 13.
19 Report about the reasons for separating the WW's drafting office from the WW, Foundation Collection Kamm, Zug.
20 Letter from Moser to Carl O. Czeschka from 17 Oct 1913, in: Spielmann 2019 (see note 1), 287.
21 Noever, Peter (ed.), *Yearning for Beauty: The Wiener Werkstätte and the Stoclet House*, exh. cat. MAK, Ostfildern-Ruit 2006, 226 ff.
22 Draft contract between the WW G.m.b.H. and Prof. J. Hoffmann from 1 Apr 1914, Foundation Collection Kamm, Zug.
23 Noever 2006 (see note 21), 230 f.

Fig. 1 JH, dining hall at Sanatorium Westend, Purkersdorf, 1904
View toward the music room
MAK/WWF-102-87-1

Otto Kapfinger

Anatomy of Catharsis

Concrete Structure as a Formative Factor for the Purkersdorf Sanatorium

15 p. 88
40 p. 79

Already in 1901, Josef Hoffmann conceived a three-story studio wing with coffered ceilings in reinforced concrete with a cascade-like glass façade along the north face as an expansion of the Imperial Royal School of Arts and Crafts. A second, much larger project planned for the School of Arts and Crafts in 1904/05 is similarly progressive in terms of its structure. Either of these projects, if built, would have been among the incunables of architecture in early 20th-century Europe.[1]

For the sanatorium, there are drafts from 1903; the project developed over two, three stages until its final version in 1904. In the first sketch, the volume is 41 meters long, twelve meters wide, and has two main floors above the basement level, which is raised above ground. The rooms are 4.5 meters wide. The outer walls, and the inner walls that accommodate the central corridor, are each 45 centimeters thick; all walls stand above one another on the floors; a large hipped roof with wooden truss sits on top: everything was easily buildable at the time, and conventional in terms of interior spatial organization.[2]

In 1904, everything changed radically—in proportions and dimensions. Maintaining the same length, the volume expanded to a width of 18 meters. Furthermore, a third floor with apartments was added, and in this new upper level, the outer wall was set back two meters on two-thirds of the building length, giving the rooms on the eastern side a front terrace. The famous dining hall is now on the floor below—22 meters long, over seven meters wide. However, now, above the garden-facing third of the 3.8-meter-high space's ceiling was the previously mentioned 45-centimeter-thick outer wall. Based on the building regulations in place at that time, a hall of this dimension with asymmetrical ceiling load would not have been allowed in a traditional brick construction with wood beam ceilings. One would have had to plan a reinforcement with diagonal walls every six meters. Moreover, adding a level—if it were to be executed with a steep hipped roof—would have brought the volume proportionally out of balance, and its height would not have been approved in the context of the surrounding buildings and based on the authorized zoning.

Due to a lack of sources, we are unable to reconstruct what was pivotal: the architect's search for a technology that would allow for a new, low-cost spatial concept in the specified area, contact with the company director Eduard Ast, rapidly rising in Vienna in matters of reinforced concrete construction and present among the Secession crowd, or more likely—the client's wishes, which called for an original combination and integration of spatial concept and building method.

Becoming manifest in this reversal from the envisaged brick to a building much more demanding in volume, use, and spatial character: Hoffmann's magnificent "cast" was possible only through the reinterpretation of the building structure in reinforced concrete—with a corresponding flat roof that drained inward, into the center of the building! The frequently described, stressed T-beam ceiling in the dining hall, for example—where the new technology was shown, in a defining moment, for the first time in a representative context outside of an industrial or commercial structure—is the logical consequence of the previously outlined parameters: a 22-meter-long, 55-centimeter-wide, and 40-centimeter-high "girder" on the garden side of the hall supports the outer wall situated exactly one floor above. Nonetheless, in favor of the space's character in terms of visual balance and symmetry, Hoffmann allowed himself the creative freedom (and sense of purpose) to identically repeat this massive concrete beam in the direction of the hall's inner wall—although no comparable load from above is present there.[3] Furthermore, he designed—until now, rarely mentioned in the critique—a change of rhythm in the structurally necessary transverse ribs: only every second one had the same profile as the main support, with a recessed "shadow groove" on the underside, the others are only half as wide.

The coordination of the dimensions of this subtly excessive cassette-like ceiling, a tenacious latticing with varying mesh widths and dimensions, additionally, accords accurately with the door axes from the corridor, as well as with doors, windows (and wall sections) of the veranda connecting on the garden side. Below the impression of a thoroughly orderly regularity of the space vibrates a barely perceptible systemic elasticity: the entire ceiling has no exact square mesh; the gaps between the crossbeams also vary by a few centimeters, arranging themselves to conform with door and

1

Fig. 2 JH, Sanatorium Westend, Purkersdorf, draft perspective, west side, 1903/04
Ink with traces of graphite
Private collection

window axes; and last but not least, the doubled cross beams bond exclusively to massive, floor-to-ceiling wall sections on the garden wall, while the narrow crossbeams always appear on the "fragmented," statically more "fragile" wall sections near doors and windows.[4]

Eduard Ast & Co. Concrete Construction Company

As mentioned, the participation of the firm Eduard Ast & Co. was paramount for the Sanatorium. The company was responsible for the static calculation of the new technology and dimensioning it for official approval, as well as for the concrete realization. Its role was lost sight of in the course of the architectural reception as all of the documents from the submission plan disappeared from the building archive of the municipality of Purkersdorf; and furthermore, no company archives from Ast & Co. are available for research.

We can only guess when and how Eduard Ast (1868–1945), who was trained as a civil engineer, and Hoffmann, two years his junior, met. The firm Ing. Ed. Ast – J. Chaillys Nachfolger, founded in early 1898, continued to operate the factory yard and staff of a construction firm located in Vienna's Döbling district, while Eduard also took over the license procured by his father (Ing. Wilhelm Ast, construction director employed by Emperor Ferdinand's Northern Railway and landowner) for use of the "Hennebique system" concrete construction patent, and at the time, held the exclusive agency for Austria.[5]

One of Ast's first independent jobs as construction supervisor was completion of the interior wall cladding of the light urban railway station by Otto Wagner at Karlsplatz in 1898—within view of the construction site at the Secession. Joseph Maria Olbrich, as Wagner's employee, was also involved with details on the design of the Karlsplatz pavilion. From 1900 to 1904, Ast, together with Julius Mayreder, realized several primary stages of concrete technology in Viennese high-rise construction: the Herrnhuter-Haus on Neuer Markt (Ast-concrete ceiling), the office and workshop building of the Hutter & Schrantz company in Gumpendorf (street façade: set concrete; yard wing: pure skeleton construction), and the building at Bognergasse 5 (concrete façade up to first floor). Mayreder was among the first members of the

Secession, built a studio building for Carl Moll in 1894, and was originally designated, along with Olbrich, Hoffmann, and Friedrich Ohmann, to participate in an internal competition for the Secession building. Already in 1899, Ast realized the first multistory building with a concrete skeleton construction—for the Druckerei Gistel & Cie. on Münzgasse—with a design by Gustav Orglmeister. On 5 December 1899 he presented an introduction to the Hennebique system in the hall of the Österreichischer Ingenieur- und Architektenverein (Austrian Engineering and Architecture Association) for the elite of the local professional world, which is still worth reading today. In 1902, the firm published a reference book with three-dozen built examples of civil engineering and bridge construction, in industrial as well as residential and commercial buildings.[6]

Moreover, Ast & Co. had particular expertise for completing a sanatorium with hydro- and electrotherapeutic treatments. Between 1899 and 1902, the firm completed five bathing facilities in Vienna; and the municipal spa in Baden near Vienna planned by the architects Krauss & Tölk, with facilities nearly identical to those in Purkersdorf. The exterior of the 80-meter-long, three-story building in Baden's Kurpark (demolished in the 1960s) was clad in a Neobaroque façade, "adapted" to the local ambiance and clientele. Nevertheless, inside, Ast & Co. demonstrated advanced applications of the Monier and Hennebique systems with the ceiling and stairway structures and the recessed water basins.[7] In 1905, Hoffmann designed a signet for the firm to use as a "logo," or as a stamp for the plans; the drafts for it are preserved in the MAK collection.[8]

During the planning and realization of the Purkersdorf Sanatorium from 1903 to 1905, Ast & Co. was also involved in the following projects: with Krauss & Tölk, the Zacherlhaus by Josef Plečnik at Wildpretmarkt (concrete skeleton construction for the shop and mezzanine levels, concrete structure of the roof); the first stage of construction of the Postal Savings Bank by Otto Wagner (concrete ceilings; ribbed concrete slab basement for safes and post office); and in 1905, the building planned by Leopold Simony for Rohrer, a major printing house, in the center of Brno, with the first application in the monarchy's history of spiral-reinforced concrete columns.[9]

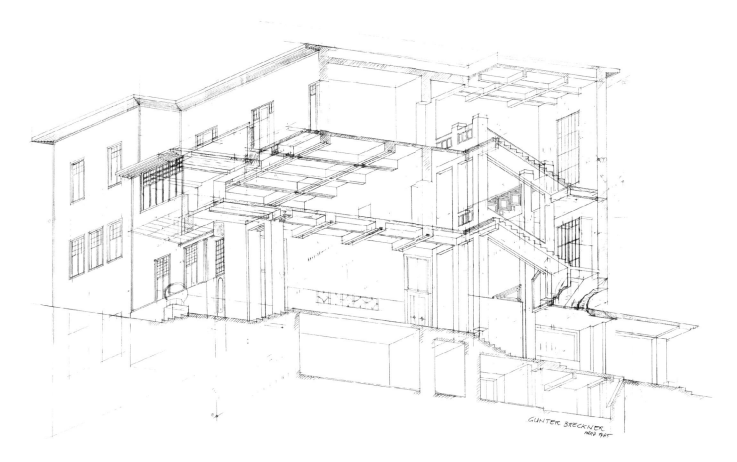

Fig. 3 Gunter Breckner, axonometric section through the central axis, 1985
Pencil on paper
© Gunter Breckner

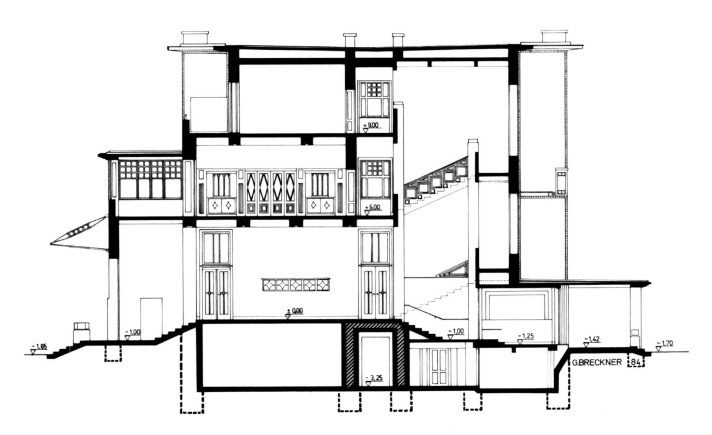

Fig. 4 Gunter Breckner, cross section through the central axis,
reconstruction of the original condition, 1982
© Gunter Breckner

Tectonics and Aesthetics

Aside from the rhythm of the dining hall ceiling, Hoffmann guided the strict economy of Ast's framework to finely tuned variations throughout the entire building in Purkersdorf. First of all, a distinction can already be sensed with the rising brick walls. From the 80-centimeter standard of the outer walls in the cellar and on the ground floor, the wall of the eastern façade tapers to 65 centimeters on the first floor—above the dining hall ceiling, large loads must be integrated and dissipated here—while the thickness of the western façade and corridor walls is reduced to 45 centimeters—smaller ceiling span widths and more reinforcing shear walls are present here, the outer walls of the western façade are above one another on the first and second floors—here, the guest rooms do not have terraces.

8   The ceiling division of the music room that adjoins to the south of the dining hall is interesting. Here, the single cross-beams are missing; two of the double beams crossing the main girder are set in such a way that four square ceiling fields arise in the corners of the space—and between them, a double-size field. In the relatively small space, the reason for this is based not only in visual relaxation, but also static logics. Since there are no terraces on the floor above, the outer walls are on top of another, but in return, diagonally overhead is a room divider, whose load is carried below exactly by the cross beam on the hall side. Through the expansion effect of the massive wall corners, the static situation of this end room is additionally supported. And in this way, Hoffmann can break the previously discussed rule here and allow the broad end-crossbeam to latch on over the window opening—precisely at its central axis, of course.

It is worth looking at these matters closely and analyzing them: in Purkersdorf, Hoffmann proves to be not only the much-celebrated (and also chastised) virtuoso of beautiful surfaces, of graphic-ornamental expression—here, at the height of his purist-geometric phase—but also presents himself as a sovereign designer who "demonstrates" in a novel context, the technique recently mastered by Eduard Ast (with partner Ing. Hugo Gröger) in large formats and multistory industrial buildings, unfolding it as physique, as anatomy of a complex building structure in delicate modularity.[10]

In the entrance hall with the stairway, the play of geometry and tectonics is even more complex than in the dining room. From the high, garden-side foyer, the space rises three floors, up to below the roof. For the first time, this type of vertical 27 p. 73 structure of reinforced concrete is consciously guided to an aesthetic event, to the sculptural effect of pure forms. The flooring of black-and-white tiles in a checkerboard pattern suggests complete control over the three-dimensionally developed grid—including the sequence of the six pillars, the side cheeks of the stairway with a concordant relief, and the evenly crossed ceiling beams. However, here, too, dissonances relax the geometry. For example, the pillars in the foyer are slightly wider than those of the staircase. Why? Because much more weight from above falls onto the foyer. In the stairway, on the other hand, the front pillars carry only the ceilings of the floors, which attach on one side, and the next pair of pillars supports only the flight of stairs—all four ends open at the top with attachments for flower arrangements. As mentioned, coming from the foyer, the room narrows by 80 centimeters, and the pillar dimensions are, additionally, coordinated with this.

Contrary to some descriptions, the geometry of the tiled floor also does not match that of the ceiling beams and pillar axes. Small shifts are present for good reason. The longitudinal beams thus meet, on the one hand, axially on the aisle-side stairway pillars—in concordance with the tiled floor—but on the other hand, flush on the slightly wider foyer pillars. The floor of the foyer hall is divided into five fields, the structure of the ceiling has only four fields longitudinally, and also transversely its geometry differs from that of the floor pattern.

The double beams of the foyer ceiling correspond only partially with the positions of the beams in the dining room above: the two outer ones underpinned by wall loads coming from above, the two inner ones bringing conflicts between the standard measure of their spacing and the symmetrical frames of the floor-to-ceiling door openings, to a balance, which while visually coherent, is nonetheless not "100-per- 7 cent accurate" in terms of dimension. These beams, although they have the same width, are much higher than those in the hall, statically reflecting the larger loads, and also visually accounting for the room height in the foyer. The grooves of the undersides here are thus wider and deeper than above. This shadow grooving, which "relaxes" the structure, also has functional reasons. Strips were inserted already in the concrete formwork, for embedding in the grooves, the electrical cables for the hanging lamps mounted in the notches. During the finishing of the concrete surfaces with fine plaster, these cables or the pipework were covered over.

We could continue to pursue such creative finesse and freedoms within the regularity of the whole in many details. They are typical of the tension between the geometries of a *planning concept*—without material strengths—and the facts and constraints of structural implementation: a phenomenon known from the Doric corner conflict of Greek temples, which looms through to the ominous "wall protrusions" of the Wittgenstein House in Vienna.[11]

The closer one looks, the more apparent it becomes that the sanatorium building has an easily underestimated material-technical logic: a reality that was experimental at the time, with special moments of resistance, which Hoffmann then brings to decidedly non-Constructivist elegance, lightness, and novel expression in his detailed art (with Koloman 3 Moser). Mediating this coherence of structure and spatial design as though in an X-ray image is an isometric sectional drawing through the main axis of the sanitorium, created by Gunter Breckner in 1985 as a supplement to his diploma thesis, which contributed fundamentally to the rescue of the building and its revitalization in 1994.[12]

Autonomy of Surface—Freedom of Ornamentation

In Purkersdorf, in 1904/05, Hoffmann, with Koloman Moser and the Wiener Werkstätte, is as "close" to Loos as he would ever be. We turn from the interior spaces outward, and based on the façades, examine to what extent this claim holds true there, too. The minimalist plaster skin of the volume, superbly reconstructed in the mid-1990s, is seamlessly applied with lime mortar in the then-progressive technique of crushed plaster (*Quetschputz*). With side lighting, the building shell looks like a surface of water rippled by the wind. These are 9 10 traces of materialization from the hand of the mason, created by means of trowel and pressing board in a rhythmic application, a structural "decoration" of the otherwise smooth surface—without the insertion of any formal tradition, any art historical design gesture, freed of all the imitated tectonics characteristic of historicist plaster façades. And the combi-

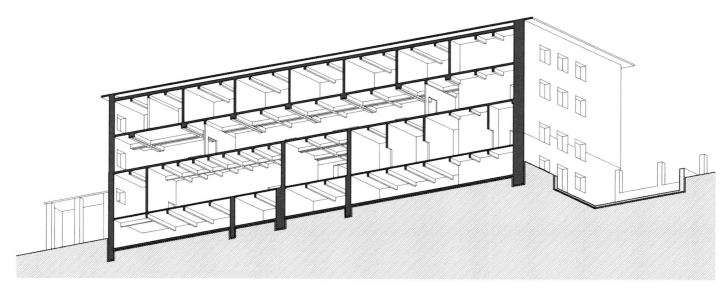

Fig. 5 Manuel Kainz, axonometric longitudinal section, sequence of the rooms, and
differentiation of the ceiling structures in reinforced concrete, digital reconstruction, 2020
© Manuel Kainz

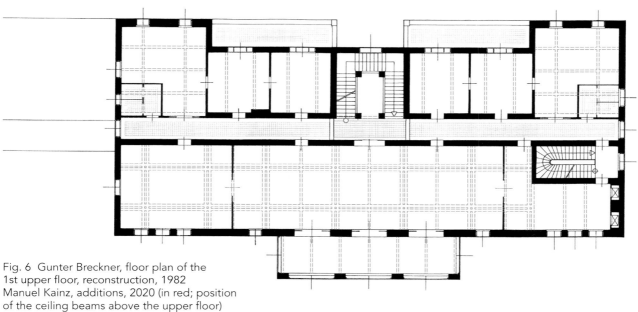

Fig. 6 Gunter Breckner, floor plan of the
1st upper floor, reconstruction, 1982
Manuel Kainz, additions, 2020 (in red; position
of the ceiling beams above the upper floor)
© Gunter Breckner, Manuel Kainz

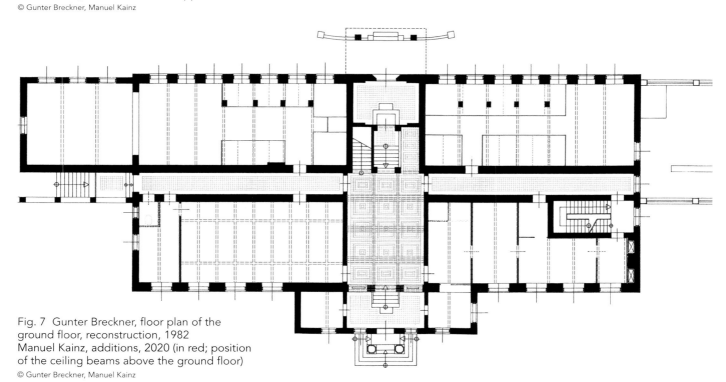

Fig. 7 Gunter Breckner, floor plan of the
ground floor, reconstruction, 1982
Manuel Kainz, additions, 2020 (in red; position
of the ceiling beams above the ground floor)
© Gunter Breckner, Manuel Kainz

nation of this plaster skin with the geometrically strict, visually flickering technique of the blue-and-white tile strips at all edges, is technically *and* formally coherent.[13]

As continuation of the interior structure, Hoffmann used the concrete technique also for the exposed parts of the façade's brick walls. Corresponding with the lack of brick arches inside, also the architraves of all openings in the outer walls are straight, concrete lintels reinforced with iron. Accordingly, Hoffmann's deletion of traditional façade details pursued a logic by which all physically exposed parts of the outer wall, that is, those exposed to rain, and the forces of erosion and use, were "armored" with the high-tenacity wall tile technology developed in the Wagner circles. All of the normal façade syntax thereby disappears. In the traditional canon of forms, even with the simplest Biedermeier plaster façades, the framing, weather-protecting window, door, and corner details were formed sculpturally in plaster as transformation of historical stone structures (hood molds, cornices, wall plates, jambs, and pilasters). Hoffmann reduced that down to frames with ribbons of glazed tiles laid with press joints—flush with the terse plaster skin. The roof cornice also corresponded formally with the technical novelty of the reinforced concrete panels. Different than Wagner, whose coffered awnings still allowed a sense of the rhythm of rafters; and different than Loos, who completed the façade on the Goldman & Salatsch building smoothed over with fine plaster, with a classically contoured cornice, the view from below of the overhang in Purkersdorf shows the statically logical, two-dimensionally staggered tapering of the concrete panel from the wall to the edge of the roof.[14]

The pattern of the plaster skin and the blue-white of the tiles evoke, among other things, the element *water*: the checkerboard pattern as geometricized form of the wave movement. And water plays a central role in the sanatorium, a *hydrotherapy spa*. For this first major project of the Wiener Werkstätte, Hoffmann cooperated with Koloman Moser through to the configurations of the furniture and details. And it was Moser, who ca. 1900, abstracted Jugendstil's formal energy through his reciprocal vegetal patterns and spatial divisions—in the orthogonal geometry of the purist, "constructive" phase of the Secession. Moser began with oscillating strips and checkerboard patterns within the graphic milieu. With these edgings and vignettes, he marked or defined areas of different significance.[15] Checkerboard lineaments possess this energetic, ambiguous emblematics. On the one hand, they have been apotropaic symbols since time eternal. They signalize *end, border, stop, defense, attention.* Their uses traverse millennia, from heraldic and military spheres, through to musical and athletic contexts. On the other hand, their oscillating appearance also seems antiperspectival: hierarchies of front and back, of figure and base are suspended, the pattern radiates in multiple directions, sutures/reinforces exposed edges—or it integrates opposites similar to a yin-yang symbol. At the 18th exhibition of the Vienna Secession, Moser decorated all of the space's edges with such borders. In this way, the walls themselves seem auratic, dematerialized—as ideal frames for Klimt's paintings.

Hoffmann acted simultaneously with Moser during this phase—and made the gridded network the omnipresent base of his designs. In Purkersdorf something else was added, which stimulated him in his passion as master of atectonic, ornamental *Flächenkunst* (art of the surface) from an entirely different aspect: from 1899, the Viennese pioneers of reinforced concrete had propagated in their lectures and writings one quality, among others, of the new technology:

the artificial stone made from natural materials—a connection of visible pressure mass and invisible reinforcement against tensile forces—eliminates the notorious problems of fixed connection of vertical and horizontal elements, or only complexly combinable dispersed building materials: stone, brick, wood, and iron. Architecture's entire constructive syntax and formal grammar developed from this challenge of merging heterogeneous elements: pillars and columns rest below with bases in pedestal sections but receive the loads and shearing force of beams and ceiling from above through special joints, capitals. Now, due to the homogeneous structure of the reinforced concrete, this is no longer necessary. From now on, monoliths cast without joints could prop up continuously force-fit structures across several floors, bevels and arches could combine in one lineament with verticals or horizontals.[16]

This type of rational skeleton construction was a monolith of "pure" surfaces independent of the genealogy of forms and liberated from "academic" problems of form. Hoffmann, who did not really appreciate the Renaissance or Baroque on his Mediterranean study trips, discovered there in anonymous rural structures his ideal for future creation: freedom from the ballast of any type of historical form. And now the reinforced concrete technique allowed, or even constituted in a technically new way, precisely this freedom.[17]

A skeleton structure (interior) such as the sanatorium, as an "architectural site," now had only the edges of the equalized surfaces. With it, Hoffmann and Ast had achieved the zero-point of constructive-formal rhetoric. The surfaces are now autonomous; the edges are the exposed afterglow of a dead, shaken-off linguisticality. And with accompanying lines in a checkerboard mode, Hoffmann gives the mute edges—as Moser did the pages of a book or the edge of furniture—the discrete comment: there is no longer a hierarchy between supports and surfaces, between above and below, compression and tension, supporting and loading; depiction of the constructedness becomes obsolete, but autonomous surfaces remain, freed for Hoffmann's innermost artistic desire: ornament, extensive patterns, ornamental intensity, joyful coloring…

The focus of the interior space of the *Kurhaus*, whose program was to offer a healing touch, cleansing, and liberation from the city's nervous complexities, was, of course, analogously, the purification and absolute catharsis of a materiality brought to near transparency—most clearly in the reception area, where the black-and-white lineaments meander free and detached in all directions across the white surfaces, sweeping across the tectonics like tender ant tracks. In the hall, it is a bit more elegant, as here, Hoffmann entwined the edges of the concrete beams with colorful leaf patterns: the naturally stylized ornamentation offers a dialectical border to the materially dense, laconic facts—a fine, final greeting from the rank vegetal line-growths of *Ver Sacrum*. On the exterior of the building, assailed by elemental forces, Hoffmann moved the accompanying border directly on and over all building edges and materialized this profile in one of the oldest and most enduring natural materials cultivated by humans—hard-fired, glazed ceramics.

It is possible to say that this transformation of building form into pure surfaces separated, or sewn by checkerboard-pattern ornamental ribbons on its edges, presents Hoffmann's response to Moser's interiors at the 18th Secession exhibition. My reading is that Hoffmann, as well as Moser, treated the edging of the spacious surfaces as *seams*, as stitches, which points to textile patterns and connected with

Fig. 8 JH, music room at Sanatorium Westend, Purkersdorf, 1904
MAK, WWF-102-98-1

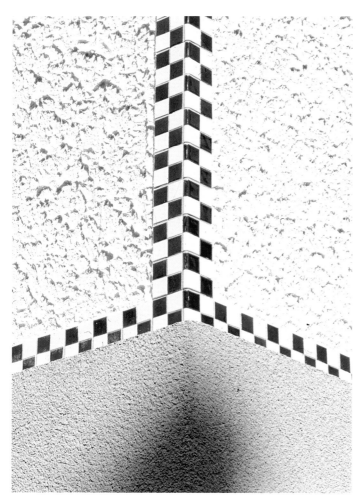

Figs. 9, 10 JH, Sanatorium Westend, Purkersdorf,
restoration of the plaster façade and the tiled frames, 1996
© BDA/Martina Oberer-Kerth

that, to wickerwork and borders, which since time eternal have offered and actuated the technical and formal occasions for ornamentation. In this way, Hoffmann/Moser provide a different reading of Gottfried Semper's theoretical writings than that of Wagner or Loos. Hoffmann thereby always seeks—in his ornamental and formal impulse—these impacts and edges, to then treat and honor them technically and formally as decorative lines for his forms.[18]

Hoffmann had a top structural engineering education, a foundation in "state of the art" at the Staatsgewerbeschule (State Technical School) in Brno, which along with Vienna's School of Arts and Crafts, certainly offered the best training of this kind far and wide. Among his contemporaries in Brno were Adolf Loos, Hubert Gessner, Leopold Bauer, and Alois Ludwig. Yet his design Eros never focused on promotion of the constructive, demonstrative "exhaustion" or furthering of such aspects. For him, construction was self-evident "craft" of the highest possible level, the basis for his artistic desire, which was located elsewhere: for the constantly varied playful element; for the stage-like, formulated setting of spaces; for the condensing of instruments and furniture to the beauty of the object. Even an unparalleled expert such as Eduard F. Sekler was tempted by an enigmatic sheet in the preliminary drafts of the sanatorium, to interpret Hoffmann's concern as a "radical utilization" of the reinforced concrete technology and to interpret "an almost continuous band of windows" in the basement level as anticipation of the upcoming Modernism. This sketch, however, does not imagine a 20-meter-long ribbon window, but instead, is merely the suggestion of a long veranda. Its thin, shallow roof is carried on the sides by massive walls, framed left and right by squared tendrils, whereby the windows and door openings planned for the façade behind are simply not drawn in. The oft-invoked anticipation of composition principles of De Stijl or Bauhaus can therefore not be maintained.[19]

As shown here, the Hoffmann/Moser motifs were different; the autonomy of *their* planar compositions comes from and goes elsewhere. For Hoffmann, the abstraction of the surfaces and their stitching, freed from tectonics, quasi "graphic and ornamented" (as Loos mocked) comes to the construction figure or object design from outside, which in this way makes the casket character discernible at all dimensions. When the spatial surfaces become autonomous with Frank Lloyd Wright, when the edges of the space dissolve with the Wagner students and with De Stijl, this is motivated from within—from the desire for static liberation of the façade through the separation (taking-inward) of supporting structure from shell, which can therewith become a "transparent" membrane. And in contrast to Otto Wagner's "masculine" tectonics, in which the construction, the "supporting line," clearly dominates the paneling of the latticed surfaces, Hoffmann cultivates this—quasi-"femininely" expressive *entanglement* of all shapes.

Conversely, Wagner realized *his* version of the framing lineaments in the Postal Savings Bank, and uses the motif there extensively on the interior walls realized in polished gypsum plaster, covering also the smooth court-side façade

Fig. 11 JH, design for the monogram
logo of the developer Eduard Ast & Co,
ca. 1905/10
MAK, KI 8857/2

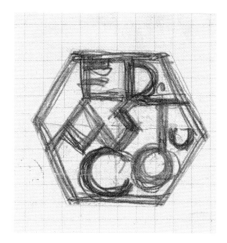

with black-and-white tiles—and takes these details along with him through to the façades on his last urban home on Neustiftgasse.

From the new, monolithic consistency of reinforced concrete, Hoffmann draws entirely different conclusions than those of the great Auguste Perret—which is explicable in light of what has been compactly presented here. Perret, the concrete construction pioneer who was active in Paris at the same time, tried his entire life to grasp the historical syntax of bearing and loading, of columns, pillars, and beams in a new form adequate for the new building material—and arrives at results that are fascinating, but different than Hoffmann's concise conclusions in Purkersdorf. It is no contradiction when Hoffmann quickly moves past these "stages" and then also once again cultivates classicist motifs, without ever again proposing them seriously structurally or dramatically, but rather, as material to play with for his own, individual ornamentation of area values liberated from the everyday of the constructive. A mere five years after Purkersdorf, he shows how that looks when pushed to the extreme—no least with Eduard Ast as client and executor—in the exterior design of Ast's villa in Döbling.[20]

1   Kapfinger, Otto/Boeckl, Matthias, *Abgelehnt: Nicht Ausgeführt. Die Bau- und Projektgeschichte der Hochschule für angewandte Kunst in Wien 1873–1993*, Vienna 1993, 19–25, 74–79.
2   Eduard F. Sekler includes six sheets of the preliminary drafts in: *Josef Hoffmann: The Architectural Work*, Princeton, NJ 1985, 67–72 and CR 84, 285–288; an additional seven in: Galerie Metropol (ed.), *Josef Hoffmann. Sanatorium Purkersdorf. Documentation by Gunter Breckner*, New York 1985.
3   Plan-based reconstruction of the original state: Gunter Breckner, thesis at the TU Wien, 1980–1982; rendition in Galerie Metropol 1985 (see note 2); for the revitalization of 1993–1995 (headed by architect Sepp Müller), Vasko+Partner issued a static assessment with drill core sample; copies are in the archive inventory of the BDA Landeskonservatoriat Niederösterreich, Krems a.d. Donau; the east-side longitudinal balcony in the dining hall is intensively reinforced with iron, the west-side balcony, which is the same size, only minimally.
4   Created on the basis of the mentioned building documentation from Breckner, with numerous illustrations, published in *Steine sprechen* (XXIV/1) 79 1985, 20–37; a sectional axonometry drawn by Breckner in 1985 first published in: Klaus AG (ed.), *Hoffmann-Bau. Purkersdorf bei Wien*, Purkersdorf 1995, 20. Also: dimensionally exact depiction of all ceiling constructions in the permit application for an unrealized revitalization by the architectural firm Hlaweniczka+Partner 1993, copies of the ground plan 1:100 in the Gunter Breckner archive.
5   Barnick-Braun, Kerstin (ed.), *Eduard Ast & Co. Das Hundert-Jahre-Buch 1898–1998*, Vienna/Graz 1998; also: *Die Bauunternehmung Ed. Ast & Co. Ingenieure*, Vienna et al., 1926.
6   *Eduard Ast & Co. Ingenieure, Concessionaires du Système Hennebique. Unternehmung für Beton-Bau, Monier-Bau, Wasserkraftanlagen*, Vienna 1902; expanded in 1904; updated in 1906. Ast, Eduard, "Das System Hennebique" (lecture), in: *Zeitschrift des Österreichischen Ingenieur- und Architekten-Vereins* (LII) 13 1900, 209–214.
7   "Bade- und Heilanstalt der Stadt Baden bei Wien," in: *Wiener Bauindustrie-Zeitung* (XXI) 33 1904, 257–261.
8   Hand drawing 6.2 x 6.2 cm; MAK, KI 8857-3.
9   Printing building of Rudolf M. Rohrer in Brno, in *Der Bautechniker* (XXVI) 9 1906, 169–173.
10 Analysis based on the quoted literature of the reconstruction plans by Gunter Breckner, from original photos available mainly in the MAK's Wiener Werkstätte Archive, and from visits to the site. Recent additions by Manuel Kainz with the author, visits on 29 Jul 2020.
11 See Turnovský, Jan, *Die Poetik eines Mauervorsprungs*, Braunschweig/Wiesbaden 1987.
12 Construction drawing in pencil on transparent paper, 50 x 76 cm; version in ink on transparent, design print 70 x 100 cm; Gunter Breckner archive.
13 Bundesdenkmalamt (ed.), *Putzfassaden in Europa um 1900. Studien zur Technologie, Restaurierung*, Vienna 1999.
14 See also Kapfinger, Otto, "Dionysus speaks through Apollo: On the source of the *Gesamtkunstwerk* in Olbrich, Hoffmann, Moser," in: Thun-Hohenstein, Christoph/Witt-Dörring, Christian/Schmuttermeier, Elisabeth (eds.), *Koloman Moser: Universal Artist between Gustav Klimt and Josef Hoffmann*, Vienna/Basel 2019, 100–109. Trans. Maria Slater.
15 See on this Franz, Rainald, "The Secession, sewn up—Koloman Moser, the Secessionist: From the surface to the space," in ibid., 162–186.
16 The most important theorist and publicist in the pioneer days of the concrete era was Univ.Doz. Dr.Ing. Fritz v. Emperger. He edited the international quarterly *Beton und Eisen. Le Béton armé. Concrete-Steel* from 1900, in which also further reports from/about Ed. Ast & Co. were published. See on this, also Pauser, Alfred, *Eisenbeton 1850–1950. Idee, Versuch, Bemessung, Realisierung. Unter Berücksichtigung des Hochbaus in Österreich*, Vienna 1994.
17 Hoffmann's statements in his report, "Architektonisches aus der österreichischen Riviera" read like a stenograph for the sanatorium: "Other than columns, which, however, in most cases originate in earlier structures, one finds nearly no singly explicit architectural form, such as cornices, pilaster, and the like. The windows are simply enclosed in smooth stone frames [...] the roof is very flat, widely protruding [...] the plastered wall surfaces are without any decoration." Published in: *Der Architekt* (1) 1895, 37.
18 See on this, also Topp, Leslie, *Architecture and Truth in Fin-de-Siècle Vienna*, Cambridge 2004; Blackshaw, Gemma/Topp, Leslie (eds.), *Madness & Modernity. Kunst und Wahn in Wien um 1900*, Vienna 2009; Thun-Hohenstein, Karin, *Josef Hoffmann – Sanatorium Purkersdorf (1904–1905)*, thesis at the University of Vienna, 2012; Thomas, Lil Helle, *Stimmung in der Architektur der Wiener Moderne. Josef Hoffmann und Adolf Loos*, Vienna/Cologne/Weimar 2017 (around 100 pages on Purkersdorf Sanatorium).
19 Sekler 1985 (see note 2), 70–72. Façade and related ground plan seen together, explain the huge horizontal opening, the "ribbon window" as a veranda placed in front of the building, open toward the garden, covered with flat wood or metal roof; realized, it would have definitely become thicker than the simple line on the frontal view of the plan.
20 Ibid., 135–143 and WV 134, 332–336. Also, see note 2 in the article "Hohe Warte: From Life Reform to Bourgeois Daily Life" by Matthias Boeckl in this catalog.

1907
1910

Fig. 1 JH, étagère for the living
area in Eduard Ast's villa, 1910
Marquetry made of Makassar
ebony and boxwood
Galerie Yves Macaux, Brussels
© Photo Studio Philippe de Formanoir/
Paso Doble

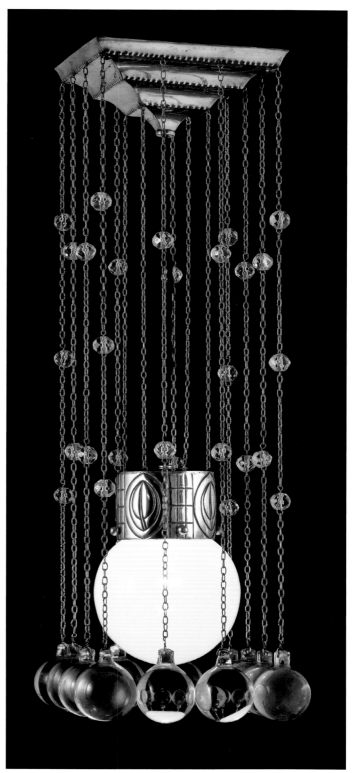

Fig. 2 JH, pendant light for the library in Dr. Hermann and Lyda Wittgenstein's apartment, executed by the Wiener Werkstätte, 1905
Brass, nickel-plated, glass
Galerie Yves Macaux, Brussels
© Photo Studio Philippe de Formanoir/Paso Doble

Fig. 3 JH, pendant light for the hall of Stoclet House, executed by the Wiener Werkstätte, 1908
Galerie Yves Macaux, Brussels
© Photo Studio Philippe de Formanoir/Paso Doble

Figs. 4a, b   JH, exhibition building for the Kunstschau, Vienna, 1908
Der Architekt XIV, 161; MBF (7) 1908, 363

Fig. 5 JH, electric samovar from a tea and coffee set,
executed by the Wiener Werkstätte, 1909
Silver, ivory
Private collection
© MAK/Georg Mayer

Fig. 6 JH, samovar owned by Dr. Hermann and
Lyda Wittgenstein, executed by the Wiener
Werkstätte, 1909
Silver, ivory
MAK, GO 2010
© MAK/Katrin Wißkirchen

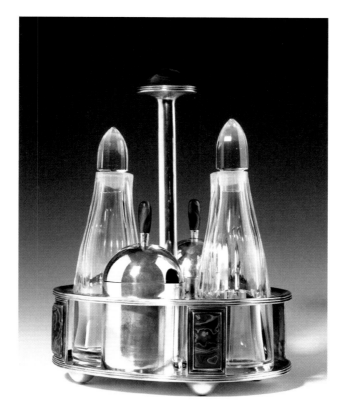

Fig. 7 JH, vinegar/oil
carafe, executed by the
Wiener Werkstätte, 1909
Silver, malachite, glass
bel etage Kunsthandel GmbH

Fig. 8 JH, vase,
executed by the Wiener
Werkstätte, 1909
Silver
MAK, WI 970
© MAK/Georg Mayer

Fig. 9 JH, brooch, executed by
the Wiener Werkstätte, 1909
Silver, gold-plated, coral, lapis lazuli,
malachite, and opal
GALERIE BEI DER ALBERTINA · ZETTER

Fig. 10 JH, brooch, executed
by Eugen Pflaumer, 1908–1910
Silver, gold-plated, agate, amethyst,
bloodstone, jasper, turquoise,
moonstone, and coral
Private collection

Fig. 11 JH, linoleum sample panel, design no. 1402, Erste
österr. Linoleumfabrik, Trieste, 1910
Technisches Museum, Vienna, 60581/12

Fig. 12 JH, linoleum sample panel, *Inlaid II*,
Delmenhorster Linoleumfabrik, 1910
Stadtmuseum Delmenhorst (DE)

Fig. 13 JH, wall-all-mounted
vitrine from the staircase in the
Ast villa, 1910
Makassar ebony, brass, glass
THE OTTO SCHOENTHAL COLLECTION
© Aslan Kudrnofsky/MAK

Fig. 14 JH, fabric *Jagdfalke*
[Hunting Falcon] on a Wiener
Werkstätte sample card, 1910/11
Silk, printed
MAK, T 10621-31
© MAK/Nathan Murrell

Fig. 15 JH, fabric *Kohleule*
[Cabbage Moth] on a Wiener
Werkstätte sample card, 1910–1915
Silk, printed
MAK, T 10621-19
© MAK/Nathan Murrell

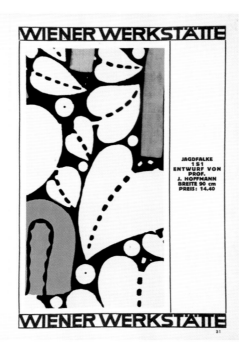

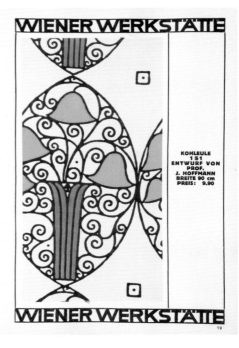

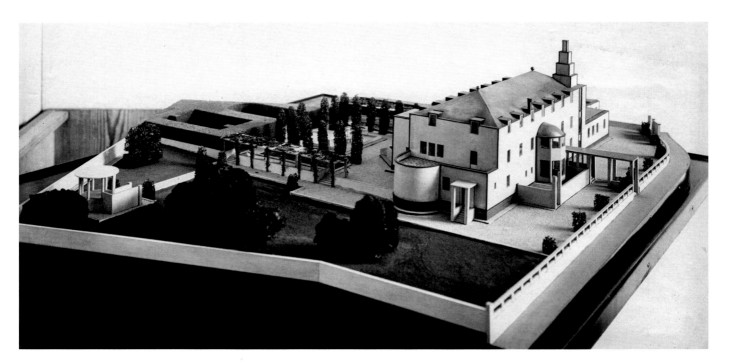

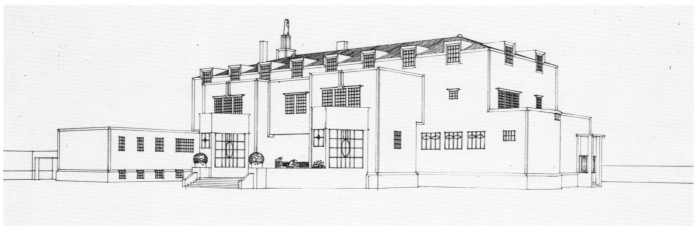

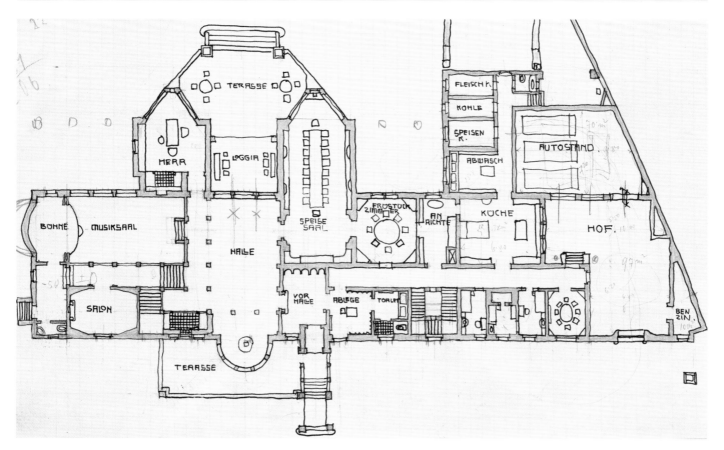

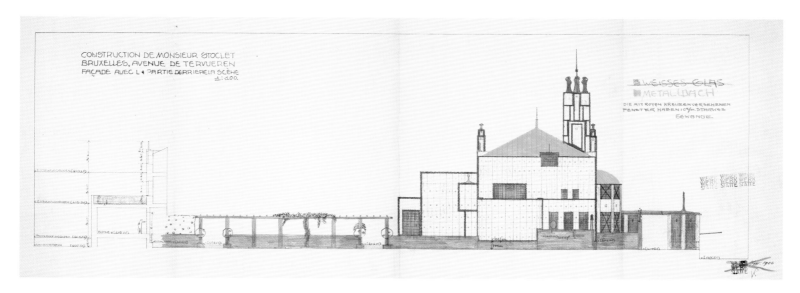

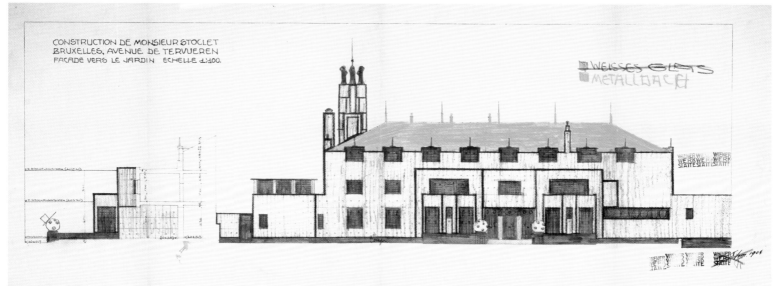

Figs. 19, 20 JH, Stoclet House, 1905–1911,
east and south view (garden side) with corrections
(façades of white glass crossed out, metal roof), 1 Aug 1906
MAK

<
Figs. 16, 17 JH, Stoclet House, 1905–1911, model view
and garden perspective, before summer 1906
MAK

<
Fig. 18 JH, Stoclet House, 1905–1911, ground floor plan,
before summer 1906
National Gallery Prague, K 17736

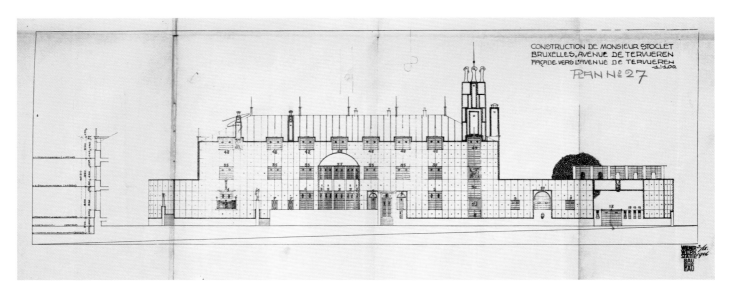

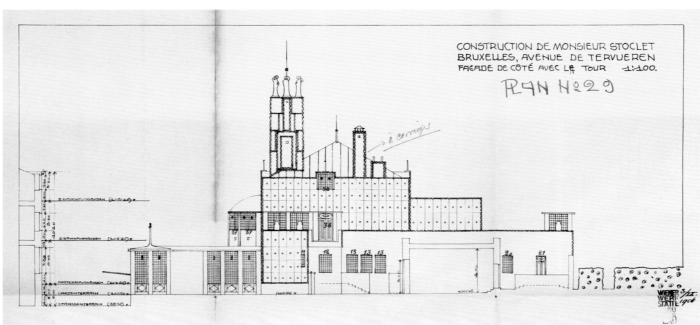

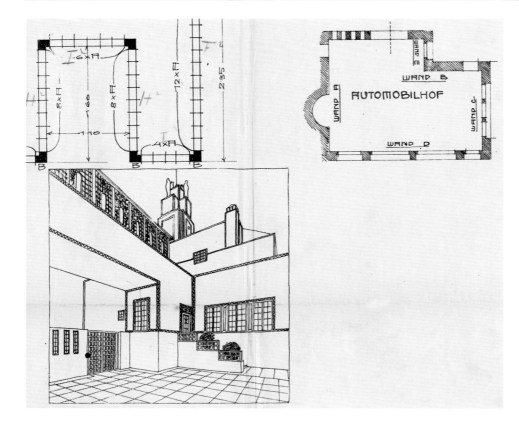

Figs. 21, 22 JH, Stoclet House,
1905–1911, north view (street side)
and west view (garage area), façades
with suggestion of bolt fittings,
3 Sep 1906
MAK

Fig. 23 JH, Stoclet House, 1905–1911,
parking yard, perspective and
ground plan, 1906
MAK

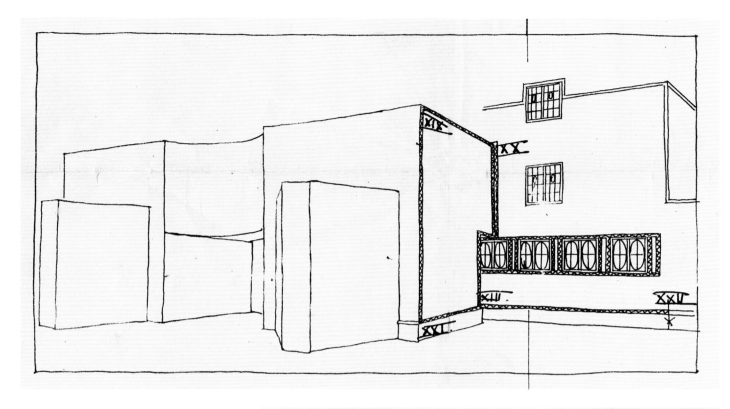

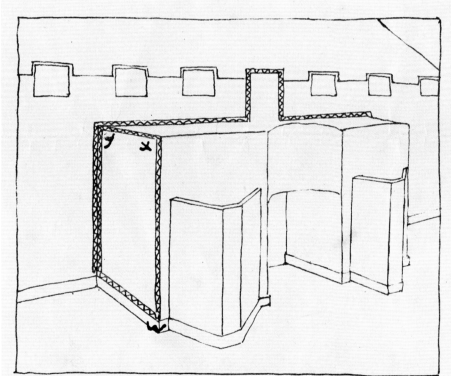

Figs. 24, 25 JH, Stoclet House,
1905–1911, south façade (garden side)
with bay windows, metal profiles in
repoussé work to frame the façades
made of white Norwegian marble, 1906
MAK

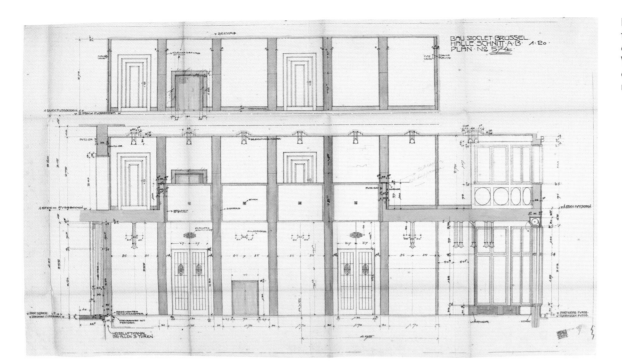

Fig. 26 JH, hall section A–B toward the vestibule and the dining hall, Stoclet House, Wiener Werkstätte's construction drawing office, 1908
MAK

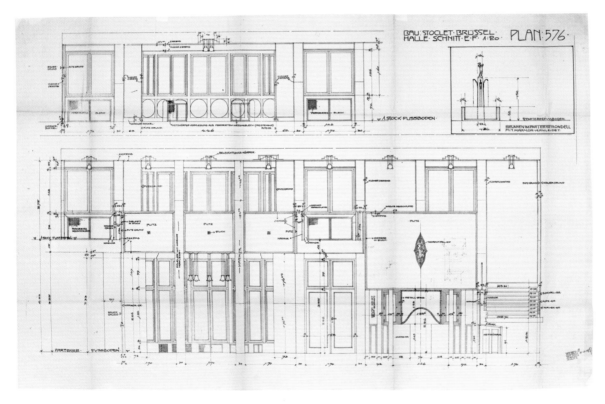

Fig. 27 JH, hall section E–F toward the street and the fountain bay, 1908
MAK

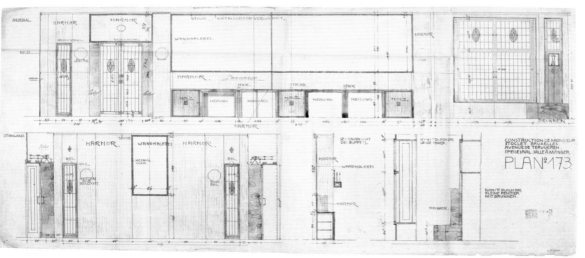

<
Fig. 28 JH, interior elevation and section through the fountain bay of the dining hall, 1907
MAK

>
Fig. 29 JH, living area looking toward the fountain bay, Stoclet House, 1905–1911
MBF (13) 1914, 15

>
Fig. 30 JH, dining hall with the mosaic frieze by Gustav Klimt
MBF (13) 1914, plate 4

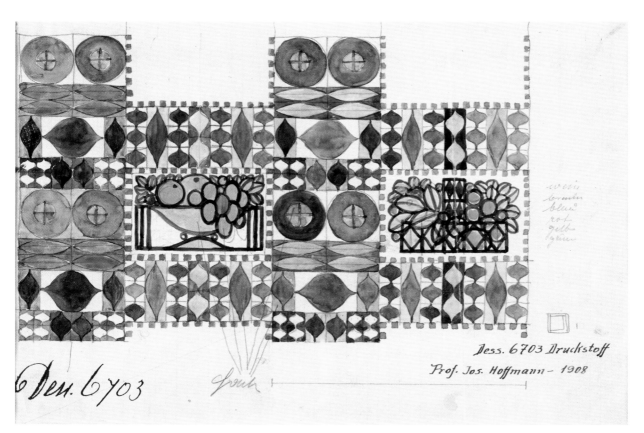

Fig. 31 JH, design for
a printed fabric, design
no. 6703, executed by
Backhausen & Söhne
for the Wiener
Werkstätte, 1908
Backhausen Archive, BA05647

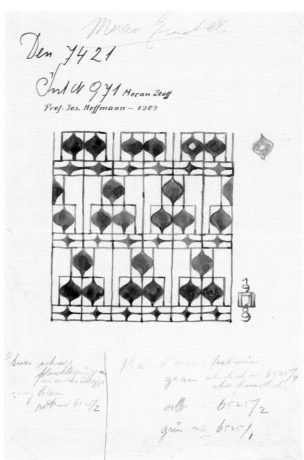

Fig. 32 JH, design for a woven fabric for
Backhausen & Söhne and the Wiener
Werkstätte, 1909
Backhausen Archive, BA03722

Fig. 33 JH, design for a printed fabric, design
no. 7421, executed by Backhausen & Söhne
for the Wiener Werkstätte, 1909
Backhausen Archive, BA05644

Fig. 34 JH, Wiener
Werkstätte postcard no. 67,
Cabaret Fledermaus,
bar area, 1907
MAK, WWPKE 1-1

Fig. 35 JH, design for a universal decorative
border for the poster and programs
of Cabaret Fledermaus, 1908
MAK, WWE 252

Fig. 36 JH, Wiener Werkstätte postcard no. 75,
Cabaret Fledermaus, theater, 1907
MAK, KI 13748-15

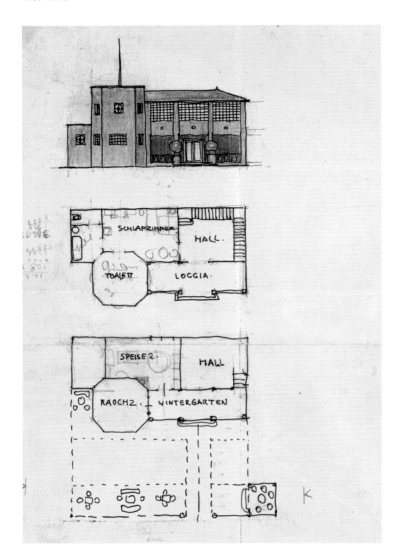

Fig. 38 JH, *Kleines Landhaus* [Small Country House] at the Kunstschau, Vienna, 1908, view of the interior
MBF (7) 1908, 370

Fig. 37 JH, design for the small country house at the Kunstschau, Vienna, 1908
Foundation Collection Kamm, Zug, K.Z. 2039

Fig. 39 JH, room of the Wiener Werkstätte at the Kunstschau, Vienna, 1908
MAK, WWF 103-172-1

Fig. 40 JH, shop of the Wiener Werkstätte on the Graben, 1907
MAK, WWF 103-177-1

Josef Hoffmann
1907
1910

JH, pillow design, lady's bedroom,
Prof. Pickler's villa, 1909
MAK, WWE 178-1

1906–1907

At the same time as Stoclet House, Hoffmann plans the house for Helene Hochstetter and the second house for Carl Moll on the Hohe Warte. In 1907 Koloman Moser withdraws from the Wiener Werkstätte after disputes over Fritz Waerndorfer's administration of funds and in the conviction that the WW's business model has no financial chance of survival, in order to devote himself entirely to painting. Eduard Josef Wimmer-Wisgrill, a student of Hoffmann, joins the WW and grows the fashion department, which he runs successfully for many years. Founding of Cabaret Fledermaus, a nightclub on Vienna's Johannesgasse/Kärntner Straße, which is intended to serve the "culture of entertainment." The complete interior design of the bar with stage and auditorium is the work of

Hoffmann together with artists like Gustav Klimt, Oskar Kokoschka, Bertold Löffler, and Emil Orlik. Poets like Peter Altenberg, Egon Friedell, or Alfred Polgar read their works there, the Wiesenthal sisters dance, and the mixologist at the bar comes specially from America. Furnishing of the WW's shop on the Graben. The young Swiss architect Charles-Édouard Jeanneret (aka Le Corbusier) visits Hoffmann in his studio. He does not accept Hoffmann's invitation to work together, but he draws the completed Cabaret Fledermaus in his travel notes. Hoffmann cofounds and becomes a board member of the German Werkbund. Interior decoration of a dining room for Sonja Knips, business premises for the Imperial Royal Court and State Printers at Seilerstätte 24/Johannesgasse 19.

1908

On the lot of what is now the Konzerthaus in Vienna, the 1908 Kunstschau takes place, which is planned as a comprehensive presentation of the artistic worldview of the Klimt Group after their departure from the Secession. Hoffmann designs its temporary exhibition building, some interiors, and a model country home complete with furnishings. The Kunstschau includes the first public display of work by Oskar Kokoschka. Meets the Parisian fashion designer Paul Poiret in Vienna. Joseph Maria Olbrich, creator of the Vienna Secession building and the Mathildenhöhe artists' colony in Darmstadt, dies in Düsseldorf.

JH, business premises of the Imperial Royal Court and State Printers, Vienna, 1907
MAK, WWF 104-216-1

JH, interior of the business premises of the Imperial Royal Court and State Printers in Vienna, 1907
MAK, WWF 104-218-1

JH, Prof. Pickler's villa, in Budapest, 1909
MAK, WWF 104-230-1

Wiener Werkstätte postcard no. 74,
Cabaret Fledermaus, 1908
MAK, KI 13748-15

1909–1910

The transportable hunting lodge for Alexander Pazzani is constructed in the environs of Vienna. For this wooden house Hoffmann uses a kind of prefabricated construction style for the first time. For the industrialist Heinrich Böhler, he furnishes a country house in Baden and constructs a garden pavilion. The last and largest of the houses on the Hohe Warte, the villa of the building contractor Eduard Ast, is built using a partly classicizing design vocabulary. In 1909 Adolf Loos gives his legendary lecture "Ornament und Verbrechen" (later translated as "Ornament and Crime") for the first time in Berlin, which is only published in French in 1913. In Budapest Hoffmann converts and redecorates a villa for Prof. Pickler. First contacts with the major industrialist and banker from Olmütz/Olomouc Otto Primavesi, at the instigation of his friend, the sculptor Anton Hanak. For Otto Primavesi Hoffmann will subsequently construct a country house in Winkelsdorf/Kouty nad Desnou, Moravia, and for his cousin Robert a villa in Vienna. Like many of Hoffmann's customers, Primavesi has exceptionally good contacts among modern Viennese artists. For example, he has Gustav Klimt paint portraits of his wife and daughter. The Austrian Werkbund is founded. Josef Hoffmann begins to focus intently on designs for glass; a long-lasting collaboration with the glassware commissioning retailer J. & L. Lobmeyr begins. ∎

JH, transportable hunting lodge for Alexander Pazzani, 1909/10
© Wolfgang Woessner/MAK

Fig. 1 JH, Stoclet House, Brussels, 1905–1911, street façade on
the Avenue de Tervueren, soon after the building's completion
Bildarchiv Foto Marburg, FN 1061761

Matthias Boeckl

Between Surface and Space

Atectonic Architectural Innovations at Stoclet House

The architecture of Stoclet House "eludes a search for immediate comparisons with any other building one has seen."[1] In many regards it has remained a unique phenomenon of its period, for example, in its uncompromising artistic permeation of every single detail of this very large house, which comprises some 1 500 m² usable floor area spread across three stories, as well as coherently designed gardens of almost 4 000 m²; in the revolutionary atectonic "peculiarity" of Hoffmann's design method; but also in the general ambiguity of the project, which systematically thwarts clear assignment to known building types, styles, or content. To this was added the extremely private nature of this stately house for a collector specialized "in the archaic and the exotic"[2] art of antiquity, his equally art-loving Parisian wife, and their three children. Finally, the historical context in which the house was built has proven unrepeatable, as the social system from which it stemmed ceased to exist with the outbreak of World War I just three years after the building's completion. Thereafter, any broad discussion or reception of Stoclet House in the international architectural discourse was prevented for decades by the adverse political conditions of the postwar period. On many levels, the project's unique constellation is similarly ambivalent, with an architect and designer whose only artistic strategy consisted in boundless individual creativity, and a building owner who, despite the project vastly exceeding its budget and missing every deadline, believed unwaveringly and unshakably in the relevance of this anti-industrial artistic approach even though his own fortune had grown out of precisely such major and global industrial enterprises.

The ambiguities begin with the construction task itself. The commission called for the relatively rare building type of a "sizeable detached town house,"[3] which combines middle-class elements (gainful employment in the nearby city, hence suburban location) with aristocratic building traditions (stately residence on a sizable, privately owned estate). To accommodate his lifestyle as a manager, art enthusiast, and father, the client had envisaged from the outset—and all the more since his discovery of Hoffmann's villas on the Hohe Warte in Vienna—an inhabitable artwork comprising a house and garden on the edge of town. What options were available to him for these particular requirements around 1900? Having profited from industrialization, the new middle classes were in most cases finding their place in society by adopting traditional representative styles, purchasing former aristocratic residences, or building new properties in historicizing styles.[4] Few tycoons of the mid-19th-century *Gründerzeit* period, and even fewer of their children, dared to express their individual lifestyles in a "peculiar" way.[5] In the case of Adolphe Stoclet, this desire appears to go back to, inter alia, a certain distancing from his father, who is said to have been skeptical about Adolphe's marriage to the daughter of the Parisian art dealer Arthur Stevens and niece of two painters. In Brussels the famous Art Nouveau pioneer Victor Horta would have been able to fulfil Stoclet's desire for individual expression to a high artistic standard; his striking town houses *Tassel*, *Horta*, *van Eetvelde*, and *Solvay* were built from 1892 and were undoubtedly familiar to the art enthusiast Adolphe Stoclet. However, when he first dreamed of building a house around 1903, Stoclet was expecting to spend many years in Vienna and had therefore already chosen Josef Hoffmann as his architect when the death of his father Victor Stoclet in 1904 called him back to Brussels.

That this decision remained unchanged even after his return to Belgium, testifies to his deep-seated belief in Hoffmann. The latter continued to encourage his client to turn away from traditional representative styles, which meant a radical rejection first of historicizing stylistic forms and second of all those building types by young architects in Continental Europe that were associated with those forms, such as the popular French- or Italian-inspired mansion styles. But what were the alternatives? There was still no established and independent Modernist representative style upon which Hoffmann could have drawn. Contemporary artists' houses like the imaginative Munich villas of Franz von Lenbach (Gabriel von Seidl, 1887–1891) and Franz von Stuck (own design, 1897/98) constitute on a functional level alone a completely different type from the house of a businessman and collector. Hence the idea immediately suggested itself to Hoffmann to use in the first instance the English model—embodied by the industry-skeptical Arts & Crafts movement and considered the prototype of modern lifestyles by young architects and designers since 1900—as the starting point for his

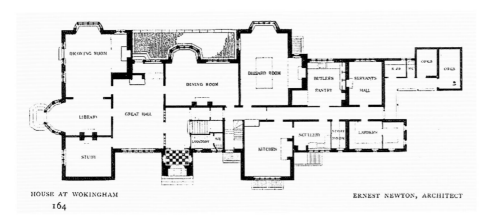

Fig. 2 Ernest Newton, *House at Wokingham*, 1899, ground floor plan
The Studio (XVII) 77 1899, 164

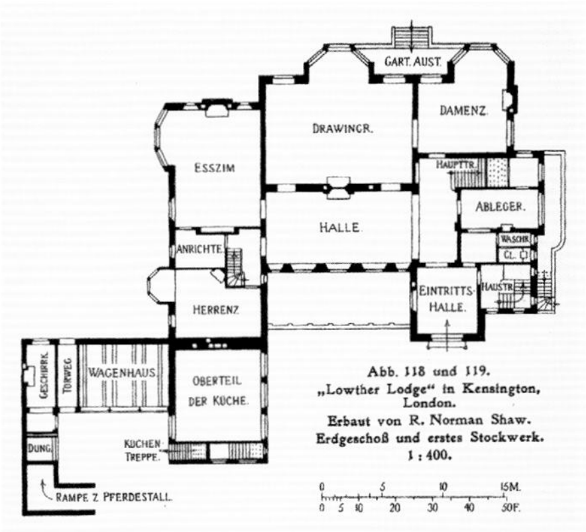

Fig. 3 Norman Shaw, Lowther Lodge, Kensington, London, 1874, ground floor plan
H. Muthesius, *Das englische Haus II*, 1904–1905, 143

creative development of this first (and final) Modernist middle-class mansion. Yet even the architects in the British motherland of this movement like M. H. Baillie Scott, C. F. A. Voysey, or Charles Rennie Mackintosh—a friend of Hoffmann's since his inclusion in the 1900 Secession exhibition—had not yet had the opportunity to construct a "sizeable detached town house" for an art enthusiast. The particular way in which they expressed their anti-industrial attitude had initially developed out of their contact with the preindustrial architectural history they idealized. This is shown by, for instance, William Morris's programmatic conversion of *Kelmscott Manor*, built in West Oxfordshire in the 16th century, into his home and workshops from 1871. It is also for this reason, namely the only slowly emerging independent modern means of expression, that the German publisher Alexander Koch held the "Haus eines Kunstfreundes" ("house for an art enthusiast") competition in his magazine *Innendekoration* in 1901; among the entries, the famous design by Charles Rennie Mackintosh supplied the first authentically modern possible solution to a novel construction commission.

However, in every regard—the size of the house, typological roots, artistic permeation—the dimensions of Hoffmann's designs for Stoclet House eclipse Mackintosh's sketch. This led to the improbable isolated case of the realization

of a major construction job living up to the ideal to a vastly greater extent than even the boldest visions drawn on paper by ambitious architects. In this regard, too, Stoclet House remains unrepeatable and unique.

Hoffmann started his design work five years after Mackintosh's project, initially by looking to the English country house. In the 19th century its typical room layout with a double-height hall, drawing room with bay window and direct access to the garden, pantry, and separate domestic wing in a loosely functional layout had been transferred to the emerging modern metropolis without any radical changes. At the time, only a few architects interpreted this construction task as an independent building type. This is observed by Hermann Muthesius, for example, a board member of the German Werkbund from 1908, in his famous three-volume work *Das Englische Haus* from 1904/05 (published in English as *The English House*, abridged in 1979 and in full in 2007):

> "Of the few [sizeable town houses, author's note] that have fallen into the hands of modern architects, but two have been chosen here: Lowther Lodge in Kensington, built by Norman Shaw in 1874, and the house constructed for Lord Windsor on Mount Street near Hyde Park by F. B. Wade in 1896."[6]

As the latter is not freestanding, it is only worth considering the layout of *Lowther Lodge*: as in Stoclet House there is a central hall, two wedge-shaped avant-corps protruding into the garden (here for the drawing room and boudoir), a dining room with bay window, and a domestic wing adjoining the side of the building for the garage and staff. *Lowther Lodge* was undoubtedly part of the international professional discourse, bearing in mind it and its floor plans were published in the magazine *The Building News*.[7]

In the 1890s Norman Shaw's student Ernest Newton continued the tentatively burgeoning modern interpretation of a large house with garden. In 1899 *The Studio*, an art magazine that was widely read in Vienna, published eight of his exemplary suburban houses with gardens.[8] Although Newton's rather rigid structures fall far short of Voysey's or Hoffmann's distinctive independent creativity,[9] the floor plan types printed in this publication nevertheless clearly prove that there was an awareness of the modern English interpretation of a stately suburban home with garden in Vienna around 1900. In its partly symmetrical layout and sequence of rooms—vestibule, great hall complete with adjoining staircase to the side, dining room, and drawing room—in the round apse of the library (at Stoclet in the theater/music

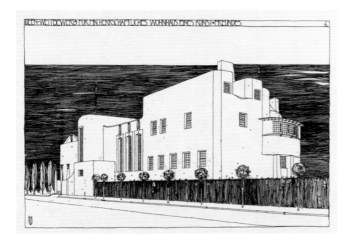

Fig. 4 Charles Rennie Mackintosh, house of an art enthusiast
Meister der Innen:Kunst 2: Charles Rennie Mackintosh – Glasgow. Haus eines Kunstfreundes. 18 Cartons Architekturen Farbige Innenräume mit Text, einen herrschaftl. Landsitz in allen Teilen darstellend, Darmstadt 1902

Fig. 5 JH, Stoclet House, Brussels,
1905–1911, preliminary design,
ground floor plan, prob. 1905
E. F. Sekler, *Josef Hoffmann*, 77

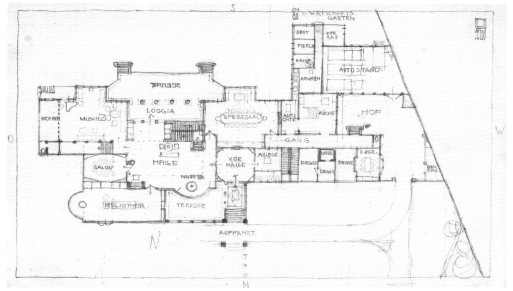

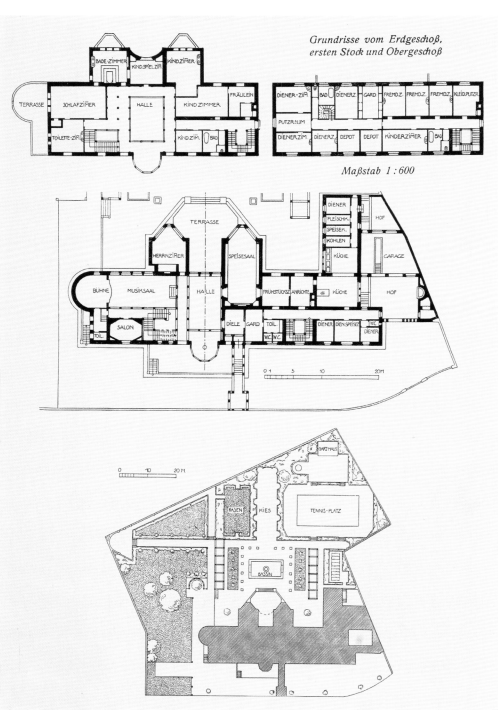

Fig. 6 JH, Stoclet House,
floor plans and site plan
MBF (13) 1914, 6

STOCKLET-HUIS   TE BRUSSEL

JOSEF HOFFMANN DOOR MAX EISLER
1870————————————————1920

15 December wordt Josef Hoffmann, de Weensche Meester, die in zijn werk op zoo voortreffelijke wijze architectuur en kunsthandwerk tot een zuivere eenheid heeft ontwikkeld, 50 jaar.
Op dien dag zullen in den engen kring van zijn vrienden, die het karakter van den kunstenaar het best kennen, geen woorden gesproken worden, zooals dat anders bij zulke feesten gewoonte is. Want deze man wil niet „gewaardeerd", noch minder „gehuldigd" worden. Noch voor zijn persoon, noch voor zijn werk.
„De kunstkritiek", zoo ongeveer liet hij zich eens uit, „is er alleen voor om het publiek te irriteeren. Zij heeft dus haar doel volkomen bereikt, wanneer zij Jan Publiek alleen maar duidelijk heeft gemaakt, dat de kunst onafhankelijk van zijn oordeel, onbekommerd en niet in de war gebracht door zijn Ja of Neen, de wegen volgt die

haar als noodzakelijk zijn aangewezen".
Deze uitlating is voor iemand van zijn karakter vanzelf sprekend en in 't geheel niet aanmatigend of ook maar bitter gedacht. Toch heeft juist zijn naaste omgeving hem genoeg aanleiding voor verbittering gegeven, hem genoeg steenen in den weg geworpen en toch heeft zij — wat wel het ergste en smartelijkste geweest is — het edele karakter van den kunstenaar en mensch steeds weer door haar troebel oordeel trachten te kleineeren. Maar dat alles kon geen macht over hem krijgen. Hij is — naar buiten en binnen — vrij en vroolijk gebleven. Want hij kende en kent maar een moreelen eisch: het werk. Woorden laten hem onverschillig, zij komen zwaar en moeielijk uit zijn mond en maken op hem slechts een pijnlijken indruk, wanneer hij ze van anderen hooren moet. Of ze hem prijzen of berispen, maakt geen verschil, want alleen het scheppen schenkt hem geluk en volkomen bevrediging. Hij verheugt zich niet eens over wat hij

Fig. 8   JH, Stoclet House, 1905–1911, garden side with bay windows and loggia
Bildarchiv Foto Marburg, FM 419349

Fig. 7   Max Eisler's report in the Dutch magazine *Wendingen*, 1920
Wendingen (3) 8–9 1920

room), and in the central hallway that leads to the sprawling lateral domestic wing, the floor plan of Newton's house in Woking, for example, bears conspicuous parallels to Hoffmann's final floor plan for Stoclet House. What is remarkable here is that this final design (with a tower and wedge-shaped structural components on the garden side) only arose after much floundering and perhaps also after much research: Hoffmann's preliminary designs still show hard and flat rectangular protrusions into the garden instead of the later "English" solutions with bay windows. It can therefore be assumed that between his first sketches from 1904/05 and the final plan from 1906 Hoffmann immersed himself in back issues of *The Studio* and in Hermann Muthesius's recently published book *Das Englische Haus*, finding in them exemplary solutions to his extravagant design task.

However, in his final design Hoffmann far surpasses all the models mentioned above. The chief architectural innovations consist in a new, "abstract" understanding of space, which obscures the traditionally clearly legible configurations of the structural elements (beams and pillars, walls, floors, and ceilings). For example, by optically combining elements that have nothing to do with one another from a structural perspective (such as the joint framing of the hall's upper-story parapet and the ceiling of the ground floor, as described below). This invention was only built on a decade later and under entirely different circumstances by Le Corbusier's Purism and the De Stijl group around Piet Mondrian and Theo van Doesburg in the way they played with free surfaces in the space. At Stoclet House Hoffmann achieved numerous artistic discoveries in the incorporeal, unfixed terrain between space and surface. They are based on his "atectonic" design method that applies square modules,[10] which Eduard F. Sekler described in detail:

"Hoffmann's rejection of tectonic expression as an artistic means may be explained at least partly by his turning toward elementary

geometrical forms, above all the square, […] in connection with the *sopraporta* relief of the fourteenth Secession exhibition. Square and cube have this in common: they are inherently non-directional and therefore without dynamic effect. Something of the feeling that static elements have been joined additively remains as typical for the Stoclet House as the patent negation of any strong tectonic expression."[11]

These "abstract" space and surface innovations can best be observed inside in the great hall and outside on the façades. It has often been described how the elements of the hall, alternating between body and surface, "glided past each other"[12]—specifically the marble-clad, two-story pillars and pilasters on a square floor plan and the parapet fields and undersides framed in decorative borders. The decorative borders and materiality combine the individual surface elements into novel and autonomous features, which are entirely emancipated from their tectonic function. It is a similar case with the surfaces of the façade, which comprise completely smooth marble panels and are edged in "tectonically neutral" metal profiles on all sides. In the upper edge of the façade in the eaves section, they distance themselves from the façade surface to incorporate the eaves windows in the surface image.[13] On the corners of the building, where the façades meet at a right angle, they do not, as one might expect, share an edge profile, but rather each continues its own, with the result that double "borders" emerge there, which emphasize to an even more extreme degree the surface and picture character of the façades when viewed from an oblique angle. On the garden side this develops into a concave curved façade section, which resembles a bent playing card and also possesses its own complete "picture frame."

It was only possible to document the completed house along with its gardens in detail—with photographs, plans, and texts—in 1914 in the specialist magazines *Moderne Bau-*

Fig. 9 JH, design for the hall of Stoclet House in Brussels, 1905/06
mumok – museum moderner kunst stiftung ludwig wien, G 144/49

Fig. 10 Le Corbusier and Pierre Jeanneret, Villa La Roche, Paris, 1923–1925, hall
© ADAGP, Fondation Le Corbusier

formen and *The Studio*.[14] This extremely unfavorable point in time at the beginning of World War I, the German occupation of Belgium, and the pan-European economic and social inconceivability of comparable projects in the postwar years prevented any broad reception of Hoffmann's artistic discoveries at first. Not long after, however, the Netherlandish avant-garde movement and eponymous magazine *De Stijl* emerged in 1917 and was followed in 1918 by the magazine *Wendingen*, whose April issue in 1920 (*W* (3) 2 1920) was dedicated to Gustav Klimt and November issue (*W* (3) 8–9 1920) to Josef Hoffmann.[15] The October issue in 1922 (*W* (4) 11 1921) presented Frank Lloyd Wright; the cover was designed by the Russian Constructivist El Lissitzky. This soon had repercussions in France. It is thus no coinci-

dence that an indirect second reception path for Hoffmann's discoveries was suddenly laid in Parisian Purism via Belgium and Holland after Le Corbusier's visit to Vienna in 1908: its emergence has often been explained as a consequence of people's enthusiasm for De Stijl and its milieu. On the other hand, the Constructivist experiments of the architecture class at Vienna's School of Arts and Crafts, which were probably likewise influenced by De Stijl and were launched in 1924/25 by Oswald Haerdtl as Hoffmann's assistant, ultimately prove that Hoffmann unreservedly supported the logical next step from his innovations at Stoclet House, namely the complete liberation of the surface from its framework and the construction of space using unbounded surfaces floating freely in the space.

1   Sekler, Eduard F., *Josef Hoffmann: The Architectural Work*, Princeton, NJ 1985, 80. Trans. Eduard F. Sekler and John Maass.

2   Ibid., 98.

3   Muthesius, Hermann, *Das Englische Haus*, vol. II, 1910[2], 141: "The detached town house is of course home to the wealthiest social class, which is in the position to not only possess a large private house in town but also to have so much land and space that it is secluded from its environs in a most noble fashion."

4   For example, the Rothschild family built in the Neobaroque style in Vienna with the French architects Gabriel-Hippolyte Destailleur and Jean Girette. Later they purchased medieval castles like that in Waidhofen an der Ybbs. In England Ferdinand Rothschild constructed—again with Destailleur—*Waddesdon Manor*. In France James and Betty Rothschild built *Château de Ferrières* with the engineer Joseph Paxton in the "goût Rothschild."

5   Exemplary Austrian role models for this are Karl

Wittgenstein, his children Margaret Stonborough-Wittgenstein, and Ludwig and Paul Wittgenstein.

6   Muthesius vol. II, 1910[2] (see note 3), 142.

7   *The Building News* 25 Jun 1875.

8   "Some Country and Suburban Houses designed by Ernest Newton," in: *The Studio* (17) 77 1899, 157–164. *The Studio* was regularly discussed, for example in Otto Wagner's master school and studio, and was also available in several Viennese coffeehouses, meaning that Hoffmann was very familiar with its content.

9   "[…] he has not perhaps proceeded so far as Mr. C. F. A. Voysey for example, but nevertheless he has succeeded in retaining his own individuality," ibid., 164.

10 "The proportional scheme of the layout is determined in a simple manner by the square. One square of approximately 12m x 12m corresponds to the size of the great hall on the second floor; three squares of the same size form the rectangle of the total of the second floor, exclusive of the thickness of the outside walls. The square asserts

itself in many places of the details of the plan as well as in elevation, notably in the shape of windows and visually important subdivisions of surfaces," Sekler 1985 (see note 1), 78.

11 Ibid., 84.

12 Ibid.

13 This "medieval" motif was used in England around 1900, in particular by R. S. Lorimer for his renovations of old country estates and when designing new houses, cf. *Earlshall* in Fife (Muthesius vol. I 1910[2] [see note 3], 80–81) and his projects *Argaty Hall*, *Glendoe Lodge*, *Colinton Cottages*, and *Kellie Castle*.

14 Levetus, A. S., "Das Stoclethaus zu Brüssel," in: *Moderne Bauformen* (XIII) 1914, 1–34; id., "A Brussels Mansion designed by Prof. Josef Hoffmann of Vienna," in: *The Studio* (LXI) 252 1914, 189–196.

15 On the magazine *Wendingen*, see the article "A Pioneer of Modernism: Josef Hoffmann and International Arts Journalism" by Markus Kristan in this catalog.

Fig. 1 JH, view into the music room at Stoclet House showing the architectural framing
of Fernand Khnopff's painting *I Lock My Door Upon Myself*, 1905–1911
MBF (13) 1914, 20

Christian Witt-Dörring

Stoclet House:
A Gesamtkunstwerk

The Shared Fate of Adolphe Stoclet and the Wiener Werkstätte 1905–1911

During the realization of Stoclet House both the contractor and the customer are stretched to their psychological and financial breaking points. Both are devoted to an idea that is founded on the quality criteria of the Arts & Crafts movement; this results in a shared fate that will last an unforeseen six years, from 1905 to 1911. The Wiener Werkstätte figures as contractor, with Fritz Waerndorfer as the project's business executive and Josef Hoffmann as its artistic director, and their customer is Adolphe Stoclet, the Belgian heir to a large fortune. On 15 January 1903 he moves his family from Milan to Vienna with the intention of attending to his father's Austrian investments:[1] shares in the Vienna–Aspang railroad, which when fully complete is intended to extend as far as Thessaloniki, in the Schneeberg railroad, and in the Wiener Lombard- und Escompte-Bank. Tradition holds that while out walking on the Hohe Warte the young family admires the villas that were constructed there according to Hoffmann's designs in the years 1900–1902. This is when the desire to have a house built for the family after plans by Hoffman is said to have arisen. Yet in October 1904—less than two years after having arrived in Vienna—Adolphe Stoclet is obliged to return to Brussels after the death of his father in order to take over and run the Stoclets' ramified empire of finance and investments.[2] The generous financial resources now available to him as a result of his patrimony[3] and the necessity to create a new, stately home for himself, his wife, and their three children in Brussels, lead him in 1905 to resume the plan to have a house built by Hoffmann. The final decision to commission the Wiener Werkstätte must have been taken in April 1905 at the latest, because a kind of character reference exists from that month with a description of Stoclet's professional activities, living conditions, and creditworthiness, which is delivered to the Wiener Werkstätte. That same month Waerndorfer congratulates Stoclet on his decision and gushes with enthusiasm for his appreciation of art:

"There are no words to express what bliss it would be if you, with whom we are in harmony in all our views and ideas, lived in Vienna. The only thing in which one can take comfort is that you are accomplishing a mission in Belgium, as today you are absolutely the only man in Belgium who knows his age and is a century ahead of his compatriots. That sounds strange, but it is genuinely so and has always been so, because ONE MAN who was ahead of his contemporaries has always done the preliminary work for thousands and his work later becomes the model for several thousand. If the collaboration between Klimt, Khnopff, and Moser succeeds in the way you envisage, then you will have a house the likes of which have not been made for perhaps 4 000 years, because I don't like any of the Renaissance houses and palaces and of course our age chiefly gave birth to them again rather than giving birth to them afresh. I am also thoroughly convinced that we will not build another house similar to yours because Hoffmann is now at the height of his ability and you are the first to set him a task of this nature. And from the outset the way in which you and your beautiful wife approached us with your commission is the most stimulating for any artist. You would not believe how deeply glad Klimt is with the idea of being able to achieve something powerful in a Hoffmann room, because you are the first since the Klinger exhibition to set Klimt such a task for an interior scheme and the first ever to ask of him not a portrait or picture of some sort, as one can buy in an exhibition, but rather something that is to be made for you, for your room designed by Hoffmann."[4]

Stoclet House is considered the paragon of the Gesamtkunstwerk—or total work of art. For Josef Hoffmann and the Wiener Werkstätte, it is the chance of a lifetime to realize—unconditionally—a stately suburban residence with garden in accordance with their artistic and qualitative beliefs. This opportunity arises at a time when the Wiener Werkstätte—after being in business for just two years—has already gained a national and international reputation for supreme, refined, modern aesthetics. Their customer's enormous financial means enables the Wiener Werkstätte for the first and—to this extent—last time to create a Gesamtkunstwerk from its architectural design down to the minute details of its interior decoration, such as the house's guest book, in line with purely artistic quality criteria. The ambitions of the customer and contractor alike were tremendous. Under Hoffmann's artistic direction, the Wiener Werkstätte grasps the opportunity with zeal, without fully realizing the financial consequences of its self-defined quality standards. The company's desire to finally prove of what supreme achievements it is capable, makes its managers disregard any financial prudence and agree a flat rate. Consequently, the project becomes simultaneously their artistic poster child and their

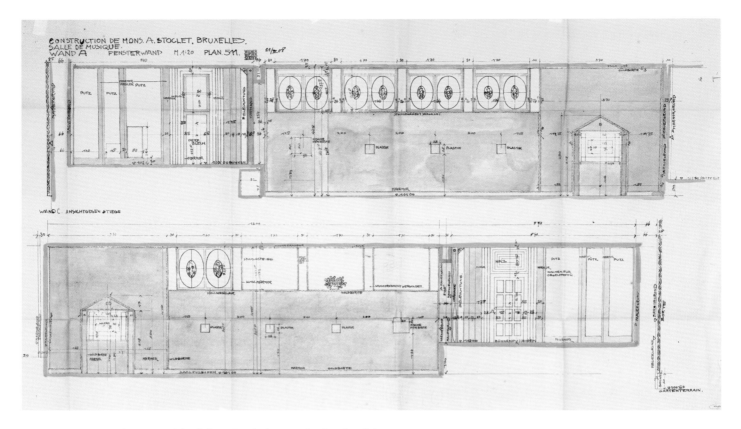

Fig. 2 JH, interior elevation of the left and right longitudinal walls of the music room at Stoclet House with the architectural framing of the Khnopff painting, 1907, Wiener Werkstätte's construction drawing office, 1908
MAK

financial death blow. It can be said that Adolphe Stoclet and the Wiener Werkstätte have a shared fate, which rests on an unshakable faith in Hoffmann's genius and the qualities of the Wiener Werkstätte. Thus, after five years of construction work without an end in sight and after costs skyrocketing for the nth time, Adolphe Stoclet writes:

"I have contemplated our conversation a great deal and as I told you, it is my sincere wish to achieve the completion of my building according to Hoffmann's ideas—a building that should remain an enduring monument to the glory etc. of its architect and the WW. I am therefore prepared to make the possible sacrifices and give my utmost to achieve this aim."[5]

In January 1912 the installation of the panels of Klimt's frieze could begin at last; two years later, upon Stoclet's invitation, Klimt can finally admire his complete frieze, framed in Hoffmann's architecture, on 18 May 1914.[6]

The magazines Moderne Bauformen and The Studio each publish richly illustrated articles in 1914.[7] The palpably proud Adolphe Stoclet informs Hoffmann of the cultural correspondent and adult educator Amelia Sarah Levetus's visit to the house:

"Ms. Levetus was also thoroughly enchanted and will hopefully write you a nice article about it. Have you seen the photographs that Hoffmann had made for a publication? They are truly wonderful—and I expect a genuine rush on the house as soon as the issue has been released."[8]

With the invasion of neutral Belgium by the troops of the German Reich, Austria-Hungary's ally in World War I, in August 1914, contact with the once dynastically and culturally closely connected Austria and the Wiener Werkstätte is lost. Despite repeated invitations[9] by Stoclet, Hoffmann will only be able to experience his epic masterpiece in its completed form on the occasion of the house's semicentennial on 4 October 1955, a year before his death. ■

1   Dumoulin, Michel, Les Stoclet. Microcosme d'ambitions et de passions, Brussels 2011, 148 f.
2   Ibid., 159.
3   Ibid., 169.
4   Letter from Fritz Waerndorfer to Adolphe Stoclet from 28 Apr 1905; private collection.
5   "J'ai beaucoup réfléchi a notre conversation et comme je vous l'ai dit, j'ai le désir sincère d'arriver à terminer ma construction suivant les idées de Hoffmann – construction qui doit rester un monument impérissable de gloire etc pour son archi-

tecte et pour le WW. Je suis donc disposé à faire tous les sacrifices possibles et à donner le maximum de mon effort pour atteindre ce but." Letter from Stoclet to Waerndorfer from 28 Jun 1910; private collection.
6   Husslein-Arco, Agnes/Weidinger, Alfred (eds.), Gustav Klimt. Josef Hoffmann. Pioniere der Moderne, Munich/London/New York 2011, 235.
7   Levetus, A. S., "Das Stoclethaus zu Brüssel," in: Moderne Bauformen (XIII) 1914, 1–34; id., "A Brussels Mansion designed by Prof. Josef Hoff-

mann of Vienna," in: The Studio (LXI) 252 1914, 189–196.
8   Letter from Stoclet to Josef Hoffmann from 22 Jul 1913; the Hoffmann named in the letter is either a mistake by the author or an unknown photographer; private collection.
9   Letter from Stoclet to Waerndorfer from 11 Jun 1912 and letter from Hoffmann to Stoclet from 19 Jun 1913; private collection.

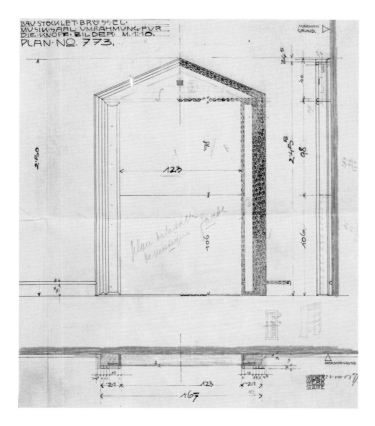

Fig. 3 JH, working drawing for the architectural framing of the Khnopff painting in the music room at Stoclet House, Wiener Werkstätte's construction drawing office, 1908
MAK

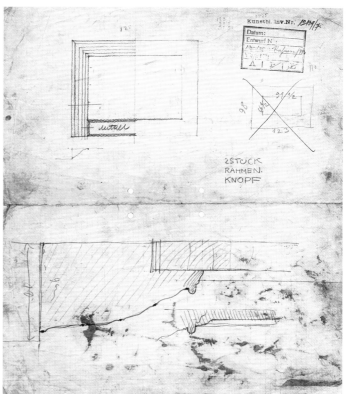

Fig. 4 JH, design for a picture frame for the two Khnopff paintings in the music room at Stoclet House, 1908
MAK, KI 12139-7

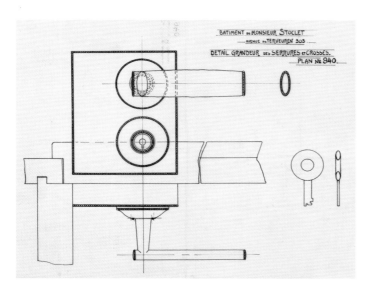

Fig. 5 JH, working drawing for the door lock cases and handles in Stoclet House, 1907, Wiener Werkstätte's construction drawing office, 1908
MAK

Fig. 1 JH, plant stand, executed by the Wiener Werkstätte, 1905
MAK, WWF 132-37-1

Anette Freytag

Plant and Square

The Gardens of Josef Hoffmann

There was lasting enthusiasm when Josef Hoffmann opened an exhibition with the simple title *Gartenkunst* [Garden Art] in the drafting room of the Wiener Werkstätte's construction drawing office on Neustiftgasse in 1907.[1] On the walls he presented ornately drawn garden designs by his colleagues Karl Bräuer, Oskar Barta, and Robert Farsky, his students at the School of Arts and Crafts Paul Roller and Franz Lebisch, as well as his own designs for the gardens of the Beer-Hoffmann, Hochstetter, and Stoclet residences. In showcases and on tables there were arrangements of flower baskets, vases, and plant pots—mostly whitewashed metal objects with squares punched out of them, of which Hoffmann would design a great number. The full length of the entrance area in front of the construction drawing office was adorned with such plant pots and metal trellises; the visitors were greeted by climbing plants that defied the rigid square and rectangle forms in and around which they grew. This interplay of strict geometry and rebellious, living nature was part of Hoffmann's interest in gardens and plants. The resulting contrasts underline the qualities of the antipodes nature and architecture. The tables of this *Gartenkunst* exhibition, at which the visitors could flick through design portfolios, as well as folios and books on the history of garden art, were hedged with groves of small long-stemmed trees with spherical topiary crowns, as if of sculpted nature. The aim of the exhibition was to propagate a new style of garden that would cause a furor until the outbreak of World War I: the "architectural garden." "[T]he combination of architecture and landscape" requires the "transition, fusion, brief organic collaboration of both elements," Ludwig Hevesi summarizes in his review of the exhibition:

> "The architectural element has namely been lost entirely; the house stands in the middle of the landscape garden like the wooden plant marker next to the flower in the garden pots. It is now of the essence to seek solutions, using the topography, terracing, hedgerows, buildings in the light garden style, such as arbors, pergolas, etc."[2]

Josef Hoffmann and his colleagues had answered this call—and furthermore had done so in keeping with the stylistic program for the architectural garden that was propagated between 1904 and 1914 in the *Österreichische Garten-*

Zeitung and in the magazine *Hohe Warte*.[3] Key inspiration in this regard came from the Arts & Crafts movement and its champions on the Continent like Hermann Muthesius and Henry van de Velde, as well as from the floor plans and design vocabulary of Otto Wagner and Friedrich Ohmann and a revival of Biedermeier and Baroque garden art. The design of the garden for what is probably Hoffmann's most famous work, Stoclet House (1905–1911), clearly illustrates the principles that reappear in variations in his other architectural gardens:[4] the house and garden are conceived as a unit. The house's orthogonal axes are continued in the garden or applied in parallel to the house. Covered walkways, loggias, terraces with steps mediate between inside and out, with the transitions occurring incrementally between completely open and completely closed. The house is pushed as close as possible to the street[5] so that there is plenty of space for a garden at the back of the house, where it is entirely concealed from view. Immediately in front of the garden façade lies the sunniest and most strictly architecturally designed section of the garden. In the case of the Stoclet garden, topiary box and yews flank the garden terrace. In front lies a rectangular pond whose width is the same as that of the central hall of the house from which one steps out onto the garden terrace. The pond is encircled by two times eight cylindrical treillages with ivy climbing up them. Positioned to their left and right are rose beds; each contains five tall-stemmed rose bushes and two strips of ground-covering roses. Adjoining these on both sides are pergolas covered in climbing roses, which lead away from the house into the more remote parts of the garden. Sunlight and shadows of wooden or metal latticework, the atmospheric effects of raindrops that hang from it and refract the light after the rain has passed, as well as the effects of artificial light, are all fundamental aspects of the impact made by Hoffmann's gardens.

The more remote sections of the garden—more shaded, mostly flowerless, and often planted with deciduous trees—lie somewhat higher or lower. Every transition from one area of the garden to the next is accompanied by terracing—howsoever subtle. In the Stoclet garden topiary hedges form new garden rooms from which—as in Baroque bosquets—large deciduous trees rise up whose crowns can grow freely. They surround spaces like a tennis court, a bowling green

Fig. 2 Detail from the garden of
Dr. Henneberg's house, 1901
DI (4) 1903, 125

for croquet and boccie games, as well as raised seating and pavilions. Small topiary trees and niches cut into hedges for sculptures, adorn the paths. Dispersed throughout the garden are elegant garden furniture and plant pots. All these elements were designed by Hoffmann himself and executed by the Wiener Werkstätte.

Composed exclusively in the colors green, white, black/gray, and the pink shades of the roses, the Stoclet garden is Hoffmann's most aesthetically radical. It is also the only garden in which fruit espaliers, berry bushes, grapevines, and fruit trees—otherwise commonplace in his private gardens—are omitted (though there is a kitchen garden). That the garden design and features should all be devised by one and the same person, was as much a requirement for the architectural garden as the fruit and vegetable garden and sport and leisure areas would prove near the functional

area of the house (at Stoclet opposite the servants' quarters) and the ornamental gardens near the prestigious section for the family and their guests.[6]

With arbors, pergolas, niches, sculptures, and seating, the architectural garden revives the private gardens of the Biedermeier period. Baroque garden design was a second source of inspiration. Hoffmann had a special affinity for both: his parents' house in Pirnitz/Brtnice (CZ) had a Biedermeier garden that Hoffmann redesigned in 1907,[7] and one of his favorite walks in Vienna regularly took him to the Baroque gardens of the Belvedere.[8] Hoffmann had a fondness not only for topiary hedges and trees, but also for the typical topological and phenomenological amusements of the Baroque period, which he incorporated both in his gardens and in his buildings. They include long axes that open unexpectedly and surprise visitors, making buildings and

6

279

Fig. 3 *Gartenkunst* [Garden Art] exhibition curated by Hoffmann in the drafting room of the Wiener Werkstätte's construction drawing office, 1907
MAK, WWF 103-140-1

Fig. 4 JH, design for plant stands for the Wiener Werkstätte, 1905/06
MAK, KI 12134-7

Fig. 5 View of Stoclet garden from the garden terrace, ca. 1914
Bildarchiv Foto Marburg, 620.288

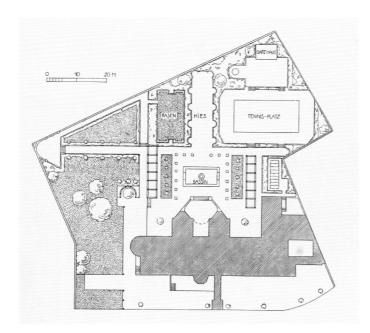

Fig. 6 Site plan of the garden for Stoclet House (1905–1911),
1914. The pergolas shown on the garden plan are drawn
incorrectly: they each have seven compartments.
MBF (13) 1914, 6

Fig. 7 View of the seating area in the southeast of Stoclet garden.
The tree left standing in the middle of the perfectly straight axis
becomes a picturesque element.
MBF (13) 1914, 33

Fig. 8 Garden side of the Ast villa, 1909–1911
The fascination with cast shadows and reflections, as well as the ubiquity of floral motifs, even on façades, is clearly visible.
MAK, KI 8951-3

Fig. 9 Greenhouse at the Skywa-Primavesi villa, 1913–1915
Hoffmann positions it as close as possible to the existing trees. Fruit espaliers can be found along the garden wall.
E. F. Sekler, *Josef Hoffmann*, 369

gardens seem more spacious. Moreover, he employed parallaxes: while moving around certain objects or designed spaces, such as a staircase with freestanding pilasters, the objects themselves—in this case the pilasters—seem to move. In places Hoffmann's consistently rhythmic compositions thus take on a dance-like quality, which one does not anticipate considering his proclivity for strict forms. Another element is the so-called Baroque fold: One sees something interesting at the other end of the garden that seems very close. Along the paths that lead to this goal, one becomes aware that it is much further removed than initially presumed. [5] [6] Space seems to unfurl. What is important here is the journey and the experiences along the way, not the destination itself.

Hoffmann is an architect for amblers. His architecture only takes full effect while walking, when it provokes manifold intuitive reactions, of both a physical and psychological nature.[9] In addition to "picturesque strolls"[10] and unusual, choreographed interiors, another central motif in Hoffmann's oeuvre is his obvious interest in atmospheres—or more precisely, changing weather conditions and the resulting effects for his architecture of sunlight, altitude of the sun, shadows, [8] [9] gathering clouds, and lasting raindrops. They are all taken into consideration in the arrangements of floor plans and front elevations, in the molding on façades and the choice of windows, in the interior compositions and the design of furnishings.[11]

Gardens and flowers are ubiquitous in the works of Hoffmann and the Wiener Werkstätte: as fabric and carpet patterns, as fire screens, as wood carvings for furniture and wall panels, as flower-filled vases and baskets, but also as stone façade features—lush garlands, leafy arabesques, and decorative reliefs. Added to these are ornately wrought metal fences with stylized flowers and trees, sundry sculptures, and perhaps as the pièce de résistance the design of the Stoclet tower with a crown of roses and laurel and floral garlands that seem to cascade down the sides, while inside the house Gustav Klimt created a magnificent, never-wilting art garden with his *Tree of Life* frieze for the dining room.

For the Wiener Werkstätte, which chose a stylized rose as its registered trademark, gardens, plants, and flowers had a deeper meaning. They symbolize *ver sacrum*, the sacred spring for the art of youth. The private paradises for the upper middle class were intended to transcend their inhabitants' everyday lives and make them better people by virtue of art and handicraft. With the Wiener Werkstätte Hoffmann wanted to "contribute to a healthy life, with all its needs and spiritual and material desires."[12] The rhetorical focus on what is beautiful, healthy, and ameliorative in nature later and in other contexts opened an abyss, much as the idea of the Gesamtkunstwerk—or total work of art—had always entailed the threat of sliding into the totalitarian. Complicated political questions are also raised by Hoffmann's comparison, published in 1920, of the work of the Wiener Werkstätte—making objects for individual needs by hand—with that of a gardener:

> "Everything that is like a template, prescribed, every foreseen method is presumptuous of a *Menschenmaterial* [human material], which grows like a colorful bed of various flowers and requires particularly loving and wise care."[13]

Austrofascism was still in the distant future at this point, but the very politically diverse life reform movement had long been active. Its ambivalent program between the liberation of the body on the one hand and the total control of the spiritually and physically "healthy" lifestyle on the other, can be found in many aspects of the work of Hoffmann and the Wiener Werkstätte, from the significance of walking to ungirded women's clothing.

From the 1930s into the 1950s, a period in which Hoffmann became a mere footnote in the international architectural debate,[14] he adopted the style of the modern outdoor living space for his houses but seemed to have lost his interest in a sophisticated spatial differentiation. In the Werkbund estates, the connection between house and garden was just as important as in the gardens of the Gesamtkunstwerke, but for a different reason. In the Austrian Werkbund movement Hoffmann had represented the conservative wing from the late 1920s at the latest, Josef Frank—who was active in the world of housing developments and community gardens—the liberal left wing.[15] Hoffmann's designs for the outdoor spaces in his housing developments were extremely reserved, with one exception: In an undated design for a multistory residential building, all maisonettes are connected by a spiral staircase, glazed, and have their own garden. The garden plan shows dense planting and a hedged walkway to a seating area. The front elevation suggests that the garden is equipped with trellises for climbers, fountains, and sundry garden furniture—a generation before Friedensreich Hundertwasser would invite the *Baummieter* (tree tenants) to move into apartment complexes in 1972. ■

10

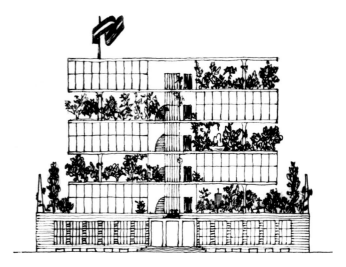

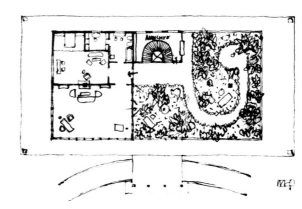

Fig. 10 JH, design for a multistory apartment building with gardens on the upper floors. Floor plan and façade, undated (due to the flag flying from the roof, prob. after May 1945).
E. F. Sekler, *Josef Hoffmann*, 464

1   Hevesi, Ludwig, "Wien eine Gartenstadt," in: *Fremdenblatt* 6 Apr 11907, 39, WWAN 81.
2   Ibid.
3   See Olbrich, Joseph Maria, "Der Farbengarten," in: *Hohe Warte* (2) 1905–1906, 184–189; esp. also the articles published from 1904 by *Hohe Warte*'s editor Joseph August Lux, which he compiled in the book *Die schöne Gartenkunst* (Esslingen) in 1907, as well as Jordan, Max, "Gartenmöbel," in: *Österreichische Garten-Zeitung* (8) 1913, 11–17.
4   In-depth analysis: Freytag, Anette, "Josef Hoffmann's unknown masterpiece: the garden of Stoclet House in Brussels (1905–1911)," in: *Studies in the History of Gardens & Designed Landscapes* (30) 4 2010, 337–372.
5   Mostly just the legally required distance.
6   See "Die Villengarten-Konkurrenz," in: *Österreichische Garten-Zeitung* (2) 9 1907, 298–308: 305.

7   See Witt-Dörring, Christian, *Josef Hoffmann: Interiors, 1902–1913*, exh. cat. Neue Galerie, New York 2006; picture in the photo album of the Hoffmann family Hoffmann, Muzeum Josefa Hoffmanna, Brtnice (CZ).
8   Sekler, Eduard F., *Josef Hoffmann: The Architectural Work*, Princeton, NJ 1985, 9. Trans. Eduard F. Sekler and John Maass.
9   Peter Behrens describes, for example, how the design of the entrance to the hall of Stoclet House made him whisper. Behrens, Peter, "The work of Josef Hoffmann," in: *Architecture* 2 1923, 589–599: 594.
10 Bois, Yve-Alain, "A Picturesque Stroll around *Clara-Clara*," trans. John Shepley, in: *October* 29 1984, 32–62.

11 See e.g., Thomas, Lil Helle, *Stimmung in der Architektur der Wiener Moderne: Josef Hoffmann und Adolf Loos*, Vienna 2017.
12 From Josef Hoffmann's speech at the academic function at Stoclet House on 4 Oct 1955, UAA, Archive and Collection, inv. no. 4437/Aut/4a.
13 From: *Over de Toekomst van Weenen Door Josef Hoffmann [Edition for Hoffmann's 50th Birthday]*, *Wendingen* (3) 8–9 1920, 21–26.
14 Sekler 1985 (see note 8), 244 f.
15 See e.g., Posch, Wilfried, "Die Österreichische Werkbundbewegung 1907–1928," in: *Wissenschaftliche Kommunikation zur Erforschung der Geschichte der Republik Österreich* 10 (1986), 279–312: 311.

Fig. 1 JH, table for the exhibition booth of the printers Christoph Reisser & Söhne
at the BUGRA exhibition in Leipzig, executed by Jakob Soulek, 1914
Oak, stained black, pores chalked white
Galerie Yves Macaux, Brussels
© Photo Studio Philippe de Formanoir/Paso Doble

Christian Witt-Dörring

The Viennese Style

Interiors 1900–1918

"At first it was no easy task and lots went wrong and had to be tackled anew. Nevertheless, one did not give up":[1] looking back, this is how Hoffmann characterizes the situation during those initial years of searching between 1900 and 1902, during which he finally establishes the main features of his modern Austrian interiors and practical objects. When reading contemporary reviews or descriptions of Hoffmann's houses and interior designs from this period, the term "tradition"—which has positive connotations at the time—frequently makes an appearance. Lost in the course of the Industrial Revolution, this tradition symbolizes a design vocabulary that grows naturally out of the local culture, serves citizens' daily needs, and is honestly and modestly pleasing. The tradition being referred to is the preindustrial so-called Biedermeier period, in which form was still in harmony with everyday life—in contrast to the Historicist period. Hoffmann's critics do not consider its qualities to have been copied but rather updated. For example, Joseph August Lux writes:

> "In the rooms created by Prof. Hoffmann, that atmosphere of the Biedermeier interior is captured and recorded, that spirit of gemütlichkeit and hospitality—in a nutshell the genius loci—and in it there is no table, no chair, no cabinet, no practical object that does not bear the spirit of our ancestors and hence through its constructive simplicity and expediency appears to vanquish our general modern culture."[2]

Here Lux, the future editor of the art and culture magazine *Hohe Warte*, is referring to rooms that Hoffmann decorated in 1901 and 1902 for Helene Hochstetter, Dr. Hugo Koller, and Gustav Pollak; they are all in rental apartments. That means that Hoffmann not only has to fit his furnishings into existing spaces but is also confronted with their prior aesthetics, like stucco ceilings or window and door proportions. For them he draws inspiration from interior designs by the English Arts & Crafts movement and endeavors to produce a structural unity between wall and storage furniture, which leaves the center of the room as free as possible, or rather not obscured. This is mostly achieved by means of wainscoting whose height echoes that of the storage furniture and doors. The result is a clear horizon, which continues along all four walls of the room. Examples are the

dining room and anteroom for Gustav Pollak or the bedroom for Helene Hochstetter; this structural element can be found in Hoffmann's interiors until around 1910. What is new compared with the fashion in interior design during the second half of the 19th century, is the intentional contrast between light wall and dark furniture, or vice versa. This experimentation with contrasting colors continues in the choice of furniture upholstery. Both are typical of the interior design of the Empire and Biedermeier periods and of a style that grants the constructive element an aesthetic effect. This is especially true of Hoffmann's furniture designs. Unlike in the years before 1900, furniture is no longer defined by the prominent plank and hence by individual surfaces, but now emerges as a cohesive entity indebted to geometric forms. In seating this also has a consistent impact on the type of upholstery that is chosen. As is common in Empire and Biedermeier styles, Hoffmann adopts the classicist angular upholstery that is clearly defined by means of welts, designing in most cases not only the fabric but also the welts themselves. When it comes to lighting the rooms, Hoffmann exploits the new opportunities offered by electric light, opting for closed or downward-facing light fixtures for better illumination. The artistic light source is now no longer concentrated in the center of the room but is distributed across the entire surface of the ceiling. In the case of the dining room for Gustav Pollak's apartment, wall lights in the form of round mirrors are also added, in front of each of which there is a lamp that is connected to the ceiling circuit. For the aforementioned interior decoration jobs, Hoffmann designs the carpets in addition to the complete furnishings and light fixtures. These are his first designs for textiles; they lay the foundation for a longstanding and fruitful collaboration between him and the J. & J. Backhausen company, with which Koloman Moser had already been working since 1898.

Coinciding with these interior decoration jobs, Hoffmann is able for the first time to put into practice his idea of a holistically designed architectural framework and associated interior, which is described by Lux "as Modernism's greatest progress."[3] In the context of the villa "colony" on the Hohe Warte in Vienna, for example, the period between 1900 and 1902 sees the creation of two houses conceived as a duplex for Carl Moll and Koloman Moser (1900/01), a villa for the

Fig. 2 JH, dining room in Gustav
Pollak's apartment, 1901/02
Furniture and wainscoting made of
richly inlaid pitch pine; dark red
leather coverings; yellow-gray walls;
fittings made of patinated copper
ID (13) 1902, 146

natural scientist and photographer Hugo Henneberg (1901/02), and another for the photographer Victor Spitzer (1901/02)—each with gardens likewise designed by Hoffmann.

Josef Hoffmann has the floor plans—including the placement of furnishings—of the Henneberg and Spitzer houses published.[4] This alone proves just how novel this unit of interior and exterior must have been for his contemporaries. Furthermore, the color palette of both houses' interiors—which cover over 60 pages—is explained in great detail. The palette that Hoffmann uses here is not muted or subdued; rather—as in the apartments described above—it revolves around strong contrasts. What is new here is the choice of roughcast walls in the living area—probably a reference to the houses' rural location. Unlike the urban rental apartment in which the individual rooms are traditionally arranged as an enfilade, in his villas Hoffmann follows the

English model, opting for a central living room, often stretching across two stories, with an open staircase from which the other ground-floor rooms can be reached. The gas fireplace plays a key role here both as a focal point and as a relaxation area. In line with the Arts & Crafts movement's ideas of social reform, Hoffmann's formal aesthetic concept intentionally extends into the ancillary rooms like the kitchen and servants' quarters. As for the storage furniture, while it is partly grouped together along the rooms' walls, it can also be arranged as a room within the room, as in the living room in Dr. Spitzer's house. This is interpreted by Hoffmann's contemporaries as a throwback to the multifunctional rooms typical of the Biedermeier period, which prioritized homeliness over prestigious representation. Another trait borrowed from the Biedermeier can be found in the bedroom of the Henneberg house: Hoffmann covers the bed with the aid of a bedspread or a *Couvertrahmen* (wooden frame over

Fig. 3 JH, bedroom in Helene
Hochstetter's apartment, 1901/02
ID (13) 1902, 142

Fig. 4 JH, washstand niche in the bedroom of
Helene Hochstetter's apartment, 1901/02
White walls, lower wall covering with green and gray
pattern, dark blue flooring; maple stained light blue;
dark squares are maple polished dark blue; fittings
made of chased iron
ID (13) 1902, 141

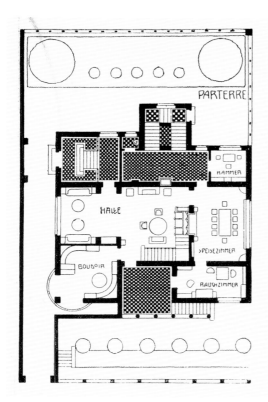

Fig. 5 JH, Dr. Spitzer's house, 1901/02,
floor plan and furnishing scheme of the
ground and upper floors,
as well as the attic
DI (4) 1903, 184

Fig. 6 JH, hall in Dr. Hugo Henneberg's house, 1900/01
DI (4) 1903, 134

Fig. 7 JH, view into the hall from the top of the hall
staircase in Dr. Henneberg's house, 1900/01
DI (4) 1903, 137

Fig. 8 JH, cook's room in Dr. Spitzer's house, 1901/02
Spruce, stained yellow
DI (4) 1903, 159

Fig. 9 JH, kitchen in Dr. Henneberg's house, 1900/01
White walls, sideboard painted white, white marble
DI (4) 1903, 150

Fig. 10 JH, vanity with seat in the guest
room of Dr. Spitzer's house, 1901/02
Spruce, stained black
DI (4) 1903, 183

Fig. 11 JH, dining room in Dr. Henneberg's
house, 1900/01
Wood painted white, furniture polished
black, green leather upholstery; gray
flooring
DI (4) 1903, 141

Fig. 12 JH, bedroom in Dr. Henneberg's
house, 1900/01
DI (4) 1903, 143

which a bedspread is hung), as was common around 1800/30. This guarantees that the bed's architecturally block-like character is preserved in its entirety and is not interrupted by the soft contours of the bedclothes underneath.

In 1902, the year before the Wiener Werkstätte is founded, Hoffmann is able to realize three more interior design commissions. For the families of Dr. Johannes Salzer, Max Biach, and Fritz Waerndorfer, ensembles are created in existing houses and a rental apartment that build on the aforementioned characteristics of Hoffmann's Modernism. For instance, the concept of islands can be found as a seat-[16] ing area in the living room and as a combined washstand [17] and vanity unit in the bedroom of the Salzer apartment, and [15] as an inglenook in the games room and as an alcove for the [14] bed in one of the bedrooms of the Biach house. An empha-

sis of the horizontals by arranging storage furniture in a line [13] can be found in the dining room of the Biach house and [19] with particular success in the dining room for Fritz Waerndorfer. This horizontal structural element can be interpreted as an intermediary between the comparatively low storage furniture and the high ceilings; it is a counterbalance that rectifies proportions that would otherwise have gotten out of hand. While the furniture already features modern proportions, the ceiling heights still correspond to the traditional room concept. When comparing Hoffmann's dining room with Mackintosh's music room for Waerndorfer, the efficacy [18] of this device—borrowed from Anglo-Saxon culture—becomes clear. Hoffmann uses it among other places in the living room of the first Moll house, where he introduces a frieze comprising decorative nails hammered into the wall at regular intervals at the same height as the room's doors.

Fig. 13 JH, dining room in
Max Biach's house, 1902/03
Art et Décoration 1904, 70

Fig. 14 JH, bedroom in Max Biach's house, 1902/03
The Art-Revival in Austria. The Studio. Special Summer Number, 1906, C 23

Fig. 15 JH, inglenook in the games room
of Max Biach's house, 1902/03
ID (16) 1905, 49

Fig. 16 JH, living room suite in Dr. Johannes
and Johanna Salzer's apartment, 1902
DI (4) 1903, 5

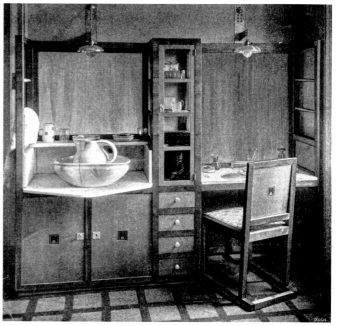

Fig. 17 JH, washstand and vanity set in the
bedroom of Dr. Salzer's apartment, 1902
DI (4) 1903, 6

Fig. 18 Charles Rennie Mackintosh, music room in Fritz Waerndorfer's house, 1902
The Studio (57) 1913, 72

While planning the interior decoration jobs for Max Biach and Fritz Waerndorfer, Hoffmann must have had greater freedom. In both cases he is permitted to make structural interventions to realize his ideal spatial concepts. In the Biach house, for example, he is able to achieve a symmetrical division of the rooms by relocating doors or straightening walls.[5] In both cases he has arrived at a new clarity and subjective individual harmony in comparison with previous works—a harmony that results from a tension between surface and space. Hoffmann manages to interpret space as surface and surface as space, to upend proportions that have been an established component of the aesthetic canon for centuries—and to make all this appear natural. Exploiting different ambiguities in this way will be one of Hoffmann's creative trademarks until well into the 1930s and is manifest

in a wide range of media and expressive forms, whether in architecture or in a vase. In a talk given in 1911, he describes the light-bulb moment that he had in this regard in Paestum and Pompei:

"I saw the Doric temple, and suddenly it fell from my eyes like scales why I did not like the stuff learned at school. There we learned only the proportions of the average of fifty temples and their columns and their columns and their entablatures. Here I saw columns with capitals almost as wide as the height of the column, and I was simply transfixed with admiration."[6]

The decor for Biach is a novelty in Vienna: It is the first interior design to be almost entirely—furniture, doors, and windows—limited to white, with just occasional accents in color. Not only the ancillary rooms and bedrooms, but also

Fig. 19 JH, dining room in Fritz Waerndorfer's house, 1902
MAK, WWF 101-8-1

Fig. 20 JH, dining room in Waerndorfer's house with George Minne's sculpture *Adolescent*, 1902
MAK, WWF 101-12-1

the rooms where guests are received, like the living and dining room, are furnished with white-painted wood and white marble. The walls are partly covered with colored stenciled patterns. It is in the bedrooms that Hoffmann first divides wall surfaces above the introduced horizon into individual fields; he uses borders comprising a checkerboard pattern to frame these fields

With Waerndorfer's dining room Hoffmann creates his most consistent and most radical interior to date in the modern Viennese style. His client's unconditional commitment undoubtedly contributed to this: Waerndorfer did not recoil at the thought of having new door and window formats installed in an old building. The latter can be sunken into the wall as in a train compartment and when open do not stand in the room. Consequently, this is the first time that Hoff-

mann's spatial concept can become a reality without facing any restrictions. The room is decorated in white, black, and silver. Out of a black-and-white marble floor, white marble walls ascend whose height is defined by the doorways, the buffet, the wall vitrines, and the lower third of the wide window. Above, the remaining wall and the ceiling are executed in silvered roughcast. Against each end wall Hoffmann stands two tall marble pedestals for—again white—marble sculptures by George Minne, behind which there are recessed mirrors in the marble walls.[7] The realization of this project was only possible thanks to the relentless efforts of Hoffmann and the client himself at persuading the various craft companies involved to execute the project. Once the room's shell with its built-in fixtures and movables had been realized in late 1902, the furnishings necessary for a modern

Fig. 25 JH, writing room at Sanatorium Westend,
Purkersdorf, 1904
MAK, WWF 102-92-1

Fig. 26 JH, office at the Schwestern Flöge fashion salon, 1904
MAK, WWF 101-21-2

Gesamtkunstwerk—or total work of art—now had to be procured: light fixtures, silver dinnerware, and flatware. This
was the project that led to Hoffmann and Moser as artistic
directors and Waerndorfer as financier resolving to establish
a manufacturing facility that would be independent of
middlemen's interventions and that would be able to guarantee the desired artistic and artisanal quality in direct contact with the craftspeople and customers. The result was the
founding of the Wiener Werkstätte (WW) in May 1903. Initially comprising only a metalworking shop, from 1904 the
WW would finally make it its business to design every single
aspect of people's everyday lives. Among other things, from

1904 it would realize for Waerndorfer the first modern
Viennese cutlery after a design by Hoffmann, the so-called
"flat model".

With the founding of the Wiener Werkstätte and its
Gesamtgestaltung—or total design—mission, Hoffmann relocates his architecture office to the company's headquarters
at Neustiftgasse 32–34. Alongside the workshops, the address also houses the salesrooms and offices designed by
Moser and Hoffmann. For Hoffmann and modern Austrian
design, the new working conditions made possible by
Waerndorfer mean the gift of a seemingly boundless testing
ground. They enable Hoffmann—initially with Moser's sup-

18 p. 69

21 22
23 24

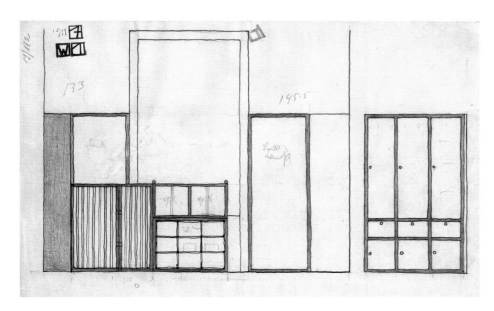

Fig. 27 JH, interior elevation for
the office of the Schwestern Flöge
fashion salon, 1904
GEORG KARGL FINE ARTS

Fig. 28 JH, inglenook in the living
room of Ing. Alexander Brauner's
house, 1905
MAK, WWF 102-107-1

Fig. 29 JH, living room in
Ing. Brauner's house, 1905
MAK, WWF 102-107-2

Fig. 30 JH, bedroom in
Ing. Brauner's house, 1905
MAK, WWF 102-113-1

Fig. 31 JH, dining room in Sonja Knips's apartment, 1907
MAK, WWF-104-199-1

Fig. 32 JH, dining/living room at
Hochreith hunting lodge, 1905/06
MAK, WWF 103-121-1

Fig. 33 JH, living room and study in
Hugo Marx's house, 1911
ID (27) 1916, 130

port—to systematically build on the artistic ideas that had been fought for up to that point, while enjoying the protection afforded by a so-called brand operation. The approach to room and furniture or rather space and surface that he had been testing out on an individual basis, will essentially remain largely unchanged into the 1920s. Time and again in Hoffmann's oeuvre, there is an ambivalent relationship between space and surface. Whether framed or free flowing, Hoffmann deliberately applies the surface as an architectural raw material. With its help the architect can define volumes. So vehemently criticized by Loos, his decorative arts approach liberates the surface from its tectonic constraints and gives it a life of its own. Hoffmann does this by suggesting the possibilities that reside inside it. This is how he manages to actively involve the viewer and resident of his spaces in what is going on. By doing so, he takes a step toward Modernism—but an even larger step toward Post-modernism.

During the WW's first large construction and decoration commission, Purkersdorf Sanatorium, in 1904, Hoffmann still uses the emphasis of the horizontals as the dominant organizing principle to which everything else is subordinate: the furniture, wall openings, wall decoration, light fixtures, and even the pictures are hung on the upper height. In the large dining hall the height of the transom windows determines the height of the doors, the narrow stenciled wall frieze, and where the wall lights and pictures are hung. Jointly realized with Moser that same year, the decoration of the Flöge sisters' fashion salon, like that of the house for Ing. Alexander Brauner from 1905, is similarly still entirely committed to this design principle. Especially in the living and bedrooms of the Brauner house, the consistently applied vertical horizon is the unifying structural element in the rooms, whose palette—with the exception of the textile furnishings and the decorative wall stencil—is exclusively white. For the Berlin apartment of the recently married couple Jerome and Margaret Stonborough-Wittgenstein, Hoffmann decorates the dining room, among other areas. He removes the stucco decoration on the ceiling dating from the 1880s and confines his spatial intervention to the wall design. He frames every wall in a black-and-white geometric border, enabling it to be experienced for itself while also reducing the mass and volume of the space. The same treatment is given to the white linen drapes of the large window. Every single bolt of fabric is framed in a black-and-white border. When closed, the lengths of curtain—as they are conceived without folds—create a large translucent surface. As in all rooms where guests will be received in the apartment, the furniture is worked from black-stained oak

1 p. 108

20 p. 70

28 29 30

26 27 28
pp. 72, 73
8 p. 95

26 27

Fig. 35 JH, dining room in the Ast villa, 1909–1911
MBF (12) 1913, 15

Fig. 34 JH, boudoir in Ing. Eduard Ast's villa
with Gustav Klimt's *Danae*, 1909–1911
MBF (12) 1913, 15

>
Fig. 36 JH, living area in the Ast villa, 1909–1911
MBF (12) 1913, 13

with white rubbed into the pores and is typical of the works from the period between 1905 and 1907.

Around 1905/06 Hoffmann's approach to space and furniture changes. Previously dominated by horizontals, the organizing principle behind the relationship between space and content is now gradually replaced by the grid as a virtual spatial definition. Thanks to its even proportions and free combinability, Hoffmann's trademark—the square—possesses a degree of formal neutrality that makes it predestined for impartial expression. It alone delimits the space: Arranged in a row, the square grids and fragments the surface. Where gridded surfaces are used to define the space, they harbor the virtual potential to fragment the space and hence to communicate between inside and outside. On a small scale this can be understood as an external boundary on the basis of Hoffmann's practical objects made of perforated metal or occasional pieces of furniture. On a large scale and as an internal boundary, they can be seen in a series of his interiors; for example, in the living/dining room of the Hochreith hunting lodge, which is extended in 1905/06 for Karl Wittgenstein. The room's walls and ceiling are veneered with shiny, polished, reddish brown verawood. The walls are divided into individual squares outlined with water-gilt molding. The dividers between the squares are black. This makes

the raised gold molding stand out sculpturally against the black background, which functions like an artificial shadow. Due to this three-dimensional grid and the wainscoting's surface being as smooth as glass, the wall's flat surface is intentionally disrupted, giving rise to an obscuring flicker that sets the room in permanent motion. Like a modular construction system, it can be rearranged at any time. When the room is completed, Waerndorfer remarks in a letter to Hoffmann:

> "[…] on Wednesday the room will be handed over done and dusted to the Wittgensteins—who will arrive on Wednesday—and it is simply beautiful beyond measure, absolutely not pretentious. Once does not at all notice the gold of the moldings separately; I could well imagine someone greatly admire the room and then respond to the question how he liked the gold moldings that he had not even noticed them […]."[8]

The horizontal organizing element is still present but loses its dominant character by structuring the surface of the wall but no longer emerging as a spatial design aspect. Examples are the dining room for Sonja Knips from 1907 or the living room/study in the Marx house from 1911. Concomitant with this is the structural and decorative uncoupling of furniture from the wall. The room no longer constitutes a wealth of details; instead, the walls become the dominant conveyor

Fig. 37 JH, music room at Stoclet House, 1905–1911
MBF (13) 1914, 21

Fig. 38 JH, dining hall at Stoclet House, 1905–1911
MBF (13) 1914, 19

Fig. 39 JH, breakfast room at Stoclet House, 1905–1911
MBF (13) 1914, 24

Fig. 40 JH, parents' bedroom at Stoclet House, 1905–1911
MBF (13) 1914, 27

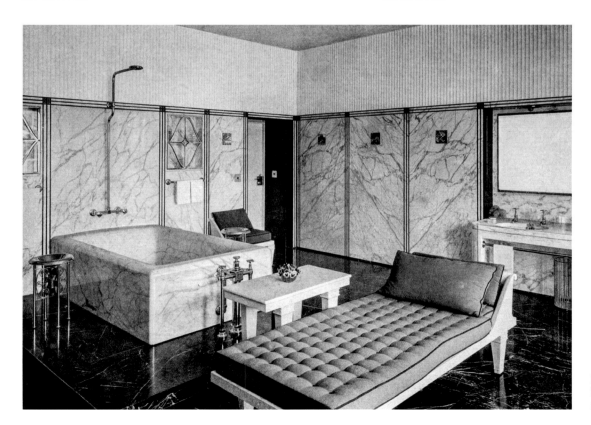

Fig. 41 JH, bathroom at
Stoclet House, 1905–1911
MBF (13) 1914, 26

Fig. 42 JH, cloakroom in the Primavesi
country house in Winkelsdorf/Kouty nad
Desnou, 1913/14
DKuD (38) 1916, 203

Fig. 43 JH, dining room, spring
exhibition at the AMAI, 1912
DKuD (31) 1912/13, 182

Fig. 44 JH, living room in Paul
Wittgenstein's apartment, 1915–1917
Courtesy of the Michael Huey and
Christian Witt-Dörring Photo Archive

Fig. 45 JH, dining room in the
Skywa-Primavesi villa, 1913–1915
DKuD (37) 1915/16, 239

Fig. 46 JH, living room in Sonja Knips's
apartment, 1915/16
DKuD (41) 1917/18, 121

Fig. 47 JH, wall decoration in one of the houses at
the Kaasgraben villa colony, 1912/13
UAA, Collection and Archive, 19.029/11/FW

and interspersed decorative details, the room is never lost in them but rather radiates a monumentality that exudes more a grounded calm than power.

In the years after 1905/06 Hoffmann's approach begins to change—not only to the elements of spatial design, but also to the surface itself. Used provocatively since 1900 as the quintessence of modern design, the smooth, undecorated surface of practical objects assembled from simple geometric shapes now becomes a playground for contemporary ornamental invention. Concurrent with the deliberate endeavor of formally emerging tectonic principles, the surface becomes the bearer of revived old craft techniques that were commonplace during the Empire and Biedermeier periods. They include carved decoration, marquetry, cameo glass, and prismatic cutting. Hoffmann taps the full potential of these techniques, primarily in connection with a monumental classicism, the epitome of tectonic expression, to arrive at untectonic solutions. For example, he uniformly covers a table from 1914, which clearly comprises bearing and load elements, with cannelures without differentiating between these two tendencies, namely the table's apron and legs. The result is a destabilizing flatness; and to emphasize this fact neither its beginning nor its end is clearly defined. Furthermore, the tabletop is offset from the edges, giving the grooved surface of the legs and apron the impression of a thin, not bearing skin that might flake off at any moment. It is not easy to account for this audacious form—unique in the Western world at that time—without Hoffmann's eureka moment during his travels in southern Italy discussed at the beginning of this article.

After the close financial intertwinement of Josef Hoffmann's architectural agendas with the Wiener Werkstätte comes to an end in 1912 and the long-term Stoclet House project is completed in 1913, the architect accepts a series of large private architectural and interior design commissions shortly before the outbreak of World War I, including the Kaasgraben villa "colony" in 1912/13, the Primavesi country house in Winkelsdorf/Kouty (now in the Czech Republic) in 1913/14, and the Skywa-Primavesi villa in 1913–1915, interior decoration jobs for Otto Zuckerkandl in 1912/13, Moritz Gallia in 1913, Sonja Knips in 1915/16, and Paul Wittgenstein in 1916/17, as well as a range of mock-up rooms in the context of exhibitions. All of these works are characterized by

of atmosphere. Their entire surfaces are covered either with a pattern or with a natural material like wood or marble. Each individual wall may be framed or merely completed with a border that is flush with the ceiling or divided into individual fields by means of open or closed frames. In the interiors of Stoclet House realized between 1906 and 1911, starting with the vestibule, then the hall, the smoking room, the theater hall, the dining room, the breakfast room, the parents' bedroom, and the bathroom, Hoffmann investigates these various possible wall treatments. Rich in material stimuli

Figs. 48, 49 JH, wall decorations in one of the houses at the Kaasgraben villa colony, 1912/13
DKuD (35) 1914/15, 309

Fig. 50 JH, table for the smoking room of Prof. Otto Zuckerkandl's apartment, 1912/13
Oak, stained black, with pores chalked white

Courtesy Yves Macaux, Brussels
© Photo Studio Philippe de Formanoir/Paso Doble

the classicist design vocabulary described above that provides the framework for ornamental invention. This ornament has become increasingly important since the years around 1908 and consists of geometric and vegetal forms. Hoffmann's enormous creative potential in plumbing the depths of surface decoration and space is documented by the wall designs he produces for the wide variety of rooms in the Kaasgraben villa colony.

From the 1910s a new generation of young architects is already coming of age in Vienna. They are able to build on the Secessionists' victories in the fight for individual artistic expression and are unabashed about using details from historic styles. Under Hoffmann's management, and especially in collaboration with Dagobert Peche, the modern and bourgeois Viennese style can evolve at the Wiener Werkstätte in accordance with the ideas of the Arts & Crafts movement.

47 48 49

1   Hoffmann, Josef, "Österreichisches Kunstgewerbe" (manuscript), October 1928, MAK, KI 23506-7.
2   Lux, Joseph August, "Innen-Kunst von Prof. Joseph Hoffmann," in: Innendekoration (13) 1902, 129–132: 130.
3   Lux, Joseph August, "Villenkolonie Hohe Warte," in: Das Interieur (4) 1903, 121–184: 139.
4   Ibid., 152 and 184.

5   Witt-Dörring, Christian, "Four interiors by Josef Hoffmann," in: id., Josef Hoffmann: Interiors 1902–1913, Munich/London/New York 2006, 151–173.
6   Hoffmann, Josef, "Meine Arbeit," talk given on 22 Feb 1911, translated as "My Work" in: Sekler, Eduard F., Josef Hoffmann: The Architectural Work, Princeton, NJ 1985, 486–492: 488. Trans. Eduard F. Sekler and John Maass.

7   The art critic and champion of the Secessionists Ludwig Hevesi describes the fairy-tale atmosphere of these rooms on the occasion of a dinner in: Hevesi, Ludwig, "Haus Wärndorfer (26.11. 1905)," in: id.: Altkunst – Neukunst. Wien 1894–1908, Vienna 1909 (reprint: Klagenfurt 1986), 221–227.
8   Noever, Peter (ed.), Der Preis der Schönheit. 100 Jahre Wiener Werkstätte, Ostfildern-Ruit 2003, 105.

Fig. 1 JH and Anton Hanak, left tympanum
of the street façade, Skywa-Primavesi villa, 1914
Cast stone
© Michael Huey

Rainald Franz

"Homely Concept of Housing" versus "Decorating over the Bad Skeleton of a Building"

From Rental Villa to "Festival Building"

In the first two decades of his career, Josef Hoffmann gained extensive experience of construction. Of the buildings he created, his villas are particularly exceptional; they became "seismographs" in their creator's oeuvre of his stylistic development.[1] The starting point for Hoffmann's solutions to the construction requirements of a modern *villa urbana* or *suburbana* is to be found in the travel sketches made by the architect during his travels in Italy in 1895/96, which were funded by the Rome Prize awarded by Otto Wagner's specialized school. These sketches, which Hoffmann was able to exhibit in the Aula Magna of the Academy of Fine Arts Vienna upon his return, caused a sensation and were discussed extensively.[2] Hoffmann comments on them himself in his essay "Architektonisches von der Insel Capri." In it he says:

> "In my opinion, despite the excessive number of newer villa developments, we certainly have not yet succeeded in creating even a single really suitable type of modern country house for our conditions, our climate, our environment."[3]

In light of this deficit, Josef Hoffmann does not advocate the imitation of folksy construction styles but rather recommends that the "homely concept of housing" be awakened in architects, "which consists not in decorating over the bad skeleton of a building with ridiculous ornaments of cast cement produced in the factory, nor in forced-on architecture of the Swiss or gable house type."[4] Despite having only just joined the private studio of Otto Wagner, here the emerging architect has already formulated the reformist approach to simplification that will lead to his first proposed solution: the *Entwurf für ein Mährisches Landhaus* [Design for a Moravian Country House] from 1899.[5] Produced in connection with Hoffmann's illustrations to accompany excerpts from Alfred Lichtwark's *Palastfenster und Flügelthuer*[6] in *Ver Sacrum*, this design features a projecting half-hipped roof, a porch—again with a hipped roof—and windows divided into squares, a large gate opening onto the back garden, and a small front garden with another, smaller gate. In the catalog of the 8th Secession exhibition in 1900, there are vignettes with three depictions of country houses, again characterized by tall roofs, in one case with half-timbering, and dynamically designed porch roofs.[7] Inspired by rural

architecture, this building type is taken up again by Hoffmann in his country house study for *Ver Sacrum* in the calendar sheet for June 1901 called *Landruhe* [Country Rest].[8] Yet again he chooses an oblique view, showing us the house's façade through the garden gate, as it were; like the other country houses, there is a half-hipped, projecting roof, which in this case covers a narrow terrace on the first floor. Here Josef Hoffmann is refining a type that he had already put into practice for the by now completed conversion of the Bergerhöhe country house near Hohenberg in Lower Austria; he is presenting a country house style oriented toward the English model but whose autochthonous roof shapes clearly root it in Austria.[9] The border vignettes framing the *Entwurf für ein Mährisches Landhaus* in *Ver Sacrum* quote the Secessionist ceiling decoration on the undersides of the interiors of the country house for Paul Wittgenstein and hence reference the connection between ideal view and execution. Impressions from his intensive contact with Charles Rennie Mackintosh during the 8th Secession exhibition in Vienna and from his travels in Great Britain with Felician von Myrbach and Fritz Waerndorfer in 1900 are immediately put to paper by Hoffmann in his ideal villa plans. Up to this point, Hoffmann the architect had taken a back seat behind Hoffmann the furniture and interior designer of ephemeral exhibition architectures. Unjustly, according to art critics:

> "I really would like to see a house by Josef Hoffmann. How come Hoffmann still isn't getting to build anything? After all, he is the man of the matter for Vienna. He is one of those people who must make the latest Vienna, and from whom it should be ordered in good time."[10]

The commission for the villa colony on the Hohe Warte in 1900 finally helped the architect achieve his breakthrough. Berta Zuckerkandl, whose brother-in-law would commission Hoffmann with Sanatorium Westend in Purkersdorf near Vienna, which was constructed entirely of cubic and panel-shaped elements in 1904, viewed the Hohe Warte villas as follows: "The architectural form is strictly constructive. The external appearance of every building has grown tightly out of its ground plan. In their profiling, in their silhouette, these homes have an uncommonly harmonious impact."[11]

11 p. 23

18 p. 26

Fig. 2 JH, three architectural studies
VS (1) 7 1898, 19

With Joseph Maria Olbrich having left for Darmstadt, it became possible for Hoffmann to roll out his formal repertoire for villas, which met a need that had arisen throughout Europe at this time. From now on his villas appear in every magazine, from *Hohe Warte* to *The Studio*; even the national and international publications on the fashionable topic of country houses and villas are inconceivable without a mention of Josef Hoffmann's buildings: a vignette of the villa for Hugo Henneberg and over 30 pictures of villas by Hoffmann illustrate Joseph August Lux's publication *Das Moderne Landhaus. Ein Beitrag zur neueren Baukunst*. Lux, from 1905 also the editor of the magazine *Hohe Warte*, followed the construction of the new city district as a writer on culture. "Suburbs of villas, that is the latest growth ring being formed around the metropolises. Where urban and rural culture meet, they emerge as an intermediary," Lux analyzed.[12]

The series of villas built between 1899 and 1911 on the Hohe Warte also includes—if at some geographic distance—the Legler house[13] constructed in 1905–1907, a model of his versatile architecture for peri-urban villas. Wilhelm Legler, a painter and student of Carl Moll, for whom Hoffmann had built the first villa on the Hohe Warte, married Margarethe Schindler, Moll's adopted stepdaughter and Alma Mahler's sister, and probably the illegitimate daughter of fellow Secessionist painter Victor Berger. In the community of reform-minded Viennese artists around Moll, it appears to have been a sign of good etiquette to a certain extent to have a villa by Josef Hoffmann to call one's own. From the outset

Hoffmann arranges the rooms in the system of strictly quadratic floor plans such that the three-story villa with a studio for the owner on the top floor can be divided into small apartments if necessary, meaning that the house can be transformed into a rental villa. Façade elements like the hipped roof with large dormer window, the projecting eaves section on all sides, roughcast, and windows with trim and glazing bars complete the typical style of the time. At this point Hoffmann had already perfected his "villa building blocks": the configuration of rooms and choice of decorative details on the façade and in the interior are adapted according to each client's wishes and financial means. Here, too, Hoffmann proves that he truly is a student of Otto Wagner, continuing the "systemic Modernism" in villa construction that the latter established in Vienna: creating building solutions customized down to the last detail to his clients' synesthetic demands. Many of Hoffmann's villas are reproduced in Arnold Karplus's *Neue Landhäuser und Villen in Österreich*, published in 1910. Karplus, himself an architect, wanted to enlighten his readership about how country houses should be created to serve their true purpose: in his words, they have to "be buildings that, situated in the garden, are a cozy, homely site of healthy living." Above all, Karplus wants to put an end to the deplorable custom of the "apartment villa, a characterless halfway house between a bad country house and a worse apartment building." Instead, architects should "build multifamily houses with individual, healthy, comfortable, and intimate apartments in such a way that several families reside in a single house without disturbing one another."[14]

Villa Colony in Kaasgraben:
Using the Villa Building Blocks

A suggested solution to this construction task was presented by Josef Hoffmann in the Kaasgraben villa colony, which was constructed in 1912/13.[15] Comprising eight single-family homes paired off as duplexes with almost square floor plans, the site owes its development to the initiative of Emil and Yella Hertzka. Emil Hertzka (1869–1932) was the director of Universal Edition, Austria's most important music publishing house at the time; founded in 1901, the company's portfolio featured—alongside Classical and Romantic works—avant-

4 5 6

Fig. 3 JH, calendar page for June 1901,
Landruhe [Country Rest]
VS (4) 1 1901, 12

Fig. 4 JH, duplex at the
Kaasgraben villa colony,
1912/13
MAK, KI 8969-9

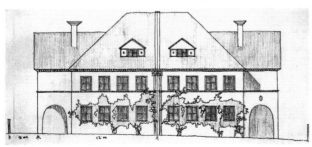

Fig. 5 JH, Kaasgraben villa colony, 1912/13,
view and façade design
© Wolfgang Woessner/MAK

Fig. 6 JH, preliminary design for the Kaasgraben
or Hertzka villa colony, 1912/13
Der Architekt (XIX) 1 1913

Fig. 7 JH, Primavesi country house in Winkelsdorf/Kouty nad Desnou, 1913/14
DK (18) 1915, 233

garde composers like Gustav Mahler, Arnold Schönberg, Egon Wellesz, Alban Berg, and Anton Webern. Yella Hertzka (1873–1948), a Zionist feminist and trained horticultural expert, founded the first horticultural high school for girls in Austria-Hungary in 1912. It was also she who initiated the founding of the "Familienhäuserkolonie" (colony of family homes), commissioned Josef Hoffmann, and provided the initial finance for the buildings. The grounds in Kaasgraben originally also accommodated the horticultural school's boarding house. On the lot owned by the Hertzkas that was parceled in 1912, properties were subsequently acquired by music historians, composers, poets, and high cultural officials: Adolf Drucker, Egon Wellesz, Hugo Botstiber, Adolf Vetter, Robert Michel, and others. Critics soon called the buildings the

> "colony of the Wiener Werkstätte. His task was not to create precious, proud rental or 'stately' villas, but to design simple private homes that would not put too great a strain on their owners' purses, in which nevertheless people of taste, advanced education, and accordingly not low standards in terms of art and domestic culture would live and feel at home."[16]

Despite following English garden-city models in terms of location and requirements, the house types developed by Josef Hoffmann bear Classicist features. The houses with basements, two main stories, and a finished attic were brick built with wooden trusses; the façades feature fine-quality stucco with vertical cannelures in the upper stories; the

hipped roofs with dormers are tiled. In contrast to the individually planned villas of the Hohe Warte, Hoffmann standardized the buildings in Kaasgraben. All the façades have a strongly projecting, convex main cornice with several rows of horizontal fluting and a string course running under the upper-story windows. Only verandas, terraces, loggias, and bay windows individualize the garden façades of each home. Sloping down toward the city, the lot was built on in such a way that there is a closed-off green space in the center—originally a tree nursery belonging to the school run by Yella Hertzka. In the houses a central staircase or hall with wooden stairs provides access to the living areas, with Hoffmann taking care to ensure a compact arrangement with a minimum of corridor spaces. The design of the rooms with simple tiled floors, rolled wall decorations, and plain furniture conformed entirely to the style of the Wiener Werkstätte (WW). With the Kaasgraben villa colony Hoffmann matured the façade system of rhythmized plaster that he had developed for the Ast villa, which was completed shortly beforehand, while the interiors took on new optical qualities thanks to his use of the latest WW patterns for the stenciling. Contemporary critics detected

> "atmospheric reminders of traditional native building designs […]. Outward-opening double windows after the so-called Hellerau model merge with the wall level, giving the façade an appearance reminiscent of familiar old Viennese houses."[17]

The Primavesi Country House versus the Skywa-Primavesi Villa: *Villa rustica* versus *Villa suburbana*

Inspiration from folk art and peasant architecture threads its way through Josef Hoffmann's country house plans. It is tangible in buildings like the Wittgensteins' country houses Bergerhöhe (1899) and Hochreith (1905/06), the entrance pavilion to the Kunstschau of 1908 with its hipped roof and the country house there that Josef Hoffmann designed as a demonstration building for the bentwood furniture company J. & J. Kohn, the transportable hunting lodge for Alexander Pazzani near Klosterneuburg (1909/10), the Böhler country house in Baden (1909/10), the villa for Dr. Hugo Koller in Oberwaltersdorf (1912–1914), as well as particularly trenchantly in the Primavesi country house in Winkelsdorf/ Kouty nad Desnou (1913/14) and the house for Sigmund Berl in Freudenthal/Bruntál (1919–1921): they are pieces of architecture that either combine features of English country houses with Austrian elements of Biedermeier villas or have façade decorations reminiscent of folksy carvings, in the style of a rural Neo-Palladianism, with traditional thatched roofs and folksy interior decoration or column cladding bearing comparison with rustication. They contrast with decidedly urban villas, which thwart any rustic inspiration, such as those of Dr. Richard Beer-Hofmann in Vienna (1905/06), Prof. Pickler in Budapest (from 1909), or Edmund Bernatzik in Vienna (1912/13).

Two exceptional buildings exemplary of these parallel aspects of his villa architecture were created by Josef Hoffmann within just a few years of one another for a single family. The "country house in Winkelsdorf near Mährisch-Schönberg" (Kouty nad Desnou near Šumperk), as it is introduced in a contemporary article in *Deutsche Kunst und Dekoration*, was conceived as a Gesamtkunstwerk—or total work of art—by Hoffmann.[18] It constitutes the folkloric counterpart to the house completed shortly beforehand for Adolphe Stoclet in Brussels in the chic surface style and the Austrian House completed that same year in an expressive Neoclassicism for the 1914 Werkbund exhibition in Cologne.

Had the building not been destroyed in a fire in 1922, we would have in it a textbook example of the ornamental adoption of folk art in Austrian Modernism. Otto Primavesi (1868–1926), a major industrialist and banker from Olmütz/Olomouc, and his wife "Mäda" Eugenie became crucial to the commercial development of the WW between 1914 and 1930. Contact with the Primavesis had been established intentionally, with efforts to do so necessitated by financial difficulties at the WW: with Otto via the sculptor Anton Hanak (befriended with Hoffmann since the international art exhibition in Rome, 1911) and with Mäda via Gustav Klimt, who had painted her portrait in 1903. In 1913 Josef Hoffmann constructed the Primavesi country house in Winkelsdorf, which was decorated by the WW; in 1914 he furnished two rooms in the Primavesi villa in Olmütz and remodeled the Primavesi bank in Olmütz in 1913/14.[19] Again in 1913, construction begins on the Skywa-Primavesi villa in Vienna for Josefine Skywa and her partner Robert Primavesi (1854–1926), Otto's cousin and brother-in-law, a member of the Austrian house of representatives, big landowner, and major industrialist.[20]

Contemporary descriptions, designs by Josef Hoffmann, his colleagues at the WW, and his students at the School of Arts and Crafts, photographs, and comments by critics from the time all prove that the construction of the Primavesi country house was taken as a guideline in terms of the aesthetic direction taken by the Wiener Werkstätte. In Winkelsdorf, 75 km north of Olmütz, Otto Primavesi had acquired a large lot on a southeastern slope at the end of the valley formed by the river Tess/Desná in the High Ash Mountains (Altvater-Gebirge/Hrubý Jeseník). At its highest point Hoffmann planned a villa, which he describes as follows:

"This house would be built entirely of wood, on stone foundations and with a thatched roof. The inner rooms, too, would be fitted out in wood in a great variety of colour combinations and

Fig. 8 JH, Skywa-Primavesi villa, Vienna, 1913, model
MAK, LI 1081

include wood carvings, the intention being to promote merry and healthy country living."[21]

The architect delivered two designs for the Primavesi country house, which was customized to the needs of the four-person family and their large number of servants. It quoted parts of previously realized buildings: In the first design, published in *Der Architekt* in 1914, with three gables facing the southeastern slope and dominating central lookout, there are ideas—like the rectangular floor plan and glazed connecting corridor to the summer house—that Hoffmann had realized in Sanatorium Westend in 1903 and in the Böhler house in Kapfenberg in 1909.[22] New features of this initial design are the complete division of the main façade with a colossal order of 14 pillars and the plan to follow the Slavic tradition of a frame construction infilled with vertical planks. In the ultimately executed second design, the building becomes a *villa rustica* constructed in the Neo-Palladian style, resembling local log houses with a portico with eight oak columns and a projecting thatched hipped roof on a thick base of rubblework. Discontinuities of materials and folkloric quotations characterize the house inside and out: colorful carvings on walls and doors, painted furniture, hand-printed linen and silk fabrics for bedclothes, curtains, and carpets after patterns by the Wiener Werkstätte, masonry heaters by Anton Hanak, and the *Gesamtgestaltung*—or total design—from flatware to bedclothes produced by artists of the WW in a rural style to Josef Hoffmann's specifications. Hoffmann even specially designed gowns of hand-printed silk for guests. Yet all of this was in a strictly proportioned structural shell, whose room symmetries and portico integrated in the façade are reminiscent of Andrea Palladio's villas and palaces in and around Vicenza.

If one assesses the building according to ornamental criteria overall, one must declare that a decorative system envelops the building from the bowling alley and the basement den to the guest rooms in the attic: in line with the Vitruvian concept of decorum, designs are developed that are appropriate to the purpose of each room.[23] Observing the building in this way, it becomes clear that the Primavesi country house is not a thoughtless adoption of indiscriminately collected folkloric motifs, but rather an attempt at total design that seeks synthesis between folkloric motif and urban decor while in a sense constrained by the corset of Neoclassicism. In light of this circumstance, the genesis of the Primavesi villa can be interpreted in many ways: as a brilliant coup for the Wiener Werkstätte's new sponsors, or as a model building of a new aesthetic oriented toward folklore, which Hoffmann intended to develop at the WW and the School of Arts and Crafts, to a certain extent as a way out of the ossified geometrism of the early years of the WW.

In the publication *Österreichische Werkkultur*, edited by Max Eisler from the Austrian Werkbund in 1916, the Primavesi country house is compared with the Skywa-Primavesi villa, complete with extensive illustrations, under the title "Der Künstler":

"The best kind of wealth of solutions will be found precisely where the creator is permitted the greatest freedom, and here in turn where he likewise designs the exterior himself, has built the rooms of the house himself, and hence is responsible for the congruence of the whole. And of the furniture it can be said that the word 'beautiful' no longer applies here in its old, still far too common sense; everything external takes a back seat, the decorative accepts a subordinate role, and form becomes as crucial

to the value of what has been achieved as the designed room is to the house."[24]

At almost the same time as the land was acquired for Otto Primavesi's country house in the High Ash Mountains, Josefine Skywa, Robert Primavesi's partner, purchases two lots on Vienna's Gloriettegasse. Skywa and Primavesi became the joint owners of the lots and commissioned the last stately villa that Josef Hoffmann was able to build in Vienna before the outbreak of the First World War.[25] Josef Hoffmann remembers that

"[b]etween 1913 and 1915, the time of the building work in Winkelsdorf, I was asked to build for a member of the Primavesi family a large villa and garden in Hietzing; this was to be a comfortable place to live but also a place of dignity where large festivities could be held."[26]

And Berta Zuckerkandl stated: "The monumental character of the Hietzing house brings to mind the beautifully structured Austrian festival building at the Werkbund exhibition in Cologne."[27] In his autobiography, Hoffmann speaks of the house being one of the "very few commissions I was allowed to carry out in Vienna without much influence from outside. I designed [it] inside and out to the smallest detail and with great delight."[28] Some 30 meters long by 27 meters wide, the floor plan is based on forms used for Stoclet House and the Ast villa, which was completed shortly beforehand. With its piers fluted from the base to the main cornice and hanging flowers and bouquets applied in yellowish fine-quality stucco, the structuring of the façade incorporates profiles from the Werkbund building in Cologne. The north/southeast/west access to the building separates a prestigious section of the main floor with large hall, dining hall with office, salon and library, games room, sunroom, and garden terrace from the servants' rooms and guest rooms in the attic, which can be accessed via a staircase, and the private living area, which runs along the south façade. Here there is a large bathroom with loggia, two bedrooms, a dressing room, and a study. The south façade is divided into eleven axes, five of which are in the central section and three each in the slightly protruding, gable-topped lateral avant-corps. Whereas Hoffmann had used Palladian forms to structure the façade of the villa in Winkelsdorf, here he chooses the motif of a recessed central avant-corps familiar from buildings dating from Vienna's Biedermeier period, in this case structured with sculpture-bearing piers. Compared to the roof section, the walls appear to be recessed; a double vertical wave as a cornice motif above a rounded profile with foliage motifs runs around the tympana with recumbent figures in the ancient style after a design by Anton Hanak. The cannelures continue into the gables of the hipped roof. The dual-height windows break up the wall patterns. Even the garden walls, latticework, and gates—again designed by Hoffmann—pick up the foliage and cannelure motifs of the walls. There are two gardens, one prestigious front garden and a private terraced garden with a teahouse with pergola and water basin. "[T]he Primavesi villa in the Gloriettegasse had to be dignified and respectable,"[29] writes Josef Hoffmann.

In the Skywa-Primavesi villa Josef Hoffmann's pre-WWI villa plans reached their absolute climax, both regarding the level of aestheticization of life and the employment of design, craft, and material. While he had developed a folkloric decorative system to permeate the Primavesi country house, at almost the same time he invented a similarly harmonious, classicizing, atectonic decorative system for the

32 p. 198

S. 3

9

10 p. 189

33 p. 199

35 pp. 200/201

Fig. 9 JH, Skywa-Primavesi villa,
1913–1915, street façade
© Michael Huey and Christian Witt-Dorring
Photo Archive

Skywa-Primavesi villa that saturates every detail of the building inside and out and forms a coherent whole. The suitability of the selected forms depends on the construction task: *villa rustica* or *suburbana*. That "ornaments of cast cement"—which he had reviled in 1897—were used for the Skywa-Primavesi villa, is a different matter entirely, but it is indicative of Hoffmann's creative flexibility.[30] The art historian Dagobert Frey viewed Hoffmann's villas from this period as follows:

"With almost no exception Hoffmann created works from two building categories: exhibition buildings and villas [...] and yet this seems to have been no mere coincidence but characteristic of the nature of his art. Exhibition buildings, meaning festival buildings, which provide the decorative framework for a unique, higher-minded purpose in life. [...] If in this sense his exhibition buildings should well-nigh be called living areas, then some of his villas almost appear to be exhibition buildings. It is certainly a prestigious aspect that lends the Stoclet, Ast, or Skiwa [sic] villas a monumentality that raises them above the character of intimate homes."[31]

1   Compare the articles "Hohe Warte: From Life Reform to Bourgeois Daily Life" and "Between Surface and Space: Atectonic Architectural Innovations at Stoclet House" by Matthias Boeckl, and "Stoclet House: A Gesamtkunstwerk. The Shared Fate of Adolphe Stoclet and the Wiener Werkstätte" by Christian Witt-Dörring in this catalog. For this reason, this article intentionally omits these buildings.

2   Pozzetto, Marco, *Die Schule Otto Wagners 1894–1912*, Vienna 1980, 17. See also the article "Josef Hoffmann: Studies at the Vienna Academy. From Carl Hasenauer to Otto Wagner's Specialized School, Rome Prize" by Rainald Franz in this catalog.

3   Hoffmann, Josef, "Architektonisches von der Insel Capri – Ein Beitrag für malerische Architekturempfindungen," in: *Der Architekt* (III) 1897, 13, reprinted under the title "Architectural Matters from the Island of Capri" in: Sekler, Eduard F., *Josef Hoffmann: The Architectural Work*, Princeton, NJ 1985, 479. Trans. Eduard F. Sekler and John Maass.

4   Ibid.

5   Illustrated in: Sekler 1985 (see note 3), CR 44, 262–263; preliminary drawing in the MAK Collection, KI 10439-4, illustration in *Ver Sacrum* (III) 5 1900, 67.

6   Alfred Lichtwark, the first director of the Hamburger Kunsthalle, published a collection of essays under the title *Palastfenster und Flügelthuer* in 1899. Josef Hoffmann became familiar with his writings during his travels through Germany with Koloman Moser. See his statement in the lecture *Meine Arbeit* from 1911, reprinted as "My Work" in: Sekler 1985 (see note 3), 486–492: 488: "On a journey with him through Germany I first en

countered the writings on Lichtwark and experienced them like a divine revelation."

7   Illustrated in the catalog accompanying the 8th Secession exhibition in 1900 and in *Das Interieur* (I) 1900, as well as in Sekler 1985 (see note 3), CR 48, 265–266.

8   Hoffmann, Josef, architectural sketch *Landruhe* [Country Rest], in *Ver Sacrum* (IV) 1 1901, 12.

9   See the article "Protestant Materialism Meets Catholic Emotions: The English Exemplar" by Christian Witt-Dörring in this catalog.

10   Hevesi, Ludwig, "Die Ausstellung der Secession (12. Januar 1900)," in: *Acht Jahre Secession*, Vienna 1906, 213 ff.

11   Zuckerkandl, Berta, "Josef Hoffmann," in: *Dekorative Kunst* (XII) 1 1903, 1–15. See the article "From Life Reform to Bourgeois Daily Life: The Villa Colony on the Hohe Warte" by Matthias Boeckl in this catalog.

12   Lux, Joseph August, *Das Moderne Landhaus. Ein Beitrag zur neueren Baukunst*, Vienna 1903, 3.

13   Armbrustergasse 22, 1190 Vienna, see Sekler 1985 (see note 3), CR 103, 299.

14   Karplus, Arnold, *Neue Landhäuser und Villen in Österreich*, Vienna 1910.

15   Kaasgraben villa colony, 1912/13, at Kaasgrabengasse 30, 32, 36, 38/Suttingergasse 12, 14, 16, 18, in Vienna's 19th district; "Eine Villenkolonie von Prof. Josef Hoffmann in Wien," in: *Der Architekt* (XIX) 1913 1, plates 8–12 ("Villenkolonie Hertzka in Wien XIX").

16   H. K., "Die Villenkolonie im Kaasgraben in Wien. Erbaut von Architekt Regierungsrat Josef Hoffmann," in: *Österreichische Wochenschrift für den öffentlichen Baudienst* XXIII (32), 1917, 397–399, plates 50–52.

17   See note 15, 398.

18   Franz, Rainald, "Die 'disziplinierte Folklore' Josef Hoffmann und die Villa für Otto Primavesi in Winkelsdorf," in: Aigner, Anita (ed.), *Vernakulare Moderne. Grenzüberschreitungen in der Architektur um 1900. Das Bauernhaus und seine Aneignung*, Bielefeld 2010, 161–177.

19   Sekler 1985 (see note 3), CR 179, 360–362, CR 181, 362.

20   Ibid., CR 185, 365–370.

21   Noever, Peter/Pokorný, Marek (eds.), *Josef Hoffmann. Selbstbiographie/Autobiography*, Ostfildern 2009, 101. Trans. Bernd Magar and Andrew Oakland.

22   *Der Architekt* (XX) 1914/15, plate 80; original design in the MAK Collection, KI 16814.

23   In his architectural treatise *De Architectura libri decem*, Vitruvius defines decorum as the adequate appearance of a building modeled on tried-and-tested conventions: "Decor autem est emendatus operis aspectus probatus rebus compositis cum authoritate" (p. 22). As such, Vitruvius applies "decorum" or "decor" to the building as a whole and not to features subsequently applied to it.

24   Eisler, Max, *Österreichische Werkkultur*, ed. by Österreichischer Werkbund, Vienna 1916, 11, 14.

25   Zuckerkandl, Berta, "Josef Hoffmann. Wien," in: *Deutsche Kunst und Dekoration* XXXVII 1915/16, 228 ff., LXVIII 1931, 31 ff.

26   Noever/Pokorný 2009 (see note 21), 102.

27   Zuckerkandl 1915/16 (see note 25), 230.

28   Noever/Pokorný 2009 (see note 21), 102.

29   Ibid.

30   See note 3.

31   Frey, Dagobert, "Josef Hoffmann zu seinem 50. Geburtstag," in: *Der Architekt* (XXIII) 1920, 65–72: 69.

Fig. 1 JH, drawing room at the Kunstschau, Vienna, 1908, mural by Anton Kling
Zeitschrift für bildende Kunst (43) NF19, 1908, 254

Rainald Franz

"Chief Architect of the Show of Force of Austrian Ambitions in Art"[1]

The 1908 Kunstschau in Vienna

Eleven years after the founding of the Union of Austrian Artists Secession, whose appearance Josef Hoffmann shaped right from the start, Hoffmann was offered the opportunity to participate in creating an entire "exhibition city" in the center of Vienna as exhibition architect and graphic designer. Hoffmann dominated the exhibition committee[2] founded for the planning of Vienna's Kunstschau set for 1 June to 15 November 1908—the climax and end of Viennese Secessionism, which Hermann Bahr had already presented in his reviews as everyday fashion.[3] Differences on artistic and financial matters had caused the "stylists" to split from the "painters" within the Secession, which led to the departure of Klimt and the entire group around him[4] in 1905. The newly formed Klimt Group, with sixteen members, comprised mainly instructors at the Academy of Fine Arts and the School of Arts and Crafts and artists in the circles of these institutes: Otto Wagner, Alfred Roller, Koloman Moser, and Josef Hoffmann were part of the core around Klimt. This association, as well as the founding of the Wiener Werkstätte in 1903, assured the artists and architects who had left the Secession brisk popularity among the circles of students and staff at these institutes. Planning for the realization of an extensive exhibition of Austrian art began in 1907. A working committee was formed on 30 October 1907.[5] The exhibition was meant to guarantee the Klimt Group presentation and sales opportunities, which had been lacking since the break with the Secession. Gustav Klimt understood the orientation as follows:

> "The new Vienna Kunstschau in 1908 will include only a small amount of paintings and sculptures, and a much larger amount of architecture and all of those objects that one tends to summarize under the names, 'decorative arts,' 'industrial arts,' 'arts and crafts,' and the like. As the guiding concept behind this event is to show that the serious, truly modern art has already established itself in all areas of public and private life."[6]

On 16 November 1907 Josef Hoffmann would take over responsibility for setting up the building. Also carried out at the meeting was a first distribution of the spaces to be assigned to the participating artists (in the end, 130), programmatically from architecture to painting, graphic arts, sculpture, through to advertising and gardening, art for children,

a section for theater, and one for modern dress.[7] In January 1908, upon request, Gustav Klimt was able to secure the "building lot reserved for the Sängerhaus Verein (Association for a Singers' House) on Heumarkt during the coming summer for the purpose of the art exhibition that he and his colleagues were planning," as the new concert hall would first be built on this site in autumn 1908.[8] Hoffmann seems to have already begun with the planning of the building. Freed from his responsibilities at the Secession, along with his teaching, he was able to focus his attention on the Wiener Werkstätte, where the Purkersdorf Sanatorium was completed in 1905 and major commissions were being embarked upon, such as the house for Adolphe Stoclet in Brussels. The founding of Cabaret Fledermaus likewise occurred in this period.[9] The projects and the artist colleagues involved overlapped with the 1908 Kunstschau. Within the overall planning for the Kunstschau, Josef Hoffmann used two unrealized design commissions from 1908: The design of a pavilion for Emperor Franz Josef in 1908 and designs for the exhibition structures of the decorative arts at the *Kaiser-Jubiläumsausstellung*, the jubilee exhibition for the emperor planned for 1908 in Vienna's Prater park.[10] The pavilion designed for the Lower-Austrian industrial association[11] in 1907 for the emperor's jubilee exhibition, with its strict symmetry, was influenced by the preplanning of Stoclet House, as well as by elements of English and Scottish architecture, for example, in the monumental bay windows inserted in the façade. Hoffmann would reuse the hipped roof and connection between wall and protruding pavilion in the entry pavilion for the Kunstschau, as well as the graphical-geometric decorative elements on the façade and the use of sculptures. For the Kunstschau planning, Hoffmann adopted from the unrealized pavilion for the festive procession for the emperor in 1908, the connection between sculpture and wall surfaces dissolved by relief.[12] The submission plans for the temporary pavilions were dated 17 March 1908. Hoffmann worked together with other students of Wagner and was also able to include his own students in the cooperation, which lent homogeneity to the entire complex.[13]

Berta Zuckerkandl wrote: "With his ground plan for the exhibition structures, Josef Hoffmann enabled all versions of a great, unified, decorative overall art."[14] He is able to

Fig. 2 JH, design for exhibition buildings for decorative arts at the *Kaiser-Jubiläumsausstellung*
[Imperial Jubilee Exhibition] planned for 1908 in Vienna's Prater park
Jahrbuch der Gesellschaft Österreichischer Architekten, Vienna 1908, 20

Fig. 3 JH, courtyard view of the entrance pavilion to the Kunstschau, Vienna, 1908
Zeitschrift für bildende Kunst (43) NF19, 1908, 246

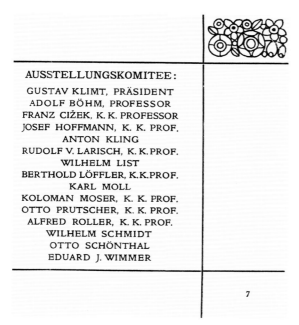

Fig. 4 Catalog of the 1908 Kunstschau,
designed by Anton Kling, names of the
exhibition committee members
MAK BI-25789-8

Fig. 5 Emil Hoppe, small concrete courtyard at the
Kunstschau, Vienna, 1908
Hohe Warte (4) 1908, 221

implement the leitmotif of "offering art for life."[15] And Emil
Utitz commented: "If we want to sum it up briefly, then this
presents architecture's conquest of the applied arts."[16]

Construction of the exhibition buildings began six weeks
before the opening of the exhibition. The completed plan
is dated 17 April 1908.[17] Building shells for the ephemeral
wood constructions were completed two weeks later. Hoffmann's basic concept envisioned an inwardly turned, orthogonal complex with a succession of pavilions, courtyards,
and gardens. The main component of the planning was symmetry: Hoffmann overrode the asymmetry of the building
site by dividing the exhibition district into two areas whose
central axes approached one another toward Schwarzen-
bergplatz. The part facing Lothringerstraße comprised pavilions and courtyards, the area toward Heumarkt was taken
up by the *Kleines Landhaus* [Small Country House], the café
with terrace, and the garden and garden theater. The entry
façade was a consecrated area, resembling a temple complex, windowless and structured solely by prominent gable
fronts and recessed outer walls.[18] Only the central entry pavilion was illuminated, which Hoffmann made the event's
signatory building, and which very quickly also surfaced on
Wiener Werkstätte postcards: an oscillating hipped roof,
flanking flagpoles, semicircular niches in the cornice zones
with sculptures (allegories of the arts) contrasting the otherwise closed front, which was actually the entry, accessible
via three steps and a podium. Flanking both sides were the
areas of writing designed by Rudolf von Larisch, his colleague
at the School of Arts and Crafts.[19] Surface patterns by Josef
Hoffmann and Anton Kling animated the interior of the entry

Fig. 6 JH, courtyard of the small country house for the
J. & J. Kohn company at the Kunstschau, Vienna, 1908
DKuD (23) 1908, 37

hall and the *Kleiner Hof* [Small Courtyard], which Hoffmann had designed together with Otto Schönthal.[20] Sparing use of colors heightened concentration on the exhibited artworks. The second autonomous piece of architecture by Hoffmann on the grounds of the Kunstschau, for which he designed the interior and exterior, was the *Kleines Landhaus,* a show house with furnishing from the bentwood furniture firm J. & J. Kohn.[21] English-Scottish architectural details inside and outside, from towerlike building parts with an octagonal ground plan, total fenestration reminiscent of Mackintosh villa through to the hall characterize the building, which "should cost only 7,000 kronen with full furnishings"— an "inexpensive building" with the sheen of the Hohe Warte villas.[22] In the space of the Wiener Werkstätte, Hoffmann revealed his talent for the staging of valuable decorative-art objects by means of a reduction to black and white and grid patterns, from the showcase through to the fitted carpets around the silver display cases by Carl Otto Czeschka at the center, which Ludwig Wittgenstein purchased from the Wiener Werkstätte for 30,000 kronen. Hoffmann adorned

the walls and columns with linear decorative ornaments that he designed himself. The reserved design accentuated the selected pieces from the offer of the Wiener Werkstätte. In spite of immense interest from the media, an intense program of events with theater, five o'clock teas, etc., and scandals, for example around Oskar Kokoschka's premiere of his play *Murder, Hope of Women,* the Vienna Kunstschau in 1908 was not a financial success. But through the exhibition, Expressionism became "socially acceptable" in Austrian art and Josef Hoffmann had passed his baptism by fire as multifunctional general organizer in the circles of his artist friends. Hermann Muthesius remarked:

> "The architectural sense has developed to maturity here, the sublime taste elevated to the highest refinement; the artistic aspirations of this group are entirely universal and extend to all visible human expressions, however always emanating from architecture […]. This modern Viennese art is perhaps the most uniform and complete that has been brought forth by our era until now."[23]

Fig. 7 Emil Hopppe, Wiener Werkstätte postcard no. 1
JH, entrance pavilion at the Vienna Kunstschau, 1908
MAK, WWPKE 225-1

Fig. 8 Emil Hoppe, Wiener Werkstätte postcard no. 2
JH, entrance courtyard at the Vienna Kunstschau, 1908
MAK, WWPKE 297-1

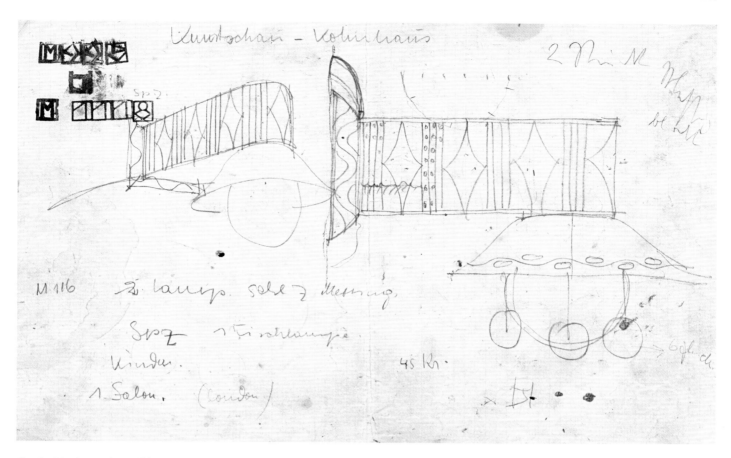

Fig. 9 JH, design for wall lighting, small country house—Kohnhaus
[Kohn House]—at the Kunstschau, Vienna, 1908
MAK KI 12112-10-1

1   Gustav Klimt, opening speech for the Vienna
    Kunstschau, 1908, printed in the exhibition cata-
    log in 1908.
2   Kristan, Markus, *Kunstschau Wien 1908*, Weitra
    2016; Husslein-Arco, Agnes/Weidinger, Alfred
    (eds.), *Gustav Klimt und die Kunstschau 1908*,
    Munich 2008.
3   Bahr, Hermann, "Die falsche Secession (1899),"
    in: Pias, Claus (ed.), *Hermann Bahr. Secession*,
    Weimar 2007, 139–148. Bahr already spoke back
    then of a "nascent battle of the true against the
    false Secession." The 1908 Kunstschau was also
    put in quotation marks as the "New Secession,"
    "Kunstschau 1908. Eine neue Sezession," in:
    Neues Wiener Journal 8 Mar 1908, 12.
4   Natter, Tobias, *Die Galerie Miethke. Eine Kunst-
    handlung im Zeitraum der Moderne*, Vienna 2003.
5   On the genesis of the preparations, see the
    written protocols of the secretary Otto Prutscher
    from Oct 1907 to Feb 1908, privately owned,
    Vienna. On the prehistory, see also Kristan 2016,
    9 ff., Husslein-Arco/Weidinger 2008, 14–18 (for
    both, see note 2). Belonging to the exhibition
    committee were Josef Hoffmann, Koloman Moser,
    Alfred Roller, Wilhelm List, Eduard Josef Wimmer-
    Wisgrill, Otto Prutscher, Wilhelm Schmidt, Carl
    Moll, Adolf Böhm, Bertold Löffler, Anton Kling,
    and Otto Schönthal with Gustav Klimt as presi-
    dent.
6   Gustav Klimt, letter to the State Assembly of the

    Grand Duchy of Austria below the Enns. Sub-
    mitted on 10 Mar 1908 (GZ: 76, Reg. Z. XXVIII/
    433).
7   Quoted by Weidinger, in: Husslein-Arco/Weid-
    inger 2008 (see note 2), 16. The following artists
    and artist groups were to be given spaces: Franz
    Metzner, Otto Prutscher, Wilhelm Schmidt, Otto
    Schönthal, Oskar Kokoschka, Bertold Löffler, Emil
    Orlik, the German-Bohemian artists, Fritz Zeymer,
    Koloman Moser, the Wiener Werkstätte, Otto
    Wagner, Carl Otto Reichel, and Eduard Josef
    Wimmer-Wisgrill.
8   Memory of an advisor concerning the realization
    of the exhibition of the Klimt Group in 1908, in:
    AVA, Ministry of Culture and Education, Vienna,
    4 Jan 1908.
9   On this, see the articles "Anatomy of Catharsis:
    Construction of a Formative Factor for the Purkers-
    dorf.
10 Sekler, Eduard F., *Josef Hoffmann: The Architec-
    tural Work*, Princeton, NJ 1985, 115 f., CR 118
    and 120, 321 f. Trans. Eduard F. Sekler and John
    Maas.
11 Perspective view in *Jahrbuch der Gesellschaft Ös-
    terreichischer Architekten*, Vienna 1908, 21.
12 *Der Architekt* (XVII) 1911, plate 17.
13 See, e.g., the article "In the Modernist Laboratory:
    Josef Hoffmann's Architecture Class at the Vienna
    School of Arts and Crafts" by Matthias Beockl in
    this catalog.

14 Zuckerkandl, Berta, in: *Wiener Allgemeine Zeitung*
    1 Jun 1908, 3.
15 Zuckerkandl, Berta, "Die Kunstschau 1908," in:
    Arbeiter Zeitung 24 May 1908, 4.
16 Utitz, Emil, in: *Deutsche Kunst und Dekoration*
    (XXIII) 1908–1909, 68–77: 74.
17 The plans are in the Municipal and Provincial
    Archives of Vienna, MA 8. Illustrated in: Husslein-
    Arco/Weidinger 2008 (see note 2), 41, 50.
18 Sekler had already pointed to the given model-
    effect of the Minoan art of the Mycenaeans, which
    were intensely reported on through the then-cur-
    rent excavations and publications of Sir Arthur
    Evans in artist and architectural circles. Sekler 1985
    (see note 10), 119n45.
19 With quotes from Francis Bacon, Thomas Carlyle,
    J. W. Goethe, Ouckama, J. A. Lux, Michelangelo
    Buonarroti, William Morris, John Ruskin, and
    Oscar Wilde.
20 Sekler 1985 (see note 10), CR 121, 322 ff.
21 Ibid., CR 123, 325.
22 Hevesi, Ludwig, "Kunstschau Wien 1908," in:
    *Zeitschrift für bildende Kunst mit den Beiblättern
    Kunstchronik und Kunstmarkt. Neue Folge* (XIX)
    1908, 245–354, quoted by Kristan 2016 (see note
    2), 137.
23 Hermann Muthesius, quoted by L. W. Rocho-
    wanski in the catalog of the 1927 Kunstschau in
    Vienna, Austrian Museum of Art and Industry (to-
    day's MAK), Vienna 1927, 12.

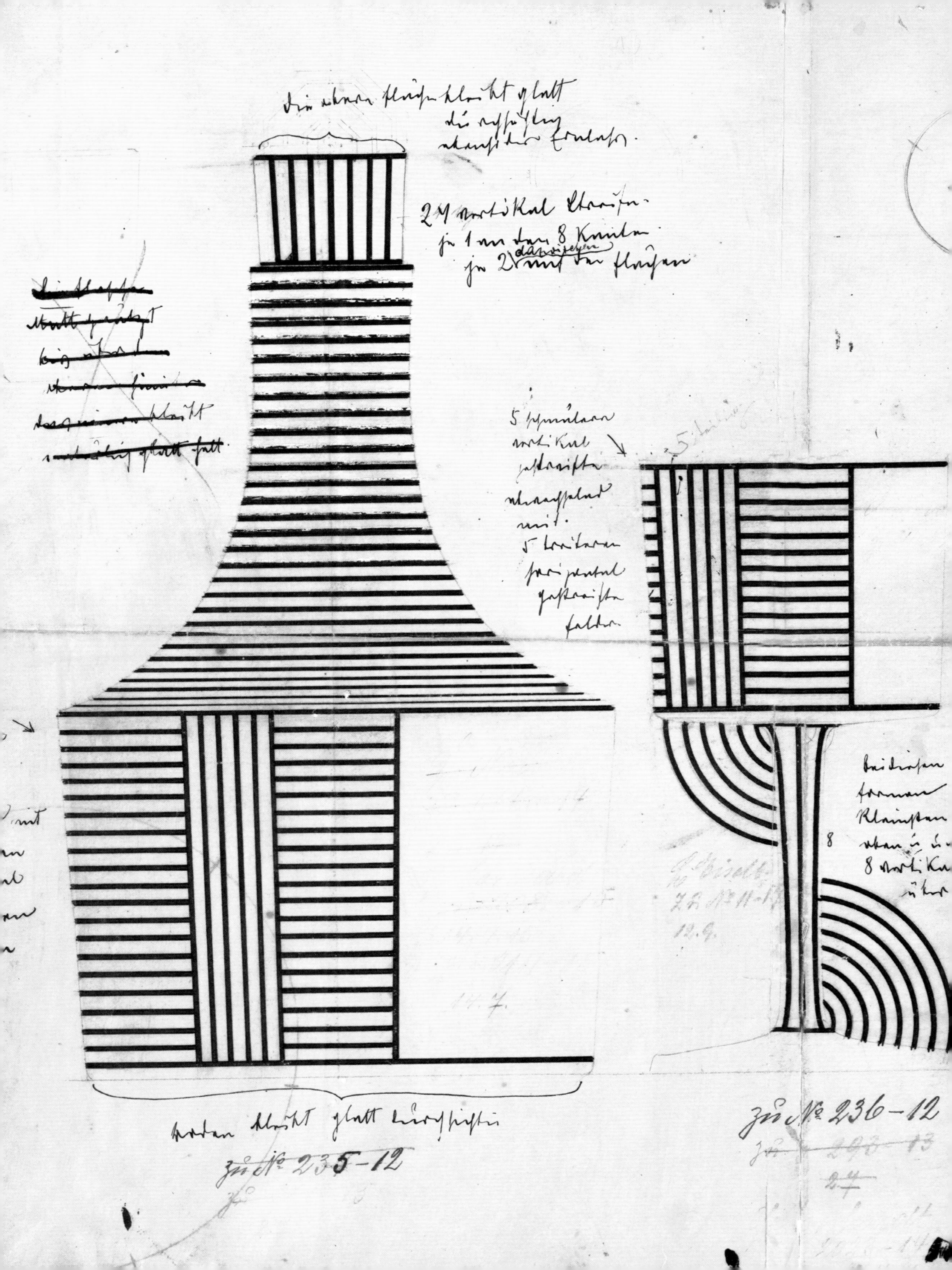
24 vertikal Streifen
je 1 neben den 8 Kanten
je 2 dazwischen mit den Flächen
5 schmalen vertikal gestreiften abwechselnd mit 5 breiten horizontal gestreiften Falten
zu № 236–12
zu № 235–12

1911
1918

JH, designs for a flacon, wine glass, and champagne bowl
with bronzite decoration, 1910
J. & L. LOBMEYR

Fig. 1 JH, coffee set, executed by the Wiener Werkstätte, 1918
Silver, ivory, and ebony
GALERIE BEI DER ALBERTINA · ZETTER

Fig. 2 JH, tea set, executed by the Wiener Werkstätte, 1927
Silver and ivory
MAK, GO 2035
© MAK/Georg Mayer

Fig. 3 JH, smoking room in Prof. Dr. Otto Zuckerkandl's apartment, 1912/13
DKuD (34) 1914, 140

Fig. 4 JH, salon in Erwin Böhler's apartment, 1917/18
Courtesy of the Michael Huey and Christian Witt-Dörring Photo Archive

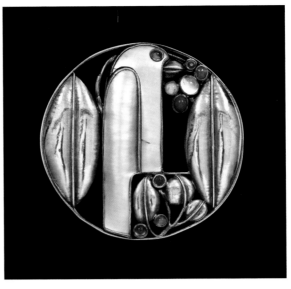

Fig. 5 JH, brooch, executed by the
Wiener Werkstätte, 1912
Silver and malachite
Private collection

Fig. 6 JH, brooch owned by Emilie and Gertrude Flöge,
executed by the Wiener Werkstätte, 1910
Gold, mother-of-pearl, moonstone, opal, lapis lazuli,
tourmaline, garnet, and chrysoprase
Private collection, courtesy of the Klimt Foundation, Vienna

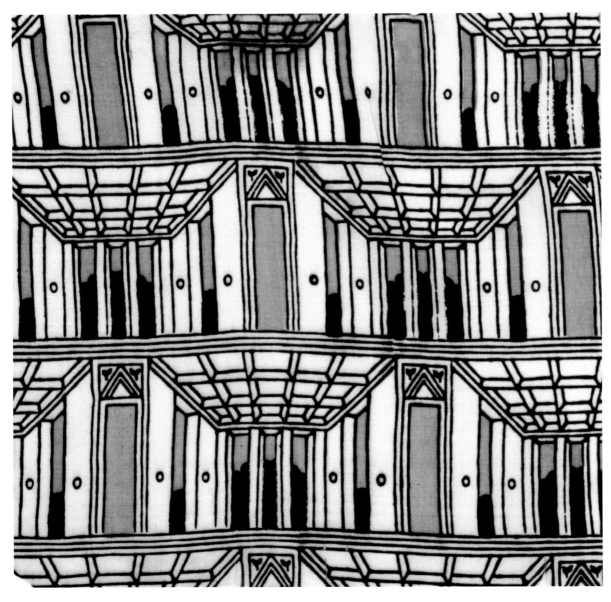

Fig. 7 JH, fabric *Theben* [Thebes], executed by the Wiener Werkstätte, 1910
Silk, printed
MAK, WWS 784

Fig. 8 JH, preliminary project for Dr. Otto Böhler's villa, Kapfenberg, 1910
Der Architekt (17) 1911, 14

Fig. 9 JH, terrace on the 2nd floor of the Ast villa, 1909–1911
Courtesy of the Michael Huey and Christian Witt-Dörring Photo Archive

Fig. 10 JH, Skywa-Primavesi villa, Vienna, 1913–1915,
vehicle entrance
MAK, KI 8969-2

Fig. 11 JH, wallpaper *Leipzig*,
executed by Max Schmidt,
Vienna, ca. 1914
MAK, WWTAMB 2-4
© MAK/Aslan Kudrnofsky

Fig. 12 JH, pattern design for the wall stencil
in the son's room, Vetter house in the Kaasgraben
villa colony, 1913
National Gallery Prague, K 17708

Fig. 13 JH, design for a fabric pattern, 1911
Backhausen Archive, BA03876

Fig. 14 JH, champagne glass, executed by a
Bohemian manufactory for J. & L. Lobmeyr, 1911
Colorless glass, etched, bronzite decoration
MAK, WI 1633-5
© Peter Kainz/MAK

Fig. 15 JH, vase, executed by a Bohemian
manufactory for J. & L. Lobmeyr, 1913
Colorless glass, etched, bronzite decoration
MAK, GL 3404
© Peter Kainz/MAK

Fig. 16 JH, glass goblet, executed by Meyr's Neffe, Adolf bei
Winterberg/Adolfov ve Vimperk, via J. & L. Lobmeyr, 1910
MAK, WI 1630-4
© Peter Kainz/MAK

Fig. 17 JH, glass goblet, executed by Meyr's Neffe, Adolf bei
Winterberg/Adolfov ve Vimperk, via J. & L. Lobmeyr, 1910
MAK, WI 1630-2
© Peter Kainz/MAK

MOTTO:
PAME.

Fig. 18 JH, design for Paul Poiret's Atelier Martine
on Avenue d'Antin, Paris, 1912, motto: PAME
MAK, WWGP 1998

Fig. 19 JH, armchair for the living area of Moritz and
Hermine Gallia's apartment, 1913
Wood, stained black; renewed leather cover
bel etage Kunsthandel GmbH

Fig. 20 JH, fauteuil, executed by J. & J. Kohn for
the German Werkbund exhibition in Cologne, 1914
Beech and plywood, bent, stained black; original blue leather
upholstery
MAK, H 2990
© MAK/Georg Mayer

Fig. 21 JH, armchair for the smoking room of Prof. Dr. Otto Zuckerkandl's apartment, 1912/13
Oak, stained black, with pores chalked white, recontructed upholstery
Courtesy of Yves Macaux, Brussels
© Photo Studio Philippe de Formanoir/Paso Doble

Figs. 22, 23 JH, designs for the city hall in Ortelsburg/Szczytno (PL), 1916–1918
National Gallery Prague, K 17754-755

Fig. 24 JH, design for the city hall in Ortelsburg/Szczytno, 1916–1918
Bauhaus-Archiv, Berlin, 297

Fig. 25 JH, vase, executed by Meyr's Neffe, Adolf bei Winterberg/Adolfov ve Vimperk, for the Wiener Werkstätte, 1915
Blue glass, cut
GALERIE BEI DER ALBERTINA · ZETTER

Fig. 26 JH, vase, executed by Meyr's Neffe, Adolf bei Winterberg/Adolfov ve Vimperk, for the Wiener Werkstätte, 1915
Purple glass, cut
Private collection
© MAK/Georg Mayer

Fig. 27 JH, vase, executed by a Bohemian manufactory for the Wiener Werkstätte, 1915
Violet glass, cut
MAK, GL 3111
© MAK/Katrin Wißkirchen

Fig. 28 JH, lidded handleless cup with decoration by Hilde Jesser, executed by Johann Oertel & Co, Haida/Nový Bor, for the Wiener Werkstätte, 1917
Blue glass, diamond-cut decoration
MAK, GL 3477
© MAK/Katrin Wißkirchen

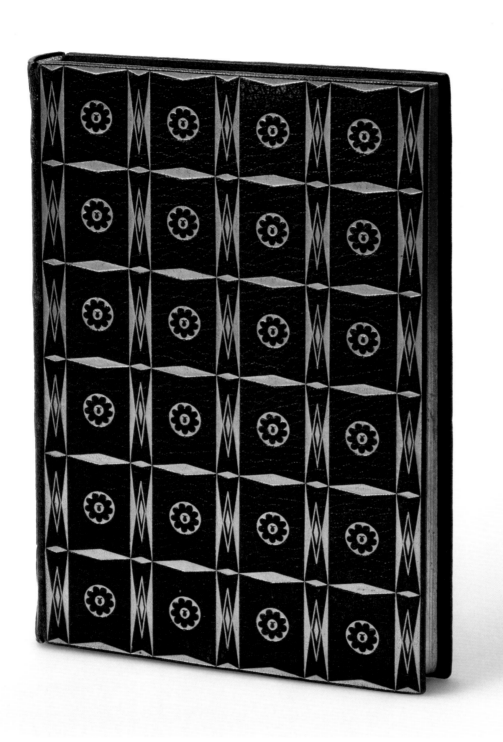

Fig. 29 JH, book cover for Edgar Allen Poe, *Der Goldkäfer und andere Novellen*, executed by the Wiener Werkstätte, ca. 1910/14 Levant Morocco leather, gold embossing
MAK, BI 21176

Fig. 30 JH, buffet, executed by Jakob
Soulek after a design for the dining
room in the spring exhibition at the
AMAI, 1912
Pearwood, stained black, partly carved;
printed linen fabric *Vorgarten* [Front
Garden] after a design by Wilhelm
Jonasch, 1910 (reproduction)
bel etage Kunsthandel GmbH

Fig. 31 JH, table for the drawing room
of the Austrian House, German Werkbund
exhibition, Cologne, 1914
Pearwood, stained black
Galerie Yves Macaux, Brussels
© Photo Studio Philippe de Formanoir/Paso Doble

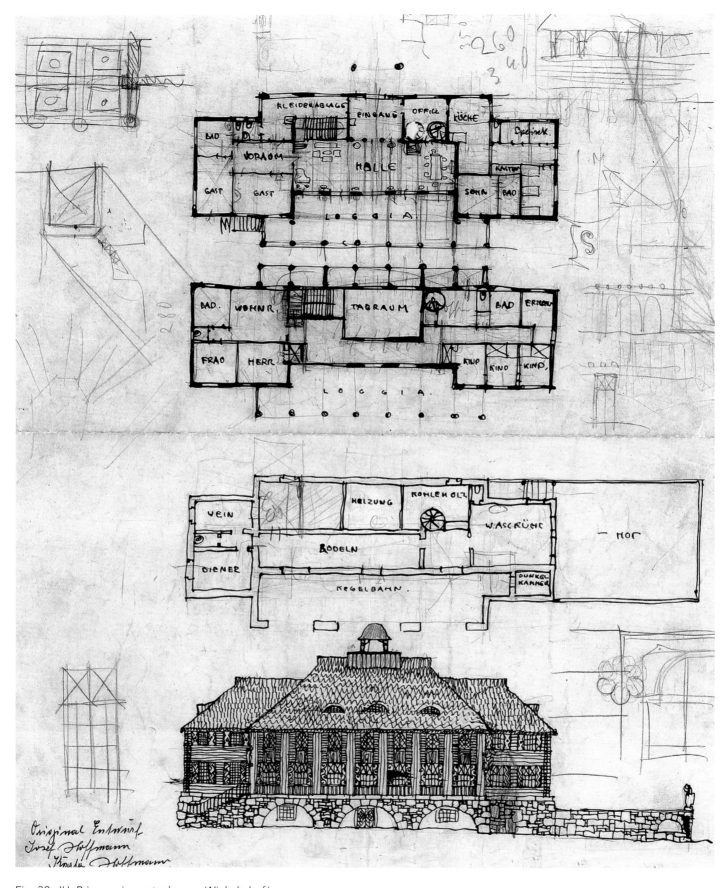

Fig. 32 JH, Primavesi country house, Winkelsdorf/
Kouty nad Desnou, 1913/14, second design

Fig. 33 JH, small tea temple
and pergola in the garden
of the Skywa-Primavesi villa,
Vienna, 1913–1915
ANL, Picture Archives, 105.670-C

Fig. 34 JH, Austrian House at
the German Werkbund
exhibition, Cologne, 1914
Der Architekt (20) 1914/15, plate 81

Fig. 35 Entrance gate, Skywa-Primavesi villa, 1914/15
© Michael Huey

Josef Hoffmann

1911
1918

Otto Wagner and
Josef Hoffmann, 1911
MAK, LI 10921

1911–1912

After the death of his parents, Hoffmann remodels his family home in Brtnice as a summer residence for himself and his sisters in 1907. The design in the taste of the WW, incorporating his parents' Baroque and Biedermeier furniture, is published in the magazine *Das Interieur*. Numerous designs for memorials and gravestones are produced, including for the composer Gustav Mahler who died in May 1911. Hoffmann occupies himself with interior decoration jobs, including for Hugo Marx in Hinterbrühl near Vienna and for Mimi Marlow, the diseuse at Cabaret Fledermaus. Design of the exhibition space for the sculptor Anton Hanak at the major art exhibition in Dresden, façade and interior design of the Grabencafé, and design for the drawing room in the exhibition *Österreichisches Kunstgewerbe* [Austrian Decorative Arts] at the AMAI, Vienna. Austrian pavilion at the *International Fine Arts Exhibition* in Rome. Josef Hoffmann plans a city palace for the fashion designer Paul Poiret in Paris.

1912–1914

First design for an Austrian Biennale pavilion in Venice, which will only be built in 1934. The administration building of the Poldihütte steel plant in Kladno is constructed after Josef Hoffmann's design. Interior designs for the industrialist Moritz Gallia in Vienna and for the painter Ferdinand Hodler in Geneva, which document Hoffmann's classicizing style characteristic of the years 1910–1914. In 1912 Josef Hoffmann is a founding and board member of the Austrian Werkbund. He separates his construction drawing office from the Wiener Werkstätte and sets it up at the School of Arts and Crafts. Work starts on the Kaasgraben villa colony; the eight pairs of single-family homes are a kind of continuation of the houses on the Hohe Warte and, in contrast to the latter, are inserted into their surroundings in the Classicist tradition. Major stylistic commonalities can also be found in two other construction projects of this period: in the villa for Josefine Skywa and Robert Primavesi on Gloriettegasse in Vienna's Hietzing

JH, view of the building site of the Austrian pavilion at the *International Fine Arts Exhibition*, Rome, 1911
Kunsthandel Widder, Vienna

district (with gatekeeper's lodge, green-house, and pavilion) and in the Austrian House at the German Werkbund exhibition in Cologne (collaboration with the sculptor Anton Hanak and the architect Oskar Strnad), which bear typological parallels: gable-crowned lateral avant-corps and façade dissolved in pilasters. In 1912–1914 the Viennese rooms of the Poldihütte are also realized; the project comprises the prestigious rooms of the general directorate, the offices, and the central sales office at Invalidenstraße 7. The financier of the Wiener Werkstätte, Fritz Waerndorfer, is bankrupt and leaves for America. His role is taken over by Otto and Mäda Primavesi, who appoint a commercial director and in 1915 Dagobert Peche as artistic director, who will be responsible for an entirely new style at the company.

1915–1918

The years 1915/16 are characterized above all by interior decoration jobs, such as those for Anton and Sonja Knips in Vienna, for Heinrich Böhler in Munich and St. Moritz, for Berta Zuckerkandl and Paul Wittgenstein Sr, and the interior design of some Wiener Werkstätte salesrooms: the fashion department on Kärntner Straße together with Eduard Josef Wimmer-Wisgrill and the fabric, lace, and lighting department on Kärntner Straße/Führichgasse, as well as the Marienbad branch. In Burghausen am Inn a factory complex is created for Dr. Alexander Wacker (electrochemical in-

JH, drawing room, office of the Poldihütte steel plant in Vienna, 1912–1914
DKuD (35) 1914/15, 360

dustry). Dagobert Peche's influence on the Wiener Werkstätte's style and not least on Hoffmann's design vocabulary becomes increasingly apparent; the painterly element seems to supersede the strict structures of Hoffmann's early designs. Peche takes a stand against the ideal of industrial production and hence the demands of the Werkbund. During the First World War, Josef Hoffmann designs patriotic war glasses and war cemeteries for the WW. The ever-more noticeable shortage of materials

and labor caused by the war is to be counteracted at the WW by employing more and more women artists, largely students of Josef Hoffmann at the School of Arts and Crafts. In 1916 the free Künstlerwerkstätte (Artists' Workshop) is set up with a kiln on Neustiftgasse. In Kladno a grocery and clothing shop is built for the steelworks, as is a villa for the director of the Poldihütte Franz Hatlanek. In 1918 Otto Wagner, Gustav Klimt, Egon Schiele, and Koloman Moser die.   ∎

JH, Graben Café, Vienna, 1912
MAK, WWF 105-5-1

JH, drawing rroom, Austrian House, German Werkbund exhibition, Cologne, 1914
Pearwood, stained black
DKuD (34) 1914, 360

Fig. 1 View of the terrace of the Austrian pavilion at the
International Fine Arts Exhibition, Rome, 1911
Kunsthandel Widder, Vienna

Rainald Franz

A Truly Effective Culture of Taste in Atectonic Classicism

The Exhibitions in Rome (1911) and Cologne (1914)

The Viennese art critic and historian Max Eisler observed in 1916 that it was the duty of exhibitions to impart a "truly effective culture of taste." This definition of exhibitions can be found in the publication released by the Austrian Werkbund that year. Published in the middle of the First World War, it contained a "Report on What Has Thus Far Been Desired and Achieved."[1] Alongside various interiors and buildings by Josef Hoffmann, the publication also gives visual and textual prominence to two exhibition pavilions by this cofounder of the Austrian Werkbund: the Austrian pavilions at the *International Fine Arts Exhibition* in Rome in 1911 and at the Werkbund exhibition in Cologne in 1914.

The Austrian Pavilion at the International Exhibition in Rome in 1911

> "In 1912 [sic], I was given the task of building in Rome the exhibition building of Austria; this allowed me to exhibit work, most significantly that of Hanak, in a courtyard which was bounded on three sides by simple loggias. Of the painters, Gustav Klimt came before an international public for the first time."[2]

This is how Josef Hoffmann recalled his participation in yet another exhibition project of national importance: together with Dr. Friedrich Dörnhöffer, the director of the Moderne Galerie[3] (now The Austrian Gallery Belvedere) in Vienna, Josef Hoffmann was supposed to "plan the pavilion and develop the interior furnishings and the decorative principles of the display of the artworks," as the exhibition catalog states.[4] The construction of the building on-site would be the responsibility of his student Karl Bräuer, with whom he was simultaneously working on the construction of Stoclet House. The *International Fine Arts Exhibition* in Rome in 1911 would coincide with an international art congress taking place in the Italian capital in the context of the celebrations to mark 50 years since the birth of the Kingdom of Italy.[5] The Austrian members of the honors committee at the art congress in Rome were Ludwig Baumann and Otto Wagner.[6] Whereas the World's Fair held in Turin that same year was an *International Exhibition of Industry and Labor*, in Rome the focus was on fine arts. On the exhibition grounds in Valle Giulia in the center of Rome, which had been terraced es-

pecially for the event, the Austrian pavilion stood in a prominent position near the main entrance. Its foundation comprised a terrace supported by rubblework. There were various preliminary studies for the pavilion; Eduard F. Sekler points to a plan drawn in 1910 that was probably connected with the *Exposición Internacional del Centenario* in Buenos Aires, in which Hoffmann had already opted for the basic principle of three wings—lateral wing with two flanking branches—that he would later employ for Austria-Hungary's pavilion in Rome.[7] For Rome Hoffmann chose a U-shaped floor plan open toward the front around a cour d'honneur. For Vienna's Moderne Galerie, which had been initiated by the Secessionists and founded in 1903, this exhibition was the first opportunity to present its collection to an international public. The experience that Josef Hoffmann had gained designing the Secession exhibitions and at the Kunstschau in Vienna in 1908 are bound to have come in handy here. Furthermore, he was friends with and had worked on joint projects with many of the exhibiting artists, including Carl Moll, Anton Hanak, Gustav Klimt, and Franz Metzner.[8] The central room of the pavilion would display monumental paintings; the peristyle and the forecourt would be adorned with monumental sculptures.

The design of the building, whose layout is simple but whose impact is striking, came to be quite significant in Hoffmann's oeuvre, bearing in mind that this ephemeral pavilion for Rome was the first time that the impact of a specific vocabulary, which the architect had developed for projects around 1910, was revealed in a realized design: The façade decoration is dominated by classical quotations, with a critic writing of Hoffmann's idea: "Perhaps the artist of the site where his work would rise up owes it to the Roman soil itself: Hoffmann's artistic eye may have retained the peristyle of a Pompeiian-Roman country house as a visual memory."[9] It is certainly possible that Hoffmann had been reminiscing about his time in Rome in 1896 after completing his studies.[10] He employs the technique of repeatedly using slim, vertical rectangles that form the façade. They are all arranged systematically and sculpturally, though only with even-surfaced, flat modeling, "[…] as if every possible competition with the monumental weight and three-dimensional, curvy modeling of the sculptures to be exhibited should be avoided," as

p. 202

1

2 3

Fig. 2 View of the building site of the Austrian pavilion at the *International Fine Arts Exhibition*, Rome, 1911
Kunsthandel Widder, Vienna

Sekler observed, an "arrangement in the service of differentiation" between support and wall to give rise to a sense of lightness.[11] In the process, Hoffmann has negated the tectonic in his response to the classic architectural problem of bearing and loads. Seen in this way, the pavilion in Rome is a link in a chain of buildings that also includes the Ast villa in Vienna and Stoclet House in Brussels. Hoffmann gave new meaning to tectonic forms of expression: Cannelures as vertical arranging elements are no longer found only on supports, but also on horizontal undersides of the roof structure and base design; there are fluted columns without bases or capitals and an entablature that is so low compared to the width of the columns that the viewer is not conscious of the load it bears. The various functions of supports or non-bearing cladding are amalgamated, parapets are combined with pedestals, optical groupings arise with girders. The pavilion in Rome constituted an important milestone on the path to the horizontally defined "striped façades" of the 1920s to 1930s in Hoffmann's oeuvre, as systematically executed in the pavilion for Paris in 1925, for example.[12]

Hoffmann was behind not only the classically inspired plans for the Austrian pavilion, but also its "interior furnishings and the decorative principles of the display of the artworks."[13] In seven galleries, in the courtyard, and in the garden, Hoffmann staged an overview of Austrian art from the second half of the 19th century into the 20th century. Loans came from the Moderne Galerie and Austrian collections, as well as from the Modern Gallery in Prague, the National Museum in Warsaw, and the museum in Lviv. The approaches to the pavilion via two landings were dominated by the monumental sculpture by Anton Hanak (*Österreich, Symbol der schöpferischen Kraft* [Austria, The Creative Forces]) and Ferdinand Andri's hanging figure *St. Michael*, flanked by two flagpoles and various other sculptural works located in the portico and in the building's courtyard.

All the large rooms inside were equipped with skylights; in the smaller rooms, for example in gallery I, paintings from the first half of the 19th century were accompanied by appropriate furniture from the period and complete furnishings down to the wall coverings, similar to the solution in the Austrian pavilion at the World's Fair in Paris in 1900. Hoffmann staged the sequence of rooms as an intensification from the outer galleries in the wings to the central room, which could not be entered from outside: visitors arrived from the side via the steps on the terrace, moving from there to the open loggia and finally into the interior. In comparison with the preliminary design, Hoffmann replaced the originally planned octagonal central room with two spatial elements: a rectangular room and a semicircular apse room. A low tripartite opening connects the two in such a way that separate vistas are possible without them merging into a unit. Whereas the remaining galleries were executed in a linear design reminiscent of Hoffmann's Secession exhibitions, for the final room, gallery VII (graphic and decorative arts), the architect chose a two-story solution with staircase and triple arcade above the gallery that invites comparison with English halls. The catalog was part of this concept; designed by Hoffmann himself, it was printed with decorative gold borders and contained photographic views of the building's interior and exterior.

Critics and the public alike reacted very positively to the overall design of the pavilion in Rome, which was opened in spring 1911. Georg Biermann wrote:

> "One perambulates these rooms with an awareness that Austria possesses that splendid culture of taste that the Wiener Werkstätten [sic] reawakened and one is delighted to encounter this great cultural document of applied art in Rome, too. No pavilion is more finely and artistically arranged than the Austrian exhibition."[14]

The Austrian House at the German Werkbund Exhibition in Cologne in 1914

> "In 1915 [sic], I built in Cologne the Austrian pavilion for the Werkbund exhibition. Here we had the opportunity to show the progressive work of the Austrian skilled crafts in its entirety, exhibiting our best practitioners, most notably Strnad, to great effect. Unfortunately, because of the outbreak of the First World War this widely-recognized [sic] achievement did not have much effect. But contact had been established with creative forces in Germany and the sincere interest of wide circles of art-lovers had been won."[15]

In old age, this is how Hoffmann himself viewed his participation in the largest exhibition yet held by the German Werkbund, which had been founded in October 1907. Josef Hoffmann, one of the cofounders of the German Werkbund together with Peter Behrens and Richard Riemerschmid, had also made a vital contribution to the founding of the Austrian Werkbund in 1912.[16] The *Deutsche Werkbund-Ausstellung. Kunst in Handwerk, Industrie und Handel, Architektur* [German Werkbund Exhibition: Art in Craft, Industry, and Trade, Architecture] was opened in Cologne in 1914. According to the official catalog, the show that ran from May to October "would attempt for the first time to put on display for the general public of our people and of foreign countries the aim of the German Werkbund to induce a refinement of German trade and industrial work through collaboration with the artist."[17] The Cologne exhibition, the final major social event before the First World War, was conceived as a joint presentation by the German and Austrian Werkbund. Alongside Hoffmann, other founding members of the Secession like Gustav Klimt, Wiener Werkstätte employees, and teaching staff from the Vienna School of Arts and Crafts were among the original members of the Werkbund. Art historians like Arthur Roessler, Hans Tietze, Berta Zuckerkandl, and Max Eisler had also joined the Austrian Werkbund, thereby ensuring the intellectual potential for disseminating its principles through the printed word. The engagement of the Austrian ministry of public works had also encouraged the participation of major industrialists in the founding of the Austrian Werkbund, who already had longstanding connections with these exponents of stylistic reform.

The first and most important prestige project by the new Austrian Werkbund would be the construction of the Austrian pavilion at the Werkbund exhibition in Cologne, for which Josef Hoffmann was commissioned. A prominent lot on the grounds, opposite Peter Behrens's festival hall, managed to be secured for the building.[18] Ideas from the plans for the Roman pavilion completed only shortly beforehand were incorporated in the plans for Cologne; Josef Hoffmann's aforementioned "atectonic Classicism" would culminate in its model building here. The monumental structure (29.4 m wide x 52 m long), executed in gray granular Terranova plaster on a wooden lattice, evolved from preliminary designs; the U-shaped ground plan arrangement from Rome that opened to the front makes a reappearance, as does the manifold use of columns without capitals or bases. According to Eduard F. Sekler, in Josef Hoffmann's plan for the Cologne pavilion "the historical stimulus was transmuted into something genuinely new. […] Hoffmann's success in Cologne was so complete because he had finally shut the rulebook of classical orders he had mastered in his youth."[19] This meant that he could apply a very thin cornice profile to the archaic-looking columns on the external façade instead of an entablature, with which he completely negated classical tectonics. In contrast, the pyramid of the three-stepped Attic story positioned above, with the archaically steep tympana above that, appears bulky, heavy, and matches the colossal columns. Looking at them, one is reminded of exaggerations of the form of French Neoclassicism around the time of the revolution, yet here Hoffmann created his own entire architectural system without any direct lodestar, the result of many years studying classical forms. The quotations from texts by Franz Grillparzer on the attic story are also fitting in this regard: In letters after a design by Hoffmann's fellow professor at the School of Arts and Crafts Rudolf von Larisch, one could read: "Science convinces us with reasons, art should convince us with its existence … It is not the thought but the depiction of the thought that makes the artwork. Beauty is the complete concord between the sensory and the spiritual." 14 columns on the front bore the entablature and the triangular gable towering over the side wings; as the main entrance, the central room was supported by four pairs of pillars. The two triangular gables, each with a wreath in its tympanum, were towered over by the gable of the main building with the same inclination; the gable roofs of the side wings tailed off into its tympanum. Toward the back, the gable roof was hipped. In front of the main façade stood the two sculptures by Anton Hanak: *Mann* [Man] and *Frau* [Woman].

Together with his fellow professors from the School of Arts and Crafts Oskar Strnad and Heinrich Tessenow, as well

Fig. 3 JH, the Austrian pavilion at the *International Fine Arts Exhibition*, Rome, 1911, before its opening
Kunsthandel Widder, Vienna

as his colleagues from the Wiener Werkstätte Dagobert Peche, Carl Witzmann, and Eduard Josef Wimmer-Wisgrill, Hoffmann also designed the galleries inside. The Imperial Royal Austrian Museum of Art and Industry (today's MAK) was directly involved in the preparations for the exhibition. In the MAK's archive there is the floor plan for furnishing the building delivered by Josef Hoffmann: in its room layout, this floor plan documents the diversity of the groups of artists, institutions, and nations united in the Austrian Werkbund. The building's interior courtyard was dominated by a stela with the *Herkules* by Franz Barwig. Designed as an entrance room by Oskar Strnad, the "representative room for painting, sculpture, and architecture" housed, in a central position against the front wall, Gustav Klimt's design for the *Expectation* at Stoclet House as the sole representative example of Austrian painting alongside works by sculptors like Anton Hanak and Robert Obsieger. The drawing room designed by Josef Hoffmann was adorned with the picture *Houses by the Sea* by Egon Schiele from Josef Hoffmann's private collection on walls paneled in white-painted wood and framed in black wooden borders. The galleries dedicated to general decorative arts were dominated by manufacturers with whom Hoffmann collaborated, as well as his colleagues from the Wiener Werkstätte and the School of Arts and Crafts: Jakob & Josef Kohn, Joh. Backhausen & Söhne, Oscar Dietrich, Emmy Zweybrück, Adele von Stark. The galleries for glass and ceramics were adorned with works designed by Michael Powolny and produced in Gmunden, in addition to ceramics by Hugo Kirsch, glasses and ceramics after designs by Josef Hoffmann and his students made by Josef Böck and J. & L. Lobmeyr in Vienna, by Johann Lötz Witwe, the Imperial Royal Specialist School in Steinschönau/ Kamenický Šenov, the Imperial Royal Specialist School in Haida/Nový Bor, Meyr's Neffe in Adolf bei Winterberg/Adolfov ve Vimperk, and Carl Schappel in Haida, all in Bohemia.

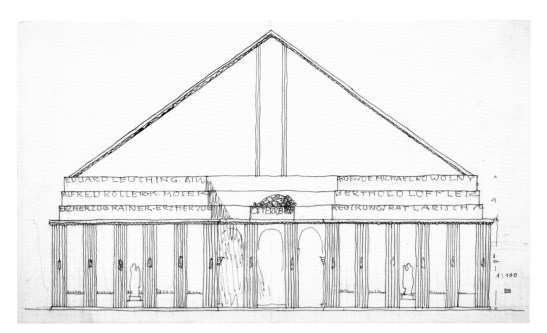

Fig. 4 JH, preliminary design for the Austrian House, German Werkbund exhibition, Cologne, 1914

Leopold Museum, LM 6004

Designed by Wimmer-Wisgrill, gallery XI was exclusively dedicated to the Wiener Werkstätte; alongside Hoffmann, works were also presented by Koloman Moser, Otto Prutscher, Carl Otto Czeschka, and colleagues. Codesigned by Josef Hoffmann as the architect, the Poldihütte crucible steel plant near Prague showed in one exhibition room "how the principles of the Werkbund also find radical application in major industry," as the catalog states.[20] By way of an extreme contrast, four galleries in the Neoclassicist—yet only wooden and gray cement-plastered—architecture by Josef Hoffmann are dedicated to the Bohemian Werkbund known as Svazčeského díla. In architecture by Otakar Nowotny and Josef Gočar, the rooms presented works by the Czech Cubists and the Artel group.

At the Werkbund exhibition in Cologne in 1914, Josef Hoffmann succeeded in making the Austrian House a unit and in doing so demonstrated once again his integrative talent as a promoter of widely divergent creative approaches: from the Rococoesque subtlety of Dagobert Peche's creation of spaces to the dynamism of the Czech Cubists. Around the central room of the Vienna School of Arts and Crafts lay the chain of rooms jointly created by its professors and students. With its two wings, the pavilion could also be interpreted as a metaphor for the dual monarchy of Austria-Hungary. Peter Jessen celebrated the Austrian House as a "genuine exhibition building by the master Josef Hoffmann. There was no building in which all the hopes and desires of the Werkbund had come closer to fruition" than this.[21] In the abstractness of its design vocabulary, Josef Hoffmann's "new Classicism"—as exemplified in the Austrian pavilion—approximated Modernism more closely than its historical exemplar and over the coming decades of the architect's career, it would prove its practicability and variability time and again. ■

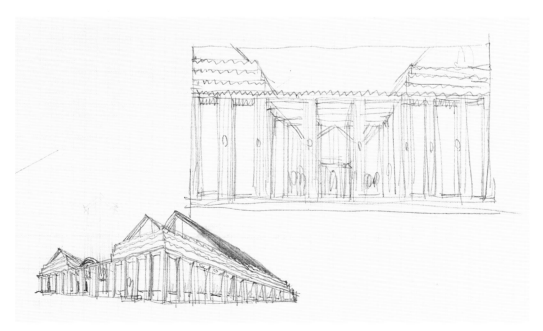

Fig. 5 JH, design for the Austrian House, German Werkbund exhibition, Cologne, 1914

Leopold Museum, LM 1731

Fig. 6 JH, entrance to the Austrian House,
German Werkbund exhibition, Cologne, 1914
MAK, KI 8951-66

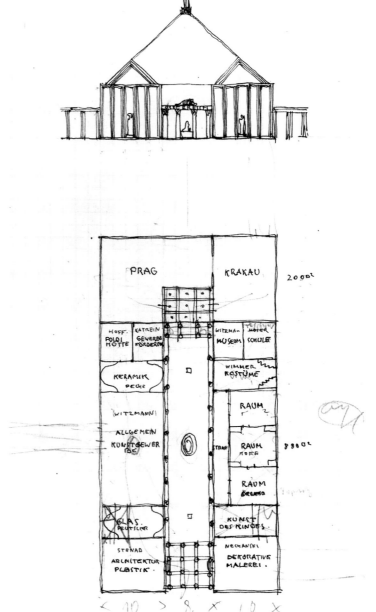

Fig. 7 JH, preliminary design for the façade, floor plan,
and room sequence for the Austrian House, German
Werkbund exhibition, Cologne, 1914
National Gallery Prague, K 17760

1   Max Eisler in: *Österreichische Werkkultur*, Vienna 1916, 38. See also the article "Josef Hoffmann and the Austrian Werkbund" by Andreas Nierhaus in this catalog.

2   Noever, Peter/Pokorný, Marek (eds.), *Josef Hoffmann. Selbstbiographie/Autobiography*, Ostfildern 2009, 102. Trans. Bernd Magar and Andrew Oakland.

3   Founded in 1903, the Moderne Galerie was renamed the k. k. Österreichische Staatsgalerie (Imperial Royal Austrian State Gallery) in 1912 and was the precursor of the Austrian art collection now at the Belvedere.

4   *Internationale Kunstausstellung, Österreichischer Pavillon nach Plänen von Architekt Professor Josef Hoffmann, Rom 1911*, exh. cat., Vienna 1911, 8.

5   Sekler, Eduard F., "Josef Hoffmanns Österreichischer Pavillon auf der internationalen Kunstausstellung in Rom 1911," in: *Österreichische Künstler und Rom. Vom Barock bis zur Secession*, exh. cat. Akademie der bildenden Künste, Vienna 1972, 81–84.

6   *Wiener Bauhütte* (V) 3 1911, 33.

7   Sekler, Eduard F., *Josef Hoffmann: The Architectural Work*, Princeton, NJ 1985, CR 135, 336, CR 141, 338–339. Trans. Eduard F. Sekler and John Maass.

8   See the articles "'Chief Architect of the Show of Force of Austrian Ambitions in Art': The 1908 Kunstschau in Vienna" by Rainald Franz and "Interior Design as a Work of Art: From 'Brettlstil' to Viennese Style" by Christian Witt-Dörring in this catalog. For Gustav Klimt this was the second international exhibition in which he had taken part after the first, a solo show, in the context of the 9th Venice Biennale in 1910 at the invitation of the Munich Secession. See: Sharp, Jasper (ed.), *Austria and the Venice Biennale 1895–2013*, Vienna 2013, 146 ff.

9   Rathe, Kurt, "Österreich auf der internationalen Kunstausstellung in Rom 1911," in: *Die Kunst für Alle* (XXVII) 4 1911, 78.

10   See the article "'It Was No Simple Matter to […] Reach an Understanding on the Real Sense of Building.' Josef Hoffmann: Studies at the Vienna Academy" by Rainald Franz in this catalog.

11   Sekler 1972 (see note 5), 81.

12   See the article "'A Shrine of a Thousand Treasures to Admire and Stroll Through.' The Austrian Pavilion at the International decorative Arts Exhibition in Paris in 1925" by Rainald Franz and Markus Kristan in this catalog.

13   Exh. cat. *Rom 1911* (see note 4).

14   Biermann, Georg, "Römische Ausstellungen. II. Die internationale Kunstausstellung in Valle Giulia," in: *Cicerone, Halbmonatsschrift für die Interessen des Kunstforschers und Sammelns* (3) 10 1911, 421–425: 423.

15   Noever/Pokorný 2009 (see note 2), 102–103.

16   See the article "The Decorative Arts Destroyed? Josef Hoffmann and the Austrian Werkbund" by Andreas Nierhaus in this catalog.

17   *Offizieller Katalog Deutsche Werkbundausstellung Cöln 1914*, Cologne 1914, V.

18   Sekler 1985 (see note 7), CR 182, 362–364.

19   Ibid., 160.

20   See note 16.

21   Jessen, Peter, "Deutsche Werkbundausstellung Köln 1914," in: *Deutsche Form im Kriegsjahr. Die Ausstellung Köln 1914*, yearbook of the German Werkbund, Munich 1915, 8.

Fig. 1 Suzanne and
Adolphe Stoclet
MAK

Fig. 2 Otto and Mäda Primavesi
MAK

Fig. 3 Margaret
Stonborough-Wittgenstein
Private collection

Fig. 4 Leopoldine
and Karl Wittgenstein
Courtesy of the Michael Huey and
Christian Witt-Dörring Photo Archive

Fig. 5 Fritz and Lili Waerndorfer
MAK/WWF-213-4

Fig. 6 Helene Hochstetter
MAK, WWF-213-4

Ursula Prokop

Josef Hoffmann's Customers as a Reflection of Social Change at the Fin de Siècle

Alongside Josef Hoffmann's various public projects, the social conditions of his age are reflected not least in his vast number of private customers. Concentrating primarily on the period prior to the First World War, this will be illustrated by a closer look at (a necessarily limited selection of) his principal patrons.

Few other architects were able to carve out a career as quickly as Josef Hoffmann. In 1897, just under two years after completing his training, the 27-year-old became a founding member of the Secession artists' union and played a significant part in its exhibitions, which would soon lead to a paradigm shift in the aesthetics of the time. Before long the success of this reform movement, which proved especially popular among the upper middle class who had been craving new representative styles, also yielded commissions for Hoffmann. In addition to some smaller interior decoration jobs for friends, he received his first construction contracts above all from the Wittgenstein family, who together with their numerous relatives comprised an extensive clan.[1] Through their involvement with big industry—especially in the coal and steel sectors—they were among the richest families in the Austro-Hungarian Monarchy at that time.

Crucial in this regard were most notably the brothers Paul Sr. (1842–1928) and Karl (1847–1913), who in quick succession commissioned Hoffmann with adapting the Bergerhöhe country house and constructing the Wittgenstein Forestry Administration building (both in Hohenberg, Lower Austria) in 1899/1900. Despite mostly being known for their interest in music prior to that point, the Wittgensteins had in fact been in close contact with the Secession movement from the outset. Both Paul Sr. and his niece Hermine, Karl's oldest daughter, were enthusiastic amateur painters and friends with founding members of the Secession including Franz Hohenberger, Viktor Krämer, and Rudolf von Alt.[2] For this reason, the Wittgenstein family soon became important patrons of Viennese Modernism[3] and customers of Hoffmann, who in essence worked as the "family architect" for the Wittgensteins and their extensive relations. Added to this is their substantial circle of friends and acquaintances, such as Alexander Pazzani, who worked as a director in the Wittgenstein companies and for whom Hoffmann also carried out some projects. Remarkably for the age, the female members of the clan also commissioned several buildings. Margaret Stonborough (one of Karl's daughters) and Helene Hochstetter (Paul Sr.'s sister-in-law), as well as her niece Anna Schmedes, independently awarded Hoffmann commissions.[4] Of the numerous interior decoration jobs, villas, country houses, administrative buildings, gravestones, and other objects that Hoffmann designed for the Wittgensteins, the hunting lodge on the Hochreith (ca. 1905) and above all the Protestant church in St. Aegyd, Lower Austria, deserve special mention. Constructed around 1902, the church is paid astonishingly little attention despite the fact that its simplicity was groundbreaking for modern church architecture; its accomplishment is surely due in no small part to the fact that both the Wittgensteins and Hoffmann were themselves Protestant.[5] Only after the death of Karl Wittgenstein in 1913 did the younger generation of the family—influenced by Ludwig Wittgenstein, the youngest son and later philosopher—abandon the idea of the Hoffmannesque Gesamtkunstwerk—or total work of art.

In addition to this significant—from a numerical perspective alone—group of customers, the members of the inner circle of the Secession and Wiener Werkstätte were of course among Hoffmann's early patrons. Their commissions include interiors for the painter Max Kurzweil; for the textile industrialist, friend of Hoffmann, and director of the Wiener Werkstätte Fritz Waerndorfer; and for the graphic artist and Koloman Moser's sister-in-law Magda Mautner-Markhof, as well as her mother Editha. The Schwestern Flöge fashion salon for Emilie Flöge, Gustav Klimt's close confidante, and her sisters, as well as the pair of semi-detached houses for the painter Carl Moll, to name but a few, can likewise be ascribed to this milieu. All these projects were realized within just a few years around 1900.[6]

Among the important customers from Hoffmann's early period are also Mr. and Mrs. Knips, with a pivotal role being played by Sonja Knips in particular, who was born into the nobility. Having had her portrait painted by Klimt as early as 1898, she was associated with Viennese Modernism from the outset. As a metal industry magnate, Anton Knips had the necessary means to underwrite his wife's generous patronage.[7] In 1903 the Knipses engaged Josef Hoffmann to decorate their city apartment in Vienna and to construct a country house for them in Carinthia. This would be followed by numerous other commissions. Alongside the repeated redecoration of their Viennese apartment, he was permitted in 1919 to design the gravestone for their son who had been killed in action and in 1925 to build the Knips villa in Vienna's Döbling district, which occupies an important position in Hoffmann's oeuvre of the interwar period. Mr. and Mrs. Knips continued to live in the homes decorated by Hoffmann until after the Second World War.[8]

The journalistic propagators of Viennese Modernism, like Hermann Bahr and Berta Zuckerkandl, played an important part as middlemen. For example, the group of literary figures around Bahr included the poet Richard Beer-Hofmann. The remarkable villa that Josef Hoffmann built for Beer-Hofmann around 1905 in Vienna's Währing district is one of the major works of the architect's early period.[9] In turn, Berta Zuckerkandl established contact between Hoffmann and her brother-in-law Victor Zuckerkandl (1851–1927), who commissioned the construction of Sanatorium Westend (1904). As a magnate in the German steel industry, he certainly had ample financial resources at his disposal. In addition to a substantial art collection, he invested his money in several sanatoriums, including the famous Westend in Purkersdorf, Lower Austria, which as the paradigm of a Gesamtkunstwerk is one of Hoffmann's most progressive projects. Zuckerkandl commuted between Vienna and Berlin and as a confidant of Walter Rathenau during the First World War was instrumental in the economic cooperation between Austria-Hungary and the German Empire. After his death in 1927 his extensive art collection was auctioned.[10] Victims of dispossession and murder, the Shoah had an especially large impact on the Jewish Zuckerkandl family, for whom Hoffmann had also realized some other projects.[11]

In the broadest sense the inner circle of Viennese Modernism must also include the construction engineer Eduard Ast (1868–1945). Approximately the same age as Hoffmann, they met in the late 1890s when Hoffmann was temporarily engaged in Otto Wagner's studio after his studies and was working on the pavilions of the Viennese Stadtbahn (light urban railway), on whose execution Eduard Ast's construction company was involved.[12] Ast had only founded his company in 1898 and, after acquiring the patent for the "Hennebique" system, specialized in the then incipient reinforced concrete construction method.

Subsequently both Hoffmann and Ast became beneficiaries of the modernization drive that occurred in both an aesthetic and an architectural regard in the early 20th century and that would define their collaboration. Evidence of this closeness is a logo designed by Hoffmann for the Ast company in 1902.[13] Together they were able to realize numerous significant projects of Viennese Modernism, including the aforementioned Sanatorium Westend and ultimately the great Kunstschau of 1908. As a successful entrepreneur and devoted art enthusiast, one year later Ast commissioned Hoffmann with the construction of his villa in Vienna's Döbling district, which would become one of the pièces de résistance in Hoffmann's oeuvre. They would work together on various projects in the years to come. In 1923 Ast commissioned the architect to construct a country house in Velden on Lake Wörthersee and the gravestone of his young son. However, the financial crisis and the weak construction market in the early 1930s hit Ast particularly hard; he lost practically his entire fortune and was forced to sell his villa,[14] which was ultimately purchased by Alma Mahler and would become a center of intellectual life in Vienna until her emigration.

Josef Hoffmann's rapid success led to him soon becoming known beyond this inner circle, by wealthy businessmen and financiers. They included the Belgian Stoclet family, who worked in the banking and railroad sector and had close business ties with Austria. Victor Stoclet was both co-owner of the Aspang-Bahn railroad and a board member of the Österr. Escompte-Bank. His son Adolphe (1871–1949), who lived in Vienna and frequently visited Secession exhibitions, was allegedly introduced to Hoffmann by Carl Moll, whose villa he admired.[15] However, after the sudden death of his father in 1904, Adolphe Stoclet had to abandon his desire to have the architect build a neighboring house for him on the Hohe Warte and was obliged to return to Brussels. This led to Stoclet House, Hoffmann's most lavish and spectacular building, being constructed in the Belgian capital. Inexhaustible financial resources, which probably stemmed from the colony in the Belgian Congo, facilitated the ultimate realization of an exquisite Gesamtkunstwerk ideal.

The cousins Robert and Otto Primavesi likewise came from the banking and industrial sector. As the vice president of the Moravian Chamber of Commerce and representative of the Austrian Werkbund, Otto (1868–1926) in particular also came face to face with the new art movement in a professional capacity.[16] His direct contact with Hoffmann must have been contrived by the sculptor Anton Hanak during the art exhibition in Rome in 1911. Hanak, who had frequently worked with Hoffmann, had already executed various art objects for the Primavesis in Olmütz/Olomouc, Moravia, now Czech Republic, on several different occasions. Within a short period of time, Hoffmann received several commissions from the banking family. For Otto Primavesi he decorated some rooms in the city villa in Olmütz and adapted the bank building in the city center, before finally being awarded the large commission in 1913 to build a country house in Winkelsdorf//Kouty nad Desnou. Constructed in a synthesis of rural architecture and classicizing elements and with all of its rooms styled by the Wiener Werkstätte, the building became a popular venue for artists' parties for a number of years, with a not insignificant role in this being played by the homemaker Mäda (Eugenia Primavesi), as well as by the protagonists' shared Moravian background.[17] In Vienna the Primavesis' cousin Robert (1854–1926) commissioned Hoffmann in 1913 to adapt an older villa for his partner Josefine Skywa, for whom he had a grand villa built on Gloriettegasse in Vienna's Hietzing district shortly thereafter, which is regarded as the glittering conclusion to Hoffmann's pre-WWI oeuvre. Hoffmann remained close to the Primavesis until well after the war. When the Wiener Werkstätte was liquidated and refounded as an operating company in 1914, Otto Primavesi joined the company as its manager along with his wife Mäda and cousin Robert by investing capital amounting to 200,000 kronen.[18] However, the financial crisis in the early 1930s spelled ruin for the family-owned bank and subsequently the Wiener Werkstätte itself.

Another family that was actively involved in the world of Viennese Modernism from the outset were the Böhlers. Industrialists with a main factory in Kapfenberg, Styria, as well as numerous other companies, they played an important role in the monarchy's arms and iron industry; their interest in art is explained by the fact that many of the family's far-flung members were themselves artists. Otto Böhler Sr (1847–1913), co-owner of the Böhler-Werke, had made a name for himself as a silhouettist, especially for his portraits of famous musicians.[19] This fondness for the arts was passed on to the next generation: both his son Hans (1884–1961)

Fig. 7 The WW's stall at the artists' garden party at Weigls Dreherpark in Vienna's Meidling district on 6 and 7 June 1907. Sonja Knips (far left), Lili Waerndorfer (2nd from right), Berta Zuckerkandl (far right)

MAK, KI 13744-11-2

and his nephew Heinrich (1881–1940) worked as painters. The latter in particular awarded Hoffmann countless commissions from 1909: in addition to some interior decoration jobs, he engaged him time and again for various conversions of his villa in Baden near Vienna until well into the 1930s.[20] However, alongside other family members who had their apartments and studios decorated by Hoffmann, it was Otto Jr (1878–1946) who awarded him the most significant commission. In 1909/10 he had Hoffmann build a country house in Kapfenberg, where he worked in the Böhler-Werke until after the Second World War; this building constitutes a paragon of Hoffmann's virtuosity in synthesizing local style and prestigious representation.[21] A theater was planned as another joint project for Kapfenberg, though it was never realized.

This small sample of Hoffmann's most important clients, all of whom were embedded in the Viennese art world, reflects the social conditions of the time: The role played by the old nobility is negligible; the affluent upper middle class has now assumed the responsibility of art patronage. It is worth noting that even parts of the population who had previously been marginalized, who—like Jews, women, and their intersection, Jewish women—did not have (full) legal capacity only a short time ago, now became important stakeholders. All of them were willing to break new ground that would fundamentally change the aesthetics of the 20th century. ▪

1   The Wittgensteins' relatives also include the Hochstetter, Figdor, and Salzer families, for whom Hoffmann likewise worked.
2   See Prokop, Ursula, Margaret Stonborough-Wittgenstein, Vienna et al. 2003, 36 ff.
3   Karl Wittgenstein was also instrumental in financing the Secession building.
4   For a list of Hoffmann's commissions, see Kamenicek, Elisabeth, "Die Wittgensteins als Sammler, Bauherren und Mäzene," in: Fetz, Bernhard (ed.), Berg, Wittgenstein, Zuckerkandl, zentrale Figuren der Wiener Moderne, exh. cat. Austrian National Library, Vienna 2018, 123 ff.
5   Though of Jewish descent, this was already the second generation of Wittgensteins to be baptized, married to Christians, and not to consider themselves "Jewish" in the traditional sense.
6   See catalogue raisonné in Sekler, Eduard F., Josef Hoffmann: The Architectural Work, Princeton, NJ 1985. Trans. Eduard F. Sekler and John Maass.

7   Sonja Knips was born Baroness Potier des Echelles, see: Natter, Tobias/Frodl, Gerbert, Klimt und die Frauen, exh. cat. The Austrian Gallery Belvedere, Vienna, Cologne 2000, 84 ff.
8   Anton Knips died in 1946; Sonja Knips's last residence was her country house in Carinthia.
9   The villa was demolished in 1970.
10 Victor Zuckerkandl's obituary, Wiener Zeitung 11 Jul 1927, 9.
11 The family comprised four brothers: Emil (anatomist) who married Berta Szeps, Otto (urologist), Victor (industrial magnate), and Richard (lawyer).
12 Ed. Ast u. Co., Ingenieure, Vienna 1903, 24.
13 My thanks to Otto Kapfinger for noticing that the layout of the company publications (see note 12) also appears to stem from Hoffmann.
14 My thanks to Judith Pavelak-Ast (Eduard Ast's grandniece).
15 Sekler 1985 (see note 6), 97.

16 Zatloukal, Pavel, "Anton Hanak und die Mäzenatenfamilie Primavesi," in: Grassegger, Friedrich/Krug, Wolfgang (eds.), Anton Hanak, Vienna et al. 1997, 112 ff.
17 The Primavesis (who were of Lombardian origin), Anton Hanak, and Josef Hoffmann all came from Moravia.
18 On the exact course of events, see Noever, Peter (ed.), Der Preis der Schönheit. 100 Jahre Wiener Werkstätte, Ostfildern-Ruit 2003, 226 ff.; Neiss, Herta, "Unternehmensgeschichte WW," in: Parnass (23) 4 2003, 28 f. In 1925 Otto Primavesi withdrew from the company and relinquished all his shares to his wife.
19 See Beyer, Andreas/Savoy, Bénédicte/Tegethoff, Wolf (eds.), Allgemeines Künstlerlexikon Online, 2009.
20 The last adaptation took place in 1934.
21 The house no longer stands.

Fig. 1 Shop window of the Dresdner Werkstätten für Handwerkskunst
with products by the Wiener Werkstätte, ca. 1906
Price book *Dresdner Hausgerät*, Dresdner Werkstätten für Handwerkskunst, Dresden 1906, 81

Klára Němečková

Freedom from Patronage

Josef Hoffmann and the Deutsche Werkstätten Hellerau

"Young firms—they call themselves Werkstätten, as distinguished from furniture warehouses or factories—have united with artists. Their aim is to offer the German home purposeful, dignified, and contemporary furnishings. Through Werkstätten, the artists are assured a broad impact; the customers, a connection with the artists."[1]

Thus explains the *Preisbuch der Deutschen Werkstätten* the goals of the "Werkstätten" or "workshops," which also feature furniture designs by the Wiener Werkstätte. The Dresdner Werkstätten für Handwerkskunst, later the Deutsche Werkstätten Hellerau, founded by Karl Schmidt in 1898, were among the earliest reformist manufacturers of furniture and interiors in the German-speaking area. From the outset, its founder's concern was with a wide-ranging effectiveness of his ideas for designs of premium quality and aesthetics.

Already in the first years after founding of the firm, Schmidt sought contact with kindred spirits, endeavoring to create an international network of renowned artists of the reformist movement, and their designs, with which he could situate the Werkstätten within a larger context. In this way, Charles Rennie Mackintosh, Mackay Hugh Baillie Scott, Richard Riemerschmid, and many hitherto little-noticed women designers, such as Marie von Geldern-Egmond and Gertrud Kleinhempel, joined the Werkstätten's artistic staff.

In a letter to Josef Hoffmann, precisely the wide appeal of serially produced and affordable designs is highlighted as the major difference to the Wiener Werkstätte, cofounded by Hoffmann:

"A significant difference has always existed between the Wiener and the Deutsche Werkstätten to the extent that: apart from textiles, the Wiener Werkstätte tried to manufacture primarily individual pieces and certainly not large quantities. The Deutsche Werkstätten have eight of their own retail shops and are represented by thirty of the largest and best furniture dealers in Germany. […] In some cases, more than 100 orders have been placed for a room, a piece of furniture, or an arts-and-crafts object."[2]

Based on Hoffmann's involvement in the German arts-and-crafts movement, it is possible to show in what follows that he was definitely not loath to the idea of a wide appeal.

First Contacts

In 1904, the Dresdner Werkstätten für Handwerkskunst began to distribute products from the Wiener Werkstätte, which had emerged the previous year. The designs' radically new and daring aesthetics most definitely offered the Dresdner audience an entirely unfamiliar image of decorative arts. The immediate inclusion of the products in the firm's repertoire signalized Schmidt's resolve to assert a new style in the arts and crafts, above and beyond his own firm. Products made of punched sheet iron and silver, in particular, were presented in the shops of the Dresdner Werkstätten—thus cleverly moving the motif of the square to the center of design; as is evident, for example, in contemporary depictions of the showcase window, in which, clearly recognizable among other objects are planters and an inkwell based on designs by Josef Hoffmann. Documents in the Wiener Werkstätte Archive confirm that nearly 120 models from the metal workshop were delivered to Dresden as consignment goods, primarily in the years 1904 and 1905.[3] The reason for this might have been that the Dresdner Werkstätten did not yet operate its own metal workshop at the time.

Founding of the German Werkbund

The relationship to the Wiener Werkstätte seemed to intensify in 1907, the year the German Werkbund was founded. It can be assumed that at the very least, discussions were carried out over a closer cooperation of the two workshops, that is, more than an acquisition of finished products.[4] Schmidt's thoughts in the preliminary stages of founding the Werkbund began from the premise that only in a larger network of different Werkstätten can reformist ideas be effectively established and the area of influence expanded. At the time, he was involved in negotiations with the Vereinigte Werkstätten in Munich, which were nonetheless unsuccessful. Instead, he was able to initiate a cooperation with Karl Bertsch's Werkstätten für Wohnungseinrichtung in Munich, which led the firm to change its name to Deutsche Werkstätten für Handwerkskunst.

At the same time, the Wiener Werkstätte was also negotiating with Munich's Vereinigte Werkstätten for an acquisition of products. Mentioned as an actor in negotiations was Fritz Waerndorfer, who in a correspondence wrote that a great ring of Werkstätten could emerge.[5] The situation of the reformist Werkstätten seemed to have stabilized in the wake of the *Dritte Deutsche Kunstgewerbeausstellung* [Third German Decorative-Arts Exhibition] organized in Dresden in 1906.

Fig. 2 JH, bedroom no. 77,
Deutsche Werkstätten Hellerau, ca. 1913
Price book *Das deutsche Hausgerät*, Deutsche Werkstätten, 11th edition, 1913

Fig. 3 JH, dining room no. 9,
Deutsche Werkstätten Hellerau, ca. 1913
Price book *Das deutsche Hausgerät*, Deutsche Werkstätten, 11th edition, 1913

Each of the firms was looking for a form of organization that would lend it a stronger influence and promote the implementation of its economic and artistic interests. Josef Hoffmann as artist and the Wiener Werkstätte as enterprise, thus became founding members of the German Werkbund along with Karl Schmidt and his Werkstätten.

Designs for Serial Production

The Deutsche Werkstätten presented their first renowned Maschinenmöbel (machine-made furniture) at the *German Decorative-Arts Exhibition*. In still the same year, 1906, its operation as "Dresdner Hausgerät" (Dresden Household Furnishings) began, based exclusively on designs by Richard Riemerschmid. Yet just a few years later, consumers were offered a selection from a remarkable array of designs by numerous other designers, such as Peter Behrens, Lucian Bernhard, Heinrich Tessenow, Margarete Junge, Marie von Geldern-Egmond, and even Josef Hoffmann.

The first furniture pieces by Hoffmann and Koloman Moser included in the *Preisbücher der Deutschen Werkstätten für Handwerkskunst*, were, by no means exclusive designs for the firm. Both the *Damenzimmer* [Boudoir] and the *Ping-Pong-Zimmer* [Ping-Pong Room], for example, which

were published in the handmade furniture catalog in 1909, date back to individual interiors of the Wiener Werkstätte—such as Purkersdorf Sanatorium[6]—designed between 1903 and 1906. The furniture was illustrated using documentary photographs. The inclusion of the furniture models in the sales catalog signalized their orientation on serial production and the associated surrender of exclusivity, which entailed an adaptation of dimensions and materials. A key factor in the orientation on the Deutsche Werkstätten for manufacture was certainly the disbanding of the Wiener Werkstätte's own carpentry workshop, and the vision of new sales markets. The fact that this is what was actually intended, is shown by further product offers beginning in 1913. While only one design from Moser—the library cabinet designed for Margaret Stonborough's Berlin living room in 1905—was adopted nearly identically in the German household furnishings catalog,[7] three complete room furnishings based on designs by Hoffmann were offered.[8] Hoffmann specially adapted the dining room no. 9 and the bedrooms nos. 76 and 77 for serial production[9].

2 3

For bedroom no. 76 he implemented the clearly framed surfaces and their relationship to one another as a means of design. The smooth surfaces of the doors and bed faces are offset by simple circumferential edging. The design refrains

4

Fig. 4 JH, bedroom no. 76,
Deutsche Werkstätten Hellerau, ca. 1912
Price book *Das deutsche Hausgerät*,
Deutsche Werkstätten, 10th edition, 1913

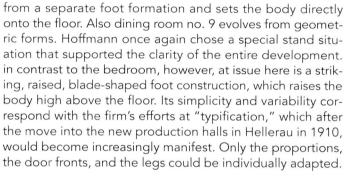

Fig. 5 JH, bedroom no. 40303,
Deutsche Werkstätten Hellerau, ca. 1938
HStADD, 11764, Deutsche Werkstätten Hellerau, F 3004

Fig. 6 JH, dining room no. 40307,
Deutsche Werkstätten Hellerau, ca. 1938
HStADD, 11764, Deutsche Werkstätten Hellerau, F 2473

from a separate foot formation and sets the body directly onto the floor. Also dining room no. 9 evolves from geometric forms. Hoffmann once again chose a special stand situation that supported the clarity of the entire development. In contrast to the bedroom, however, at issue here is a striking, raised, blade-shaped foot construction, which raises the body high above the floor. Its simplicity and variability correspond with the firm's efforts at "typification," which after the move into the new production halls in Hellerau in 1910, would become increasingly manifest. Only the proportions, the door fronts, and the legs could be individually adapted.

Designs by Hoffmann for textiles and carpets can also be verified, in addition to the furniture.[10] In 1907, the Deutsche Werkstätten entered into an exemplary cooperation, as defined by the German Werkbund, with the carpet manufacturer Erismann & Cie., which manufactured machine-produced carpets based on artists' designs. Among the early patterns, two motifs based on designs by Hoffmann can be identified. Specifically, one is a variation of the *Efeu* [Ivy] pattern realized by the Austrian firm Backhausen as textiles. The other reveals motifs typical of the Wiener Werkstätte and especially Hoffmann, such as small squares, a geometric division of planes into rectangles, and a stylized leaf.

Late Work of the Deutsche Werkstätten Hellerau

In 1944, the cooperation between the Deutsche Werkstätten Hellerau and Josef Hoffmann was again clarified in a contract.[11] Most likely, the collaboration was similar to the one around 1911. Explicit reference was made to the exclusivity of the designs and the payment of a corresponding premium:

> "For the duration of this agreement, your designs for furniture and interior work will be manufactured by the Deutsche Werkstätten; for interior work, to the extent that your clients do not explicitly stipulate other suppliers."

The artist's fee was calculated as net-invoice revenue. The payment was two percent for serially produced furniture and five percent for handmade, or bespoke furniture.

The contract has been preserved in the firm's archive, as have photos of two interiors.[12] Bedroom no. 40303 and dining room no. 40307 reveal dignified designs from a collaboration in the 1930s before this contract had been signed. Although the contract mentions an advertisement in the catalog, that would not come about. The upheavals of the postwar period brought an end to the collaboration. What remains remarkable is Hoffmann's initiative in networking with the firm and actively contributing to the realization of the workshop idea.

1 *Handgearbeitete Möbel*, catalog of the Deutsche Werkstätten für Handwerkskunst, Leipzig 1909, 5.
2 Letter from the Deutsche Werkstätten Hellerau to Josef Hoffmann from 20 Dec 1944; HStADD, 11764 company archive of the Deutsche Werkstätten Hellerau no. 559, contracts, agreements, and written correspondence with Prof. Josef Hoffmann, Vienna, n.p.
3 I would like to thank Elisabeth Schmuttermeier, MAK Vienna, for this information, based on the silver and metal model books.
4 See Němečková, Klára, "Internationale Netzwerke von Karl Schmidt," in: *Dresdner Kunstblätter* (62) 3 2018, 12–21; id., "Knotenpunkt 'Deutsche Werkstätten' zwischen Glasgow, Bedford und Wien – Internationale Verortung einer Dresdner Vision," in: König, Susanne/Lupfer, Gilbert/Obenaus, Maria (eds.), *Drehscheibe Dresden. Lokale Kunstszene*

und globale Moderne, Dresden 2018, 24–32.
5 On the efforts of Fritz Waerndorfer and the improvement of the financial situation of the Wiener Werkstätte, see Witt-Dörring, Christian, "Furniture," in: Witt-Dörring, Christian/Staggs, Janis (eds.), *Wiener Werkstätte 1903–1932: The Luxury of Beauty*, Munich 2017, 212–259: 217 f.
6 See *Handgearbeitete Möbel* 1909 (see note 1), 22, 41. With the interiors, at issue are the furnishings of the Purkersdorf Sanatorium.
7 In contrast to the *Handgearbeitete Möbel* catalog, *Das deutsche Hausgerät* was the catalog for machine- or mass-produced furniture, which was manufactured by the Deutsche Werkstätten Hellerau in a much larger edition to have in stock.
8 See *Das Deutsche Hausgerät* catalog, Deutsche Werkstätten Hellerau, 10th, 11th, and 12th editions, 1913.

9 Witt-Dörring explains that only Hoffmann's bedroom no. 77 was specially designed for the Deutsche Werkstätten. See Witt-Dörring 2017 (see note 6).
10 See Němečková, Klára/Stöver, Kerstin, "Erismann & Cie. – Künstlertapeten für die Deutschen Werkstätten," in: *Dresdner Kunstblätter* (62) 3 2018, 32–39: 35.
11 HStADD, 11764 company archive of the Deutsche Werkstätten Hellerau no. 559 (see note 2).
12 These photographs are probably ensembles intended but not acutally used for the 1938 catalog of the Deutsche Werkstätten Hellerau *Handgearbeitete Möbel*. It can only be conjectured whether the National Socialists' lacking appreciation of Hoffmann may have been the reason.

Fig. 1 Carl Bergsten, furniture and interior design, exhibited at the General Swedish
Exhibition of Arts and Crafts and Art Industry in Stockholm, 1909

Bendix, Carl L., and Folcker, Erik G. (eds.), *Det svenska konsthandtverket 1909: allmänna svenska utställningen
för konsthandtverk och konstindustri i Stockholm*, Stockholm 1910; © National Library of Sweden

Jan Norrman

A Cheerful and Capricious Energy

Josef Hoffmann and the Wiener Werkstätte in Sweden

The influence of Josef Hoffman and the Wiener Werkstätte on Swedish design and consumer goods can be traced back to two main sources: Swedish architects finding inspiration on the Continent, and a series of department store and art exhibitions that resulted in an enduring interest among consumers.

Josef Hoffmann visited Sweden on at least three occasions: twice in conjunction with the *Österrikisk konstutställning* [Austrian Art Exhibition] at Liljevalchs konsthall in 1917, and once during the summer of 1930 when visiting the *Stockholm Exhibition*.

Immediately after the Austrian exhibition at Liljevalchs in 1917, the *Hemutställningen* [Home Exhibition] opened, with furnishings for the working class, without a luxury approach. This exhibition would lead the way for Sweden in the decades to come. Manufacturers, artists, and architects came together in search of "Vackrare Vardagsvara" ("better things for everyday life"),[1] promoted by the Svenska Slöjdföreningen (Swedish Arts-and-Crafts Society, similar to the German Werkbund). Out of this came the Swedish Functionalist movement, which was devoid of the luxury associated with the Wiener Werkstätte.

Carl Bergsten and Inspiration from Vienna

The new trends from Vienna were first introduced in Sweden by architects returning from scholarship trips.[2] When Carl Bergsten (1879–1935) returned from travels through Germany and Austria in the summer of 1904, he reworked a proposal for exhibition architecture for the *Norrköping Exhibition of Art and Industry* of 1906. This was the first and most inspired example of the Viennese style of Hoffmann and Otto Wagner in Sweden.[3] The egg-shaped cupola of the main hall bore these impressions with its bolted decorations, and the shape of the art hall entrance echoed the Ernst Ludwig House in Darmstadt, but with peacock ornaments in the Viennese style. The café with "its orange-yellow walls, green flooring, and decorations in black and cold gray" was reminiscent of Vienna.[4] The chairs designed by Bergsten resembled Hoffmann's chairs for Cabaret Fledermaus and are early examples of bentwood furniture manufactured in Sweden.[5]

At the 1909 *Allmänna svenska utställningen för konsthandtverk och konstindustri* [General Swedish Exhibition of Arts and Crafts and Art Industry] in Stockholm, Bergsten presented an interior with the hallmarks of Hoffmann: exclusive materials, cubic furniture in polished wood with quadratic decoration, and polished marble blocks surrounding the fireplace. However, Carl Bergsten's attempts were rather isolated (they might even have hindered his career) and the architectural influences from Vienna did not produce followers.[6]

Nordiska Kompaniet, 1916

The first exhibition with objects by the Wiener Werkstätte (WW) and Josef Hoffmann was held at the newly opened department store Nordiska Kompaniet. More than 2 000 objects by 150 exhibitors were shown during one week in April 1916, in a state-run effort to promote Austrian fashion and applied arts.[7] Fashion shows were accompanied by possibilities to meet fashion industry representatives, including the WW. Apparently the textiles and the glass sold well: the exhibition raised 20,000 Swedish kronor in just the first days.

Preserved photos from the exhibition show glass and ceramics on top of draped textiles, both printed and laces. J. & L. Lobmeyr was honored with its own display case and the WW probably had several. Some of the identifiable objects were also shown in the *Ausstellung österreichischen Kunst- und Exportglases* [Exhibition of Austrian Art and Export Glass] at the Imperial Royal Austrian Museum of Art and Industry (today's MAK) in Vienna in 1915. Josef Hoffman's jardiniere was sold together with two vases from the series *Achteckig Schwarzbronzit* [Octagonal Black Bronzite].[8] The success of and demand for Wiener Werkstätte products is apparent—in the following years regular advertisements announced that local shops had the latest fashion from the WW, both batik and laces.[9]

Austrian Art Exhibition, 1917

Josef Hoffmann was appointed to curate the *Austrian Art Exhibition* at Liljevalchs konsthall in 1917.[10] He spent a busy summer finding the right artists and firms for the show, and

2 3

Figs. 2, 3 Display cases at Nordiska kompaniet, 1916
MAK, KI 9972-8, KI 9972-3

it was finally possible to install the exhibition in September.[11] As with the exhibitions at Nordiska Kompaniet in 1916 and later in 1930, the Austrian state provided financial and organizational support.

Viennese fashion had been in demand since the show at Nordiska Kompaniet in 1916, and therefore fashion companies, including the WW, advertised to urge contact with importers.[12] The fashion was presented with 18 mannequins during an eventful week; the program also included concerts and a lecture on Austrian art by the painter Ernst Wagner (1877–1951).

The layout of the exhibition can be reconstructed.[13] Over 1 000 objects were shown, including 240 entries of paintings, drawings, and sculpture. The applied arts were concentrated in the main hall close to the entrance. In 16 vitrines covered with *Semiramis* by Dagobert Peche,[14] a wide spectrum of Austrian applied art was presented. The major glass manufacturers from Bohemia exhibited objects next to artisanal textile works by young female artists. Lobmeyr had two display cases and the Wiener Werkstätte used four in the far end of the hall, with some sculptural works lining the walls, as well as four long printed textiles hanging from ceiling to floor.

The preserved receipts allow us to analyze what was sold at the exhibition.[15] Otto Lendecke's *The Empress Zita* was the most expensive artwork at 3,300 Swedish kronor; in total 19 artworks brought in 8,000 kronor. No painting by Klimt, Schiele, or Kokoschka found a buyer in Stockholm, but the Nationalmuseum did purchase a Klimt drawing. The Stockholm press mentioned that the "big collectors" were absent during the opening. The applied art, on the other hand, found its way to the Stockholmers; 4 096 visitors came between 8 and 30 September.[16] Each customer was recorded with their title and address, and objects were listed with their actual model numbers. The buyers mainly came from the nearby Östermalm, a well-to-do part of Stockholm. Surprisingly many are listed as Miss, buying just a single glass from glass sets by Lobmeyr, or laces. A total of 3 079 applied art pieces were sold to 335 different customers. Lobmeyr sold 2 240 glasses, mainly from glass sets, and the WW sold 449 objects for 4,459 kronor—an average price of 10 kronor (approximately two days' salary for an industrial worker at the time). Around 70 percent of the sales were works of applied arts.[17]

The success for the glass manufacturers is evident; not only the glass from Lobmeyr but also that from Friedrich Pietsch and Joh. Oertel & Co. sold widely. This is even clearer when analyzing the WW's sales. Many of Josef Hoffmann's designs found buyers, mainly the colored, cut glass from Ludwig Moser & Söhne (64 sales). Many of the models were brand new in September 1917. The Swedish architects

Fig. 4 View of Liljevalchs konsthall by Carl Bergsten, 1916
Stockholms Stadsmuseum, ArkDes, ARKM.1962-101-0933

Fig. 5 Display cases at
Liljevalchs konsthall, 1917
MAK, KI 9982-1-1

Fig. 6 The Wiener Werkstätte's
vitrines at Liljevalchs konsthall, 1917
MAK, KI 9982-2-2

Fig. 7 Exhibition design
at Nordiska kompaniet, 1930
Nordiska museets arkiv, archive 167:1, K 1 d vol. 23
Österrikisk utställning 1930

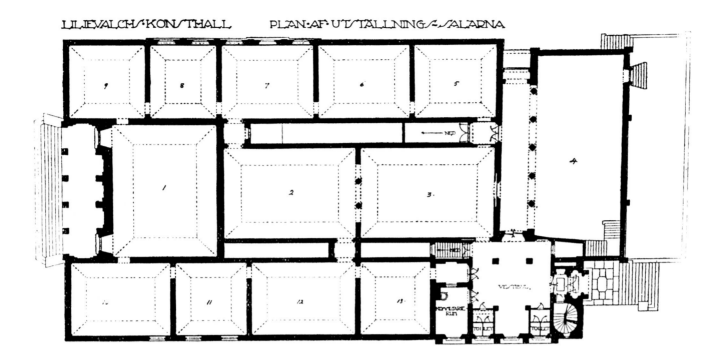

Fig. 8 Floor plan of the exhibition at Liljevachs konsthall, 1917
Österrikiska konstutställningen, exh. cat., September 1917, Stockholm
Liljevalchs konsthall katalog n:o 8, 75
Private collection

visiting the exhibition preferred the Wiener Werkstätte, with Sigurd Lewerentz buying a large ceramic sculpture for 423.50 kronor. Carl Bergsten and Gunnar Asplund also purchased applied art objects. Finally, it should be noted that Orrefors glassworks bought glasses from the exhibition.[18] These might have gone on to serve as inspiration for the newly recruited artists Edward Hald and Simon Gate.

Not everything ran smoothly. It is possible to trace the difficulties in delivering the ordered pieces in the correspondence after the exhibition.[19] Nevertheless, parts of the exhibition traveled on to Copenhagen in late 1917.[20]

Art Exhibitions

Two other exhibition projects in Stockholm should be mentioned, in which fewer applied artists participated.

In January–February 1917 the Vereinigung bildender Künstlerinnen Österreichs (VBKÖ, Austrian Association of Women Artists) was invited to exhibit together with the Association of Swedish Women Artists at Liljevalchs konsthall. The Swedish-born VBKÖ representative Edith von Knaffl-Granström stated that they found the courage to send the fragile artworks through Europe after noticing the success of the applied arts at Nordiska Kompaniet in 1916.[21]

Another art exhibition was arranged by the artist Lucy Karrach at the Konstnärshuset (home to the Swedish Artists' Association) for three weeks in the autumn of 1922. The profits would help artists in need in Austria, and she gathered works by renowned painters to support the cause: Oskar Laske, Robin Christian Andersen, Egon Schiele, and drawings by Gustav Klimt, to mention but a few. Three Laske paintings were sold, as were two works by Schiele: *City on the Blue River* and *The Krumau Town Hall*.[22] Unsold works were sent to a public auction.

In the years after the war, Sweden helped the suffering Austrian population, inviting children to come to Sweden for a few years, and sending nurses and doctors to Austria. To show its gratitude, the Austrian state offered a silver vase designed by Josef Hoffmann to the city of Göteborg in 1923, the 300th anniversary of its founding.[23]

Nordiska Kompaniet, 1930

In January 1930 the next large Austrian exhibition took place at Nordiska Kompaniet. Seven rooms were dedicated to the show, and Josef Hoffmann designed the WW exhibit.[24] The newspapers predicted success for "Hagenauer's small and grotesque brass figurines"; again, as in 1916 and 1917, the comments state that it was an "occasion to buy cheap pieces of art." A large public—30 000 visitors in three weeks—saw what a critic described as "a radiant energy in form, and a cheerful, capricious, but tenacious energy, which in the midst of the difficulties and labors of everyday life knows how to create a more beautiful, happier, more joyous world with the help of fantasy."[25]

Josef Hoffmann visited the *Stockholm Exhibition* in the summer of 1930.[26] There he experienced the more austere Swedish design that focused on standardization and design for the masses. Axel Romdahl's description of the works by the WW as "a serious game […] somewhat whimsical" in 1929 demonstrates that they no longer had any relevance in Sweden. Already in 1932 Uno Åhrén, the leading Swedish Functionalist, stated that the movement had proven victorious. Indeed, when Josef Frank published his criticism of Functionalism, with its lack of understanding for personal style and taste, in Sweden, he was met by silence.[27] From now on, Functionalist austerity dominated Swedish design, and there was no place for the playfulness of the Wiener Werkstätte.

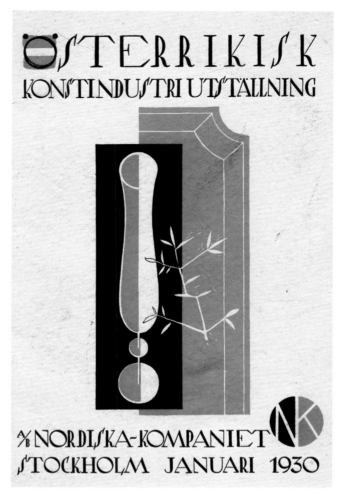

Fig. 9 Catalog cover *Österrikisk konstindustriutställning*, Nordiska Kompaniet, Stockholm, January 1930
Private collection

1   This was the title of a seminal text by Gregor Paulsson from 1919, translated into English in: Creagh, Lucy/Kåberg, Helena/Miller Lane, Barbara, *Modern Swedish Design: Three Founding Texts*, The Museum of Modern Art, New York 2008, 72–125. Trans. David Jones.

2   *Teknisk tidskrift. organ för Svenska teknologföreningens afdelning för husbyggnadskonst Arkitektur* (32) 3 1902, 40: The architect C. J. Forsberg discussed the artists' colony in Darmstadt. Axel Lindgren wrote on modern jewelry in the April 1902 edition, (32) 4, 50–54, mentioning Otto Prutscher.

3   *Teknisk tidskrift* (35) 3 1905, 44–51.

4   Johansson, Bengt O. H., *Med egna vågor om Carl Bergsten arkitekt 1879–1935*, Stockholm 2019, 201 ff.

5   *Gemla fabrikers aktiebolag, Diö: Möbler af helböjdt virke, s. k. Wienermöbler*, 1914, without the chairs by Bergsten but with 192 pieces of furniture in bentwood; many are copies or influenced by Thonet or Kohn.

6   Eriksson, Eva, *Den moderna staden tar form: Arkitektur och debatt 1910–1935*, Stockholm 2001, 59, 118.

7   *Neues Wiener Tagblatt* 6 Apr 1916, 10–11.

8   MAK, WI 1674 is shown in the photograph MAK, KI 9972-3. Also Bertold Löffler's *Erster Krinolinen-Jahreszeitenzyklus* [First Crinoline Cycle] for Wiener Keramik was shown next to a vase by Pavel Janák.

9   First advertisement in *Svenska dagbladet* 22 May 1916, the last in 1923.

10 Sign. E. K—n, *Svenska dagbladet* 5 Sep 1917;

Clegg, Elizabeth "War and Peace at the Stockholm 'Austrian Art Exhibition' of 1917," *The Burlington Magazine* (154) 1315 2012, 676–688. The article mainly discusses the fine art, much less the applied art.

11 Board minutes from 31 May 1917, para. 3, and 13 Jun 1917, para. 4, Stadsarkivet [Stockholm City Archive] SE/SSA/1265/A1/2. Liljevalchs konsthall was made available for free, with a commission of 10 percent to be paid on sold items. The catalog and poster (150 printed) were funded by Liljevalchs konsthall.

12 Advertisement in *Dagens Nyheter* 13 Sep 1917.

13 Exhibition photos in Stadsarkivet SE/SSA/1265/K1a/8 and MAK, KI 9982, together with Clegg 2012 (see note 10) and *Österrikiska konstutställningen: september 1917*, no. 8, exh. cat. Liljevalchs konsthall, Stockholm 1917. The reader is given a tour of the exhibition in: *Stockholms dagblad* 8 Sep 1917.

14 Information kindly provided by Christian Witt-Dörring.

15 Sales records, Stadsarkivet SE/SSA/1265/G 7/1.

16 *Stadskollegiets utlåtanden och memorial 1923*, no. 154, attachment A, 619, Stockholm, 1923.

17 The works by Michael Powolny also found several buyers, including for two each of *Putto mit Flöte* [Putto with Flute] and *Putto mit zwei Füllhörnern* [Putto with Two Cornucopias], and seven *Steigendes Pferd* [Rearing Horse].

18 Ricke, Helmut/Anderbjörk, Jan Erik/Dahlbäck Lutteman, Helena (eds.), *Glas in Schweden: 1915–1960*, Munich, 1986, 32–33.

19 Letters from the director Sven Strindberg to rep-

resentatives of the Austrian state and different firms, Stadsarkivet SE/SSA/1265/E1/3; finally on 17 Mar 1918 he wrote to Hoffmann "canceling every order not yet delivered."

20 *Østrigsk Kunstudstilling (Maleri, plastik, kunstgenstande), December 1917–Januar 1918: Den frie udstilling*, n.d. n.p.; the catalog lists 116 paintings and works on paper; 26 sculptures; and 27 exhibitors of applied arts and architecture.

21 *Föreningen Svenska konstnärinnor och Vereinigung bildender Künstlerinnen Österreichs: Januari–Februari 1917*, Stockholm 1917. 900 works of art were exhibited, of which 80 were sold in the first week. Three ceramic artists participated: Helena Johnová, Ida Schwetz-Lehmann, and Johanna Meier-Michel.

22 *Aftonbladet* 28 Sep 1922, 5. Swedish titles: *Staden vid den blåa floden* and *Rådhuset i Kruman* [sic].

23 *Aftonbladet* 31 Aug 1923, 2. The silver vase has an inscription stating it is from the AMAI collection.

24 Sekler, Eduard F., *Josef Hoffmann: The Architectural Work*, Princeton, NJ 1985, CR 322, 420. Trans. Eduard F. Sekler and John Maass. Photos at Centrum för Näringslivshistoria, SE/CFN/HUF_7924-1 K1a:18

25 Wåhlin, Hans, "Österrikisk konstslöjd," *Aftonbladet* 2 Feb 1930.

26 "Sweden does not need functional furniture," *Svenska dagbladet* 17 Jul 1930, 10.

27 Frank, Josef, "Rooms and Furnishings," trans. David Jones, in: Bojankin, Tano/Long, Christopher/Meder, Iris (eds.), *Josef Frank: Writings. Published Writings 1931–1965*, vol. 2, Vienna 2012, 288–305.

1919
1925

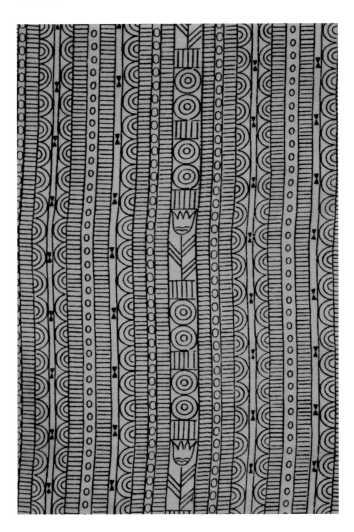

Fig. 5 JH, pastry bowl, executed by
the Wiener Werkstätte, 1919
Silver
MAK, GO 2079
© MAK/Katrin Wißkirchen

Fig. 6 JH, tea set, executed by
the Wiener Werkstätte, 1923
Silver and ivory
bel etage Kunsthandel GmbH

Fig. 7 JH, tea set, executed by
the Wiener Werkstätte, 1923
Brass and ebony
MAK, ME 846
© MAK/Tamara Pichler

Fig. 8 JH, table lamp, executed by the
Wiener Werkstätte, 1925
Brass, silk
MAK, ME 867
© MAK/Georg Mayer

Fig. 11 JH, centerpiece,
executed by the Wiener
Werkstätte, 1924
Brass
MAK, GO 1987
© MAK/Georg Mayer

Fig. 9 JH, vase, executed by the
Wiener Werkstätte, 1923
Brass
Wien Museum, 53.805

Fig. 10 JH, vase, executed by the
Wiener Werkstätte, 1922
Brass
GALERIE BEI DER ALBERTINA · ZETTER

Fig. 12 JH, vase, executed by
Johann Oertel & Co, Haida/Nový Bor,
for the Wiener Werkstätte, 1921
Green glass, cut
GALERIE BEI DER ALBERTINA · ZETTER

Fig. 13 JH, vase, executed by Ludwig Moser & Söhne,
Karlsbad, for the Wiener Werkstätte, 1923
Violet glass, cut
GALERIE BEI DER ALBERTINA · ZETTER

Fig. 14a JH, vase, executed by
Ludwig Moser & Söhne, Karlsbad,
for the Wiener Werkstätte, 1923
Radon-colored glass, mold-blown
MAK, GL 3785
© MAK/Georg Mayer

Fig. 14b JH, footed dish, executed by
a Bohemian manufactory for the
Wiener Werkstätte, 1922
Iridescent glass, mold-blown
MAK, GL 3309
© MAK/Georg Mayer

Fig. 15 JH, freestanding chest of drawers for a
smoking room, *International Exposition of Modern
Decorative and Industrial Arts*, Paris, 1925
Walnut wood
Private collection
© MAK/Georg Mayer

Fig. 16 JH, book cover, executed by
the Wiener Werkstätte, ca. 1922
Snakeskin
Dr. E. Ploil Collection
© MAK/Georg Mayer

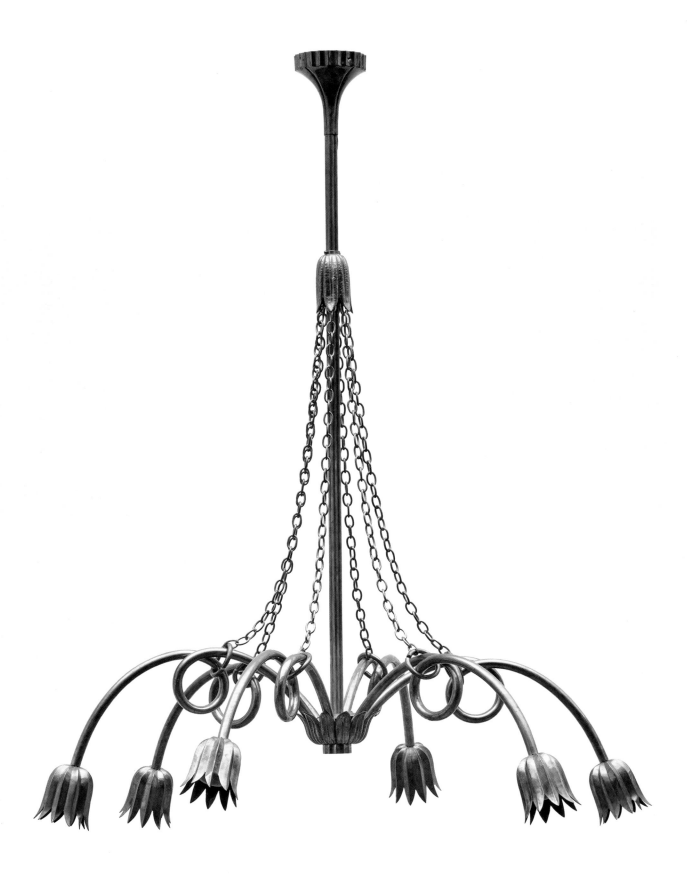

Fig. 17 JH, 6-branch chandelier, executed
by the Wiener Werkstätte, 1923

Galerie Yves Macaux, Brussels
© MAK/Georg Mayer

Fig. 18a JH, Fritz Grohmann's house, Würbenthal/Vrbno pod Pradědem, 1920/21
MAK, KI 9951-78

Fig. 19 JH, worker's houses for the Grohmann company, Pochmühl bei Würbenthal/
Vrbno pod Pradědem, 1922/23, multifamily home with barrel roof
© Jan Šafář and Irena Perničková, Moravská galerie v Brně

Fig. 18b JH, Fritz Grohmann's house, Pochmühl
bei Würbenthal/Vrbno pod Pradědem, 1920/21
Kunsthandel Widder, Vienna

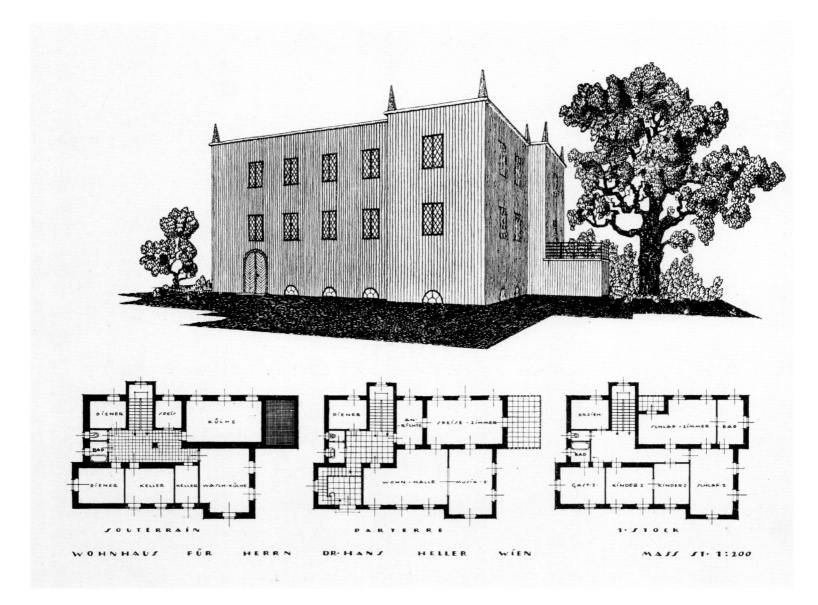

Fig. 20 JH, project for Dr. Hans Heller's villa, Vienna, 1923
Perspective and floor plans
DKuD (53) 1923/24, 37

Figs. 21, 22 JH, Eduard Ast's country house, Aue near
Velden on Lake Wörthersee, 1923/24
ID (38) 1927, 54

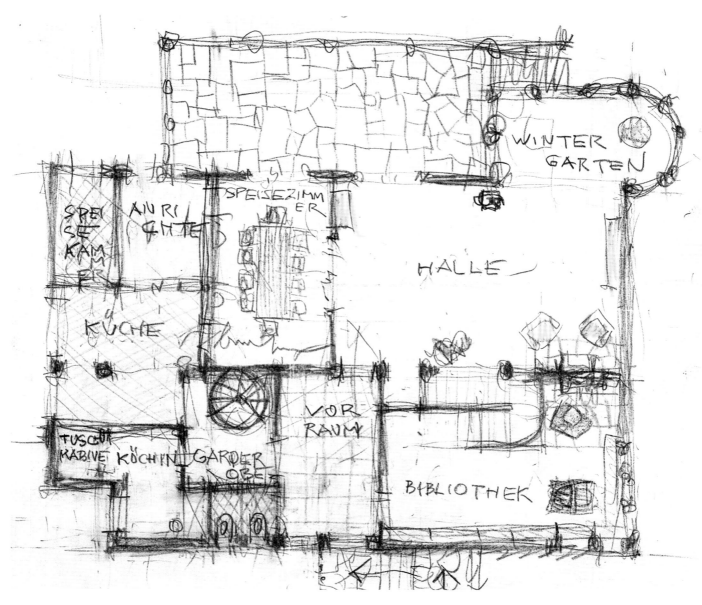

Fig. 23 JH, Ast country house, Aue near
Velden on Lake Wörthersee, 1923/24
Floor plan sketch
MAK, KI 8802-2-1

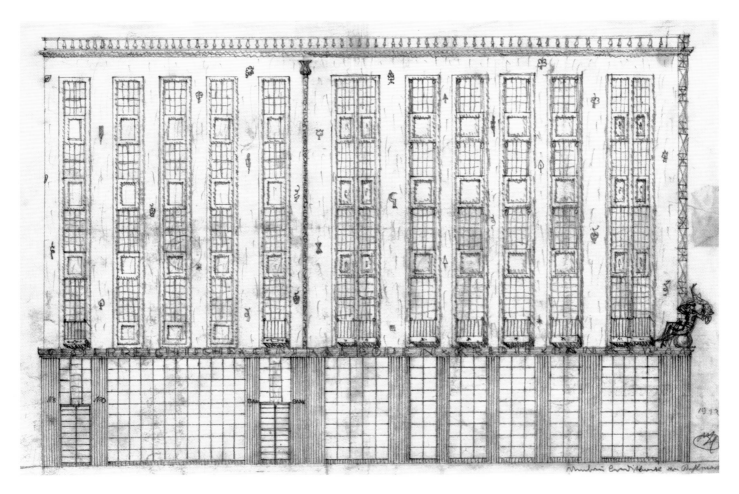

Fig. 24 JH, Central Boden Credit Bank, 1924,
project for a façade design
MAK, KI 8800

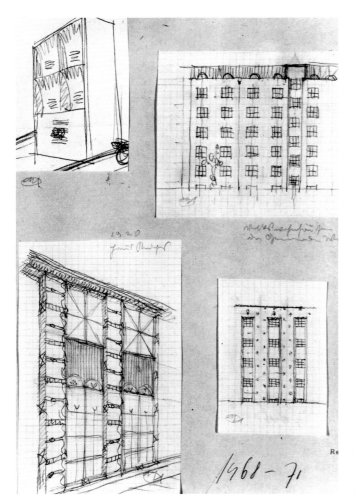

Fig. 25 JH, portfolio, compiled in 1925/26 for an acquisition by the
National Gallery Prague, with façade studies for a monument (top left),
a *Volkswohnhaus der Gemeinde Wien* [People's House of the
Municipality of Vienna] (prob. 1923 for the Klosehof, top right), the
Knips house (1920, bottom left), and a multistory house (bottom right)
National Gallery Prague, K 17781-84

Fig. 26 JH, Klosehof, housing complex for the municipality
of Vienna, Philippovichgasse, 1923–1925, inner courtyard
MAK, LI 10886-1

Figs. 27, 28 JH, Sonja Knips's house, Vienna, Nußwaldgasse, 1919
Façade designs
MAK, LI 10888

Fig. 29 JH, Sigmund Berl's house, Freudenthal/Bruntál, 1919–1922,
garden side
MBF (24) 1925, 289

Fig. 30 JH, Sigmund Berl's house,
details of the garden side
MAK, LI 10885-1

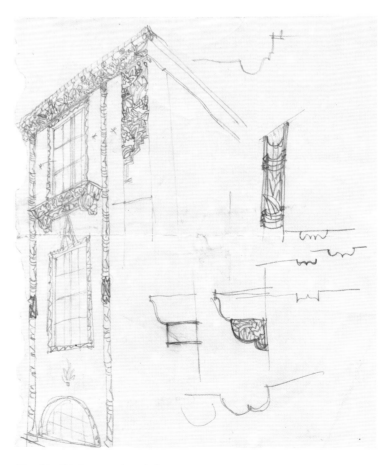

Fig. 31 JH, Sigmund Berl's house,
designs for façade details, 1919–1922
UAA, Collection and Archive, 1830

Figs. 32, 33 JH, Austrian pavilion at the *International Exposition
of Modern Decorative and Industrial Arts*, Paris, 1925
Entrance area and inner courtyard
MAK, KI 10147-150, -148

Josef Hoffmann

1919
1925

Josef Hoffmann, ca. 1925
MAK, WWF 218-7

1919–1925

First plans for a villa for Sonja Knips, which only receives planning permission in 1924 due to the postwar shortage economy. In 1920 Hoffmann delivers a design for a festival hall for Salzburg (artist's impression). Joseph Urban, a Viennese architect who has lived in the USA since 1911, opens the "Wiener Werkstätte of America" on 5th Avenue in 1922 with showrooms where arts-and-crafts works by Hoffmann can be bought. His architectural clients of the postwar period mostly come from Austria's more economically powerful successor state, Czechoslovakia. In the health spa of Groß-Ullersdorf/Velké Losiny, Hoffmann converts the Elisabeth Sanatorium. He builds a house for the textile industrialist Fritz Grohmann in Würbenthal/Vrbno pod Pradědem and for Sigmund Berl in Freudenthal/Bruntál, which are typological continuations

of prewar solutions (block shape with structured avant-corps and hipped roof). In contrast, for the Ast country house on Lake Wörthersee, his first large postwar commission in Austria, Hoffmann uses a flat roof and designs the greatly admired arch-shaped arbor in concrete—Eduard Ast was a pioneer of the reinforced concrete construction method in Austria. From 1922 a workers' settlement is constructed for the company Grohmann & Co in Vrbno pod Pradědem. Fritz Grohmann becomes another financier of the Wiener Werkstätte. Together with Peter Behrens, Oskar Strnad, and Josef Frank, Hoffmann designs the Austrian pavilion for the *International Exposition of Modern Decorative and Industrial Arts* in Paris in 1925, which—due to Germany's absence at this World's Fair—unofficially comes to represent both German-

speaking countries (Behrens's part of the building) and is thus the object of particular attention from the specialist media. Adolf Loos, who is living and working in Paris at this time, rejects an offer to participate in the undertaking. Nevertheless, the art and architecture critic celebrates the pavilion as one of the most original creations in the exhibition. Hoffmann shows the *Ruheraum einer Dame* [Lady's Relaxation Room], a new type of room between boudoir and bedroom in the 1920s style, which had already been shown at the AMAI in 1923 and will be put on public display once again in 1928 at Macy's Department Store in New York. Hoffmann is at the height of his international success, not only being awarded the French Legion of Honor but also being invited to write the entry on modern interior design for the 14th edition of the *Ency-*

JH, Winarskyhof, housing complex by the municipality of Vienna, Stromstraße, 1924
Architekturzentrum Wien, Achleitner Archive

Josef Hoffmann's architecture studio at the Vienna School
of Arts and Crafts at Stubenring 3, ca. 1924
Josef Hoffmann Museum, Brtnice

clopedia Britannica. The City of Vienna
commissions Hoffmann with planning
the housing complex Klosehof (Vienna's
19th district, 140 apartments, 1923–
1925) and a section of the Winarskyhof
(20th district, 76 apartments, 1924/25),
on which Peter Behrens, Oskar Wlach,
Josef Frank, and Oskar Strnad also
collaborate. Hoffmann marries Karla
Schmatz; his second wife is a model at
the Wiener Werkstätte. ■

Invitation to view the Wiener Werkstätte
and houses by Hoffmann, 1923
MAK, KI 13743

JH, Central Boden Credit Bank, 1924, façade design
Österreichs Bau- und Werkkunst (2) 1925, 57

Fig. 1 JH, Sonja Knips's villa, street view shortly after completion in 1926
MAK, KI 8951-62

Rainald Franz

Continuing to Build for Patrons

Josef Hoffmann's Villas 1918–1933

After the First World War and the collapse of the Habsburg Monarchy, Josef Hoffmann had to come to terms with different conditions in the world of construction. In the new Austrian Republic, most of his former clients were initially either not willing to build or impoverished. The ledger of plans from Hoffmann's architecture studio records a mere fraction of the projects for villas and country houses for the years until 1933 compared to the prewar period from 1900.[1] In approximately the decade and a half after the end of the war, it is also possible to observe how Hoffmann's construction work diversified as a result of an increasing number of social housing projects being added to his commissions for villas and exhibition buildings.[2] However, with his villas Hoffmann also took a unique position in the discourse around the design of 20th-century bourgeois houses that defined the interwar period.[3] To a certain extent, the way that Hoffmann taught architecture at the School of Arts and Crafts during this period went against the new movements represented by young professors like Josef Frank or Oskar Strnad. He pursued his own version of the "Arts-and-Crafts architecture of traditionalist Modernism," while also incorporating elements of the International Style in his system, which in his class would be advocated above all by Oswald Haerdtl.[4]

Freudenthal/Bruntál and Würbenthal/Vrbno pod Pradědem: "Hipped-Roof Modernism" against the Suppression of All Regionalisms

Between the end of the war and the mid-1920s, Josef Hoffmann was mainly able to realize villa projects in northern Moravia and the Moravian-Silesian Region. The newly founded, economically relatively strong and prosperous Czechoslovakia was home to the new financiers of the Wiener Werkstätte (WW), industrialists and German nationals who would soon commission villas and country houses.[5] The Primavesi and Grohmann families, related by marriage like the Wittgenstein and Salzer families during the WW's founding years, now decided the financial fate of the new Wiener Werkstätte GmbH in Vienna. Jindřich Vybíral characterized the typological relationship between the villas that Josef Hoffmann developed for the northern Moravian industrial

elite as "block-like volumes, crowned in a hipped roof, and the axial symmetry of the main façades' composition, which roughly correspond to a symmetrical arrangement of the interiors in three strips around the ground-floor hall."[6] As early as 1918 Fritz Grohmann, a member of one of the most important textile producing families in the monarchy and a spinning mill owner who was married to Susanne Primavesi, commissioned Josef Hoffmann to construct a prestigious manufacturer's villa. Only completed in 1922 due to administrative delays, the *Neues Herrenhaus* [New Manor] stood in the immediate vicinity of the factory in Würbenthal/Vrbno pod Pradědem.[7] Compared with the decorative eccentricity of the Primavesi country house in Winkelsdorf/Kouty nad Desnou (1913/14), the central portion of the building under a tall hipped roof and the two short adjoining side wings, which flank a terrace in the style of a cour d'honneur, are kept very simple. Half-round windows open up the façade on the ground floor; the rectangular windows on the upper floor reach up to the cornice. Sparse stucco decoration emphasizes the window axes. Inside, the rooms on the ground and upper floors are arranged around the dominant hall with staircase.

Fritz Grohmann's brother Kuno commissioned Hoffmann to convert a house in Pochmühl bei Würbenthal/Pocheň near Vrbno pod Pradědem in 1922.[8] In his adaptation of the—at its core Baroque—building, Hoffmann expressed his commitment to the historical and regional form. This can also be said of the house he built in 1919–1922 for the timber merchant and sawmill owner Sigmund Berl in Freudenthal/Bruntál in Silesia. Here, too, Hoffmann varied classical motifs but included them in his form of "hipped-roof Modernism."[9] However, in the Berl villa the classical elements of pilasters and entablature were no longer converted into a single homogenous and abstracting modern texture as in the exhibition buildings from 1911 and in the Viennese villas like that for Eduard Ast, but treated in a nuanced way: The eaves cornice bears a richly molded relief of arabesque and foliage shapes, while the pilasters are kept in the typically Hoffmann-style horizontal profiles throughout of fluting, bulges, and ridges with regularly applied foliage motifs.[10] The heavy, large forms of the cubic and sculptural flower boxes on consoles, of the hipped roof, and of the dormers appear to

18a, b
p. 233

4

29 30 31
p. 239

Fig. 2 JH, Ast country house, façade design, 1923
MAK, KI 8802/1

heighten this intended solidity, which was likewise sought by the building's owner.[11]

Regularly schematized hip-roofed country houses, now almost without any classicizing façade structure, were built at almost the same time as Josef Hoffmann by Mies van der Rohe in Berlin in the form of the houses Riehl in Neubabelsberg (1907), Perls (1910/11), Urbig (1915–1917), Feldmann (1922), and Mosler (1924–1926). Similar forms can also be found in the early villas by Peter Behrens and the projects from the romantic early period of Le Corbusier's oeuvre.[12] Due to their significance for the pronouncedly avant-garde aspiration of Bauhaus and New Objectivity, these buildings—frequently omitted in older biographies—can nevertheless serve as examples of the importance of this construction type in the original construction practice of these later Functionalist and equally doctrinaire and anti-traditionalist masterminds of Modernism. That Mies of all people pursued both styles in parallel for a time is illustrated by the contemporary modernity of the hipped-roof building type, as well as the embedding of traditionalist reform in the context of the generally recognized Modernism, and relativizes the later apparent irreconcilability of construction attitudes.[13]

"Purposeful and Steadfast Intent"[14]: The Villa for Sonja Knips (1924–1926)

Hoffmann's buildings in Moravian-Silesia were "ostensible outposts of metropolitan taste," as Vybíral so trenchantly characterized them.[15] One house that was intended to embody the best of this metropolitan taste was realized by Josef Hoffmann in the mid-1920s on Vienna's Nußwaldgasse for the longstanding customer and financier of the Wiener Werk-

stätte Sonja Knips.[16] Initial plans for the villa date back to 1919, showing a monumental hipped-roof house with a main façade with nine axes and a garage building clad in trellis reminiscent of the Skywa-Primavesi villa.[17] In the executed villa, the original L-shaped ground plan remains with a single-story elongated domestic wing and two-story main house, but the building's core was reduced from nine to six axes and the columns were omitted. "The basic form of the house is defined by its cubic layout and wide sloping roof," analyzed Max Eisler, "the stockiness of the whole recurs in the individual parts."[18] Josef Hoffmann himself speaks in his autobiography of the country house for Sonja Knips on Nußwaldgasse being one of the "very few commissions […] in Vienna […] I designed inside and out to the smallest detail and with great delight. […] the villa in the Nusswaldgasse was intended to provide the Knips family, and first and foremost Mrs Sonja Knips, with a milieu that was comfortable in every way and consistent with the baroness's noble and artistic disposition."[19] Eisler describes it thus in his richly illustrated article from 1927:

> "In other ways, too, every motif is clearly worked out: the entrance and the open stairs at grade, next to them the pillar-like projecting windows over the basement arches, above the others in a stout format and recessed in the brickwork. This ascending arrangement with slim and then shortened verticals sets a horizontal limit to the energetic entablature of the eaves."[20]

The contrast between the light plastered wall area and the gray slate of the hipped roof is accompanied by the window and door frames ornamented with chip carvings. Furthermore, diamond and grape motifs distributed symmetrically in the stucco of the façade, combined with the muntins, are responsible for the impression of the "pure embedded

Fig. 3 JH, Fritz Grohmann's house, Würbenthal/
Vrbno pod Pradědem
© Jan Šafár and Irena Perničková, Moravská galerie v Brně

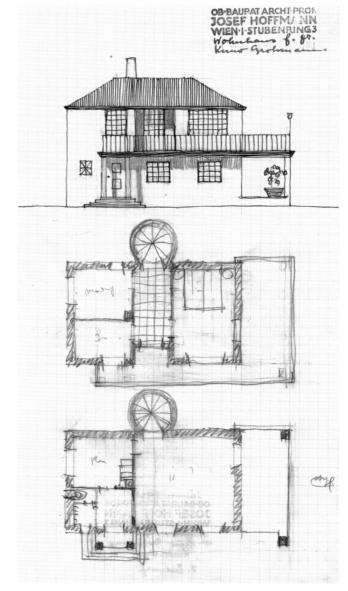

tranquility."[21] Such interspersed grand decorative motifs on
the façade can also be found in the simultaneous projects
for the Paris pavilion, the Klosehof, and the Boden-Credit
Anstalt bank. The garden side contrasts with the protruding
street façade. Hoffmann himself describes his solution thus:

> "I suggested we did without a front garden, which is rarely con-
> venient, so as to build the house up to the street, where a small
> space remained between the house next door to the front, which
> protruded onto the street, and an enormous, old, sheltered walnut
> tree at the back. By demolishing the dilapidated old building it
> proved possible to build the house on street-level, with a large
> terrace at its back which made immediate use of the rubble. From
> this terrace a long flight of steps led to the rest of the garden,
> which was also levelled, and which, by using the trees and veg-
> etation at hand, was transformed into avenues, paths, lawns,
> open spaces and specially designed areas for seating. Every re-
> markable tree was spared; we were fortunate to be in a position
> to have a finished garden as the construction work on the villa
> was completed. By this time the back wall of the demolished
> building had been put to use as the terrace wall, while part of
> the cellar could be used as a cool, enclosed space against the
> garden's lower path. As all the sitting- and bedrooms faced the
> garden, the situation was one of great tranquility; there were no
> neighbouring buildings to disturb the greenery."[22]

25 26 p. 236

Fig. 4 JH, second project for a house for Dr. Kuno Grohmann,
Würbenthal/Vrbno pod Pradědem, 1923/24
Front elevation, floor plans (ground floor, 1st floor)
MAK, KI 8809

1 p. 250

Whereas the ground floor is dominated by an open floor plan, as was propagated at this time by Le Corbusier and Mies van der Rohe for rooms serving social functions, the rooms on the attic floor convey privacy and are "compartments entirely tailored to the needs of their inhabitants."[23] The last suburban villa planned entirely by Hoffmann with the involvement of the Wiener Werkstätte became an often-published model building, which was admired by its frequent visitors like Emilie Flöge, Helene Klimt, Carl Moll, Peter Behrens, and Henry van de Velde. Leopold Kleiner appears to be speaking about the Knips villa in his Hoffmann monograph when he writes that Hoffmann's houses

> "arose from studying the life of the people for whom he was building. Out of their habits and demands, he created rooms for them. Out of their correct arrangement emerged the organic structure of the floor plan and layout, as well as ultimately the house itself, whose outer beauty resulted not from an outwardly decorative will but from knowledge of the dimensional ratios between cube, wall, and window."[24]

"The Knips house comes from Hoffmann's maturity. As ever, it is a productive plethora," confirmed Max Eisler.

Approximating "Cubic" Modernism[25]: Eduard Ast's Country House and the Project for Dr. Hans Heller's Villa

2

At almost the same time as the villa was being constructed for Sonja Knips in Vienna, Josef Hoffmann starts working again for Eduard Ast, for whom he had built a villa on the Hohe Warte. In 1923 Ast decided to have a summerhouse built in the community of Auen on Lake Wörthersee.[26] Hoffmann designed the three-story villa building on a hill overlooking the lake and a porter's lodge on the main road, but also included the garden and the accompanying lakeside lot on the other side of the road in his plans. A preliminary design for the building has survived.[27] It shows a façade profile reminiscent of mock embossing. The façade of the main building that was ultimately executed is smooth, structured only with horizontally positioned, multiple profiling comprising double stucco stripes—a solution that Hoffmann would

return to in a slightly altered form for the pavilion of the international exhibition in Paris in 1925.[28] The floor plan and front elevation in the preliminary drawing show the building as being assembled from geometric shapes like cubes and cuboids. The internal organization of the house sees all the rooms arranged around a central hall; in the completed building, a portico is situated in front of the main entrance whose solid cornice is adorned with a frieze with dancers by Anton Hanak. Hoffmann's first villa with a flat roof featured a glazed children's playroom on the roof terrace with fluted pillars and a hipped roof. In the concrete pergola located in the garden, Hoffmann adopts forms from the technical structural designs of his client's construction company. Here Hoffmann combines his typical elements of horizontal façade structuring with reductionist volumes, of course without failing to quote a hipped roof at least in the rooftop structure. The original arrangement of the interiors around the double-height living area corresponds to his plans for his hipped-roof villas.[29]

21 22 23 p. 235

4

Hoffmann takes a similarly adaptive approach to the topic of cubic structural forms in the project for a villa for Dr. Hans Heller.[30] For this young married couple, Hoffmann plans a two-story garden villa with a flat roof. "A flat roof for the sun-worshipping residents" is the description in the review by Richard Ernst. The long oblong building shape is enriched with irregularly arranged cubic avant-corps on all four sides. The façade exhibits vertically fluted stucco throughout, with white window frames, "white-painted wooden latticework with rhomboid panes," and small obelisks as crowing finishing touches on the flat roof. Richard Ernst, then a custodian at the Austrian Museum of Art and Industry (today's MAK) in Vienna, describes Hoffmann's buildings from these years in *Deutsche Kunst und Dekoration* as follows:

20 p. 234

> "The delightful arrangement of the rooms, surrounded by a simple casing, which deliberately exposes the aristocracy to true culture, the integrity of an art that disregards fibbing pomp and pretension; a simplicity whose natural beauty remains hidden from miseducated or stupid eyes until familiarization or history has taught them to love the obvious and natural. Josef Hoffmann's recently completed buildings in Silesia, his recent Viennese interiors take the same direction; they show the master's interminable creative force at the peak of perfection."[31]   ■

Fig. 5 Pergola and Eduard Ast's country house near Velden on Lake Wörthersee, 1923/24
MAK, KI 8951-25

1   Ledger of plans from Josef Hoffmann's construction studio. Now in the estate of Camilla Haerdtl, Architekturzentrum Wien, collection.

2   See the article "The Social Question: Josef Hoffmann's Municipal Apartment Complexes and Housing Developments before 1933" by Matthias Boeckl in this catalog.

3   Hirschfell, Marc, "Das ist das Haus vom Nikolaus. Die Geschichte des Walmdachhauses als Urform und Idealtyp," dissertation at the Martin Luther University Halle-Wittenberg, Halle 2005, .

4   Ibid., 68; see also the article "In the Modernist Laboratory: Josef Hoffmann's Architecture Class at the Vienna School of Arts and Crafts, 1899–1918" by Matthias Boeckl in this catalog; Müller-Wulckow, Walter, Architektur 1900–1929 in Deutschland, Königstein 1999. On Josef Hoffmann's early villas, see the articles "From Life Reform to Bourgeois Daily Life: The Villa Colony on the Hohe Warte" and "In the Modernist Laboratory: Josef Hoffmann's Architecture Class at the Vienna School of Arts and Crafts" by Matthias Boeckl and "'Homely Concept ofHousing' versus 'Decorating over the Bad Skeleton of a Building': From Rental Villa to 'Festival Building'" by Rainald Franz in this catalog.

5   Ploil, Ernst, "Economics," in: Witt-Dörring, Christian/ Staggs, Janis (eds.), Wiener Werkstätte 1903–1932: The Luxury of Beauty, Munich/London/New York 2017, 20–31; Pese, Claus, "Ein Ruin für die Kunst. Kuno Grohmann (1897–1940) und die Wiener Werkstätte," manuscript online, n.d., http://archiv.ub.uni-heidelberg.de/artdok/6810/1/Pese_Ein_Ruin_fuer_die_Kunst_Kuno_Grohmann_2020.pdf; Franz, Rainald, "Unternehmensphilosophie Gesamtkunstwerk. Die Wiener Werkstätte

1903–1932 im Kontext der Reformkunstbewegungen der ersten Hälfte des 20. Jahrhunderts," in: Natter, Tobias (ed.), Klimt, Hodler und die Wiener Werkstätte in Zürich, 2021, forthcoming; on the economic situation: Neiß, Herta, 100 Jahre Wiener Werkstätte. Mythos und ökonomische Realität, Vienna 2004, 93, 94.

6   Vybíral, Jindřich, Junge Meister. Architekten aus der Schule Otto Wagners in Mähren und Schlesien, Vienna 2007, 241.

7   Sekler, Eduard F., Josef Hoffmann: The Architectural Work, Princeton, NJ 1985, CR 231, 385–386. Trans. Eduard F. Sekler and John Maass; Vybíral 2007 (see note 6), 235. The house is published in: de Fries, Henry, Moderne Villen und Landhäuser, Berlin 1925. Noever, Peter/Pokorný, Marek (eds.), Josef Hoffmann. Selbstbiographie/Autobiography, Ostfildern 2009, 132–133. Trans. Bernd Magar and Andrew Oakland.

8   Sekler 1985 (see note 7), CR 283a, 386.

9   Ibid., CR 226, 382–384; Vybíral 2007 (see note 6), 239–241; Hirschfell 2005 (see note 3), 113.

10 "The foliage […] almost appears to be floating on a calm water surface"; Vybíral 2007 (see note 6), 246.

11 Ibid., 260.

12 Krohn, Carsten, Mies van der Rohe. Das gebaute Werk, Basel 2014, 20 ff.

13 Hirschfell 2005 (see note 3), 113–114.

13 Josef Hoffmann on Sonja Knips in a letter to her, 26 Jan 1926, quoted by von Miller, Manu, Sonja Knips und die Wiener Moderne, Vienna 2004.

15 Vybíral 2007 (see note 6), 255.

16 Sekler 1985 (see note 7), CR 265, 400–402; Miller 2004 (see note 13), 85 ff.

17 Published in: Moderne Bauformen (XXV) 1926, 353.

18 Eisler, Max, "Neue Werke von Josef Hoffmann," in: Moderne Bauformen (XXVI) 1927, 161.

19 Noever/Pokorný 2009 (see note 7), 102. On the interior design, compare the article "The Viennese Style: Interiors 1900–1918" by Christian Witt-Dörring in this catalog.

20 Eisler 1927 (see note 18), 161.

21 Ibid.

22 Noever/Pokorný 2009 (see note 7), 102.

23 Miller 2004 (see note 13), 98.

24 Kleiner, Leopold, Josef Hoffmann, Berlin 1927, XXVI.

25 Senarclens de Grancy, Antje, Keine Würfelwelt. Architekturpositionen einer "bodenständigen" Moderne. Graz 1918–1938, Graz 2007.

26 Sekler 1985 (see note 7), CR 254, 391–394; Noever/Pokorný 2009 (see note 7), 132–135.

27 MAK, KI 8802/1,2.

28 See the article "'A Shrine of a Thousand Treasures to Admire and Stroll Through': The Austrian Pavilion at the International Decorative Arts Exhibition in Paris in 1925" by Rainald Franz and Markus Kristan

29 The Knips country house was converted by Josef Hoffmann in 1934 for the general manager Friedrich Meyer-Helbeck, during which time the roof terrace was replaced with an upper story.

30 Sekler 1985 (see note 7), CR 252, 390–391; façade design and floor plans for the construction of the garden villa in Ober St. Veith in Vienna published in: Deutsche Kunst und Dekoration (LIII) 1923/24, 36–37.

31 Ernst, Richard, in: Deutsche Kunst und Dekoration (LIII) 1923/24, 36.

Fig. 1 JH, design drawing for the dining room of the Knips villa, 1924/25
The Studio (97) 1929, 385

Christian Witt-Dörring

Luxury Put to the Test

The Wiener Werkstätte and Hoffmann's Interior Designs 1919–1932

Due to his authority in the field of Austrian culture—which is occasionally even recognized by the state—Josef Hoffmann feels obliged to comment on Vienna's seemingly desperate situation as early as 1919[1]:

> "We have become poor and small. We cannot predict where great misery will yet lead us. Chasms are open before us, yet do we dare hope for a better future? This poor, intimidated Vienna, can it ever rise again, can it hope to experience a better, a great time?"[2]

One must permit the right men, of whom there are ample numbers in the country, to act freely, he continues. Neither institutions nor statutes would tip the balance, but rather individual creative talents. This is an appeal that Hoffmann has repeated since time immemorial and that he will continue to repeat like a mantra, regardless of the ruling political system, until his death: Time and again he speaks out against the uninformed omnipotence of state bureaucracies; to him they are the obstacle that prevents great ideas. By way of example he states that Vienna has turned its back on the Danube and by doing so has foregone the opportunity to integrate the Danube into urban planning; another example he names is the reconstruction of the palace of justice after the fire of 1927, which he holds to be both functionally and architecturally misguided.[3] At the same time, however, he points the way to a better future—if only the right forces are given the opportunity of completely free, unhindered development. In utter devastation he sees the opportunity and the possibility for a new start. He offers the help of Vienna's artistic elite, whose creative roots go back to the endeavors and ideology of Vienna's art spring beginning in 1897. This elite had made Vienna famous beyond the country's borders as an alternative modern art destination. It was a matter of intertwining art and everyday life, from which a general aesthetic consciousness, a sense of beauty could emerge, a remedy to heal wounds. When Vienna faces another new beginning after the Second World War, Hoffmann will once again foreground aesthetic arguments in his reconstruction plans.[4] They are in keeping with the vision of Vienna that he had developed in 1935, according to which the city would have blossomed in "orderly beauty" in the year 2000.[5]

In Hoffmann's vision of a better future for Vienna, he ac-cords the Wiener Werkstätte (WW) and Viennese arts and crafts in general a major part in rebuilding the economy and creating a sense of identity. For him, the two go hand in hand. Vienna's altered role from capital of an empire and seat of imperial power to capital of a microstate makes it necessary to determine and build on effective symbols of identity that can be capitalized on both domestically and abroad. This will draw the attention of the world to Austria—and especially Vienna with its cultural offerings—as a tourist destination. Accordingly, in 1919 Hoffmann's criticism is directed at, among other things, the resumption of construction work inside the corps de logis of the Neue Burg Palace:

> "On the Burgplatz the delayed building should be finally begun. Since we cannot afford luxury, there—integrated into the architectural setting, i.e., fitting into the main massing—one should finally erect the Vienna Hotel that invites the stranger to the best place, as befits a civilized city. This hotel should have no equal in the world; it should truly represent us."[6]

The economic significance of Viennese arts and crafts for the Austrian tourist industry is repeatedly emphasized by Hoffmann. It supports his defense of his own artistic work and ideological conviction in the face of his rivals, who like Adolf Loos want to deprive the decorative arts of their right to exist in the modern world and in the everyday life of the old social order.[7] It is to this end that Joseph Roth makes use of the old Baroness Trotta in his novel *The Emperor's Tomb*. When her son returns from imprisonment after the First World War and asks her how his wife has fared in his absence, she responds:

> "'No, you can't imagine,' my mother persisted. 'Guess what she has become!' I worked out the worst, or what would in my mother's eyes seem the worst. 'A dancer?' I enquired. My mother shook her head gravely. Then she said sadly, almost mournfully, 'No—a craftswoman. Do you know what that is? She designs, or rather carves[…]. Worse than that, boy! When people start using worthless material to make something which looks as if it has some value where will it all stop?'"[8]

A draft letter by Hoffmann to the Austrian tourist board from December 1927 starts with the sentence "If we ask which things repeatedly steer foreigners to our homeland,

Fig. 2 Joseph Urban, shop of the Wiener Werkstätte of America in New York, 1922
MAK, WWF-137-91-1

>
Fig. 4 JH, design for the adaptation of the living and dining rooms in Dr. Kuno Grohmann's house in Würbenthal/Vrbno pod Pradědem, 1921/22
Gregor Grohmann Collection
© MAK/Georg Mayer

Fig. 3 JH, dining room in the Ast country house in Aue near Velden on Lake Wörthersee, 1923/24
ID (38) 1927, 64

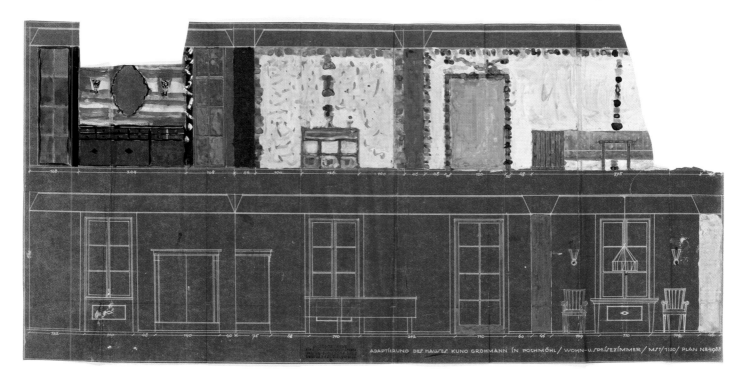

then alongside many other things the decorative arts are sure to play a major role."[9] The draft subsequently details and extols the merits of and the range of wares by the domestic decorative arts and is hence an eloquent testament to the marriage of convenience between tourism and the decorative arts entered into under Hoffmann.

The question is to what extent a producer of luxury goods like the WW can realize Hoffmann's vision in times of financial hardship after the lost war. Who is its clientele? After Waerndorfer's departure in 1915, the WW's new investor is Otto Primavesi, the industrial magnate and banker from Olmütz/Olomouc (now in the Czech Republic), who starts to instigate the necessary reforms from 1919. They are intended to make the company viable again after its longstanding operating deficit. The suggestions include transforming the WW from a purely arts-and-crafts enterprise into an arts-and-crafts and industrial enterprise.[10] Negotiations launched in 1920 with Hoffmann's former student and

assistant Philipp Häusler lead to his appointment in 1921 as the coordinator of all WW operations in an organizational, artistic, and technical capacity in consultation with the commercial and artistic managers.[11] Additionally taking over responsibility for the WW's artistic program from 1922, Häusler's attempts to reconcile the individual ambitions of the artistic employees with the economic reality in the country and to boost serial production, lead to friction between him and Hoffmann, as well as Mäda Primavesi, Otto Primavesi's wife. In due course a succession of artists leaves the WW,[12] which at this point employs 120 staff members and 250 workers.[13] Häusler must have been contemplating the WW's future prospects at the same time. He receives a memorandum in this regard from Norbert Bischoff,[14] legation councilor at the federal ministry of the exterior; dated 2 June 1922 it pertains to the significance of the decorative arts in Austria. In it Bischoff analyzes among other things the WW's current situation; to exploit its potential he proposes its continued

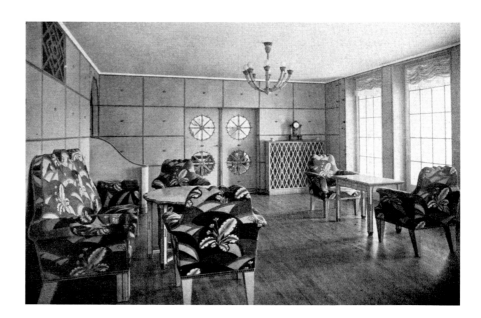

Fig. 5   JH, living area in Sigmund Berl's house in Freudenthal/Bruntál, 1919–1924
MB (24) 1925, 294

Figs. 6, 7, 8 JH, bedroom in Dipl.Ing. Ernst Bauer's apartment, 1927,
mural by Maria Strauss-Likarz
DKuD (61) 1927/28, 454, 455, 459

>
Fig. 9 JH, dining room in the
Lengyel house in Bratislava, 1929
DKuD (68) 1931, 34, 36

Fig. 10 JH, living area in the
Lengyel house in Bratislava, 1929
DKuD (68) 1931, 32

Fig. 11 JH, library room in the
Panzer house, 1929
DKuD (68) 1931, 45

operation as a state manufactory working not for profit but without a deficit.[15] Then in 1926 Hoffmann himself contemplates the WW being taken over by the municipality of Vienna.[16] Finally, in 1923 the WW publishes its first printed sales catalog. Thereafter the WW produces special designs that are intended for execution in larger numbers. They include mold-blown glasses produced in Bohemian glassworks, objects worked from brass, leatherware, wallpapers, and above all clothing and decorative fabrics. However, in addition to these designs suited to serial production, the WW continues to serve the luxury segment, for which primarily the architect Dagobert Peche—permanently employed at the WW since 1915—assumes responsibility. A parallel universe of forms thus emerges alongside Hoffmann's dominant aesthetic. Continuing until 1923 and Peche's untimely death, it is tantamount to an artistic innovation but leaves Hoffmann unaffected. For example, it calls for the triumph of aesthetics over utility and hence a separation of art from function.[17] Immediately after the end of the war, the WW redoubles its participation in exhibitions in German industrial museums (Stuttgart and Cologne in 1920, and Hannover in 1922) and in trade fairs (Leipzig in 1919 and 1920, Frankfurt in 1920 and 1921, and Vienna in 1921).

In 1921 Joseph Urban visits his former hometown of Vienna, where he experiences the hardships of the postwar period and the demise of the once resplendent metropolis first-hand. Trained as an architect at the Academy of Fine Arts Vienna, Urban knows the Secessionists from his time in the capital as a member of the Siebener Club and as a founding member of the Hagenbund. Having emigrated to the USA in 1911, he has had a successful career as an architect and scenographer for the Boston Opera House, the Ziegfield Follies, the Metropolitan Opera, and William Randolph Hearst's Cosmopolitan Film Company, among others. Confronted with the Viennese artists' fight for survival due to a lack of commissions, he composes his letter of thanks to Häusler on 27 July 1921 before he has even left Vienna; in it he writes: "Do not forget me if you think that I can help. Consider it my duty to help! While you all suffered and are still suffering from the war, I was able to work without worry—so it is only natural for me to do my part as far as I am able!"[18] This offer gives rise to the idea of setting up a branch of the WW in New York; designed by Urban, it opens on 9 June 1922. Yet its existence is short-lived: just 18 months after opening its doors, it has to close them for good in December 1923.[19]

Against all the odds, such as mass unemployment and hyperinflation in Austria since 1922, Hoffmann strives to keep Vienna's art world alive. For instance, he is of the opinion that, "to maintain the interest of both the artists and the

14a, b p. 230
9 11 p. 229
1 2 p. 226

Fig. 12 JH, sideboard, ca. 1925
MBF (27) 1928, 71

Fig. 13 JH, *Ruheraum einer Dame* [Lady's Relaxation Room],
Österreichisches Kunstgewerbe [Austrian Decorative Arts]
exhibition at the AMAI, 1923
DKuD (54) 1924, 34

public, exhibitions are among the most important undertakings."[20] Although Hoffmann has regularly availed himself of this medium since the Secession was founded, its importance grows in the face of the almost complete absence of art patronage compared with the prewar period. Of similar importance in this climate are public appearances, which give Hoffmann the opportunity to develop and show new creations. The financial and creative effort expended by the designers and the executing companies for these temporary presentations is remarkable.

Among his prewar circle of patrons, Hoffmann can still rely on commissions from the Primavesi, Knips, and Ast families. While Otto Primavesi steps down as the WW's manager for financial reasons in 1925, his wife Mäda carries on the business as its main shareholder until 1926/27. Due to the loss of one of its biggest patrons and the generally poor economic situation, the WW is forced to make redundancies. This leads to staff numbers reaching their lowest level since the WW's founding with just 66 individuals able to remain in work. The larger construction and interior decoration jobs undertaken for longstanding patrons in these years include the villa on Vienna's Nußwaldgasse for Sonja Knips in 1924/25 and the country house in Aue near Velden on Lake Wörthersee, Carinthia, for Eduard Ast in 1923/24. Among Hoffmann's new customers are first and foremost Mäda Primavesi's nephews by marriage, the brothers Fritz and Kuno Grohmann. While just one villa complete with furnishings is created for Fritz in Würbenthal/Vrbno pod Pradědem (now in the Czech Republic) in 1920/21, Kuno Grohmann commissions the WW not only with converting and decorating a villa in Würbenthal according to plans by Hoffmann in 1921/22 but also with planning workers' houses for the same location in 1922/23, some of which would be realized at a later date, as well as a series of other construction projects that did not come to fruition. Moreover, his financial engagement helps to keep the WW afloat until 1930: necessitated by the bankruptcy of the Primavesi bank, when the WW's composition proceedings are completed it is Kuno Grohmann who invests in the WW as a partner and majority shareholder in 1927. However, after further recapitalization attempts he withdraws from the company in 1930 in the course

1
27 28 p. 238

3
21 22 23 p. 235

4 5
18a, b p. 233

19 p. 233

Fig. 14 JH, music room, *Wiener Raumkünstler* [Viennese Room Artists] exhibition at the AMAI, 1930
MAK, KI 9230-5-1

Fig. 15 JH, exhibition space of the Austrian publishing and printing institutions, *International Exposition of Modern Decorative and Industrial Arts* at the Grand Palais in Paris, 1925
Art et Décoration (68) 1925, 129

Fig. 16 JH together with Oswald Haerdtl, D train, 2nd-class carriage, for the Österreichische Bundesbahnen, 1927–1936
DKuD (67) 1930/31, 420

of the Great Depression. This post-WWI and pre-Wall Street Crash period sees a villa complete with interior decoration constructed after plans by Hoffmann for Sigmund Berl in Freudenthal/Bruntál (now Czech Republic) in 1919–1922 and a number of Viennese interior decoration jobs realized for Dr. Baru (1921), Dr. Reinhold (1926), Dipl.Ing. Bauer (1927), Dr. Lengyel (1929), and Dr. Panzer (1929).

In addition to these interior designs that were produced for specific customers, it is predominantly in the interiors created especially for exhibitions—whose designs in part also come from Hoffmann[21]—that he can give free rein to his ideas.[22] Displayed between 1920 and 1932 in the ephemeral context of temporary exhibitions, these room and furniture creations serve Hoffmann as a testing ground for his further formal stylistic development, which is characterized by explosive form-finding as if he were reinventing himself. Hoffmann's unwavering quality awareness remains unaffected by political, economic, or social upheavals. At the same time, however, his aesthetic path that had been so clear prior to the First World War now gives way to a wealth of new formal aesthetic possibilities. They permit the simultaneous coexistence of decorated and plain, soft and hard surfaces or of curved and straight contours. Cannelures become folds made of fabrics and ribs and gadroons made of metal. On the other hand, patterned woven fabrics and increasingly the vibrant grain of wood veneers or colorfully lacquered or painted surfaces are used where well into the 1910s the dominant palette was black and white or white combined with a contrasting color. A room's harmony is now no longer produced by a uniform decorative concept, for example a set of furniture, but rather arises from the diverse range of home furnishings that are brought together by the unifying element that is Hoffmann's artistic individuality. For instance, he now directs his attention more and more to designing stand-alone pieces of furniture. In the context of the interior, they take on a sculptural, often almost monumental expression that emphasizes their volume. In line with the diktat of the age and people's preference for homeliness over prestigious representation, Hoffmann reinterprets space itself. The walls and ceiling are no longer divided into horizontal and vertical structural elements; instead, the ceiling is used as "total architecture of the interior."[23] Examples include the

Ruheraum einer Dame [Lady's Relaxation Room] in the *Ausstellung Österreichisches Kunsthandwerk* [Exhibition of Austrian Arts and Crafts] at the Austrian Museum of Art and Industry (AMAI, today's MAK) in 1923, the tearoom for the Austrian furniture industry's presentation at the Galerie des Invalides and the WW's long hall in the Austrian pavilion for the *International Exposition of Modern Decorative and Industrial Arts* in Paris in 1925, the bedroom in Dr. Bauer's apartment in 1927, the D train's second-class carriage for the Österreichische Bundesbahnen (Austrian national rail company) in 1927–1936, the powder room for Macy's in New York in 1928, the library room for Dr. Panzer in 1929, and the living area and dining room in the Lengyel house in 1929. The aforementioned wealth of material and formal stimuli applied indiscriminately here is the expression of his irrepressible individualistic creative drive. For consumers it entails the risk of a bewildering mixture of tastes. Yet if they engage with these designs, they will still discover Hoffmann's customary discipline and rigor when it comes to function and use of material, as well as his confident sense of proportion. They are rewarded with the novel in the familiar.

As the artistic director of the Austrian pavilion at the *International Exposition of Modern Decorative and Industrial Arts* in Paris in 1925, Hoffmann is afforded the opportunity to present this entire spectrum of artistic expression to an international audience with the collaboration of as diverse a group of artists and designers as Josef Frank, Oskar Strnad, Peter Behrens, and many others, as well as a great number of graduates from the School of Arts and Crafts. Adolf Loos, who is living in Paris at the time, declines Hoffmann's invitation to contribute to in Austria's display.[24] Despite the artistic success of the Austrian pavilion, the country's participation in Paris is a commercial failure, which prompts Loos to once again voice his biting criticism of the Wiener Werkstätte as a misguided Modernist concept.[25] On 20 April 1927 he causes a scandal with his talk "Das Wiener Weh (Die Wiener Werkstätte). Eine Erledigung" ("Viennese Woe (The Wiener Werkstätte): A Settlement of Accounts") in the Großer Saal of the Musikverein.[26] A year later, on 31 May 1928, the WW is able to celebrate its 25th anniversary in the presence of Federal President Michael Hainisch with a ceremony in the Hall of the Muses at the Albertina. At the

5
29 30 31 p. 239

6 7 8
9 10 11

10 p. 229
5 6 7 p. 227
11 p. 229
15 16 p. 231
14

1 p. 280

13

14 p. 277
6 7 8

16
11
9 10

Fig. 17 Vally Wieselthier, front book cover for the anniversary publication *Die Wiener Werkstätte 1903–1928. Modernes Kunstgewerbe und sein Weg*, 1929

MAK, BI 18873-2
© MAK/Georg Mayer

suggestion of Josef Hoffmann, this occasion is marked by a commemorative publication called *Die Wiener Werkstätte 1903–1928. Modernes Kunstgewerbe und sein Weg*, which is realized by Mathilde Flögl. It is an artist's book with a layout that changes from page to page and a cover designed by Vally Wieselthier and Gudrun Baudisch that is executed in papier-mâché and impression printed in color. Extremely complicated to print, this book produced in silver, gold, red, and black should be interpreted as an expression of the will to survive of a company alive to its artistic vitality and innovative force that had just been saved from composition proceedings by Kuno Grohmann. Yet as soon as 1930 the WW again needs new capital to avoid closure; a financial syndicate around Alfred Hofmann and Georges Oeri, the principal agents of the Swiss wallpaper company Tekta & Salubra, takes over almost all the shares in the business.[27] Despite major recapitalization efforts and an even stronger focus on mass production, the WW ultimately has to be liquidated in 1932. That same year the unemployment rate in Austria amounts to between 21.7 and 27 percent among the non-self-employed. The following year Alfred Hofmann, the last shareholder and financier of the Wiener Werkstätte, attempts to prevent the WW's creative potential from forever falling into oblivion. He turns to the architect Philipp Häusler, who had taken over the central management of the WW in 1920, with the intention of reorienting the WW's manufacturing in order to achieve wider appeal and standardization. However, Häusler is resignedly forced to declare:

"I have spoken with my industrialist friends who come into consideration in this regard and have gained the impression that the erstwhile unquestionably extant interest in the artistic values of the Wiener Werkstätte no longer exists. It could also be observed—and this made a considerable impression on me—that Vienna's current artistic production is unknown in the milieu of this industry."[28]

17

Fig. 18 Mathilde Flögl, layout of the anniversary publication *Die Wiener Werkstätte 1903–1928. Modernes Kunstgewerbe und sein Weg*, 1929

MAK, BI 18873-2
© MAK/Georg Mayer

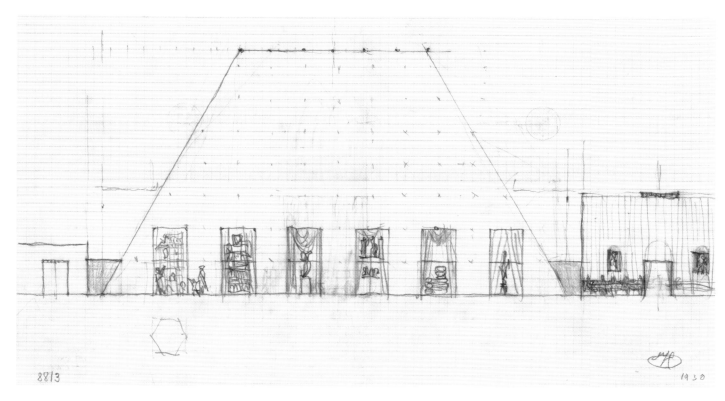

Fig. 19 JH, design for the central room of the Werkbund exhibition at the AMAI, 1930
MAK, KI 8813

Fig. 20 JH, design for an interior elevation in the nursery with
foldaway bed in Dipl.Ing. Ernst Bauer's apartment, 1927
MAK, KI 8819-12

Fig. 21 JH, corridor of Wiener Werkstätte display cases, Werkbund exhibition at the AMAI, 1930
DKuD (66) 1930, 309

Fig. 22 JH and Oswald Haerdtl, salesroom for the Altmann & Kühne confectionery on Kärntner Straße, ceiling painting by Mathilde Flögl, 1928
MB (27) 1928, 467

Fig. 23 JH, living room, *Raum und Mode* [Room and Fashion] exhibition at the AMAI, 1932
MAK, *Raum und Mode*, exh. cat.

Fig. 24 JH, tearoom, *Die neuzeitliche Wohnung* [The Contemporary Home] exhibition at the AMAI, 1928, mural by Mathilde Flögl
DK (32) 1929, 15

Fig. 25 JH, Wiener Werkstätte shop in Berlin, 1929
DKuD (65) 1929/30, 327

1   For example, the imperial royal ministries of the exterior and trade, as well as the imperial royal war press bureau, approach Hoffmann in 1917 with the request to establish a branch of the WW in Zurich and to organize art exhibitions in Copenhagen, Stockholm, and Amsterdam to present Austria-Hungary on neutral territory as a cultural nation by way of a propaganda exercise.

2   Hoffmann, Josef, "Wiens Zukunft," *Der Merker* Dec 1919. Translated as "Vienna's Future" in: Sekler, Eduard F., *Josef Hoffmann: The Architectural Work*, Princeton, NJ 1985, 492–493: 492. Trans. Eduard F. Sekler and John Maass.

3   Hoffmann, Josef, undated manuscript on the reconstruction of Vienna's palace of justice, MAK, KI 23506-11.

4   Hoffmann, Josef, "Gedanken zum Wiederaufbau Wiens I u. II," *Wiener Zeitung* 23 Dec 1945 and 21 Apr 1946. Translated as "Thoughts on Vienna's Reconstruction" I and II in: Sekler 1985 (see note 2), 501–503.

5   Hoffmann, Josef, "Wiener im Jahre 2000," *Neues Wiener Journal* 17 Feb 1935. Translated as "Viennese in the Year 2000" in: Sekler 1985 (see note 2), 500–501: 500.

6   Hoffmann 1919, in: Sekler 1985 (see note 2), 493.

7   Transcript of a letter from Josef Hoffmann written on the occasion of the proceedings in the Austrian Werkbund in March 1933, a facsimile of which was sent by Max Welz to the members of the Werkbund. In: Sekler 1985 (see note 2), 498–500.

8   Roth, Joseph, *The Emperor's Tomb*, New York 2002, 76 f. Trans. John Hoare.

9   Draft letter entitled "Österreichisches Kunstgewerbe!," MAK, KI 23506.

10   Noever, Peter (ed.), *Der Preis der Schönheit. 100 Jahre Wiener Werkstätte*, Ostfildern-Ruit 2003, 276 ff.

11   Manuscript Department of the Vienna City Library, Philipp Häusler estate.

12   In 1920 Vally Wieselthier is among those to leave the WW and though Dagobert Peche resigns, he is convinced to stay. In 1922 Eduard Josef Wimmer-Wisgrill leaves the WW and Hoffmann and Peche once again contemplate leaving the WW.

13   Noever 2003 (see note 10), 295.

14   Norbert Bischoff was consular attaché at the consulate general in Cologne in 1919/20, when Häusler was teaching at the trade school there.

15   Philipp Häusler estate (see note 11).

16   Hoffmann, Josef, undated handwritten manuscript, MAK, KI-23506-10.

17   Noever, Peter (ed.), *Dagobert Peche und die Wiener Werkstätte*, Ostfildern-Ruit 1998.

18   Philipp Häusler estate, 2.1.3.10.5.12-25 (see note 11).

19   Witt-Dörring, Christian/Staggs, Janis (eds.), *Wiener Werkstätte 1903–1932: The Luxury of Beauty*, exh. cat. Neue Galerie, Munich/London/New York 2017, 468 ff.

20   Hoffmann, Josef, "Kunst in Not," *Neue Freie Presse* 3 Sep 1920, 5, column 2. My thanks to Markus Kristan for this reference. Letter from Philipp Häusler to Alfred Hofmann from 23 Apr 1933, Philipp Häusler estate (see note 11).

21   Room of the Austrian publishing and printing industry in the Grand Palais and the long halls of the Wiener Werkstätte, the textiles and papers and the reception room in the Austrian pavilion at the *International Exposition of Modern Decorative and Industrial Arts* in Paris in 1925, Austrian section of the *Ausstellung Europäisches Kunstgewerbe* [Exhibition of European Decorative Arts] at the Grassi Museum in Leipzig in 1927, Austrian Werkbund exhibition at the AMAI in 1930.

22   *Ruheraum einer Dame* [Lady's Relaxation Room] displayed in 1923 in the *Ausstellung Österreichisches Kunsthandwerk* [Exhibition of Austrian Arts and Crafts] at the AMAI, a smoking or writing room and a tearoom for the anniversary exhibition of the Österreichischer Kunstgewerbeverein (Austrian Arts-and-Crafts Association) at the AMAI in 1924

and for the *International Exposition of Modern Decorative and Industrial Arts* in Paris in 1925, a living room with adjoining sunroom for the 1927 Kunstschau at the AMAI, mock-up room for the social housing at the exhibition *Wien und die Wiener* [Vienna and the Viennese] at Vienna's Messepalast in 1927, a tearoom for the exhibition *Die neuzeitliche Wohnung* [The Contemporary Apartment] at the AMAI in 1928, the lady's relaxation room already exhibited in Paris and a powder room for the exhibition *Art in Industry* at Macy's Department Store in New York in 1928, a music room for the exhibition *Wiener Raumkünstler* [Viennese Room Artists] at the AMAI in 1929, the coffeehouse in the Werkbund exhibition at the AMAI in 1930, the inglenook of a living room for the exhibition *Raum und Mode* [Space and Fashion] at the AMAI in 1932.

23   Copy of a typescript of a radio lecture given by Josef Hoffmann on 9 Oct 1930, Eduard Sekler estate, private collection, soon in the collection of the University of Applied Arts Vienna.

24   Anonymous, "Wer ist an der österreichischen Kunstpleite in Paris schuld? Professor Hoffmann schreibt der 'Stunde' über seine Tätigkeit in Paris – Josef Hoffmann, Meine Gegner und ich," *Die Stunde* 10 Jan 1926, 6. My thanks to Markus Kristan for this reference.

25   Thun-Hohenstein, Christoph/Boeckl, Matthias/Witt-Dörring, Christian (eds.), *Ways to Modernism: Josef Hoffmann, Adolf Loos, and Their Impact*, exh. cat. MAK, Basel 2015. Trans. Eva Ciabattoni, Anthony DePasquale, and Maria Slater.

26   A. [Ankwicz-Kleehoven, Hans], "Vortrag Adolf Loos," *Wiener Zeitung* 22 Apr 1927, 5. My thanks to Markus Kristan for this reference.

27   Noever 2003 (see note 10), 397.

28   Letter from Philipp Häusler to Alfred Hofmann from 23 Apr 1933 (as note 20), Philipp Häusler estate (see note 11).

Fig. 1 Oswald Haerdtl, design of the architecture exhibition by the School of Arts and Crafts at the AMAI, 1924
DKuD (54) 1924, 334
© TU Wien, library

Matthias Boeckl

Presence despite Permanent Crisis

Josef Hoffmann and the Vienna School of Arts and Crafts 1919–1938

Notwithstanding entirely new political parameters, new prevailing social building tasks, and thus, also new educational objectives, the program at the School of Arts and Crafts remained virtually unchanged at the start of the young republic in 1918/19. Two architectural classes continued to be taught—in addition to Hoffmann's own, now also that of Oskar Strnad[1]—and the curriculum also remained practically the same. Hoffmann was still able to run his private architecture office in the school's spaces.[2] As before, he consistently deployed his national and international networks for his school's media presence, and for a number of appearances at important exhibitions. He further involved successful students and employees in his own planning assignments and instruction at the school, whereby the borders remained fluid. He was even able to expand his position at the School of Arts and Crafts by taking on further teaching duties: from 1923 to 1936, he additionally managed the workshops for enameling, metal design, and metalwork.

Of the assistants in Hoffmann's office and school during this time, first and foremost was Oswald Haerdtl, who after his studies with Strnad, assisted Hoffmann from 1922 until taking over his own architecture class in 1935. In Hoffmann's private architecture office, Haerdtl also rose from assistant (1922–1928), to office manager (1928–1932), to partner (1932–1938). In addition to Haerdtl, also other influential architects were active in Hoffmann's specialized class and/or office for shorter or longer time periods until his final retirement in 1937: Max Fellerer, who had already worked in the architecture office and in the Wiener Werkstätte in 1913/14, was chief architect in Hoffmann's office from 1919 to 1926; and after interludes in the master school and office of Clemens Holzmeister (1927–1934) returned to the School of Arts and Crafts on Stubenring as director in 1934–1938 and again in 1945–1954. Leopold Kleiner, former student of Hoffmann, architect, and publicist who was forced to flee to New York in 1938, where he continued to write about Viennese Modernism, was an assistant in the specialized class from 1919 to 1923. He regularly published articles about Hoffmann and the School of Arts and Crafts in daily newspapers and specialized media, crowned by the first Hoffmann monograph, which was published in 1927 by the Verlag Ernst Hübsch in Berlin.[3] In 1936, the former Strnad

student and collaborator Hans Adolf Vetter[4] worked as an assistant and in 1937, also briefly as successor to Hoffmann at the School of Arts and Crafts. Other active young architects in the circle were Hoffmann's student Philipp Häusler, as well as Strnad's students Hans Bichler and Gabriel Guévrékian. Häusler was pushed by Hoffmann into the position of school director for a short time during the Nazi era;[5] Guévrékian worked at Hoffmann's office in 1922 and was subsequently a key contact in the circles around Le Corbusier in Paris; meanwhile, Bichler played an ambivalent role as Hoffmann's central "tool" during this time, as head of the Wiener Kunsthandwerkverein (Viennese Association of Arts and Crafts) from 1938 to 1945, and at the school as successor to Otto Prutscher, a former student of Hoffmann who had been dismissed, from 1941 to 1944. Hoffmann's son Wolfgang, who had studied in the Strnad class, also worked temporarily in the office in 1922 before leaving for America. Finally, Josef Kalbac, a student of Strnad, also occasionally worked in the architecture office and from 1938 to 1956, was Hoffmann's partner at the new office in the Viennese Association of Arts and Crafts at Kärntner Straße 15.[6]

What was everyday life like in the architecture class?[7] Former student Herbert Thurner, who likewise worked in Hoffmann's architecture office from 1933 to 1935, explains: "We had no lessons in the conventional sense. There were no lectures and there was no 'program' with agonizing deadlines. All work was geared toward unfolding the talent and specific character of each individual." Lillian Langseth-Christensen outlines Hoffmann's teaching method: "Hoffmann taught us nothing. If teaching meant the imparting of knowledge, then he was not a teacher. Hoffmann believed that what we could become lay within ourselves, that we could not learn it, he could not teach it, but he could discover it."[8] Despite the extreme freedom, in the Hoffmann class of this time, alongside the continued exercise of diverse design tasks, such as fabric patterns, posters, book covers, jewelry, furniture, toys, glass and ceramic dishes, wallpaper, fashion, etc.—several emphases typical of the era can be recorded in the architectural field. From 1922 onward, housing developments and garden cities, townhouses, single-family homes, bathing facilities, country homes and boat houses, cinemas, and

Fig. 2 JH, Austrian pavilion at the *International Exposition of Modern Decorative and Industrial Arts*, Paris, 1925, display cases with painting by female students of Hoffmann's specialized class at the Vienna School of Arts and Crafts
MAK, WWF 137-11-1

>
Fig. 5 Anton Z. Ulrich (Hoffmann's specialized class), design for a club and boathouse for the Zagreb rowing club H.V.K., 1927
MBF (26) 1927, 379

Fig. 3 Leopold Kleiner, living room, Kunstschau, AMAI, 1920
MBF (26) 1927, 391

Fig. 4 Oswald Haerdtl, decorative-arts room with view to the architecture room, Breslau/Wrocław, 1926
MBF (26) 1927, 395

hotels were designed, for the most part under the direction of Hoffmann's assistant Oswald Haerdtl. Focal points of the social construction tasks (supplemented with crematoria projects, resulting from a Viennese competition, the first of its kind to be held in Austria, in 1921), display a telling balance with structures for leisure activities and tourism, which was becoming increasingly more important for Austria. Almost all projects were worked out not only in drawings, through to representative and artistic color perspectives, but also in cardboard models, which were often exhibited, photographed, and published, for the most part with texts by Max Eisler.[9] Among the most active students of the 1920s and 1930s were Camilla Birke, Lilly Engel, Philipp Ginther, Julius Jirasek, Lillian Langseth-Christensen, Walter Loos, Karl Panigl, Hilde Polsterer, Carmela Prati (married: Haerdtl), Simon Schmiderer, Stefan Simony Jr, Alfred Soulek, Herbert Thurner, Rudolf Trostler, and Anton Z. Ulrich.

In addition to the publications in international specialized media, the Hoffmann class also attracted public attention through numerous exhibitions. The most important involvements took place in Vienna in 1924, in Paris in 1925, and again in Vienna in 1929. In May 1924, the two architectural classes of the School of Arts and Crafts presented themselves together in the neighboring Austrian Museum of Art and In-

dustry (today's MAK). Assistant Oswald Haerdtl designed the small exhibition in clear response to the De Stijl movement as a free composition of horizontal and vertical planes in the space. On the one hand, these served as pedestals and vertical planes for models and drawings, but on the other hand—similar to Friedrich Kiesler's *Internationale Ausstellung neuer Theatertechnik* [International Exhibition of New Theater Technique], which arose parallel in Vienna in 1924 and his *Raumstadt* [City in Space] (Austrian theater contribution, Paris 1925)—as depictions of the avant-garde vision of architecture's emancipation from gravity. In addition to students' works, the architecture presentations of the School of Arts and Crafts always showed works by the two specialized class instructors, Hoffmann and Strnad. In 1924, for example, exhibited alongside a model of Stoclet House by Hoffmann, were house designs by Otto Niedermoser and Julius Jirasek.[10] The same models were presented at the Austrian architecture exhibition in the context of the *International Exposition of Modern Decorative and Industrial Arts* in Paris in 1925 in the Grand Palais together with works by Oskar Wlach, Josef Frank, and many others. Kiesler's *Raumstadt*[11] was in the adjoining room. Finally, the most extensive exhibition of student works from the two departments led by Hoffmann at the School of Arts and Crafts took place in

Fig. 6 Rudolf Trostler (Hoffmann's specialized class), design
for the model of a middle-class colony, 1927
MBF (26) 1927, 386

Fig. 7 Karl Panigl (Hoffmann's specialized class),
design for a country house, 1927
MBF (26) 1927, 379

1929. At the anniversary exhibition at the Austrian Museum
of Art and Industry, one could admire exemplary, clear, objective solutions for the social and touristic tasks of the era
with Alfred Soulek's large model of a housing development
and Philipp Ginther's terrace hotel for the Lapad peninsula
near Dubrovnik, but in large wall display cases, also numerous products from Hoffmann's workshops for enamel and
metalwork.[12]

The impact of Hoffmann's architecture instruction and
the special model of the Vienna School of Arts and Crafts
was displayed especially on an international level after 1918.
While Hoffmann's graduates from the period before World
War I were still able to help in visibly shaping Austria's architectural and design landscapes as teachers, designers, and
architects between 1905 and 1933, the careers of many students and assistants from the interwar period were already
gravely affected by crises and war, persecution and exile.
Until the expulsions of the Nazi era, the international impact
of Hoffmann's teaching developed along the usual paths:
Philipp Ginther, for example, taught interior design in Istanbul
from 1929 and Anton Ulrich was one of the most influential
and active architects of Croatian Modernism from the 1930s
onward. The Vienna Secessionists' modern art education
developed into an important influence at the Bauhaus in

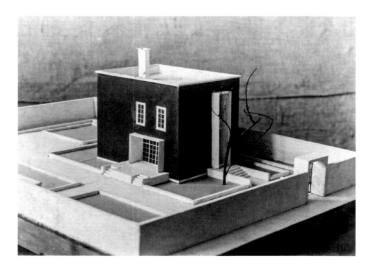

Fig. 8 Hilde Polsterer (Hoffmann's specialized class),
design for a country house, 1925
MAK, KI 8961-102

Fig. 9 Oswald Haerdtl, design of the School of Arts and Crafts's anniversary exhibition at the AMAI, 1929, architecture section with the model of a country house on a coastal cliff by Alfred Soulek (Hoffmann's specialized class)
UAA, 11142-F-W-24

Weimar and Dessau. Walter Gropius's reform of the united Dresden schools of art and applied arts (Henry van de Velde had run the latter from 1907 to 1919) under the ideal image of "building" as a symbol and form of a modern unity of the arts can undoubtedly also be traced back to Gropius's intimate knowledge of Viennese Modernism by virtue of his marriage to Alma Mahler (1915–1920). The Bauhaus curriculum with preliminary courses, specialized departments, and workshops is clearly modeled on the Vienna School of Arts and Crafts with its general department, the specialized classes, and workshops. Gropius documented this himself in 1925 by publishing several works by Viennese students in his first Bauhaus book.[13]

After 37 years of devoted and influential teaching, Hoffmann's departure from the School of Arts and Crafts proceeded in a nearly traumatic way. In September 1936, the now 65-year-old was meant to retire permanently in keeping with the law, but against his will. Numerous interventions

followed, including a request by Max Fellerer to employ Hoffmann in the school year 1936/37 for twelve hours per week as an assistant teacher for decorative arts in his former specialized class, which was now being led temporarily by Hans Adolf Vetter, and finally from 1937 to 1967 by Franz Schuster, a former student of Heinrich Tessenow, "because no other teacher is available who could take over the decorative arts department of Professor Hoffmann's specialized class."[14] The Ministry of Commerce, which was in charge of the matter, approved the application, but only for the winter semester.[15] With the definitive retirement of Hoffmann in 1937, the era of Secessionist art education reform came to an end, with its ideal of the unity of the arts, which had made it possible to teach architecture in a former class for furniture design, and then in this architecture class, teach almost all of the other decorative arts techniques. In 1938, Haerdtl opened the new age of industrial design, with a new class in commercial and industrial design, which he taught in addition to his architecture class. Hoffmann himself made a

Fig. 10 Oswald Haerdtl, design of the School of Arts and Crafts's anniversary exhibition at the AMAI, 1929, workshops for enamel- and metalwork (Josef Hoffmann)
MBF (28) 1929, 404

Fig. 11 Oswald Haerdtl, design of the
Austrian architecture section at the
*International Exposition of Modern
Decorative and Industrial Arts* at the
Grand Palais in Paris, 1925, with models
incl. from the School of Arts and Crafts
MAK, KI 8961-107

final—failed—attempt at restitution of Secessionist, craft-
oriented ideals in 1938 with two concepts for art school reform for the Nazi authorities.[16] Instead, in 1941, the School
of Arts and Crafts became the "Reichshochschule für angewandte Kunst" (Reich College of Applied Art).

From 1938, a number of Hoffmann's former students were
affected by flight and expulsion. Walter Loos, Simon Schmiderer, Stefan Simony, and Rudolf Trostler, for example, had
to leave Austria due to "racial" and/or political persecution,
and head to Argentina, the U.S., Turkey, or Israel where they
were, in part, able to realize major building oeuvres—especially Schmiderer in the U.S. and Trostler in Israel.[17] Alfred
Soulek, on the other hand, remained at the school from 1935
to 1979 as an instructor, while after 1945, Herbert Thurner
and Friedrich Euler were able to realize several major residential and school buildings.

Fig. 12 Alfred Soulek (Hoffmann's specialized class),
desk of gray varnish with bookshelf on the back, 1929,
executed by J. Soulek furniture factory, Vienna
MBF (28) 1929, 403

1   A third class of architecture taught by Heinrich
    Tessenow came to an end after he returned to
    Germany in 1919.
2   Hoffmann ran another architecture office, that of
    the Wiener Werkstätte, on Neustiftgasse.
3   This monograph may have been available to Adolf
    Hitler when he reviewed Hoffmann's work together
    with Albert Speer in 1940, see the article "Josef
    Hoffmann and National Socialism: An Evaluation"
    by Elisabeth Boeckl-Klamper in this catalog.
4   Son of the Werkbund board member and head
    of the Austrian state-run theaters Dr. Adolf Vetter,
    for whom Hoffmann had built one of the houses
    in the villa colony Kaasgraben, 1912–1923. Dr.
    Vetter headed the Trade Advancement Bureau
    prior to 1918 and in 1925 was acting director of
    the Austrian contribution to the *International Ex-
    position of Modern Decorative and Industrial Arts*
    in Paris.
5   See Boeckl-Klamper (note 3) in this catalog.
6   Hoffmann used this office until his death in 1956;
    see the stamps on the submission plans for the
    municipal housing complex of the City of Vienna
    at Heiligenstädter Straße 129, 1953–1954, City
    of Vienna, MA 37, EZ 557.

7   Kapfinger, Otto/Boeckl, Matthias, "Vom Interieur
    zum Städtebau. Architektur am Stubenring 1918–
    90," in *Kunst: Anspruch und Gegenstand. Von
    der School of Arts and Crafts zur Hochschule für
    angewandte kunst in Wien 1918–1991*, Vienna/
    Salzburg 1991, 102–108.
8   Ibid., 102. Furthermore, Herbert Thurner reports
    that the class was regularly visited by international
    architecture stars, including André Lurçat, Le Cor-
    busier, and Frank Lloyd Wright. Cf. Thurner, Her-
    bert, "Zum 100. Geburtstag Josef Hoffmann," in:
    Der Bau 1970, 21. Herbert Thurner also reports
    that the class was frequently visited by interna-
    tional star architects, including André Lurçat, Le
    Corbusier, and F. L. Wright. Cf. Thurner, Herbert,
    "Zum 100. Geburtstag Josef Hoffmann," in: Der
    Bau 1970, 21.
9   For example, 28 illustrations of models and plans
    by the students Anton Z. Ulrich, Karl Panigl, A.
    Fischer, Rudolf Trostler, Philipp Ginther in: Eisler,
    Max, "Josef Hoffmann und seine Schule," in:
    Moderne Bauformen (26) X 1927, 373–387.
10 Kapfinger/Boeckl 1991(see note 7), 98–99.
11 Peter Behrens' master school at the Academy of
    Fine Arts held another important presentation

abroad of the young Viennese Modernism; at the
Brooklyn Museum in New York in 1930, arranged
by the American William Muschenheim, a student
of Bauhaus and of Behrens, who also worked in
Joseph Urban's studio in New York from 1930 to
1933. Cf. Grimme, Karl Maria (ed.), *Peter Behrens
and his Academic Master-School, Vienna*, Vienna
1930.
12 Eisler, Max, "Neues aus Wien und Brünn," in:
    Moderne Bauformen (28) X 1929, 393–432: 404.
13 Gropius, Walter (ed.), *Bauhausbücher 1, Interna-
    tionale Architektur*, 1st edition, Munich 1925, 70–
    71, with illustrations of projects by Niedermoser
    and Jirasek. These projects were no longer in-
    cluded in the 2nd edition in 1927.
14 Zl. 136/1936 from 9 Sep 1936; UAA, Collection
    and Archive.
15 ASA, AdR, Commerce, Zl. 138.303/14 A-36.
16 Cf. Boeckl-Klamper (see note 3) in this catalog.
17 See Boeckl, Matthias (ed.), *Visionäre & Vertrie-
    bene. Österreichische Spuren in der modernen
    amerikanischen Architektur*, Berlin 1995.

Fig. 1 JH, stationery room at the end of the showcase room in the Austrian pavilion at the
International Exposition of Modern Decorative and Industrial Arts, Paris, 1925
MBF (24) 19295, plate 62

Rainald Franz, Markus Kristan

"A Shrine of a Thousand Treasures to Admire and Stroll Through" Max Eisler

The Austrian Pavilion at the International Decorative Arts Exhibition in Paris in 1925

With the commission to design an Austrian pavilion for the *International Exposition of Modern Decorative and Industrial Arts* that would take place in Paris in 1925, Josef Hoffmann returned to a very familiar construction task: designing prestigious buildings for the nations and institutions to which he belonged. The original plan was in fact to work side by side on both the Paris exposition and the Werkbund exhibition in Cologne, for which Hoffmann would conceive his *Österreichisches Haus* [Austrian House] and which would open in 1914. In 1911 notices in newspapers had celebrated France's intention to organize an international exhibition for modern decorative arts in Paris in 1914 or 1915. This would replace the canceled World's Fair in Paris: despite only having been scheduled to take place in 1920, preparations had already begun in 1911.[1] In France it was hoped that the exhibition would create "a 20th-century style,"[2] since the success of the Munich decorative arts exhibition in the Parisian *Salon d'Automne* of 1910 had opened the French people's eyes to "how far behind the modern decorative arts are there."[3] Indeed, the motivating force behind the event came from an alliance of three Parisian decorative arts societies: the Union centrale des arts décoratifs, the Société des artistes décorateurs, and the Salon des artistes décorateurs.[4]

However, with World War I forcing the cancelation of the Parisian decorative arts exhibition of 1916, a plan was devised in 1919 to host an international decorative arts exhibition in Paris in 1922.[5] The French government decided to exclude Germany, its wartime enemy, from this exhibition.[6] Then in July 1923 the Austrian Federal Chancellery was informed that the opening of the major *International Exposition of Modern Decorative and Industrial Arts* in Paris had now been postponed to the year 1925.[7] The desire was expressed that there would be a dedicated pavilion "to show off Austrian individuality to the full."[8] Dedicated to Dagobert Peche who had died earlier that same year, the fall exhibition at the Austrian Museum of Art and Industry (today's MAK) in 1923 featured works by several architects, including Josef Hoffmann,[9] Hugo Gorge, Josef Frank, and Peter Behrens: every one of them a teacher at Vienna's architecture schools, their contributions would go on to define the Austrian presentation in Paris in 1925.[10] By early 1924 Austria's preparations for the Parisian exhibition were well underway. Indus-

trialists and companies working in the decorative arts invited Austrian artists to deliver designs that they would produce.[11]

The site for the exhibition was settled that March: it would be held on the grounds of the previous World's Fair in Paris in 1900, including the Grand Palais, the Cours la Reine, the Quai d'Orsay, and the Esplanade des Invalides.[12] The federal government, the municipality of Vienna, the Vienna Chamber of Commerce, and the Bankenverband (Banking Federation) all made several billion kronen available for Austria's participation in the exposition. Josef Hoffmann was appointed the head architect and was required to submit a design for the pavilion to the exhibition committee forthwith.[13] In June 1924 Hoffmann traveled to Paris in order to make all the necessary arrangements with the French exhibition commission. Austria was allocated a parcel of land for its prestigious pavilion on Cours la Reine very close to Pont Alexandre III. Furthermore, Austria was also allotted a large space in the halls that were to be constructed on the Esplanade des Invalides. The Austrian decorative-arts schools would present their creations on the first floor of the Grand Palais.[14] Josef Hoffmann published one of his few articles in the *Neues Wiener Journal* of 6 July 1924, in which he reported on "The Coming World's Fair in Paris."[15] At the end of his remarks, he writes:

> "The Austrian pavilion, which will cover an area of approximately 400 square meters and has been given one of the exhibition's most advantageous locations for its construction, and which I have the honor to build, will hopefully be the star attraction of the exhibition. We artists will certainly do everything that is in our hands to make this wish a reality. Hopefully those at home who will have to collaborate on the work, will support us in this desire. We *need* global success and we *must* achieve it!"

At first the plans for the Austrian pavilion in Paris, which Josef Hoffmann was able to present at the Chamber of Commerce as early as July 1924, were not published or described so as "not to damage Austria's precedence," as Berta Zuckerkandl writes.[16] "That Josef Hoffmann's genius will also have a formative influence on this exhibition as a Gesamtkunstwerk [or total work of art] of Austrian expressive sculpture, however, and that it promises the utmost success, can already be predicted."

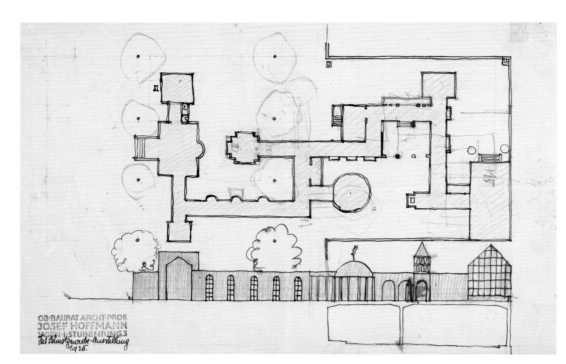

Fig. 2 JH, preliminary
design for the floor plan
and the façade elevation of
the Austrian pavilion at the
*International Exposition of
Modern Decorative and
Industrial Arts*, Paris, 1925
Canadian Centre for Architecture,
Montreal, DR 1985:0057

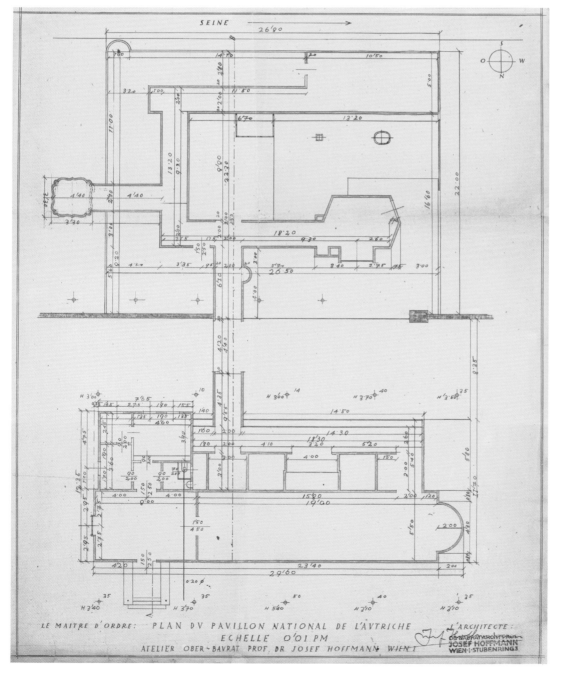

Fig. 3 JH, *Plan du pavillon national
de l'Autriche*, Paris, 1925, working
drawing, floor plans
Belvedere, Vienna, AKB_KD-8-S-8-2

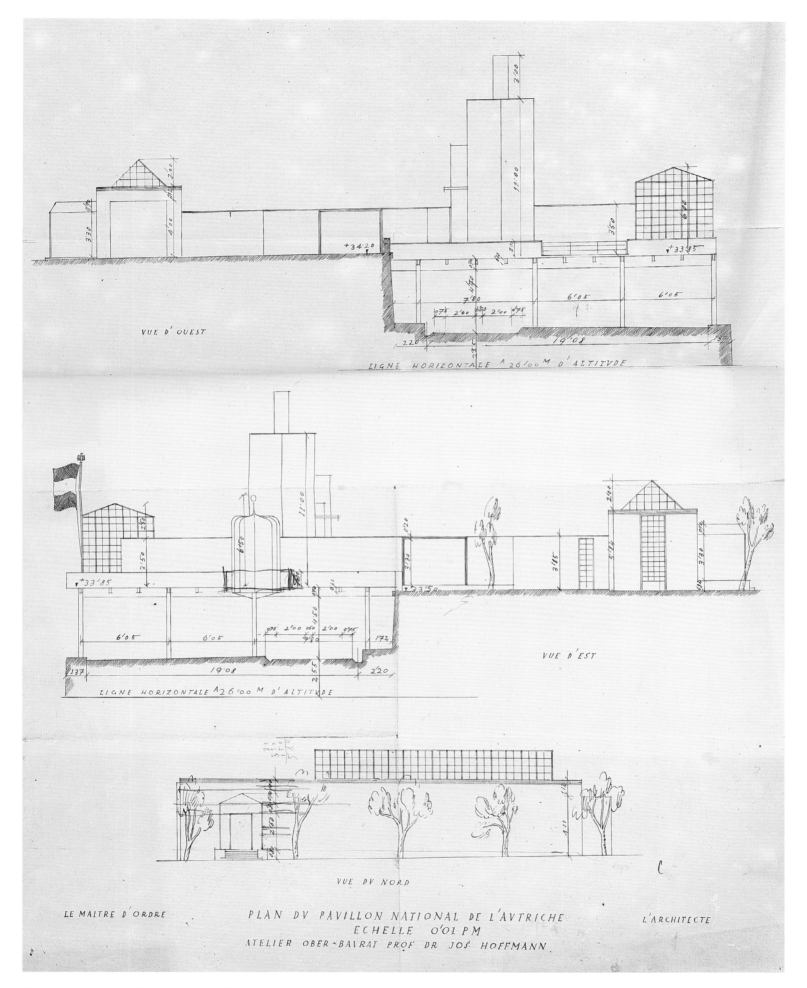

VUE D'OUEST

LIGNE HORIZONTALE A 26·00 M D'ALTITVDE

VUE D'EST

LIGNE HORIZONTALE A 26·00 M D'ALTITVDE

VUE DV NORD

LE MAITRE D'ORDRE

PLAN DV PAVILLON NATIONAL DE L'AVTRICHE
ECHELLE 0·01 PM
ATELIER OBER-BAVRAT PROF DR JOS HOFFMANN

L'ARCHITECTE

Fig. 4 JH, *Plan du pavillon national de l'Autriche*, Paris, 1925,
working drawing, sections
Belvedere, Vienna, AKB_KD-8-S-8-3

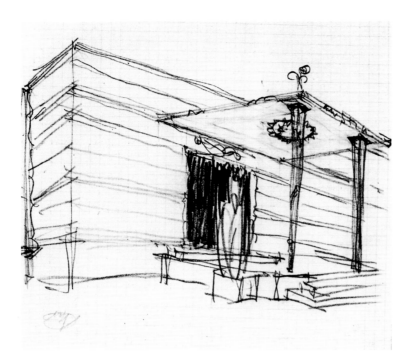

Fig. 5 JH, preliminary design for the entrance to the Austrian pavilion at the *International Exposition of Modern Decorative and Industrial Arts*, Paris, 1925
National Gallery Prague, K 17802

Fig. 6 JH, design for the drawing room of the Austrian pavilion, Paris, 1925
National Gallery Prague, K 17801

3 Hoffmann's design for the Austrian pavilion reacts to the
4 confined space on the banks of the Seine. For the building he develops a 30-meter-long and 20-meter-wide terrace, which in two places breaches the quay walls and projects into the river on slender concrete pillars. This enlarges the available floor area to 1 230 square meters, of which 974 square meters would be built on. In contrast to the pavilions
10 in Rome in 1911 and in Cologne in 1914, Hoffmann refrains from emphasizing the verticals and axial symmetry as design elements. Instead, he structures the complex with a molding that runs horizontally around the buildings, a "recumbent cannelure," and thus creates the wall decoration that would define the pavilion's external appearance. The surviving de-
5 sign drawings from Hoffmann's hand for the entrance and
6 the side façade already apply this stylistic feature. Over a
7 low, whitish-gray-colored basement, the façade—in the final

version rendered in pale pink—oscillates back and forth with multiple rhythmically arranged horizontal stripes. The bulges in the upper and lower areas of the stripes and arrises give the viewer the impression of a strikingly rippled surface. This horizontal molding was a motif that Hoffmann had used successfully in various designs—such as back in 1914 in the furniture for the *BUGRA*, the international book trade fair in Leipzig, as well as in the Berl house and in the design for altering the Österreichische Boden Credit-Anstalt bank in 1924—and now monumentalized here to arrive at an animated interplay of light and shade.[17] The structure of the façade is more ephemeral, in keeping with the building's purpose: "[…] a lath structure with thin walls of slats, plaster, and render," as Leopold Bauer describes it in his critique of the exhibition.[18] On the façade Bauer writes: "It was a simple, plain cuboid building, only these cuboids were given a mod-

32 33 pp. 240, 241

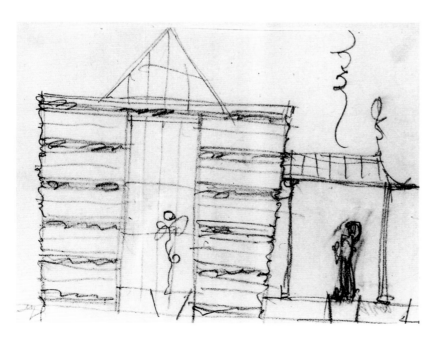

Fig. 7 JH, preliminary design for the drawing room of the Austrian pavilion at the *International Exposition of Modern Decorative and Industrial Arts*, Paris, 1925
National Gallery Prague, K 17803

Fig. 8 JH, main entrance to the
Austrian pavilion, Paris, 1925
MAK, KI 8961-60

Fig. 9 JH, drawing room with bronze statue *Der brennende
Mensch* [Man Burning] by Anton Hanak
MAK, KI 10147-63

Fig. 10 JH, preliminary drawing for the façade
of the Austrian pavilion, Paris, 1925
MAK, KI 8806-2

Fig. 11 Oskar Strnad, organ tower of the
Austrian pavilion, Paris, 1925
MAK, KI 10147-147

ern style."[19] The floor plan of the two-part pavilion, on the
8 quay and on the terrace over the Seine, enables a 76-meter-
long meandering tour through the twelve connecting rooms
arranged like links in a chain. An open passage as a thor-
oughfare for visitors to the exhibition coming from a promenade on the quayside, provides access to the parts of the
building on the shore and on the terrace. The individual
rooms are connected inside by galleries and separated outside by garden courtyards. The wing on the quay of the
Seine is designed as a building with two different heights
14 and a large gable skylight, structured by an apse and a large
display window, both part of the so-called "showcase room"
2 p. 264 for objects by the Wiener Werkstätte and the Austrian Werkbund. By way of decoration the names of men who contributed to Austria's glory are embedded in the pink render
in cement relief: Schubert, Beethoven, Mozart, etc. Each
name is accompanied by an appropriate symbol: Mozart by
1 a sphinx, Schubert by panpipes, etc. The terrace wing of
the pavilion comprises various building shapes: low galleries,
the second part of the section planned by Hoffmann, the
organ tower after a design by Oskar Strnad, the Café Vien-
12 nois by Josef Frank, and the Expressionistic glass house by
Peter Behrens.
13   Not only the pavilion's architecture, but also the overall
artistic management of the entire exhibition is placed in the
hands of Josef Hoffmann.[20] In keeping with his functions as
a professor at the School of Arts and Crafts, as an artistic
director of the Wiener Werkstätte, and as a board member
of the Austrian Werkbund, the Austrian exhibition in Paris
would focus on the work of these three institutions. A choice
that would lead to severe criticism in the course of the exhibition.[21] As in Cologne in 1914, the job of prestigiously

uniting seemingly utterly divergent aesthetic approaches in
a single building again falls to Josef Hoffmann. And once
again Hoffmann would prove himself to be a designer and
organizer who was open to quality in every area and aspect
of applied art and architecture.

In the fall of 1924 the City of Vienna held a music and
theater festival. In the course of this the *Internationale Ausstellung neuer Theatertechnik* [International Exhibition of
New Theater Technique] designed by Friedrich Kiesler was
shown in the Wiener Konzerthaus. The highlight was its
Raumbühne [Space Stage] constructed in the Mozartsaal,
with which he anticipates the *Raumstadt* [City in Space] that
he would show in Paris in 1925.[22] A couple of days after the
theater technique exhibition started, the *Jubiläumsausstellung des Wiener Kunstgewerbevereins* [Anniversary Exhibition of the Viennese Arts-and-Crafts Association] was
opened in the Austrian Museum of Art and Industry to commemorate the 40th year since its founding.[23] Many artists
who would participate in the exhibition in Paris the following
year showed works at this exhibition.[24] Its designer was Hoffmann's colleague and fellow professor at the School of Arts
and Crafts Otto Prutscher.

In Austria's provinces and provincial capitals, the deadlines for Austrian artists to register their interest in participating in the decorative arts exhibition in Paris gradually
passed. Companies were given the opportunity to contact
Josef Hoffmann directly.[25] France's keen interest in Austria's
participation was evidenced in the fact that the Austrians
were not charged rent for their exhibition areas and that the
French railroad company granted them free return transport
for their exhibits.[26] Even the Austrian national railway supported the enterprise with a generous reduction in transport
costs.

In December 1924 Dr. Adolf Vetter, former president of
the state theater administration, was appointed the Austrian
general commissioner of the decorative arts exhibition in
Paris—an auspicious choice for Josef Hoffmann.[27] Just one
month later, in late January 1925, the Austrian pavilion was
loaded onto 17 freight cars and shipped to Paris, as Berta
Zuckerkandl-Szeps reports, where it would be erected in
situ next to the Pont Alexandre III.[28] In her essay Zuckerkandl
provides an initial characterization of Hoffmann's pavilion:

> "When I spent some time in Paris a few weeks ago, a French
> member of the exhibition commission called on me. 'I congratu-
> late you as an Austrian,' he said, 'on the superb floor plan solution
> found by Josef Hoffmann. I admit that we did not find the narrow
> strip, intersected on one side by the public promenade and li-
> mited on the other by the quay walls of the Seine, especially fa-
> vorable to a possible development. Who could have anticipated
> that Josef Hoffmann would propose the bold intention to breach
> these quay walls in two places and build a 30-meter-long, 20-
> meter-wide cement terrace that would project mightily into the
> Seine? It really is a unique solution, which, besides the significant
> enlargement of the space available, guarantees that the Austrian
> pavilion will be a special attraction. Because this terrace that pro-
> jects into the Seine will be an oasis providing the nerves with
> unexpected and welcome relaxation in the middle of the fair-
> ground noise of this so widespread exhibition.'"

The exhibition was opened on 28 April 1925 by the
French president Gaston Doumergue. However, the Austrian
pavilion remained closed as the surrounding buildings and
streets were still not finished.[29] Only on 8 May 1925 did the
Austrian general commissioner Dr. Adolf Vetter finally declare
it officially open together with its artistic director and archi-

tect Josef Hoffmann. Paul Clémenceau said of the pavilion: "It is more than art that the Austrian pavilion, this precious box, proffers us. It is the World's Fair of an ingenious people."[30] In honor of the opening the organ in the organ tower was played by the multitalented artist and Polish Austrian Jan Śliwiński, in whose apartment at 20 Quai d'Orléans on the Île Saint-Louis Adolf Loos—Hoffmann's great adversary—was living at this time. Loos had left Vienna in a rage in 1923 and refused to take part in the Austrian exhibition in Paris. Josef Hoffmann reported how this had come to pass:

> "My plan thus immediately kicked off with me encouraging other artists to take part. [...] Loos told me that he wanted nothing to do with Vienna, that he himself was a Czechoslovakian citizen and would at most exhibit with Prague. He had left Austria for good. Every connection appeared to have gone sour. Unfortunately, as a Czechoslovakian citizen he would not have been able to exhibit with us anyway and so it was a futile affair."[31]

And what did Adolf Loos have to say about the building?

> "The architecture of the Austrian pavilion? It is so simple that one cannot criticize it at all. You see a kind of small African desert redoubt, but one made of concrete with wide horizontal wavy lines. This kind of wavy line is new to the Austrians and has grown dear to them."[32]

These spiteful comments were not able to detract from the pavilion's popular success. Max Eisler praised the building in *Moderne Bauformen* in 1925; Hoffmann had transformed the modern world of exhibiting in Austria

> "from a decorative matter to an architectural matter [...]. A man of 53 [sic] years, Hoffmann has remained the master of youthful freshness and imagination and design. His new building similarly combines grace with strength and has a thoroughly original form—which has become so rare in architecture and is unlikely to be seen a second time even in Paris."[33]

According to Eisler the pavilion is defined by its location and purpose. For him the pavilion is a "burgeoning, austerely branched plant, inserted into and empathizing with the landscape; indeed, virtually entangled in it." Hoffmann had "set himself the goal of providing a total presentation of our diverse handicrafts [...]. Here, too, he has remained true to his tradition, the best spirit of Austrian exhibition culture." To reduce costs, Hoffmann had foregone opulently filling the space,

> "but not the organic unity of building and forming, and not that which makes us contemplate them: spatial art. Opened up with tall windows, with arcades, courtyards, and passages, his house became a shrine of a thousand treasures to admire and stroll through. His leitmotif—in Rome the loggia, in Cologne the courtyard—was the 'passage,' in terms of both approach and traverse."[34]

Indeed, Eisler believed Hoffmann had conditioned the visitors to the pavilion through the sequence of rooms: "They fall into the slightly liberated, finely restrained Viennese rhythm." The twelve rooms of the pavilion, the "exciting house of the Austrians tells of part of the whole, of the highly talented hybrid of these 'frontier Germans.' And shows that this section of the competition of precious works still leads the way, that—despite hardship and revolution—it remains a joy-giving force of general culture."

The pavilion in Paris would become a reference project for Josef Hoffmann's career in the 1920s, bearing in mind the appearance he had architecturally staged for the politically young Austria in Paris had caused a controversy in which Hoffmann himself and the architects, artists, art historians, and art writers close to him from the milieu of the School of Arts and Crafts, Wiener Werkstätte, and Werkbund each spoke out in turns against the enterprise's critics in the newspapers—indeed, they downright fought a verbal duel.[35] The building would go on to be cited many times in Art Deco architecture.[36] As Eduard F. Sekler observed, with the

Fig. 12 JH and Josef Frank, terrace of Café Viennois on the Seine, Paris, 1925
MAK, KI 10147-111

Fig. 13 Peter Behrens, greenhouse on the Seine,
Austrian pavilion, Paris, 1925
MAK, KI 8961-51

"[Josef Hoffmann] has all of a sudden become greater than Vienna can bear, and it is obliged to fear he might ultimately become as strong as his great teacher Otto Wagner. […] The world is the oyster of an architect of such high status, especially now after receiving public approval as a result of his great success in Paris. If he calmly goes to Berlin, Holland, or America, then two years later Vienna will lionize and enthuse over him and only him."[39]

Bahr's "right man for America" himself, by now decorated as a Knight of the French Legion of Honor, has a cool-headed response to several articles opposing the Paris pavilion and Hoffmann himself that were published in *Die Stune* under pseudonyms of the poster designer Julius Klinger, a supporter of Adolf Loos. In 1926 Hoffmann replies under the title "Meine Gegner und ich" ("My Opponents and I"):

"It pleases Mr. Julius Klinger as an advertising expert to introduce a new, in his opinion American, touch to our different-natured art world by occupying himself with public attacks directed primarily against myself, most of which are teeming with such venom and—in the basics—with such invalidity that it is impossible to respond. […] The coming new issues of our age preoccupy us all immensely and I do not believe that a fair judge can consider our school backward in this relationship. We look to America with the greatest interest […]. Similarly, the Bauhaus movement in Germany, the young art from France and Russia is also very dear to us. Obviously, it is nevertheless our intention to give our kin their own unique appearance. It pleases Mister Klinger to praise me as an organizer. I would be glad if he were right, because I have always held every organizational task in the highest respect, I judge it to be the most important matter imaginable—indeed, to be the actual creative Americanism. Unfortunately, I fear I am unable to agree with him in this regard either."[40]

Yet the architect and organizer Josef Hoffmann had succeeded in Paris in 1925 by charging an exhibition pavilion with aesthetics and drawing a close cultural portrait of Austria with his design work for the young First Republic in a way that could be easily conveyed in the media. The reviews, even the negative ones, found in his favor. ∎

pavilion Hoffmann had found "a way to come to terms with the Modern Movement without surrendering his artistic integrity" in the years after 1925.[37]

Hans Tietze calls Josef Hoffmann's pavilion "a work by our artistic field staff, those artists who come to mind every time that Austria needs worthy representation abroad";[38] Hermann Bahr even recommends he leave the country:

1   "Pariser Warenhäuser," in: *Vorarlberger Landes-Zeitungen* 6 May 1911, 9.
2   "Eine Ausstellung für dekorative Kunst in Paris," in: *Neues Wiener Journal* 12 Apr 1911, 6.
3   "Eine internationale Kunstgewerbe-Ausstellung in Paris," in: *Prager Tagblatt* 17 May 1911, 9.
4   "Projekt einer Internationalen Ausstellung für Kunstgewerbe, Paris 1914," in: *Wiener Montags-Zeitung* 3 Jul 1911, 11.
5   "Internationale Kunstgewerbeausstellung in Paris 1922," in: *Pester Lloyd* (evening edition) 5 Dec 1919, 6.
6   "Eine gute Antwort nach Paris," in: *Linzer Tages-Post* 7 Feb 1920, 3.
7   "Internationale Kunstgewerbe-Ausstellung in Paris 1925," in: *Christliche Kunstblätter* (64) 7–9 1923, 111.
8   "Plan einer kunstgewerblichen Ausstellung in Paris," in: *Neues Wiener Journal* 5 Oct 1923, 10.
9   Exhibited works by Josef Hoffmann include the *Ruheraum einer Dame* [Lady's Relaxation Room], which was shown in Paris again two years later. Peter Behrens' *Gelehrtenstube* [Scholars' Room], exhibited in 1923, atmospherically anticipates

that which Behrens once again realized in "his" glass house in Paris in 1925.
10 See e.g.: H. T., "Unser Kunsthandwerk. Zur Eröffnung der Ausstellung im Österreichischen Museum für Kunst und Industrie," in: *Neues Wiener Tagblatt* 30 Sep 1923, 9.
11 "Ausstellung des modernen Kunsthandwerkes in Paris," in: *Wiener Zeitung* 7 Feb 1924, 6.
12 "Die Pariser Ausstellung," in: *Neues Wiener Tagblatt* 2 Mar 1924, 9.
13 "Die Beteiligung Österreichs an der Pariser Kunstgewerbeausstellung," in: *Neues Wiener Tagblatt* 19 Apr 1924, 20. A fundamental publication on this topic is: Kristan, Markus, *L'Autriche à Paris 1925 – Österreich auf der Kunstgewerbeausstellung 1925*, Weitra 2018.
14 "Internationale Kunstgewerbeausstellung Paris 1925," in: *Wiener Zeitung* 28 Jun 1924, 8.
15 Hoffmann, Josef, "Die kommende Weltausstellung in Paris," in: *Neues Wiener Journal* 6 Jul 1924, 17–18.
16 Zuckerkandl, Berta, "Das österreichische Kunstgewerbe in Paris," in: *Neues Wiener Journal* 30 Jul 1924, 4–5.

17 Sekler, Eduard F., *Josef Hoffmann: The Architectural Work*, Princeton, NJ 1985, 184 f. Trans. Eduard F. Sekler and John Maass.
18 Bauer, Leopold, "Österreich und die Pariser Ausstellung für moderne dekorative Kunst, Ein Nachwort von Oberbaurat Leopold Bauer," in: *Wiener Sonn- und Montags-Zeitung* 25 Jan 1926, 7.
19 See note 17.
20 His fellow professor at the Vienna School of Arts and Crafts, the sculptor and painter Eugen Steinhof, remarked: "The artistic direction lies in the hands of the chief construction counselor Professor Hoffmann, a true creative soul; all mental acrobatics that lead to formless nothingness are far from his thoughts. As such no true achievement will go unnoticed, and as a result Austria will win first place." Steinhof, Eugen, "Österreich auf der Kunstgewerbeausstellung in Paris 1925," in: *Neues Wiener Journal* 15 Nov 1924, 5.
21 See Kristan 2018 (see note 13).
22 "Internationale theatertechnische Ausstellung," in: *Linzer Tages-Post* 23 Jul 1924, 7; K. Sfd., "Die illusionslose Bühne. Zur bevorstehenden internationalen Ausstellung neuer Theatertechnik," in:

Fig. 14 JH, long hall of the Austrian pavilion at the *International Exposition
of Modern Decorative and Industrial Arts*, Paris, 1925
MAK, KI 10147-154

Neue Freie Presse 6 Sep 1924, 8; -ld, "Das ent-
fesselte Theater. Internationale Ausstellung neuer
Theatertechnik," in: *Neues Wiener Tagblatt* 24
Sep 1924, 8.

23 "Jubiläumsausstellung des Wiener Kunstge-
werbevereines," in: *Wiener Zeitung* 27 Sep 1924,
10–11.

24 Ankwicz-Kleehoven, Hans, "Vierzig Jahre Wiener
Kunstgewerbeverein. (Die Jubiläumsausstellung
im Österreichischen Museum)," in: *Wiener Zeitung* 2 Dec 1924, 1–3.

25 "Internationale Kunstgewerbausstellung in Paris,"
in: *Reichspost* 22 Nov 1924, 11.

26 E.g.: "Internationale Kunstgewerbausstellung
Paris 1925," in: *Tagblatt* (Linz) 22 Oct 1924, 5.

27 "Der Vertreter Österreichs auf der Pariser Kunstgewerbausstellung," in: *Neues Wiener Journal*
12 Dec 1924, 9. Adolf Vetter (1867–1942) was well
known to Josef Hoffmann, considering he was one
of the co-initiators and board members of the Austrian Werkbund and in that position sought to
spread an understanding of art and the decorative
arts, as well as to establish further collaboration
between artists, artisans, and industrialists.

28 Zuckerkandl-Szeps, Berta, "Die Pariser Ausstellung 1925. Der österreichische Pavillon. – Das internationale Theater. – Ausstellungsfeste," in:
Neues Wiener Journal 10 Feb 1925, 7–8.

29 "Österreichische Künstler auf der Pariser Kunstgewerbausstellung," in: *Neues Wiener Journal*
26 Apr 1925, 23.

30 Paul Clémenceau to the Austrian trade minister
Hans Schürff, quoted in Kristan 2018 (see note
13).

31 "Wer ist an der österreichischen Kunstpleite
schuld? Professor Josef Hoffmann schreibt der
'Stunde' über seine Tätigkeit in Paris – Josef
Hoffmann, Meine Gegner und ich," in: *Die Stunde*
10 Jan 1926, 6.

32 Saint-Macret (possibly a pseudonym of Adolf
Loos), "Une heure de promenade aux Arts
décoratifs. Premier coup d'œil. –En Autriche," in:
L'intransigeant 7 Jun 1925. A German translation
of the French can be found in Adolf Loos's written
estate in Vienna.

33 Eisler, Max, "Österreich in Paris," in: *Moderne
Bauformen* (VIII) 1 1925, 249.

34 Ibid.

35 The most important essays can be found in Kristan 2018 (see note 13), 109–273.

36 On this see the article "Beauty in Utility: The
Reception of Josef Hoffmann in Belgium and
France" by Adrian Prieto in this catalog, and
Sekler 1985 (see note 17), 186 ff.

37 Sekler 1985 (see note 17), 190.

38 Tietze, Hans, "Das österreichische Kunstgewerbe
in Paris," in: *Neues Wiener Tagblatt* 26 May
1925, 7.

39 Bahr, Hermann, "Tagebuch," in: *Neues Wiener
Journal* 25 Dec 1925, 14.

40 Hoffmann 1926 (see note 31).

1926
1933

R. Lechner (Wilhelm Müller), Josef Hoffmann, 1931
Kunsthandel Widder, Vienna

Fig. 1 JH, cabinet, executed by Anton Pospischil,
displayed at the Kunstschau at the AMAI in 1927
Wood, painted orange
Private collection

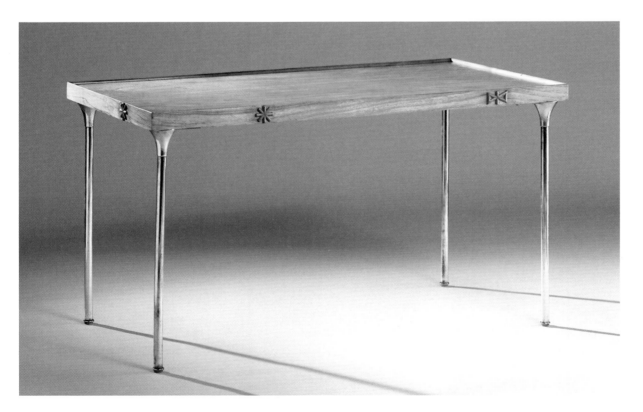

Fig. 2 JH, table for a tea salon, executed by Jakob Soulek, displayed in the exhibition
Die neuzeitliche Wohnung [The Contemporary Home] at the AMAI in 1928
Walnut and brass
MAK, H 3332 – dedication Dr. E. Ploil
© MAK/Georg Mayer

Fig. 3 JH, letter-paper box, executed by the Wiener Werkstätte, 1926
Leather, gold embossing
Dr. E. Ploil Collection

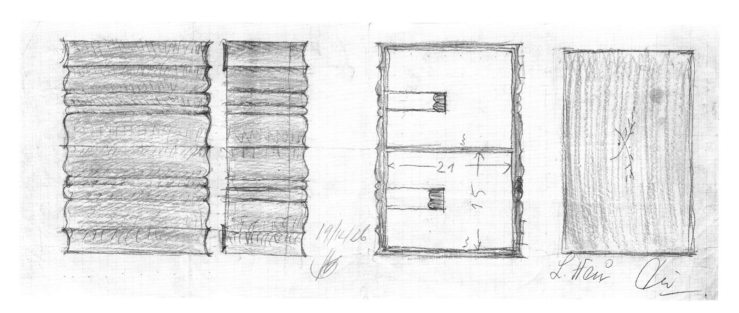

Fig. 4 JH, design for a letter-paper box for the Wiener Werkstätte, 1926
MAK, KI 12046-23-1

Fig. 5 JH, design for a sideboard, ca. 1930
UAA, Collection and Archive, 109

Fig. 6 JH, design for a coffeepot and matching coffee cup, 1928
MAK, KI 8844-1

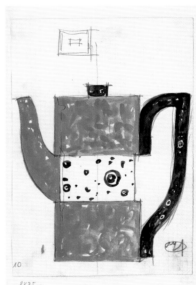

Fig. 7 JH, design for a coffeepot, 1928
MAK, KI 8835

Fig. 8 JH, fabric *Tenor*, executed by the Wiener Werkstätte, 1928
MAK, WWS 762
© MAK/Branislav Djordjevic

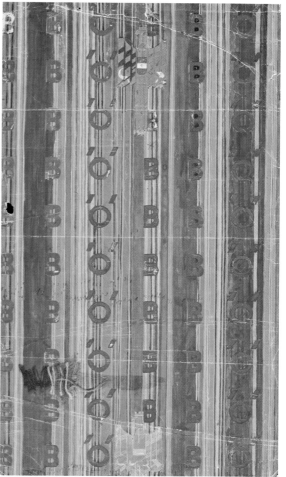

Fig. 9 JH, working drawing for the fabric covering of the 1st-class coach of the ÖBB, executed by J. & J. Backhausen (design no. 10416), 1930
Backhausen Archive, BA 05665

Fig. 10 JH, cup with saucer, executed by the Augarten Porcelain Manufactory (set form no. 18, decoration no. 5544), 1929
Porcelain, glazed white, red and black decoration
Wien Museum, 58339/1 & 2

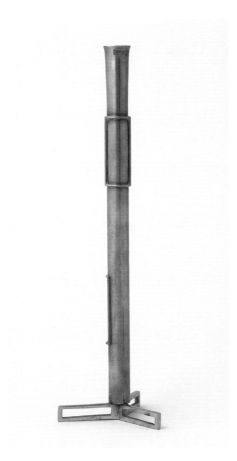

Fig. 11 JH, vase, executed by the
Wiener Werkstätte, 1929
Brass
Wien Museum, 53736/1

Fig. 12 JH, vase, executed by the
Wiener Werkstätte, 1928
Brass
Private collection
© MAK/Georg Mayer

Fig. 13 JH, trophy for the winner of
the 1930 polo game, executed by
the Wiener Werkstätte, 1929
Silver
MAK, GO 1798
© MAK/Katrin Wißkirchen

Fig. 14 JH, 5-branch candelabra,
executed by the Wiener Werkstätte, 1930
Nickel silver
MAK, GO 2018
© MAK/Aslan Kudrnofsky

Fig. 15 JH, 6-branch candelabra,
executed by the Wiener Werkstätte, 1928
Silver
MAK, GO 1796
© MAK/Katrin Wißkirchen

Fig. 16 JH, coffee set, executed by
the Wiener Werkstätte, 1929
Silver, rosewood
Wien Museum, 53.708/1-6

Fig. 17 JH, espresso set, executed by
the Wiener Werkstätte, 1928
Silver, ebony
MAK, GO 1797
© MAK/Georg Mayer

Fig. 18 JH, tea set, executed by
the Wiener Werkstätte, 1928
Silver, ebony
MAK, GO 2008
© MAK/Georg Mayer

Fig. 19 JH, housing complex for the municipality of Vienna, Anton-Hölzl-Hof (future designation),
Laxenburger Straße 94, 1928–1932, courtyard with sculpture by Otto Fenzl
MAK, KI 8951-43

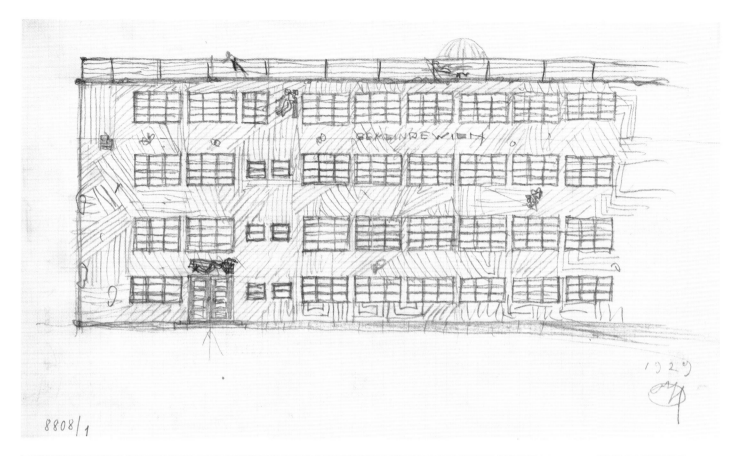

Figs. 20, 21 JH, design for an apartment complex for Vienna's
Werkbundsiedlung on the Laaerberg, façade sketch, 1929, and model, 1930
MAK, KI 8808-1, 8969-7

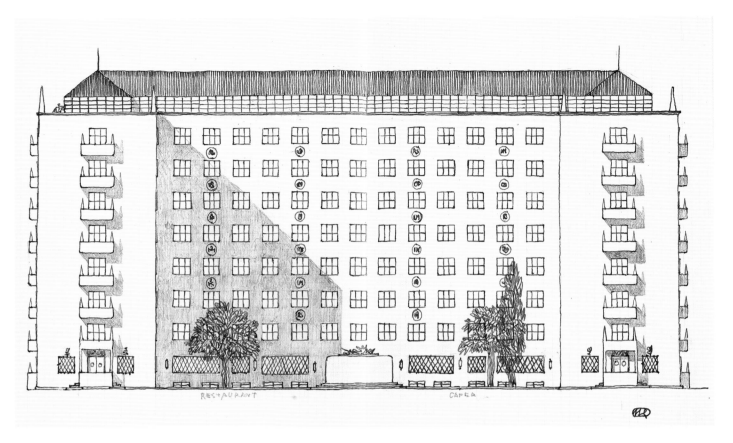

Fig. 22 JH, design sketch for a municipal apartment building, n.d.
Kunsthandel Widder, Vienna

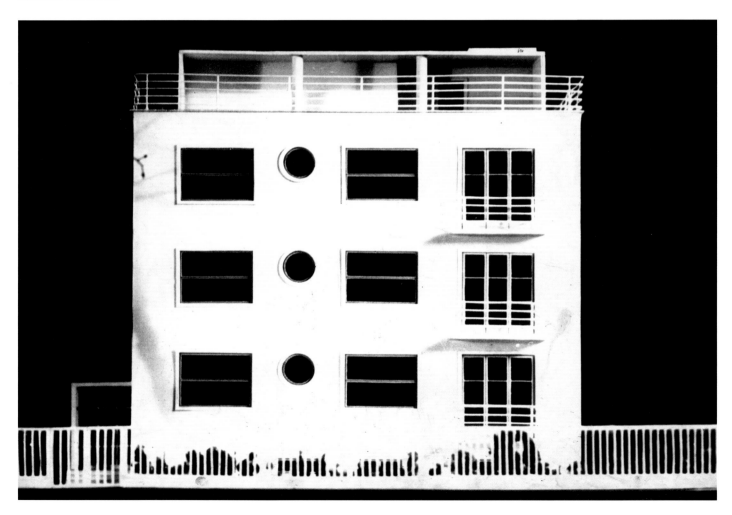

Fig. 23 JH, design for a multistory house, before 1931
Model view
MAK, KI 8969-10

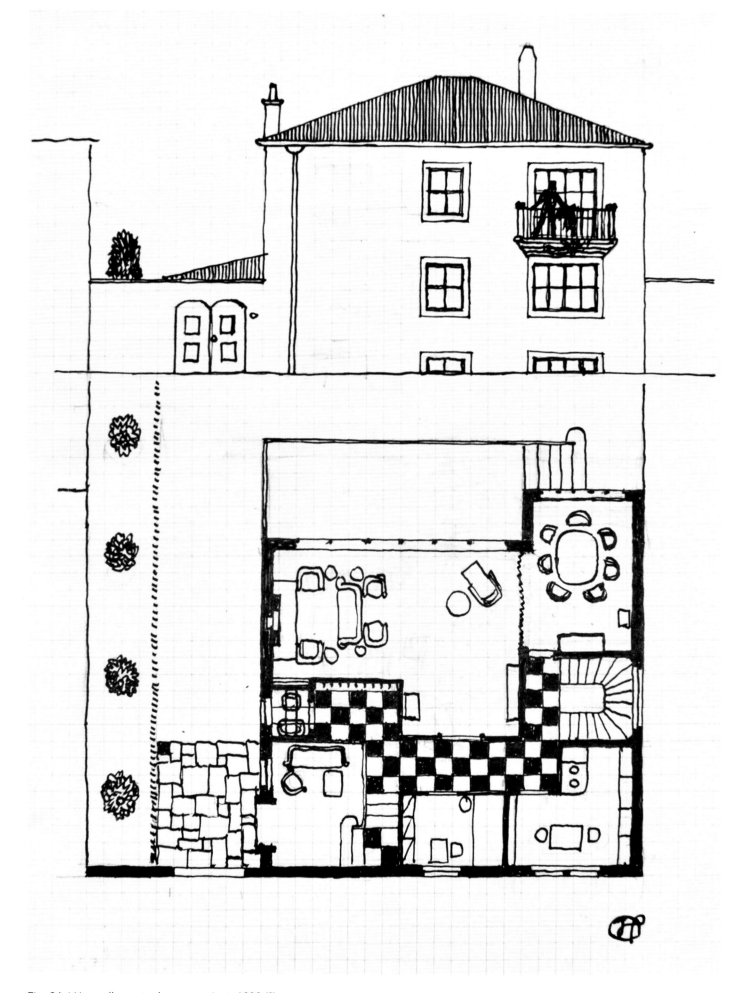

Fig. 24 J H, small country house, project, 1932 (?)
Graphic Collection, Academy of Fine Arts Vienna, HZ 26310

Fig. 25 JH, festival hall or *Welttonhalle* [World Concert Hall] for Gustav Mäurer's Welt-Musik-
und-Sanges-Bund (World Music and Song Association), Vienna, Augarten, 1927, main hall
MBF (26) 1927, 168

Figs. 26, 27 JH, steel house for the Vogel & Noot company, 1928, prototype
MBF (28) 1929, 77–78

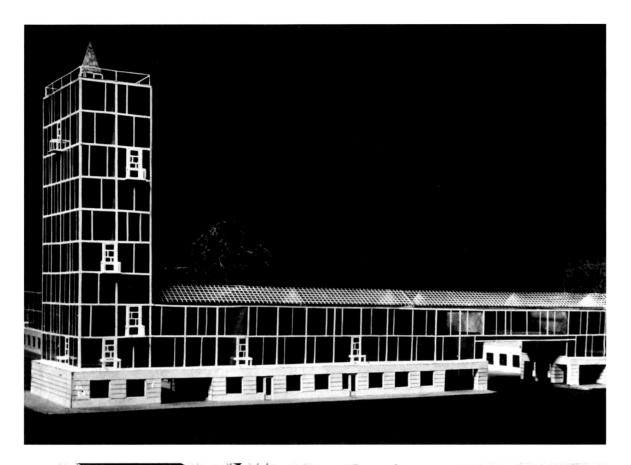

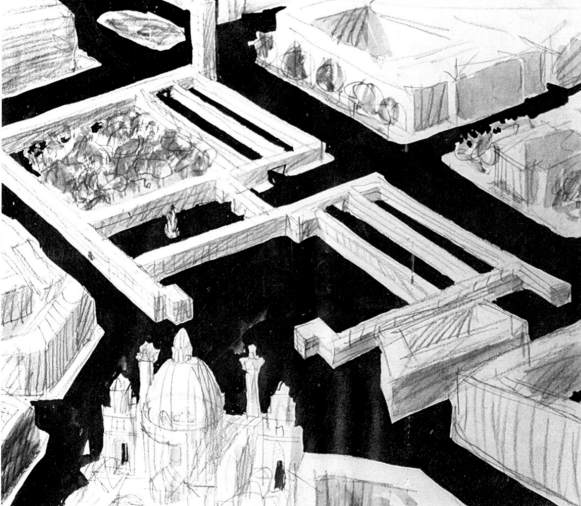

Figs. 28, 29 JH, art and exhibition hall for Vienna, Karlsplatz, 1928/29,
model view and bird's-eye view
MAK, KI 8951-74; ANL, Vienna 8410795

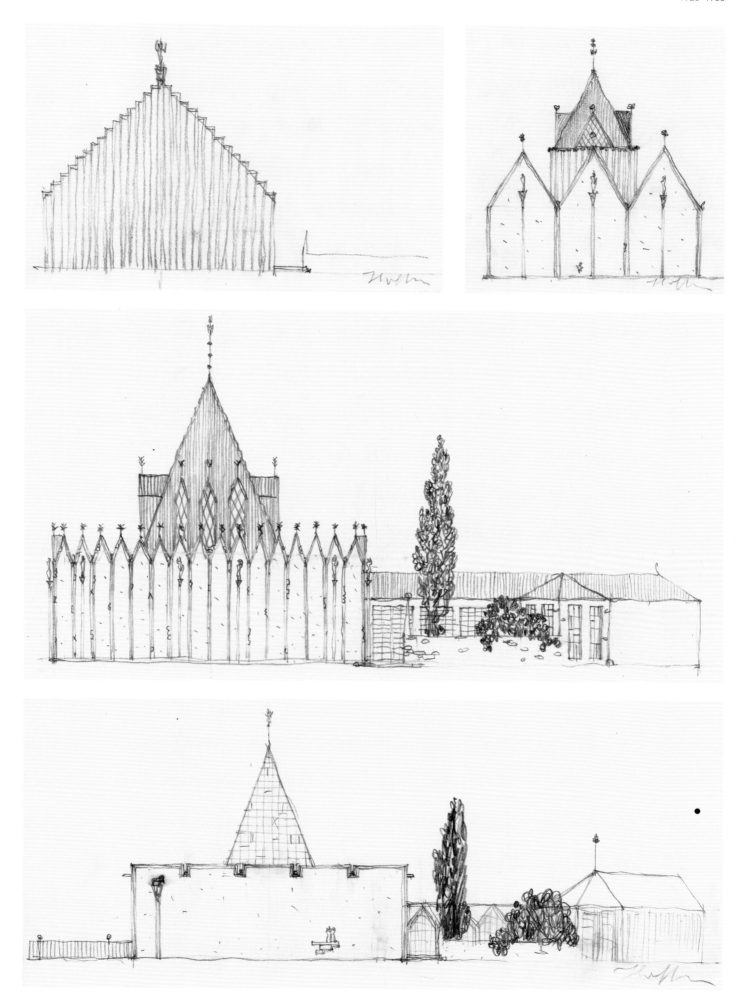

Fig. 30 JH, competition project for the synagogue in Sillein/Žilina (SVK), 1928, design sketches
Graphic Collection, Academy of Fine Arts Vienna, HZ 26314-26317

Josef Hoffmann
1926
1933

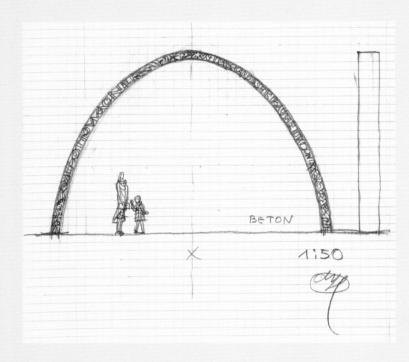

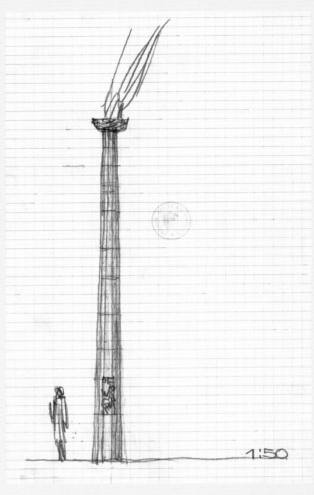

JH, two designs for the Otto Wagner
monument on Heldenplatz, Vienna, 1929
MAK, KI 8815-9, -6

1927

At the Kunstschau at the AMAI in 1927, which is organized by Oswald Haerdtl, Hoffmann shows two decorated and furnished rooms. Interior decoration job for Ernst Bauer in Vienna. The Wiener Werkstätte is once again in financial straits and has to commence composition proceedings. The acrimonious antagonism of Adolf Loos, who lambasts the "eclecticist bric-a-brac art" ("Das Wiener Weh [Wiener Werkstätte] – Eine Abrechnung," *Neue Freie Presse* 21 Apr 1927, 67) of the WW in lectures and newspaper articles, and his supporters plunge Hoffmann into depression. The first monograph on Hoffmann's creative work is written by his assistant Leopold Kleiner. Hoffmann becomes a corresponding member of the American Institute of Architects.

1928–1930

House for Isidor Diamant and office building for Industria Sarmej S.A. in Klausenburg/Cluj-Napoca, Romania. Project for a *Welttonhalle* [World Con-

cert Hall] for Vienna's Augarten park. Competition design for the synagogue in Sillein/Žilina (now in Slovakia), which is later built by Peter Behrens. In 1928 Hoffmann is awarded the Golden Coin of Honor by the Österreichischer Ingenieur- und Architektenverein (Austrian Association of Engineers and Architects), whose member he becomes in 1931. To celebrate 25 years since the founding of the Wiener Werkstätte, a comprehensive retrospective is presented in the form of the volume *Wiener Werkstätte. Modernes Kunstgewerbe und sein Weg*—commonly known as the "Kachel-Katalog" (so-called tile catalog)—which was designed and edited by Mathilde Flögl and had a papier-mâché binding reminiscent of tile patterns, which was designed by Vally Wieselthier and Gudrun Baudisch. In it Le Corbusier describes Josef Hoffmann as a "steadfast seeker, a true trailblazer," to whom he wants to "pay thanks." In 1929 Hoffmann furnishes the villa that was constructed by Fried-

rich Weinwurm for the attorney Arpad Lengyel in Bratislava. In Vienna he produces the interior design for the Doblinger phonograph shop at Dorotheergasse 10. Redesigns rooms in the former Skywa-Primavesi villa. Shop furnishings for the new WW branch in Berlin. Design of the music room at the exhibition *Wiener Raumkünstler* [Viennese Room Artists] at the AMAI. With 332 apartments Hoffmann plans his largest municipal housing project for the City of Vienna on Laxenburger Straße in 1928–1932. Nominated as a juror for the Palais des Nations competition in Geneva by the Austrian federal government. Hoffmann is busy with major projects and house building. The International Style, Le Corbusier, and the Bauhaus become his inspiration. Works on a series of urban planning projects, including an art and exhibition hall on Karlsplatz in Vienna. Hoffmann delivers plans for the redevelopment of Vienna's old town and for a monument to Otto Wagner for Vienna's Heldenplatz. Shop furnishings and portal of the Altmann & Kühne confectionery together with Oswald Haerdtl, with whom he also redesigns the Grabencafé. Entire layout of the Austrian Werkbund exhibition at the AMAI in 1930. Vice president of the Austrian branch of the Werkbund. Armand Weiser's book on Josef Hoffmann is published in Geneva in 1930 as part of the series "Meister der Baukunst" ("Masters of Architecture"). The Triennale in Monza honors Hoffmann, as well as Frank Lloyd Wright, Ludwig Mies van der Rohe, and Le Corbusier, with a solo show. That same year, the AMAI dedicates an anniversary exhibition to him for his 60th birthday. In the model housing development built by the Werkbund in Vienna, Hoffmann builds four row houses (until 1932).

1932

The row houses in the Werkbundsiedlung (Werkbund Estate) exceed all expected costs. The controversy leads Hoffmann to withdraw from the Werkbund. The Wiener Werkstätte is forced to register bankruptcy; Hoffmann is not kept on as its artistic director. Liquidation of the Wiener Werkstätte and auctioning of all remaining stock. At Vienna's spring fair, Josef Hoffmann presents the prototype for a "growing house" made of prefabricated steel components, which was jointly developed with the structural steelwork engineering company Vogel & Noot. Oswald Haerdtl becomes a partner at Hoffmann's studio. ■

JH, housing complex for the municipality of Vienna, Laxenburger Straße 94, 1928–1932, courtyard with sculpture by Otto Fenzl
Kunsthandel Widder, Vienna

Oswald Haerdtl, design of the Hoffmann retrospective at the AMAI, Vienna, 1930/31
Photo: Oswald Haerdtl, UAA 1978, 30

15

Fig. 1 JH, unexecuted design for the Vienna Secession room,
pavilion at the Louisiana Purchase Exposition, St. Louis, 1904

Vereinigung bildender Künstler Österreichs Secession, *Ver Sacrum: Die Wiener Secession
und die Ausstellung in St. Louis*, Vienna 1904, 15

Christopher Long

From Vienna to Hollywood

Josef Hoffmann and America

In late May 1956, the *New York Times* published a short notice of Josef Hoffmann's death in Vienna, at the age of 85.[1] The information concerning his passing came from Leopold Kleiner, who had once been Hoffmann's student at the Vienna School of Arts and Crafts and, later, his *Assistent*.[2] In the wake of the Anschluss, Kleiner had immigrated to the United States and was then living in New York. The brief obituary was his way of honoring his long-term mentor.[3]

It is not clear whether the *Times* would have run an obituary had Kleiner not made the effort. Hoffmann's reputation, by 1956, was in nearly full eclipse. He represented a generation of Modernists whose time had long since passed, and he had produced little work of importance for more than a decade. Still, the old architect's connections to New York—and, for that matter, to the American design world—had once been extensive. He was the most renowned and influential of the Viennese designers of his time in the United States. Even more, he had contributed in far-reaching ways to the rise and development of American Modernism.

Scarcely any of that, however, comes through in the *Times* obituary. It notes merely that Hoffmann was "a pioneer in modern architecture and design," and that he had been a "founder and leader for thirty years of the Wiener Werkstaette [sic], a famous artcraft center." About his place in American Modernism, there is only silence.[4]

Hoffmann's impress on America extended for most of the first three decades of the 20th century. What he contributed came in the form of a plea for a new and powerful aesthetic, not in words to be sure, since he wasn't a confident or fluent writer, but through his extraordinary designs. It was a vision more than a few found inspiring, and it would not be an exaggeration to say that there was more than a fine streak of the Hoffmannesque running through much of early American Modernism.[5]

Unlike Adolf Loos, Hoffmann never visited the United States. Although he had several opportunities, he never took them up.[6] But Hoffmann's influence in the United States began early. He came to the notice of the most perceptive American observers already in the late 1890s, in publications, such as *Ver Sacrum* or *Der Architekt*, and to those who ventured to Vienna around the turn of the century and encountered his work there. To those who followed the European art scene closely, the advent of the Secession, and Hoffmann's role in it, was evident nearly from the outset. It would be several more years, though, before anyone living in America had the chance to see Hoffmann's work. His first appearance on the American scene did not come until 1904, at the Louisiana Purchase Exposition in St. Louis.

Austria almost turned down the invitation to erect a pavilion, but when it was learned that among the major powers only the Ottoman Empire was not intending to send an exhibit, plans were hastily formed to submit an entry. The initial scheme for the Austrian pavilion in St. Louis had called for Hoffmann to design a room for the Vienna Secession, in which, above all, Gustav Klimt's paintings were to be presented. Hoffmann wanted the room to be a true temple of art. He produced a spare and elegant design that provided prominent spaces for several of Klimt's works (including his controversial university paintings, *Philosophy*, 1900, and *Jurisprudence*, 1903), as well as pedestals displaying sculptures by Franz Metzner.[7]

Dominating Hoffmann's composition, as was so often the case in his interiors of those years, is an insistent and evocative rectilinearity applied to all of the framing surfaces—walls, floors, and ceiling. The design, however, angered many within the Secession's membership, especially the more traditional easel painters, who vehemently protested their exclusion. Government officials attempted to find a compromise, but the leaders of the Secession objected to their interference. In the end, the group withdrew, and the design was never executed.[8]

Hoffmann did have the opportunity to design another room, a smaller space devoted to the Vienna School of Arts and Crafts.[9] Even more than his original conception, it presented an image of refinement and modern astringency. The color palette was highly controlled, limited to black, white, and gray. Vitrines placed in niches and a few tables set off to the side displayed works by the school's students and faculty. Most of the room, however, was left open. The overwhelming impression was conveyed through Hoffmann's restraint. It was a compelling essay in reduction and geometric purity, one that was wholly new to Americans.

The reactions in the American press mostly stressed the colorfulness of the pavilion's other displays. But at least one

1

2

Fig. 2 JH, Vienna School of Arts and Crafts room in the Austrian
pavilion at the Louisiana Purchase Exposition, St. Louis, 1904
Joseph Urban Collection, Performing Art Collections, Rare Books and
Manuscript Library, Columbia University, New York.

observer, Frank Lloyd Wright, saw the inherent lessons. After touring the Austrian exhibits, he was so impressed that he paid the train fare for one of his draftsmen, Barry Byrne, to see the spaces.[10]

Wright would find in the stylistic language of the Secessionists ideas he would incorporate in his own work. A few others, such as the New York architects Robert D. Kohn and Emery Roth, Chicago architect George W. Maher, and St. Louis architect Thomas P. Barnett, appropriated elements of the new Austrian design for their buildings.[11] But more significant, perhaps, were two other young Americans who spent time in Vienna. There they encountered—and were directly influenced by—Hoffmann's designs.

One of them was the Ohio-born graphic artist Dard Hunter. Hunter was so taken with Hoffmann's work from publications he saw that he decided to spend part of his honeymoon in Vienna, in 1908. Two years later, he returned to attend courses at the Graphische Lehr- und Versuchsanstalt (Graphic Teaching and Experimental Design Institute). After he went back to the US, working mostly on his own, he developed a highly purified design language that reproduced some elements of Hoffmann's work.[12]

In those same years, another young American, Edward Aschermann, also undertook an extended trip to Vienna.[13]

The son of German immigrants, Aschermann had grown up in Milwaukee, Wisconsin. Around the turn of the century, he studied art at the Académie Julian in Paris. While in Vienna, he acquired a more than superficial understanding of Hoffmann's aesthetic, which he subsequently displayed in a series of drawings he made for Box Furniture, a book by social reformer Louise Brigham.[14] Later, between 1912 and 1916, Aschermann and his wife, Gladys, made and installed various Hoffmann-inspired interiors in apartments and houses in New York.[15]

The works of Hunter and the Aschermanns remained mostly out of the public eye, but eight years after the St. Louis exposition, in 1912, John Cotton Dana at the Newark Museum of Art put together a traveling exhibition of German and Austrian designs, including works by Hoffmann, for the Wiener Werkstätte.[16] The show made stops in Newark, Chicago, Indianapolis, Pittsburgh, Cincinnati, and St. Louis, attracting throngs of visitors along the way.

Americans—at least those who had a sophisticated understanding of the design scene in Europe—also continued to read about Hoffmann and his designs in The Studio and other art publications.[17] The years of World War I, however, brought a cessation to direct American contacts with Vienna, and it was not until Joseph Urban launched the Wiener Werk-

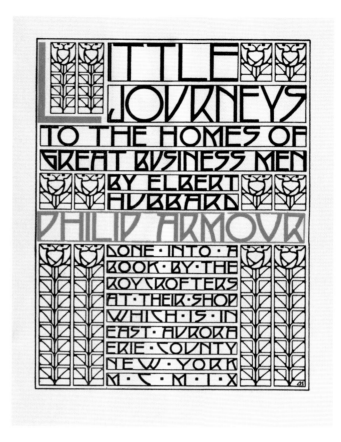

Fig. 3 Dard Hunter, book cover for Hubbard, Elbert, *Little Journeys to the Homes of Great Businessmen: Philip Armour*, New York 1909
Private collection

stätte of America in New York in 1922, that most of the public had the opportunity to see Hoffmann's more recent designs firsthand.[18]

The Wiener Werkstätte of America, Inc., proved to be a spectacular failure. It lasted barely a year and a half before quietly closing, nearly bankrupting Urban in the process. Even so, many of those who visited the remarkable interiors Urban had installed in his gallery at 581 Fifth Avenue (and at the Art Institute of Chicago, where he mounted a brief exhibition) were awed. Sales, however, were disappointing. Most of the public found the objects strangely exotic and overwrought.

Nonetheless, the impact of Urban's effort resounded for some time. Several Austrian-born designers, including Urban and Paul T. Frankl, were able to translate Hoffmann's design mannerisms in a way Americans found more acceptable. Frankl, in particular, became extraordinarily successful selling Viennese-inspired pieces at his Frankl Galleries at 4 East 48th Street in Manhattan.[19] And a few others, including Rena Rosenthal, sister of the prominent architect Ely Jacques Kahn, sold Hoffmann's designs in her exclusive shop on Madison Avenue.[20]

Throughout the 1920s, better-off Americans were again making the trek to Vienna. A few visited (and bought articles at) the Wiener Werkstätte shop on the Neustiftgasse. And at least one young woman, Lillian Langseth-Christensen, studied with Hoffmann in those years.[21] His greatest moment of visibility, though, came in another exhibition, the *International Exposition of Art in Industry*.

The show was held at Macy's New York department store in May 1928. Hoffmann was in excellent company: among those non-Americans contributing were Bruno Paul and Gio Ponti.[22] He installed two spaces, a boudoir and a powder room.[23] The boudoir was an older design, the *Ruheraum einer Dame* [Lady's Relaxation Room], he had first exhibited at the Austrian Museum of Art and Industry (today's MAK) in 1923.[24] Executed in polished walnut by August Ungethüm, it featured a striking and elegant daybed set into a deep niche and surrounded with shelving, a desk, and painted panels resembling inlay work from Maria Strauss-Likarz. (Hoffmann recycled the design, with small variations, at the 1925 Paris exposition and then at Macy's.[25])

Fig. 4 Edward Aschermann, *A Corner of the Nursery*, frontispiece from Brigham, Louise, *Box Furniture: How to Make a Hundred Useful Articles for the Home*, New York 1909
Private collection

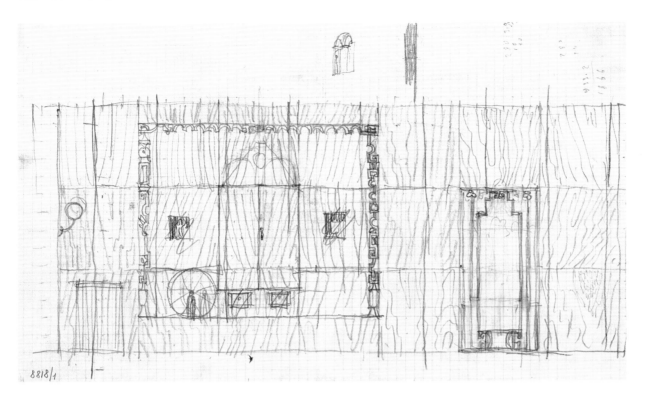

Fig. 5 JH, original sketch for a boudoir
(*Ruheraum einer Dame* [Lady's Relaxation Room]), 1925
MAK, KI 8818-1

Fig. 6 Josef Hoffmann, powder room, exhibited at
the *International Exposition of Art in Industry*, Macy's
Department Store, New York, 14–26 May 1928
Courtesy of Macy's East, Inc., New York

It was the second of these spaces, the powder room, however, which attracted far greater attention. It was a new design for Hoffmann, a creative imagining of the possibilities of combining glass, mirrors, and chromed metals. He arranged the room with glass or mirrors on the floors, walls, and ceiling in such a way, as one observer noted, "to allow a visitor to see herself or himself in ten separate images."[26] So popular was the space, a reporter for the *New York Times* wrote, that "yesterday afternoon the crowds in front of this room had to be held back."[27] Elisabeth L. Cary, the reviewer for the *Times*, offered a more sober and insightful statement: "Austria's representation includes two rooms by Josef Hoffmann [...] whose designs for textiles and furniture have been marked by the peculiar elegance of Viennese art in its higher manifestations. The inclusion of these countries [here she is referring to Austria and Germany] ont [sic] only brings into the exhibition dominant factors in the development of modern design, but it will also indicate to acute observers sources of influence in our own rapidly unfolding fabric of industrial art."[28]

Cary was entirely correct in pointing to the broad influences of Central European Modernism in the United States. What she failed to note was the reason, perhaps because it was so well known at the time: a sizeable number of the important modern designers in New York, Chicago, Los Angeles, and elsewhere had come from the region, and most had been stimulated by, or had at least partially drawn their individual styles from, Hoffmann. (The membership of the leading organization of US designers at the time, the American Union of Decorative Artists and Craftsmen, or AUDAC, was so heavily German-speaking that at their luncheons German could be heard nearly as often as English.)[29]

Frankl, who was the founder of AUDAC, knew very well Hoffmann's importance; he frequently included photographs of Hoffmann's recent designs in his publications and lectures.[30] But even if Frankl had not acknowledged the debt

Fig. 7 Wolfgang Hoffmann, coffee table,
manufactured by the Howell Company,
Geneva, IL, ca. 1930
Chrome-plated steel, glass
Courtesy of Wright, Chicago

he and others had to Hoffmann, his presence in the American scene was embedded in countless designs. It came out most visibly in a penchant for pure geometries and simplified floriferous motifs. Hoffmann also had some part in awakening the popularity of the modernized Classicism that ran through so much of the American scene.

In the later 1920s and 1930s, one could see echoes of Hoffmann in the works shown at the American Designers' Gallery, in the various AUDAC exhibitions and publications, and in interiors and galleries in New York, Chicago, Los Angeles, and other cities.[31] Hoffmann's ideas were also carried directly to the United States through the work of his son Wolfgang, Wolfgang's wife Pola (née Josefine Pola Weinbach, later Pola Stout), and several of his students from the School of Arts and Crafts or former coworkers from the Wiener Werkstätte (among them Vally Wieselthier, Susi Singer, and Joseph Binder), who had emigrated from Austria to the U.S. in those years.

Wolfgang Hoffmann worked initially in New York, but he settled in Chicago, where he produced designs for sundry furniture manufacturers.[32] His pieces were gracile and lovely, and more than a few reproduced the refined geometries of his father. Yet the younger Hoffmann's influence was limited, his pieces rarely produced in large numbers. Pola, who after divorcing him had married the writer Rex Stout, had the greater impact in her later career as a textile designer. True to her beginnings as one of Hoffmann's students, she continued to refine a design vocabulary based on angular lines and pure geometries. Many of the leading fashion designers of the 1940s and 1950s employed her fabrics, and they appeared in Hollywood films of the time.[33]

Josef Hoffmann's own impact in the Hollywood of the 1920s and 1930s had been considerable, in part because so many Austrians and Germans were involved in the film industry and knew and admired his works.[34] Ofttimes, his impact was not explicit, but the taste that so many set de-

signers and directors had for sharp contrasts and lighting, and clear, astringent forms, undoubtedly owed at least something to his aesthetic.

He made one more work for the American context, a house for Alma Morgenthau-Wertheim, sister of the U.S. Secretary of the Treasury. Hoffmann prepared a project for a two-story, flat-roofed structure, with planar walls and large surfaces of glass. While the work was ongoing, Alma married one of Wolfgang's friends, Paul Lester Wiener, who redesigned the house, wrapping it with a smooth, streamlined envelope, almost completely obliterating Hoffmann's scheme.[35]

Hoffmann's presence on the American design scene declined gradually over the course of the 1930s, as his work began to appear dated and political events interceded. But near the height of his popularity, in the summer of 1930, Walter Rendell Storey, the longtime design critic for the *New York Times*, visited the Austrian Werkbund exhibition in Vienna. In his extensive review of the show, he offered a radiant portrait of Hoffmann and his ideas, one that summed up well the American view:

"Known more in America for his architecture and his decorative art than for his educational work, Professor Hoffmann of Vienna has also been from the early years of his career an important force as a teacher. The pupils of his classes […] are encouraged from their first entry to develop along the lines in which they are interested. Being an architect, and one noted throughout the world, Professor Hoffmann sees decorative furnishings as integral parts of the dwelling in which they are ultimately introduced […]. To interview Professor Hoffmann is a difficult task. He is so modest that instead of discussing his work he leads others to become with him enthusiastic over the work of his pupils. But it is through this hour of inspection of their work and in looking with him at the studies that some of his pupils have brought to him for criticism that one gains another inkling of the source of this wealth of decorative art which one sees in the Werkbund exhibition and in the shops of Vienna […]. To him it is very important that the designer of today be sensitively alert to the life around him […]. His individual but always appropriate touch is everywhere evident."[36]

A fitting denouement to the story comes from Frankl, who on his last trip to Vienna in 1954 paid a courtesy visit to Hoffmann. As he told a reporter afterward, he was surprised to find the grand old man of Austrian design still active, still producing new designs.[37] But by then Hoffmann's attachments to America were far in the past. ■

I would like to thank Linda Lackner for her kind assistance with the research for this piece.

1 "Josef Hoffmann Dies: Architect and Designer, 85, Headed Center in Vienna," New York Times 26 May 1956, 17.
2 Ibid.
3 Kleiner spoke or wrote often about Hoffmann during his time in New York. See his brief biography in Boeckl, Matthias (ed.), Visionäre und Vertriebene: Österreichische Spuren in der modernen amerikanischen Architektur, Berlin 1995, 336.
4 The obituary also notes that Hoffmann was survived by his "widow and son"—without mentioning that the son in question was the designer and photographer Wolfgang Hoffmann, then living in Chicago. See note 1.
5 On Hoffmann's influence, see Sekler, Eduard F., "Josef Hoffmann, Adolf Loos und die Vereinigten Staaten," in: Liskar, Elisabeth (ed.), Wien und die Architektur des 20. Jahrhunderts, Vienna 1986, 125–135.
6 Sekler points out, quite correctly, that the relationship Loos and Hoffmann had with America was very nearly opposite. Loos spent almost three critical years of his early life in the United States, and he was deeply affected by the experience. Yet, Loos's influence in America, prior to the 1960s, was nearly zero. Hoffmann, by contrast, never set foot in the country, yet he would come to have a significant role in American design in its early phase. Ibid., 125.
7 Vereinigung bildender Künstler Österreichs Secession, Die Wiener Secession und die Ausstellung in St. Louis, Vienna 1904. See also: Sekler, Eduard F., Josef Hoffmann: The Architectural Work, Princeton, NJ 1985, CR 85, 289. Trans. Eduard F. Sekler and John Maass.

8 See Forsthuber, Sabine, Moderne Raumkunst: Wiener Ausstellungsbauten von 1898 bis 1914, Vienna 1991, 101–102.
9 Sekler 1985 (see note 7), 289.
10 Brooks, H. Allen, The Prairie School: Frank Lloyd Wright and His Midwest Contemporaries, New York/London 1996, 91. Wright was especially attracted to the work of Joseph Maria Olbrich, then living in Darmstadt, who had contributed a suite of six rooms and a courtyard to the German pavilion. But Wright was also fascinated with Austrian design, Hoffmann's room, it seems, included. On Wright's reactions to the St. Louis exposition, see Alofsin, Anthony, Frank Lloyd Wright: The Lost Years, 1910–1922, Chicago 1993, 2–16. On the responses to the Austrian displays in the American press, see, for example, "Austria's Pavilion Formally Opened," Missouri Republic 3 Jun 1904; and "Austria Opens Her Colorful Building," St. Louis Dispatch 3 Jun 1904. On the larger influences of Austrian design at the time, see Long, Christopher, "The Viennese Secessionsstil and Modern American Design," in: Studies in the Decorative Arts (14) 2 2007, 8–17; and Topp, Leslie, "Moments in the Reception of Early Twentieth-Century German and Austrian Decorative Art in the United States," in Price, Renee/Kort, Pamela/Topp, Leslie, New Worlds: Austrian and German Art, 1890–1940, exh. cat. Neue Galerie, New York 2001, 572–582.
11 Long 2007 (see note 10), 18–19.
12 Baker, Cathleen A., By His Own Labor: The Biography of Dard Hunter, New Castle, DE, 2000, esp. 33–43. After returning to the United States, Hunter worked for a time for Roycroft, Elbert Hubbard's Arts & Crafts colony, in East Aurora, New

York. Later, he set up his own design and papermaking enterprise.
13 Edward H. Aschermann later claimed to have studied with Hoffmann, but there is no evidence that he ever did so. It is quite possible, though, that he sat in Hoffmann's studio informally as an observer.
14 Brigham, Louise, Box Furniture: How to Make a Hundred Useful Articles for the Home, New York 1909. On Brigham and her work with Aschermann, see LeFarge, Antoinette, Louise Brigham and the Early History of Sustainable Furniture, Cham 2019, esp. 21, 40, 56, 100, 110.
15 Gladys Goodwin grew up in Halifax, Nova Scotia, and moved to New York to study design. After she married Aschermann in 1911, they established the Aschermann Studio, using their apartment on 31st Street as a showcase for their work. They produced interiors and objects for clients in and around New York in a markedly Secessionist style until about 1919, when they bought a house in Olgunquit, Maine, splitting their time between there and New York. McClain, Aurora/Long, Christopher, "The Aschermanns: The Forgotten Beginnings of Modern American Design," in: The Magazine Antiques (178) 1 2011, 222–231; "Mr. and Mrs Aschermann's Studio Decorations," New York Times 16 Apr 1914, 8. See also Adler, Hazel H., The New Interior: Modern Decorations for the Modern Home, New York 1916; and "Interior Decorations," in: MAC [Modern Art Collector]: A Monthly Collection of Modern Designs 1 1915, 9.
16 Anonymous, German Applied Arts: Touring Exhibition of the Deutsches Museum für Kunst im Handel und Gewerbe Hagen I. W., with the co-

Fig. 8 Promotional photograph of Rosalind Russell (with Cary Grant) in the film *His Girl Friday* (1940), wearing a suit designed by Robert Kalloch made from one of Pola Stout's textile designs
Columbia Pictures, Los Angeles

operation of the Oesterreichisches Museum für Kunst und Industrie in Wien: Newark, Chicago, Indianapolis, Pittsburgh, Cincinnati, St. Louis, 1912–1913, exh. cat. Newark Museum of Art, Newark 1912; and Shifman, Barry, "Design for Industry: The 'German Applied Arts' Exhibition in the United States, 1912–13," in: *Journal of the Decorative Arts Society* (22) 1988, 19–31.

17 For instance, a selection of Hoffmann's work is presented in Home, Charles (ed.), *The Art-Revival in Austria*, London 1906. From time to time, U.S. publications also offered coverage of how Americans were adapting to Secessionist architecture. See, for example, Price, C. Matlack, "Secessionist Architecture in America: Departures from Academic Traditions of Design," in: *Arts and Decoration* (3) 12 1912, 51–53.

18 Staggs, Janis, "The Wiener Werkstätte of America," in Witt-Dörring, Christian/Staggs, Janis (eds.), *Wiener Werkstätte 1903–1932: The Luxury of Beauty*, exh. cat. Neue Galerie New York, Munich 2017, 468–505.

19 See Long, Christopher, *Paul T. Frankl and Modern American Design*, New Haven/London 2007.

20 Stern, Robert A. M./Gilmartin, Gregory/Mellins, Thomas, *New York 1930: Architecture and Urbanism between the Two World Wars*, New York 1995, 554. On Rosenthal and her shop, see Stern, Jewel/Stuart, John A., *Ely Jacques Kahn, Architect: Beaux-arts to Modernism in New York*, New York 2006.

21 Langseth-Christensen recounted her experiences in detail in her later memoir. Langseth-Christensen, Lillian, *A Design for Living: Vienna in the Twenties*, New York 1987.

22 Anonymous, *An International Exposition of Art in Industry, From May 14 to May 26, 1928, at Macy's, 34 Street & Broadway, N. Y.*, exh. cat. Macy's, New York 1928.

23 Sekler 1985 (see note 7), CR 292, 410.

24 Ankwicz-Kleehoven, Hans, "Ausstellung von Arbeiten des modernen österreichischen Kunsthandwerks Wien 1923," in: *Deutsche Kunst und Dekoration* (54) 1924, 19 ff.

25 Sekler 1985 (see note 7), 180–81, CR 247, 389–90.

26 Leach, William, *Land of Desire: Merchants, Power, and the Rise of the New American Culture*, New York 1993, 318–319.

27 "Design Exposition Visited by 100,000: City Apartment Exhibit and the Austrian Boudoir Centre of Crowds," *New York Times* 20 May 1928, 25.

28 See also Cary, Elisabeth L., "International Exhibition of Art in Industry Opens: Six Countries Exhibit," *New York Times* 13 May 1928, 18.

29 Many other American designers, like Eugene Schoen or Ely Jacques Kahn, were of German heritage and had traveled to Austria, where they likewise drew from Hoffmann's ideas. And there were also those Americans who were not of Central European heritage and had not traveled in the region but were nonetheless influenced by him. Sekler mentions, for example, the young architect Bruce Goff, who in the later 1920s was working in Tulsa, Oklahoma, and whose Page Warehouse (1927) seems to have borrowed its exterior cladding from Hoffmann's use of multiple frame motifs. Sekler 1986 (see note 5), 132.

30 See, for example, Frankl, Paul T., *The Arts and Decoration Practical Home Study Course in Interior Decoration*, New York 1928, Lesson 1, 9–15, Lesson 4, 68; and *Form and Re-Form: A Practical Handbook of Modern Interiors*, New York 1930, figs. 20, 40.

31 See Marilyn F. Friedman's works, "Defining Modernism at the American Designers' Gallery, New York," in: *Studies in the Decorative Arts* (14) 2 2007, 79–116; *Selling Good Design: Promoting the Early Modern Interior*, New York 2003; and *Making America Modern: Interior Design in the 1930s*, New York 2018; and Stern/Gilmartin/Mellins 1995 (see note 20), 336–346. For contemporary examples, see Leonard, R. L./Glassgold, C. A., *Modern American Design: American Union of Decorative Artists and Craftsmen*, exh. cat. Brooklyn Museum, New York 1930.

32 Boeckl 1995 (see note 3) 333–334; and https://modernism.com/designers-and-manufactures/wolfgang-hoffmann [21 May 2020].

33 Boeckl 1995 (see note 3), 333–334.

34 See Ulrich, Rudolf, *Österreicher in Hollywood*, Vienna 2004.

35 Sekler 1985 (see note 7), CR 343, 426–427; and Boeckl 1995 (see note 3), 334.

36 Storey, Walter Rendell, "Applied Arts Quicken Life in Vienna: New Developments in Decoration Are Shown at the Exhibition of The Austrian Werkbund," *New York Times* 3 Aug 1930, 74–75.

37 "Nothing for Us in Europe," *Grand Rapids* [Michigan] *Herald* 26 Jul 1953, 26.

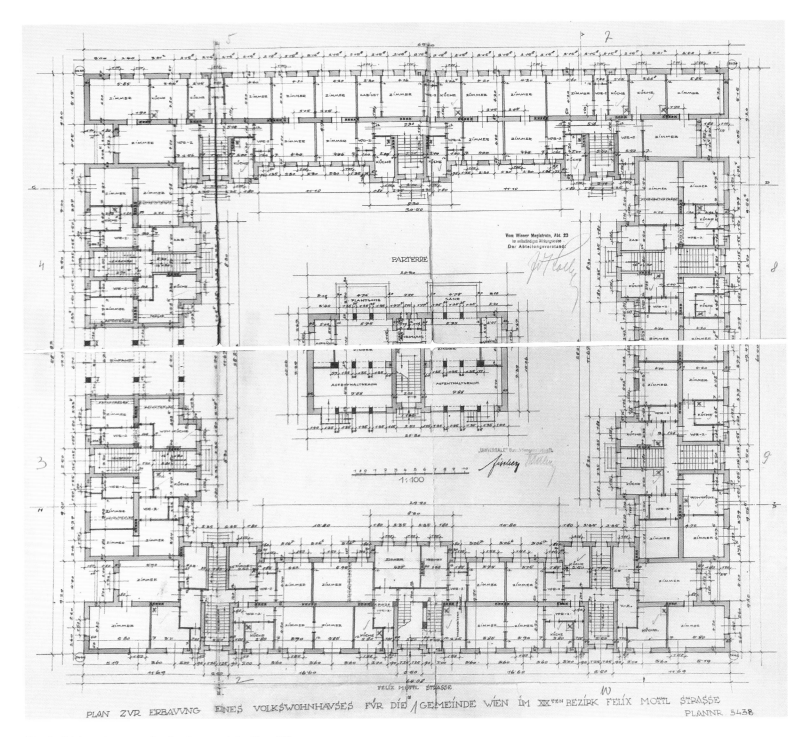

Fig. 1 JH, housing complex for the municipality of Vienna,
Klosehof (future designation), Philippovichgasse 1, 1923–1925
Ground floor plan

Matthias Boeckl

The Social Question

Josef Hoffmann's Municipal Apartment Complexes and Housing Developments before 1933

The upheavals of World War I propelled a henceforth dominant subject into the heart of the international architectural debate: public housing—in all its variants from small-scale housing projects to entire *Siedlungen* (housing developments) and large high-rise apartment complexes. While the avant-garde in France and Germany had already applied themselves to this issue before 1918,[1] in Austria the leading architects still had not produced any large public housing projects at this time.[2] The Secessionists self-critically recognized this deficiency and in 1913 appointed Heinrich Tessenow from Dresden to the Vienna School of Arts and Crafts to fill this gap in modern architecture training.[3]

In the milieu of the Secession, the "housing question" had mainly been addressed from an aesthetic perspective and for bourgeois target groups prior to 1918. Like Otto Wagner his students created numerous apartment buildings and single-family houses for the middle class in Vienna and other cities. Even bourgeois garden-city-like *Siedlungen* were on their agenda, such as Joseph Maria Olbrich's Cobenzl-Krapfenwaldl "Villenstadt" (villa town) conceived in 1896. Yet concepts for workers' settlements were limited to the experimental stage in architecture schools. In roughly 1906/07 Josef Hoffmann analyzed the issue of company towns with his students at the request of the national railroad company "to facilitate the proposal of potential beautifications and improvements in this all too important area."[4] However, in contrast to the interwar period when Hoffmann's students designed multiple public housing projects and exhibited them on a number of occasions,[5] the results of this analysis appear not to have been published.

Siedlungen

With the abrupt system change and the social crisis of the years 1918/19, an enormous demand arose for public housing that could be erected rapidly. Possible construction types were on the one hand sprawling, suburban, low-rise *Siedlungen* in the form of row houses or duplexes, with accessible open spaces that could be farmed—which had proved successful in the international garden-city movement for 20 years—and on the other hand large, inner-city, high-rise apartment complexes with up to 1 000 apartments, which were accredited primarily with greater economic efficiency. A political dimension proceeded from the issue of ownership:

in the long term apartments in housing cooperatives become the property of their inhabitants, hence making them independent lower-middle-class property owners, whereas high-rise apartments always remain the property of the building's original owner and as such the tenants remain dependent. It was for this reason that "Red Vienna" ceased constructing its own *Siedlungen*[6] in 1925—which led to intensive debates with the architectural community[7]—and exclusively built high-rise apartment complexes until 1933. Of the 60 000 apartments built in total in the years between 1919 and 1933, many of the most prominent complexes were planned by students of Otto Wagner like Karl Ehn (in the municipal construction bureau), Hubert Gessner, Josef Hoffmann, Rudolf Perco, Emil Hoppe, and Otto Schönthal (as freelance architects). They were intentionally constructed using traditional craft techniques in order to increase employment. The industrialization of public housing demanded by the avant-garde was out of the question in Vienna at that time.

Many of Vienna's modern architects took part in both public housing programs.[8] The *Siedlungen* were mostly commissioned by nonprofit housing cooperatives. Around 1922 Josef Hoffmann designed two alternatives for an exhibition building in a *Siedlung*—perhaps intended for presentations of construction projects and practical objects—for the Österreichischer Verband für Siedlungs- und Kleingartenwesen (Austrian Housing Development and Allotment Association),[9] which had been founded two years previously under Otto Neurath, a member of the Vienna Circle of philosophers, and his planning officer Franz Schuster, a former Tessenow student at the School of Arts and Crafts. Two years later he planned a *Siedlung* concept for the cooperative Aus eigener Kraft (Under Our Own Steam); the sculptural roof gardens of the row houses are clearly reminiscent of Le Corbusier, while the community center takes an elegant abstract Classicist form in the style of Heinrich Tessenow. After the customer rejected the design, the *Siedlung* was "built by Franz Schuster and Franz Schacherl in the more familiar forms of vernacular architecture."[10]

Moravian-Silesia: Hoffmann's First Realized *Siedlung*

The first realization of a *Siedlung* concept by Hoffmann began in 1922 in the new Czechoslovak Republic. Since planning the Primavesi country house in Winkelsdorf/Kouty

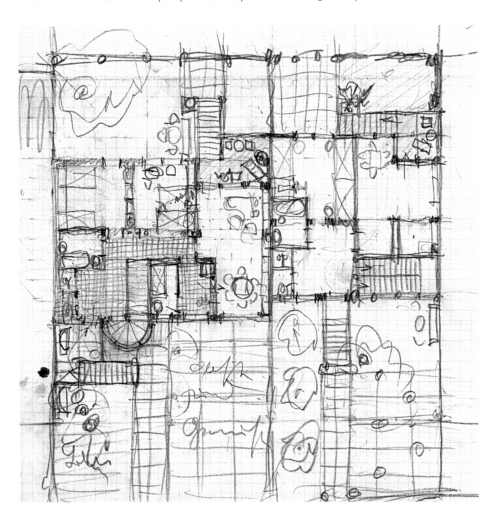

Fig. 2 JH, row houses in Vienna's
Werkbundsiedlung, 1930–1932, floor
plan sketches
MAK, KI 8812-4

nad Desnou in 1913 thanks to a recommendation from the sculptor Anton Hanak, Hoffmann—himself born in southern Moravia—had regularly been commissioned with building houses by some cultivated entrepreneurs in Silesia[11]—comparable to Adolf Loos's commissions from acquaintances of the Hirsch family in Pilsen.[12] The young industrialist Kuno Grohmann (1897–1940), who was actively engaged in social and artistic issues, was the majority shareholder at the Wiener Werkstätte from 1927 to 1929, and lived in a house by Hoffmann in Vienna from 1937,[13] started building a workers' settlement in Würbenthal/Vrbno pod Pradědem in 1922 based on the model garden city of Hellerau in Dresden. With their bull's-eyes and dormers, bell and hipped roofs, Hoffmann's designs for its single- and two-family houses, on which Max Fellerer also collaborated,[14] possess a playful diversity and charm that are still very much palpable today.[15] In another project in 1931 Grohmann promoted his social concept of modern-day housing by appealing to the citizens of Würbenthal and having brochures specially printed[16] in reaction to the unemployment caused by the Great Depression. With houses that would eventually have become the property of their inhabitants featuring a minimalist design vocabulary so atypical of Hoffmann, the never-realized plans for this housing development project show—like the earlier Neustraßäcker housing development project for Vienna—the clear influence of the International Style, which can be traced back to the collaboration on the project of Hoffmann's assistant Oswald Haerdtl.[17]

Hoffmann's other *Siedlung* projects reveal his constant endeavor to wrest a modicum of aesthetic dignity from the small houses and meager construction budgets. This was by no means limited to decorative façade elements but rather included diverse building shapes, for example the addition of tower-like elements, protrusions and recesses, balconies and (roof) terraces, spacious living areas, and practical but beautiful furniture. The catalogue raisonné names 13 other designs for houses in *Siedlungen* besides the four plans mentioned above,[18] though of them it was possible to realize only a single project—Hoffmann's four houses in Vienna's Werkbundsiedlung (Werkbund Estate).

Four Houses in Vienna's Werkbundsiedlung

In 1929–1932 an international model exhibition on building modern *Siedlungen* was held in Vienna,[19] which was organized by the Austrian Werkbund on the initiative of Josef Frank with the municipality's own Gemeinwirtschaftliche Siedlungs- und Baustoffanstalt (GESIBA, the Institution for Public Housing and Construction Materials) under Hermann Neubacher[20] as the construction company. Prior to this Frank had been the only Austrian participant in the German Werkbund's housing exhibition in Stuttgart, run by Ludwig Mies van der Rohe (1927), and the only Austrian (and Functionalism-critical) founding member of the Congrès Internationaux d'Architecture Moderne (CIAM, 1928). Therefore, he was predestined to offer an alternative to the nascent Functionalist dogmatism. This Viennese alternative consisted in a limitation to low-rise *Siedlungen* (in Stuttgart Mies van der Rohe had also constructed a large high-rise apartment complex) and in the presentation of select undogmatic concepts. As such, from the international community Frank invited for France not Le Corbusier but André Lurçat and Gabriel Guévrékian, for the Netherlands not Mart Stam but Gerrit Rietveld,

Figs. 3, 4 JH, workers' housing for the Grohmann company,
Würbenthal/Vrbno pod Pradědem, 1922/23
© Jan Šafář and Irena Perničková, Moravská galerie v Brně

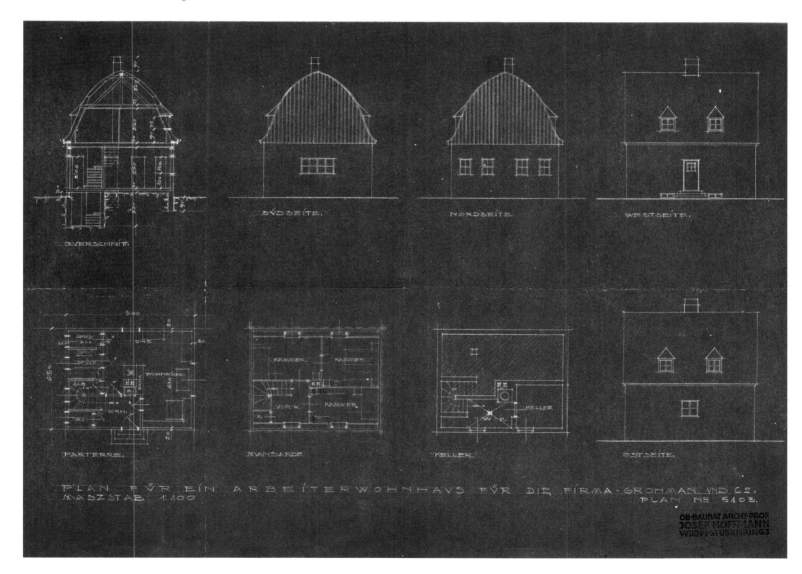

Fig. 5 JH, worker's house for the Grohmann company, Würbenthal/Vrbno pod Pradědem, 1922/23
Elevations and floor plans
Gregor Grohmann Collection
© MAK/Georg Mayer

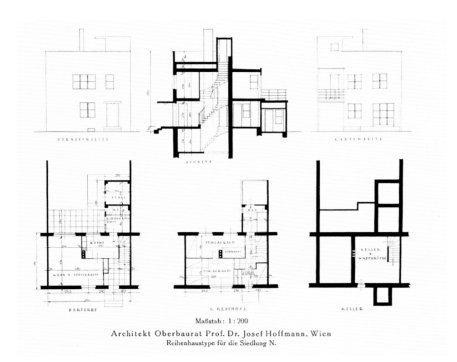

Figs. 6–8 JH, designs for the Neustraßenäcker housing development,
Vienna's Stadlau neighborhood, 1924
Row house types and perspective of the main square
MBF (26) 1927, 373–375

for Germany not Mies van der Rohe but Hugo Häring, and
for the first time guests from the USA in the form of the Austrian emigrants Richard Neutra and Arthur Grünberger. Almost all established modern architects from Austria were
represented, including Adolf Loos, Clemens Holzmeister,
Josef Hoffmann, and Frank himself. However, it was also important to him to give the younger generation a chance,
which is why names that would later become so famous like
Ernst A. Plischke, Margarete (Schütte-)Lihotzky, Karl Augus-
tinus Bieber, Max Fellerer, and Otto Niedermoser were able
to build their first houses here.

The four row houses that Hoffmann planned for the Werkbund Estate, display an exerted effort to give the small buildings a consistent style and equip them with higher-quality
elements like terraces and perrons, lavishly glazed staircases,
accessible roofs with different shapes, and well-made furniture. Documented in two color drawings,[21] the early design
stages reveal Hoffmann's great pleasure in designing with
their playful tower finials and elegant, vertically grooved
façades.[22]

Three High-Rise Apartment Complexes
for the City of Vienna

Hoffmann's involvement in the high-rise apartment building
program of "Red Vienna" began some six years before the
Werkbundsiedlung. These projects gave him the opportunity
to probe the highly contentious issue of (traditional) beauty
in practical social policy. That the relevance of aesthetics
was very highly valued by the social democratic Viennese
politicians as a means to ensure the inhabitants identify with
their homes and hence to achieve broad political acceptance
of the construction program, is demonstrated primarily by
the early projects, whose romanticizing towers and loggias,
stone sculptures in green inner courtyards, and lots of decorative arts like wrought ironwork in the gates and ceramics
on the façades conformed entirely with Hoffmann's views.[23]
However, the basic parameters of density, standards, and
building types were strictly stipulated as the central component of social democratic local politics.[24] As such the architects' creative possibilities were limited to modeling the
mass of the buildings, solving individual layout issues, and
designing furnishings.

With its intelligent distribution of building mass, its
high-quality artistic interiors, and its elegant proportions,
Hoffmann's first *Gemeindebau* (municipal housing project)

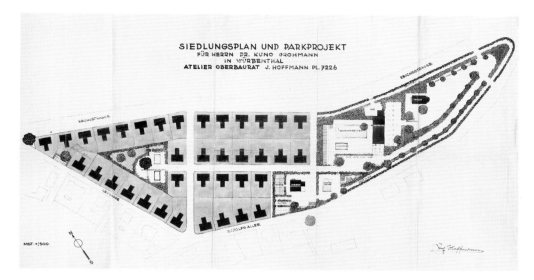

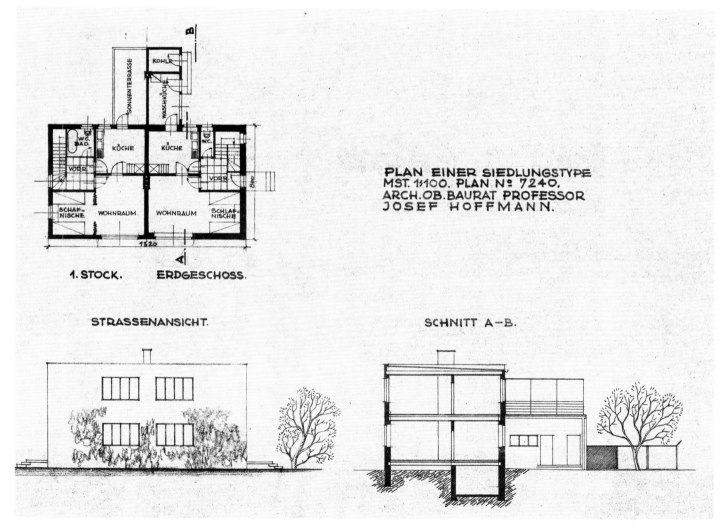

Figs. 9–11 JH, housing development and house for Dr. Kuno Grohmann,
Würbenthal/Vrbno pod Pradědem, 1931, site plan, brochure, and house types
Gregor Grohmann Collection
© MAK/Georg Mayer

is simultaneously his most advanced. The Klosehof on Philippovichgasse (1923–1925)[25] distributes its substantial cubature for 140 apartments across a five-story perimeter block closed on four sides and a six-story tower-like building in the center of the inner courtyard. Sculptural accents are added to the exterior with recessed loggias and a large gateway to the east; classicizing elements appear on the portals, whose cornices bear two sculptures of fruit bearers by Anton Hanak. Details like subtly proportioned door and window muntins, as well as oculi, amplify the building's sophisticated appearance. Yet the aesthetic pinnacle is undoubtedly the towering cube in the inner courtyard; with its two triple openings on the ground floor, its central rows of bull's-eyes, and its flush window glazing installed sym-

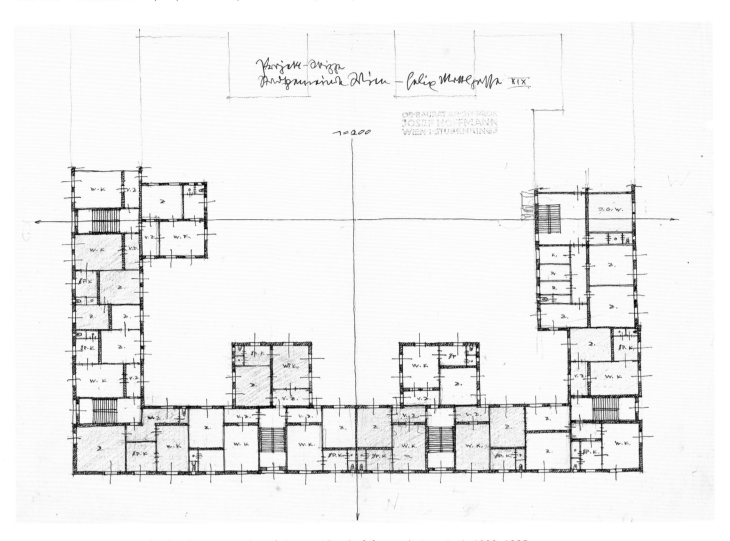

Fig. 12 JH, housing complex for the municipality of Vienna, Klosehof (future designation), 1923–1925,
preliminary design without the tower wing in the courtyard
Kunsthandel Widder, Vienna

metrically in twos, it gives the impression of a manifesto for
the Italian Razionalismo movement. For this reason this
masterpiece of abstract surface art is also the most frequently published detail of Hoffmann's *Gemeindebauten*.

24 p. 242   Hoffmann had to be prepared to accept considerably
more compromises for the two other residential buildings
that he planned for the municipality of Vienna before World

War II. The Winarskyhof was conceived in 1924 as a collective showpiece for Vienna's foremost modern architects,
whose diverse design strategies would be exemplified in a
large complex together with the neighboring Otto-Haas-
Hof while complying with the city's building stipulations
described above. It was with this project that Adolf Loos's
participation in the City of Vienna's high-rise apartment com-

Figs. 13, 14 JH, sample rooms for the houses for the municipality of Vienna, 1927
MBF (26) 1927, 399

Figs. 15–18 JH, housing complex for the municipality of Vienna, Klosehof (future designation), 1923–25, model of a preliminary design and three views shortly after completion

Kunsthandel Widder, Vienna

Figs. 19, 20 JH, housing complex for the municipality of Vienna, Klosehof, 1923–1925, portal sculptures by Anton Hanak, views of the courtyard
© private

>
Fig. 22 JH, housing complex for the municipality of Vienna, Anton-Hölzl-Hof, 1928–1932, ground floor plan
City of Vienna, MA 37, E.Z. 1438 NZ
© Kerstin Bauhofer

plexes failed, as his proposal for a split-level house, which was incompatible with the aforementioned sociopolitical specifications, was not realized. The other invited architects planned a wing of the site each: in addition to the prestigious street-side section for 76 apartments designed by Josef Hoffmann (Stromstraße 36–38),[26] there were perimeter blocks and courtyard developments by Peter Behrens, Oskar Strnad, Josef Frank, Oskar Wlach, Franz Schuster, Margarete Lihotzky, and Karl Dirnhuber. Hoffmann would have liked to produce more elaborate façades and crenellated eaves.[27] The two gables, the semicircular arched gates, and the cornice over the rectangular gateway between that were ultimately built, nevertheless exude metropolitan grandeur. With its 332 apartments, the Anton-Hölzl-Hof (Laxenburgerstraße 94, 1928–1932)[28] is Hoffmann's largest Gemeinde-

bau. Once again, the five-story complex with partially converted attics is a perimeter block, though this time with an open, spacious, and green inner courtyard. The need to economize is again balanced with the complex's subtle splendor. With minimal means Hoffmann applied masterful highlights, such as an emphasized corner of the building with tall triple openings on the ground floor that are also used in the Klosehof, or numerous partial symmetries. On the south and east sides of the complex, balconies add a regular structure to the façades. Otto Fenzl's sculptural group of two workers towers over the center of the inner courtyard on a tall plinth. The building was even publicized during the Nazi period as an exemplary "people's house"[29] and remains a well-functioning example of public housing to this day.   ◼

18 19
    20

Fig. 21 JH, housing complex for the municipality of Vienna, Anton-Hölzl-Hof (future designation), Laxenburger Straße 94, 1928–1932, street view
© private

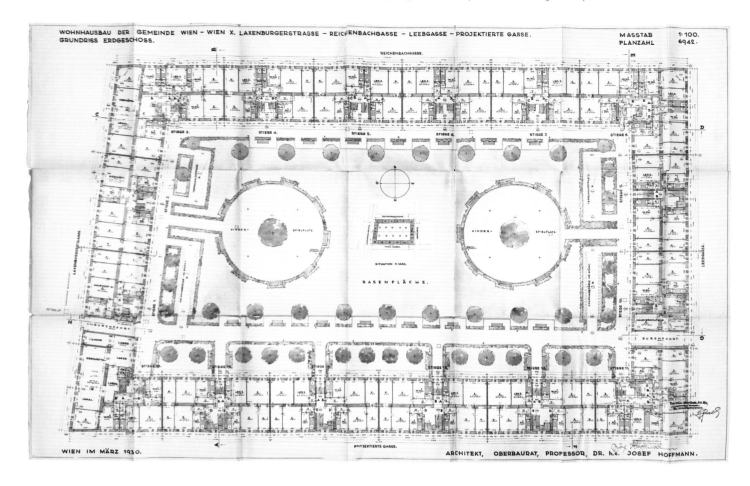

1   Such as in the Staaken Garden City near Berlin by
    Paul Schmitthenner, in the Hellerau Garden City
    in Dresden by Richard Riemerschmid, Heinrich
    Tessenow, and others, and in Tony Garnier's con-
    cepts for a *Cité industrielle*, which included exten-
    sive residential quarters for workers.
2   In Austria the tradition of company towns was domi-
    nant, which socially minded industrialists mostly
    built with local builders or which large companies
    had planned by their employees (like the Südbahn-
    gesellschaft [Southern Railroad Company] with
    Wilhelm von Flattich).
3   Boeckl, Matthias, "Von der Kunstrevolution zur
    Lebensreform. Heinrich Tessenow und die Integra-
    tionsstrategien der Wiener Moderne," in: Reinhold,
    Bernadette/Kernbauer, Eva (eds.), *zwischenräume
    zwischentöne. Wiener Moderne, Gegenwartskunst,
    Sammlungspraxis. Festschrift Patrick Werkner*,
    Berlin/Boston 2018, 142–149.
4   Hoffmann's annual report from 1906/07, UAA,
    Collection and Archive.
5   In Paris in 1925 and in other exhibitions, models
    with elaborate consistent styles were presented,
    such as by Anton Ulrich with housing development
    types (1925) or by Alfred Soulek with a row house
    complex (1927). Cf. Kapfinger, Otto/Boeckl, Mat-
    thias, "Vom Interieur zum Städtebau. Architektur
    am Stubenring 1918–90," in: *Kunst: Anspruch und
    Gegenstand. Von der Kunstgewerbeschule zur
    Hochschule für angewandte Kunst in Wien 1918–
    1991*, Salzburg/Vienna 1991, 102–108.
6   There was a temporary housing development office
    in the Vienna City Administration from 1921, which
    was founded by Max Ermers, run by Hans Kampff-
    meyer, and briefly advised by Adolf Loos as the
    head architect. See esp. Kapfinger, Otto, "Stadt-
    baukunst von unten," in: Thun-Hohenstein, Chris-
    toph/Czech, Hermann/Hackenschmidt, Sebastian
    (eds.), *Josef Frank. Against Design*, exh. cat. MAK,
    Basel 2015, 86–117.
7   Nierhaus, Andreas, "'Ein Werk der Kultur, das wei-
    terbestehen wird in der Geschichte.' Der Karl-Seitz-
    Hof und das Wohnbauprogramm des Roten
    Wien," in: Schwarz, Werner M./Spitaler, Georg/
    Wikidal, Elke (eds.), *Das Rote Wien 1919–1934.
    Ideen, Debatten, Praxis*, exh. cat. Wien Museum,

Basel 2019, 192–197: 194. However, the cooper-
    atives' construction of *Siedlungen* continued to be
    supported.
8   Adolf Loos planned some *Siedlungen* and hoped
    in vain to introduce his split-level house concept in
    the high-rise apartment complex. Josef Frank built
    both *Siedlungen* and "people's houses." Cf. e.g.,
    Blau, Eve, *The Architecture of Red Vienna 1919–
    1934*, Cambridge, MA 1999, 113 ff.
9   Designs in the National Gallery Prague, inv. nos.
    K 17742 and 17743.
10 Sekler, Eduard F., *Josef Hoffmann: The Architectural
    Work*, Princeton, NJ 1985, CR 257, 396. Trans.
    Eduard F. Sekler and John Maass.
11 Including Sigmund Berl's house in Freudenthal/
    Bruntál (CZ, 1919–1922) and Fritz Grohmann's house
    in Würbenthal (1920/21). Vybíral, Jindřich, *Junge
    Meister. Architekten aus der Schule Otto Wagners
    in Mähren und Schlesien*, Vienna/Cologne/Weimar
    2007; Noever, Peter/Pokorný, Marek (eds.), *Josef
    Hoffmann. Architekturführer*, Ostfildern 2010,
    30–75; Boeckl, Matthias, "Avantgarde und Identität.
    Vorgeschichte und Nachwirkungen der Otto
    Wagner-Schule in Tschechien," in: *Umeni a evoluce
    sazba, Festschrift Jindřich Vybíral*, Prague 2020.
12 Domanický, Petr/Jindra, Petr (eds.), *Loos – Plzeň –
    souvislosti/Loos – Pilsen – connections*, exh. cat.
    Západočeská Galerie/Gallery of West Bohemia,
    Pilsen 2011.
13 Grohmann, Kuno, *Eine kurze Biographie*, brochure,
    ed. by the Wiener Werkstätte, Vienna 1928; Groh-
    mann, Kuno, "Der Investitionswechsel. Die univer-
    selle Finanzierungsmethode für öffentliche und pri-
    vate Investitionen zum Zwecke der Arbeitsbeschaf-
    fung grossen Stils," n.d. (ca. 1933–1938), unpub-
    lished typescript, private collection; Ploil, Ernst,
    "Economics," in: Witt-Dörring, Christian/Staggs,
    Janis (eds.), *Wiener Werkstätte 1903–1932: The
    Luxury of Beauty*, Munich/London/New York 2017,
    20–31; Pese, Claus, "Ein Ruin für die Kunst. Kuno
    Grohmann (1897–1940) und die Wiener Werk-
    stätte," n.d., online manuscript.
14 Correspondence between Fellerer (for Hoffmann's
    office) and Grohmann, 1922, Grohmann archive,
    private collection.
15 Sekler 1985 (see note 10), CR 246, 389; Noever/

Pokorný 2010 (see note 11), 72–75; planning docu-
    ments in the Grohmann archive, private collection.
16 *Emil Grohmann-Siedlung. Siedlungsverein Würben-
    thal, seinen Mitbürgern gewidmet von Dr. Kuno
    Grohmann*, self-published, 1931.
17 Sekler 1985 (see note 10), CR 336, 424.
18 Sekler (ibid.) names 12 projects: CR nos. 302, 333,
    334, 349, 367, 408, 413–416, 494, and 495. Georg
    Rizzi later identified a 13th project in the form of an
    undated housing development plan by Hoffmann
    for the Böhler Works in Kapfenberg, which is not
    yet listed in Sekler.
19 Nierhaus, Andreas/Orosz, Eva-Maria, *Werkbund-
    siedlung Wien 1932: Ein Manifest des neuen Woh-
    nens*, exh. cat. Wien Museum, Vienna/Salzburg
    2012; see also the article "The Decorative Arts De-
    stroyed? Josef Hoffmann and the Austrian Werk-
    bund" in this catalog; www.werkbundsiedlung-
    wien.at/en/ [30 Jul 2020].
20 The illegal National Socialist Neubacher later be-
    came the first Nazi mayor of Vienna (1938–1940)
    and in that role supported many projects by Hoff-
    mann.
21 MAK, KI 8812-3 and -4.
22 Three of these houses by Hoffmann were recently
    restored—along with other houses in the Werkbund-
    siedlung—by the Viennese P.GOOD (Praschl &
    Goodarzi) architects.
23 An exemplary *Gemeindebau* is e.g., the Reumann-
    hof on Margaretengürtel by Hubert Gessner, 1924–
    1926.
24 Considerably lower densities and larger green
    spaces dissociated these projects from speculative
    private housing. The old "Bassena" standard with
    only one point of access to running water and shared
    toilets on each floor was replaced by a WC and
    running water in every apartment, as well as central
    laundry and bathing facilities. Five- to six-story peri-
    meter blocks were the preferred building type.
25 Sekler 1985, 1985 (see note 10), CR 255, 394 f.
26 Ibid., CR 264, 400.
27 Hoffmann produced a number of decorative façade
    sketches for all of his municipal projects.
28 Ibid., CR 307, 415 f.
29 "Arbeiten von Prof. Josef Hoffmann, Wien," in:
    Moderne Bauformen (XLI) 8 1942, 277–296.

Fig. 1 JH, Austrian pavilion, *International Fine Arts Exhibition*, Rome, 1911
Kunsthandel Widder, Vienna

Valerio Terraroli

A New Classicism

Josef Hoffmann and His Reception in Italy

Clarity, geometric simplicity, sobriety, elegance, sophistication, extravagance, and balance: it is with these terms that the Italian critics describe Josef Hoffmann's style at the turn of the 20th century. A style so characteristic and innovative that—in contrast to the developments in Italy—it moves from a radically Secessionistic interpretation of Modernism, metamorphoses, and from the 1910s is courageously enriched with Classicist elements, then—primarily in the interwar period—integrates quotations from art history, and hence becomes a benchmark for Italian architects and designers in the 1920s and 1930s. Hoffmann's relationship with Italian culture is one of give and take that begins during his training and intensifies from the 1910s when Hoffmann increasingly turns to the "Italian model." Remembering his travels through Italy in 1895/96, the Viennese architect writes:

"From the first I […] was overcome by the onrush of impressions […]. Nevertheless, as the school of Otto Wagner intended to keep us from falling sacrifice to the blind style copyism […] [p]erhaps my appreciation of the simple yet peculiar Italian building style most prevalent in the country, which was an antithesis to the great, official architecture, came of its own accord. In any case, it had far more to impart for our endeavours to give shape to purpose and material."[1]

In 1911 Hoffmann reestablishes contact with Italy when he designs the Austrian pavilion at the *International Fine Arts Exhibition* in Rome; in 1933 a solo show is organized at the Milan Triennial, and the following year he constructs the Austrian pavilion for the Venice Biennale. Nevertheless, just like the novel ideas proposed by the Vienna Secession, the innovations in his architectural and decorative-art vocabulary have no immediate influence on the Italian architects, artists, and designers of the early 20th century, who only investigate the Hoffmann model in the late 1910s and early 1920s. At this time Hoffmann and the Vienna Secession finally become the main source of inspiration for Italian Art Deco and early, nascent Modernism, and even go on to have an impact on the clear and elegant Rationalism of the likes of Carlo Scarpa.[2] Despite Art Nouveau being at the peak of its expansion at the time of the *First International Exhibition of Modern Decorative Art* in Turin in 1902, Josef

Hoffmann's style has still had no considerable or at least no explicit or discernible influence on Italy. However, a certain interest in Hoffmann and the Viennese tradition can be identified in the newspaper articles published that year, in which astute and informed intellectuals discuss Modernism and the merits of the new style. Vittorio Pica, for example, writes:

"The new Austrian interior decoration, above all for schools, newspaper editorial offices, and art exhibitions, brings to light such a sophisticated gracefulness and ingenious elegance that the eye of the art afficionado is instantly captivated. All those who had not been following the regular exhibitions of the Vienna Secession since 1897, were astonished and delighted by the exquisite and playful novelty of the overall decoration of the rooms in the Austrian fine arts section at the Paris World's Fair of 1900 […]. The ensemble truly did have a rare charm with its expert interplay of green and gold with white and black, with its subtle emphasis of every arabesque and every stylized figural or tree motif on the monochrome walls. Josef Hoffmann's absence from the exhibition in Turin is thus deeply regrettable, since none other than he conceived, designed, and had executed these gorgeous rooms; he is undisputedly the most sagacious, most rational, and most original master of interior decoration […]. He would have given the Italian public the opportunity to appreciate his value to one of the most interesting and characteristic aspects of Austria's current renaissance in the decorative arts; he would have made them understand that those same snapped off lines and those same mascarons with long hanging ribbons, with exaggerated dimensions […] that seem quite tiresome on the exteriors of buildings, can in fact, when tastefully and discerningly arranged inside a room, appear eminently graceful."[3]

These observations are evidently the result of an intimate familiarity with Austrian innovations and the leading role of Viennese architects. One of the most vociferous advocates of Italy adopting the Modernist style, Enrico Thovez publishes a long article in the magazine *L'Arte decorativa moderna* entitled "L'Arte decorativa austriaca" in 1903. Referring to the World's Fair in Paris in 1900, he declares: "With regard to design, novelty, skill, harmony of forms, and exquisitely elegant taste, the rooms furnished by Austria were superior to those of all other nations,"[4] and continues:

Fig. 2 Giovanni Greppi, house at Via Statuto 12, Milan, 1919
Private archive

Fig. 3 Giovanni Greppi, Irpinia (Avellino) pavilion, Milan,
Fiera Campionaria, 1928
Private archive

>
Fig. 4 Music room in
Alberto Grubicy's house
on Via Carlo Ravizza,
Milan, 1908
Alberto Previati's estate

"The editions of the magazine *Der Architekt*, as well as the volumes published under the title *Aus der Wagnerschule*, have made us aware of names and works, above all those of Joseph Maria Olbrich and Josef Hoffmann.[5] [...] The Austrian furniture shown in our pictures corresponds to the commercial model commonplace in Viennese homes. In contrast to the furniture designed by Olbrich, Hoffmann, Bauer, and other Secessionists, it is not the product of any particular innovation. It is simply English furniture, but developed, made robust and more practical [...]. Incidentally, its success at the exhibition in Turin in 1902 is the best proof that even the general public has acquired a taste for it."[6]

This confirms that the Italians are aware that Hoffmann has created a coherent architectural/decorative syntax and show their immediate interest, yet his impact on Italian art occurs only later, even if within the diverse panorama of Art Nouveau a fondness for abstract geometric forms can already be discerned among some Italian artists, predominantly among those artists who were raised as citizens of the Austro-Hungarian Empire and were shaped by Viennese culture: Pietro Marussig, Ugo Zovetti, Adolfo Levier, Carlo Crampa, Vittore Zanetti Zilla, Alfeo Argentieri, and Luigi Bonazza. However, their abstract geometricity often and readily yields to floral shapes, naturalistic ornaments, or eclectic/Classicist quotations. Yet no homogeneous modern style ever emerges in Italy; instead, Modernism is interpreted individually, with each artisan, artist, and architect's approach being conditioned by their own strengths and regional traditions. In a nutshell, a very eclectic interpretation of Modernism as opposed to the rigor of the Secession. Nevertheless, there are some Modernist markers: For example, the influence of Hoffmann can be identified in the furnishing of the music room commissioned by the famous Milanese gallerist Alberto Grubicy for his daughter (and which survived unchanged until 1922, the year the gallerist died). In 1907/08 Grubicy commissioned Gaetano Previati to produce a cycle of six paintings devoted to music for the villa on Via Carlo Ravizza in Milan; the villa no longer stands, but a photo from 1908 shows a room with contemporary furnishings that are unequivocally influenced by the Secession. The wooden wainscoting that frames Previati's paintings and divide the room, as well as the panels that separate the room proper from

the piano room, the parallelepiped furniture with rectangular recessed fittings, the deep, quadrilateral chairs, the drop-leaf table likewise influenced by the ornamental motif of the square (five white, quadrilateral intarsias on ebony wood): all this points to Hoffmann and Vienna, despite the fact that the furniture was most likely produced in Milan, by the company Quarti or Ceruti.[7]

Only at the Venice Biennale in 1910, when the famous solo show of 22 paintings by Gustav Klimt was held in the Austrian room of the central pavilion designed by the Austrian architect Eduard Josef Wimmer-Wisgrill, did the Italians fall in love with the Vienna Secession once and for all, specifically with the paintings and interior design, as the works by Galileo Chini and Vittorio Zecchin prove. Klimt can build on his success in Italy at the 1911 *International Fine Arts Exhibition* to commemorate the half centenary of the Kingdom of Italy, while Josef Hoffmann designs the now demolished Austrian pavilion in Vigna Cartoni, which hosted another solo show with twelve Klimt paintings. The building, U-shaped around a courtyard, incorporates classical forms in a sophisticated and simplified way: These can be seen in the high base, in the monumental windows with geometric jambs, in the plain, fluted pilasters of the cloister, as well as in the interior, which is conceived as a sacral, white, open space suffused with natural light whose only decoration consists in the rhythmic repetition of the straight line, the rhombus, the acute angle. All these elements are part of the Art Deco stylistic vocabulary and are used unambiguously in 1920s Milan in the projects of Giovanni Muzio, Gio Ponti,

Emilio Lancia, Tomaso Buzzi, and Giovanni Greppi. The rectangular splayed window reveals on the ground floor, the strict geometricity of the apertures, the T-shaped section of the main entrance, and not least the sharply triangular bay window of the building constructed by Greppi at Via Statuto 12 in Milan in 1919, all reveal allusions to Hoffmann's oeuvre. These elements are taken up again by Greppi in 1928 in the Irpinia (Avellino) pavilion at the *Fiera Campionaria di Milano* [Milan Trade Fair], though this time accompanied by classical allusions like Tuscan columns, spheres, and cornucopian vessels. What is impressive about Milanese Art Deco is its intelligent fusion of Hoffmann's square and linear forms with sophisticated historical allusions, from Mannerism to Neoclassicism. As, for example, in the so-called "Ca' Brütta" by Giovanni Muzio (1919–1923), in the house on Via Randaccio built by Gio Ponti (1924–1926), in Palazzo Borletti on Via San Vittore, which was similarly designed by Ponti but in 1928, and the headquarters of the Banca Popolare di Milano, which was constructed by Giovanni Greppi (1928–1930) and in which Neoclassical elements coalesce with vast columns of cipollino marble furnished with architraves, familiar from the Looshaus in Vienna, which was built by Adolf Loos between 1909 and 1911.

Once a version of Modernism finally emerges in Italy that rejects all Naturalist, Historicist, and Eclecticist compromises, Hoffmann is credited as its role model. The main points of reference are Stoclet House and his creations for the Wiener Werkstätte, in which he incorporates Baroque and Rococo

elements in his repertoire, though not without first simplifying and flattening their lines, such as in the Austrian pavilion for Paris in 1925: "It is an architecture of furniture that is inspired by Baroque forms; extraordinary architecture, the fruit of sophisticated taste and therefore interesting as an elegant game."[8]

Roberto Papini provides a striking definition that gives an indication of how the ideas of Hoffmann and the Wiener Werkstätte were perceived in Italy:

> "Austria has been the avant-garde for three decades […] the Austrian artists work metal and jewels, wood and glass, wire and ceramic with exceptional skill; one indulges their every caprice because it is always contained within the limits of a strict, if not obvious logic. The rooms created by Hoffmann, Strnad, and Gorge in the Austrian section constitute a fascinating compromise between whimsy and equilibrium. Woe betide anyone who dares imitate the Austrian architects and decorators without possessing their expert taste: the result would be ungainly and grotesque."[9]

Furthermore, Papini emphasizes Hoffmann's genius in the decorative arts:

> "This style is shaped by few artists and almost exclusively by architects, with Josef Hoffmann at the forefront […]. Clarity and geometric simplicity of forms indisputably dominate Austrian production; maximum frugality with adornments is accompanied by the simplification of form. Even if neither gold nor silver, the materials are precious thanks to the way they are worked: the obvious hammering, the care and expertise with which reliefs, repoussage, rough and smooth surfaces, perfect contours,

harmonious curves are created. Artisans who are such masters of their tools, such experts in every technique, are guided by a natural sense of elegance and sophistication. Certain things might go against our Italian taste, which is hostile to excesses even of sophistication; yet [among the Austrians' products] there is nothing vulgar or careless, nothing that does not comply with general contemporary taste."[10]

In *Le arti d'oggi. Architettura e arti decorative in Europa*, a comprehensive overview of Italian and international Art Deco published in Milan in 1930, Papini frequently cites Hoffmann. In the richly illustrated section, he compares him with Ponti and Lancia, attempting to prove that Italian architecture and decorative arts—despite their individuality—have reached the same level as their Austrian exemplars. Papini concludes his visionary and dreamlike account, which precedes the illustrated section and is dedicated to life in Universa—a metropolis that arose from the ruins of war—with praise for the "new Classicism" in contrast to Modernism: "The young people of Universa are not ashamed to admit that they live in an archaic age. It is an age in which people are starting over. […] Founding a new Classicism, means returning to order, measure, form, style."[11] These are the watchwords of Italian Art Deco, whose protagonists were Muzio, Greppi, Ponti, Buzzi, Lancia, Portaluppi, Andloviz, Zecchin, Martinuzzi, Chini, the early Scarpa and whose absolute lodestar in the field of both architecture and the decorative arts was Josef Hoffmann, the embodiment of the Secession.

Fig. 6 Piero Portaluppi, interior view of the Fagianaia Reale, 1928–1930
Monza Park, Golf Club headquarters
Milan, Piero Portaluppi Foundation

1   Noever, Peter/Pokorný, Marek (eds.), *Josef Hoffmann. Selbstbiographie/Autobiography*, Ostfildern 2009, 90. Trans. Bernd Magar and Andrew
Oakland.

2   Franz, Rainald, "'La viennesità evidente.' Immagini
da un'architettura mitteleuropea: Hoffmann e
Vienna nell'opera di Scarpa." in: Tegethoff, Wolf/
Zanchettin, Vitale (eds.), *Carlo Scarpa. Struttura e
forme*, Venice 2007 (Studi su Carlo Scarpa 6).

3   Pica, Vittorio, *L'Arte Decorativa all'Esposizione di
Torino del 1902*, Istituto Italiano d'arti grafiche,
Bergamo 1903, 159–160.

4   Thovez, Enrico, "L'Arte decorativa austriaca," in:
L'Arte decorativa moderna (II) 5 1903, 129.

5   Ibid., 136.

6   Ibid., 139.

7   The photo of the music room at the Grubicy villa

dates from 1908 (Eredi Alberto Previati archive).
See Staudacher, Elisabetta, "Le suggestioni di
Previati per il salone musicale di casa Grubicy,"
in: Vorrasi, Chiara (ed.), *Tra simbolismo e futur-
ismo. Gaetano Previati*, exh. cat Castello Estense,
Ferrara 2020, 69. My thanks to Dr. E. Staudacher
and Dr. M. Vinardi for procuring this photo for me.

8   Papini, Roberto, *Le arti d'oggi. Architettura e arti
decorative in Europa*, Milan/Rome 1930, fig. XLIII.
Works by Hoffmann can also be seen in the following photographs: architecture and furniture:
XXXVII–XL (together with the graphic arts pavilion
by Ponti and Lancia at the exhibition in Milan in
1927), XLII, XLIV, XLVI (Paris 1925), LXXXIV (together with Muzio's Villa Minetti), XCVII (with the
vestibule from the Domus Nova series for the La
Rinascente department store designed by Ponti

and Lancia in 1927), CXIII–CXIV, CXXIII (interiors),
CXXXV (collector's cabinet, together with a desk
by Buzzi), CLV (table, together with a table by
Buzzi), CLXIX–CLXX (interiors); metalwork: CLXXX–
CLXXXII (lamps by the Wiener Werkstätte), CXCI–
CXCII, CXCIV–CXCVII (coffee and tea sets and
cups by the Wiener Werkstätte), CXCIX–CC (vases
by the Wiener Werkstätte).

9   Papini, Roberto, "Le arti a Parigi nel 1925. II: gli
interni e I loro mobili," in: *Architettura e arti decorative* (V) V 1925, 357, 360.

10 Papini, Roberto, "Le arti a Parigi nel 1925. III: I
metalli," in: *Architettura e arti decorative* (VI) I
1926, 22, 24.

11 Papini 1930 (see note 8), 22.

Fig. 1 The original, six-man adjudicating panel for the Palais des Nations in Geneva, 1925/26, from left: Victor Horta (Belgium),
Attilio Mùggia (Italy), Karl Moser (Switzerland), Charles Lemaresquier (France), Bernardo Attolico (Deputy Secretary-General
of the League of Nations), Josef Hoffmann (Austria), and James Burnet (United Kingdom)
gta archive/ETH Zurich, Karl Moser

Matthias Boeckl

At the Zenith of His International Influence

Josef Hoffmann and the Competition for the Palais des Nations in Geneva

One of the positive consequences to emerge from the devastation of the First World War was the founding of the League of Nations (LON) by 32 states on 28 April 1919 in the context of the Paris Peace Conference. The city of Geneva in the Francophone region of neutral Switzerland was chosen for the organization's headquarters. Five years later the League of Nations decided to stage an international architectural competition for the construction of a new assembly building. Erected between 1930 and 1936, the result—a monumental site after plans by an international team of architects comprising Henri-Paul Nénot, Julien Flegenheimer, Carlo Broggi, Giuseppe Vago, and Camille Lefèvre—is a combination of Neoclassicism, Beaux-Arts architecture, and Art Deco. Its conservative style illustrates Modernism's (as yet) weak status in the European culture and politics of the 1920s. Despite this being the third decade of the movement's existence, it was still far from being the dominant style for general construction work on the continent. The avant-garde had often declared itself the movement's mouthpiece, even though it had much less "majority appeal" than the comparatively accepted approaches of pioneers like Auguste Perret in France, Victor Horta in Belgium, or Josef Hoffmann in Austria.

Setting the Scene

In this sense the second of the three great international "defeats of Modernism"—the first was the competition held by the *Chicago Tribune* in 1922 and another would follow in 1930 with the *Palace of the Soviets*—was in actual fact a defeat of the avant-garde and as such to be expected. Indeed, it was arguably inevitable from the outset: a complex project for a client that comprised representatives of dozens of state governments divided into several committees requiring unanimity, the procedure by definition allowed for nothing but a compromise supported by a broad consensus and—in terms of modernity—a kind of lowest common denominator. In this regard the avant-garde thoroughly misjudged the political reality—or intentionally ignored it to gain more ground. It would only receive the reward for its efforts after the Second World War when the new headquarters of the United Nations, the successor to the failed League of Nations, was built in New York by a team of architects around Le Corbusier, Oscar Niemeyer, and Wallace Harrison and the UNESCO building in Paris was constructed by Bernard Zehrfuss, Marcel Breuer, and Pier Luigi Nervi.

Under Sir James Eric Drummond, the British secretary-general from 1920 to 1933, the League of Nations with its mere 60 employees first moved into Geneva's Hôtel national, which had been built in 1873–1875. The global organization was clearly dominated by European countries, especially the victors of World War I—though without the USA, which never joined this first global organization. Germany only became a member in 1926 and left again in 1933. Consequently, significant parameters of the construction project had in essence already been decided beforehand: no resolution could be passed against France, Italy, and the United Kingdom, meaning that the only architectural approach that could win the competition for this prestigious construction project in 1927 was one with which the governments of these countries and its jurors could identify.

The Power of the Jurors

At its fifth general assembly in 1924, the League of Nations adopted the resolution to build a new headquarters and announced the architectural competition for its design. Thereafter the LON's Executive Council[1] established two committees to realize the project, which was initially limited to a *salle des assemblées*. A construction committee comprising a citizen of the city of Geneva, three delegates from neighboring countries, two members of the LON secretariat, and a member of the likewise Geneva-based International Labor Organization (ILO) would oversee the project. In addition to this there was a five-member expert panel that was to be made up exclusively of architects. The first step was to select the members of this powerful panel. With the rather superficial argument that the jurors should not have to travel too far to attend the numerous anticipated meetings, the council opted to ask Switzerland, Italy, and France, but also the further removed United Kingdom, to nominate jury members. After vehement intervention from the Belgian chair of the Executive Council—which required unanimity—Belgium was also accorded the right to nominate a jury member. Subse-

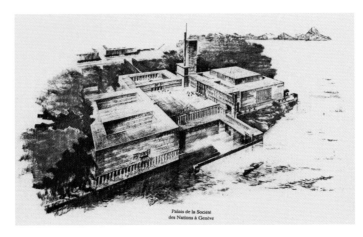

Figs. 2–5 Competition for the Palais des Nations in Geneva, first prizes: projects by Emil Fahrenkamp and Albert Deneke from Düsseldorf (top left), Giuseppe Vago from Rome (top right), Broggi/Vaccaro/Franzi from Rome (bottom left), and Nénot/Flegenheimer from Paris/Geneva (bottom right), 1926
Société des nations, Concours d'architecture, Geneva 1926

quently the council decided to also "include an additional member from a Central or Eastern European country, with Austria being their selection."[2]

At the request of Secretary-General Drummond from 11 November 1924, each of the aforementioned six governments finally nominated an architect who in their opinion had enough prestige and international experience for this high office: the United Kingdom delegated the 68-year-old Sir James Burnet, Belgium the 64-year-old Art Nouveau pioneer Victor Horta, France the conservative 55-year-old Beaux-Arts architect Charles Lemaresquier, Switzerland the 65-year-old professor at the ETH in Zurich Karl Moser, and Italy the 64-year-old engineer Attilio Mùggia. In the 55-year-old Josef Hoffmann the Austrian federal government with its Christian Social politicians Rudolf Ramek (federal chancellor) and Heinrich Mataja (in charge of external affairs) had nominated the second youngest of the original six jurors whose average age was roughly 62. After the death of Otto Wagner in 1918 and before the ascent to architectural celebrity of the 39-year-old Clemens Holzmeister and the 40-year-old Josef Frank, Josef Hoffmann was the country's only experienced and active (modern) architect with a high international reputation. Moreover, the government had just commissioned him to plan the Austrian pavilion for the *International Exposition of Modern Decorative and Industrial Arts* in Paris: in effect, there were no alternatives to his nomination.

Shortly thereafter massive diplomatic pressure led to further jury members being nominated by the Netherlands, Spain, and Sweden—namely the 69-year-old Hendrik Petrus Berlage, the 48-year-old Antonio Flórez Urdapilleta, who

was later replaced by Carlos Gato Soldevila, and the 47-year-old Ivar Tengbom. Consequently, seven of the nine jurors belonged to "an older generation of architects whose work was associated with the architectural achievements and developments of the late 19th century."[3]

In the course of this politically and artistically explosive process with which the League of Nations was entering uncharted territory, the expert panel under its resolute chair Victor Horta was gradually granted comprehensive responsibilities more or less against its will: they ranged from formulating the competition brief to determining the appropriate site for the new building and advising the Executive Council, which at times only accepted the experts' suggestions under protest.[4]

Steinhof and Berlage: The Centralized Plan as a Symbol

Between the first meeting in January 1925 and the last in May 1927, the jury assembled a marathon 63 times. Thematically, these meetings began by debating the future building's location,[5] then moved on to formulating the competition brief and the budget, as well as—after the deadline in January 1927—discussing the merits of the submitted projects, coming to a final decision, and making a recommendation to the Executive Committee. The Viennese architect and sculptor Eugen Steinhof wielded a certain influence on the competition brief. Speaking fluent French after having studied philosophy at the Sorbonne, he taught a sculpture class, among other things, at the Vienna School of Arts and Crafts from 1923 to 1932 and often substituted for his col-

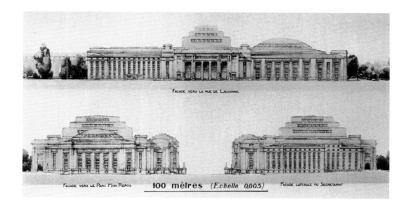

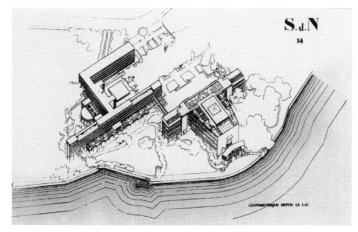

Figs. 6–9 Competition for the Palais des Nations in Geneva, first prizes: projects by Camille Lefèvre from Paris (top left), Georges Labro from Paris (top right), Nils-Einar Erikson from Stockholm (bottom left), and Le Corbusier and Pierre Jeanneret from Paris (bottom right), 1926
Société des nations, Concours d'architecture, Geneva 1926

league Josef Hoffmann as his officially appointed deputy at the jury meetings in Geneva—undoubtedly in close consultation with and simultaneously as a spokesman for Hoffmann. "In addition to the sufficiently discussed technical and administrative problems, the competition brief thus far lacked an ideational concept," is Katrin Schwarz's summary of Steinhof's remarks at the 9th meeting of the jury on 15 January 1926. The subject of that meeting was the project's symbolism and typology, which were intended to express brotherhood and peaceful cooperation between the member states, and would be best achieved with a centralized plan—the opposite of the free-flowing asymmetrical volumes of International Modernism: "Steinhof declared his preparedness to collate his thoughts in a kind of manifesto. Hendrikus Petrus Berlage also agreed in principle with this statement." After debates about whether "palace" as a term and building type was appropriate to the project, the jury finally reached a consensus about a passage in the brief on the intended building:

> "[...] that its composition would translate the lofty aims into a monument whose free style and harmonious forms seem destined to symbolize the peaceful ideals of the 20th century."[6]

377 Projects, 63 Meetings, 27 Prizes

The invitation to tender was announced on 25 July 1926 and contained unusually rigid formal conditions, which in no way corresponded to the notion of a competition of ideas.[7] Entries were to be submitted within half a year. As such, the jury was clearly steering toward the swift selection

of a detailed project whose realization would supposedly be expeditious. For reasons of pragmatism or political ambition, the jury waived the option of including new ideas in a multistage process, which might have altered the official functional brief, the future building's location, or the project's budget.

Although the jury's decisive final minutes are nowhere to be found, the adjudication of the 377 projects that passed the preliminary examination—entrants from Austria include Clemens Holzmeister with Ernst Egli, Oskar Strnad with Felix Augenfeld, Josef Frank with Oskar Wlach and Lois Welzenbacher, as well as the Austro-Americans Richard Neutra and Rudolph M. Schindler[8]—is well documented.[9] Due to fierce resistance from the conservative jury members from the Romance-speaking countries to the suggestion by Moser, Tengbom, Berlage, and Hoffmann from 18 April 1927 to award a single first prize,[10] especially to the project by Le Corbusier that was nominated for first place by Karl Moser,[11] it was not possible to arrive at an agreement for a single project but only for the noncommittal compromise of a complex prize-winning panel of 27 awards (nine each for first prize, first mention, and second mention). In the 2–10 final round of voting on 2 May 1927, each juror could nominate a project for each of these three prize categories. A surviving note by Karl Moser documents how the members voted.[12]

The friends Moser and Hoffmann might have come to an agreement that the former would cast his vote for Le 10 Corbusier, while the latter would select the project by Erich zu Putlitz/Rudolf Klophaus/August Schoch from Hamburg featuring a block closed on four sides and surrounded by

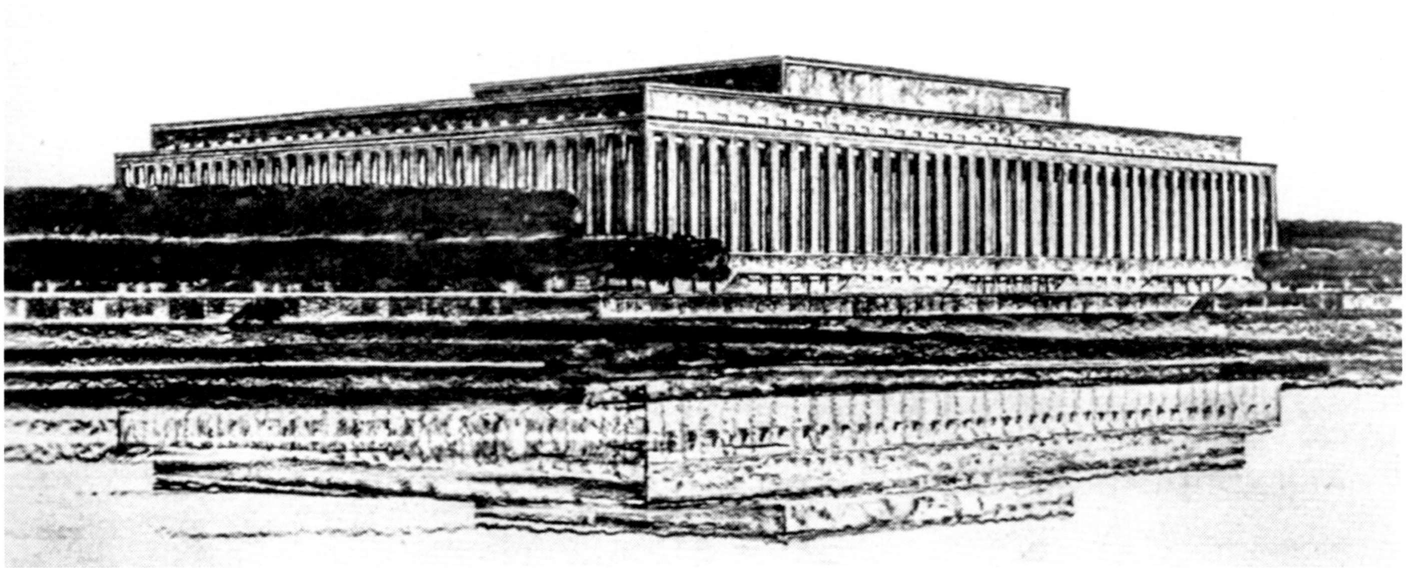

Fig. 10 Competition for the Palais des Nations in Geneva, first prizes:
project by Putlitz/Klophaus/Schoch from Hamburg, 1926
Société des nations, Concours d'architecture, Geneva 1926

a monumental colonnade, with the assembly hall in the inner courtyard.[13] That also seems consistent with the aforementioned Steinhof statement, namely that the intended symbolism could only be achieved with a centralized plan—and is entirely in compliance with Hoffmann's own monumental projects of this period, such as that for a festival hall or world concert hall from that same year.[14] Ultimately the jury recommended delegating the building design to yet-to-be-selected architects from among the first-prize winners (Broggi/Giuseppe Vaccaro/Gino Franzi from Rome, Putlitz/Klophaus/Schoch from Hamburg, Nils-Einar Erikson from Stockholm, Camille Lefèvre from Paris, Emil Fahrenkamp and Albert Deneke from Düsseldorf, Le Corbusier and Pierre Jeanneret from Paris, Giuseppe Vago from Rome, Georges Labro from Paris, and Nénot/Flegenheimer from Paris/Geneva). After numerous political and artistic interventions, in the end four of them—namely Nénot/Flegenheimer, Broggi, Vago, and Lefèvre—were commissioned with the implementation planning by a "Comité des cinq" from the Economic and Financial Section of the League of Nations, to which the diplomats Štefan Osuský (CZ), Mineitciro Adatci (JP), Nikolaos Politis (GR), Francisco José Urrutia Olano (CO), and Edward Hilton Young (GB) belonged. Le Corbusier, who thereupon launched his "crusade,"[15] left empty-handed, as did his fellow winning architects Erikson, Putlitz/Klophaus/Schoch, Labro, and Fahrenkamp.

Hoffmann's Summary

How did Josef Hoffmann experience this pinnacle of his international influence? What conclusions did he draw from the elaborate tendering and adjudication process? Did he share the avant-garde's assessment that the process had been a "chronique scandaleuse"?[16] Immediate impressions upon his return from Geneva were captured in a report by the famous art publisher Leopold Wolfgang Rochowanski, which was released as early as 13 May 1927:

"There were also many fights for the artistic, and between sense of national identity and quality, between conservatism and the modern spirit it was not always possible to decide in favor of the

latter. It had almost, as Professor Hoffmann described, come to an unresolved conclusion and to a new competition being announced. A great burden for all, both the artists and the members of the jury, was the tremendously complicated tender requirements, which demanded not only drawings of the building but also some fifty details of floor plans and façades. This meant for the submitting architects an exorbitant waste of work that devoured millions for each of them. Hoffmann himself had proposed an open competition in which each applicant would only submit their picture, one of their best achievements to date, and a sketch of the project—a method that would have been much better, simpler, and less expensive. […] During the comprehensive assessment work, two groups soon formed. Those who were opposed to everything outmoded and academic, impersonal, and wrongly borrowed and who strove to assert the new, good, and clear, included Professor Josef Hoffmann, Dr. H. B. Berlage, Professor Tengbom from Stockholm, and Professor Moser from Zurich. They also succeeded in helping a large portion of their intentions to triumph."[17]

In his own manuscript[18] Hoffmann summarizes almost objectively:

"Actually at the last major exhibition [Paris in 1925] the overview of the state of modern-day architecture was quite apparent and in point of fact the decision had already been made then and there: the states whose buildings came first at that exhibition also performed best in Geneva. For the first time after the war Germany was represented on the international stage and was not out of place with its excellent works. […] The work of the Swiss-French Corbusier struck us—I mean Berlage, Tengbom, Professor Moser, and me—as refreshing and new, with agreeable simplicity. […] It was probably intentional that the architects of the École des Beaux-Arts passed by all the movements of recent decades. But nothing special was submitted in terms of the usual names either. Likewise, the Italians did not supply anything of note. […] It remains to be seen whether such an interesting modern institution as the League of Nations will be generous enough to be guided by quality and good taste in its selection. It would obviously be marvelous if a distinguished man could be the builder. That would also be the surest and noblest propaganda for the League of Nations itself."

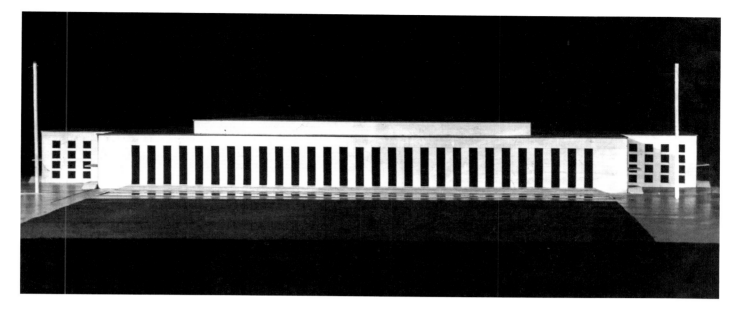

Figs. 11, 12 JH, festival hall or *Welttonhalle* [World Concert Hall] for Gustav Mäurer's Welt-Musik-und-Sanges-Bund (World Music and Song Association), Vienna, Augarten park, 1927, model views
MAK, KI 8951-23 and KI 8951-13

1   In 1924 four permanent members (United King-dom, France, Italy, and Japan) and four temporary members (Belgium, Brazil, Czechoslovakia, and Spain) sat on the Executive Council.
2   Schwarz, Katrin, *Bauen für die Weltgemeinschaft. Die CIAM und das UNESCO-Gebäude in Paris*, Berlin 2016, 203. My thanks to the author for her support with the artwork.
3   Ibid.
4   Ibid., 198–247.
5   With its recommendation to purchase an alter-native lot to that previously chosen, the jury was able to triumph over the Executive Committee.
6   Schwarz 2016 (see note 2), 208–211.
7   The "type and number of all drawings, elevations, and sections [was stipulated], likewise the format of the plans and the drawings' scale on graph paper. Even the ink to be used and the amount of wash were standardized by the jury to guaran-tee the comparability and equivalence of all pro-jects" (ibid., 204).
8   Kapfinger, Otto/Stiller, Adolph, "Neutra und Schindler. Zwei Europäer in Kalifornien," in: Boeckl, Matthias (ed.), *Visionäre und Vertriebene.*

Österreichische Spuren in der modernen ameri-kanischen Architektur, Berlin 1995, 124–128.
9   Steinmann, Martin, "Der Völkerbundspalast: eine 'chronique scandaleuse,'" in: *werk archithese* (65) 23–24 1978, 28–31; Oechslin, Werner (ed.): *Le Corbusier & Pierre Jeanneret. Das Wettbewerbs-projekt für den Völkerbundpalast in Genf 1927. A la recherche d'une unite architecturale*, Zurich 1988; Schwarz 2016 (see note 2), 213n54.
10 Oechslin 1988 (see note 9), 99.
11 "Thus the design number 273 fell victim to the machinations that stemmed from the 'Academy' and France (France's representative, Briand, threw his weight at the League of Nations behind them). On the other hand, these machinations had the effect that the representatives of the new architecture—termed 'barbarism'—banded to-gether 'to support one another,' as it says in the declaration that they made at the Congrès inter-national d'architecture moderne between 26 and 29 June 1928 in La Sarraz," Steinmann 1978 (see note 9), 29.
12 Oechslin 1988 (see note 9), 101.
13 For first prize Berlage voted for Fahrenkamp/

Deneke, Burnet for Vago, Gato Soldevila for Nénot/Flegenheimer, Lemaresquier for Labro, Horta for Lefèvre, Mùggia for Broggi/Vaccaro/Franzi, and Tengbom for Erikson.
14 Sekler, Eduard F., *Josef Hoffmann: The Architec-tural Work*, Princeton, NJ 1985, CR 279, 407–408. Trans. Eduard F. Sekler and John Maass.
15 Le Corbusier, *Une maison – un palais*, Paris 1928; Roth, Alfred, "Der Wettbewerb, die Projektbear-beitung und Le Corbusiers Kampf um sein preis-gekröntes Projekt," in: Oechslin 1988 (see note 9), 20–29.
16 Steinmann 1978 (see note 9).
17 Rochowanski, L. W., "Der Wettbewerb um das neue Völkerbundgebäude. Gespräch mit Archi-tekten Josef Hoffmann, Mitglied der internation-alen Jury," in: *Neues Wiener Journal*, 13 May 1927, 7–8: 7. My thanks to Markus Kristan for this reference.
18 MAK, KI 23506-12. My thanks to Christian Witt-Dörring for this reference. Cf. Sekler 1985 (see note 14),

Fig. 1 JH, houses in Vienna's Werkbundsiedlung (Werkbund Estate), 1932
ANL, Picture Archives, 423015-D, photo: Julius Scherb, Vienna

Andreas Nierhaus

The Decorative Arts Destroyed?

Josef Hoffmann and the Austrian Werkbund

"Under all circumstances, as long as there is still a homeland for us, we do not want our creative forces to perish, even in the worst times. [...] Let others philosophize, display their vehement knowledge, let them misguidedly or deliberately spew poison and gall over such developments; we must detach ourselves and learn to bear it. We want to keep the respect for every creative work and seek nothing else. We must time and again seek to strengthen faith in that [which] through its true distinctiveness [is] novel and creates value, and in its striving for its own means of expression. It is healthy, not degenerate, humanity in the best sense."[1]

With these words, in March 1933 in a letter addressed to Max Welz, who in turn, forwarded a copy to the members of the Austrian Werkbund, Josef Hoffman turns against the representatives of a "purely speculative intelligence" who prevent the unfolding of the country's creative forces. The target of Hoffmann's attack was Josef Frank, who had increasingly distanced himself with critique of the decorative arts; in summer 1932, the bankruptcy of the Wiener Werkstätte seemed to prove Frank right. The letter marked a climax in the long-smoldering conflict over the direction of the Werkbund between arts and crafts and industry, which soon led to a polarization of "vernacular" traditionalism and "international" Modernism, and was accompanied in the press by blatant anti-Semitism against Jewish Werkbund members.[2] The founding of the conservative "New Austrian Werkbund" in 1934 toed the line of the new political conditions in the authoritarian corporative state, but was also the end result of irreconcilable differences that had shaped the work of the Werkbund from the start. Hoffmann's equal involvement in the founding and the fatal split of the Austrian Werkbund reveals his deeply ambivalent relationship to the association's goals.[3] As representative of a version of arts and crafts still rooted in the 19th century, which was elite but also heavily shaped by ethics, he was only moderately interested in the issues of industrial production current at the time. Was his involvement in the Werkbund in the end, a grave misunderstanding?

Between Precious Goods and Mass Products

"'Ennobling of industrial work in a cooperation of art, industry, and crafts'—is that necessary?" Yes! was the reply to the rhetorical question with which Adolf Vetter, director of the Imperial Royal Trade Advancement Bureau, began his opening lecture for the fifth annual meeting of the German Werkbund in June 1912 in Vienna.[4] In addition to economic advantages from the work of the Werkbund in Austria, Vetter also expected the opportunity for greater cooperation among the people in the monarchy, and thereby regeneration from within of an increasingly fragile major power internally divided by ethnic conflicts, which in mutual competition for high-quality work could find new unity. However, the political demands placed on the Austrian Werkbund already before its founding would prove to be too great; despite lengthy negotiations, Vetter's goal of a transnational Austrian Werkbund could not be realized.[5] It therefore took until 30 April 1913 for the Austrian Werkbund to meet for its first general assembly.[6] Ennobling the commercial and suppressing the purely mechanical work, production of plain, simple, and inexpensive but exquisite products, in a collaboration of artists, artisans, industry, and consumers; promotion of domestic culture, social reform work, finally, the ideal of "making good and beautiful things" were the basic points of the programmatic speech by the president, Baron Adolf Bachofen von Echt, Jr.[7] Josef Hoffmann, already involved in the founding of the German Werkbund in 1907, was elected to the board. Through the Wiener Werkstätte, he was among the first to have again reunited high-quality artistic design and arts-and-crafts production after the industrial disassociation of the 19th century, with the claim of a comprehensive aesthetic renewal—albeit with a total neglect of the issues of serial and mass production.[8] Hoffmann thereby left himself open to accusations of not only acting naïvely in terms of business (which the persistent financial difficulties of the Wiener Werkstätte would prove), but also of ignoring the demands and needs of the nascent modern consumer society. Hoffmann, on the contrary, considered the mutual enrichment of artist and artisan a counterpoint to soulless, inhuman machine work.[9]

Fig. 2 JH, central hall of the Werkbund exhibition at the AMAI, 1930, Vienna
ANL, Picture Archives, 95.539-C

Fig. 3 Otto Prutscher, showcase by the Wiener Werkstätte in
the Kunstschau at the AMAI, 1920, with objects by Dagobert
Peche, Josef Frank, Josef Hoffmann, and others
MAK, WWF 137-68-1

This romantic ideal image was bound to collide sooner
or later with 20th-century reality. Nonetheless, at first Hoffmann was still able to celebrate absolute success in the context of the Werkbund. At the Werkbund exhibition in Cologne in 1914, the German colleagues were enthusiastic in
their reception of the Austrian pavilion that he designed together with Oskar Strnad:[10] nowhere else, wrote Peter
Jessen, had the hopes and wishes of the German Werkbund
come so close to being fulfilled.[11] For Max Eisler, the Austrian
decorative arts in Cologne had proven,

> "that its special nerve is handicrafts, industry, its secondary area,
> thus precisely the reverse relations as in Imperial German cre-
> ation. Perhaps that is a detriment economically, but artistically
> it is most certainly an advantage."[12]

However, the collapse of the monarchy, and the collateral
loss of important production areas and sites would soon
pose entirely new challenges for the work of the Werkbund.

Contradictions and Conflicts

Hoffmann's corporative-influenced belief in the ethical significance of the handicrafts and the thereby associated responsibility of the designing artist survived undamaged
through the end of the war and Austria's political reorganization. In a text on "Vienna's Future" written in December
1919, he once again emphasized the impact that the manufacture of aesthetic, high-quality practical objects had on
the artisan who made them: "This beautiful and good work
reflects on these people and gives them that cheerful temper
which rightly delights everyone."[13] Machines and industrial-

Fig. 4 Monument to
Otto Wagner on Vienna's
Heldenplatz, 1930
Österreichische Lichtbildstelle,
Wien Museum, 79.000/6314

ization had, indeed, led to a brutalization, "yet the old forces still work within these people and can always be awakened." In the material, social, and intellectual destitution of the postwar era, this romantic, even naïve perspective invited opposition. Likewise in December 1919, the art historian Hans Tietze, a member of the Werkbund from the very start, subjected the local decorative arts to fundamental critique. The occasion was the *Ausstellung österreichischer Kunstgewerbe* [Exhibition of Austrian Decorative Arts] at the Austrian Museum of Art and Industry (today's MAK), which set itself apart "from the deadly earnestness of the present time" with its "thousand amiable trifles… untimely, even eerie."[14] The decorative arts serve only "a handful of connoisseurs," and evoke "a fictional culture of victory that has no roots"; the Werkbund is "deeply entangled in this quaint episode," and must be brought back "to sober work." Just a few days later, Tietze put more coal on the fire and demanded the "reorientation and reorganization of crafts-based work, as a whole."[15] Hoffmann felt justifiably duped, but could argue little more than make the escapist and debunking remark that the uniqueness of Viennese arts and crafts, which is found "in its pleasantness, its delicate sensibility, in the ease and grace of their creativity," would be "destroyed" by consideration of present-day needs.[16]

The next opportunity for Tietze to offer a fundamental critique came in summer 1920, when the Kunstschau designed by Carl Witzmann, under Hoffmann's guidance, offered an overall survey of current trends in the fine arts and handicrafts.[17] Despite prominent individual achievements of fine artists, such as Anton Hanak, Gustav Klimt, Oskar Kokoschka, and Egon Schiele, to whom entire halls were devoted, for Tietze, the decorative arts determined the overall impression:

> "The spirit of the Kunstschau is completely imprisoned in this delicate soap bubble. […] The exhibition is […] like a dream, colorful, fantastical, and consequently: the decorative-arts products […] are the most dreamlike blossoms in this enchanted world; orchid-like whimsical entities; highly cultivated, absolved of purpose, magical as pure enjoyment, with their unhealthy hothouse culture, the characteristic product of unhealthy conditions […]."[18]

In this, Tietze saw one cause of the "destruction of the Austrian Werkbund" that was underway, "which was just now in the process of dividing into two groups." The bone of contention was Hoffmann's desired closure of the sales shop of the Werkbund, which in his opinion, sold too many low-quality decorative arts;[19] in truth, however, as Arthur Roessler suspected, the competition that the commercially successful operation gave to the Wiener Werkstätte, also helped tip the scales.[20] Following Adolf von Bachofen-Echt Jr's resignation from office as president, Josef Hoffmann replaced him, but then resigned from the Werkbund just a few weeks later along with the majority of the board.[21] Tietze saw on the one side—around Josef Hoffmann—the "temple servants," who ascribed to the arts and crafts great ideational power, while on the other side—in the circle around Robert Oerley—those who were devoted to current needs.[22] Even when Tietze emphatically called on the two parties to cooperate, the division could no longer be stopped: in May 1921, Hoffmann founded the Vienna Werkbund, which he integrated as an association into the German Werkbund, and whose first president was Margaret Stonborough-Wittgenstein, the sister of the philosopher Ludwig Wittgenstein.[23] For Hans Tietze, the situation in 1921 presented itself as such: on the one side, the "old" Austrian Werkbund, which bowed down to the hardships of the era, and placed the material promotion of its members at the forefront; on the other side, the "new" Vienna Werkbund around Josef Hoffmann, Anton Hanak, and Adolf Vetter, which "from the monstrous task that the Werkbund concept had once posed, singled out only the intellectual elements."[24] In the division, Tietze recognized a symptom of the times: in the German Werkbund, too, sooner or later, the fateful question would be whether the material or the ideal moments should determine its further development.

In the 1920s, "fragmentation of the powers of the Austrian Werkbund movement"[25] took its course—at precisely the moment when, in connection with the new political, economic, and cultural start, united Werkbund work would have been necessary. Even Austria's successful participation in the *International Exposition of Modern Decorative and Industrial Arts* in Paris in 1925 under Hoffmann's guidance

SANATORIUM PURKERSDORF   1904

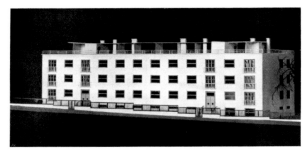

MIETHAUS, PROJEKT FUR WIEN XIX.   1930

Fig. 5 Comparison of Sanatorium Westend
(1904) and a project for an apartment
building (1930)
Leopold Kleiner, *Festschrift für Josef Hoffmann*, n. p. (33)

could not hide the fact of this shortcoming.[26] By May 1926, however, the differences had been overcome and the announcement could be made of the reentry of the group gathered in the Vienna Werkbund into the Austrian Werkbund.[27] Negotiations for the unification of the two associations dragged on for more than two years due to differences in terms of doing business, and the board of the Austrian Werkbund first constituted itself on 29 November 1928: Hermann Neubacher, head of the influential Gemeinwirtschaftliche Siedlungs- und Baustoffanstalt (GESIBA, the Institution for Public Housing and Construction Materials) and later Vienna's first Nazi mayor was made president; Josef Hoffmann and Josef Frank, vice presidents, whereby the presidium was ideally staffed in terms of business, design, and theory.[28] The following four years mark the most important phase in the history of the Austrian Werkbund—Hoffmann, as doyen of modern architecture, took center stage in the activities time and time again.

Werkbund Exhibition 1930, Werkbund Estate 1932

"Every single thing should be made as well as it can be made"—under this only apparently simple motto, Josef Frank was able to unite the in part strongly diverging views within the Werkbund during this decisive phase when mutual work was being carried out on the most ambitious project in the history of the association: For the year 1930, they had invited the German Werkbund to hold its annual convention in Vienna. Josef Hoffmann, who celebrated his 60th birthday in the same year, played a key role in the activities planned in this context: not only was a major exhibition at the AMAI put together under his guidance, he also provided the design for a memorial for Otto Wagner, and, last but not least, would be represented with a large residential home in the exhibition of housing developments conceived by Josef Frank, whose realization, however, had to be postponed for organizational reasons.[29] Nonetheless, the Werkbund offered

Hoffmann a large stage in 1930. While he was able to display his mastery in the dramatic staging of exhibitions in the tent-like design and furnishing of the large central space in the Austrian museum, the radical abstracted monolith that he designed as a memorial to Otto Wagner, seemed to refer back to the purist early period of his oeuvre.[30] While the Werkbund unequivocally made their German friends aware of Austria's leading historical role in the fundamental renewal of architecture with this monument for the pioneer of Modernism, with his concept, Hoffmann was also able to present himself as a founder of modern design. The Festschrift published by the Werkbund for Hoffmann's 60th birthday in December 1930, with tributes by Erik Gunnar Asplund, Hendrik Petrus Berlage, Le Corbusier, Walter Gropius, and many others, also pursued this intention: placed below the photo of the Purkersdorf Sanatorium is the photo of a model of an elegantly proportioned residential building,[31] which with large window openings and a continuous roof terrace, blends perfectly into the image of contemporary International Modernism, and has been conclusively identified by Otto Kapfinger as a variant for the Werkbundsiedlung (Werkbund Estate).[32] With the visual correspondence, a formal continuity extending across decades is created, staging Hoffmann—beyond all twists and turns in terms of design—as still active pioneer of Modernism.[33]

At this time, it was already clear that the residential building Hoffmann had planned would not be built in the Werkbund Estate in this form. The multistory housing by Hoffmann, Josef Frank, André Lurçat, and Walter Sobotka in the estate's first overall plan was conceived as response to the housing program of Red Vienna, and was thereby, "definitely the most polemical part of the action."[34] After the City of Vienna—most likely for fear of overt criticism of "thoughtless"[35] urban residential building—withdrew from direct funding of the project, the estate was realized in the context of GESIBA's home-building aid program and the building site moved from Wienerberg to Lainz. That led to the multistory residential buildings being replaced by housing de-

Fig. 6 JH, sketch for
a multifamily house in
Vienna's Werkbund-
siedlung, 1929/30
MAK, KI 8812-1

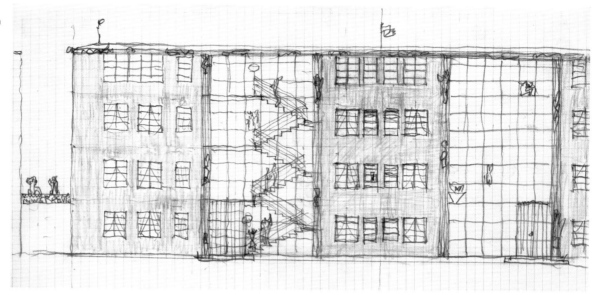

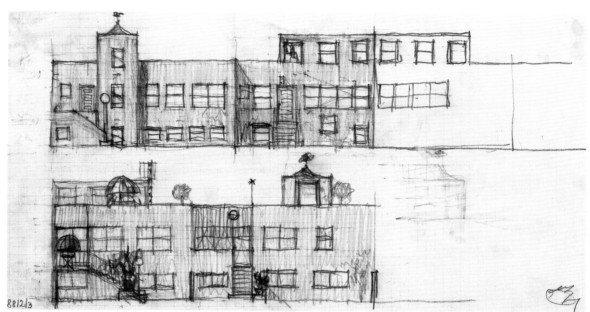

velopment homes and forced Hoffmann to create a completely new design. Along with the strictly "sober" solutions
for the multifamily homes published in the Festschrift, he
also had versions designed with entirely glazed staircases
and opulent sculptural framing, meant to combine monumentality with playful elegance. Initially, he laid out the housing development homes as romantic country estates *en
miniature* with richly structured building volumes, small
towers, terraces, and stairs. The realized homes have entirely
glazed staircases on the street side, while terraces, and open
stairways mediate toward the garden, and the roofs are
designed as sun terraces.[36] Hoffmann furnished two of the
four houses himself for the duration of the exhibition.

Finale

The Werkbund Estate was the final great international showcase of the Austrian Werkbund. Already in summer 1932,
Josef Frank withdrew from the board; in January 1933, Hoffmann scathingly turned his back on the Werkbund, as he
felt slighted by the decision to entrust Oskar Strnad rather
than him with the design of the Austrian section of the Triennale in Milan.[37] However, the driving force behind the divi-

sion taking place was not Hoffmann, but rather, Clemens
Holzmeister, who fostered a deep aversion to Frank and at
a meeting of the Werkbund in February 1933 openly refuted
the latter's artistic ability.[38] In June 1933, when Hermann
Neubacher then also stepped down from his office as president, the Werkbund's division could no longer be stopped.
On 24 February 1934, the "New Austrian Werkbund" was
founded, with Clemens Holzmeister as president and Josef
Hoffmann and Peter Behrens as vice presidents. The intention was to accentuate "Austrian work and Austrian talent,"
with the "revival of the old Werkbund program," and "become Austria's cultural conscience."[39] The closer orientation
on traditional handicrafts and a supposed "vernacular" culture met the new political conditions: however, contrary to
claims made otherwise, the association was not at all anti-
Semitic[40]— the Jewish publishing house owner Sigmund
Rosenbaum, for example, was on the board.[41] For Hoffmann,
however, the division of the Werkbund was a Pyrrhic victory,
as under the new powers, rather than he, the politically well-
connected Holzmeister should take over the leading role in
the cultural field. The "old" Austrian Werkbund, extremely
weakened in its possibilities through the division, tried to
further demonstrate intellectual and cultural openness under

its new president Hans Tietze. Oskar Kokoschka and Ernst Křenek were admitted to the Werkbund already in 1933. The Werkbund's final public activities included a lecture by Robert Musil entitled "On Stupidity" in March 1937.[42]

After the Anschluss in 1938, both Werkbunds were dissolved by the new powers in the course of "coordination," and their Jewish members banished or murdered. Hermann Neubacher became the first Nazi mayor of Vienna in 1938 and procured several contracts for Josef Hoffmann: furnishings for the "House of Fashion" in Palais Lobkowitz[43] (1938), a project for a guesthouse for the City of Vienna[44] (1938 or 1939), and the design for a mausoleum for the Albanian national hero Georg Kastriota, alias Skanderbeg, including a

showcase for his insignia[45] (1944), which would have hardly come about otherwise. Shortly before his death, Hoffmann would design a city hall for Addis Abeba in 1954/55, where the former high Nazi official Neubacher, was meanwhile working as advisor to the emperor Haile Selassie.[46]

Eduard F. Sekler appropriately ascertained that Hoffmann's insistence on a traditional concept of arts and crafts "does not reveal a genuine ideological coming to terms with the great technological, economic, and social changes that profoundly altered the Europe of the 1930s."[47] Hoffmann was disinterested in, or even lacked understanding of the potential of the work of the Werkbund beyond the promotion of the arts and crafts—there is no other way to explain his repeated active involvement in the division of the association. Moreover, Hoffmann's stalwart generation of new artistic forms unfazed by sociopolitical and economic transformations would inevitably clash with Josef Frank's talk about the "destruction of form"[48] as the essential task of the present. Unperturbed by the pressing issues of the day, the apparently playfully accomplished high quality of Hoffmann's works, while not contributing to the problem-conscious and purposeful work of the Werkbund, at least contributed significantly to a sustained high respect for Austrian decorative arts in the final phase of his history. ∎

Fig. 8 JH, living room in house no. 8 of Vienna's Werkbundsiedlung, 1932
ANL, Picture Archives, 423011-D
Photo: Julius Scherb, Vienna

1   Josef Hoffmann to Max Welz, March 1933, quoted by Sekler, Eduard F., *Josef Hoffmann: The Architectural Work*, Princeton, NJ 1985, 498. Trans. Eduard F. Sekler and John Maass. Also the following quotes.

2   "Ausschaltung der Juden im Werkbund," in: *12-Uhr-Blatt* 23 Dec 1933, see Welzig, Maria, *Josef Frank 1885–1967. Das architektonische Werk*, Vienna/Cologne/Weimar 1998, 163; Posch, Wilfried, *Clemens Holzmeister. Architekt zwischen Kunst und Politik*, Salzburg 2010, 243–244.

3   On the history of the Austrian Werkbund, see Achleitner, Friedrich, "Der Österreichische Werkbund und seine Beziehungen zum Deutschen Werkbund," in: Burckhardt, Lucius (ed.), *Der Werkbund in Deutschland, Österreich und der Schweiz. Form ohne Ornament*, Stuttgart 1978, 102–113; Gmeiner, Astrid/Pirhofer, Gottfried, *Der Österreichische Werkbund. Alternative zur klassischen Moderne in Architektur, Raum- und Produktgestaltung*, Salzburg/Vienna 1985; Posch, Wilfried, "Die österreichische Werkbundbewegung 1907–1928," in Ackerl, Isabella/Neck, Rudolf (eds.), *Geistiges Leben im Österreich der Ersten Republik*, Vienna 1986, 279–312; id., "Köln – Paris – Wien. Der Österreichische Werkbund und seine Ausstellungen," in: Nierhaus, Andreas/Orosz, Eva-Maria (eds.), *Werkbundsiedlung Wien 1932. Ein Manifest des Neuen Wohnens*, exh. cat. Wien Museum, Salzburg 2012.

4   Vetter, Adolf, "Die Bedeutung des Werkbundgedankens für Österreich," in: *Zur fünften Tagung des Deutschen Werkbundes Wien 6.–9. Juni 1912*, Vienna [1912], n.p.; subsequently also the following quotes. On the prominent audience of the

meeting, see *Deutscher Werkbund: Liste der Teilnehmer an der Wiener Jahresversammlung d. Deutschen Werkbundes 6.–9. Juni 1912*, n.p.

5   See Posch 1986 (see note 3), 291.

6   Ibid.

7   "Die Schaffung des österreichischen Werkbundes," in: *Neues Wiener Tagblatt* 1 May 1913, 12.

8   On the history of the Wiener Werkstätte see most recently, Witt-Dörring, Christian/Staggs, Janis (eds.), *Wiener Werkstätte 1903–1932: The Luxury of Beauty*, exh. cat. Neue Galerie New York, Munich/London/New York 2017.

9   See among others, Hoffmann, Josef, "My Work," lecture given on 22 Feb 1911 at the Niederösterreichischer Gewerbeverein (Lower Austrian Trade Association), manuscript quoted by Sekler 1985 (see note 1), 486–492: 490.

10 On this see the article "A Truly Effective Culture of Taste in Atectonic Classicism: The Exhibitions in Rome (1911) and Cologne (1914)" by Rainald Franz in this catalog.

11 Jessen, Peter, "Die deutsche Werkbundausstellung Köln 1914," in: *Jahrbuch des Deutschen Werkbundes 1915*, Munich 1915, 1–42: 8.

12 Eisler, Max, *Österreichische Werkkultur*, ed. Austrian Werkbund, Vienna 1916, 54.

13 Hoffmann, Josef, "Wiens Zukunft," in *Der Merker*, December 1919, quoted by Sekler 1985 (see note 1), 492–493: 492.

14 Tietze, Hans, "Ausstellung österreichischer Kunstgewerbe," in: *Der neue Tag* 11 Dec 1919, 4. Also following quotes. See also Posch 1986 (see note 3), 301.

15 Tietze, Hans, "Österreichisches Kunstgewerbe," in: *Der neue Tag* 25 Dec 1919, 8–9: 8.

16 "Zitat der Replik von Josef Hoffmann," in: Tietze, Hans, "Die Frage des österreichischen Kunstgewerbes," in: *Der neue Tag* 1 Feb 1920, 5–6: 5.

17 *Kunstschau 1920, Juni – September*, exh. cat. AMAI, [Vienna 1920], 5 and 7.

18 Tietze, Hans, "Die Wiener Kunstschau, die Wiener Werkstätte und der Österreichische Werkbund," in: *Kunstchronik und Kunstmarkt* (55) 46 1920, 892–895: 892.

19 Posch 1986 (see note 3), 299.

20 Ibid., 301–302.

21 Ibid., 300.

22 Tietze 1920 (see note 18), 894.

23 Posch 1986 (see note 3), 300.

24 Tietze, Hans, "Werkbund Wien," in: *Kunstchronik und Kunstmarkt* (55) 41/42 1921, 765–766: 766. Subsequently also the following quotes.

25 Posch 1986 (see note 3), 305.

26 On this see the article "'A Shrine of a Thousand Treasures to Admire and Stroll Through': The Austrian Pavilion at the International Decorative Arts Exhibition in Paris in 1925" by Rainald Franz and Markus Kristan in this catalog.

27 Posch 1986 (see note 3), 311.

28 Ibid., 311; Posch 2010 (see note 2), 237.

29 On the Werkbund Estate, see Krischanitz, Adolf/Kapfinger, Otto, *Die Wiener Werkbundsiedlung. Dokumentation einer Erneuerung*, Vienna 1985; Nierhaus/Orosz 2012 (see note 3); Kapfinger, Otto, "Anspruch und Ausgang. Zur Projekt- und Baugeschichte der Internationalen Werkbundsiedlung Wien 1932," in: ibid., 36–57.

30 On the memorial for Otto Wagner, see Nierhaus, Andreas, "Josef Hoffmanns Denkmal für Otto Wagner. Zu einer Neuerwerbung des Wien

Fig. 9 JH, houses in Vienna's Werkbundsiedlung, 1932
ANL, Picture Archives, 423013-D
Photo: Julius Scherb, Vienna

Museums," in: *Wiener Geschichtsblätter* (64) 2 2009, 1–11.

31 Sekler 1985 (see note 1), CR 326, 422.

32 Kapfinger 2012 (see note 29), 45. In addition to the localization "Wien XIX" (Vienna, 19th district) in the picture caption, arguing against such an identification, is that a photo of the model in the estate of Oswald Haerdtl, who was apparently involved in the project, is listed as "Wohnhaus Franz Humhal" or "Franz Humhal's house" (Stiller, Adolph, *Oswald Haerdtl: Architekt und Designer 1899–1959*, Salzburg 2000, CR 65). In light of the accordance with the other designs for the Werkbund Estate, which reached through to the slightly sloping topography of the original building site, it is, however, possible that Hoffmann only slightly adapted the project already largely worked out for the Werkbund Estate for the new, potential clients. In a contribution on Hoffmann in *Deutsche Kunst und Dekoration* (67) 1930/31, 278, with the model photo likewise programmatically placed before it, the location information is missing for the illustration.

33 Österreichischer Werkbund (ed.), *Josef Hoffmann zum sechzigsten Geburtstag 15. Dezember 1930* (special publication of the journal *Almanach der Dame*, Vienna), [Vienna 1930].

34 Kapfinger 2012 (see note 29), 44.

35 At the start of the planning, it was said that a model estate for Vienna was "especially important. As here, a turbulent building activity of grandiose scale often impairs the consideration of the problems of modern building methods." "Mitteilungen des Österreichischen Werkbundes," in: *Die Form* (4) 22 1929.

36 Sekler 1985 (see note 1), CR 333, 423 f.; Kapfinger, Otto, "Haus 8/9/10/11. Josef Hoffmann, Wien," in: Nierhaus/Orosz 2012 (see note 3), 120.

37 The newspapers provided detailed reporting, among others: "Konflikt im Werkbund," in: *Der Tag* 19 Jan 1933, 3; "Professor Hoffmann und der Werkbund," in: *Die Stunde* 21 Jan 1933, 5; Max Eisler, "Konflikt im Werkbund," in: *Der Morgen* 24 Jul 1933, 9–10; "Prof. Strnad über die Werkbund-spaltung," in: *Der Abend* 13 Dec 1933, 3. See also Sekler 1985 (see note 1), 209; Gmeiner/Pirhofer 1985 (see note 3), 182.

38 Posch 2010 (see note 2), 241–242.

39 Neuer Werkbund Österreichs (statement), in: *Profil* (2) 3 1934, VII.

40 Achleitner 1978 (see note 3), 111.

41 Posch 2010 (see note 2), 246. In addition to the printing press brothers Rosenbaum, also the designer Emmy Zweybrück-Prochaska belonged to the preparation committee of the New Austrian Werkbund (printed call, UAA, Archive and Collection, 2734/Q/1).

42 Musil, Robert, *Über die Dummheit* (On Stupidity), Vienna 1937.

43 Sekler 1985 (see note 1), 221 and CR 382, 439 f.

44 Ibid., 220 and CR 384, 440 f.

45 Ibid., 223 and CR 393, 444 f.

46 Ibid., 225–226 and CR 403, 449.

47 Ibid., 210.

48 Frank, Josef, "Architecture as Symbol. Elements of the German New Building," trans. John Sands, in: Bojankin, Tano/Long, Christopher/Meder, Iris (eds.), *Josef Frank: Writings. Vol. 2: Published Writings 1931–1965*, Vienna 2012, 173.

Fig. 10 Josef Hoffmann at the opening of Vienna's Werkbundsiedlung
Die Bühne 331, July 1932, 16, photo: Franz Mayer

Fig. 1 JH, design for a gown for a masked ball, executed by the Wiener Werkstätte, ca. 1910
MAK, T 11827
© MAK/Georg Mayer

Lara Steinhäußer

Women's Clothing as Another Surface

Josef Hoffmann and Fashion

In his monograph Eduard F. Sekler verified Josef Hoffmann's enduring interest in the phenomenon that is fashion and attributed this to his claim to the total design of all aspects of life; characteristic of the contemporary avant-garde, this claim was already pronounced in Hoffmann's oeuvre by the turn of the century and can be traced all the way through to his late work.[1] Indeed, it is possible to identify several aspects of his career that demonstrate his affinity for fashion. On the basis of the key facts[2] outlined here, his role as a networker in the promotion of fashion and his own design work in this sector, predominantly in the area of clothing, will become apparent.

Josef Hoffmann designed fashionable accessories made of silver or leather for the Wiener Werkstätte (WW) from the outset, including hatpins, belt buckles, wallets, and handbags.[3] Many of his fabric designs for the WW—which could also be purchased retail—were employed not only for interiors but also for clothing designs. For instance, in 1912 one of his classics, the pattern *Apollo*, was used together with other WW fabrics by Remigius Geyling, who like Hoffmann was a member of the Klimt Group, for Iphigenie Buchmann's costume in *Caesar and Cleopatra*.[4] What is striking about these costumes is that their straight cut appears to be based on that of the famous Hoffmann dresses realized around 1910.

A handful of designs prove that Hoffmann was himself a designer of dresses. They can all be traced back to a simple basic pattern that emphasizes the surface, which—in accordance with the dress reform trends of the early 20th century—hangs loosely around the waist and does not restrict the wearer's movements. The only part of the known models that varies is the length of their sleeves. Hoffmann's design principle of foregrounding decoration through reduced basic forms can be found in dresses predominantly structured using (graphic) patterns or black-and-white contrasts, as well as in accessories like the famous little bags with gold embossed leather.[5]

The execution of the earliest surviving design for a dress, dated 1904,[6] is documented by two photographs in the WW Archive at the MAK.[7] Handwritten notes by Eduard Josef Wimmer-Wisgrill, who was head of the WW fashion department from at least 1911 and was responsible for most of the designs,[8] allow us to identify two other dresses as Hoffmann's designs.[8] Its structuring by means of three-dimensional fabric roses, which gather individual sections, sets one of these designs apart from the other known models whose surfaces are primarily conceived as being two-dimensional. Two more sketches have been preserved in the National Gallery Prague.[9] The execution of one of these two appears certain due to an illustration in *Wiener Mode*, which was printed in 1911 in the context of a report on WW fashion and in which another design by Hoffmann is also depicted.[10] The second Prague sketch resembles Hoffmann's gown for a masked ball for two cousins of the Wittgenstein family, one of which survives as the only dress after his design.[11] Despite being considerably lengthened and partly gathered around the chest, the always slightly varied cut is reminiscent of a type of North Indian tunic, which was not only collected and worn by Alfred Roller's wife Mileva at this time, but had also been displayed during the major costume exhibition at the Austrian Museum of Art and Industry (AMAI, today's MAK) as early as 1891 and subsequently acquired for the museum's collection.[12] There is also a theoretical basis to support this connection, considering that in 1898 Hoffmann had praised Indian clothing on account of its individual surface design in his article "Das individuelle Kleid" on artistically designed clothing.[13] More evidence attesting to Hoffmann's enthusiasm for Indian fabrics is his own textile collection, which includes examples of Indian clothing alongside pieces from the Austro-Hungarian Monarchy.[14]

Another drawing in the MAK collection, presumably a costume design, shows a kind of coat dress with geometric ornaments. A single newspaper article is the only written evidence of Hoffmann's design work in this area. In 1918 the *Montagsblatt* mentions that the costumes of Leopoldine Konstantin in *Das Weib und der Hampelmann* had been designed by Hoffmann for the WW.[15] In addition to the ladies' dresses and costumes, around 1914 he is said to have designed the gentlemen's leisurewear for the inhabitants of the guest rooms at the Primavesi country house in Winkelsdorf/Kouty nad Desnou (CZ) in the same patterns as those rooms' wallpapers.[16] All in all, Hoffmann's clothing designs can largely be dated to the early 1910s.[17] However, Janis Staggs speculates that Hoffmann—like his colleague Koloman Moser—might have created reform dresses for his first wife, Anna Hladik, prior to this period.[18] While there is not yet any evidence to substantiate this theory, a remark by Adolf Loos during the WW's early period that Hoffmann should found a ladies' fashion department, could be interpreted as an allusion to design activities of this kind.[19]

Fig. 2 JH, dress design
Mode photo book, ca. 1910
MAK, WWF 169-15

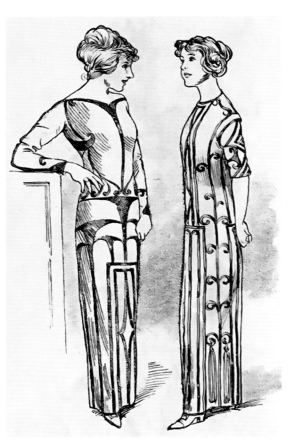

Fig. 3 Anonymous, illustration with dress designs
by Josef Hoffmann for the Wiener Werkstätte
Wiener Mode (24) 16 1911, 930

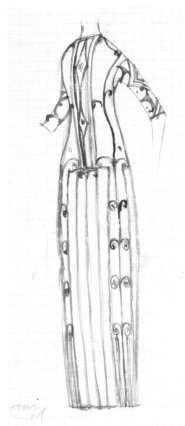

Fig. 4 JH, sketch
National Gallery Prague, K 17713

Fig. 5 Poiret fashion show in Vienna, staged with cushions
made of WW textiles and putto by Powolny
Světozor. Světová kronika současná slovem i obrazem. časopis pro zábavu i ponaučení (12), 7 Dec 1911, 356

Fig. 6 JH, sketch (possibly for a costume), ca. 1910
MAK, KI 11916

Fig. 7 Heinrich Böhler (photo), the dancer Stacia Napierkowska in a dress after a design by Josef Hoffmann, Vienna 1910
Museo d'arte Mendrisio, Donazione Fondazione Gino e Gianna Macconi

The link between architecture/interiors and fashion in the early 20th century[20] is a well-known phenomenon proven by countless theoretical and practical examples—like Hermann Muthesius, Henry van de Velde, or Frank Lloyd Wright, and in Vienna primarily Adolf Loos or indeed Hoffmann. Around 1900 designing the architectural surface was frequently understood as being similar to designing a dress. The foundation of this connection between textiles or dresses and architecture had been laid in the mid-19th century with Semper's "Bekleidungsprinzip" (principle of dressing); at the turn of the century it had effectively become a kind of trend for architects to occupy themselves with the modern design of not just the naked wall but also the reform dress. In this context Hoffmann's encouragement of an alliance between the WW and the Parisian fashion designer Paul Poiret should be mentioned. Poiret took the opposite route by proceeding from fashion to then explore interior design when he started emulating the examples of Franz Čižek's class and the WW

that he had encountered in Vienna; he subsequently founded the interior design company Martine, which worked on the basis of designs by freely taught, young girls. Poiret and the WW planned wide-ranging collaborations, with Poiret purchasing a dress by Hoffmann as a prototype, for example.[21] Hoffmann assumed the artistic direction of Poiret's fashion shows in Vienna,[22] as the use of WW textiles proves, and planned a—never realized—business premises with integrated living quarters and "theater,"[23] whose previously lost plans were only discovered in the course of research for this article. The "Motto: PAME" is probably an abbreviation referring to the first letters of the individual areas of Poiret's palace: Atelier, Maison, and École.[24]

This network made a significant contribution to the WW's international standing and, alongside Hoffmann's own creative work, probably also helped him to establish a name for himself as a fashion expert, which led to him being deemed an appropriate choice as a member of the jury for

5

9 10

18 p. 190

the Jung Wiener fashion prize in 1913[25] and as the artistic director of the *Modeausstellung* [Fashion Exhibition] at the AMAI in 1915/16. These two initiatives served to establish Austrian fashion on the international stage, Vienna's reputation as a fashion capital, and "artists' fashion" as the blueprint for fashion companies.[26] As can be inferred from the minutes of the meetings of the Imperial Royal Trade Advancement Bureau, "Councilor Hoffmann" was a member of the "committee for the preparation of a Viennese fashion show" as the "representative of the artists involved." At his suggestion a separate *Spitzen- und Zubehör-Ausstellung* [Lace and Accessories Exhibition] was organized as part of the fashion exhibition. In charge was the director of the Trade Advancement Bureau, Adolf Vetter, who like Hoffmann had been involved in founding the Austrian Werkbund in 1913. In 1925 their paths would cross again, when Hoffmann as the artistic director and Vetter as the general commissioner were both involved in organizing the Austrian contribution for the *International Exposition of Modern Decorative and Industrial Arts* in Paris.[27] It is therefore hardly surprising that

Vetter even became a member of the supervisory board in the final years of the WW.[28]

As these key facts have demonstrated, Hoffmann was able to establish himself as a fashion promoter as a result of his own independent design work in the field of fashion and with the aid of his personal network. In the interests of the Gesamtkunstwerk—or total work of art—he also made it possible for numerous students[29] to turn their hand to clothing design. The fruits of this labor were presented in some exhibitions like that with students' fashion drawings at the AMAI in 1924[30] or the show *Raum und Mode* [Room and Fashion] at the same venue in 1932.[31] Some architectural work, like the Schwestern Flöge fashion salon, the shop of the Otto Beyer publishing house's fashion plate and sewing pattern department,[32] and the *Haus der Mode* [House of Fashion],[33] illustrate the extent to which Hoffmann's expertise in this area and his symbolic power as a representative of a Viennese style or rather of a Viennese fashion were appreciated.

Fig. 8 Caricature of the week, Privy Councillor Dr. Adolf Vetter
Der Morgen 6 Mar 1916, 5

1   Sekler, Eduard F., *Josef Hoffmann: The Architectural Work*, Princeton, NY 1985, 220 f. Trans. Eduard F. Sekler and John Maass.
2   Among the numerous links with the production of textiles and fashion, the following details can be found in Hoffmann's biography: his family had shares in the Collalto'sche Kattunmanufaktur (cotton manufactory) in Brtnice and his second wife, Karla Schmatz, was a WW model. See: Franz, Rainald, "Die Restaurierung des Geburtshauses von Josef Hoffmann in Brtnice/Pirnitz, Tschechien," in: *Österreichische Zeitschrift für Kunst und Denkmalpflege* (58) 2004, 116–132: 117; Sekler 1985 (see note 1), 235.
3   Even a women's hat after his design can be found in: *Deutsche Kunst und Dekoration* 27 1910, 180.
4   *Linzer Tages-Post* 3 Sep 1911, 10; cf. e.g., Theatermuseum, Vienna, FS_PU264084.
5   Cf. Buxbaum, Gerda, *Mode aus Wien*, Salzburg/Vienna 1986, 265.
6   The design is now preserved in the Foundation Collection Kamm under K.Z 2136. For an illustration, see: Sekler 1985 (see note 1), 221.
7   For this comparison, see also: Völker, Angela, *Moda. Wiener Werkstätte*, Florence 1990, 7. Cf. also: MAK, WWF 124-20-5.
8   A sketch for a dress by Wimmer-Wisgrill; MAK, KI 13267-4, which resembles that in fig. 2, moved Völker to doubt the later added notes by Wimmer-Wisgrill. Cf. Völker, Angela, *Wiener*

Mode und Modefotografie. Die Modeabteilung der Wiener Werkstätte 1911–1932, Munich 1984, 10–20.
9   Fig. K 17713, see: Thun-Hohenstein, Christoph/Völker, Angela (eds.), *The Unknown Wiener Werkstätte: Embroidery and Lace 1906 to 1930*, Vienna 2017, 30.
10 A coat by Hoffmann is also reported on here: *Wiener Mode* (24) 16 1911, 930.
11 Cf. Thun-Hohenstein/Völker 2017 (see note 9), 28.
12 Cf. k. k. Österreichisches Museum für Kunst und Industrie (ed.), *Führer durch die Costüm-Ausstellung*, Vienna 1891, 28.
13 Hoffmann, Josef, "Das individuelle Kleid," in: *Die Wage* (1) 15, 9 Apr 1898. Cf. also Staggs, Janis, "The Inside: A Female Realm. Abandoning the Corset to Express Individual Character," in: id./Witt-Dörring, Christian (eds.), *Josef Hoffmann: Interiors 1902–1913*, exh. cat. Neue Galerie, New York/London/Munich 2006, 99–127: 99 f. It appears that the article was a response to an article by Loos published shortly beforehand, which praises the non-artistic clothing on graphics by Myrbach. Shapira, Elana, "Die kulturellen Netzwerke der Wiener Moderne. Loos, Hoffmann und ihre Klienten," in: Ottillinger, Eva B. (ed.), *Wagner, Hoffmann, Loos und das Möbeldesign der Wiener Moderne: Künstler, Auftraggeber, Produzenten*, exh. cat. Hofmobiliendepot, Vienna 2018, 123–133: 125. The WW's work program also includes general theoretical remarks on the production of clothing as early as 1905.
14 They include a blouse and a fragment of a headdress. Parallels to these pieces can be found in a similar blouse fragment, which, repurposed as a cushion, is part of the textile collection of Gustav Klimt or rather Emilie Flöge. Cf. Franz, Rainald, "Gustav Klimt und Josef Hoffmann. Als Reformer der grafischen Künste und der Raumkunst in der Gründungsphase von Secession und Wiener Werkstätte," in: Husslein-Arco, Agnes/Weidinger, Alfred (eds.), *Gustav Klimt – Josef Hoffmann. Pioniere der Moderne*, exh. cat. Belvedere Vienna, Munich/London/New York 2011, 38–49: 43–46.
15 Cf. *Montagblatt* 8 Jan 1918, n.p.; MAK, WWAN 83-190. An illustration in: *Sport und Salon* 18 Dec 1918, 11, might show one of the aforementioned costumes by Hoffmann.
16 One of these "cassocks" for Hanak has survived. See: Buxbaum 1986 (see note 5), 266. Hoffmann had already commented on menswear in his text "Das individuelle Kleid."
17 Under inventory number 1002304/KOS-1998-0037 a black evening gown from the late 1920s

has survived at the Kunstmuseum Den Haag, which is said to have been designed by Josef Hoffmann.
18 Staggs 2006 (see note 13), 102 f.
19 Cf. ibid., 120; Schweiger, Werner, *Wiener Werkstätte. Kunst und Handwerk*, Vienna 1982, 223.
20 Cf. esp. Wigley, Mark, *White Walls. Designer Dresses. The Fashioning of Modern Architecture*, Cambridge 1995.
21 *Neue Freie Presse* 2 Dec 1911, 10; *Wiener Sonn- und Montagszeitung* 4 Nov 1911, 6.
22 *Neues Wiener Tagblatt* 12 Nov 1911, 12; *Neues Wiener Journal* 19 Nov 1911, 11.
23 Zuckerkandl, Berta, "Paul Poiret und die Klimt-Gruppe," in: *Neues Wiener Journal* 25 Nov 1923, 5.
24 Goss, Jared, "Paul Poiret and the decorative arts," in: Koda, Harold/Bolton, Andrew (eds.), *Poiret*, exh. cat. Metropolitan Museum of Art, New York, New Haven/London 2007, 43–44: 43.
25 *Neue Freie Presse* 11 Jul 1913, 11.
26 It is also in this context that Hoffmann's initiative for the work *Mode Wien 1914/5*, published by Eduard Kosmack, should be seen for which numerous artists created graphics.
27 *Die Stunde* 17 Jun 1925, 6.
28 *Neue Freie Presse* 30 Apr 1931, 9.
29 Hence Leopold Kleiner reported in his memories of Josef Hoffmann, directed toward Wilhelm Mrazek, in 1975 on his architecture class at the School of Arts and Crafts: "[…] peacefully the fashion artist worked there alongside her male colleague, who was planning the design for a residential building on his drafting table […]." An almost identical description can also be found here: A. K., "Professor Dr. Ing. E.h. Josef Hoffmann Wien. 60 Jahre," in: *Deutsche Kunst und Dekoration* (67) 1930/31, 280. According to Kleiner, the then "Hoffmann school" had only just earned the name "Applied Art." Cf. also: "Kunstgewerbeschüler beim Schneidern," in: *Neues Wiener Journal* 7 Jan 1916, 6–7.
30 *Der Morgen* 14 Feb 1924, 7.
31 In the context of the exhibition *Raum und Mode* at the AMAI, fashion shows under the artistic direction of Wimmer-Wisgrill and Hoffmann were launched by the Trade Advancement Bureau of the Vienna Chamber of Commerce and the exhibition managers; cf. *Der Tag* 20 Dec 1932, 5.
32 Buxbaum 1986 (see note 5), 266.
33 As early as 1936 Hoffmann had argued the case for a fashion authority in an article. Cf. Sekler 1985 (see note 1), 221; see also the article "'The Leadership's Will': Hoffmann's Projects under National Socialism" by Matthias Boeckl in this catalog.

Fig. 9 JH, design for the floor plan
of Paul Poiret's Atelier Martine,
Paris, 1912, motto: PAME
MAK, WWGP 1999

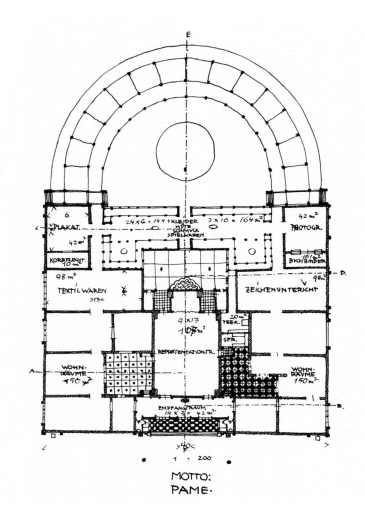

Fig. 10 JH, designs for the façades
of Paul Poiret's Atelier Matine,
Paris, 1912, motto: PAME
MAK, WWGP 2000

Fig. 1 Francis Jourdain, design for a nursery for Mme Rothschild
Drawing on paper with collages, colored inks, india ink and gouache, 1920
Musée d'art et d'histoire, Saint-Denis

Adrián Prieto

Beauty in Utility

The Reception of Josef Hoffmann in Belgium and France 1900–1939

Investigation of what remains of the complex and disjointed convergence of Paris and Vienna between 1900 and 1939 confirms what others have already suspected about the meaningfulness of a critical confrontation with this uncertain period. It would be naïve to assume that the development and reception of Josef Hoffmann's oeuvre played no role in those transcultural dynamics. Eduard F. Sekler, in his masterful work on the architect originally published in German in 1982, suggests that: "it has been too little noticed what an immense influence on the French decorative arts movement was exerted by Hoffmann, his school, and the Wiener Werkstätte."[1] Today this hypothesis maintains all its historiographical validity, pointing to the manifold resonances the architect's ideals and design experience triggered on various personalities and events in the francophone context, and especially in Paris. Nevertheless, is it possible to determine how, and to what extent, his relevance actually materialized beyond one-off encounters and several obvious stylistic elements? Did Hoffmann really play an important role in the shaping of modern French decorative arts and vice versa; did these events leave a mark on his own work? Those who attempt to draft an answer must first review the undisputed place of Modernism in France and the legitimacy of a canonic narrative that no longer seems entirely correct today, or, like everything that is presented without being questioned, at least suspicious. Geopolitical tensions and a radicalization of nationalist sensibilities have led to a routine disregard of the convergences between the two capitals, and often their reduction to mere anecdotes.[2] Under these conditions, which are inseparably tied to the history of the European avantgarde's origins, Hoffmann's oeuvre is likely to be perceived as floating between events and ideologies. In this regard, investigations by numerous historians and researchers into the axis of transfer between Vienna and Brussels provide an important reference for proposing a transregional reading of the architect's oeuvre without resorting to a rhetoric founded in territorial loyalty.

Since the 1976 publication of the article "Léon Sneyers ou la sécession importée,"[3] significant progress has been made within the context of research on the visual representation of the Vienna Secession and the impact of its symbolic power emanating from Stoclet House (1905–1911) on the development of Belgian Modernism. The French context, however, is determined by very diverse structural conditions, in which the ideological dominance of the discipline of the École des Beaux Arts and the misunderstandings surrounding tradition allow only a limited reception and visibility of foreign ideas. Of course, these circumstances did not preclude the reception of Hoffmann's ideals in a variety of ways and intensities. On the one hand, the suggestive power of his practice and the radical creative imagery of the Wiener Werkstätte influenced the shaping of a decorative taste à la mode, which became manifest especially among the heterogeneous group of designers known as les coloristes. One of the most representative proponents of this is the couturier Paul Poiret (1879–1944), who, after a visit to Vienna in 1911, founded Atelier Martine (1911–1929) following the precedent of the Wiener Werkstätte.[4] On the other hand, references to Vienna, and particularly to Hoffmann, were important guidelines for those who aligned their principles and personal visions in opposition to the dogmatic Rationalism that would be ascribed to modern architecture in France from 1925 onward, with Le Corbusier as the archetype of a modern architect. Two figures stand out as particularly sensitive to these vicissitudes in the reception of Hoffmann's ideas: the architect Robert Mallet-Stevens (1886–1945) and the painter and designer Francis Jourdain (1876–1958). Through their practice, they both became mediators between the two different approaches to Modernism, drawing attention to visions from outside the Parisian context. The intensity with which they adopted a series of recognizable principles from Hoffmann—primarily in the areas of formal abstraction, spatial representation, and composition—are notable for a particular attitude toward design. Through these connections, we are able to trace the lineage of Modernism from its roots in the Arts & Crafts movement that branched out in the direction of Vienna, a fact that has been overlooked in the chronology of sources of French Modernism. Related aesthetic traits are visible in many projects by Mallet-Stevens and his circle, which define, in their own ways, the narrative of France's modern architecture and decorative arts.

Participation in the 1900 Paris Exposition offered Hoffmann the first opportunity to confront an international and cosmopolitan audience with the formal simplicity and

Fig. 2 Robert Mallet-Stevens, design for a country house for M. Écorcheville, 1914
Musée des Arts Décoratifs, Paris, 38608 A3

meticulous realization of his works from this period. Thanks to the international distribution of the magazine *Ver Sacrum* (1898–1903), his name was known in French intellectual circles and among a handful of connoisseurs as being associated with the spirit of renewal of the Secession style (1897).[5] In Paris, one of his contributions was exhibited in the hall of the Vienna School of Arts and Crafts, "in that charming Austrian wing, which presents us with the country's modern decorative-arts movement."[6] It resonated greatly with the audience and international critics alike.[7] The space, pointedly symbolic, was conceived as "a grove of the muses,"[8] and gathered together numerous works by his students. It is not surprising that one of the first critical reactions in France focused precisely on educational reform, or what the artist and designer M. P. Verneuil identified in his article as "L'Enseignement des Arts Décoratifs à Vienne."[9] The report mentioned the class of Professor Hoffmann, which he had taught since 1899, and contained numerous illustrations of works by his students, including several drawings by Max Benirschke (1880–1961), who stood out by virtue of his talent in the graphic arts. Of course, many of Benirschke's colleagues shared this talent. Between 1900 and 1919 they would produce some of the most radical and avant-garde works of their era,[10] although their significance has been underestimated to the present day. The style of teaching, which did justice to the life of modern people,[11] was for the most part practical, favoring intuition over doctrine. Yet Hoffmann's advancement of his teaching activities and desire to pave the way for an international style through the commercial ambitions of the Wiener Werkstätte, while striving for universal applicability, remained simultaneously obliged to the values closely associated with the idiosyncrasies of a local bourgeoisie. A tension that became evident in the rigor of his creative process and his inability to react to the surrounding trends can be seen in a letter written by Fritz Waerndorfer, founder and patron of the Wiener Werkstätte, during a stay with Hoffmann in Paris in 1906: "Hoffmann did not see a single building in Paris that could have interested him in the slightest, and so we lived in the Musée Cluny, where we studied the tapestries very thoroughly."[12] These contradictions are important in the analysis of Hoffmann's international significance—especially between 1900 and

1925—with regard to an idealized representation of his work from the irreducible "French view." This becomes clear with various critical voices whose one-sided opinion succumbs to the wish to emphasize merely the decorative aspects of his art, as occurred in the article "Quelques interieurs à Vienne, par Josef Hoffmann"[13] published in 1904, amply furnished with illustrations of the four villas on the Hohe Warte in Vienna. It is easy to imagine how Hoffmann's elegant designs might evoke a certain dismissal among those who emphasized the "bon goût français"[14] as their stylistic reference. The situation was different for Dagobert Peche, Hoffmann's admired colleague in the Wiener Werkstätte, whose playful designs corresponded more with Parisian preferences, and toward whom, according to Sekler, Hoffmann was not entirely indifferent.[15] Nonetheless, such approaches from the French perspective disregarded the comprehensiveness and steady transformation of Hoffmann's architecture by equating his vision after 1911 exclusively with the archetypal Modernism presented by Stoclet House. The reception of Hoffmann's work in France relied on fragmented resonances, based largely on a sporadic exchange of images and for the most part lacking a critical/theoretical apparatus and first-hand experience. Thus, once again, the crucial role played by publications and photography is a trait paradoxical to the cause of Viennese Modernism—specifically in the development of creative processes in Belgium and France.

In 1911, the Austrian magazine *Der Architekt* published a drawing entitled *Projekt einer Brücke über die Seine* [Project for a Bridge on the Seine].[16] What might well be a utopian vision by a student at the School of Arts and Crafts in Vienna is actually a design by the architect Mallet-Stevens. Apart from its potential as metaphor, this project marks the beginning of a period that would last until 1921 (i.e., the start of Mallet-Stevens's construction of a house for Paul Poiret[17]), during which the architect settled—in line with Hoffmann's ideal—on a response to a series of intuitive realizations that had occupied him during the course of his education at the École Spéciale d'Architecture.[18] His exercises on paper are defined by freedom in dealing with dynamic shapes, colors, and proportions. Their masterful execution and playful grace are demonstrated in the publication *Une Cité Moderne* (1917–1923).[19] Here Mallet-Stevens

3

calls for a modern utopian community based on an ideal of formal beauty, which, as is the case with Hoffmann, is conceived as a medium for progress and social development. This Viennese period is generally interpreted under the questionable notion of "influence" as contextualized within Mallet-Stevens's relationship to the Stoclet family,[20] which allowed him the privilege of witnessing the materialization of Hoffman's ideal in Brussels. While this does not entirely explain his involvement in the Viennese situation and precise knowledge of it, nor address the full extent of his inquisitive search for and subsequent spreading of architectural concepts beyond his Parisian milieu, it does explain why he focused his full attention on Vienna. Mallet-Stevens's proposals make no secret of projects such as the Ast villa (1909–1911), the entrance to the Kunstschau pavilion (1908), and the pavilion of the *International Fine Arts Exhibition* in Rome (1911); neither do they fail to acknowledge works by students of Hoffmann, such as Emanuel Margold (1888–1962).[21] Furthermore, he promoted values and solutions formulated by Hoffmann in numerous articles published in French and Belgian magazines, for example, in "Le noir et le blanc" (1911)[22] and in "Une cuisine moderne" (1913).[23] Through all of this, he would become the sole representative of this school in France: an exceptional phenomenon when one considers that, contrary to many speculations and myths[24] fueled by the lack of archival material, there is little possibility that he studied with Hoffmann in Vienna. Francis Jourdain, his colleague and friend, likewise maintained a graphic style very close to Hoffmann's, manifested chiefly in the color palette and composition of the interior space. In the materialization of his vision, however, it became evident early on that Jourdain attributed great significance in his designs to then-current debates about the ornament. We are thus talking about two pioneers of Modernism of the French interwar period whose connection to Vienna in each case shaped a perspective and a career, not to mention its subsequent historical reception. Furthermore, their special sensitivity offers the chance to investigate how deftly they transferred some formal concepts to other artists—for example, Djo-Bourgeois or René Gabriel, who belonged to a later generation and apparently had no direct relationship to the Viennese mindset.

At the *International Exposition of Modern Decorative and Industrial Arts* in Paris in 1925, it became obvious how diversely the positions had evolved since 1900 and how greatly they reflected the distress and problems of the period. Hoffmann, who meanwhile enjoyed great international esteem, had designed the Austrian pavilion, which was enthusiastically received by critics and the audience and was seen as a contribution of the highest quality in the realm of modern decorative arts. The momentary expectations, however, gave way to the discomfort and disappointment of those who envisioned a different type of Modernism. An article by Mallet-Stevens about Stoclet House, published anonymously, expressed—despite great admiration—a general mood regarding Hoffmann's architecture:

> "Since 1907 great technological advances have been made: reinforced concrete allows for unimagined audacity, a new aesthetic is born. The architecture of tomorrow will invariably differ from Hoffmann's concepts—the unornamented Viennese architecture of Loos is gradually moving away from Hoffmann's [...]."[25]

The wave form on the façade of the Austrian pavilion—one of Hoffmann's frequently employed leitmotifs—is dismissively described as a decorative gesture and his compact with the beautiful seen as something that radically differentiates him, both socially and ideologically, from other forms of Modernism. Unable to react to new expectations of—and decorative trends for—contemporary architecture, Hoffmann reaffirmed his conviction that form was essential, not doctrine, whereby, as Sekler explains,[26] he apparently invoked no longer appropriate pre-industrial values. And like a circle that draws to a close, the same French critic who had visited the School of Arts and Crafts in 1902 wrote a new article in which he points out Hoffmann's estrangement with regard to contemporary expectations: "In instruction and in the essence of the works of the students, no changes whatsoever can be recognized in comparison with 20 years earlier."[27] Nonetheless, he emphasizes the exceptional quality of student works exhibited in the wing of the Grand Palais designed by Oswald Haerdtl, Hoffmann's confidant, who at the time had recently taken over directorship of the master's studio. The forms and geometric volumes of Haerdtl's 1925 Parisian project responded to the entrance of the tourism pavilion designed by Mallet-Stevens, only meters away, as though by osmosis. In this, an interesting development toward a De Stijl-movement-inspired vectoral architecture becomes clear—something identified by the architectural historian Bruno Reichlin[28] as "Viennese Cubism," by which he was referencing Hoffmann's formal abstraction, such as in the prophetic bas-relief on the portico of a side room during the 14th exhibition of the Secession in 1902.

As a result of diverging trends within the European avantgarde, characterized by the dominance of Rationalism after 1925 and focused on the illusion of an historical rupture commonly associated with the Modernist movement—a situation accentuating Hoffmann's progressively diminishing relevance and banishing him to the sphere of compromised Historicist—Hoffmann's fidelity to form was seen as a reason to question his devotion to the Modernist cause. Increasingly, it distanced him from international debates and events pertaining to the future of architecture. The connections with Paris became limited to isolated encounters, for example with André Lurçat and Gabriel Guévrékian during their participation in creation of the Vienna Werkbundsiedlung

Fig. 3 Robert Mallet-Stevens, project for a bridge over the Seine, 1911
Der Architekt (XVII) 1911, 76

Fig. 4 Leon Sneyers,
illustration *L'intérieur
moderne*
The Home, June 1914.
CIVA Collection, Brussels

(Werkbund Estate) in 1932. Guévrékian transformed himself into an authentic advocate for the relationship between Paris and Vienna, becoming an essential figure for the group of Austrian emigrants that included Hans Vetter, Jean (Hans) Welz, Adolf Loos, and himself. After the enthusiastic reaction to many of the objects shown in Paris in 1925, the Austrian Chamber of Commerce commissioned Guévrékian with the design of Le Studio Viennois, a sales branch (and, moreover, cultural showcase) presenting objects from the Wiener Werkstätte, Hagenauer, and Haus und Garten, and intended to provide a lexicon of Viennese taste of the period. But in 1933—perhaps due to the difficulty of winning over the Parisian clientele, the economic and political crisis, or the dissolution of the Wiener Werkstätte (in late 1932)—the shop made way for a small café. The walls were painted with idyllic mountain landscapes and traditional specialties were served—a metaphor for a near future when the motto "Austria as holiday destination" would define the program of the national pavilion at the *Brussels International Exposition* of 1935 as well as in Paris at the 1937 *International Exposition of Art and Technology in Modern Life*. Both pavilions were designed by Haerdtl, who found it easier to keep step with developments, and who had officially become Hoffmann's successor as the country's spokesperson in decorative and architectural matters.

Nikolaus Pevsner, in his book *Pioneers of Modern Design. From William Morris to Walter Gropius* (1936), leaves no doubt that Hoffmann played a transcendental role in the history of Modernism in the early 20th century; however, the historian's vision of design as anchored in historical continuity and interdisciplinarity, neglects the specific conditions of the era and simplifies the nuances of transnational approaches to Modernism. Repetition of such handed-down views has perpetuated a complacent misconception, which, among other things, has led to an overlooking of the obvious evidence of Hoffmann's significance in the francophone context. Thus, to return to the questions posed at the outset, it seems evident that, as in Belgium, references to Hoffmann's oeuvre shaped various attitudes within French Modernism, while not always being cited as features of decorative taste. Nonetheless, a critical examination of the facts is necessary to determine the extent to which this synergy between Paris and Vienna actually became manifest. The results of such an examination will depend on the extent to which it is possible to integrate the various personalities and specific historical conditions. Ultimately, the results must be subordinated to the capricious variability of Hoffmann's oeuvre, the image and perception of which depend on the position and perspective from which they are viewed. Meanwhile, it seems certain that the beauty of his creations and his ideals became an essential guide for the feverish intuitions of all who were seeking their own way through the uncertainties of the period, simply striving to be modern.   ▪

Fig. 5 Oswald Haerdtl,
room of the architecture
class of the School of
Arts and Crafts at the
*International Exposition
of Modern Decorative
and Industrial Arts*, Paris,
1925

MAK, KI 23086-56

1   Sekler, Eduard F., *Josef Hoffmann: The Architectural Work*, Princeton, NJ 1985, 186. Trans. Eduard F. Sekler and John Maass.
2   The continued tension and political hostility between the two countries resulted in a succession of patriotic gestures from the Viennese intellectual circles in favor of the cultural independence of Austria from the tyranny of French taste. After the outbreak of the war in 1914, the Austrian critic Berta Zuckerkandl, among others, insisted in the *Wiener Allgemeine Zeitung* on a "Freedom from Paris," in order to allow the demand for a national taste, in which the Wiener Werkstätte should have a decisive role. See Hess, Heather, "Producing Fashion. Commerce, Culture and Consumers," in: *The Wiener Werkstätte and the Reform Impulse*, VI, University of Pennsylvania, 2008.
3   Culot, Maurice, "Léon Sneyers ou la sécession importée," in: *Bulletin des A.A.M.* 8 1976.
4   On a tour through central Europe, Paul Poiret stopped in Vienna in November 2011, to hold three eagerly awaited lectures.
5   The Viennese artists were represented in several of the Grand Palais's spaces; Hoffmann designed the entryway and two exhibition spaces, which, in relation to the exhibited objects and works, underscored the complicated and harmonious polychromy of the ensemble.
6   "Quelques Intérieurs à Vienne, par Josef Hoffmann," in: *Art et Décoration* (XVI) Jul–Dec 1904, 61.
7   In 1902, the magazine *Innendekoration* published in Darmstadt by Alexander Koch devoted a long article to him, written by the critic Joseph August Lux, which emphasized the quality of Hoffmann's work and pointed to the new orientation that he had triggered in German arts and crafts. A fact that was also insinuated by Charles-Edouard Jeanneret (Le Corbusier) in his 1912 publication, *Étude sur le mouvement d'art decoratif en Allemagne*, where he wrote, "Vienna provided a sensitive soil [...] Joseph Hoffmann imposed his undeniable personality, and became the soul of an unparalleled speculative enterprise—the Wiener Werkstätte—that brought Vienna attention unequaled to this day."
8   Sekler 1985 (see note 1), 36.
9   "L'Enseignement des Arts Décoratifs à Vienne," in: *Art et Décoration* (XI) Jan–Jun 1902, 143–164.

10   Students, such as Hans Scharfen, Johann Stubner, Georg Winkler, and Carl Witzmann, etc., who are hardly known due to the lack of available records, or because they were no longer productive after their education. Their designs possess a radicalness, which in some cases, anticipated the formal compositions and colorfully designed spatial representation methods that developed in the second half of the 1920s in the trends of the avant-garde in Europe. See: *Raummalerei – Spatial Painting. Künstler um Josef Hoffmann 1900–1910/Artists in the Josef Hoffmann Group*, Galerie Metropol, Vienna/New York, 1987.
11   Sekler 1985 (see note 1), chapter 1.
12   Letter from Fritz Waerndorfer to Adolphe Stoclet, 22 Nov 1906, quoted by Witt-Dörring, Christian, "Palais Stoclet," in: id./Staggs, Janis (eds.), *Wiener Werkstätte 1903–1932: The Luxury of Beauty*, Munich/London/New York 2017, 385.
13   "Quelques Intérieurs à Vienne" 1904 (see note 6), 61–70.
14   As is evident from a letter to Hoffmann sent in 1920 by the French architect René Allard, who, after receiving several objects from the Wiener Werkstätte for sale in France, expressed his dismay, describing the pieces as grotesque and unsuccessful. However, Allard reminded him how pleased he was with the ceramics by Michael Powolny, which were closer to the Expressionist French taste. In: René Allard to Josef Hoffmann, Nov 1920; Prof. Häusler's archive, Vienna.
15   See Sekler 1985 (see note 1), 166–167: "Peche's [...] influence in the Wiener Werkstätte and on Hoffmann himself was very significant and lasted beyond his death in 1923."
16   *Der Architekt* (XVII) 76 1911. In 1914 two projects were again published. For a young French architect that is unusual, and can possibly be explained through mediation by Hoffmann, who had connections to the magazine.
17   In 1912, Poiret commissioned Hoffmann with a residential structure. However, the project never materialized, see Sekler 1985 (see note 1), 349. The original plans for that project were first found again in the course of this research, see the article "Women's Clothing as Another Surface: Josef Hoffmann and Fashion" by Lara Steinhäußer in this catalog. The construction work by Robert Mallet-Stevens in Mézy began in 1921 and lasted until

1923; the work had to be stopped due to the designer's bankruptcy. The photographs of the exposed concrete structure have usually been interpreted as the first modern ruins.
18   Founded 1865 and led by Émile Trélat, on the foundations of rationalist thinking by Viollet-le-Duc.
19   Mallet-Stevens, Robert, *Une cité moderne*, Paris 1922.
20   The architect is the nephew of Suzanne Stevens, who married Adolphe Stoclet in 1896. From 1904 Robert Mallet added the name Stevens to his signature. On the affiliations of the architect and his Belgian connections, see Culot, Maurice Robert, "Mallet-Stevens, reporter, critique d'art, décorateur. 1907–1914," in: id. (ed.), *Robert Mallet-Stevens. Itinéraires: Paris–Bruxelles–Hyères*, Paris 2016.
21   The work of both architects reveals strong parallels in many aspects and characteristics of its graphic production. In 1930 Margold wrote an introduction on Mallet-Stevens's work, for the publication Mallet-Stevens, Robert, *Dix années de réalisations en architecture et décoration*, Paris 1930.
22   Mallet-Stevens, Robert, "Le noir et le blanc (Lettre de Paris)," in: *Tekhné* 34 1911.
23   Mallet-Stevens, Robert, "Une cuisine moderne. Architecture et Décoration," in: *La Petite Illustration* 9 1913.
24   The recent discovery of a letter by Adolphe Stoclet to Fritz Waerndorfer from 1911, in which he announces the upcoming visit of his nephew to Vienna, debunks the numerous hypothesis made previously about Mallet-Stevens's possible residency in Vienna, and a collaboration in Hoffmann's studio. See Witt-Dörring 2017 (see note 12), 405.
25   Anonymous (Mallet-Stevens, Robert), "Le Palais Stoclet à Bruxelles," *L'Architecte* Jan 1924.
26   Sekler 1985 (see note 1), 190.
27   "L'enseignement de l'Art Décoratif en Autriche," in: *Art et Décoration* (XLIX) Jan–Jun 1926, 85–96.
28   See Reichlin, Bruno, "De Stijl aus Wien. Die Architekturausstellungen in Wien 1924 und Paris 1925," in: Stiller, Adolph, *Oswald Haerdtl. Architekt und Designer, 1899–1959*, Salzburg 2000, 60–67. On Mallet-Stevens see Reichlin, Bruno, "Mallet-Stevens versus De Stijl," in: Bois, Yve-Alain/Reichlin, Bruno/Troy, Nancy J. (eds.), *De Stijl et l'architecture en France*, Brussels 1985.

1934
1938

Benedikt Fred Dolbin, caricature of Josef Hoffmann, 1932
Johannes Spalt, *Josef Hoffmann. Porträts – Signets – Stempel*, Vienna 2002, 63

Fig. 1 JH, vitrine, executed by Franz Konecny for the *Das befreite Handwerk* [The Liberated Handicraft] exhibition at the AMAI in 1934
Walnut wood, glass
MAK, H 2156
© MAK/G. Nimatallah

Fig. 2 JH, cabinet, ca. 1935
Wood, painted
GALERIE BEI DER ALBERTINA · ZETTER

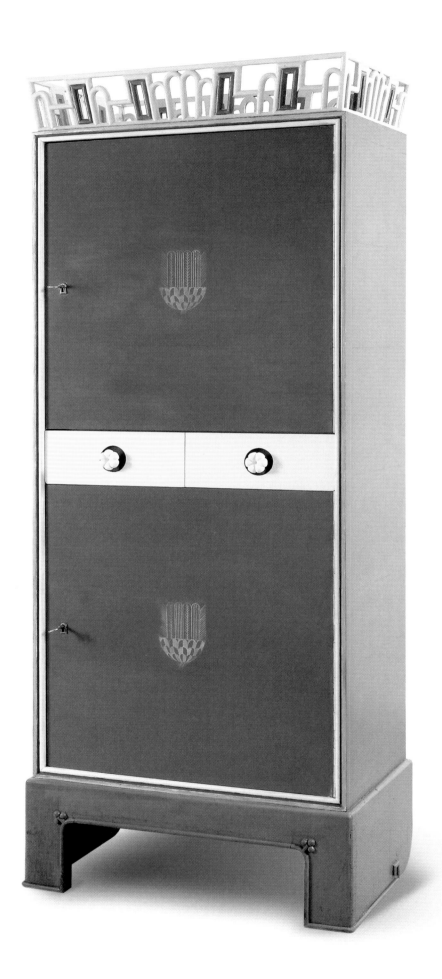

Fig. 5 Reconstruction of the *Boudoir d'une grande vedette* [Boudoir for a Big Star] shown at the World's Fair in Paris in 1937, executed in the MAK's conservation workshops in 2014
Wood, milled and silver-plated with metal leaf; metal, cast; plastic; plate glass
MAK, H 3815 and H 2058-61
© MAK/Georg Mayer

Fig. 3 JH, small table, ca. 1930
Rosewood, partly carved and gold-plated
bel etage Kunsthandel GmbH

Fig. 6 JH, daybed, *Boudoir d'une grande vedette* [Boudoir for a Big Star], executed by Max Welz (woodwork and plating) and Hedwig Pöchlmüller (embroidery), World's Fair, Paris, 1937
Wood, carved and silver-plated, woolwork
MAK, H 2059
© MAK/Nathan Murrell

Fig. 4 JH, chair, executed by Jakob Soulek for the *Das befreite Handwerk* [The Liberated Handicraft] exhibition at the AMAI in 1934
Walnut, partly carved, original leather upholstery
MAK, H 1701
© MAK/Nathan Murrell

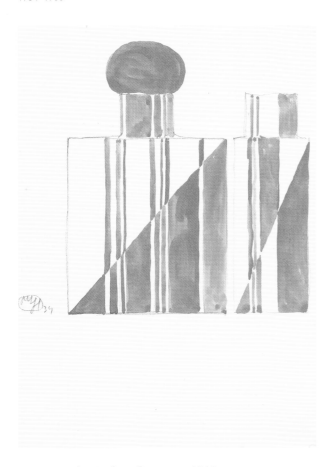

Fig. 7 JH, design for a flacon, ca. 1935
Kunsthandel Widder, Vienna

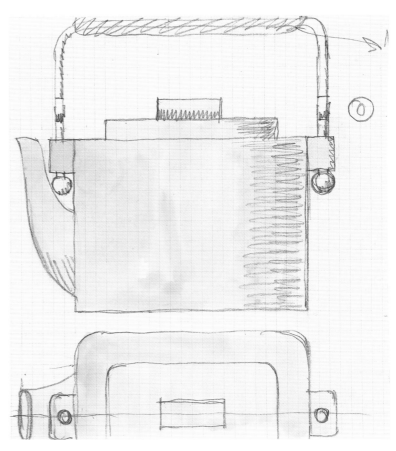

Fig. 8 JH, design for a porcelain teapot, ca. 1935
Kunsthandel Widder, Vienna

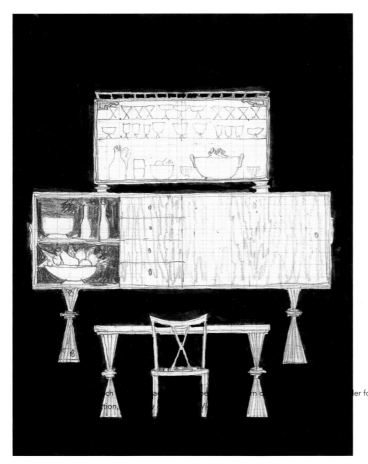

Fig. 9 JH, design for a buffet with a top-mounted
vitrine, table, and chair, ca. 1935
Kunsthandel Widder, Vienna

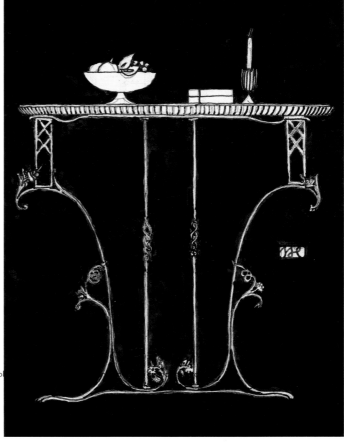

Fig. 10 JH, design for a wrought iron console table, ca. 1935
Kunsthandel Widder, Vienna

Fig. 11 JH, exhibition design, *50 Jahre Wiener Kunstgewerbeverein*
[50 Years of the Viennese Arts-and-Crafts Association] at the AMAI, 1934
Profil (2) 6 1934, 183

Fig. 12 JH, decorative-arts room at the *Austria in London* exhibition, 1934
Profil (2) 5 1934, 51

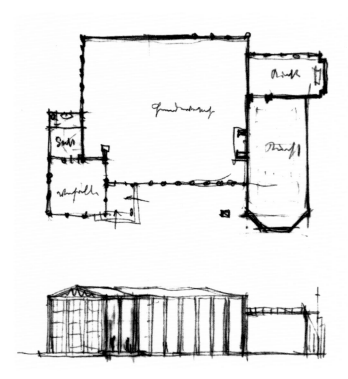

Fig. 13 JH, design study for the Austrian
pavilion for Brussels, 1934
E. F. Sekler, *Josef Hoffmann*, 429

Fig. 14 JH, competition project for the Palace
of the Great National Assembly of Turkey,
Ankara, 1936, sketch of a flagpole
Donation from Wittmann Möbelwerkstaetten GmbH
MAK, KI 23086-56

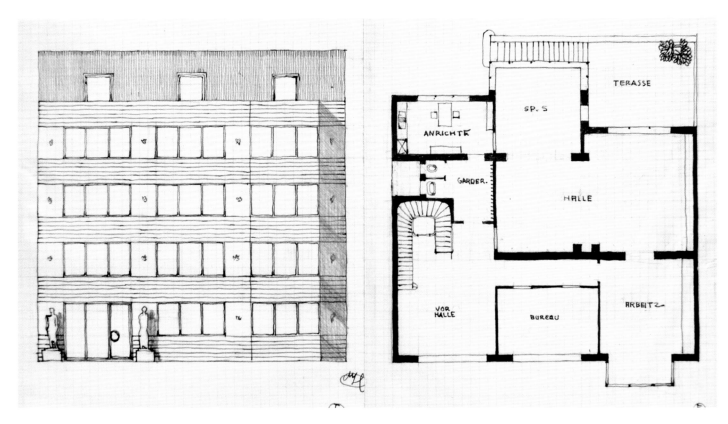

Fig. 15 JH, small urban house in Vienna's Landstraße district,
project, 1935 (?), façade and floor plan
Graphic Collection, Academy of Fine Arts Vienna, HZ 26309

Fig. 16 JH, competition project for the Palace
of the Great National Assembly of Turkey,
Ankara, 1936, façade study

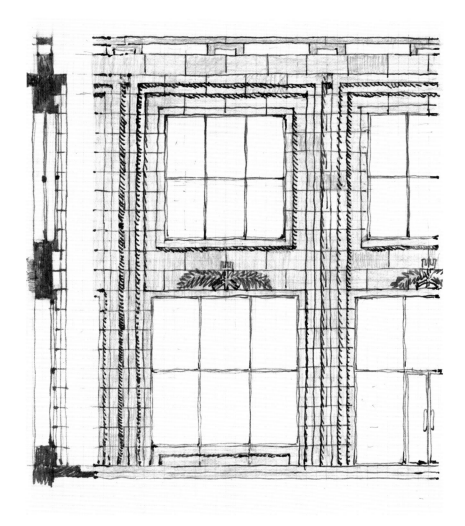

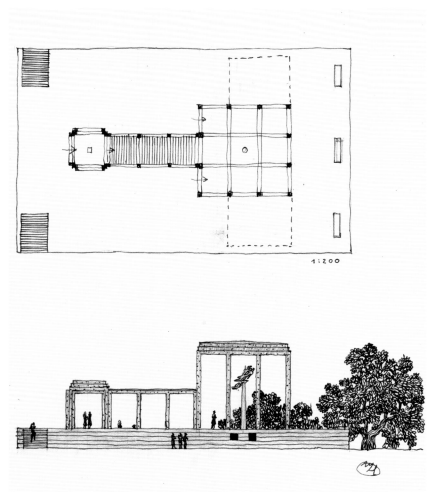

Fig. 17 JH, project variant for a hall of fame and
vault of Austrian composers in Vienna's
Volksgarten park, 1935, floor plan and view

Josef Hoffmann
1934
1938

1934–1937

In 1934 the Austrian pavilion for the Venice Biennale is constructed. For the *Austria in London* exhibition, Hoffmann designs the arts-and-crafts gallery. Interior design of the exhibition *50 Jahre Wiener Kunstgewerbeverein* [50 Years of the Viennese Arts-and-Crafts Association] at the AMAI. That same year, a schism emerges in the Austrian Werkbund, which culminates in the founding of the New Austrian Werkbund under the leadership of Clemens Holzmeister (president), Peter Behrens and Josef Hoffmann (vice presidents). The 1934/35 Christmas exhibition at the AMAI is organized around the theme of revival: *Das befreite Handwerk. Geschmack und Wohnkultur* [The Liberated Handicraft: Taste and Domestic Culture] presents a new support policy by the authoritarian Ständestaat (corporative state) regime. Alongside Oswald Haerdtl, the chairman of the decorative-arts branch of the group of cooperatives and the organizer of the exhibition, Josef Hoffmann masterminds the concept for the exhibition. Their explicit objective is to reinvent an "Austrian style." The aim is to deliver designs that would offer craftspeople like gilders, carvers, upholsterers, and passementerie makers to show off their skills—a trade-oriented aesthetic and attitude in contrast to the works shown at the Werkbund exhibition of 1930. From the outset, the principle is "to once again exhibit richer and more artistically substantial creative works, which guarantee better employment for the decorative trades and other branches of the decorative arts" (Hertl, Oswald, *Das Befreite Handwerk*, exh. cat., Vienna 1933). In 1936 Hoffmann retires from the

JH, small pieces of furniture, *Das befreite Handwerk* [The Liberated Handicraft] exhibition at the AMAI, 1934
MAK, KI 9197-4-2

School of Arts and Crafts and is made an "adjunct professor," meaning that he continues to manage the decorative-arts department of his former architecture class in the winter semester of 1936/37. Hoffmann now also has to close his architecture studio at the School of Arts and Crafts—the heads of the New Austrian Werkbund, Holzmeister, Haerdtl, and Max Fellerer, dominate architecture and the decorative arts in the Austrian corporative state. From now on, Hoffmann mainly produces projects and studies, for example a competition project for the *Palast der Großen Nationalversammlung der Türkei* [Palace of the Great National Assembly of Turkey] in Ankara, the project for a *Ruhmeshalle und Gruft für*

österreichische Musiker [Hall of Fame and Vault for Austrian Composers] for a Viennese park, and studies for the Austrian pavilion for the World's Fair in Paris in 1937, which will later be planned by Oswald Haerdtl, where Hoffmann's *Boudoir d'une grande vedette* [Boudoir for a Big Star] will once again be exhibited. Redesign of various rooms in the casino in Baden, again with Oswald Haerdtl. Furnishing of the publishing house and printing office of the Schroll-Verlag in Vienna's Margareten district. Josef Hoffmann's final attempt to reestablish the Wiener Werkstätte, which had been liquidated in 1932, in the corporative state with Friedrich Nerold and Franz Hollmann fails.

Josef Hoffmann (left) with Karla Hoffmann
(center), Ernst Huber, Fritz Wotruba,
Max Fellerer, at a function by the School
of Arts and Crafts, 1937
Kunsthandel Widder, Vienna

1938

The arrival of German troops and Austria's Anschluss with the National Socialist German Reich in March 1938 is viewed by Hoffmann as an opportunity for a new beginning for Viennese decorative arts. He applies for membership of the NSDAP, but his application is not accepted. The formerly illegal National Socialist, head of Vienna's municipal construction company GESIBA, president of the Werkbund for many years, and a good longstanding acquaintance of Hoffmann, Hermann Neubacher becomes the first Nazi mayor of Vienna. That very March, Hoffmann writes a paper on the "Neuausrichtung unserer Kunstschulen" ("Reorienting Our Art Schools") and his former assistant Philipp Häusler briefly becomes the provisional director of the School of Arts and Crafts. With Josef Kalbac, a colleague of Oswald Haerdtl and Hoffmann's future partner at their joint architectural firm, Hoffmann furnishes the shop of the Leipzig fashion publisher Otto Beyer on Singerstraße.

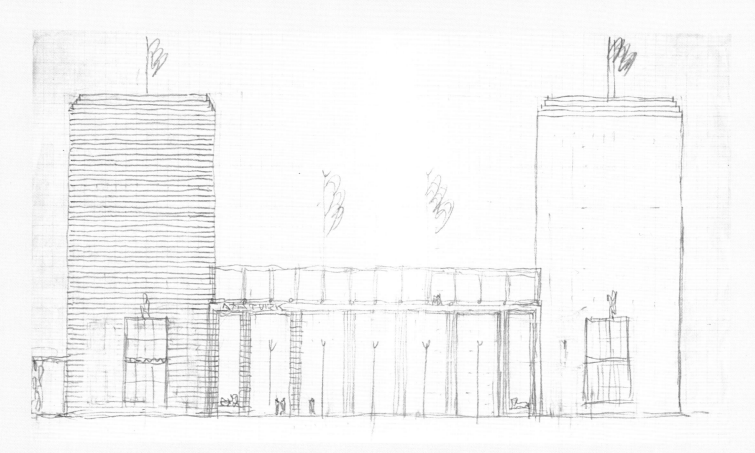

JH, preliminary design for the façade of the propylaeum of the parliament in Ankara, 1936
Donation from Wittmann Mobelwerkstaetten GmbH
MAK, KI 23086-47

Fig. 1 JH, wool velour for the seat covering of the 1st-class coach of the
Österreichische Bundesbahnen, executed by J. & J. Backhausen
(design no. 10416), 1934
Backhausen Archive, BA 03759

Elisabeth Boeckl-Klamper

Temporary Career Setback

Josef Hoffmann and the Ständestaat

The collapse of the monarchy in 1918 constituted a significant watershed in Josef Hoffmann's life. Over 15 years later he described the immediate postwar period as "disastrous," among other things, in an article published in the *Pause*,[1] despite the fact that neither poverty nor hunger were a serious concern for him thanks to his teaching position and his continued receipt of design and construction commissions even during the war. If, as he later wrote, he considered the restructuring of Europe a "fragmentation of the old world" and a "cordoning off of individual regions of an old cultural area that belonged together,"[2] then it was in part because his birthplace of Pirnitz/Brtnice, to which he felt a close connection, now lay in the new Czechoslovak Republic where the German-speaking population was occasionally subjected to harassment.

However, given that Hoffmann kept his political opinions as secret as his private life,[3] it is impossible to prove unequivocally whether he approved or disapproved of the system change. Having created a brand in the Wiener Werkstätte that perhaps more than any other was synonymous with the cultural requirements of the Viennese upper middle class or rather with "Viennese taste," it was undeniably difficult for him to live and work under such radically different social and political conditions. Even Stefan Zweig, who in principle welcomed the founding of the republic, wistfully characterized the period prior to the First World War as "the Golden Age of Security" when "[e]veryone knew how much he possessed or what he was entitled to, what was permitted and what forbidden."[4] Indeed, the loss of large regions that had been crucial to industrial and agricultural production, combined with hunger, mass unemployment, and the unbridgeable divide between the two main political camps (Christian Social Party and Social Democratic Party) made the political and financial viability of the young republic seem more than questionable. Appreciative of art and in need of representative styles, the upper middle class had seen its numbers diminish considerably as a result of the war.

An Apolitical Person?

In contrast to many other architects, Hoffmann was entrusted with prestigious construction and exhibition projects even during the economic turmoil of the 1920s. When he nevertheless describes these years as "times of economic decline"

characterized by "constant crises and commotions" and laments the "lack of any funds,"[5] this can be explained on the one hand by the difficult financial situation at the Wiener Werkstätte and on the other by the persistent debate about the very purpose of the decorative arts, which at times flared up with passionate intensity.

Hoffmann is described by both his assistant of many years Leopold Kleiner and his biographer, the architectural historian Eduard F. Sekler, as an "apolitical" person. He was in the habit of answering questions on political issues with the words "I don't understand anything about it."[6] Yet despite never having expressed or confirmed a party-political opinion at any point during his life, he was by no means blind to or naïve about political and social conditions. Rather, he strove to exploit political constellations whenever they struck him as beneficial to the realization of his artistic ideas or when they bore the promise of commissions. Accordingly, he had no qualms about working with the social democrat-dominated city administration in Vienna, who for their part profited from the cooperation as they could promote their cultural activities with the name of an architect of international standing.[7] Consequently, in 1933 Hoffmann was appointed to the Kunstbeirat zur Förderung der Gegenwartskunst (Arts Council for the Promotion of Contemporary Art); founded by the City of Vienna, it was the body that decided on the acquisition of works of fine art. Alongside Hoffmann the other members of the council were Alfred Coßmann, Carl Moll, Ferdinand Kitt, Edmund Hellmer, Fritz Zerritsch, Hans Tietze, Ludwig Graf (†), and—as the chair—Alfred Roller.[8]

To prevent the Wiener Werkstätte's bankruptcy, Hoffmann was also prepared in 1926 to negotiate with the City of Vienna about incorporating the Wiener Werkstätte into the financially successful, municipally owned Gemeinwirtschaftliche Siedlungs- und Baustoffanstalt (GESIBA, the Institution for Public Housing and Construction Materials)—a proposal that ultimately failed.[9] These contacts nevertheless proved useful for Hoffmann as they enabled him to come into closer contact with Hermann Neubacher, the director of GESIBA at the time. Two years later Neubacher was appointed president of the Werkbund and after Austria's Anschluss with Nazi Germany in 1938 he became mayor of Vienna; as such he was Hoffmann's most important contact in the National Socialist city administration.

Fig. 2 JH, exhibition design *Das befreite Handwerk* [The Liberated Handicraft], AMAI, 1934
MAK, KI 9197-1-2

Hoffmann and the Authoritarian "Christian Ständestaat"

The proclamation of the authoritarian "Christian Ständestaat" (corporative state) on 1 May 1934 brought another change in the balance of political power. Among the ideological cornerstones of the new regime were not only the rejection of parliamentary party democracy but also anti-liberalism, anti-Marxism, the "re-Christianization" of private and public life, and a societal structure organized according to professions.[10] Negating the modern industrial and class society, the "Christian Ständestaat" invoked the ideal of a seemingly medieval agrarian society structured according to guilds—illustrated by Federal Chancellor Engelbert Dollfuss, for instance, with the aid of a picture of a farmhouse in which "in the evening the farmer eats his soup from the same bowl and at the same table as the farmhands with whom he has been working."[11] The new regime glorified the monarchy in a similar way as the "good old days" and attempted to legitimize itself as its "lawful" successor. The latter is demonstrated, for example, by the construction of the heroes' memorial in Vienna's Burgtor gate (originally a memorial to the European monarchies' victory over Napoleon) or in the new national coat of arms, which again showed the old imperial double-headed eagle,[12] as well as in the—at least advertised—revival of old crafts and artisanal techniques. These were now considered "typically Austrian." In the corporative state's ideology they were therefore deemed valuable tools for building national identity.

As there are no surviving statements by Hoffmann on the Ständestaat specifically, it would be speculative to claim that he had clearly condoned it. That being said, it is beyond doubt that its ideology and propaganda contain elements that had positive associations for him—not least due to the way they harked back to the past. Aside from the fact that Hoffmann's notion of decorative-arts organizations shared certain similarities with the Austrian corporative state's ideal of organizing society into guilds, the effect on identity creation that the regime attributed to craft traditions definitely met with his approval.

Hoffmann, who in the 1920s had been treated by some colleagues with, as the short-term chair of the Werkbund Otto Lagus records in a letter, "perfidious respect […] as the representative of an effectively dead decorative era,"[13] could now expect to reprise a more prominent role in art and cultural policy. With this in mind he emphasizes in an article the "particularly improvable handicraft," which in Austria could "achieve great things as the existing workers are, in contrast to distant foreign countries, available everywhere and possess great skill and adaptability."[14]

Following the ideological guidelines of the Ständestaat, which now saw Austria's former political hegemony as stemming from its cultural life[15] and hence created the myth of Austria as a "cultural superpower," Hoffmann not only accredited arts and crafts with "exceptional obligations" that had to be satisfied "in our small but, in spite of all unjust peace treaties, important state for Europe"[16] but also attributed to "the Austrian" an "especially inherent gift for enriching and refining our environment."[17] In his endeavor to

help direct more attention to arts and crafts, he also seized
on what were frequently ideologically loaded terms like
"down-to-earth" or "blood." As, for example, when he
claimed that the machine is "mostly at the service of the not
always down-to-earth businessman who changes his occupation depending on the economic situation."[18] Or when he
said: "All attempts […] will certainly evolve and ultimately
once again lead to works that are bound to have a distinctive
character because they are in accordance with our blood,
our age, and our hereditary abilities."[19]

The Exhibition *Das befreite Handwerk. Geschmack und Wohnkultur*

It did indeed look as though Hoffmann could hope to have
both greater influence on art policy and a flourishing career
in decorative arts and architecture under the Ständestaat.
In 1934 he contributed substantially to both the *Jubiläumsausstellung des Kunstgewerbevereins* [Anniversary Exhibition
of the Viennese Arts-and-Crafts Association] and the exhibition *Das befreite Handwerk. Geschmack und Wohnkultur*
[The Liberated Handicraft: Taste and Domestic Culture],
which were shown at the Austrian Museum of Art and Industry (today's MAK). As the director Dr. Richard Ernst explained,
the latter was conceived as a "declaration of war to the increasingly reduced, naked form of the merely objective or
of that semblance of objectivity that sometimes may conceal
no less unsuitability or shallowness than the most ornate
thing."[20] On display were elaborately ornamented objects,
such as a chip-carved buffet, wrought silverwork, handwoven
carpets, etc. For the exhibition Hoffmann had designed a
liquor cabinet finely crafted from walnut wood, among other
things.[21] In the style of the Ständestaat propaganda, which
gladly underscored the Austrians' alleged fondness for the
Baroque and playful taste, Hoffmann said in the exhibition
catalog that "the decorative artists [do not want] to be forced
to cast aside valuable skills," but had to try "to revive a gift
especially inherent to the Austrian for enriching and refining
our environment in order to overcome the customary, all too
uniform, by now almost monotonous mindset and to break
new ground."[22]

Yet prior to the exhibition the director Ernst had written
a letter to the federal ministry of trade and transport dated
26 September 1934 in which he described the title of the
exhibition as "asinine" and "misleading" and firmly declared
that the museum could not agree to it.[23] As few relevant
sources survive—Hoffmann's opinions are missing entirely—
it is no longer known which arguments were able to change
Ernst's mind. What has survived is a letter from him to Hoffmann from 2 November 1935 in which he asserts that he
holds Hoffmann's work to be "a necessary prerequisite not
merely for art and the decorative arts, but also <u>ideologically</u>."
Ernst closed the letter with the words: "May you take from
my lines a sense of my wholehearted veneration and regret
for the vehemence of my resistance."[24]

The exhibition's poster showed imaginary guild crests for
various arts-and-crafts professions and was designed by Hans
Bichler, the student of Oskar Strnad and Franz Schuster. At
this point Bichler, who had collaborated on the international
Werkbund exhibition in the Austrian Museum in 1930, among
other things, and who between 1935 and 1938 worked in
the studio of Hoffmann and Haerdtl, was already a member
of the (then illegal) NSDAP.[25] He therefore played an important role in Hoffmann's professional network after the Anschluss with Nazi Germany.

Fig. 3 Corner of a room with JH's liquor cabinet covered
in red leather, executed by Johann Beran, in the exhibition
Das befreite Handwerk, AMAI, 1934
MAK, KI 9197-3-1

Fig. 4 Hans Bichler, poster for
Das befreite Handwerk, AMAI, 1934
MAK, PI 2313

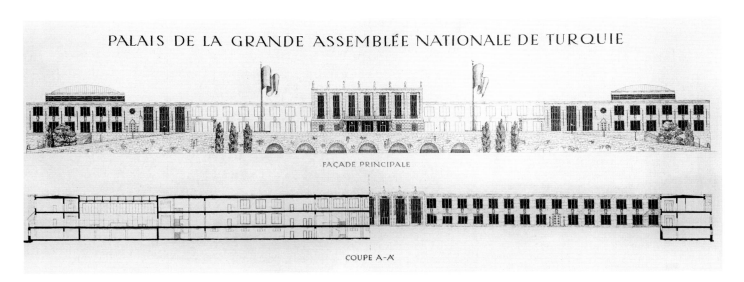

PALAIS DE LA GRANDE ASSEMBLÉE NATIONALE DE TURQUIE

FAÇADE PRINCIPALE

COUPE A-A'

Fig. 5 JH, competition project for the Palace of the Great National Assembly of Turkey,
Ankara, 1936, main view and section
Graphic Collection, Academy of Fine Arts

The Pavilion in Venice: Success for Hoffmann?

In February 1934 Josef Hoffmann was awarded the commission for the "production of designs and plans according to the authorized preliminary designs"[26] for the Austrian pavilion at the Venice Biennale. This decision had been preceded by a politically charged competition in which alongside Josef Hoffmann the architects Erich Boltenstern, Joseph F. Dex, Eugen Kastner, and Hermann Kutschera had taken part. Clemens Holzmeister held the position of chair of the jury, whose members are still unknown today.[27] Yet Hoffmann was only "conferred [the commission] with the stipulation that the architect Robert Kramreiter is enlisted to contribute to the [project's] execution."[28] Although the pavilion was subsequently constructed according to Hoffmann's design, he had no part in its construction. This approach must have hurt him deeply, because on 22 June 1936 he observed in a letter to the ministry of education in connection with structural damage to the pavilion:

> "From this it can be learned that with such an important building that is in constant competition with other nations, beyond drawing plans the architect must on all accounts be in charge of overseeing construction and contracting the construction company. As in the realization of my plans I was not entrusted with overseeing the construction, and not even with inspecting the building upon completion, I must abdicate any responsibility."[29]

In the respective deed at the ministry of education there is an explicit reference to the "entry [containing] for the most part protestations by the somewhat resentful Professor Hoffmann."[30] Evidently, therefore, the Ständestaat used Hoffmann's design and—as he also enjoyed an excellent reputation in Italy—his name but excluded him from all further stages of the project.

Hoffmann was also forced to acknowledge that though the New Austrian Werkbund he had cofounded was a successful representative of the publicized "Austrian touch" in the decorative arts and architecture between 1934 and 1938, he himself played only a peripheral role. For example, the *Neue Freie Presse* wrote on 28 January 1936 that the exhibition design "for London in 1934, Brussels in 1935, the triennial in 1936 [was placed] in the hands of the members of the New Werkbund, State Councilor Professor Dr. Clemens

Holzmeister, Professor Oswald Haerdtl, and Director Professor Max Fellerer." In all these decisions a substantial part was played by Holzmeister. Known personally to its main protagonists since his student days and friends with some of them, the Ständestaat appointed him state councilor.[31] As such he occupied a prominent and influential position, which nevertheless did not stop him from withholding from Hoffmann a fee of 300 schillings, which he had been promised for his participation in the Biennale competition, with the justification that he "as an executor will be compensated via the architect's fee."[32]

Too Little, Too Late

Clemens Holzmeister was a prominent figure in the Austrian corporative state due to not only his capacity as State Councilor but also his position in the Catholic Church. In 1933, for instance, he organized the "Catholics' Day" in Vienna, during which Engelbert Dollfuss held his programmatic speech about the future Ständestaat. The Catholic Church became the most important patron for artists and architects between 1933 and 1938. Hoffmann did not receive any of its commissions; the fact that he had been baptized a Protestant was perhaps one explanation.

Hoffmann's successes under the "Ständestaat" were largely limited to arts and crafts. Despite their valorization in the regime's propaganda, he soon came to the realization that they were by no means as well funded as he had obviously expected. In the fall of 1935 Hoffmann wrote in the *Pause*:

> "Sadly it almost seems as though our age were too lethargic to pay allegiance to newly emergent Austrian arts and crafts. [...] Lauded all over the world, the artistic and artisanal Austria might consequently be doomed to drop off the radar [...]."[33]

Hoffmann also did not succeed in reestablishing the Wiener Werkstätte, which had been liquidated in 1932. A final attempt was made in February 1938, when a former employee of the Wiener Werkstätte, the sculptor Friedrich Nerold, addressed a letter to State Councilor Guido Zernatto in which he made reference to Hoffmann and—utterly mis-

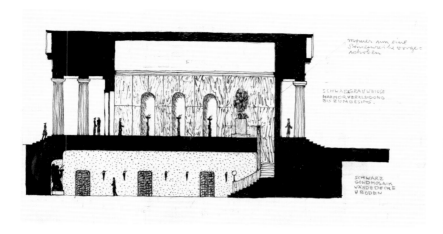

Figs. 6, 7 JH, project variants for a hall of fame and vault for
Austrian composers in Vienna's Volksgarten park, 1935
Section of the Theseus Temple, free version
Graphic Collection, Academy of Fine Arts Vienna, HZ 26301 and 26303

judging the political climate—requested financial support
for the reopening: "The absolute order and security that has
now come to pass in the country is the guarantee that the
reopening of the Wiener Werkstätte might be carried out
with complete success."[34] The letter is signed with the greeting "Austria." On 28 February 1938 Guido Zernatto en-
treated the federal leadership of the Fatherland Front in
Vienna to check "the civic conduct, the political attitude,
and membership of the following persons with regard to the
reopening of the Wiener Werkstätte, including Hoffmann,
Friedrich Nerold (sculptor), Franz Hollmann (professional
development trainer)."[35]
 Eleven days later the German troops marched into Austria.

1 Hoffmann, Josef, "Die Kräfte drängen. Weg und Schicksal des neuen österreichischen Kunsthand-werkes," in: Die Pause (1) 9 1935, 30 f.
2 Ibid.
3 Kleiner, Leopold, Erinnerungen an Josef Hoff-mann, New York, n.d. (prob. 1975).
4 Zweig, Stefan, The World of Yesterday, Lincoln, NE 1964, 1. Trans. Benjamin W. Huebsch and Helmut Ripperger.
5 Hoffmann 1935 (see note 1), 30 f.
6 Sekler, Eduard F., Josef Hoffmann: The Architec-tural Work, Princeton, NJ 1985, 219. Trans. Eduard F. Sekler and John Maass.
7 Between 1924 and 1933 Hoffmann planned a total of three large people's houses for the City of Vienna.
8 Wien Museum, records in the municipal collections, St. S. 1001/30; Moderne Welt (14) 4 1933, 30.
9 Posch, Wilfried, "Josef Frank," in: Stadler, Frie-drich (ed.), Vertriebene Vernunft II. Emigration und Exil österreichischer Wissenschaft, Interna-tionales Symposion 19. Bis 23. Oktober 1987 in Wien, Vienna/Munich 1988, 649.
10 See: Klamper, Elisabeth, "Die böse Geistlosigkeit. Die Kulturpolitik des Ständestaates," in: Tabor, Jan (ed.), Kunst und Diktatur, Architektur, Bild-hauerei und Malerei in Österreich, Deutschland, Italien und der Sowjetunion 1922–1956, 2 vols., Baden 1994, 124–133.
11 Quoted in: Talos, Emmerich/Manoschek, Walter, "Politische Struktur des Austrofaschismus (1934–1938)," in: Austrofaschismus. Beiträge über Poli-tik, Ökonomie und Kultur 1934–1938, Vienna 1984⁴, 78.

12 Feller, Barbara, "Sichtbarmachung der Vergan-genheit. Kunst-am-Bau und neue Monumente in Österreich 1930–1938," in: Tabor 1994 (see note 10), 282–287: 284.
13 Letter from Otto Lagus to the members of the Werkbund, 19 Jun 1933; Vienna City Library, Manuscript Department, Philipp Häusler estate, ZPH 833.
14 Hoffmann, Josef, "Österreichisches Kunsthand-werk," in: Moderne Welt (15) 9 1934, 38 ff.
15 Cf.: Klamper 1994 (see note 10), 126.
16 Hoffmann, "Österreichisches Kunsthandwerk," in: Moderne Welt (15) 8 1934, 36.
17 Das befreite Handwerk. Geschmack und Wohnkul-tur, Kunstgewerbeausstellung, veranstaltet von der Kunstgewerbesektion des Wiener Gewer-begenossenschaftsverbandes unter Mitwirkung des Gewerbeförderungsinstitutes der Kammer für Handel, Gewerbe und Industrie in Wien, exh. cat. AMAI, Vienna 1933, 14.
18 Hoffmann (15) 9 1934, 38 ff. (see note 14).
19 Hoffmann (15) 8 1934, 36 (see note 16).
20 Das befreite Handwerk 1933 (see note 17), 14.
21 Cf.: profil. Österreichische Monatsschrift für bil-dende Kunst, herausgegeben von der Zentral-vereinigung der Architekten Österreichs (2) 11 1934, 395.
22 Das befreite Handwerk 1933 (see note 17), 14.
23 MAK Archive, holdings 884-1934.
24 MAK Archive, holdings 929-1935.
25 Bichler had joined the NSDAP in either 1932 or 1934. The statements he made on this himself after the Anschluss in 1938 vary. Cf: ASA, AdR, gau file no. 1309: Hans Bichler.

26 ASA, education, AVA, general education (1848-194), exhibitions: abroad Venice—Zurich, 3330, Sign. 15, Fz. 2963, GZ.10858-I-6a/1934.
27 Feller, Barbara, "Venedig, 29. Jänner 1934. Öster-reich und die Biennale in Venedig," in: Tabor 1944 (see note 10), 302–307: 305.
28 ASA, education (see note 26).
29 ASA, education (see note 26), GZ.21862-I-6a/1936.
30 Ibid.
31 In the authoritarian Ständestaat the state councilor had an advisory role in relation to the government; he could not make laws himself but could examine them in camera. It was at the government's dis-cretion to what extent it would take the federal councilor's opinion into account. The members of the state council were appointed by the federal chancellor. Cf.: Wohnout, Helmut, "Im Zeichen des Ständeideals. Bedingungen staatlicher Kul-turpolitik im autoritären Österreich 1933–1938," in: Tabor 1994 (see note 10), 134–141: 139.
32 Letter from Clemens Holzmeister to the federal education ministry, attn Department Head Dr. Pernter, 14 Feb 1934, ASA, education (see note 26), GZ.4679-I-6a/1934. Hoffmann ultimately re-ceived the 300 schillings.
33 Hoffmann (1) 9 1935, 30 f. (see note 1).
34 Letter from Friedrich Nerold to State Councilor Guido Zernatto, Feb 1938, regarding the reopen-ing of the Wiener Werkstätte; ASA, AdR, BKA, 14.034/38.
35 ASA, AdR, gau file no. 4892: Josef Hoffmann.

Fig. 1 JH, Austrian pavilion at the Venice
Biennale at its opening, 1934
MAK, KI 23506

Rainald Franz

Austria's Aesthetic Self-Portrait

The Austrian Pavilion in Venice 1933–1934

"Is Josef Hoffmann's Biennale Pavilion of 1934 modern architecture? Probably not from the avant-garde standpoint of the International Style, nor from that of Le Corbusier's four composition principles. But are these criteria sufficient? Particularly from the side of Austria, several additional layers have been integrated within the 20th century. In Vienna, it was above all Josef Hoffmann whom Le Corbusier registered on his travels."[1]

The Austrian architect Hermann Czech hereby queries a structure, which along with the sanatorium in Purkersdorf near Vienna and the Stoclet House in Brussels, is generally associated with Josef Hoffmann, from an international perspective.

The ultimate solution for presenting Austrian art in the context of the Biennale d'Arte was preceded by Hoffmann's approach to the building site in the Giardini of Venice stretching across four decades, shaped by the different political goals of the respective Austrian governments. At the first Venice Biennale, the *Esposizioni internazionali d'Arte della Città di Venezia* held in 1895, the Austrian artists whom the jury had selected for participation exhibited in the Giardini pubblici in a general pavilion for all nations.[2]

When the exhibiting nations began to establish the building of individual pavilions beginning in 1907, the Austro-Hungarian Monarchy was put on the spot. From September 1912, the Austrian half of the empire projected an art pavilion for Austria on the Biennale grounds. The prospective building site was the one currently occupied by the US pavilion.[3] Josef Hoffmann, Oberbaurat (chief building officer) and professor of architecture at the School of Arts and Crafts, was asked to design a project. Eduard F. Sekler dates the receipt of the design as 1912.[4] Drawings in the Albertina, the Academy of Fine Arts Vienna, and the National Gallery Prague document this first draft for the Austrian Biennale pavilion. It is also comprehensible in a model reconstruction carried out by Hans Hollein's master class for architecture at the University of Applied Arts in 1984, and preserved by the Architekturzentrum Wien.[5] Based on structures in Ravenna, such as San Vitale and the grave of Theoderic (the Great), and the mausoleum of Diocletian in Split, Hoffmann created a central octagonal structure illuminated in the cupola by semicircular windows. An entry hall attached to the main façade, while

offset 45 degrees, a further gallery wing with two flanking exhibition halls, outside staircase, and pillar placements guarantee the structure's permeability. The site's given features necessitated breaking the symmetry axis. In the ground plan, the building appeared fully designed, through to the dimensions of the details. Two variants are provided for the building's outer façade: one, with the entry hall as a classicizing portico with eight fluted columns, triangular gables, and outside staircase—Hoffmann's design accords with his start in Neoclassicism, and to a certain extent offers a link from the pavilion in Rome in 1911 to the Austrian House at the Werkbund exhibition in Cologne in 1914. A different, most likely later variant shows the elevated, diaphanous-seeming central section, the entry closed by a flat roof, and on both sides of a further central opening in the façade, structureless wall surfaces, with a circular window incised into each; four slender supports structure the central opening. Both variants show the loggia of the gallery wing with round-arched pier arcades. Like with the pavilion in Rome, the building's sculptures also played an important role for Hoffmann: on eight sides of the central building, a figurative sculpture was planned in the middle under the cornice. In the second variant, monumental figures flank the entry. On 6 May 1914, Josef Hoffmann asked for a transfer of 1,300 kronen to finance his trip to Venice and to prepare the project of the Austrian pavilion there.[6] The outbreak of World War I thwarted his plan and the project was set aside.

The First Republic in Austria inherited the problem of deciding for or against erecting a pavilion for the *Esposizione internazionale di Venezia*. Only in 1921 did Austria receive another invitation to contribute to the 13th Biennale. Construction of a permanent Austrian pavilion was again discussed. Under the duress of the Great Depression, in 1929, the Ministry of Trade and Transport reclaimed the subvention designated for building the pavilion. In early 1932, upon request by the delegation, the money was reallocated for the support of destitute artists, since "at present, the project of erecting a pavilion in Venice doesn't even come into question."[7] Austrian artists would first exhibit at the Venice Biennale in their own pavilion in 1932, as in this year, Germany canceled their participation in the 18th Biennale and their vacant pavilion was made available to Austria. The general

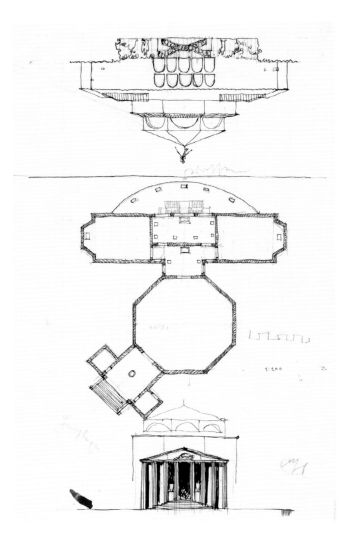

Fig. 2 JH, design for the Austrian pavilion at the Venice Biennale, 1912, published in: *Der Architekt* (XXIII) 1920, 67
National Gallery Prague, K 17741

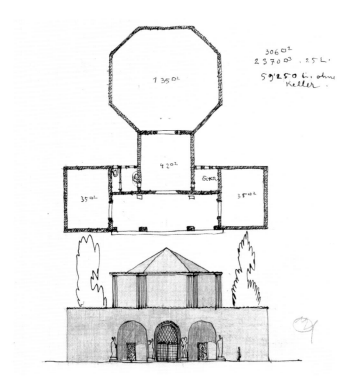

Fig. 3 JH, design for the Austrian pavilion at the Venice Biennale, 1912
National Gallery Prague, K 17762

secretary of the Biennale, Antonio Maraini, thereupon requested that Austria build its own pavilion for the upcoming Biennale in 1934.[8] For the Austrian government under Engelbert Dollfuss who had ruled since the elimination of the parliament in 1933 under the "Wartime Economy Authority Act" from World War I, and who aspired to the formation of an authoritarian corporative state, the chance to display national greatness in an Austrian pavilion at *Esposizione internazionale* was a crucial external effect. The building would be a prestige project and was taken on by Minister of Education Kurt Schuschnigg. The Dollfuss government and the Italian fascists under Benito Mussolini groomed their close relationship also in the field of culture. The *Moderne italienische Kunst* [Modern Italian Art] exhibition was shown already in 1933 at Vienna's Künstlerhaus and in early 1934, Austria was prominently represented at the *Mostra Internazionale d'Arte Sacra* in Rome. Acting as exhibition architect was Robert Kramreiter, a student of Peter Behrens at his master school of architecture at the Academy of Fine Arts in Vienna from 1925 to 1928.[9] As an architect loyal to the regime, Kramreiter was apparently also included in the planning process for Venice at an early stage. He was sent to Venice and on the plot of today's Venezuelan pavilion, laid out a ground plan for the Austrian pavilion to be built.[10] The pavilion was meant to be completed by the opening of the 19th Biennale on 15 May 1934. At first, Kramreiter operated officially as planning architect,[11] and no mention was made of Josef Hoffmann as planner. The intended completion of the building was set for 20 April 1934.[12] At this point, Kramreiter had apparently already submitted a complete design for the pavilion. Clemens Holzmeister, omnipresent and influential in the corporative state especially in matters of architecture, had clearly seen the design. "Prof. Holzmeister has rejected the project with the remark that the entry is inadequate, and structurally not possible. Apart from that, he does not like the stairs on the side," Kramreiter's office partner Leo Schmoll reported to him in Rome on 5 February 1934.[13] Holzmeister, professor and rector of the Academy of Fine Arts Vienna, influential cultural functionary and architect in the corporative state, was able to push through a new competition in Austria, where a civil war had been raging since 12 February 1934, and also determine the participants. On 14 February 1934, he sent the Federal Ministry of Education the list of those participating in the competition for the Austrian pavilion: Erich Boltenstern, assistant to Holzmeister at the academy from 1934; Joseph F. Dex, architect of a double residential home in the Werkbund Estate; Josef Hoffmann, the most prominent participant from the Vienna School of Arts and Crafts; the architects Eugen Kastner and Fritz Waage, students at Vienna's technical university, the TU Wien, and active in the Fatherland Front; and Hermann Kutschera, Holzmeister's student and employee in his studio from 1926 to 1932. He forgot to add Robert Kramreiter, an oversight that had to be corrected with a red pen: "Arch. Kramreiter is missing!"[14] A document from 14 May 1934, signed by Section Head Pernter in the ministry, recorded, "the jury has chosen the design by Oberbaurat Prof. J. Hoffmann." With an additional note to Hoffmann: "On this occasion, we would like to announce that we have chosen your submitted design for the realization of the pavilion." The building design by Hoffmann ignored the exceptional political state: Already on 1 March 1934 the Hoffmann/Haerdtl studio had submitted to Section Head Hohenauer in the Ministry of Education, "the design of the elevations of the Venice pavilion."[15] On 19 March, the studio then ultimately

Fig. 4 JH, project for the
Austrian pavilion at the
Venice Biennale, 1912
Graphic Collection, Academy
of Fine Arts Vienna, HZ 26307

asked for a written contract "for creation of the design and plan of the Venice pavilion."[16] On 11 April, the contract awarded for the creation of a design and architectural plan was regulated by an act of the federal ministry to the extent, that:

> "[…] Josef Hoffmann's design has been chosen and he has been given an oral contract for creation of the design and plan based on the approved draft plan with the stipulation that in the realization, the architect Robert KRAMREITER is to be involved. As architect's fee, Hoffmann should receive 11,000 shillings, whereby this will be paid out in the relation of 6,000 to 5,000 to the architects HOFFMANN and KRAMREITER."[17]

Thus, within their working team, Kramreiter's involvement in the realization was granted nearly equal status with Hoffmann's in terms of his share of the payment. After submitting the plans, Hoffmann did not travel to Venice and was also not on site for the opening of the pavilion in May, which gives cause to question what Kramreiter's role was after Hoffmann's nomination: Kramreiter had been originally designated for the building of the pavilion, and as an architect, was more convenient for the government. In the run-up to construction of the young Dollfuss regime's external symbol of cultural politics, pressure in the area of aesthetic politics had led to Holzmeister's intervention in the competition and to Josef Hoffmann being awarded the commission. Hoffmann was Protestant and not compliant with the government, but he was internationally renowned. Several aspects of Kramreiter's plan nonetheless found their way into the final design, especially since he was the executing architect on site. Hoffmann's winning design for the Austrian pavilion presented a Neoclassical reshaped version of the spatial concept apparently already laid out by Kramreiter in his first design: strict axial symmetrical construction with flat roofs, central portal with passageway into a courtyard, side spaces in the form of wings, and the main entry exaggerated as a portal of victory are all characteristics that were also exhibited in Kramreiter's planning. Hoffmann now gave Kramreiter's diaphanous "scaffolding" an opaque shell in the form of a travertine framing of the central portal, which cut high into the transverse rectangular main building, with the entire structure standing on a stepped base. In front, on the side

across from the entry, are two lower hall structures flanking the sculpture terraces with central fountain pools. The side structures were entirely glazed toward the terrace, but otherwise without opening and appeared laterally, somewhat before the alignment of the main building. The main building also had no openings other than the portal, but was illuminated by circumferential, entirely glazed toplighting, whereby the light was meant to be filtered inside through a velum, or a transparent ceiling. The outer walls, coated with the finishing plaster "Terranova" are grooved; the horizontal flutes seem to cover the entire building. Inside the pavilion, the passage from façade to sculpture garden is surrounded by three-part, arched pillars. One can gaze through these into the high halls on both sides of the central axis, whose floor is recessed. One door in the central axis of each annex connects it with the high halls. The only realized architectural decoration is a sgraffito on the portal's courtyard façade; there was not enough time for anything else.

On 12 May 1934, Austria's Biennale pavilion was festively opened.[18] Josef Hoffmann first stated his opinion on the building in 1936, with a critique of Kramreiter's construction management:

> "As has been told to me by various parties, at the Austrian pavilion at the Biennale in Venice, several damages to the building have become apparent. What we can see from that, is that with such an important building constantly confronted by the competition with other nations, apart from creating the design, it is absolutely necessary that also the building management and awarding of construction occur by the architect. As I was not even allowed to act as construction manager in the realization of my own design and was not even entrusted to control the completed building upon handing it over, I refuse any responsibility. I have not even been able to see my work until today. Of course, the general public cannot imagine the circumstances and will therefore have to blame me for it. Moreover, as I see in publications, someone arranged some sort of conclusion in the rear courtyard without my knowledge, with which I am not at all satisfied, and which most definitely disturbs the overall impression and with its stake-like realization cannot possibly shape a worthy conclusion. As the designer, I would have expected that additions to the plans by strangers would not have been allowed, as this presents

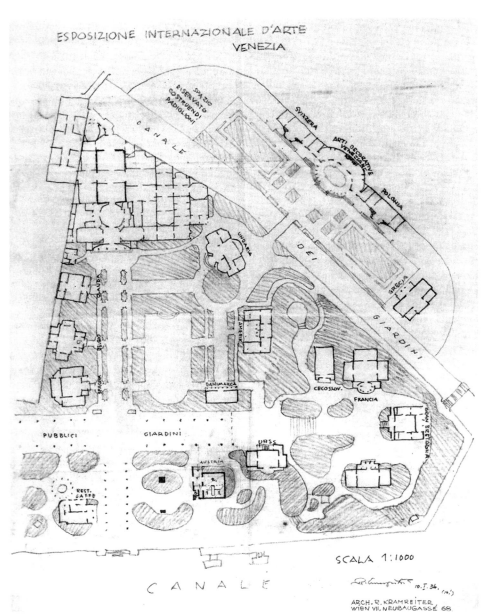

Fig. 5 Robert Kramreiter, Vienna: project
for the Austrian pavilion at the Venice
Biennale, site plan 1:1000
Pencil on tracing paper, 10 Jan 1934
Archivio Storico Arti Contemporanee, Venice,
Scatole nere padiglioni, Exp. 2/3.
© La Biennale Venezia, ASAC

an undeserved artistic compromising of my work. The entire building is composed with a sculptural emphasis on the central axis
and the present imperfect state must seem permanently inexpli-
cable […]."[19]

Hoffmann was only able to carry out several of the repairs
that he demanded after the change of power in 1938: the
panel covering and concluding wall were renovated. The
further configuration was postponed, as after the Anschluss
in 1938, the pavilion was no longer used. Austrian artists
now had to exhibit in the German pavilion. Construction on
the pavilion was first resumed in 1948, when it was again
used as a space for Austrian art of the Second Republic. The
sculpture garden was expanded in 1954; Hoffmann planned
the asymmetrical placement of a flying roof, and a curved
boundary wall and a basin were added to the yard. Based
on designs by Ferdinand Kitt, a kitchen was built from the
outside in 1956. After Hoffmann's death in 1956, the central

entry area was simplified, the roll-up doors were dismantled,
and glass doors put in.

After 50 years of existence, a first, comprehensive ren-
ovation and careful return to the original state, for example
through a rebuilding of the roll-up doors, took place under
the management of the Austrian Biennale commissioner at
the time, Hans Hollein, in 1984. Hollein sees the pavilion as
the "dream (of the Austrian) from the south" and compares
it to the open, "pleasure buildings" of the elder Fischer von
Erlach and Lucas von Hildebrandt, which did not exist north
of the Alps.[20]

This structure, which exists until today, has thus proven
to be the most enduring of all of Hoffmann's ephemeral exhibition structures. In the history of its creation in the midst
of Austrian civil war and its public utilization, it remains a
highly political building of aesthetic self-presentation of each
of the governments defining Austria.   ▪

20 p. 414

Fig. 6 JH, the Austrian pavilion in
Venice at its opening on 12 May 1934,
courtyard side
MAK, KI 23506-2-2

Fig. 7 JH, the Austrian pavilion in Venice
at its opening on 12 May 1934, inside
MAK, KI 23506-2-3

1   Czech, Hermann, "The Hoffmann Pavillon," in: commonpavilions.com/pavilion-austria.html [21 Sep 2020]; and Franz, Rainald, "The Austrian Pavilion at the Venice Biennale: 1893–2013," in: Sharp, Jasper (ed.), *Austria and the Venice Biennale 1895–2013*, Nuremberg 2013, 87–100.

2   On the use of the Biennale grounds before the building of national pavilions, see Plattner, Hansjörg, in: BMUK/Hollein, Hans (eds.), *Josef Hoffmann, 50 Jahre Österreichischer Pavillon*, Salzburg/Vienna 1984, 62, with secondary literature. Also essential: Feller, Barbara, "Venedig, 29. Jänner 1934. Österreich und die Biennale in Venedig," in: Tabor, Jan (ed.), *Kunst und Diktatur. Architektur, Bildhauerei und Malerei in Österreich, Deutschland, Italien und der Sowjetunion 1922–1956*, exh. cat. Künstlerhaus Vienna, Baden 1994, 302–307.

3   Report by Friedrich Dörnhöffer, director of the Imperial Royal State Gallery to the Ministry of Culture and Education, Vienna, 29 Oct 1913; k.k. Ministerium für Kultus und Unterricht, "Erbauung eines österreichischen Kunstpavillons in Venedig, Verwaltungsarchiv 1913 VA PAV Bau; k.k. Finanzministerium, "Erbauung eines österreichischen Kunstpavillons in Venedig," Z 74787 Supplement 25, 7 Oct 1913.

4   Sekler, Eduard F., *Josef Hoffmann: The Architectural Work*, Princeton, NJ 1985, CR 157, 347–348. Trans. Eduard F. Sekler and John Maass.

5   Albertina Vienna, projects for an exhibition building in Venice, pencil on paper, 1913; inv. nos. 8380, 8381; Academy of Fine Arts Vienna; National Gallery Prague; Model Collection, UAA; published in *Der Architekt*, XXIII 1920, 67; fig. BMUK/Hollein 1984 (see note 2).

6   Invoice from the studio of Councilor Professor Josef Hoffmann to "Herr Ministerialrat v. Foerster" at the Imperial Royal Ministry of Education, 6 May 1914; printed in BMUK/Hollein 1984 (see note 2), fig. 7, 25; administrative archive and act of the Imperial Royal Ministry of Culture and Education no. 21158, 6 May 1914, "regarding liquidation of a sum of 1,300 kronen for the conception of the project for the Austrian exhibition pavilion in Venice and the a sociated travel costs."

7   Agreement to this proposal in AVA-Finanzen, file no. 30075/32.

8   ASAC, fondo storico scatole nere padiglioni b 1 mostra austria 1934, lettera gironcoli, 7 December 1933. Furthermore, Herbert Thurner reports that the class was regularly visited by architecture stars, including André Lurçat, Le Corbusier, and Frank Lloyd Wright; cf. Thurner, Herbert, "Zum 100. Geburtstag Josef Hoffmann," in: *Der Bau* 1970, 21.

9   Vocelka, Karl, *Geschichte Österreichs. Kultur–Gesellschaft–Politik*, Graz/Vienna 2000, 289 ff. On the aesthetics of the corporative state, see also: Tabor 1994 (see note 2).

10 ASAC 1934, preliminari lettera di impresa, 19 Jan 1934 (see note 8).

11 *Gazzetta di Venezia*, 29 Jan 1934.

12 BMU 1934, Geschäftszahl 3665-I 6a, VZ 32559/29, A.E. Teilnahme Österreichs an der "Biennale" Ausstellung in Venedig ab 1934; Errichtung eines österr. Ausstellungspavillons., 6.II. 1934, ASA, AVA Unterricht UM Unterrichtsministerium, 1848–1940.

13 Letter from Leo Schmoll to Robert Kramreiter from 5 Feb 1934, property of Pedro Kramreiter. On the role of Holzmeister, see: Posch, Wilfried, *Clemens Holzmeister. Architekt zwischen Kunst und Politik. Mit einem Werkverzeichnis von Monika Knofler*, Vienna/Salzburg 2010. My special thanks go to Pedro Kramreiter for his generous transfer of documents in his possession on the construction history of the Austrian Biennale pavilion and the role of his father Robert Kramreiter.

14 Clemens Holzmeister to the BMU, 14 Feb 1934; ASA, N.Z. 4679/34.

15 Letter from studio Hoffmann/Haerdtl, 1 Mar 1934, ASA, AVA.

16 Letter from studio Hoffmann/Haerdtl, 19 Mar 1934, ASA, AVA.

17 BMU 1934 GZ 190858-I 6a, 9 Apr 1934, ASA, AVA.

18 Report of the ambassador in Rome, Rintelen to Federal Chancellor Dollfuss, 14 May 1934; ASA, AdR BKA, BKA-I Federal Chancellery-Interior, 1918–1938 (inventory).

19 Letter from Josef Hoffmann from 22 Jun 1936; AT-OeVA, Unterricht 15, no. 21862/36.

20 BMUK/Hollein 1984 (see note 2).

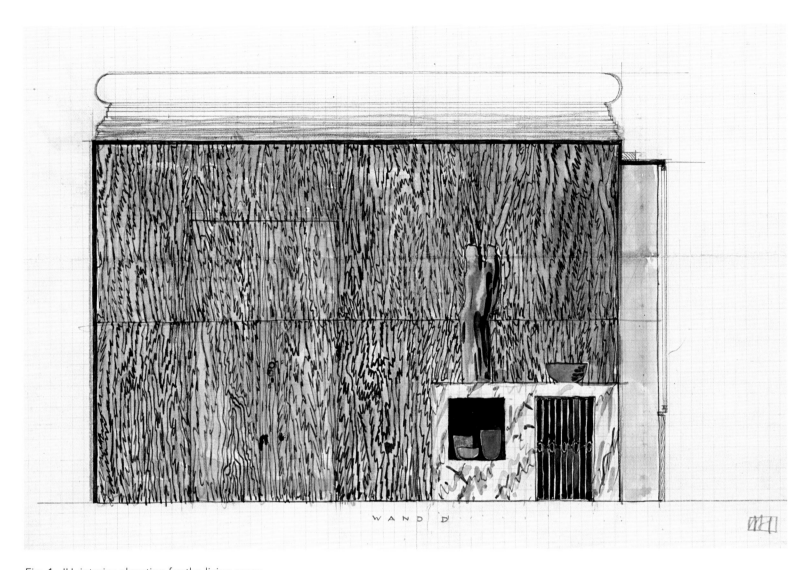

Fig. 1 JH, interior elevation for the living room
in Dr. Meyer-Helbeck's apartment, 1935
Graphic Collection, Academy of Fine Arts Vienna, HZ 27319

Christian Witt-Dörring

Working without the Wiener Werkstätte

Decorative Arts 1933–1938

The liquidation of the Wiener Werkstätte (WW) in 1932 can be considered the dominant event that will define the remainder of Josef Hoffmann's career. It deprives Hoffmann of an infrastructure that over the previous 30 years had not only permitted him to pursue formal aesthetic experiments without the burden of financial constraints, but that had also made possible their high-quality artisanal execution. Moreover, until that point the WW had simultaneously functioned as a vehicle for marketing the Josef Hoffmann brand.

The validity of the WW's code of values increasingly comes under the microscope as a result of the drastically altered economic and associated social parameters from late 1929. To this is added from the 1910s a new generation of architects and designers who take for granted the prerequisites for their work—namely the reforms and progress that had been hard fought for by the founding generation of the Secession—and who extend these reforms in line with the requirements of their time. It already becomes apparent in the course of the Werkbund exhibition in 1930 that the decorative artists of the old school only want to be beholden to the traditional ideal of quality as a premium product, whereas the exhibition organized by the Austrian Werkbund in 1931—likewise at the Austrian Museum of Art and Industry (today's MAK)—called *Der gute billige Gegenstand* [The Good, Cheap Object] and the Werkbund Estate of 1932 offer solutions that take the economic situation into account. Perforce this generational conflict is vented within the Werkbund itself. With the Austrian decorative-arts exhibition at the Milan Triennial in 1933 being awarded to Oskar Strnad and not to Josef Hoffmann, in combination with some words uttered by Josef Frank—distorted for good measure—during a talk, the blanket accusation of "hostility to the decorative arts" is leveled against the Werkbund. Josef Hoffmann subsequently declares his departure from the association and founds the New Werkbund.[1]

In addition to the decorative arts' status, Hoffmann's concept of the Gesamtkunstwerk—or total work of art— also comes under close scrutiny from society at large. In his novel *The Emperor's Tomb*, Joseph Roth creates a wonderfully atmospheric picture of the 1930s when he has the Baroness Trotta voice his own assessment of the decorative arts during a conversation with her son:

"When people start using worthless material to make something which looks as if it has some value, where will it stop? Africans

wear mussel shells, that's something else again. Let people swindle—fine. But these people [decorative artists] are earning a living from swindling, boy! No one can persuade me that cotton is linen or that you can make a wreath of laurels out of pine needles."[2]

In the six years that lie between the end of the WW and Austria's annexation by Nazi Germany in 1938, Hoffmann searches for new distribution channels—or rather public appearances—and for craftspeople who will execute his decorative arts, which are conceived as a specifically Austrian cultural achievement.[3] The year 1934 offers him several such opportunities in the context of three exhibitions that he himself designs. Hosted by the Austrian Museum, they are the show for the *50 Jahre Wiener Kunstgewerbevereins* [50 Years of the Viennese Arts-and-Crafts Association] and *Das befreite Handwerk* [The Liberated Handicraft], as well as his design of the decorative-arts room in the exhibition *Austria in London*, which is organized by the Austrian federal government. In the latter he exhibits among other things small items of furniture and frames specially developed for the frame maker Max Welz. In addition to Max Welz,[4] who had already produced a number of frames for the WW in 1922 after designs by Dagobert Peche, it is the owner of the glassware commissioning retailer J. & L. Lobmeyr, Stefan Rath Sr, who challenges and supports Hoffmann's inexhaustible creative talent during these bleak financial times. The result is an abundance of new designs, though they were sadly never executed. Due to the loss of the WW's own production facilities, Hoffmann is forced to seek direct contact with executing craft firms. He finds a suitable opportunity during the 1934 exhibition *Das befreite Handwerk*, which is initiated by the decorative-arts branch of the Wiener Gewerbegenossenschaftsverband (Viennese Association of Trade Cooperatives). It is conceived as a backlash to the Werkbund exhibition, which was similarly held at the Austrian Museum some four years previously. Due to the latter show's promotion of modern objectivity in combination with a new modesty, craftspeople working in purely decorative trades like passementerie, painting, turning, sculpture, carpentry, and gilding had felt their very existence to be threatened. The defining adjective in the exhibition's title— "befreit" or liberated—therefore refers to the desire to throw off the chains of a production process that is defined by utilitarian thinking and limited to a mere cost-benefit calculation. The chairman of the decorative arts branch Oswald

2 3

12 p. 353

4

2 p. 360

Fig. 2 JH, design for the *50 Jahre Wiener Kunstgewerbeverein* [50 Years of
the Viennese Arts-and-Crafts Association] exhibition at the AMAI, 1934
UAA, Collection and Archive, 146/2

Fig. 3 JH, design for the *50 Jahre Wiener Kunstgewerbeverein* [50 Years of
the Viennese Arts-and-Crafts Association] exhibition at the AMAI, 1934
UAA, Collection and Archive, 145/1

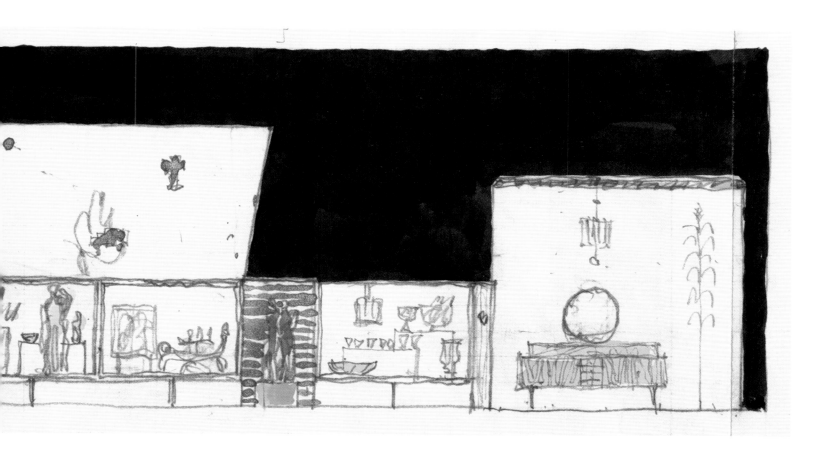

Fig. 4 Vitrine with furniture after designs by Josef Hoffmann, *Das befreite Handwerk*
[The Liberated Handicraft] exhibition at the AMAI, 1934
MAK, KI 9197-2-1

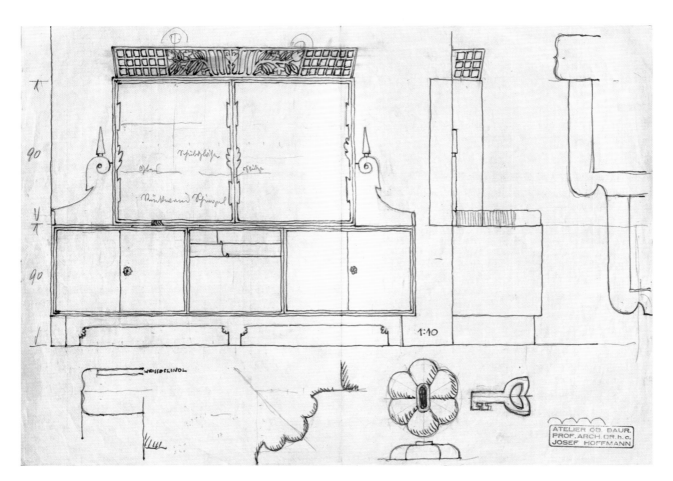

Fig. 5 JH, design for a sideboard with top-mounted vitrine, ca. 1935
MAK, KI 23086-11

Fig. 6 JH, design for an object in
remembrance of Dagobert Peche, 1938
UAA, Collection and Archive, 4287

Fig. 7 Dagobert Peche, the Wiener Werkstätte's tribute for
Josef Hoffmann's 50th birthday, 1920
Silver and ebony
MAK, GO 1788
© MAK/Georg Mayer

Hertl describes the reasons that convinced him of the
necessity of this exhibition initiative:

> "Also consider that giving and creating work is the most noble
> and most important task of our times, that even the craftsperson
> can only live and create valuable things if the style of our age
> gives them the space and opportunity to demonstrate masterful
> proficiency and sublime skill. An austere, plain, and unembel-
> lished style will never be able to do justice to this fundamental
> demand of our age."[5]

In Josef Hoffmann as the artistic director and designer
of the exhibition, Hertl finds the ideal partner to realize his
idea. He guarantees the primacy of individual artistic
expression in conjunction with superior-quality artisanal
execution. Accordingly, Hoffmann delivers a series of particularly elaborate furniture designs whose realization serves
to shine a spotlight on the expertise of the various Viennese
decorative tradespeople.

As of 30 September 1936 Hoffmann is forced to retire,
meaning that he now also loses his studio rooms in the
School of Arts and Crafts and hence another important pillar
of his infrastructure. Mäda Primavesi attempts to reestablish

the WW with German financial backing in 1937, traveling
to Munich especially for this purpose. She reports:

> "In 1937 the cultural director in Munich wanted to give large
> funds to allow the WW—with affiliated factories—to rise again;
> I wanted to provide him with all the necessary documents. When
> I arrived with the documents, one had told him—he had been in
> Vienna—that Prof. Hoffmann is not related by marriage to Jews
> and not many artists are Jewish. He suggested to me to have the
> WW financed by the Munich Workshops. We did not want that."[6]

For the Austrian pavilion at the Paris World's Fair in 1937,
the federal government chooses Hoffmann's former student,
assistant, studio manager, and since 1932 the copartner of
his studio Oswald Haerdtl as the artistic director and head
architect. Josef Hoffmann is represented by a *Boudoir d'und
grande vedette* [Boudoir for a Big Star] executed by the
Max Welz company. In remembrance of Dagobert Peche
and in the style of his design for the WW's honorary gift for
Josef Hoffmann's 50th birthday, in 1938 Hoffmann designs
an object *in memoriam Dagobert Peche*. In 1939 Oswald
Haerdtl finally leaves the studio community and founds his
own atelier.

1 p. 348
4 p. 350

5 6 p. 351

6 7

1   Printed statement by the board of the Austrian
    Werkbund "Zur außerordentlichen Vollversamm-
    lung am 20. Juni 1933," Christian Witt-Dörring's
    archive.
2   Roth, Joseph, *The Emperor's Tomb*, New York
    2002, 76 f. Trans. John Hoare.

3   See the article "Luxury Put to the Test: The Wiener
    Werkstätte and Hoffmann's Interior Designs 1919–
    1932" by Christian Witt-Dörring in this catalog.
4   See e.g., the illustrations and M.E.–Wien, "Aus
    den Werkstätten von Welz und Soulek," in: *Innen-
    dekoration* 46 1935, 132 ff., 139 f.

5   Hertl, Oswald, "Vorwort," in: *Das befreite Hand-
    werk*, exh. cat. AMAI, Vienna 1933, 6.
6   Noever, Peter (ed.), *Yearning for Beauty: The
    Wiener Werkstätte and the Stoclet House*, Ost-
    fildern-Ruit 2006, 399.

1939
1945

1939–1945

378

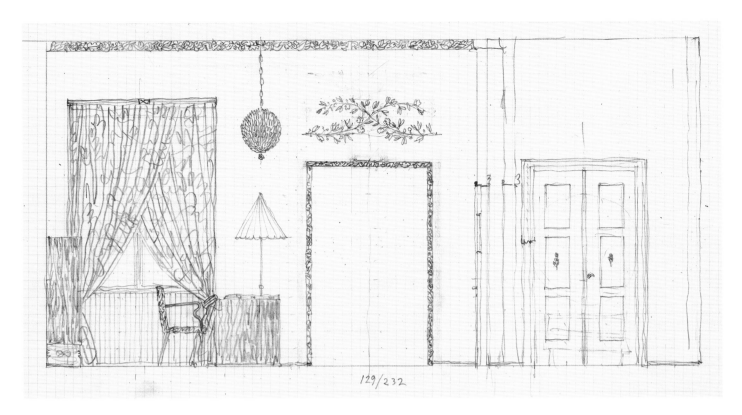

Fig. 1 JH, design for the interior elevation of a mock-up room
for the Deutsche Werkstätten in Munich, 1940
Graphic Collection, Academy of Fine Arts Vienna, HZ 26320

Fig. 2 JH, wall light for the *Haus der Wehrmacht*
[House of the Armed Forces], 1940
Limewood, gold-plated
Private collection
© MAK/Georg Mayer

Fig. 3 JH, mirror frame, executed by
Max Welz (Friedrich Nerold), 1942
Makassar ebony and African padauk, mirror
MAK, H 1949
© MAK/Georg Mayer

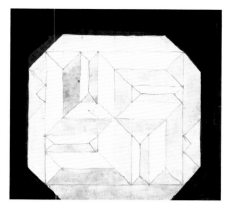

Fig. 4 JH, design for a lidded box
made of cut crystal glass, ca. 1940
Kunsthandel Widder, Vienna

Fig. 5 JH, mirror frame, executed by Max Welz, ca. 1940
Limewood, stained black, mirror
GALERIE BEI DER ALBERTINA · ZETTER

Fig. 6 JH, jug, executed by Schleiss Keramik,
Gmunden, 1939/40
Stoneware, painted and glazed
Private collection
© MAK/Georg Mayer

Fig. 7 Jug, executed by Alexander Sturm, 1942
Silver
MAK, GO 1864
© MAK/Katrin Wißkirchen

Fig. 8 JH, design for the chandelier in the showroom of the *Haus der Mode* [House of Fashion], 1938
UAA, Collection and Archive, 4000/2

Fig. 9 JH, design for
the tomb of the Flöge
family, 1943
Graphic Collection, Academy
of Fine Arts Vienna, HZ 26313

Fig. 10 JH, project for a
Skanderbeg mausoleum,
vitrine for helmet and
sword, Krujë, Albania,
1944
E. F. Sekler, *Josef Hoffmann*, 223

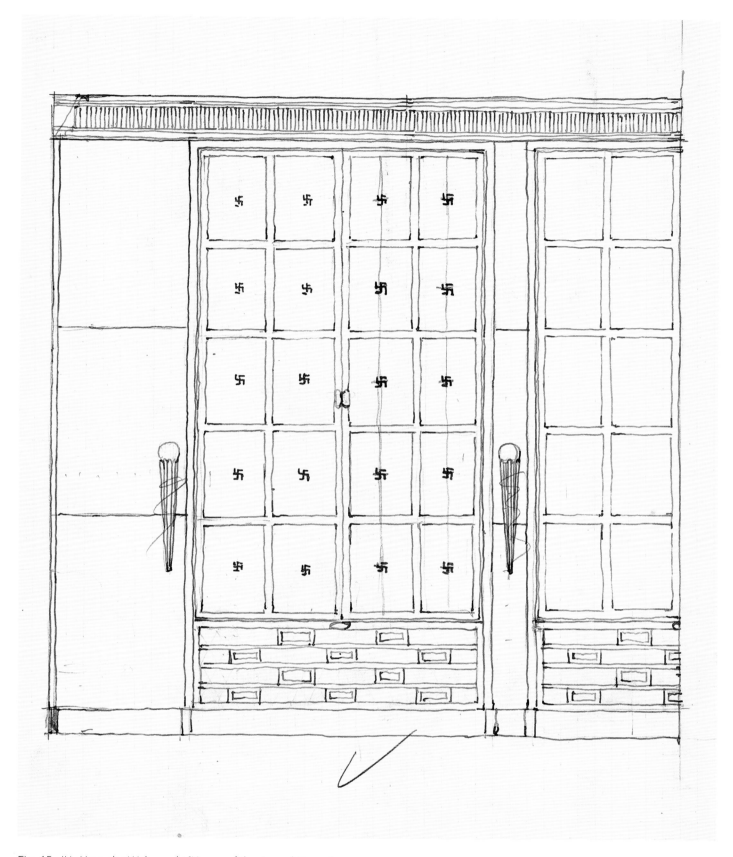

Fig. 15 JH, *Haus der Wehrmacht* [House of the Armed Forces],
Vienna, 1940, wall decoration in the ceremonial hall
Kunsthandel Widder, Vienna

<
Figs. 11–14 JH, adaptation and furnishing of the *Haus der Mode*
[House of Fashion] in Palais Lobkowitz, Vienna, 1938/39, room of the
male artistic director, drawing room of a female artistic director,
showroom, and followers' dining hall
MBF (41) 1942, 285–288

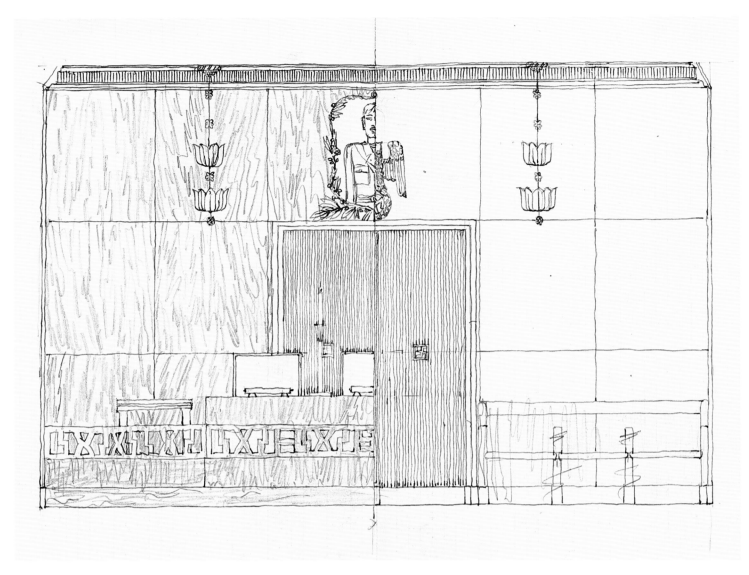

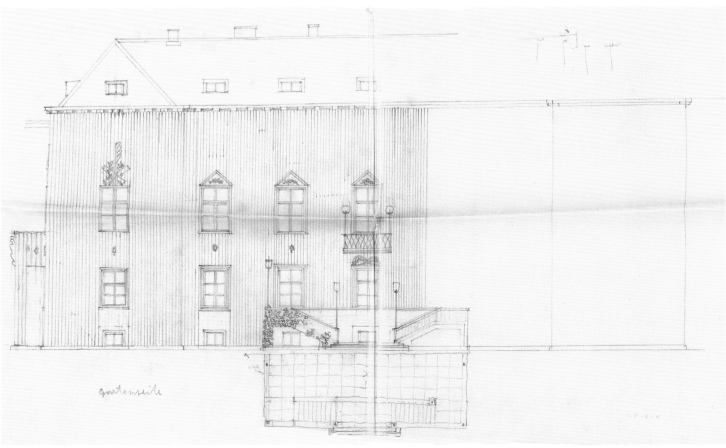

Gartenseite

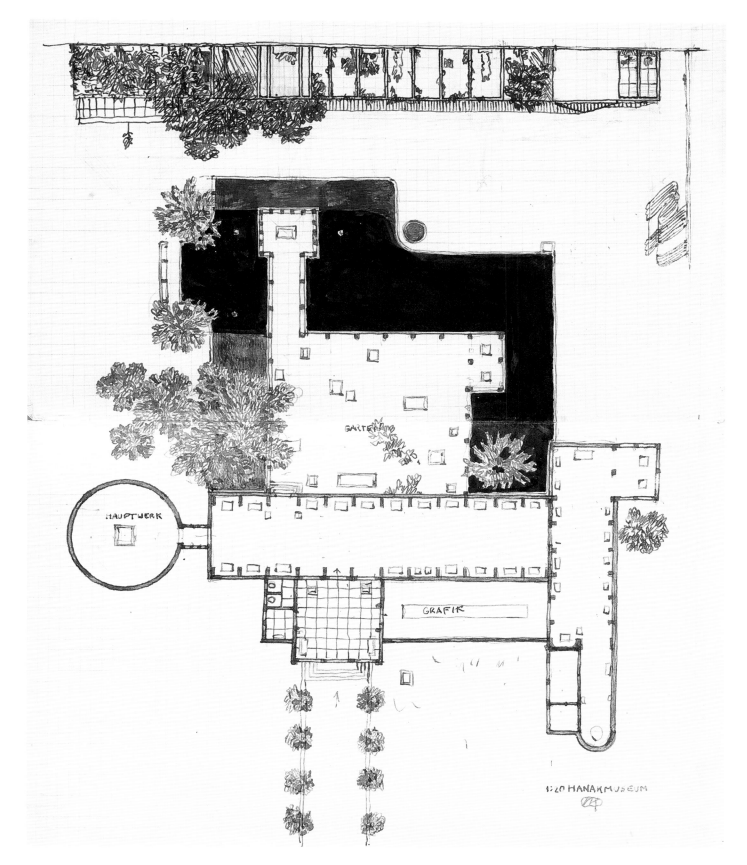

Fig. 18 JH, design for an Anton Hanak museum in Vienna's
Augarten park, prob. 1938–1940, floor plan and view
Kunsthandel Widder, Vienna

<

Fig. 16 JH, interior elevation for a paneled assembly room with podium and
seating, *Haus der Wehrmacht* [House of the Armed Forces], Vienna, 1940
Kunsthandel Widder, Vienna

Fig. 17 JH, design for the garden façade, *Haus der Wehrmacht*
[House of the Armed Forces], Vienna, 1940
Kunsthandel Widder, Vienna

Josef Hoffmann
1939
1945

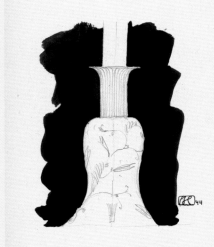

JH, design for a candlestick for the experimental workshop of the Wiener Kunsthandwerkverein (Viennese Association of Arts and Crafts), 1944
Kunsthandel Widder, Vienna

1939

Josef Hoffmann becomes honorary chairman of the Wiener Kunsthandwerkverein (Viennese Association of Arts and Crafts) that is reestablished by the City of Vienna and run by his former assistant Hans Bichler, an illegal National Socialist. The association, complete with its salesrooms, workshops, and offices, moves into the previously aryanized Zwieback department store on Kärntner Straße/Weihburggasse, where Hoffmann also runs his new architectural firm together with Josef Kalbac into the 1950s. In February 1939 the *Haus der Mode* [House of Fashion] designed by Hoffmann is opened in the rooms of Palais Lobkowitz in Vienna. Together with Josef Kalbac he converts the former German embassy on Metternichgasse, in Vienna's Landstraße district, into the *Haus der Wehrmacht* [House of the Armed Forces]. The festive decorations for Vienna's Opera Ball in 1939 are designed by Hoffmann and Oswald Haerdtl, who subsequently closes their joint studio and founds his own firm.

1940

Hoffmann develops competition projects for the trade fair grounds in Vienna's Prater park (with Haerdtl), for a guesthouse of the City of Vienna, and for an Anton Hanak museum in Vienna's Augarten park. With Kalbac he furnishes the shop of the Meissen Porcelain Manufactory on Kärntner Ring. An exhibition at the State Arts and Crafts Museum in Vienna (today's MAK) to mark his 70th birthday is postponed to 1941 as a result of differences of opinion regarding cultural policy within the Nazi administration and is a modest affair. The intention to award Hoffmann the Goethe Medal is prevented among other things by a negative assessment by Albert Speer.

1941–1945

With the new jobs for Mayor Hermann Neubacher, for the Reichsstatthalter (Reich Governor) Arthur Seyß-Inquart, and more big names in the local Nazi regime in other regions under Nazi control who were friends with Hoffmann, his planning commissions start to run dry. In 1941 he becomes an honorary member of the Academy of Fine Arts Vienna and in 1942 is awarded the City of Vienna's Honorary Prize for Arts and Crafts. Continues to produce designs for the Wiener Kunsthandwerkverein and for J. & L. Lobmeyr, the Augarten Porcelain Manufactory, the Deutsche Werkstätten Hellerau in Dresden, and the Lausitzer Glaswerke in Weißwasser. Hoffmann publishes an article on arts and crafts in the magazine *Die Pause*. In 1943 he designs a house for Baron Wieser in Vienna's Grinzing district. Created at the suggestion of the now Balkan officer Hermann Neubacher, the design for a mausoleum for the Albanian ruler Skanderbeg in Krujë, Albania, in 1944 remains unrealized.

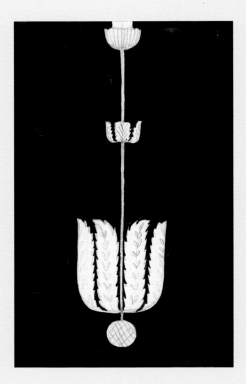

JH, design for the hanging lamp in the courtroom, *Haus der Wehrmacht* [House of the Armed Forces], Vienna, 1940
Kunsthandel Widder, Vienna

Sergius Pauser, portrait
of Josef Hoffmann to
commemorate his 70th
birthday, commissioned
by the municipality of
Vienna, 1942
Oil on canvas
Wien Museum, 73.043

JH, wall design for a
paneled assembly room
with podium and seating,
Haus der Wehrmacht
[House of the Armed
Forces], Vienna, 1940
Kunsthandel Widder, Vienna

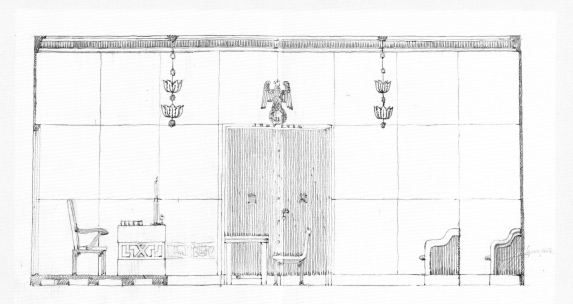

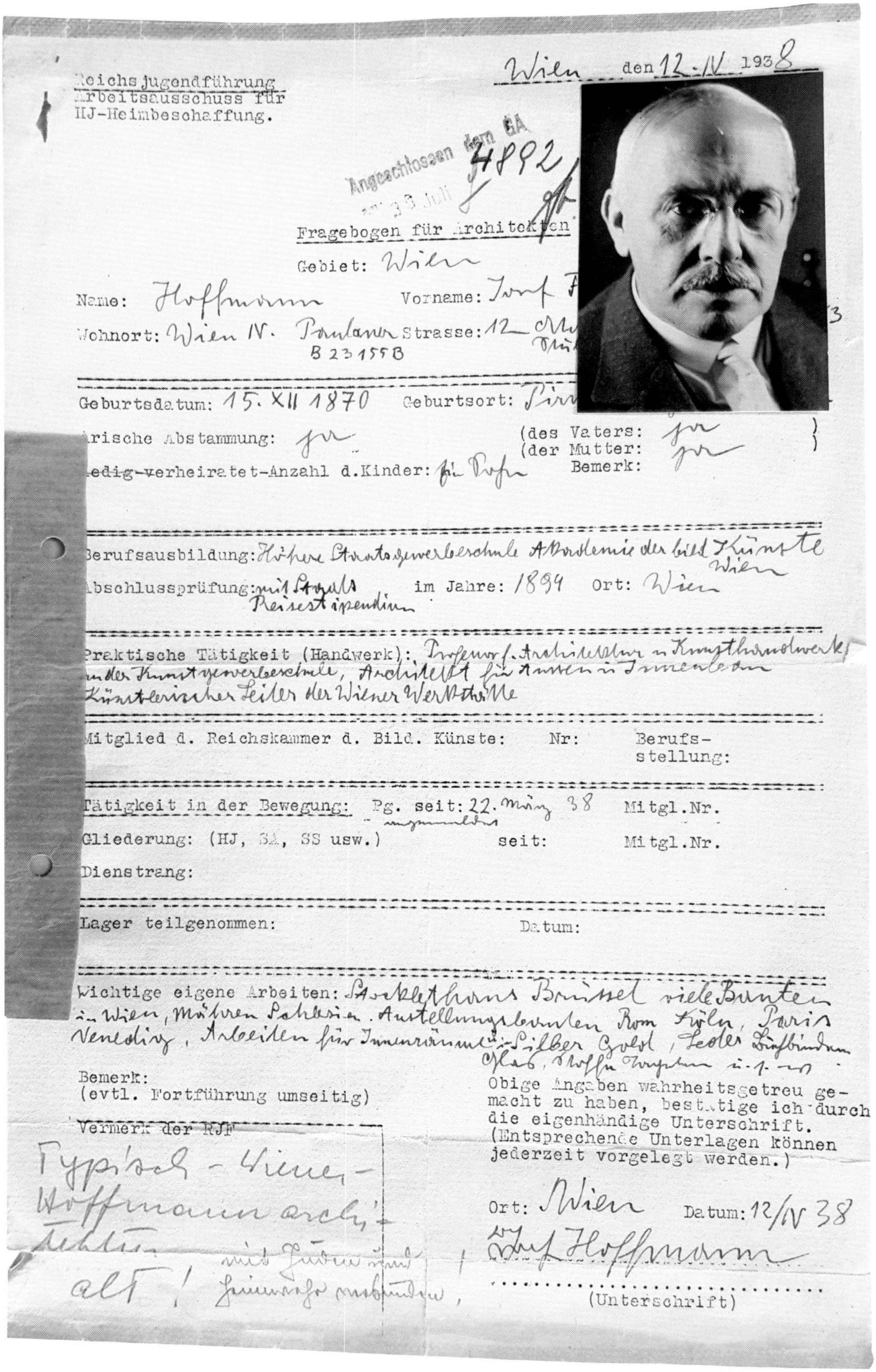

Wien den 12. IV 1938

Reichsjugendführung
Arbeitsausschuss für
HJ-Heimbeschaffung.

Angeschlossen dem GA
... 30 Juli
4892

Fragebogen für Architekten

Gebiet: Wien

Name: Hoffmann Vorname: Josef F...

Wohnort: Wien IV. Paulaner Strasse: 12 ...
B 23155 B

Geburtsdatum: 15. XII 1870 Geburtsort: Pirn...

Arische Abstammung: ja (des Vaters: ja) (der Mutter: ja)
Ledig-verheiratet-Anzahl d. Kinder: ein Sohn Bemerk:

Berufsausbildung: Höhere Staatsgewerbeschule Akademie der bild. Künste Wien

Abschlussprüfung: mit Staats Reisestipendium im Jahre: 1894 Ort: Wien

Praktische Tätigkeit (Handwerk): Professor f. Architektur u. Kunsthandwerk an der Kunstgewerbeschule, Architekt für Außen u. Innenbau, Künstlerischer Leiter der Wiener Werkstätte

Mitglied d. Reichskammer d. Bild. Künste: Nr: Berufsstellung:

Tätigkeit in der Bewegung: Pg. seit: 22. März 38 angemeldet Mitgl.Nr.
Gliederung: (HJ, SA, SS usw.) seit: Mitgl.Nr.
Dienstrang:

Lager teilgenommen: Datum:

Wichtige eigene Arbeiten: Stocklethaus Brüssel viele Bauten in Wien, Mähren Schlesien. Ausstellungsbauten Rom Köln, Paris Venedig, Arbeiten für Innenräume in Silber Gold, Leder Bucheinbänden Glas, Stoffe Tapeten u.s.w.

Bemerk:
(evtl. Fortführung umseitig)

Vermerk der RJF
Typisch – Wiener – Hoffmann architekten mit Juden und Freimaurer verbunden, alt!

Obige Angaben wahrheitsgetreu gemacht zu haben, bestätige ich durch die eigenhändige Unterschrift. (Entsprechende Unterlagen können jederzeit vorgelegt werden.)

Ort: Wien Datum: 12/IV 38

Josef Hoffmann
(Unterschrift)

Fig. 1 Reich Youth Leadership, Committee for the Creation of Hitler Youth Centers, questionnaire for architects, Josef Hoffmann, 1938
ASA, AdR, Gauakt Josef Hoffmann, no. 4892 2.S

Elisabeth Boeckl-Klamper

Josef Hoffmann and National Socialism

An Evaluation

After Austria's Anschluss with the National Socialist German Reich in March 1938, Josef Hoffmann—now 67 years old—quickly fell into line with the new political reality. For example, as early as 12 April he filled out a form "for architects" issued by the Reich Youth Leadership's Committee for the Creation of Hitler Youth Centers. In the column asking about "activities in the movement," he noted down "PG [= *Parteigenosse*, party member] since 22 March 1938," but relativized this equally premature and incorrect statement by writing "signed up" under the date. Hoffmann, who stressed throughout his life that he did not understand anything about politics,[1] evidently had no reservations about promptly putting himself at the service of the new National Socialist authorities. Like many Austrians he believed their propaganda, which promised an economic recovery and general prosperity. As such, he welcomed the "union with the Reich, which has been desired since time immemorial," as he wrote to Carl Otto Czeschka in June 1938.[2] In the same letter Hoffmann, who "[f]rom his origins among the German-speaking minority of Moravia […] was conditioned to have sympathies for the German National camp,"[3] not only expresses his delight at now being permitted "as a Sudeten German" to feel "unproblematically German," but also stresses how happy he would be to be able to become involved in "the great cause once more in my life in an artistic way."[4]

Useful Networks

Thanks to his decidedly good relationship with local proponents of the Nazi regime, especially with Vienna's National Socialist city administration, Hoffmann was soon provided such an opportunity to become involved. On 12 March 1938—the day before the Anschluss officially happened—Hermann Neubacher was appointed mayor of Vienna. Neubacher, the former director of the Gemeinwirtschaftliche Siedlungs- und Bauaktiengesellschaft (GESIBA, the Institution for Public Housing and Construction Materials), had been elected president of the Werkbund in 1928 and made a member of the Wiener Werkstätte's supervisory board in 1931. One can assume that he was by no means merely, as Eduard F. Sekler writes, an "old acquaintance" of Hoffmann,[5]

but rather that the two were friends. Neubacher awarded Hoffmann several commissions—not only during his time as Vienna's mayor until December 1940, but also later (e.g., the Skanderbeg mausoleum in Krujë/AL, 1944) when he performed various political functions in the Balkan States.

In addition to the art-loving Hermann Neubacher, another important contact within Vienna's National Socialist city administration was Johannes Cech, a nephew of Hoffmann. Cech, born in 1903, was the son of Franziska Cech, one of Hoffmann's sisters, who had occasionally worked in customer service at the Wiener Werkstätte after the First World War.[6] Johannes Cech had studied architecture and typography. He was a member of the Deutscher Turnerbund (German Gymnastics Association), the Nordische Gesellschaft (Nordic Society),[7] and from 1932 the NSDAP. His entrenchment in the party that was banned in Austria from June 1933 to February 1938 due to numerous terrorist attacks, was obviously deep. Having previously worked as a freelancer, Cech was employed as a text and graphics consultant at the Vienna Kulturamt (Culture Authority) on 1 October 1938 and as the head of the Wiener Frauenakademie (Women's Academy of Vienna) two years later as a kind of reward for his illegal Nazi activities.[8] It is not possible to reconstruct all the particulars of the professional relationships between Cech and Hoffmann and Neubacher and Hoffmann, as the Nazi-era records from the Vienna Kulturamt—with the exception of the card catalog of general business protocols—have not been preserved. However, significant proceedings were recorded in abbreviated form on these index cards, including, for example, that all matters concerning the Kunsthandwerkverein (Association of Arts and Crafts)—whose honorary chairman was Hoffmann and whose role will be discussed in more detail later—had to be presented to Johannes Cech.[9]

"Art-Egoism"

Due to his excellent relationship with Vienna's city administration, soon after the Anschluss Hoffmann was commissioned with two design projects that were as prestigious as they were lucrative. He was entrusted with converting the now obsolete German embassy into the *Haus der Wehr-*

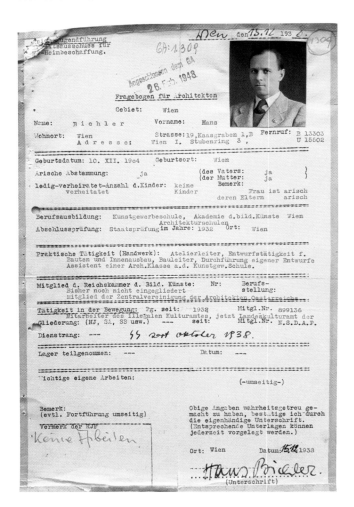

Fig. 2 Reich Youth Leadership, Committee for the Creation
of Hitler Youth Centers, questionnaire for architects,
Hans Bichler, 1938
ASA, AdR, Gauakt Hans Bichler

macht [House of the Armed Forces] and with redesigning
the interiors of Palais Lobkowitz, which had housed the embassy of the Czechoslovak Republic until the Anschluss.[10]
While the *Haus der Wehrmacht* was used as an officers' mess
from the fall of 1940, the *Haus der Mode* [House of Fashion]
was opened in Palais Lobkowitz in February 1939.[11] That
Hoffmann was commissioned with executing both of these
prominent buildings, was not just advantageous to him—in
addition to the prestige his fee for the conversion plans for
Palais Lobkowitz amounted to 20,000 reichsmarks[12]—but
also to the city administration. It could credit itself with employing an architect of international repute—a fact that
would boost the reputation of the new National Socialist
rulers both at home and abroad. After all, it was not only
abroad that the mass arrests and pogrom-like persecution
of 1938 (in which, for example, Jews were forced to scrub
the sidewalks) had called into question Germany's claim to
being a cultural nation—they had also discomfited parts of
the Viennese population.

Hoffmann, too, was aware of the growing social margi-
nalization of the Jewish population and the removal of art
that was considered "undesirable" for ideological reasons.
For example, he observed in the aforementioned letter to
Czeschka:

> "The WW's small collection in the municipal gallery was naturally
> smeared as degenerate, as were our very good modern galleries.
> All that will of course be set straight once people have had time
> to have second thoughts."[13]

Clearly with this unusual choice of words Hoffmann was
alluding to objects by the Wiener Werkstätte being vilified
as decadent by some National Socialists and hence being
removed from collections, and to the fact that galleries under
Jewish ownership—many of which had shown modern art
prior to 1938, such as Otto Kallir's Neue Galerie—had to be
closed. Like many people, however, Hoffmann underestimated the unscrupulousness and dynamism of the Nazi regime: he evidently believed that such incidents would pass
after the initial "Anschluss enthusiasm" ("once people have
had time to have second thoughts"). Also to be interpreted
in this light is the anecdote related by his former assistant
Leopold Kleiner, according to whom Hoffmann had called
out to him from the full terrace of Café Imperial on the
Opernring: "Just stay here, after all it won't last long."[14]

By all accounts Hoffmann, who "knew too much of the
world and its broad cultural spectrum not to possess a certain
tolerance and a wider perspective than was to be found
among his […] National Socialist contemporaries,"[15] was
vexed by the excesses of the new regime. It would be speculative to try to judge whether he himself was anti-Semitic.
The fact is that there is no evidence, for example, that Hoffmann made any defamatory remarks about colleagues who,
according to the Nuremberg Laws, were now considered
Jewish. When he writes in a letter to Czeschka in November
1938: "Bit by bit we are also sensing the decline in non-
Aryan competition,"[16] it can be interpreted more as a reference to Jewish artists being forced to emigrate than as
his approval of the anti-Jewish policies of the Nazi regime.

One can assume that Hoffmann was neither an adherent
of Nazi ideology nor shared the political aims of the NSDAP
and certainly did not abet the Nazi regime's art policy with
his artistic ideas. In the "gau file"[17] on Hoffmann compiled
by the administration of the gau of Vienna, a record from
April 1940 states that he was "not a party member but a
member of the Reich Chamber of Visual Arts."[18] However,
Hoffmann did strive to use the new order of Viennese cultural
politics to realize his own artistic ideals and especially to
promote the decorative arts, in part with the aid of his personal network, which extended both into the city administration and into the NSDAP. His attitude toward the Nazi regime and its proponents was not defined by ideological
premises but by that same "art-egoism" that Stefan Zweig
detected in Richard Strauss: "Through his art-egoism […]
he was inwardly indifferent whatever the regime."[19]

In order to achieve his goals, Hoffmann accepted not
only the regime's culturally conservative art policy and compulsory membership of the Reich Chamber of Visual Arts
but also ignored the fact that people were being arrested
and removed from office, and that a not insignificant proportion of his erstwhile customers were forced to flee. One
must, however, give him credit for not making any conces-
sions to the Nazi regime's artistic ideals in his own works,
with the exception of his use of expressions like "our fatherland's greatest epoch"[20] or "time of world-historic change
of unfathomed greatness"[21] in various newspaper articles.

Plans for Art Education Reform
and the Wiener Kunsthandwerkverein

Immediately after the Anschluss Hoffmann believed himself
able to use the new political situation to implement his long-
cherished plans for art education reform, which were closely
tied to his notions of the role of the decorative arts. Thus

Fig. 3   JH, design for the salesroom in the *Haus der Mode* [House of Fashion],
Palais Lobkowitz, 1938/39

Fig. 4   JH, adaptation and submission *Haus der Mode*, Palais Lobkowitz, Vienna, 1938/39,
artistic director's room, wall elevation

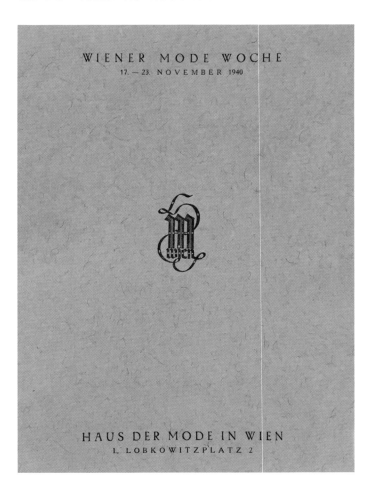

Zum Wesen der Mode gehört, daß sie sich unaufhörlich verjüngt und stets neue Schöpfungen hervorbringt. Es lag darum nahe, bei der Planung der ersten Wiener Modewoche auch den jugendlichen Nachwuchs im Bereich modischer Arbeit zu Wort kommen zu lassen.

Dadurch sollte den aufstrebenden, in den deutschen Modeschulen tätigen, jungen Kräften Gelegenheit geboten werden, vor den anläßlich der Wiener Modewoche in Wien versammelten Fachleuten ihre Leistungen zu zeigen.

Durch die Einbeziehung der Modeschulen in das Vorführungsprogramm erhält die Wiener Modewoche eine überaus reizvolle und interessante Note, da sich in ihren Schöpfungen die Kräfte zeigen, die einmal in wenigen Jahren als selbständiger Modellgestalter wertvolle Mitarbeiter im deutschen Modeschaffen sein werden.

Unserer Aufforderung haben die Deutschen Modeschulen
 Textil- und Modeschule der Stadt Berlin
 Deutsche Meisterschule für Mode, München
 Staatliche Kunst- und Fachschule für Textilindustrie, Modeschule, Plauen i. V.
 D.A.F.-Schule für Herrenschneider, Damenschneider und Putzmacher, Wien
Folge geleistet. Zu unserem großen Bedauern ist die Modeschule der Stadt Frankfurt verhindert, sich zu beteiligen

he wrote a paper dated March 1938 entitled "Neuausrichtung unserer Kunstschulen" ("Reorienting Our Art Schools"), as well as another, dated 10 April 1938 and with the title "Vorschläge zur Reorganisation des Kunstunterrichts" ("Suggestions for Reorganizing Art Education"). Hoffmann's expectations to be able to realize the suggestions these papers contained were fueled by the fact that promptly after the Anschluss two of his former assistants, Hans Bichler and Philipp Häusler, independently attempted to gain provisional control of the School of Arts and Crafts.[22] While Bichler's endeavors in this regard failed, Häusler was officially entrusted with the school's management by the Federal Ministry of Trade and Transport on 19 March 1938. During his reopening speech Häusler not only denounced the school's "spirit that has been Judaized and spoiled by cultural Bolsheviks" but also called for it to be converted into a "master school of German handicrafts." Yet even Häusler was ultimately unseated as the provisional director of the School of Arts and Crafts—despite Hoffmann intervening on his behalf with Reichsstatthalter (Reich Governor) Arthur Seyß-Inquart.[23]

Despite this setback, Hoffmann remained anxious to realize his ideas about the role of the decorative arts. Only a few months later, on 11 August 1938, the Stillhaltekommissar (Liquidation Commissioner) for Societies, Organizations, and Associations addressed an "urgent personnel request" to the Gestapo headquarters in Vienna and to various NSDAP authorities calling for information about any "concerns of a political, personal, or other nature" regarding Hans Bichler, as he was a "prospective" head of a new Wiener Kunsthandwerkverein (Viennese Association of Arts and Crafts).[24] Bichler had collaborated on Vienna's Werkbundsiedlung (Werkbund Estate) in 1930,[25] among other things, and had been employed in the studio of Hoffmann and Haerdtl between 1935 and 1938. He had also been a member of the NSDAP since 1932 or 1934—the statements he himself made in this regard vary—and a member of the SS since March 1938. A memorandum by the Gestapo headquarters in Vienna from 5 April 1944 reveals that he occasionally worked with them as one of their "volunteer workers" in "matters of the Reich College of Applied Arts and Viennese decorative arts."[26] This simply means that Bichler delivered reports on the political behavior of the persons employed there to the Gestapo.

The Wiener Kunsthandwerkverein was ultimately launched under Bichler's management in May 1939, with Josef Hoffmann as its honorary chairman.[27] The society was conceived as the continuation of the two Austrian Werkbund associations that were dissolved on 29 September 1938. Its aim was "the refinement of arts-and-crafts work in the collaboration of art, craft, and industry" and "the general fostering of taste."[28] To this end the society would give the "outstanding master artisan, to the extent that he [did not possess] sufficient design skills himself," the opportunity of "collaborat[ing] with the designer." Furthermore, it would provide support in procuring materials and workshops and promote the sales of decorative-art products.[29] Anyone could become a member "who committed to the society's aims and [worked] as a designer or executing artisan." However, Jews and "Mischlinge" ("half-castes") were barred from joining.[30] In 1939/40 the Kunsthandwerkverein, which was originally based in the Zehrgadenstiege[31] of the Hofburg Palace, was given some rooms in the building of the former Ludwig Zwieback & Bruder department store at Kärntner Straße 15 "at the request of the cultural department of the City of Vienna."[32] Its former owner, Ella Zirner-Zwieback, was con

Fig. 9 Advertisement by the Wiener Kunsthandwerkverein (Viennese Association of Arts and Crafts), 1940
Die Pause 5 1940

sidered a Jew according to the Nuremberg Laws and was thus forced to sell the building in June 1938. The new owner was now the Zentralsparkasse (municipal savings bank) of the City of Vienna, the chair of whose supervisory board was the mayor—i.e., Hermann Neubacher. The intention was for the former department store to be demolished and replaced by a new building that would house the main branch of the bank. As this plan was dashed by the start of the war, the Kunsthandwerkverein—evidently at Neubacher's behest— was supplied with several rooms "precarially, with the right to cancel at any time, and free of charge," with the Zentralsparkasse receiving "no rent but merely payment of expenses."[33] Commercial premises, office space, and finally— in the second half of 1941—several design and experimental workshops were installed across two stories in which "young talents" would be trained.[34] The workshops, which "comprised all areas of handicraft," were run by Josef Hoffmann once he had been appointed "Special Envoy of the Kulturamt to the Wiener Kunsthandwerkverein" in May 1941 in return for a monthly remuneration of 190 reichsmarks.[35]

Hoffmann was undoubtedly the *spiritus rector* behind the founding of the Kunsthandwerkverein, which for him was tantamount to a comeback of the Wiener Werkstätte (WW). Reviving the WW under its old name was not possible since it was considered "utterly Judaized."[36] That Hans Bichler, who was deeply entrenched in the NSDAP, would run the Kunsthandwerkverein, was likewise a deliberate decision, because Hoffmann was not uncontroversial within the party. The form issued by the Reich Youth Leadership's Committee for the Creation of Hitler Youth Centers mentioned at the outset, already features marginalia—in several people's handwriting—remarking "linked to Jews and the Heimwehr [Home Guard]" and "typically Viennese Hoffmann architec

9 10 11 12 13

Figs. 10, 11, 12 JH, "Wiener Kunsthandwerk," with illustration of decorative-arts objects by Hertha Bucher, Josef Hoffmann, Alfred Soulek, and Julius Zimpel, 1942
Die Pause (7) 1 1942, 12–21

ture—old." Although the assessment of Hoffmann's politics ultimately turned out positive in the previously cited gau file, it had ambivalent undertones:

> "Hoffmann was professor at the Vienna School of Arts and Crafts and gave lessons in modern art and fashion drawing [sic]. In a technical regard he is an advocate of modern art and not sympathetic to art of a National Socialist tendency. His artistic outlook is international. He therefore associated a great deal with Jews prior to the changes [i.e., the Anschluss] as he was also a member of the Wiener Werkstätte, which was utterly Judaized. […] He is a Sudeten German, has behaved indifferently in a political regard and only discovered his German heart after the changes. No hostile attitudes of a political nature toward National Socialism are known. Bearing in mind his old age, he can be considered politically unobjectionable."[37]

The "Viennese Touch"

Besides the fact that Hoffmann had an influential protector in Hermann Neubacher, he was a far too important poster child for Viennese cultural policy for a not exclusively positive political assessment to have consequences for him. The reason for this pragmatism by the local Nazi authorities can be found in the political dilemma with which they were confronted soon after the Anschluss. Before 1938 many Austrian and above all Viennese National Socialists had been under the illusion that Vienna would have the special status of an eastern capital within the Greater German Reich. However, they were soon forced to acknowledge that the decisions about Austria's future would not be made in Vienna and the city's political authority was minimal. To strengthen its reputation and political clout and safeguard Vienna from being downgraded to a provincial town, they invoked the grandeur

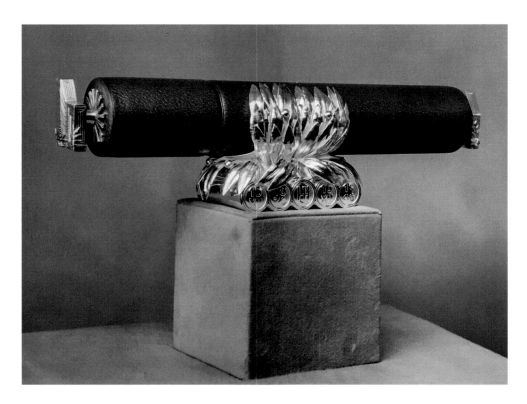

Fig. 13 Oswald Haerdtl, gift of honor from the Design and Experimentation Workshop for Arts and Crafts for Josef Hoffmann's 70th birthday, 1940
OESTERREICHISCHE WERKSTAETTEN/ Art Works Handels Gmbh

Fig. 14 Exhibition stand of the Wiener Kunsthandwerkverein
(Viennese Association of Arts and Crafts) in Leipzig
OESTERREICHISCHE WERKSTAETTEN/Art Works Handels Gmbh

of its cultural heritage and the city's intrinsically art-loving atmosphere. For example, at the opening of the *Haus der Mode* on 22 February 1939, Hermann Neubacher declared that it was "the unique artistic and creative atmosphere of the city that empowers not only the people grown from this soil to great achievements."[38] Yet Adolf Hitler, whose attitude to Vienna was ambivalent, was reluctant to recognize Vienna as a significant German city of culture as he feared that doing so might lead to the development of Austrian separatism. To avoid snubbing the Viennese population and party members too much, he tolerated the cultivation of the myth of "Vienna's cultural mission," which was invoked by local Nazi politicians in their propaganda.[39] Under these circumstances not only was Hoffmann celebrated by local cultural policy makers as the advocate of the "Viennese culture of taste" but even the "Judaized" Wiener Werkstätte was declared part of the city's unique cultural heritage.[40] The latter claim was possible because, among other things, the Nazi regime never formulated its own art program but eclectically drew on the wealth of existing practices.[41]

The Reich as a whole—and Hitler and Goebbels in particular—thought little of a specifically Viennese cultural touch. After all, besides Hitler's animosity toward Vienna this notion not only contradicted the eradication of everything Austrian as sought by the Nazi regime but was also considered suspect due to the alleged lack of seriousness of Viennese culture.[42] The latter view was something Hoffmann was obliged to discover on his 70th birthday. Although the proposal to award him the Goethe Medal[43] on his special birthday came from Adolf Ziegler, the president of the Reich

Chamber of Visual Arts, and was approved by Baldur von Schirach, who had been appointed Reichsstatthalter (Reich governor) and gauleiter of Vienna in August 1940, Hoffmann did not receive his award. The reason was, on the one hand, that in a letter to the Reich Ministry of Propaganda and Public Enlightenment—which was in charge of awarding the honor—Albert Speer stated not just that he personally held Hoffmann to be "overrated" but also that Hitler had received an "authoritative monograph on Professor Hoffmann" in which he (Hitler) "had discovered nothing worthy of special mention." In Speer's view it would therefore be "too much to call upon the Führer today to honor Hoffmann."[44] On the other hand, at almost the same time as Speer's letter, a telex arrived at the Propaganda Ministry from the Reich propaganda office in Vienna. In this it was reported that Hoffmann had "after the changes stated in front of the then provisional head of the Vienna Secession and chairman of the state administration of the Reich Chamber of Art in Vienna, the painter Revy, that one needed to show no consideration for the principles of National Socialist art policy because all that magic could not last much longer anyway."[45] This denunciation by Heinrich Revy, a former member of the Bund deutscher Maler Österreichs (Association of German Painters in Austria), which was founded in 1937, who remained largely unknown among experts even after the Anschluss, says much about envy and malevolence within the Viennese NSDAP but little about Hoffmann's political stance. One can assume that Hoffmann would not have made such a remark in the presence of a pronounced National Socialist like Revy. Consequently, for Hoffmann's

13   70th birthday there was merely a short celebration on 14 December in the Small Festival Hall of Vienna City Hall, at which the deputy mayor Hanns Blaschke gave a speech and brought a "handwritten letter from Reich Governor Baldur von Schirach and from the adjunct for architecture Dr. [Leopold] Tavs to be read aloud."[46]

The proceedings surrounding the awarding of the Goethe Medal also had an impact on the exhibition that was planned by the State Arts and Crafts Museum in Vienna (today's MAK) to mark Josef Hoffmann's birthday. Evidently Schirach had heard about Hoffmann's alleged statement and about Speer's—or rather Hitler's—disapproving attitude, because Director Richard Ernst was requested by the General Department for Promotion of the Arts, State Theaters, Museums, and Public Education, which was under the control of the Reichsstatthalter, in early December 1940 to give an account of the content of the exhibition. In his letter to the General Department, Ernst stressed that Josef Kalbac, Hoffmann's assistant, had been "instructed" to "limit himself to the wholesome and enduring in Josef Hoffmann's oeuvre and to avoid certain older l'art pour l'art things that might

not comply with the Reich's cultural policy."[47] Obviously Ernst did not manage to silence all their concerns, because the exhibition had still not opened in early February 1941, and he was once again called on to provide a "precise answer" whether "the Hoffmann exhibition was in line with national and National Socialist principles in every aspect."[48] The exhibition was opened a few days later—as yet it has not been possible to establish the exact date—without any ceremony.

The commotion both around the awarding of the Goethe Medal and around the 1940 exhibition must have greatly affected Hoffmann because he was forced to acknowledge that he had substantially overestimated his significance to the Nazi regime's cultural policy. Disillusioned, he wrote to Czeschka on 28 May 1942: "The tendency in the school is to eradicate and neutralize every memory of our proficiency. My exhibition for my 70th birthday was proscribed and almost banned. […] Nevertheless, I am still alive though I have not a single commission or any big job. […] One should not expect too much from life, and it was certainly varied enough."[49]

1   Sekler, Eduard F., *Josef Hoffmann: The Architectural Work*, Princeton, NJ 1985, 219. Trans. Eduard F. Sekler and John Maass.

2   Spielmann, Heinz, *Carl Otto Czeschka. Ein Wiener Künstler in Hamburg*, Göttingen 2019, 233.

3   Sekler 1985 (see note 1), 219.

4   Spielmann 2019 (see note 2), 234.

5   Sekler 1985 (see note 1), 219.

6   Noever, Peter/Pokorný, Marek (eds.), *Josef Hoffmann. Selbstbiographie/Autobiography*, Ostfildern 2009, 100. Trans. Bernd Magar and Andrew Oakland.

7   The Nordische Gesellschaft was a society founded and based in Lübeck in 1921, which initially focused on promoting economic and cultural ties between Lübeck and the countries of northern Europe. After the National Socialists seized power in 1933, it was "gleichgeschaltet" (coordinated) and remodeled as an instrument of National Socialist propaganda.

8   MPAV, dept. 202, A5 personnel files 1st row: Johannes Cech.

9   MPAV, M. dept. 350 MA7 card catalog on the business protocol (B1) 1941, GZ 914.

10   ASA, AdR, BKA/RST III/201 747-38.

11   Cf. *Hannoverscher Anzeiger* 23 Feb 1939, 5; Wien Museum, collection of newspaper clippings on the *Haus der Mode*.

12   ASA, AdR, ZNsZ RK matter 2100 2238/1.

13   Spielmann 2019 (see note 2), 234.

14   Kleiner, Leopold, *Erinnerungen an Josef Hoffmann*, New York n.d. (prob. 1975). Leopold Kleiner emigrated to the USA in December 1938. Cf. https://kg.ikb.kit.edu/arch-exil/356.php [12 Apr 2020].

15   Sekler 1985 (see note 1), 219.

16   Spielmann 2019 (see note 2), 237.

17   A "Gauakt" (gau, or regional, file) was compiled by the gau personnel office of the respective gau administration, chiefly when an application for membership of the NSDAP or a professional association was made.

18   ASA, AdR, gau file no. 4892: Josef Hoffmann.

19   Zweig, Stefan, *The World of Yesterday*, Lincoln/London 1964, 373. Trans. Benjamin W. Huebsch and Helmut Ripperger.

20   "Das Haus der Wehrmacht. Bemerkungen zum Umbau von Oberbaurat Prof. Dr. H. C. Josef Hoffmann," in: *Die Pause* (5) 12 1939/40, 50–51.

21   Sekler 1985 (see note 1), 220.

22   Koller, Gabriele, "Die verlorene Moderne. Von der Kunstgewerbeschule zur (Reichs-)Hochschule für angewandte Kunst, Wien," in: Seiger, Hans/Lunardi, Michael/Populorum, Peter Josef (eds.), *Im Reich der Kunst. Die Wiener Akademie der bildenden Künste und die faschistische Kunstpolitik*, Vienna 1990, 183–216: 199 f.

23   Ibid., 213 f.

24   ASA, AdR, gau file no. 1309: Hans Bichler.

25   In the Werkbundsiedlung (Werkbund Estate) Bichler designed the interior of Ernst A. Plischke's house no. 36.

26   DÖW file 20333/8.

27   MPAV, dept. 119, A32 defunct societies: 6357/1939.

28   Ibid.

29   MPAV, M. dept. 350/A 55 special repository: "Feier zum fünfjährigen Bestehen des Wiener Kulturamtes am 22.10.1943," n.p.

30   MPAV, dept. 119, A32 defunct societies: 6357/1939.

31   The Zehrgadenstiege is located in the Schweizertrakt (Swiss Wing) of Vienna's Hofburg Palace.

32   BA-CA, Z, general registry, May 1940–Dec 1940, "Bericht über den Neubau der Hauptanstalt der Zentralsparkasse der Gemeinde Wien auf dem Objekt 1, Kärntnerstraße 11, 13, und 15 und Weihburggasse 4," 25 Sep 1940.

33   MPAV, M. dept. 350/A 55 special repository (see note 29).

34   *Neues Wiener Tagblatt* (daytime edition) 18 Oct 1941, 4.

35   Ibid., and: MPAV, M. dept. 350 MA7 card catalog on the business protocol (B1) 1941, GZ 696.

Fig. 15 JH, "Das Haus der Wehrmacht. Bemerkungen zum Umbau," 1939/40
Die Pause (5) 12 1939/40, 50–51

36 From the political assessment of Josef Hoffmann by the Gauhauptstellenleiter (head of the gau main office) Franz Kamba, 13 Apr 1940, in: ASA, gau file no. 4892: Josef Hoffmann.

37 Ibid.

38 *Freiburger Zeitung* 23 Feb 1939, 5; Wien Museum (see note 11).

39 Klamper, Elisabeth, "Zur politischen Geschichte der Akademie der bildenden Künste 1918 bis 1948. Eine Bestandsaufnahme," in: Seiger et al. 1990 (see note 22), 5–64: 39.

40 *Kleine Volks-Zeitung* 31 Jul 1942, 6; Wien Museum (see note 11).

41 Cf. Werckmeister, Otto Karl, "Politische Führung und politische Überwachung der deutschen Kunst im Zweiten Weltkrieg," in: Ruppert, Wolfgang (ed.), *Künstler im Nationalsozialismus: Die "deutsche" Kunst, die Kunstpolitik und die Berliner Kunsthochschule*, Cologne 2015, 111.

42 Tabor, Jan, "Die Gaben der Ostmark. Österreichische Kunst und Künstler in der NS-Zeit," in: Seiger et al. 1990 (see note 22), 277–296: 283 f.

43 The "Goethe-Medaille für Kunst und Wissenschaft" (Goethe Medal for Art and Science) was inaugurated by Reich President Paul von Hindenburg to commemorate the centenary of Goethe's death on 22 March 1932, and was originally intended as a tribute to people who had made an outstanding contribution to the Goethe celebra-

tions in Weimar in 1932. However, Hindenburg went on to award it to a great number of artists, scientists, civil servants, and politicians. From 1934 awarding of the medal was generally limited to birthdays of elderly citizens or other important memorial days.

44 Ibid.; BA Berlin, RMfVuP-IB-1365-03-1. Unfortunately the files concerning the awarding of the Goethe Medal to Josef Hoffmann were not accessible in the Austrian State Archives/Schirach holdings.

45 BA Berlin, RMfVuP-IB-1365-03-1. Revy presumably falsified a similar statement by Hoffmann to intrigue against him. Intrigues were a widespread phenomenon within the Nazi state and party institutions, especially in Vienna.

46 Cf. *Handbuch des Reichsgaues Wien von 1941, Chronik des Handbuches*, part 2, unofficial, 12; "Ehrung Professor Josef Hoffmanns," in: *Neues Wiener Tagblatt* 17 Dec 1940, 6. In addition to the celebration at the City Hall, Sergius Pauser was commissioned with a portrait of the honoree. As early as May 1940 Hoffmann had bequeathed some 100 "old Viennese portraits" from his estate to the state collections; the portraits had been created in the period from 1740 to 1880 and were "interesting and instructive especially with regard to costume," see *Völkischer Beobachter*, Vienna edition, 10 May 1940, 4. Both the Pauser portrait

and the collection of paintings are now at the Wien Museum.

47 MAK 931-1940.

48 MAK 137-1941.

49 Spielmann 2019 (see note 2), 242. Be this as it may, Hoffmann did receive another honor when he was awarded the Alfred Roller Prize for Arts and Crafts on 2 October 1942, which had been newly created by Reich Governor Baldur von Schirach; see e.g., *Neues Wiener Tagblatt*, 3 Oct 1942, 3.

Fig. 1 JH, *Haus der Wehrmacht* [House of the Armed Forces], Vienna, 1940
Main entrance and street façade
Kunsthandel Widder, Vienna

Matthias Boeckl

"The Leadership's Will"

Hoffmann's Projects under National Socialism

Austria's Anschluss with Nazi Germany in March 1938, the Munich Agreement about the Sudetenland from September 1938,[1] and the German occupation of the whole of Bohemia and Moravia in March 1939 raised great expectations in the south Moravian Josef Hoffmann.[2] After having tended to be marginalized in the Austrian Ständestaat (corporative state)[3] and having suffered the ordeal of being permanently retired from the Vienna School of Arts and Crafts in 1937, the tables suddenly seemed to have turned. The new political situation in Central Europe and Hoffmann's close-knit personal network in the Viennese Nazi elite were a propitious starting point for potentially restoring his status in the Austrian decorative arts, in art education, and in the architecture sector: Primarily via his friend Hermann Neubacher, the former head of the Gemeinwirtschaftliche Siedlungs- und Baustoffanstalt (GESIBA, the Institution for Public Housing and Construction Materials) and first Nazi mayor of Vienna; as well as via his nephew Johannes Cech, a key functionary in the newly founded Kulturamt (Culture Authority) of the City of Vienna; and probably also via the son of one of his teachers at the grammar school in Iglau/Jihlava (CZ), Arthur Seyß-Inquart, who had been appointed federal chancellor on the eve of the Anschluss and was then Reichsstatthalter (Reich governor) until 1939; as well as via Seyß-Inquart's secretary of state for culture, Kajetan Mühlmann,[4] unexpected opportunities arose for Hoffmann to influence the cultural and architectural policies of the local Nazi authorities.

However, the hopes that the regime would adopt new aesthetic strategies, would quickly turn out to be delusive as a result of Hitler's refusal to grant Vienna or Austria as a whole any special role in the Reich, and at the latest as a result of the outbreak of war on 1 September 1939, which only permitted the construction of buildings that were essential to the war effort. In addition, the period when Hoffmann's influential friends were active in Vienna did not last long: Seyß-Inquart went to Poland as the deputy governor general as early as October 1939 and to the Netherlands as Reich commissioner in 1940; Mühlmann likewise went to Poland in 1939, in his case as "special commissioner for the protection of works of art in the occupied territories"; Neubacher was sent to Bucharest and Athens as an ambassador in December 1940 and to Belgrade as the "special envoy of the foreign office for the southeast" in 1943. As such Hoffmann's

impact was limited—with the aid of his nephew Johannes Cech—to the sphere of influence of the City of Vienna and to the decorative arts. His work in construction ended in 1940 with the conversion of the German embassy into a *Haus der Wehrmacht* [House of the Armed Forces]. That same year Baldur von Schirach, Seyß-Inquart's successor as Reichsstatthalter, appointed the Berlin architect Hanns Dustmann, an employee of Albert Speer, as the "architectural consultant for redesigning Vienna" and the city's head planner to whom all new projects had to be submitted.[5] Since Speer and his milieu had an extremely unfavorable opinion of Hoffmann,[6] his opportunities to influence the cityscape now vanished completely. For his former partner Oswald Haerdtl, in contrast, who had been running his own office since 1939, the new circumstances proved more auspicious in terms of construction contracts—though not in Vienna but in occupied Poland, where he opened his own studio in Kraków, constructed the Park- or Osthotel for the Wehrmacht in addition to some smaller buildings, and designed another hotel project for Casino G.m.b.H.[7] In general the younger generation of not-persecuted Austrian architects was able to profit considerably more from the Nazi regime than Hoffmann; they included first and foremost Alexander Popp, Hermann Kutschera & Anton Ubl, Roland Rainer, Johann Gundacker, Kurt Klaudy & Georg Lippert, Siegfried and Werner Theiß & Hans Jaksch, Josef Becvar & Victor Ruczka, Walter & Ewald Guth, and Franz Kaym & Franz Schläger. However, the biggest projects—both in the Ostmark (as Austria was now known) and in the occupied territories—were the sole preserve of German architects.

In this short window between 1938 and 1940, Hoffmann was able to realize a major conversion and four interior decoration projects in Vienna. Furthermore, he designed four more comprehensive construction projects, none of which was ultimately actualized. In 1940–1945 just one single-family house would be constructed; besides this he only produced works of decorative art.

The largest construction project to be realized was the aforementioned *Haus der Wehrmacht*, a conversion of the German embassy building, which had lost its purpose since the Anschluss, into an officers' mess.[8] The building on Metternichgasse had been planned in an Italo-French-inspired

1 2 3 4

Fig. 2 JH, conversion of the former German embassy into a *Haus der Wehrmacht* [House of the Armed Forces], 1940

Kunsthandel Widder, Vienna

Neobaroque style by Viktor Rumpelmayer in 1877, who had previously worked in the studio of van der Nüll & Sicardsburg. Hoffmann described the commission as being "on the one hand to preserve the existing building mass and windows, on the other to express in a simple, clear, military way the building's current use through its form." This design report reads like a catechism of Modernism with its necessity to reveal the building's "uniqueness" under the "excess of moldings, cornice formations, and superficial decoration [...]. Everything that is contemplated and occurs according to plan from the outset in a new building, is very much complicated when converting a building from the age of unthinking stylistic imitation." Once again Hoffmann demands the right to contemporary expression:

"If in all previous ages it seemed valid to repeatedly construct buildings of a new, strange architectural form, as a natural expression of that ever-new age, immediately next to and without any consideration for wonderful existing creations, then in this, our fatherland's greatest epoch, we must at least be granted an

attempt—as is the leadership's will—to break new ground, to give the right form to the new needs and tasks."[9]

The result consisted primarily in an elegant new façade with wide, plane wall surfaces over the window apertures, which are crowned in fine triangular pediments, with a subtly structured eaves cornice, continuous rustication on the ground floor, "which terminates in a continuous band with the motif of our uniform's epaulette instead of the customary meander pattern," as well as with a portico complete with fluted pilasters and a sculptural Reich eagle above.[10]

The unexecuted major building projects before 1940 mainly concerned proposals by the City of Vienna and can hence clearly be classed as the patronage of Mayor Neubacher. Design drawings survive for three of these projects; for the fourth there is only a text description. The three drawn designs pertain to a competition entry for the new trade fair grounds in the Prater park, for a *Gästehaus der Stadt Wien*

Figs. 3, 4 Michael Powolny, overdoor reliefs and freestanding sculptures for the *Haus der Wehrmacht* [House of the Armed Forces], 1940

MAK, KI 10321-10 and -11

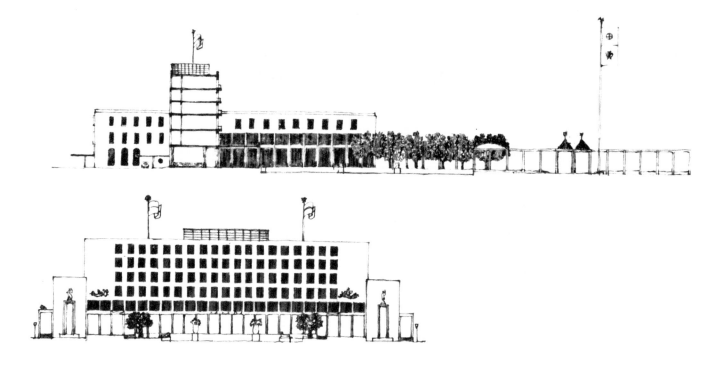

Fig. 5 JH, project for a guesthouse of the City of Vienna in the Stadtpark, prob. 1938/39
E. F. Sekler, *Josef Hoffmann*, 440

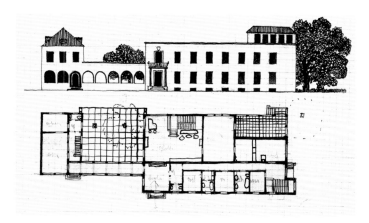

Fig. 6 JH, project for a house for Baron Wieser in Vienna's
Grinzing district, 1943, street view and floor plan
Graphic Collection, Academy of Fine Arts Vienna, HZ 26306

Fig. 7 JH, project for an Anton Hanak museum in Vienna's
Augarten park, prob. 1938–1940, two views
E. F. Sekler, *Josef Hoffmann*, 441

[Guesthouse of the City of Vienna] in the Stadtpark, and a museum for the sculptor Anton Hanak, who had died in 1934 and with whom Hoffmann had been close friends. The masterplan project for the trade fair grounds[11] was developed by Hoffmann in 1938 together with his partner Oswald Haerdtl, to whom Eduard F. Sekler attributes the majority of the design motifs.[12] The guesthouse project for the City of Vienna, on the other hand, which was also presented in the small exhibition for his 70th birthday at the State Arts and Crafts Museum (today's MAK) in 1941, envisioned in Hoffmann's typical handwriting a symmetrical structure with plane perforated façades in the multistory upper section and low wings at the back surrounding a garden—this would have replaced the Kursalon in Vienna's Stadtpark. A casual pavilion structure between trees, the design for a *Hanak-Museum* in Vienna's Augarten park similarly bears that fine poetic touch that so clearly differentiates Hoffmann from the regime's official means of expression: According to Sekler

"they prove unequivocally that in artistic matters he [Hoffmann] had considerably more character than many of his colleagues. In contrast to architects (like, for example, Fritz Breuhaus) who could not have changed their style faster to please the new regime, these two projects from the era of National Socialism [the guesthouse and the Hanak museum] do not show any striking difference from those designed in the early 1930s."[13]

In terms of realized interior designs from the Nazi period, two projects are documented that Hoffmann designed together with Haerdtl, as well as two others that he planned together with Josef Kalbac, his colleague and office partner in later years. All four concerned bourgeois and upscale lifestyles. The interior of the business premises—built in 1938— of the Leipzig-based fashion publisher Oskar Beyer on Vienna's Singerstraße[14] largely comprised display tables and chests of drawers for sewing patterns for fashion: "Ceilings and walls are white, woodwork light walnut, fabrics on brown ground patterned light gray and red. The flooring is

Fig. 8 JH, adaptation and furnishing of a shop for the Meissen Porcelain Manufactory, Kärntner Ring 14, Vienna, 1940
ID (53) 1942, 207

>
Figs. 10–13 JH, adaptation and furnishing of the *Haus der Mode* [House of Fashion] in Palais Lobkowitz, Vienna, 1938, study of the commercial director, library, room of the artistic director (seating and wall with chest of drawers)
MAK, KI 10243-1 to -5

composed of warm gray linoleum."[15] The final joint project with Haerdtl was the *Festdekoration des Wiener Opernballs* [Festive Decoration for Vienna's Opera Ball] in 1939, in which the guests were greeted by a festive portal in the form of a high pillared hall.[16] More elaborate than the business premises for the Beyer publishing house, the premises for the Meissen Porcelain Manufactory on Kärntner Ring were designed by Hoffmann together with Josef Kalbac in 1940.[17] The large salesroom was dominated by a wall of vitrines pa-

neled in mahogany that stretched the entire width of the room at whose center stood sales counters.

However, Hoffmann's most important projects during the Nazi era once again involved Austrian decorative arts. In the context of the Viennese Nazi grandees' failed strategy to make the Danube metropolis the capital of German taste, fashion played a significant part.[18] The City of Vienna correspondingly developed a comprehensive action plan that envisioned both the construction of a fashion school and the founding of a *Haus der Mode* [House of Fashion], which was responsible for marketing Viennese couture. Josef Hoffmann, who had designed the Schwestern Flöge fashion salon in 1904 and the Wiener Werkstätte's fashion shop at Kärntner Straße 41 in 1916, was undoubtedly the most suitable and most reputable local architect for such tasks in the eyes of both the city's Kulturamt (Culture Authority) and Hoffmann's nephew who worked there. Consequently, the commission to convert the newly rented Palais Lobkowitz in Vienna's inner city into the *Haus der Mode* went to him. The construction program for this "fashion authority" allowed for a showroom, a library, a dining room, offices for the artistic and the commercial director, and rooms for the mannequins. The elaborate color perspectives created for the project once again demonstrate the ease and elegance that provide a worthy and appropriate stage for the task of presenting fashion—including a showroom with floor-to-ceiling mirrors on all sides, gray plush fauteuils in the office of the artistic director, and oval mirrors in the dining room.

In addition to the *Haus der Mode*, which opened on 22 February 1939,[19] Hoffmann also developed a more comprehensive but unrealized project for the promotion of Viennese couture. In 1940 he was asked to provide his expert opinion on the intended founding of a "fashion academy and school of good taste," in the course of which he strongly advised against the planned conversion of the former headquarters of the health insurance company for the hospitality industry on Treitlstraße as the site for the teaching rooms, student apartments, event rooms, and gardens that he deemed necessary. Instead, he proposed an alternative: two houses that adjoined Palais Lobkowitz on Augustinerstraße and Dorotheergasse, which were also owned by the Lobkowicz

10 11 12 13

11 12 13 14 p. 380

Fig. 9 JH and Oswald Haerdtl, festive decoration for Vienna's Opera Ball, 1939
Photo: Julius Scherb, from: *"Wien. Die Perle des Reichs."*
Planen für Hitler, Zurich 2015, 91

Figs. 14, 15 JH and Oswald Haerdtl, shop furnishings for the
Otto Beyer publishing house's fashion plate and sewing pattern
department, Singerstraße 12, Vienna, 1938
MAK, KI 10242-1, -4

Fig. 16 JH, adaptation and furnishing of
the *Haus der Mode* [House of Fashion] in
Palais Lobkowitz, Vienna, 1938, desk and
wall-mounted vitrine MAK, KI 10243-2

Fig. 18 Wiener Kunsthandwerkverein (Viennese Association
of Arts and Crafts), Kärntner Straße 15, street façade
Photo: United States Information Service, 5 Sep 1945
ANL, Picture Archives, 687678 US 339

Fig. 17 Oswald Haerdtl, exhibition design in the Wiener
Kunsthandwerkverein (Viennese Association of Arts and Crafts), 1944
"Wien. Die Perle des Reiches." Planen für Hitler, Zurich 2015, 94

family, should be demolished and replaced with a new building so as to pool all the city's fashion activities (fashion authority, fashion school) in a single location. Furthermore, in his
report Hoffmann also suggested redesigning Augustinerstraße between Michaelerplatz and the Albertina. A new
"colonnaded walkway" for pedestrians—in continuation of
the Stallburg arcades—that would go through Palais Pálffy,
the proposed new building, and Palais Lobkowitz, was
intended to mitigate the dangerously narrow road by the
Augustinian monastery while simultaneously improving the
appearance of this core area of the historic city center.[20]

Hoffmann's numerous activities for the decorative arts—
in terms of both designing and production and sales—could
be concentrated in the rooms of the Wiener Kunsthandwerkverein (Viennese Association of Arts and Crafts), which
was newly founded by the City of Vienna in 1938 and based
at Kärntner Straße 15, in his new role as its honorary president and employee.[21] Run by Oskar Strnad's former student
Hans Bichler, the architectural design of the association's
business premises, as well as the offices and workshops, probably also came from his hand.[22] Together with Josef Kalbac
Hoffmann was able to install not only his new office headquarters here but also experimental workshops for artisans,
which continued to trade under the name Künstlerwerkstättenverein (Association of Artists' Workshops) in the postwar period. In 1948 the successor company, Österreichische

Werkstätten, took over the premises and offices. Hoffmann's
official main studio remained at this address until his death.

With Hoffmann's influential political friends starting to
depart for various German-occupied European countries
from 1940 and with the war escalating, the sources of the
70-year-old's commissions quickly disappeared. He retreat-
ed but continued to provide substantial support to Viennese
decorative arts, both in the Kunsthandwerkverein and with
several designs of his own, which were still executed by
several manufacturers—including the Deutsche Werkstätten in Dresden, with whom he signed a contract in 1944.[23]
Around 1943 he also produced a design for a house for
Baron Wieser in Vienna's Grinzing district.[24] And in 1944 a
bizarre greeting arrived from Hermann Neubacher, who was
now working in the Balkans, in the form of a commission to
design a *Mausoleum für Kruja und eine Vitrine mit Helm
und Schwert Skanderbegs als Repräsentationsgeschenk an
Albanien* [Ceremonial Gift to Albania: Mausoleum at Krujë
and a Showcase for the Helmet and Sword of Skanderbeg].[25]

Hoffmann's experience of the bombing of Vienna, which
commenced on 17 March 1944—such as that on 15 January
1945—is documented on a small piece of now rare paper
on which he tirelessly sketched design drawings for small
boxes and vessels between 5 January and 5 February 1945
and as such withdrew from a world that had become inhos-
pitable.[26]

17 18

10 p. 381

19

Fig. 19 JH, sketches for wooden jars and boxes, 5 Jan – 5 Feb 1945

Foundation Collection Kamm, Zug
© Wolfgang Bauer

1   With the Munich Agreement of September 1938, border regions in southern Moravia around Znaim/Znojmo, Nikolsburg/Mikulov, and Lundenburg/Břeclav had already fallen to Germany—but not the area slightly further north between Iglau/Jihlava and Brünn/Brno, where Hoffmann's home village of Pirnitz/Brtnice lay.

2   Hoffmann wrote to Carl Otto Czeschka in November 1938: "We are doing reasonably well; it almost looks as though there were or will be something to do. Now that we have banned many things again, we can feel reassured when looking to the future. Bit by bit we are also sensing the decline in non-Aryan competition. Although my home region is still in the Czech kingdom, the few Germans who are still vegetating there, will now be treated somewhat better after very grave dangers beforehand." In: Spielmann, Heinz: Carl Otto Czeschka. Ein Wiener Künstler in Hamburg, Göttingen 2019, 237 f.

3   Save for the Austrian pavilion at the Venice Biennale, the prestigious commissions from the Dollfuss-Schuschnigg regime between 1934 and 1938 went to Hoffmann's office partner Oswald Haerdtl (Austrian pavilions at the World's Fair in Brussels in 1935 and in Paris in 1937) or to Clemens Holzmeister (RAVAG broadcasting company's headquarters in Vienna, Salzburg Festival buildings). For other reasons, too, Hoffmann was not able to realize a single construction project between 1934 and 1938 and had to limit his activities to designs for interiors, exhibitions, and buildings, in part for competitions.

4   The art historian and Nazi politician Mühlmann was married to the graphic artist Poldi Wojtek, who had studied in Hoffmann's specialized class from 1924 to 1926.

5   Architekturzentrum Wien/Holzschuh, Ingrid/Platzer, Monika (eds.), "Wien. Die Perle des Reichs." Planen für Hitler, Zurich 2015, 218.

6   Speer had disapproved of the intention to award Hoffmann the Goethe Medal in an expert report, see the article "Josef Hoffmann and National Socialism: An Evaluation" by Elisabeth Boeckl-Klamper in this catalog, 397n43. Considering the great cultural significance that Hoffmann attributed to the Viennese cityscape and that he publicly reaffirmed immediately after 1945, he must have found this affront doubly hurtful; see Hoffmann, Josef, "Zum glücklichen Geleit," in: Oertel, Rudolf, Die schönste Stadt der Welt, Vienna 1947, 5–7.

7   Az W et al. (eds.) 2015 (see note 5), 116–119.

8   Sekler, Eduard F., Josef Hoffmann: The Architectural Work, Princeton, NJ 1985, CR 388, 442. Trans. Eduard F. Sekler and John Maass.

9   Quotes from: Hoffmann, Josef, "Das Haus der Wehrmacht. Bemerkungen zum Umbau," in: Die Pause (5) 12 1939/40, 50–51: 51.

10 Whether Hoffmann also adapted the interior, is unclear as he did not mention it and it does not feature in any known contemporary photographic documentation. As-built plans, produced in 1941 and 1943 by the army's building authority, provide no conclusive information; Berlin, Federal Archives, foreign office, B 112-280 (1955).

11 Sekler 1985 (see note 8), CR 383, 440.

12 This was followed in 1942 by a new project for the trade fair, finalized to the point of a detailed model, by Kutschera/Popp/Ubl, which was created in the context of the new development plans for Vienna by Hanns Dustmann and was likewise left unexecuted. Cf. Az W et al. (eds.) 2015 (see note 5), 124.

13 Sekler 1985 (see note 8), 220. Instead of a Hanak museum, which was only built in a reduced form in Langenzersdorf long after Hoffmann's death, Georg Lippert, one of the most active Viennese architects of the Nazi period and a party member, built the studio and later museum of the sculptor Gustinus Ambrosi in Vienna's Augarten park in

1953–1957; in 1938–1943 Ambrosi had supplied two bronze figures for the garden of the New Reich Chancellery in Berlin on commission from Albert Speer.

14 Sekler 1985 (see note 8), CR 381, 439. Between 1929 and 1943 the publishing house produced the magazine die neue linie, among other publications, on which the Bauhaus artists Moholy-Nagy, Bayer, and Gropius had collaborated before 1938.

15 "Arbeiten von Prof. Josef Hoffmann in Wien," in: Moderne Bauformen 1942, 281.

16 Sekler 1985 (see note 8), CR 386, 441.

17 Ibid., CR 387, 441 f.

18 Sultano, Gloria, Wie geistiges Kokain… Mode unterm Hakenkreuz, Vienna 1995; Mattl, Siegfried/Pirhofer, Gottfried, Wien im nationalsozialistischen Ordnung des Raums: Lücken in der Wien-Erzählung, Vienna 2018.

19 Freiburger Zeitung 23 Feb 1939.

20 ASA, AdR, ZNsZ RK, matter 2100 2238/1. The colonnaded walkway would probably also have led through Palais Fries-Pallaviccini on Josefsplatz, which is not mentioned by Hoffmann.

21 See the article "Josef Hoffmann and National Socialism: An Evaluation" by Elisabeth Boeckl-Klamper in this catalog.

22 The construction file of the building—the aryanized Zwieback department store—contains no plans from the Nazi period but does contain Hoffmann's redesign of the building entrance dating from 1956; City of Vienna, MA 37, EZ 590.

23 See the article "Freedom from Patronage: Josef Hoffmann and the Deutsche Werkstätten Hellerau" by Klára Němečková in this catalog.

24 Sekler 1985 (see note 8), CR 392, 443 f., date uncertain.

25 Ibid., CR 393, 444 f. The objects can now be found in the Kunsthistorisches Museum in Vienna, Imperial Armoury, A 550 and A 127.

26 Foundation Collection Kamm, Zug.

1946
1956

Yoichi R. Okamoto, Josef Hoffmann, 1951
UAA, Collection and Archive, 5341/2/FP

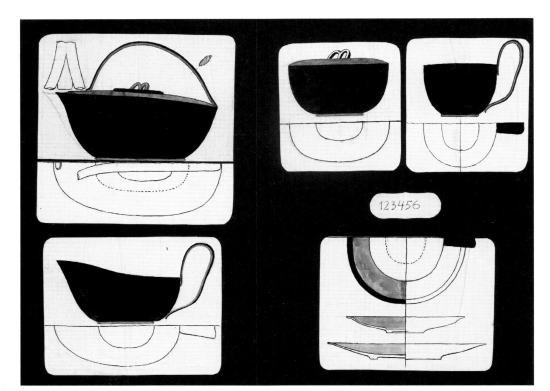

Fig. 1 JH, designs for two
different tea sets,
ca. 1950

Augarten Porcelain Manufactory
© MAK/Georg Mayer

Fig. 2 JH, catalog for the Austrian exhibition
at the 27th Venice Biennale, 1954

mumok – museum moderner kunst stiftung ludwig wien, MD 230/0

Fig. 3 JH, trunk, painted by
Franz von Zülow, 1947
Wood, painted
bel etage Kunsthandel GmbH

Fig. 4 JH, small table, painted
by Gertrude Balaban, 1947
Wood, painted
Dr. E. Ploil Collection

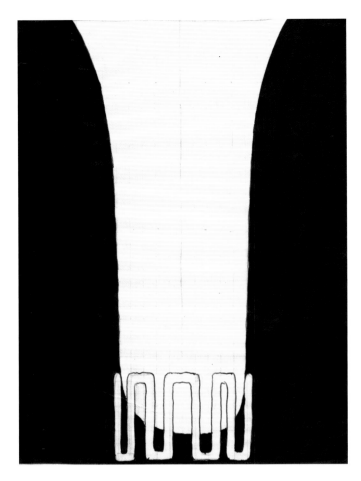

Fig. 5 JH, design for a glass vase, ca. 1950
UAA, Collection and Archive, 80/2

Fig. 6 JH, design for a cast-glass tumbler, ca. 1950
J. & L. LOBMEYR
© MAK/Georg Mayer

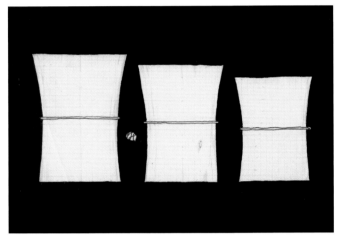

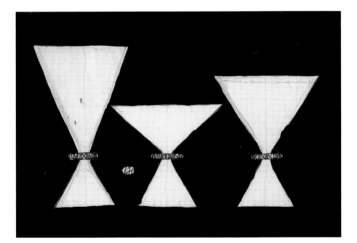

Figs. 7–10 JH, designs for glass sets, ca. 1950
J. & L. LOBMEYR
© MAK/Georg Mayer

Fig. 11 JH, glass set for the Milan Triennial, executed via J. & L. Lobmeyr, 1954
Colorless glass, cut
MAK, GL 3287
© Peter Kainz/MAK

Fig. 12 JH, flatware (model no. 86), executed by C. Hugo Pott, Solingen (DE), 1955
Sterling silver
mumok – museum moderner kunst stiftung ludwig wien, M 16/1

Fig. 13 JH, tea set, executed by Ludwig Kyral for the culture and adult
education authority—Künstlerwerkstätte (Artists' Workshops), 1947
Copper, silver-plated, rosewood
Dr. E. Ploil Collection

Fig. 14 JH, lidded box, executed by
the Österreichische Künstlerwerkstätte, 1952
Walnut wood
MAK, H 2012
© MAK/Nathan Murrell

Fig. 15 JH, cigarette case, executed by Rudolf Bojanovski
for the Österreichische Künstlerwerkstätte, 1946
Rosewood
Private collection
© Michael Huey

Fig. 16 JH, wallpaper pattern from the
artists' wallpaper collection of the Gebr.
Rasch wallpaper factory in Bramsche (DE), 1950
MAK, BI 26064
© MAK/Branislav Djordjevic

Fig. 17 JH, design for a lidded
goblet for the drafting and
experimental workshop for creative
design, 1946
Kunsthandel Widder, Vienna

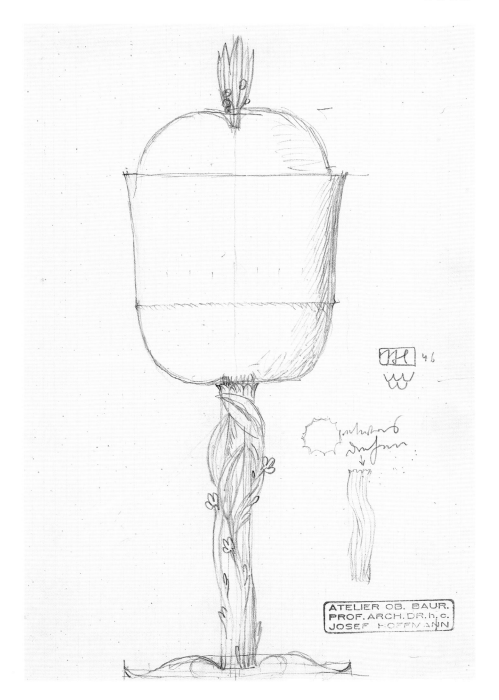

Figs. 18, 19 JH, imaginative sketches for small summerhouses, before 1947
E. F. Sekler, *Josef Hoffmann*, 445

Fig. 20 JH, annex in the inner courtyard of the Austrian
pavilion in the Giardini, Venice Biennale, 1954
© La Biennale Venezia, ASAC, Phototeca/Sharp

Fig. 21 JH and Josef Kalbac, housing complex for
the municipality of Vienna, Blechturmgasse 23–27,
1949/50, detail of the iron-barred gate
© private

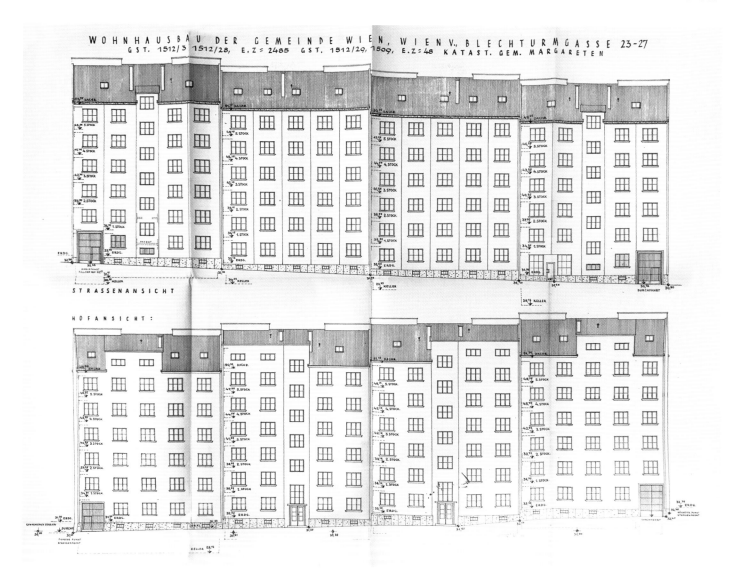

Fig. 22 JH and Josef Kalbac, housing
complex for the municipality of Vienna,
Blechturmgasse 23–27, 1949/50,
submission plan showing street and
courtyard façades
City of Vienna, MA 37, EZ 48 V
© Kerstin Bauhofer

Fig. 23 JH and Josef Kalbac, housing
complex for the municipality of Vienna,
Silbergasse 2–4, 1951/52, inner courtyard
Kunsthandel Widder, Vienna

Josef Hoffmann

1946
1956

Josef Hoffmann and Oskar Kokoschka
at a Secession opening, ca. 1955
© Franz Hubmann

1946–1956

The Wiener Kunsthandwerkverein that had been founded by the Nazi regime is converted into the Austrian Werkbund and the Österreichische Werkstätten cooperative by Josef Hoffmann's former partner Oswald Haerdtl in 1948. Hoffmann acts as a member of the executive and supervisory boards of the cooperative. His late architectural work primarily includes housing complexes for the municipality of Vienna—on Blechturmgasse, Silbergasse, and Heiligenstädterstraße—as well as numerous unrealized designs for private homes. A design for a school in Langenzersdorf near Vienna is realized in an altered form. Furthermore, Hoffmann continues to design decorative-arts objects. In 1950 he is awarded the Grand Austrian State Prize; in 1951 he is given honorary doctorates by the Technische Hochschule Wien (today's TU Wien) and the Technische Hochschule Dresden (now the Technische Universität Dresden). Hoffmann is a member of the art senate of the young Second Republic and the general commissioner of the Austrian section of the Venice Biennale; he designs a rear extension for the Austrian pavilion. Between 1945 and 1956 he is

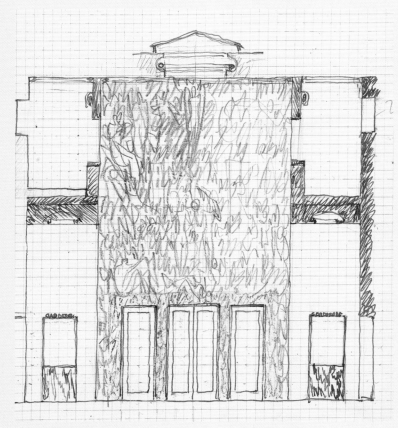

JH, design for the interior decoration of the entrance hall of the war-damaged Secession building, Vienna, 1948
Kunsthandel Widder, Vienna

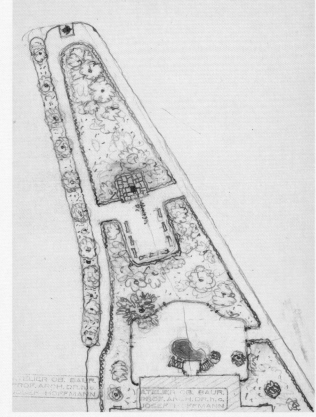

JH, ground plan design for the green space around the war-damaged Secession building, Vienna, 1948
Kunsthandel Widder, Vienna

Josef Hoffmann and Adolphe Stoclet's
granddaughter in Stoclet House,
Brussels, 1955
© Eva Ritter-Gelinek

intermittently president and committee
member of the Vienna Secession. 1954
sees a city hall project—again commissioned by Hermann Neubacher, now an
adviser to Emperor Haile Selassie—for
Addis Ababa. That same year, Josef
Hoffmann is awarded the Commenda-
tore dell'Ordine della Corona d'Italia by
the Republic of Italy. He celebrates his
85th birthday in Stoclet House in Brussels and dies shortly after, on 7 May
1956, of a stroke in Vienna. Josef Hoffmann is laid to rest in a grave of honor
designed by Fritz Wotruba in Vienna
Central Cemetery. ■

Sergius Pauser, portrait of Josef Hoffmann, 1951
Wien Museum, 104.760

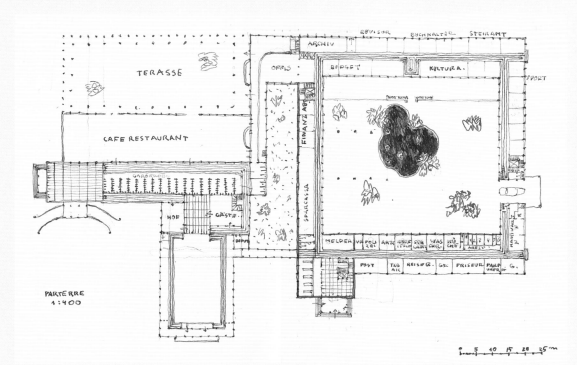

JH, project, Addis Ababa
city hall, ground plan,
1954/55
Kunsthandel Widder, Vienna

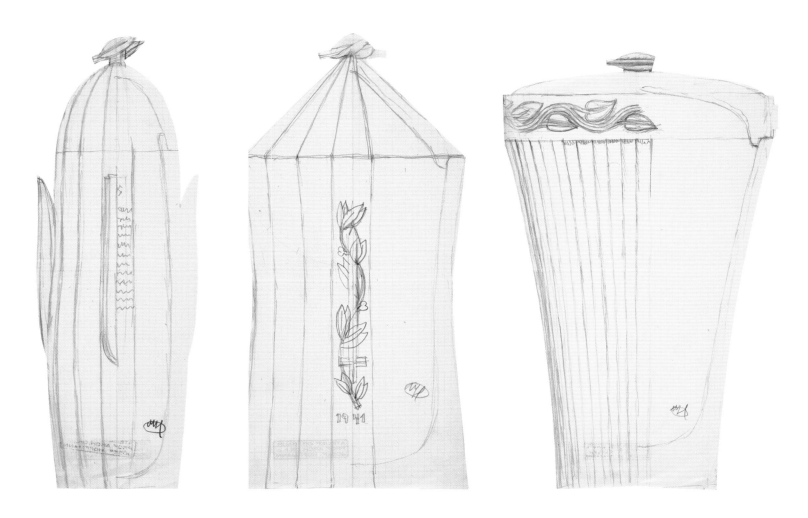

Figs. 1–3 JH, designs for lidded tumblers
for J. & L. Lobmeyr, 1941
J. & L. LOBMEYR
© MAK/Georg Mayer

Christian Witt-Dörring

Individuality versus Obligatory Conformity

Decorative Arts 1938–1956

The importance Josef Hoffmann attaches to the decorative arts as a cultural vehicle for the creation of state or societal identity is a common theme running through his entire oeuvre. It represents everyday life with confidence and on an equal footing with the expansive gesture that is architecture. The associated quality standards manage to survive not only the obligatory ideological conformity of all the German Reich's cultural affairs by Berlin, but also the wartime shortage of materials and labor.[1] Although his appointment as arts-and-crafts commissioner for the City of Vienna's Kulturamt (Culture Authority) from 1939 again gives him access to an organizational structure in the Wiener Kunsthandwerkverein (Viennese Association of Arts and Crafts), founded as the successor to all societies and associations (e.g., the Austrian Werkbund), which declares him the center of local arts-and-crafts activities, his potential to influence broad matters of cultural taste is limited. He runs the experimental workshop for creative design that is affiliated with the Kunsthandwerkverein, in which role he is intended to have an impact on design.[2] In 1946 he retrospectively describes his influence at the time as follows: "[…] the plan to ensure all artistic activities conformed to a specific, officially propagated style, was unsuccessful here; we continued—albeit in secret—going our own way and are now freed from all constraints of that kind […]."[3]

What characterizes Hoffmann's "own way" in the works executed during the Third Reich in contrast to his decorative-arts creations of the immediate postwar period? The subtextual proclivity for individual artistic expression is unmissable. A good example of this are the wall lights for the great hall of the Haus der Wehrmacht [House of the Armed Forces]. Hoffmann covers their wall brackets with a decorative band that paraphrases both the swastika and meander. In between he places scattered flowers, thereby sabotaging once and for all the originally political statement of this ultimate Nazi symbol. Hoffmann's individualistic design vocabulary manifests itself not so much in a decorative or ornamental innovation but rather in his unexpected and skillful proportional inventions, which give the cohesive form its distinctive Hoffmannesque character. However, at the same time this formal invention is overshadowed by a monumentalizing austerity prescribed by the system, which curbs its

individuality. Further testaments to this include his decoration of the Haus der Mode [House of Fashion] and designs for mock-up rooms for the Deutsche Werkstätten München, and even the designs he produced for the Lausitzer Glaswerke.[4] By the early postwar years, Hoffmann has already moved on from this curb. Now his forms, material, and decoration speak a new language of lightness, which gives expression to his skepticism about the monumentality that had recently been celebrated through frontality and symmetry.

A design produced in 1945 for a tulle embroidery with fairy-tale fantasy architecture as its motif, crowned in the reclaimed former symbols of the Austrian state, can be interpreted as evidence of this desire for innovation in line with old, tried-and-tested principles. Fritz Waerndorfer had so aptly identified them in a letter to Carl Otto Czeschka in 1910, summarizing them in the following remark: "Hoff is the only one who can pull off a new blouse as well as he can a new public building."[5]

However, there is continuity at the Kunsthandwerkverein institution. It survives the regime change after 1945 at the same address, Kärntner Straße 15, and on its first floor houses the Künstlerwerkstättenverein (Artists' Workshop Society), which has been newly founded on Hoffmann's initiative. Its task is to develop model designs for handicrafts.[6] They are realized in collaboration with Viennese craft companies like the metal workshop Ludwig Kyral, the frame maker Max Welz, and the glassware commissioning retailer J. & L. Lobmeyr, or the sculptor Karl Kirch, the carpenter R. Bojanovski, and the ceramicist Lotte Michel. They include chest models designed by Hoffmann, which are painted by various artists (Erna Rottenberg, Max Snischek, Gertrude Balaban, Franz v. Zülow).[7] The energy with which the physical and institutional reconstruction is embarked on immediately after the war has ended in May 1945, is admirable. It means that by late August it is already possible to use the exhibition space at the Kunsthandwerkverein, despite it having served as a horse stable for the German armed forces and the Russian troops.[8] In his fellow campaigner for the decorative arts, active since the 1910s, the editor and publisher Leopold Wolfgang Rochowanski who was banned from publishing by the Nazis, Hoffmann rediscovers his old advocate and finds a new customer. For the Agathon pub-

8 p. 380

11 12 13
14 p. 382

1 p. 378

5

4

13 p. 412

5 6 7 8
9 10 p. 410

15 p. 412

8

7

3 4 p. 409

3 p. 378

6 p. 420

2 p. 378

10

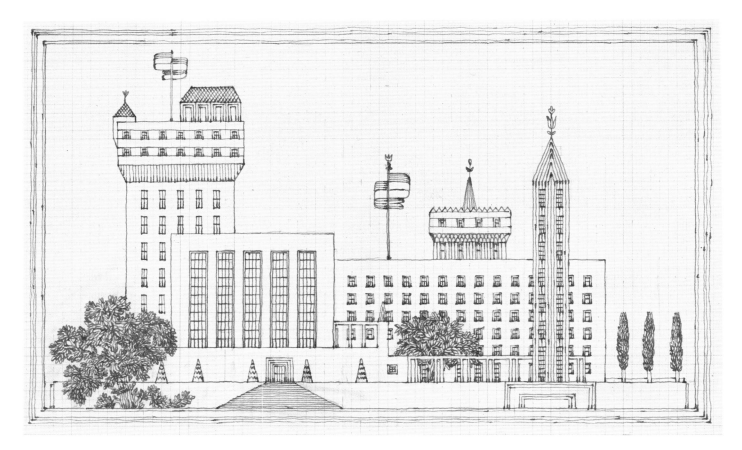

Fig. 4 JH, design for a tulle embroidery, 1945
Graphic Collection, Academy of Fine Arts Vienna, HZ 26340

Fig. 5 JH, two vases, executed by the Lausitzer
Glaswerke, Weißwasser (DE), 1939
Product catalog of the Lausitzer Glaswerke, 1939, model nos. A 45029–30
MAK, BI 22335

Fig. 6 JH, design for a coffeepot for the Augarten
Porcelain Manufactory, 1941
Graphic Collection, Academy of Fine Arts Vienna, HZ 26325

Fig. 7 JH (form), Ena Rottenberg (painting), trunk,
executed for the Kunsthandwerkverein (Association of
Arts and Crafts), 1946
Wien Museum, 211.708

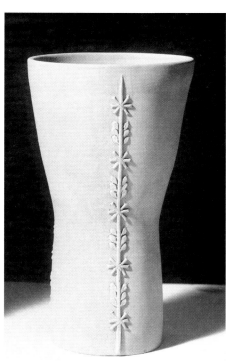

lishing house, which was founded in 1946 and closed down
just two years later in 1948 as a victim of the 1947 currency
reform and which issued not only the *Agathon Almanach*
but also the magazine *Die Schönen Künste*, Hoffmann designs book covers and illustrations. To mark Hoffmann's
80th birthday Rochowanski dedicates a Festschrift to him.[9]
Despite having been destroyed in February 1945, it is possible to move back into the Secession building as early as
January 1949.[10] Hoffmann designs very humble furnishings
for its administrative office in 1948.[11] In addition to Hoffmann's familiar aesthetic from the 1930s, he starts to develop
his typical, organic style from the 1950s onward. It can be
found alongside abstract geometric forms, whether as a wallpaper pattern for the wallpaper factory of the Gebrüder
Rasch in Bramsche (DE), as fabric patterns, as a tea set for
the Augarten Porcelain Manufactory, as silver flatware for
the Hugo Pott manufactory in Solingen (DE), or as a glass
set for the J. & L. Lobmeyr company for the Milan Triennial.
And it also dominates his "graphic fantasies" created in
1950, which may oscillate for the viewer between decorative
invention and narrative. Hoffmann himself referred to them
as poems;[12] it is his very own nonverbal language of forms.

9 11

1 p. 408

16 p. 412
12 p. 405

11 12 p. 411

p. 453

Fig. 8 JH, vases, executed by Lotte
Michel for the Kunsthandwerkverein
(Association of Arts and Crafts), 1946
Wien Museum, 211.711

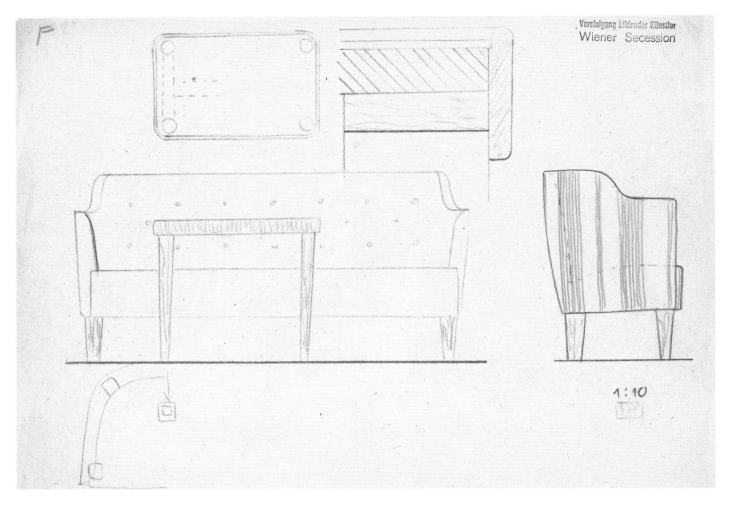

Fig. 9 JH, design for a living room suite for the office of the Secession, 1948
Donation Wittmann Möbelwerkstätten GmbH
MAK, KI 23506-1-1-11

1   Hoffmann, Josef, "Tätigkeitsbericht des Bevoll-mächtigten des Kulturamts der Stadt Wien für das Kunsthandwerk," undated typescript in Ank-wicz-Kleehoven's estate at the Belvedere Research Center, portfolio 6, no. 32.

2   Neues Wiener Tagblatt 20 Aug 1942, 3, and Ank-wicz-Kleehoven, Hans, "Die Künstlerwerkstätte Prof. Josef Hoffmann," undated typescript in Ank-wicz-Kleehoven's estate at the Belvedere Research Center, portfolio 8.

3   Hoffmann, Josef, "Kunstgewerbe – Aufgabe und Verpflichtung," in: Der Fortschritt, special issue "Kunsthandwerk in Österreich," Dec 1946, 4.

4   Typescript of an obituary of Josef Hoffmann, 1956, 6 in Ankwicz-Kleehoven's estate (see note 2). Design drawings for both works can be found in the Graphic Collection of the Academy of Fine Arts Vienna, HZ 26320 and HZ 26321.

5   Letter from Fritz Waerndorfer to Carl Otto Czeschka from 27 Oct 1910, in: Spielmann, Heinz, Carl Otto Czeschka. Ein Wiener Künstler in Ham-burg, Göttingen 2019, 180.

6   Wiener Kurier 27 Dec 1945, 4, and Noever, Peter/Pokorný, Marek (eds.), Josef Hoffmann: Autobiography, Ostfildern 2009, 104. Trans. Bernd Magar and Andrew Oakland.

7   Hoffmann 1946 (see note 3), 4–5.

8   Salzburger Nachrichten 7 Sep 1945, 4.

9   Rochowanski, Leopold W., Josef Hoffmann. Eine Studie geschrieben zu seinem 80. Geburtstag, Vienna 1950.

10   Metzger, Rainer, "Der Secessionsstil," in: Seces-sion (ed.), Secession, Vienna 2018, 109.

11   The design drawings can be found in the MAK's Works on Paper Collection, KI 23506-1-1-1 to 16.

12   Typescript (see note 4), 7.

Fig. 10 JH, detail of the wall light for the Haus der Wehrmacht [House of the Armed Forces], 1940
Limewood, gold-plated
Private collection
© MAK/Georg Mayer

Fig. 11 JH, design for the reconstruction and redesign
of the Secession's entrance hall, 1948

Kunsthandel Widder, Vienna

Fig. 1 JH, design for a housing complex for the municipality of Vienna,
Heiligenstädterstraße, 1952, street façade
Cooper Hewitt Smithsonian Design Museum, New York, gift of Marilyn Walter Grounds, 2008-20-29
© bpk/Cooper Hewitt Smithsonian Design Museum/Art Resource, NY/Matt Flynn

Matthias Boeckl

Reconstructing Modernism

Josef Hoffmann's Late Work as an Architect and Curator

The end of World War II and the liberation of Vienna by the Red Army in April 1945 brought about the fourth political transition actively experienced by Josef Hoffmann. Once again, it was accompanied by far-reaching changes to working conditions for modern architects and designers. Yet once again, Hoffmann's adherence to the necessity of beauty in our surroundings proved a timeless and crisis-proof means for continuous productivity across all caesuras. Unlike many ambitious younger architects who had aligned themselves so closely with National Socialism that many a humane basic ideal of Modernism had been sacrificed and who were temporarily banned from accepting any public contracts during the denazification of the new Second Republic, the now 75-year-old Hoffmann had not come under suspicion of having unduly served the Nazi regime.[1] Consequently, on the one hand his work at the Wiener Kunsthandwerkverein (Viennese Association of Arts and Crafts), which had been founded in 1939, was able to continue almost unaltered (its main office at Kärntner Straße 15 remained Hoffmann's official work address until his death), and on the other he had the opportunity to resume numerous official activities that had been interrupted by the Ständestaat (corporative state) and the Nazi dictatorship. They include his influential work as the new commissioner of the Austrian contributions to the Venice Art Biennales[2] and his plans for housing complexes for the City of Vienna, which he now recommended with his colleague and partner Josef Kalbac. In 1948–1949 Hoffmann also served as the president of the Vienna Secession, which he had cofounded in 1897 and which had been forcibly amalgamated with the Künstlerhaus by the National Socialists in 1939;[3] it was reestablished in 1945.

Continuity and Beauty

In a city that had been badly affected by bombardments and days of fighting, rebuilding the art industry was guided first by the notions of culture forcefully communicated by the four occupying powers and second by the older artists' desire to proceed with an "Austrian" Modernism, which would give the country a sense of identity and unity despite the Allies' massive external control. Thus, in 1952 Hoffmann's former assistant Max Fellerer, who was the director of the now Academy of Applied Arts (previously School of Arts and Crafts) in 1934–1938 and again in 1945–1954, wrote: "Today, the school's tasks are not so much rebellious as consolidatory and clarifying, based on the ideas of the previous generation."[4]

These efforts to continue pre-1938 Austrian Modernism are also evidenced by the artists whom Hoffmann nominated to represent the country at the Venice Biennale.[5] Hoffmann had jointly planned the Austrian pavilion there with Robert Kramreiter in 1934. As the first official commissioner of the Second Republic, he organized a two-person exhibition on Egon Schiele and Fritz Wotruba in 1948, a solo show on Herbert Boeckl and a group exhibition with some 50 artists of all ages in 1950, another two-person exhibition in 1952—this time on Alfred Kubin and Fritz Wotruba—and a presentation of the avant-garde Austrian Art Club in 1954.[6]

The City as a Stage

In Vienna the widespread destruction was an invitation to plan creative new approaches and comprehensive urban modernizations. In some German cities the reconstruction plans executed after 1945 had actually already been designed by Nazi architects during the wartime bombing. However, due to the city's division into four occupied sectors, no comprehensive urban development projects could be realized in Vienna at first—neither the plans for the redesign of the capital produced by Albert Speer's employee Hans Dustmann in 1940–1942 (*Führervorlage* [submission to the Führer] from 1941), nor Roland Rainer's *Grünflächenplan für Wien* [Green Spaces Plan for Vienna], which he had developed in 1940 during his research work for the Deutsche Akademie für Städtebau, Reichs- und Landesplanung in Berlin.[7] Therefore, it was possible to discuss numerous artistic visions prior to the City Council's implementation in 1952 of the "Acht-Punkte-Programm für den sozialen Städtebau" (Eight-Point Program for Social Urban Development), inspired by dogmatic Modernism and CIAM's Athens Charter from 1933.[8] Rather than planning the suburban housing developments needed to mitigate the oppressive housing shortage, they instead focused on the reconstruction and

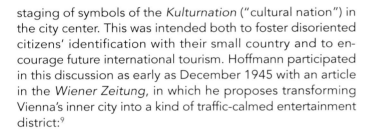

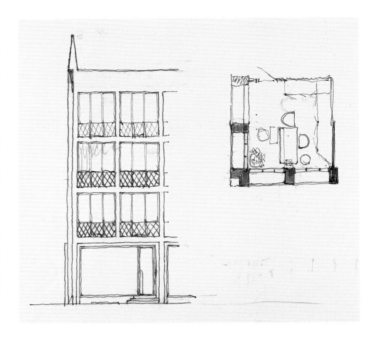

Fig. 2 JH, annex in the inner courtyard of the Austrian pavilion in the Giardini, Venice Biennale, 1954, section and floor plan
© BMUK 50 Jahre Pavillon, Salzburg 1984, 60/Sharp

Fig. 3 JH, project for a city hall in Addis Ababa, 1954/55, detail of a corner with office floor plan
Donation from Wittmann Möbelwerkstaetten GmbH
MAK, KI 23086-51

staging of symbols of the *Kulturnation* ("cultural nation") in the city center. This was intended both to foster disoriented citizens' identification with their small country and to encourage future international tourism. Hoffmann participated in this discussion as early as December 1945 with an article in the *Wiener Zeitung*, in which he proposes transforming Vienna's inner city into a kind of traffic-calmed entertainment district:[9]

> "Only artists, scholars, friends of art, and especially original people should live in this part of the city. On the ground floors only small, quality shops ought to be accommodated in the fashion typical of old Vienna. In between, places of amusement [...] in impeccable, special form; small original restaurants and wine taverns, fruit restaurants, confectioners, tearooms and cafés, fish restaurants for Danube fish, lake fish, crayfish, and the like, with every finesse in the Viennese manner, could be housed here. [...] It must be possible to find everything here that fits into the framework of our old Vienna. Thus, for example, antiquarian bookshops, art dealers, exhibitions of old and new art, small collections which here could be preserved as entities, and much else that would soon result. Driving in these quarters should be prohibited during certain hours; transportation possibly could be even by sedan chairs."[10]

Logically, Hoffmann proposes that these projects "must be under the general direction of an experienced man, an extraordinary film director would be best; he would call on our ablest artists for the many varied tasks." The dramaturge Rudolf Oertel may have felt that this remark was addressed to him personally; two years later in his book *Wien. Die schönste Stadt der Welt*, he also suggests a reconstruction of Vienna that actively involves cultural functions. In his foreword to this publication, Hoffmann wrote:

> "What we have learned in bitter experiences must prove to us that a culturally designed life appears more important than the civilizing and technical progress that ultimately brought us so close to ruin. Nothing can encourage our love of life and a nation's cultural validity more than the ever-vibrant artistic design

of all things that surround us. [...] The contempt for the cultural and the supremacy of the spiritually inferior must be categorically overcome. It is vital to nurture ambition in all sections of the population, a task that will benefit everyone, which demands not only a material but also a psychological renewal, to devote oneself to enthusiastic collaboration on it and not to forget that even in the poorest areas culture constitutes the core of humane life."[11]

Langenzersdorf and Addis Ababa

Besides an interior decoration job for the Stern family in Langenzersdorf near Vienna (around 1952)[12] and the redesign of the entrance to the Künstlerwerkstättenverein (Artists' Workshop Society)[13] building planned in 1955, Hoffmann was not able to carry out any private construction commissions after World War II. However, he continued to produce numerous unrealized projects, of which the project for a city hall in Addis Ababa was the most substantial.[14] It was the result of reactivating his old networks: Hoffmann designed it together with Anton Ubl and Franz Hubert Matuschek, who had been among the favorite architects of Hermann Neubacher, the first Nazi mayor of Vienna.[15] Neubacher had been an old acquaintance of Hoffmann since the former's stint as the head of the municipally owned Gemeinwirtschaftliche Siedlungs- und Baustoffanstalt (GESIBA, the Institution for Public Housing and Construction Materials), which had constructed Vienna's Werkbundsiedlung (Werkbund Estate) in 1929–1932, and was the key figure behind Hoffmann's brief success in 1938–1940. After Neubacher's departure to the Balkans and short imprisonment in Yugoslavia in 1951, he worked as a consultant to the Ethiopian Emperor Haile Selassie in 1954–1956 on the expansion of the capital city, for which he commissioned Hoffmann with designing the city hall. In many of its details (such as the tower and the long façades divided by vertical oblong fields), the project is reminiscent of Hoffmann's similarly unrealized plan from 1928–1929 for an exhibition hall on Karlsplatz that was to be run by the City of Vienna.[16]

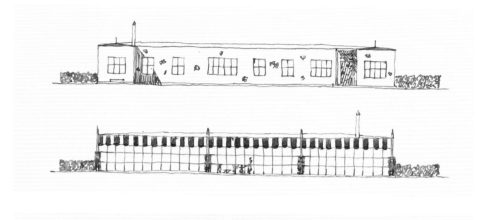

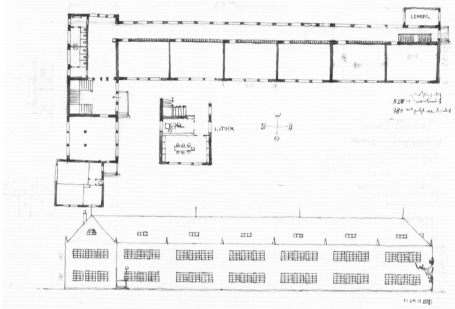

Stockerau and Vienna

The public commissions that were awarded to Hoffmann and his now partner Josef Kalbac in the postwar period comprised an elementary school in Lower Austria and three housing complexes for the City of Vienna. The elementary school for girls was planned in 1951 for the municipality of Stockerau: "The school was built according to Hoffmann's concept but with changes in detail."[17] In the three *Gemeindebauten* (municipal housing projects) for the City of Vienna, whose apartment typology and facilities standards were prescribed by the city to an even greater extent than they had been in "Red Vienna" in the 1920s, Hoffmann's handwriting is recognizable above all in the subtle modeling of the structural shell as a reaction to its location and in the artistic features. Thus, the project on Heiligenstädter Straße[18] with 46 apartments comprises three parallel structures whose staggered positions reflect the local topography; a figurative stone relief by Heinz Leinfellner has been included over the entrance to one of the buildings. Similarly, the 70 apartments on Silbergasse[19] are artfully divided into three buildings:

two low flanking structures and a taller central section. This system of towerlike concentration in a freestanding structural component had first been realized by Hoffmann in the Klosehof in 1923–1925[20] and he repeated it again in 1949/50 in the six-story courtyard wing of the apartment complex on Blechturmgasse.[21] The austere building with 81 apartments features subtle artistic accents in the structuring of the façade by means of a wide-meshed grid of fine plaster grooves, as well as star motifs in the metalwork of the large gates with their iron railings. Alternative floor plan designs, whose circulation spaces with apartment entrances on one side only would have notably differed from the standard apartment types of the Viennese public housing of the period, were never realized. Hoffmann had experimented with such variants for municipal housing projects at Vienna's Malfattigasse 31 (realized by Josef Kalbac) and in the town of Hainburg an der Donau.[22] These were his final attempts to enrich this social construction work with individual creativity.

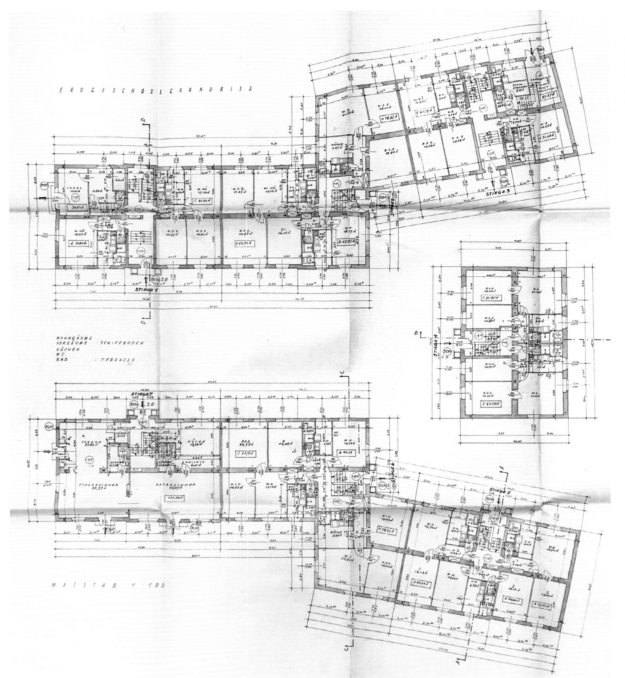

1   Hoffmann's NSDAP membership application received a negative assessment from a party functionary in 1938; see the article "Josef Hoffmann and National Socialism: An Evaluation" by Elisabeth Boeckl-Klamper in this catalog.

2   In 1934 and 1936 the former diplomat Nikolaus Post had been Austria's commissioner.

3   Hoffmann served as liquidator of the Secession's property along with Christian Ludwig Martin and Oswald Roux.

4   Kapfinger, Otto/Boeckl, Matthias, "Vom Interieur zum Städtebau. Architektur am Stubenring 1918–90," in: Kunst: Anspruch und Gegenstand. Von der Kunstgewerbeschule zur Hochschule für angewandte Kunst in Wien 1918–1991, Salzburg/Vienna 1991, 131.

5   In 1934 Hoffmann had jointly planned the Austrian pavilion there with Robert Kramreiter. See the article "Austria's Aesthetic Self-Portrait: The Austrian Pavilion in Venice" by Rainald Franz in this catalog.

6   Sharp, Jasper, Austria and the Venice Biennale 1895–2013, Nuremburg 2013, 268–311

7   Architekturzentrum Wien (ed.), Wien. Die Perle des Reichs. Planen für Hitler, Zurich 2015, 60 and 150.

8   Denk, Marcus, "Zerstörung als Chance? Städtebauliche Konzepte, Leitlinien und Projekte in Wien 1945–1958," dissertation at the University of Vienna, 2007, 147.

9   This vision became a reality in a similar form from the 1970s.

10   Hoffmann, Josef, "Gedanken zum Wiederaufbau Wiens," in: Wiener Zeitung 23 Dec 1945, quoted by Sekler, Eduard F., Josef Hoffmann: The Architectural Work, Princeton, NJ 1985, 501 f. Trans. Eduard F. Sekler and John Maass.

11   Hoffmann, Josef, "Zum glücklichen Geleit," in: Oertel, Rudolf, Die schönste Stadt der Welt – Ein utopisches Buch, Vienna 1947, 5–6.

12   Sekler 1985 (see note 10), CR 465, 468.

13   Founded in 1939, the Wiener Kunsthandwerkverein became the Österreichische Werkstätten in 1948 (see the article "On the Reconstruction of the Arts and Crafts: Österreichische Werkstätten 1948" by Eva-Maria Orosz in this catalog). The association's Versuchswerkstätten (experimental workshops) appear to have been run independently as a spin-off; in 1955 they operated under the name Künstlerwerkstättenverein (Artists' Workshop Society) which submitted the planning

application for the new entrance. Construction records of the City of Vienna, MA 37—Municipal Department of Building Inspection, Kärntner Straße 15, EZ 590.

14   Sekler 1985 (see note 10), CR 403, 449.

15   Cf. the project by Hermann Kutschera, Alexander Popp, and Anton Ubl for new exhibition and sports grounds in the Prater park, 1938–1943, and Matuschek's high-rise air-raid shelter in Aspern, 1941; Architekturzentrum Wien 2015 (see note 7), 124 and 201.

16   Sekler 1985 (see note 10), CR 287, 409 f.

17   Sekler 1985 (see note 10), CR 501, 476; six designs by Hoffmann for a school and kindergarten, Cooper Hewitt Museum, New York, gift of Marilyn Walter Grounds, inv. nos. 2008-20-22 to -27.

18   Sekler 1985 (see note 10), CR 401, 448.

19   Ibid., CR 400, 446–448.

20   Ibid., CR 255, 394 f.

21   Ibid., CR 395, 445.

22   Drawings at the Cooper Hewitt Museum, New York, gift of Marilyn Walter Grounds, inv. nos. 2008-20-3, -4, -5, -7, -8, -9, -11 (Malfattigasse), -49, -50 (Blechturmgasse), -58, -59 (Hainburg).

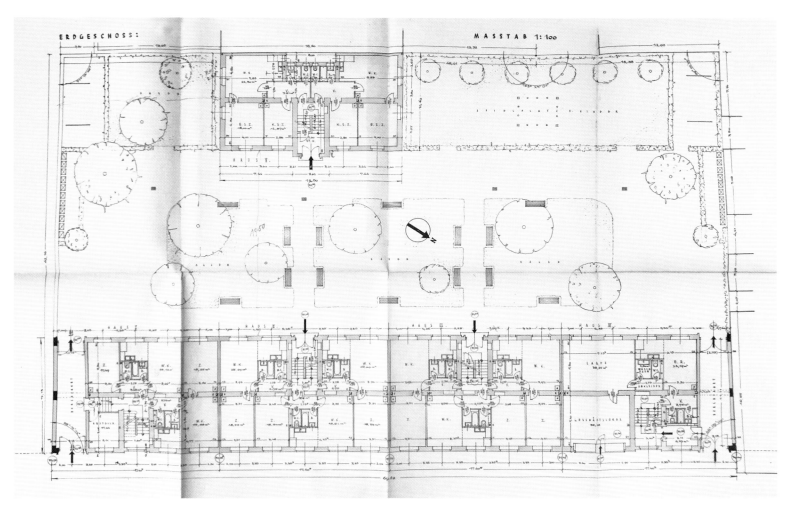

Fig. 8 JH and Josef Kalbac, housing complex for the municipality of Vienna,
Blechturmgasse 23–27, 1949/50, submission plan, ground floor plan
City of Vienna, MA 37, EZ 48 V
© Kerstin Bauhofer

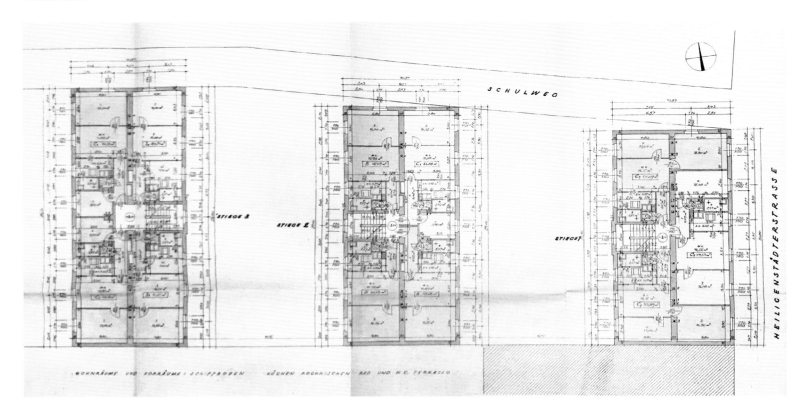

Fig. 9 JH and Josef Kalbac, housing complex for the municipality of Vienna,
Heiligenstädterstraße 129, 1952, submission plan, floor plan of the 1st upper floor
City of Vienna, MA 37, EZ 557
© Kerstin Bauhofer

Fig. 1 JH, box, executed by Rudolf Bojanovski
for the Österreichische Künstlerwerkstätte, 1950
Walnut
MAK, H 2010
© MAK/Nathan Murrell

Eva-Maria Orosz

On the Reconstruction of the Arts and Crafts

Österreichische Werkstätten 1948

After the end of the war, the new Austria set the formation of its cultural identity in the area of the applied arts on the foundation of Viennese Modernism. The aim was to link onto the former international reputation of Viennese arts and crafts—the Wiener Werkstätte—and reclaim its special position on the world market. The crafts tradition should be continued, and a typical Viennese creation of form expanded as "Austrian." This decision was understandable against the backdrop of Austria's economic situation, which in a comparison of European countries, featured more of a broad-based crafts structure rather than one of industrial production.

Josef Hoffmann no longer held any official offices after the war. Yet he still announced his idea of the future of arts and crafts in 1946 in an article. While he did show understanding for the industrial manufacture of the new era, he nonetheless adhered to the ideas of the Arts & Crafts movement: an artist's design is implemented by a craftsperson, who experiences in his or her work, a meaningful and satisfying activity. In the manufacture of perfectly formed wares, the worker becomes a transporter of culture, and offers an important contribution to society.[1] The successor generation of designers in influential positions no longer had the reformist aspect, rooted in the 19th century, in mind. Those who after 1945 wanted to free arts and crafts and product design from the ideology of the Nazi regime and set Austrian identity and product culture on a contemporary and exportable path, found themselves faced with a difficult task. Even without foresight, the increasing international switch to mass production made it possible to predict that neither arts and crafts nor veneration of the "Austrian" could actually be assured for the long term. After 1945, what voices grew louder for, was a new profession of product designers based on the international role model, which freed architects from some of the design work.

Oswald Haerdtl, professor of the spatial art, commercial and industrial design class at what was now called the College of Applied Arts, or (from 1947) Academy of Applied Arts, formerly the School of Arts and Crafts, guaranteed the desired bridge between tradition and departure after the war. As Hoffmann's office partner, he, too, had joined the New Werkbund under Hoffmann and Holzmeister in 1934. Although his roots were in craftsmanship, Haerdtl was es-

sentially future-oriented. With the support of Vienna's Kulturamt (Culture Authority), immediately after the war, he took on the revival of the Werkbund, which had been disbanded in 1938. The exhibition at the Kunsthandwerkverein (Viennese Association of Arts and Crafts) in summer 1945 thus offered the Werkbund members a forum again for the first time.[2] Proponents of the Werkbund, in addition to Haerdtl, were his colleagues from the College of Applied Arts, professors Ceno Kosak and Otto Niedermoser.[3] The official new founding, however, did not take place until 1948, and was a "denazification" measure. The arts-and-crafts association that had united all arts-and-crafts associations under National Socialism was disbanded and the Österreichische Werkstätten (ÖW) appeared in its place.[4]

The Österreichische Werkstätten collective saw itself as the Werkbund's executive business instrument, and was occupied with the purchase and sales of its members' flawlessly designed and exemplarily produced arts-and-crafts products.[5] The name was chosen in the style of the Wiener Werkstätte, and with the hope of carrying on its international reputation. The business model was similar to the Werkbund's former, independent retail shops from 1926 in the Grand Hotel on Kärntner Ring and in Red Vienna's housing advisory offices. A jury examined the members' products for quality, execution, and artistic integrity before they were put up for sale. Like in a furniture store, the goods were presented in a living ambiance—in an interplay of all of the objects of daily use.[6] In addition to textiles and furnishings departments, there was also a "low-cost department," as well as the intention of serial production, in order to make good form "affordable for the less well-off classes."[7] The first board members were Hans Harald Rath, Carl Auböck, Leopold Wieninger, Ceno Kosak, Karl Peschta, and Karl Hagenauer.[8] But since the statutes mandated that a third of the board and supervisory board members be replaced every year, soon all renowned personalities through to Josef Hoffmann, Oswald Haerdtl, and Max Fellerer were involved in the further destiny of the ÖW.[9] The roughly 100 members belonged also to the Austrian Werkbund (ÖWB)[10] and represented a wide diversity of professions, such as carpenters, shoemakers, weavers, turners, goldsmiths, jewelers, embroiderers, and bookbinders.[11]

Fig. 2 Shop of the Wiener Kunsthandwerkverein (Viennese Association of Arts and
Crafts; first address of the Österreichische Werkstätten), September 1945
ANL, Picture Archives, 687682 US 341

After 1945, the Werkbund movement failed to emerge in Vienna with any activities comparable to their prior major accomplishments. For the opening of the shop at Kärntner Straße 15, they found themselves confronted with accusations of being outmoded and having an elite attitude, as they presented the unaffordable, top-quality luxury of "something unusual, the brilliant idea" rather than solid wares.[12] In the first years after the war, there was a general lack of new and interesting products;[13] in 1950, practically no new products other than those from Auböck and Hagenauer were available at an international level, so that recourse was taken to prewar products.[14] Also the book *Wiener Möbel in Lichtbildern und maßstäblichen Rissen* published by Erich Boltenstern in 1934 was published in 1949 in an unchanged third edition.[15]

The main controversy of the Werkbund movement—individual arts-and-crafts consumer goods versus design for industrial production—was rarely discussed after 1945. However, the standpoints and future visions were more diverse than before the war. Viennese architects meanwhile continued to design every detail of their design contracts and carried forth the Viennese formal language. The ÖW con-

centrated on the traditional arts-and-crafts sector. Wolfgang von Wersin (1882–1976), an architect and designer who had become successful in Bavaria, answered the essential question—"Wozu ein Werkbund?" why have a Werkbund in Austria? The fact that the goal, the formation of an artistic culture of form from an artistically aligned community, was destined to fail with such diverse positions, was not surprising. Wersin, who managed the Neue Sammlung in Munich and organized the highly acclaimed exhibition *Der billige Gegenstand. Die Wohnung für das Existenzminimum und Ewige Formen* [The Inexpensive Object: The Home for Subsistence Living and Eternal Forms] in 1930, honored the accomplishments of Hoffmann and the Wiener Werkstätte, however pointed to a new path. His recommendation was to overcome the "expression of abundance"—an Austrian specialty—and steer all of the country's creative abilities into "design of what was essential."[16] While the Upper Austrian Werkbund was subsequently quite active under Wersin,[17] the Austrian Werkbund was calmly and quietly deleted from the register of associations. It had become inactive and no longer had an elected board of chairpersons, Ceno Kosak had been the last.[18]

Figs. 3, 4 Shop window and display of the Österreichische Werkstätten, Kärntner Straße, Vienna, after 1954
OESTERREICHISCHE WERKSTAETTEN/Art Works Handels Gmbh

1   Hoffmann, Josef, "Kunstgewerbe. Aufgabe und Verpflichtung," in: *Kunsthandwerk in Österreich. Sondernummer der österreichischen Monatsschrift Der Fortschritt*, December 1946, 4–7: 7.

2   Horwitz, G., "Der Österreichische Werkbund – neu erstanden," *Österreichische Zeitung*, 3 Jul 1945, 3.

3   Letter from the ÖWB to the security department, Vienna section, from 10 May 1948; MPAV, A32 deleted associations, file 1.3.2.119.A32.9888/1948 – 9888.

4   Through the disbanding of the arts-and-crafts association and founding of the Österreichische Werkstätten cooperative as legal successor, the member's association assets could be preserved. Protocol of the first regular general assembly of the Österreichische Werkstätten on 8 Sep 1949; Vienna, Commercial Register, FN 93466a, 38.

5   Statute Österreichische Werkstätten; ibid., 29.

6   "Handwerk zwischen Luxus, Kunst und Kitsch. Der neue Österreichische Werkbund stellt sich vor," *Neues Österreich*, 25 Sep 1948, 5.

7   "Nachfolgeschaft der 'Wiener Werkstätten,'" *Die Weltpresse*, 24 Sep 1948, 6.

8   Vienna, Commercial Register, FN 93466a, Statute.

9   Excerpt from the protocol of the regular general assembly on 7 Jan 1952; ibid., 51f.

10 Statute Österreichische Werkstätten; ibid., 13.

11 Letter from the Chamber of Commerce for Vienna to the Österreichische Werkstätten from 29 Nov 1948; ibid.

12 "Handwerk…" 1948 (see note 6).

13 Protocol for the 4th proper general assembly on 6 May 1954; Vienna, Commercial Register, FN 93466a, 76.

14 Haerdtl, Oswald, "Die Architektur von Heute und die Tendenzen der angewandten Kunst," lecture, Vienna, 16 May 1950, in: Stiller, Adolph, *Oswald Haerdtl. Architekt und Designer 1899–1959*, Salzburg 2000, 174–183: 181.

15 Witt-Dörring, Christian, "Creative Ambivalence: Austrian design mentality?," trans. Lisa Rosenblatt,

in: Beyerle, Tulga/Hirschberger, Karin (eds.), *Austrian Design 1900–2005*, Basel/Boston/Berlin 2006, 10–19: 19n2

16 Von Wersin, Wolfgang, *Wozu ein Werkbund*, Österreichischer Werkbund (ed.), Vienna 1949, 7. The text was first published in April 1948 in Goisern; Linz, Oberösterreichisches Landesarchiv (Upper Austrian State Archives), Flgs (leaflet collection) 37.

17 My gratitude to Wilfried Posch for information on the ÖWB after 1945. Grieshofer, Franz, "'Vom Adel der Form zum reinen Raum'. Franz C. Lipp und der Oberösterreichische Werkbund," in: Oberösterreichisches Landesmuseum Linz (ed.), *Der Volkskundler Franz C. Lipp (1913–2002)*, Linz 2018, 177–194.

18 Posch, Wilfried, "Die Österreichische Werkbundbewegung 1907–1928," in: Acker, Isabella/Neck, Rudolf (eds.), *Geistiges Leben in Österreich der Ersten Republik. Auswahl der bei den Symposien in Wien vom 11. bis 13. November 1980 und am 27. und 28. Oktober 1982 gehaltenen Referate*, Wissenschaftliche Kommission zur Erforschung der Geschichte der Republik Österreich, vol. 10, Vienna 1986, 279–312: 279. Letter from the Federal Ministry of the Interior to the Österreichischer Werkbund association from 12 Apr 1973; MPAV, A33 deleted associations, 2nd row, 23830/1948 –23830/48.

STAATLICHES BAUHAUS WEIMAR

Lieber Meister
Josef Hoffmann.
Mit dem Bauhaus
beglückwünscht Sie
in Freundschaft
und Verehrung
Ihr Walter Gropius.
Weimar Dezember 20.

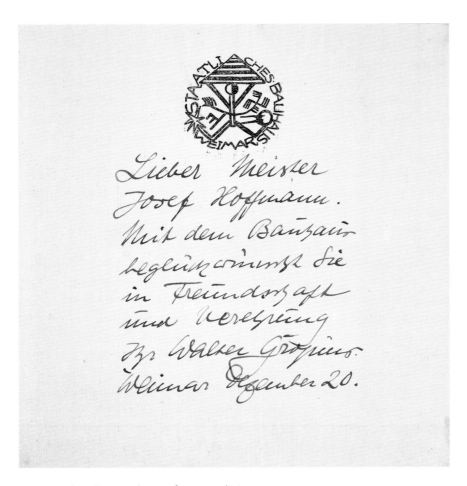

Fig. 1 Walter Gropius, letter of congratulations for Josef Hoffmann's 50th birthday, 1920
MAK, BI 121381-14

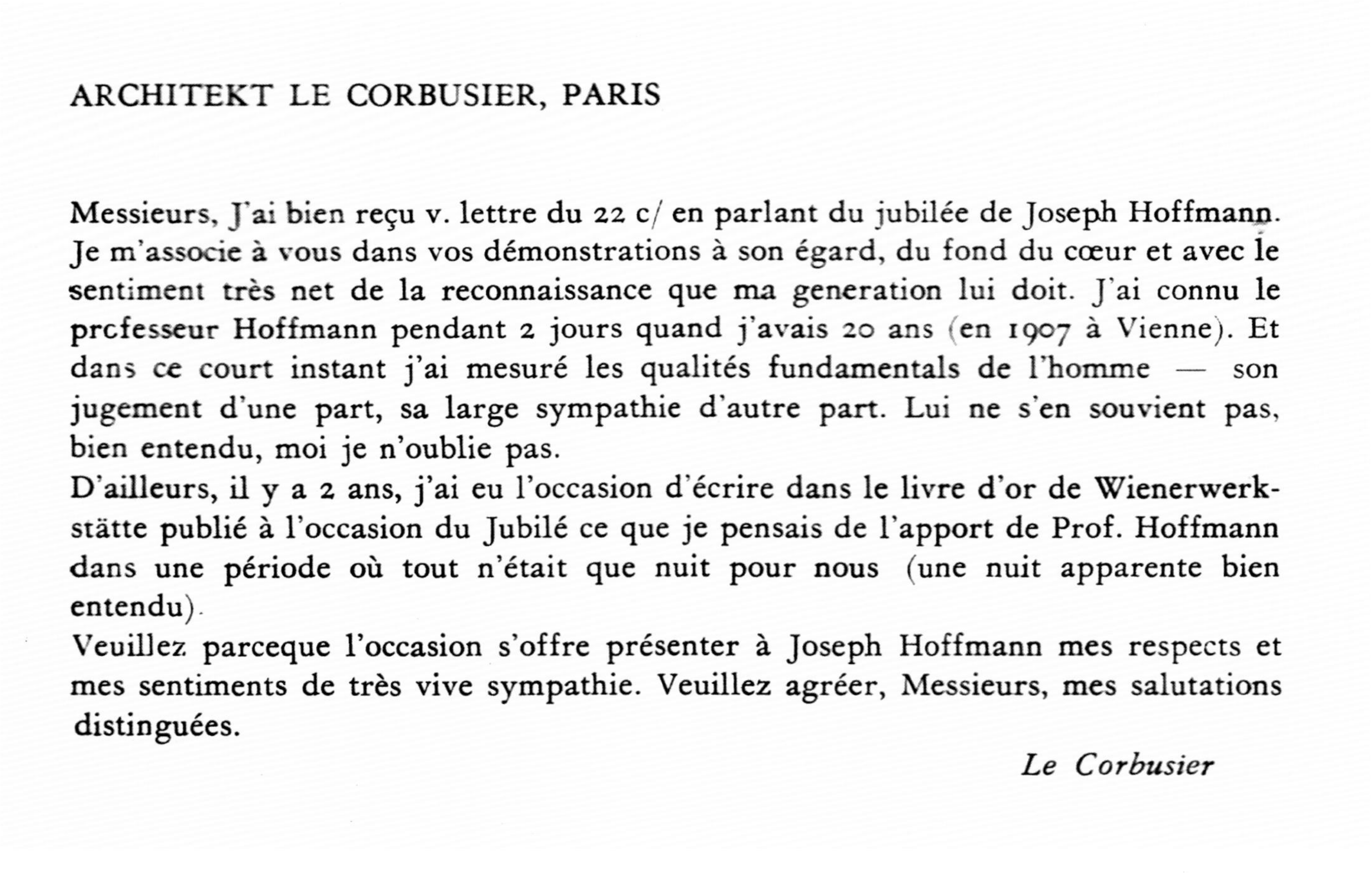

ARCHITEKT LE CORBUSIER, PARIS

Messieurs, J'ai bien reçu v. lettre du 22 c/ en parlant du jubilée de Joseph Hoffmann. Je m'associe à vous dans vos démonstrations à son égard, du fond du cœur et avec le sentiment très net de la reconnaissance que ma generation lui doit. J'ai connu le prcfesseur Hoffmann pendant 2 jours quand j'avais 20 ans (en 1907 à Vienne). Et dans ce court instant j'ai mesuré les qualités fundamentals de l'homme — son jugement d'une part, sa large sympathie d'autre part. Lui ne s'en souvient pas, bien entendu, moi je n'oublie pas.
D'ailleurs, il y a 2 ans, j'ai eu l'occasion d'écrire dans le livre d'or de Wienerwerkstätte publié à l'occasion du Jubilé ce que je pensais de l'apport de Prof. Hoffmann dans une période où tout n'était que nuit pour nous (une nuit apparente bien entendu).
Veuillez parceque l'occasion s'offre présenter à Joseph Hoffmann mes respects et mes sentiments de très vive sympathie. Veuillez agréer, Messieurs, mes salutations distinguées.

Le Corbusier

Fig. 2 Le Corbusier, letter of congratulations for Josef Hoffmann's 60th birthday, 1930
Österreichischer Werkbund (ed.), special edition of the magazine *Almanach der Dame* 1930, 12

Markus Kristan

A Pioneer of Modernism

Josef Hoffmann and International Arts Journalism

The boom in print media around 1900 is one of the main factors behind the success of modern art and architecture. Their feisty debates raged in specialist journals and even in daily newspapers from the outset. Josef Hoffmann could rely on a number of influential Viennese publicists in this regard who documented and commented on his works in great detail—they included Ferdinand Fellner von Feldegg in *Der Architekt* and Joseph A. Lux, Leopold Kleiner, Hans Tietze, Dagobert Frey, Max Eisler, and Berta Zuckerkandl in numerous other public and specialist publications. Among the prominent Viennese authors is Adolf Loos, who was embroiled in a controversial debate with Hoffmann throughout his life: Loos actually opens his piece for the Munich-based specialist journal *Dekorative Kunst* in 1898 with the words "I find it difficult to write about Josef Hoffmann."[1] It is one of the first—if not the very first—article to address Josef Hoffmann's creative output. It is also the only article by Adolf Loos in which Hoffmann's former schoolmate from Brno is inclined to analyze the oeuvre of his contemporary in a positive—if skeptical—light, though he "cannot declare [himself] in any way in agreement" with his furniture. The first anthology of essays written by Loos before 1900, *Ins Leere gesprochen*, was published in German in 1921 by Georges Crès et Cie in Paris because there was no publishing company to be found for it in Austria, as Loos complains in his foreword. He had intentionally excluded the aforementioned short essay about Josef Hoffmann, "Ein Wiener Architekt," from this publication. Yet an overview of international arts journalism proves that Hoffmann was famous far beyond Austria's borders at this time.

The Studio: Fernand Khnopff and Amelia Sarah Levetus

Among the most important periodicals for Modernism—and for Hoffmann's international reputation—was the magazine *The Studio*. Founded and edited by Charles Holme in London from 1893, one of its first reports about Josef Hoffmann and the Wiener Werkstätte was written as early as 1901 by the famous Symbolist painter Fernand Khnopff.[2] In it Khnopff describes the exhibition that Hoffmann designed for the Vienna Secession at the World's Fair in Paris in 1900. Among

other things that impressed him about Hoffmann's works were their "rational" compositions and successful proportions.[3] Khnopff was followed by Amelia Sarah Levetus, an Austro-British art historian, author, and devoted adult educator. In 1891 she moved from England to Vienna, where she taught English and started working as an arts journalist. From 1902 she regularly published long reports about Hoffmann's projects in the Austrian and German media and above all in the London-based art magazine *The Studio*. For example, in 1906 a *Special summer number* was issued that is dedicated to the *Art-Revival in Austria*. In it Levetus documents several works by Hoffmann with numerous illustrations.[4] She reports that it was Hoffmann's main objective to follow in the footsteps of John Ruskin and William Morris and create a base for modern art in Vienna where not only artists but also craftspeople might feel at home. In April 1911 an article by Levetus on the Wiener Werkstätte was printed in *The Studio*,[5] and three years later she published a longer piece on Stoclet House in Brussels.[6]

Early Reception in France and the Netherlands: Maurice Verneuil and Hendricus Theodorus Wijdeveld

Hoffmann's growing significance is also reflected in the increasing number of essays that are not in written in German and not published in the Austrian or German media. Articles about his work were especially valuable for Hoffmann's international reputation when they were written by foreign-language authors. One example is the piece by the French artist and writer Maurice Pillard Verneuil, which was published in the art magazine *Art et Décoration* in 1904.[7] Verneuil's discussion and characterization of Hoffmann's style is extremely sympathetic. The illustrations show interiors in the villas for Dr. Henneberg, Dr. Spitzer, Fritz Waerndorfer, and Max Biach. Moreover, this essay had a considerable impact on the history of Modernism: it was through this article that Le Corbusier became aware of Hoffmann.

One of the first monographic publications on Hoffmann after 1918 with ambitious graphic design standards is the August/September 1920 issue of the Dutch magazine *Wendingen. Maandblad voor Bouwen een Sieren van Archi-*

tectura et Amicitia.[8] Its editor was the Netherlandish architect and graphic designer Hendricus Theodorus Wijdeveld. Every issue is dedicated to a specific topic or personality. The Hoffmann issue contains articles by Max Eisler (in Dutch), Josef Hoffmann (in German), and some of his colleagues (Eduard Leisching, Adolf Vetter, Alfred Roller, Oskar Strnad, Anton Hanak, Rudolf von Larisch; all in German). Hoffmann's own article stemmed from the year 1919 and had already been published in the Austrian magazine *Der Merker* under the title "Wiens Zukunft."[9] This same article was published again in 1923, this time in French, in the Parisian art magazine *L'Amour de l'art* under the title "La Culture Viennoise."[10]

Peter Behrens and the Heroes of Modernism

Josef Hoffmann's friendship with Peter Behrens, the great German "painter architect"[11] and designer, began as early as 1903.[12] Behrens had been visiting Vienna in quest of teachers for the School of Arts and Crafts in Düsseldorf; his contact at the Vienna School of Arts and Crafts was Hoffmann. Then from 1921 to 1936 Behrens himself ran one of the two architecture master classes at the Academy of Fine Arts Vienna. In July 1923 a letter from Behrens was published in the English journal *Architecture, a magazine of architecture and the applied arts and crafts*, in which he discusses various aspects of modern Austrian architecture and briefly delves into Josef Hoffmann's work.[13] This letter is followed in October 1923 by an article written by Behrens that is entirely dedicated to Hoffmann,[14] whom he considers a leading light—not just among Austrian architects but among all the architects of his generation. Exactly one year later the same text by Behrens is published in the *Journal of the American Institute of Architects*.[15]

To celebrate Hoffmann's 60th birthday a solo exhibition was held in the Austrian Museum of Art and Industry in Vienna (today's MAK), accompanied by a commemorative publication edited by the Austrian Werkbund.[16] It compiles dedications and articles by—among many others—personalities from the international Modernist movement, such as Erik Gunnar Asplund (Stockholm), Peter Behrens (Berlin/Vienna), H. P. Berlage (The Hague), Le Corbusier (Paris), Josef Frank (Vienna), Walter Gropius (Berlin), Roberto Papini (Rome), Bruno Paul and Hans Poelzig (Berlin), C. R. Richards (New York), Axel L. Romdahl (Göteborg), Philip Morton Shand (London), Ivar Tengbom (Stockholm)—an impressive panorama of international appreciation.

Paris 1923–1925: Waldemar George

The influential Paris-based art critic and essayist Waldemar George, originally Jerzy Waldemar Jarociński, regularly championed Austrian art. Possibly in anticipation of the Austrian contribution to the *International Exposition of Modern Decorative and Industrial Arts* in 1925, in August 1923 he launched a series of articles about Austrian art in the art magazine *L'Amour de l'art* entitled "Le Mouvement moderne en Autriche" with contributions by Josef Hoffmann, Max Eisler, Josef Frank, and Alfred Roller. Beyond this series of articles, though closely connected to it, there is also a short essay by George about Anton Faistauer.[17] These articles are richly illustrated with works by Hoffmann, Oskar Strnad, Josef Frank, Hugo Gorge, Adolf Loos, Otto Prutscher, Oskar Wlach, Dagobert Peche, Michael Powolny, Julius Zimpel, Susi Singer, Paul Thomas, Hertha Bucher, and Anton Hanak. Josef Hoff-

mann's article had—as mentioned above—already been printed in Vienna in 1919 and in *Wendingen* in 1920 under the title "Over de Toekomst van Weenen."[18]

Le Corbusier and His Circle

Le Corbusier was another figure who repeatedly wrote about Josef Hoffmann and the Wiener Werkstätte in French—though his comments rarely contain substantive statements but rather reflect the younger architect's veneration of his elder. In 1907 he traveled on a study trip to Italy, Budapest, and Vienna with the sculptor Léon Perrin. As early as 1904 he—at that time still known by the name Charles-Édouard Jeanneret-Gris—had read the aforementioned article on Josef Hoffmann by Maruice Pillard Verneuil in the French art magazine *Art et Décoration*, which is what had drawn his attention to the Viennese architect.[19] During his six-month sojourn in Vienna, he visited Hoffmann—who promptly offered the gifted young architect a job at his studio. However, Le Corbusier declined and moved to Paris instead. In the Wiener Werkstätte's 25th anniversary book, which was published in late 1928,[20] there is a short text by him in French and German about the company and its artistic director. A longer text was published in 1930 in the Werkbund's above-mentioned commemorative publication. After Hoffmann's death in May 1956, some of Le Corbusier's memories of the Viennese master were printed in the magazine *Forum*.[21]

Josef Hoffmann also had a significant impact on Le Corbusier's students: In 1973 the Swiss architect Alfred Roth, who had been Le Corbusier's office manager for many years, dedicated a long chapter to him in his famous book *Begegnungen mit Pionieren*.[22] In it he describes an encounter in Hoffmann's apartment on Vienna's Salesianergasse in May 1947. On this occasion Hoffmann had explained why he believed that Le Corbusier had declined to work with him in 1907: "I was obviously not radical enough for him."

Fame in America: Joseph Urban and Shepard Vogelgesang

The architect and designer Shepard Vogelgesang,[23] an employee of the Austro-American architect Joseph Urban in New York, wrote a series of articles about modern architecture in the 1920s and 1930s in the American architecture magazines *Architectural Record* and *Architectural Forum*. Most of these essays are related to works by Joseph Urban or his Austrian and German friends.[24] For example, in November 1928 a representative article was published in *Architectural Forum* entitled "The Work of Josef Hoffman [sic]," which provided his American colleagues with much inspiration for advanced modern design vocabularies.[25]

Italy: Edoardo Persico and Gio Ponti

Among the international authors, the list of Italians who wrote about Josef Hoffmann before and after his death is probably the longest.[26] Only some of the most important can be mentioned here.[27] It is beyond doubt that the influential architecture and art critic Edoardo Persico was particularly significant. Between 1931 and 1935 he published the first substantial reflections on Josef Hoffmann in Italian architectural magazines,[28] as well as some noteworthy critical historical essays.[29] In 2014 Luka Skansi analyzed how Persico's judgment changed within this short period given the political developments in Italy: after his initially euphoric evaluations of Hoffmann's work, Persico's assessment became increasingly critical as the years passed.

A great admirer of Hoffmann was the eminent architect, designer, and publicist Gio Ponti. Together with Gianni Mazzocchi, he founded the famous international art, architecture, and design magazine *Domus* in 1928, which he ran—with a brief hiatus between 1941 and 1947—until he died. Even in its early years *Domus* became the main forum for Razionalismo, the Italian Modernism that abstracted classical elements into geometric basic forms, much as Josef Hoffmann had done in the 1910s. On several occasions Ponti provided space in his magazine for Hoffmann's works. In the September 1935 issue he himself wrote an article about Hoffmann.[30] Ponti finally traveled to Hoffmann's workplace in 1936 when the Italian cultural institute in Vienna commissioned him with redesigning the interior of Palais Lützow at Bösendorfer Straße 13.[31]

Eduard F. Sekler vs. International Style

The great Austro-American architect, art historian, and Harvard professor Eduard Franz Sekler devoted a substantial portion of his published research to Josef Hoffmann. An early international article about him was printed in 1967 in the book *Essays in the History of Architecture Presented to Rudolf Wittkower* under the title "The Stoclet House by Josef Hoffmann."[32] The pinnacle of research into Hoffmann to date was reached in 1982 with Sekler's large monograph. His book summarizes 25 years of research, the results of which are compiled in a catalog of architectural works comprising some 502 entries. In 1985 it was also released in English, in 1986 in French, and in 1991 in Italian.[33]

However, it is conspicuous that three of the most famous Western architectural historians of the 20th century, Sigfried Giedion, Nikolaus Pevsner, and Henry-Russell Hitchcock, only fleetingly touched on Hoffmann's oeuvre. These apologists for the International Style wrote surveys of the history of Modernism that were long considered standard reference works. What they have in common is the major influence of the Bauhaus, Mies van der Rohe, and Le Corbusier. Nevertheless a relatively detailed positioning of Hoffmann's oeuvre in the international context is provided by Hitchcock in his book *Modern Architecture*, in which the International Style is almost the sole representative of modern architecture.[34] For the movement represented by Josef Hoffmann and his work, he coins the term "New Tradition."[35]

This overview of Hoffmann's presence in the international specialist media demonstrates that his role as one of the great pioneers of Modernism was widely recognized from the outset and that his work was discussed in all European countries and in the USA. Only the dogmatic phase of Modernism in the 1930s to 1950s caused his oeuvre to temporarily take a back seat before being rediscovered under Postmodernism. His vitality and prolificacy have been evident ever since.   ∎

1   Loos, Adolf, "Ein Wiener Architekt," in: *Dekorative Kunst. Eine illustrierte Zeitschrift für angewandte Kunst* II 1898 (Munich), 227.
2   Khnopff, Fernand, "Josef Hoffmann – Architect and Decorator," in: *The Studio* (XXII) 98 1901 (London), 261–267.
3   Ibid. 264.
4   Haberfeld, Hugo, "The Architectural Revival in Austria;" Levetus, Amelia Sarah, "Modern Decorative Art in Austria," both in: Holme, Charles (ed.), *The Art-Revival in Austria. The Studio. Special summer number*, London/Paris/New York 1906.
5   Levetus, Amelia Sarah, "The 'Wiener Werkstätte', Vienna," in: *The Studio* (52) 217 1911, 187–196.
6   Levetus, Amelia Sarah, "A Brussels Mansion. Designed by Prof. Josef Hoffmann of Vienna," in: *The Studio* (61) 251 1914, 189 (numerous illustrations of Stoclet House until 197).
7   Verneuil, Maurice Pillard, "Quelques Intérieurs à Vienne par Josef Hoffmann," in: *Art et Décoration. Revue Mensuelle d'art Moderne* (XVI) 7–12 1904 (Paris), 61–70.
8   *Wendingen. Maandblad voor Bouwen een Sieren van Architectura et Amicitia*, special issue on Josef Hoffmann, (3) 8–9 1920 (Amsterdam).
9   Hoffmann, Josef, "Wiens Zukunft," in: *Der Merker. Österreichische Zeitschrift für Musik und Theater* (10) part IV 24 1919 (Vienna), 784–788.
10 Hoffmann, Josef, "La culture viennoise," in: *L'Amour de l'art. L'Architecture, les arts appliqués & l'enseignement professionnel modernes en Autriche* (4) 8 1923 (Paris), 631–632.
11 Peter Behrens had studied painting and not architecture in Karlsruhe and Düsseldorf.
12 Letter from Peter Behrens to Josef Hoffmann from 27 Apr 1903, Eduard Sekler archive, private collection. See Ehmann, Arne, "Wohnarchitektur des mitteleuropäischen Traditionalismus um 1910 in ausgewählten Beispielen," dissertation at the University of Hamburg, Hamburg 2006, n162.
13 Behrens, Peter, "A Letter from Austria," in: *Architecture, a magazine of architecture and the applied arts and crafts* (2) 7 1923 (London), 454–459.
14 Behrens, Peter, "The Work of Josef Hoffmann," in: *Architecture, a magazine of architecture and the applied arts and crafts* (2) 24 1923, 589–599.

15 Behrens, Peter, "The Work of Josef Hoffmann," in: *Journal of the American Institute of Architects* (12) 10 1924 (Washington), 421–426.
16 Österreichischer Werkbund (ed.), *Josef Hoffmann zum 60. Geburtstag. 15. Dezember 1930. Eine Übersicht anlässlich der Ausstellung im Österreichischen Museum in Wien*. Special issue of *Almanach der Dame*, Vienna 1930.
17 *L'Amour de l'art* (see note 10): 631–632 (Hoffmann, Josef, "La culture viennoise"); 633–645 (Eisler, Max, "L'architecture, la décoration intérieure et l'ameublement"); 646–652 (Frank, Josef, "Le Métier d'art"); 653–657 (Roller, Alfred, "L'Ecole des Arts Appliqués"); 658 (George, Waldemar, "Un jeune maître de la peinture autrichienne: Antoine Faistauer").
18 Hoffmann, Josef, in: *Wendingen* 21–26 (see note 8).
19 Verneuil 1904 (see note 7).
20 *Die Wiener Werkstätte. 1903–1928. Modernes Kunstgewerbe und sein Weg*, Vienna 1929.
21 Le Corbusier, "In Memoriam Josef Hoffmann," in: *Forum (Neues Forum). Internationale Zeitschrift für Dialog* (3–4) 30 1956 (Vienna), 237.
22 Roth, Alfred, *Begegnungen mit Pionieren: Le Corbusier, Piet Mondrian, Adolf Loos, Josef Hoffmann, Auguste Perret, Henry van de Velde*, Basel/Stuttgart 1973, 211–216.
23 Shepard Vogelgesang's father Carl Theodore Vogelgesang (1869–1927) was a famous admiral in the United States Navy. The unusual first name Shepard was the family name of his mother Zenaide Shepard.
24 E.g., Vogelgesang, Shepard, "The Reinhard Theatre, New York," in: *Architectural Record* (63) 6 1928 (New York), 461–465; id., "The New School for Social Research," in: *Architectural Record* (65) 4 1930, 305–309; id., "Peter Behrens. Architect and Teacher," in: *Architectural Forum* (LII) 5 1930 (New York), 715–721.
25 Vogelgesang, Shepard, "The Work of Josef Hoffmann," in: *Architectural Forum* (XLIX) 11 1928, part one, 697–712.
26 My heartfelt thanks to Professor Luka Skansi, Venice and Rijeka, for this information. See also: Skansi, Luka, "Hoffmann and Loos in Italy between 1930 and 1970," in: Thun-Hohenstein, Christoph/

Boeckl, Matthias/Witt-Dörring, Christian (eds.), *Ways to Modernism: Josef Hoffmann, Adolf Loos, and Their Impact*, exh. cat. MAK Vienna, Basel 2014, 268–273. Trans. Eva Ciabattoni, Anthony DePasquale, and Maria Slater.
27 Other essays and books that might otherwise have been discussed include those by: Vittoria Girardi, Giulia Veronesi, Maruizio Fagiolo, Daniele Baroni, Antonio D'Auria, Franco Borsi, Alessandra Perizzi, Giuliano Gresleri.
28 Persico, Edoardo, "Il gusto dell'Austria," in: *La Casa Bella* 2 1931 (Milan); id., "La nuova Architettura," in: *La Casa Bella* 5 1931; id., "Architetti a Mosca," in: *La Casa Bella* 9 1932; id., "Fine di un'azienda celebre," in: *La Casa Bella* 10 1932; id., "Errori Stranieri," in: *L'Italia Letteraria*, 28 May 1933 (Milan); id., "Decadenza di Hoffmann," in: *L'Eco del mondo* 23 Mar 1935 (Rome); id., "Trenta anni doppo il Palazzo Stoclet," in: *Casa Bella* 7 1935.
29 Persico, Edoardo, "Punto ed a capo per l'architettura," in: *Domus* 83 1934 (Milan); id., "Profezia dell'architettura," in: *Casa Bella* 2 1936.
30 Ponti, Gio, "Il gusto di Hoffmann," in: *Domus* 93 1935.
31 "Das Italienische Kulturinstitut in Wien," in: *Österreichische Kunst* (VII) 3 1936 (Vienna), 18–19 (numerous illustrations); "Das Italienische Kultur-Institut in Wien," in: *Profil* 3 1936 (Vienna), 104–107 (numerous illustrations).
32 Sekler, Eduard F., "The Stoclet House by Josef Hoffmann," in: Fraser, Douglas/Hibbard, Howard/Lewine, Milton J. (eds.), *Essays in the History of Architecture Presented to Rudolf Wittkower*, London 1967, 228 ff.
33 Sekler, Eduard F., *Josef Hoffmann: The Architectural Work*, Princeton, NJ 1985. Trans. Eduard F. Sekler and John Maass.
34 Hitchcock, Henry-Russell/Johnson, Philip, *The International Style. Architecture since 1922*, New York 1932; Hitchcock, Henry-Russell, *Modern Architecture: Romanticism and Reintegration*, New York 1929.
35 My thanks to Rainald Franz for these valuable suggestions.

Fig. 1 Hans Hollein, installation *Werk und Verhalten, Leben und Tod, alltägliche Situationen*
[Work and Behavior, Life and Death, Everyday Situations], 36th Venice Biennale,
Italy, 1972, raft with chair
Neue Galerie Graz, Universalmuseum Joanneum, loan of the Artothek des Bundes
Photo: Franz Hubmann, © Hollein Private Archive

Matthias Boeckl

The Relevance of the Beautiful

Enduring Resonances of Josef Hoffmann's Oeuvre

Josef Hoffmann's life work is a statement that has endured for more than six decades. His categorical decree: beauty is a human necessity, it thrives best through personal creativity and this becomes manifest ideally in artisanal production methods. He would not alter this fundamental conviction his entire life. It penetrates all of his manifold spatial and surface designs, and his shaping of objects and festivals, images and words. Hoffmann's aesthetic fundamentalism arose from an opposition to the early, totalitarian phase of industrialization and its counterpart in the arts, Historicism. Art reacted to this with Modernism, which Hoffmann's generation forged in the late 19th century. They offered diverse interpretations of industry's fundamental evolutionary challenge to our way of life. Two poles can be identified: on the one hand, the affirmative artistic utilization of profound mechanization and, on the other hand, the *Lebensreform* (life reform) movement, which offered a critique of civilization and sought to balance artistic creation with tradition and modernity. This movement is also an expression of the second major consequence of the Enlightenment: individualization. No artist of the 20th century could reject *all* industrial achievements or pursue *exclusively* technological solutions. Hoffmann, however, was indubitably among the most consistent advocates of an individual, creative further development of tradition and technology (Otto Kapfinger offers an illuminating insight into Hoffman's interpretation of technology in his article in this catalog). Proponents of other lines in the broad spectrum between radical "aesthetic rebellion" and equally radical mechanization of the creation of form, such as Adolf Loos, often denied this "aestheticism" any innovative power.

What influence, what opportunities, did Hoffmann's position have in the development of modern art? Here, a distinction must be made between the levels of form and system. Dissemination of a personal handwriting is, in principle, a paradox: as soon as an individual means of expression is used by anyone other than its inventor, it loses its individual character. It becomes a "style," which is stripped of its original cultural context and as mere form can no longer comprehensively define culture. However, individualization is not accomplished solely at the formal level, but rather, mainly as a system. When one views Modernism's systematic striving for individualization, it is possible to detect numerous remote effects of Hoffmann's design strategies that are able to claim major relevance today. In this interpretation, forms are always the results of a typical, basic approach of individual aesthetics. These can be observed, among others, at ten sites that will be described below—arranged along Hoffmann's chronology of works.

The Freed Form

Hoffmann's generation enjoyed the privilege of executing, as pioneers, a cultural transformation that had long been felt: namely, showing for the first time, the necessity and possibility of their own era's authentic form of expression after 60 years of the arts' industrially-induced insecurity and their normative attempts at compensation through the

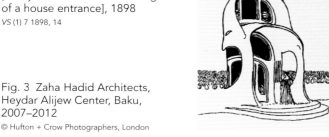

Fig. 2 JH, *Studie zur decorativen Ausgestaltung eines Hauseingangs* [Study for the decorative design of a house entrance], 1898
VS (1) 7 1898, 14

Fig. 3 Zaha Hadid Architects, Heydar Alijew Center, Baku, 2007–2012
© Hufton + Crow Photographers, London

revitalization of past cultures. Complete liberation from all formal systems and rules: the free form as expression of the free individual was born as maximum opposition to the strictly normed forms of the Revival Styles still dominant in the late 19th century. The initial euphoric eruptions were effusive: Hoffmann's organoid, curved fantastical building designs from 1898 set the standard for bold anti-mainstream architecture, the impact of which is still felt today. This is demonstrated, for example, by Zaha Hadid's curvilinear bio-morphism, shown quintessentially in her Heydar Aliyev Center in Baku (2007–2012).

2 3

aret Fledermaus (1907), and kinetic polychromes of elementary forms (Sauerbruch Hutton, installation *Oxymoron*, 2018) are consequences of this discovery that extend until the present day.

4 5

Fig. 6 JH, Sanatorium Westend, Purkersdorf, 1904, entrance hall with furniture by Koloman Moser
MAK, WWF 102-86-1

Fig. 4 JH, Cabaret Fledermaus, Vienna, 1907, Wiener Werkstätte postcard
MAK, KI 13748-4

Fig. 5 Sauerbruch Hutton, *Oxymoron*, installation at the 16th Venice Architecture Biennale, 2018
© Jan Bitter

Fig. 7 Hans Hollein, installation *Werk und Verhalten, Leben und Tod, alltägliche Situationen* [Work and Behavior, Life and Death, Everyday Situations], 36th Venice Biennale, 1972, room with ordinary objects
Photo: Franz Hubmann,
© Hollein Private Archive

Unity of the Arts

Along with the historicizing form, the young art rebels of 1900 also experienced the arts' possessive specialization as a strait jacket stifling individual creativity. Forms and technologies were restricted to their genres; an architect could not build sculptural forms, a sculptor could not create tectonically minimal figures, and a painter could not make three-dimensional forms, etc. Therefore, a large part of the art revolution comprised restoring a unity of the arts that had been self-evident in preindustrial times. Reinterpreting every design commission through forms and structures from other genres was, for example, still self-evident for Michelangelo. Elementary geometry was the perfect vehicle for the assertion of this lost unity of the arts in the modern era, as it was the easiest to apply in all media—realized exemplarily in the Purkersdorf Sanatorium. Postmodernism recalled this idea—Hans Hollein, for example, ran the gamut of the square motif in surface, furniture, and spatial designs in an installation in Venice in 1972.

1 6 7

Basic Pattern

The second step following the curvilinear effusions in Hoffmann's and his allies' modern form revolution was the discovery of elementary geometry—and not only as a strikingly "different" design strategy in the sense of a distinction from mainstream art at the time, but also as a perfectly efficient generator of form, far superior in its simple mechanics than any complexly historicizing attempt at individualization. A precursor to digitalization and genetic engineering: endless construction of identities from the clear assembly kit of square and rectangle, circle and triangle, dot and line, surface and cube. The only difference from industrial generation of form is that these patterns arise in the artists' imagination and are produced by hand. Static applications, such as Cab-

Aestheticism

Hoffmann's ideal of beauty led, among other things, to a total immersion in radically aestheticized environments. All spaces of the house of the art connoisseur and client Sonja Knips are precious art "cabinets," which can entirely absorb

8

Fig. 8 JH, Sonja Knips's house, Nußwaldgasse 22, Vienna, 1924–1925, lady's salon with Gustav Klimt's *Adam and Eve*, 1917 (Belvedere, Vienna)
MBF (25) 1926, 353

Fig. 9 Sagmeister & Walsh, *Beauty* exhibition, MAK, Vienna, 2018, color room
© MAK/Aslan Kurdnofsky

inhabitants and visitors. This concept has since been realized in countless other artists' spaces. For example, the Austro-American designers Sagmeister & Walsh traced the effects of a potential comprehensive aestheticizing of the lived environment in their exhibition *Beauty*, presented by the MAK in Vienna in 2018.

"Eigenart": Crafted Identities

The comprehensive individualization process beginning with the Enlightenment led to the necessity of demarcating every individual and every social group from all others. The artists of Josef Hoffmann's generation were the first that were able to fulfill this new imperative for individual distinction in grand style with entirely new forms, which provided clients with an aesthetically sophisticated "ready-made identity." The ideal of the Gesamtkunstwerk—or total work of art—also had its impact here, subjecting the total design of the environment, from house and garden through to the skin of the human body to a uniform, fictitious aesthetic ideal leading to the emergence of "artificial" identities handmade by designers. This was displayed by a fancy-dress ball, for example, in Hoffmann's Primavesi country house, where the family of the owners and several artists wore fantasy costumes of the same origins as the identity-generating ornamental language of the interiors. The "Conchita Wurst style" of today, among others, demonstrates the construction of a customized, yet likewise exchangeable artist identity that has been available since.

Multiplication and Variation

In the invention of geometrical design strategies, also an analogy to mechanical processes became evident, which Hoffmann and his contemporaries were perhaps not aware of. In hand-drawn designs, they varied their squares and triangles, lines and surfaces, based on their own inspiration.

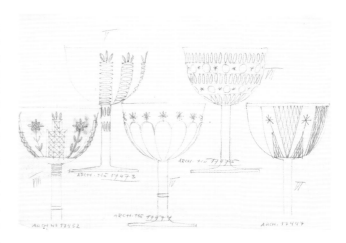

Fig. 12 JH, glass set: two glass goblets/decorative glasses; *Service 200-Dekor 4: "Porterkelch"* [Set 200-Decoration 4: "Porter Goblet"]; *Service 200-Dekor 3: "Porterkelch"*; *Service 200-Dekor 1: "Porterkelch"*; designs for the Wiener Werkstätte, before 1923
MAK, KI 11923-9

Fig. 10 "Schweindlfest" (little pig party) in the basement lounge at the Primavesi country house in Winkelsdorf/Kouty nad Desnou, 1916
MAK, WWF 137-1-6

Fig. 11 Conchita Wurst, *Black is Back*, 2013
Photo (left): © Thomas Ramstorfer/picturedesk.com
Photo (right): © Milenko Badzic/picturedesk.com

Despite the neutral basic geometric forms, this combination of individual creativity with manual processes yielded a clearly recognizable "handwriting." Can these individual influences on the creation of form be grasped in algorithms today? Can artificial intelligence learn how Hoffmann designed, and as a digital assistant, make appropriate suggestions to today's designers? Can the learning of history, in general, be delegated to machine intelligence and be called up on demand? The young architect Ben James, for example, pursues this question in his digital investigation of Hoffmann's working methods.

Fig. 13 JH, Austrian pavilion,
International Fine Arts Exhibition, Rome, 1911
MAK, WWF 105-258-1

Fig. 14 David Chipperfield Architects, James-Simon-Galerie, Museumsinsel, Berlin 1999–2018
© Ute Zscharnt for David Chipperfield Architects

Classical

After the "handling" of historicizing forms through his curvilinear and elementary-geometry design strategies, beginning in 1910, Hoffmann dared encounter the highest historical authority: the classical style. The classical era had already been reinterpreted in the Renaissance of the 16th century and in Classicism around 1800, and was also broadly implemented as a new standard for the aesthetic organization of a suddenly seemingly chaotic present. Was it also Hoffmann's intention to put order to a "chaotic art present" that he had participated in sparking with his own inventions ten years earlier? Or, in being faithful to his radical, creative individualism, did he now see even the hitherto sacrosanct classical architecture, like every other traditional architecture, as a mere "storehouse of motifs" with forms that after ele-

mentary-geometrical "cleansing" were thoroughly "useful" for certain purposes? Typical of Hoffmann's ambiguity, this question cannot be answered. And even today, classical forms can seem entirely modern, as the British architect David Chipperfield proves in prominent cultural buildings.

Atectonics: Removing Structures' Boundaries

A further central component of the modern art revolution was the (symbolic) dissolution of all spatial limitations. Behind this was the idea of a removal of gravity and the vision of a gravity-free floating through an endless space of free forms. Wassily Kandinsky realized this vision of Modernism in painting; Friedrich Kiesler, among others, worked on it in architecture in his *Raumstadt* [City in Space] from 1925. Through the use of elementary-geometric and organic patterns, in applying the ideal of the unity of the arts, Hoffmann discovered the necessity of the dissolution of spatial boundaries in the form of the usual tectonics of columns and beams, floor, wall, and ceiling. The new forms flooded all of these boundaries and shaped a new, atectonic space. The artist Peter Kogler also uses this realization in installations with serial forms that create autonomous art spaces.

Fig. 15 JH, Bauer apartment, Vienna, 1927
DKuD 1927–1928, 445

Fig. 16 Peter Kogler, exhibition installation at the ING Art Center, Brussels, 2016
© Vincent Everarts photography, Brussels

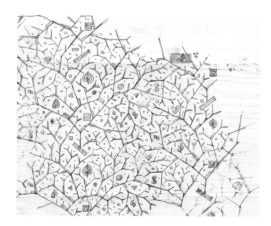 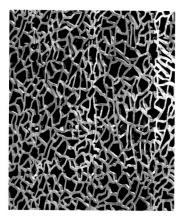

Fig. 17 JH, fabric design *Bremen*
for the Wiener Werkstätte, before 1928
MAK, KI 11869-1

Fig. 18 Rudy Ricciotti, Musée des
Civilisations de l'Europe et de la
Méditerranée (MuCEM), Marseilles,
façade detail
© Edmund Sumner, London

Organic Tissue

In the 1920s, Hoffmann became interested in naturally ac-
17 cruing patterns. The branches of a tree, for example, present
a classical example of a self-organized, constantly differentiating biological growth process. Whereas in nature one
rarely encounters explicitly geometrical structures (such as
hexagonal basalt columns), organic "patterns" are omnipresent. They form tissues, texture, and webs that work well
as surface patterns, but also as transparent shells for build-
18 ings, for example, as demonstrated by Rudy Ricciotti with
the fascinating filigree skin of the Musée des Civilisations
de l'Europe et de la Méditerranée opened in Marseille in
2013.

Cultural Nation

Josef Hoffmann was one of the main bearers of the still effective idea of Austria as a "cultural nation." The idea arose
as a reaction to the loss of nearly 80 percent of the country's
former territory, population, and industrial resources due
to the collapse of the monarchy at the end of World War I,
and the Treaty of Versailles of 1919. The small, Central European republic was thus forced to exalt potentials other than
economic or military ones as its core national expertise in
the international dialogue crucial to its survival. In this way,
the traditional art forms of the Habsburg court, nobility,
clerics, and bourgeoisie were elevated to Austria's trademark; substantial effort went into their official presentation
at numerous international events. Almost all of these, such
as the first international World's Fair after World War I in
Paris in 1925, were designed by Josef Hoffmann, who was
thus able to guarantee that also Modernism had a place in
19 the concept of Austria as a "cultural nation." This Austrian
tradition of artistically ambitious representational structures
continues today, for example, with Raimund Abraham's sen-
20 sational Austrian Cultural Forum in New York (1998–2002),
which stands out impressively within the surroundings of
standard high-rise buildings and has since advanced to become an art landmark.   ▪

Fig. 19 JH, Austrian pavilion at the
*International Exposition of Modern
Decorative and Industrial Arts*, Paris, 1925
MAK, KI 10147-146-1

Fig. 20 Raimund Abraham, Austrian
Cultural Forum, New York, 1998–2000
© david plakke media nyc 2009

Yoichi R. Okamoto, Josef Hoffmann, 1954
MAK, KI 13740-5

(Select) Bibliography

Books and Catalogs

Kleiner, Leopold, *Josef Hoffmann*, Berlin 1927

Weiser, Armand, *Josef Hoffmann*, Geneva 1930

Rochowanski, Leopold Wolfgang, *Josef Hoffmann. Eine Studie, geschrieben zu seinem 80. Geburtstag*, Vienna 1951

Josef Hoffmann: Drawings and Objects from Conception to Design, exh. cat. Goldie Paley Gallery, Philadelphia 1980

Baroni, Daniele/D'Auria, Antonio, *Josef Hoffmann e la Wiener Werkstätte*, Milan 1981

Sekler, Eduard F., *Josef Hoffmann: The Architectural Work*, Princeton, NJ 1985. Trans. Eduard F. Sekler and John Maass

Perizzi, Alessandra, *Josef Hoffmann tempo e geometria*, Rome 1982

Josef Hoffmann – Wien. Jugendstil und Zwanziger Jahre, exh. cat. Museum Bellerive, Zurich 1983

Lane, Terence, *Vienna 1913: Josef Hoffmann's Gallia Apartment*, exh. cat. National Gallery of Victoria, Melbourne 1984

Hollein, Hans (ed.), *The 50th Anniversary of Josef Hoffmann's Austrian Pavilion at the Biennale of Venice*, exh. cat. Biennale di Venezia, Salzburg/Vienna 1984

Amanshauser, Hildegund, *Josef Hoffmann Variationen*, inventory cat. Museum of the Twentieth Century, Vienna 1987

Noever, Peter/Oberhuber, Oswald (eds.), *Josef Hoffmann. Ornament zwischen Hoffnung und Verbrechen*, Vienna 1987

Vandenbreeden, Jos, *The Stoclet House*, Brussels 1988

Muntoni, Alessandra, *Il Palazzo Stoclet di Josef Hoffmann, 1905–1911*, Rome 1989

Kurrent, Friedrich/Strobl, Alice, *Das Palais Stoclet in Brüssel von Josef Hoffmann*, Salzburg 1991

Noever, Peter (ed.), *The Baroque Hoffmann: Josef Hoffmann in His Birthplace in Moravia*, exh. cat. Hoffmann House, Brtnice 1992

Noever, Peter (ed.), *Josef Hoffmann Designs*, Vienna/Munich 1992

Takyo, Shito (ed.), *Josef Hoffmann und die Wiener Werkstätte*, exh. cat. Toyota Municipal Museum of Art, Toyota 1996

Denk, Wolfgang (ed), *Josef Hoffmann und neues internationales Möbeldesign aus Österreich*, Prague 1998

Josef Hoffmann and His Native House in Brtnice, exh. cat. Spole nost Josefa Hoffmanna, Brtnice 1998

Riess, Felicia, *Ambivalenzen einer Eigenart: Josef Hoffmanns Ausstellungsbauten als Entwurf einer modernen Formensprache für Österreich*, Weimar 2000

Kristan, Markus, *Josef Hoffmann. Bauten und Interieurs*, Vienna 2002

Spalt, Johannes, *Josef Hoffmann. Porträts – Signets – Stempel*, Vienna 2002

Kristan, Markus, *Josef Hoffmann. Villenkolonie Hohe Warte*, Vienna 2004

Topp, Leslie, *Architecture and Truth in Fin-de-Siècle Vienna*, Cambridge 2004

Freytag, Anette, *"Jardin du Palais Stoclet créé par Josef Hoffmann et la Wiener Werkstätte, 1905–1911."* Etude historique pour la Direction des Monuments et Sites, Brussels 2004

Witt-Dörring, Christian (ed.), *Josef Hoffmann: Interiors 1902–1913*, exh. cat. Neue Galerie, Munich et. al 2006

Zednicek, Walter, *Josef Hoffmann und die Wiener Werkstätte*, Vienna 2006

Sarnitz, August, *Josef Hoffmann. Im Universum der Schönheit*, Cologne 2007

Noever, Peter/Pokorný, Marek (eds.), *Josef Hoffmann. Selbstbiographie/Autobiography*, Ostfildern 2009. Trans. Bernd Magar and Andrew Oakland

Witt-Dörring, Christian, *Josef Hoffmann: Interiors 1902–1913. The Making of an Exhibition*, New York 2008

Thun-Hohenstein, Christoph/Boeckl, Matthias/Witt-Dörring, Christian (eds.), *Ways to Modernism: Josef Hoffmann, Adolf Loos, and Their Impact*, exh. cat. MAK, Basel 2015. Trans. Eva Ciabattoni, Anthony DePasquale, and Maria Slater

Thun-Hohenstein, Christoph/Witt-Dörring, Christian/Schmuttermeier, Elisabeth (eds.), *Koloman Moser: Universal Artist between Gustav Klimt and Josef Hoffmann*, Basel 2019. Trans. Maria Slater

Witt-Dörring, Christian/Staggs, Janis (eds.), *Wiener Werkstätte 1903–1932: The Luxury of Beauty*, exh. cat. Neue Galerie, Munich/London/New York 2017

Book and Magazine Articles

Loos, Adolf, "Unsere jungen Architekten," in: *Ver Sacrum* (I) 7 1898, [21–23]

Loos, Adolf, "Ein Wiener Architekt," in: *Dekorative Kunst* (II) 1898, 227

Zuckerkandl, Berta, "Josef Hoffmann," in: *Dekorative Kunst* (VII) 1903, 1–15

Hevesi, Ludwig, "Neubauten von Josef Hoffmann," in: *Altkunst – Neukunst Wien 1894–1908*, Vienna 1909, 214–221

Hevesi, Ludwig, "Haus Wärndorfer," in: *Altkunst – Neukunst Wien 1894–1908*, Vienna 1909, 221–227

Hevesi, Ludwig, "Kabarett Fledermaus," in: *Altkunst – Neukunst Wien 1894–1908*, Vienna 1909, 240–245

Ascherman, Edward H., "Some Foreign Styles in Decoration and Furniture," in: *House and Garden* (24) 1913, 32–34, 56

Mallet-Stevens, Robert, "Le Palais Stoclet à Bruxelles," in: *L'Architecte* 1 1924, 21ff.

Hoffmann, Josef, "Austrian Contribution to Modern Art," in: *An International Exposition of Art in Industry*, exh. cat. Macy's, New York 1928, 8–9

Ankwicz-Kleehoven, Hans, "Josef Hoffmann," in: *Große Österreicher. Neue Österreichische Biographie ab 1815*, vol. 10, Vienna/Zurich/Leipzig 1957, 171–179

Marlier, Georges, "La première maison totalement nouvelle du XXe siècle," in: *Connaissance des Arts* (140) 10 1963, 50 ff.

Windisch-Graetz, Franz, "Das Jagdhaus Hochreith," in: *Alte und moderne Kunst* (92) 1967, 30 ff.

Hollein, Hans, "Haus Wiener (Wertheim), USA, ca. 1928. Josef Hoffmann," in: *Bau* (XXV) 1 1970, 22–27

Schachel, Roland L., "Zum 100. Geburtstag von Adolf Loos und Josef Hoffmann," in: *Steine sprechen* 31/32 1970, 2–10

Becherer, R., "Monumentality and the Rue Mallet-Stevens," in: *Journal of the Society of Architectural Historians* (40) 1 1981, 44–55

Bogner, Dieter, "Die geometrischen Reliefs von Josef Hoffmann," in: *Alte und moderne Kunst* 184/185 1982, 24 ff.

Sármány, Ilona, "A Bécsi Szecesszió Budapesti Emléke, a Pikler-Villa," in: *Ars Hungarica* (X) 2 1982, 289–296

Marchetti, Maria, "Josef Hoffmann. Ein Künstler zwischen Vergangenheit und Zukunft," in: *Wien um 1900. Kunst und Kultur*, Vienna/Munich 1984, 323–328

Gorsen, Peter, "Josef Hoffmann. Zur Modernität eines konservativen Baumeisters," in: Alfred Pfabigan (ed.), *Ornament und Askese. Im Zeitgeist des Wien der Jahrhundertwende*, Vienna 1985, 69–92

Prossinger, Cynthia, "Josef Hoffmanns Ateliereinrichtung für Ernst Stöhr," in: *Alte und moderne Kunst* 201/202 1985, 24–29

Breckner, Gunter, "Rettet das Sanatorium Purkersdorf," in: *Steine sprechen* (XXIV/1) 79 1985, 20–38

Kamm-Kyburz, Christine, "Tendenzen im Ornament Josef Hoffmanns," in: *Grenzbereiche der Architektur, Festschrift Adolf Reinle*, Basel 1985, 115–123

Moeller, G., "Peter Behrens und das Junge Wien," in: *Wien und die Architektur des 20. Jahrhunderts. Akten des XXV. Internationalen Kunsthistoriker Kongresses Wien 1983*, Vienna 1986, 77 ff.

Sármány, Ilona, "Zum Einfluss der Wiener Architektur in Ungarn um die Jahrhundertwende," in: *Wien und die Architektur des 20. Jahrhunderts. Akten des XXV. Internationalen Kunsthistoriker Kongresses Wien 1983*, Vienna 1986, 26 ff.

Hébert-Stevens, François, "La théorie architecturale de Mallet-Stevens," in: *Rob Mallet-Stevens*, Paris 1986

Braumann, A., "Vienne – Bruxelles, fragments de la modernité," in: *Vienne – Bruxelles, la fortune du Palais Stoclet*, Brussels 1987, 9–27

Witt-Dörring, Christian, "Bent-wood production and the Viennese avant-garde: The Thonet and Khon firms 1899–1914," in: Ostergard, Derek E. (ed.), *Bent Wood and Metal Furniture: 1850–1946*, New York 1987

Sekler, Eduard F., "Josef Hoffmann: Architekt als Entwerfer des Gesamtkunstwerks," in: *Wien um 1900. Klimt, Schiele und ihre Zeit*, exh. cat. Sezon Museum of Art, Tokyo 1989, 224–242

Schwarz, Mario, "Außenrestaurierung des Sanatoriums Purkersdorf vollendet," in: *Steine sprechen* 104 1996, 3–5

Topp, Leslie, "An Architecture for Modern Nerves: Josef Hoffmann's Purkersdorf Sanatorium," in: *Journal of the Society of Architectural Historians* (56) 4 1997, 414–437

Topp, Leslie, "Josef Hoffmann," in: *New Worlds: German and Austrian Art 1890–1940*, exh. cat. Neue Galerie, New York 2001, 480–486

Witt-Dörring, Christian, "Wenn Inhalte zu Informationen werden. Ein Brief Fritz Wärndorfers an Eduard Wimmer-Wisgrill," in: Förster, Wolfgang/Natter, Tobias G./Rieder, Ines (eds.), *Der Andere Blick*, Vienna 2001, 63–70

Franz, Rainald, "Eine kulturgrädige Wohnstätte patrizierhafter Leute. Josef Hoffmanns Beziehungen zu seinem Geburtshaus und die Wirkung der Herkunft auf sein Werk," in: *CD Sammelband der Beiträge des Symposions zum 10. Gründungsjubiläum der Josef-Hoffmann-Gesellschaft*, Brtnice 2002, 24–30

Asenbaum, Paul/Ploil, Ernst, "Die Ausstellungsräume der Wiener Werkstätte," in: *100 Jahre Wiener Werkstätte*, auction cat., Im Kinsky Wiener Kunstauktionen, Vienna 2003, 26–31

Franz, Rainald, "Die Restaurierung des Geburtshauses Josef Hoffmanns in Brtnice/Pirnitz, Tschechien," in: *Österreichische Zeitschrift für Kunst und Denkmalpflege* (LVIII) 2004, 116–132

Volpi, Christiana, "Formation, Influences et Premiers Travaux," in: *Robert Mallet-Stevens: L'œuvre complète*, exh. cat. Centre Pompidou, Paris 2005, 18–21

Witt-Dörring, Christian, "On the Path to Modernism: The Ambiguity of Space and Plane," in: Witt-Dörring, Christian (ed.), *Josef Hoffmann: Interiors 1902–1913*, Munich et. al 2006, 24–69

Huey, Michael, "Art Itself: The Private Lives of Josef Hoffmann," in: Witt-Dörring, Christian (ed.), *Josef Hoffmann: Interiors 1902–1913*, Munich et. al 2006, 74–97

Huey, Michael, "Hoffmann at Home," in: *The World of Interiors* 11 2006, 156–163

Franz, Rainald, "Modern Tradition: Otto Wagner, Josef Hoffmann and the Legacy of Classical Architecture," in: *Centropa: A journal of central European architecture and related arts* (6) 1 2006, 8–14

Clegg, Elisabeth, "War and peace at the Stockholm 'Austrian Art Exhibition' of 1917," in: *The Burlington Magazine* (154) 1315 (Oct) 2012, 676–688

Witt-Dörring, Christian, "The Aesthetics of Biedermeier Furniture," in: Winters, Laurie (ed.), *Biedermeier: The Invention of Simplicity*, exh. cat. Milwaukee Art Museum, Ostfildern 2006

Freytag, Anette, "Der Garten des Palais Stoclet in Brüssel. Josef Hoffmanns 'chef d'œuvre inconnu,'" in: *Die Gartenkunst* (20) 1 2008, 1–46

Franz, Rainald, "La Viennesità evidente: immagini da un'architettura mitteleuropea. Hoffmann e Vienna nell'opera di Scarpa," in: Tegethoff, Wolf (ed.), *Carlo Scarpa: struttura e forme* (= Studi su Carlo Scarpa 6), Venezia 2008, 99–113

Franz, Rainald, "Die 'disziplinierte Folklore.' Josef Hoffmann und die Villa für Otto Primavesi in Winkelsdorf," in: Aigner, Anita (ed.), *Vernakulare Moderne. Grenzüberschreitungen in der Architektur um 1900. Das Bauernhaus und seine Aneignung*, Bielefeld 2010, 161–177

Franz, Rainald, "The Austrian Pavilion at the Venice Biennale: 1893–2013," in: Sharp, Jasper (ed.), *Austria and the Venice Biennale 1895–2013*, Nuremberg 2013, 87–100

Overviews

Lux, Joseph August, *Die moderne Wohnung und ihre Ausstattung*, Vienna/Leipzig 1905

Zuckerkandl, Berta, *Zeitkunst. Wien 1901–1907*, Vienna 1908

Rochowanski, Leopold Wolfgang, *Ein Führer durch das Österreichische Kunstgewerbe*, Vienna 1930

Uhl, Ottokar: *Moderne Architektur in Wien von Otto Wagner bis heute*, Vienna 1966

Mrazek, Wilhelm, *Die Wiener Werkstätte: modernes Kunsthandwerk von 1903–1932*, Vienna 1967

Hoffmann, Werner, *Gustav Klimt und die Wiener Jahrhundertwende*, Salzburg 1970

Holzbauer, Wilhelm/Kurrent, Friedrich/Spalt, Johannes, *L'Architettura a Vienna intorno al 1900*, exh. cat. Galleria Nazionale d'Arte Moderna, Rome 1971

Johnston, William M., *The Austrian Mind: An Intellectual and Social History 1848–1938*, Berkeley 1972

Vergo, Peter, *Art in Vienna 1898–1918*, London 1975

Schorske, Carl, *Fin-de-Siècle Vienna: Politics and Culture*, New York 1979

Adlman, Jan Ernst, *Vienna Moderne: 1898–1918*, exh. cat. Cooper-Hewitt Museum, New York 1979

Asenbaum, Paul and Stefan/Witt-Dörring, Christian, *Moderne Vergangenheit 1800–1900*, exh. cat. Gesellschaft bildender Künstler Österreichs, Künstlerhaus, Vienna 1981

Behal, Vera J., *Sammlung des Österreichischen Museums für angewandte Kunst in Wien*, Munich 1981

Rukschcio, Burkhardt/Schachel, Roland, *Adolf Loos. Leben und Werk*, Salzburg/Vienna 1982

Schweiger, Werner J., *Wiener Werkstätte. Kunst und Handwerk 1903–1932*, Vienna 1982

Vergo, Peter, *Vienna 1900: Vienna, Scotland and the European Avant-Garde*, exh. cat. National Museum of Antiquities of Scotland, Edinburgh 1983

Nebehay, Christian, *Die Sessel meines Vaters*, Vienna 1983

Moravánszky, Ákos, *Die Architektur der Jahrhundertwende in Ungarn und ihre Beziehungen zu der Wiener Architektur der Zeit*, Vienna 1983

Völker, Angela, *Wiener Mode + Modefotografie. Die Modeabteilung der Wiener Werkstätte 1911–1932*, Munich/Paris 1984

Traum und Wirklichkeit – Wien 1870–1930, exh. cat. Historisches Museum der Stadt Wien, Vienna 1985

Krischanitz, Adolf/Kapfinger, Otto, *Die Wiener Werkbundsiedlung. Dokumentation einer Erneuerung*, Vienna 1985

Fliedl, Gottfried, *Kunst und Lehre am Beginn der Moderne. Die Wiener Kunstgewerbeschule 1867–1918*, Salzburg/Vienna 1986

Varnedoe, Kirk, *Vienna 1900: Art, Architecture & Design*, exh. cat. The Museum of Modern Art, New York 1986

Kallir, Jane, *Viennese Design and the Wiener Werkstätte*, exh. cat. Galerie St. Etienne, New York 1986

Clair, Jean, *Vienne 1880–1938: L'Apocalypse Joyeuse*, exh. cat. Centre Pompidou, Paris 1986

Day, Susan, *Louis Süe: Architectures*, Brussels 1986

Fischer, Wolfgang Georg, *Gustav Klimt und Emilie Flöge. Genie und Talent, Freundschaft und Besessenheit*, Vienna 1987

Oberhuber, Oswald (ed.), *Dagobert Peche 1887–1923*, Vienna 1987

Langseth-Christensen, Lillian, *A Design for Living: Vienna in the Twenties*, New York 1987

Wagner, Otto, *Modern Architecture: A Guidebook for His Students to This Field of Art*, Santa Monica 1988. Trans. H.F. Mulgrave

Moravánszky, Ákos, *Die Erneuerung der Baukunst. Wege zur Moderne in Mitteleuropa 1900–1940*, Salzburg/Vienna 1988

Wien um 1900. Klimt, Schiele und ihre Zeit, exh. cat. Sezon Museum of Art, Tokyo 1989

Völker, Angela, *Die Stoffe der Wiener Werkstätte 1910–1932*, Vienna 1990

Brix, Emil/Werkner, Patrick, *Die Wiener Moderne: Ergebnisse eines Forschungsgespräches der Arbeitsgemeinschaft Wien um 1900 zum Thema "Aktualität und Moderne,"* Vienna 1990

Achleitner, Friedrich, *Österreichische Architektur im 20. Jahrhundert. Wien 1.–12. Bezirk*, vol. III/1, Salzburg/Vienna 1990

Frottier, Elisabeth, *Michael Powolny. Keramik und Glas aus Wien 1900 bis 1950*, Vienna/Cologne 1990

Forsthuber, Sabine, *Moderne Raumkunst. Wiener Ausstellungsbauten von 1898 bis 1914*, Vienna 1991

Erika Patka (ed.), *Kunst: Anspruch und Gegenstand. Von der Kunstgewerbeschule zur Hochschule für angewandte Kunst in Wien 1918–1991*, Salzburg/Vienna 1991

Viena 1900, exh. cat. Museo Nacional Centro de Arte Reina Sofia, Madrid 1993

Natter, Tobias G. (ed.), *Broncia Koller-Pinell. Eine Malerin im Glanz der Wiener Jahrhundertwende*, exh. cat. Jüdisches Museum der Stadt Wien, Vienna 1993

Arnold, Klaus-Peter, *Vom Sofakissen zum Städtebau. Die Geschichte der Deutschen Werkstätten und der Gartenstadt Hellerau*, Dresden/Basel 1993

Festi, Roberto, *Josef Zotti 1882–1953. Architekt und Designer*, Rome 1993

Alofsin, Anthony, *Frank Lloyd Wright: The Lost Years, 1910–1922: A Study of Influence*, Chicago 1993

Achleitner, Friedrich, *Österreichische Architektur im 20. Jahrhundert. Wien 13.–18. Bezirk*, vol. III/2, Salzburg/Vienna 1995

Boeckl, Matthias (ed.), *Visionäre & Vertriebene. Österreichische Spuren in der modernen amerikanischen Architektur*, Berlin 1995

Wagner, Manfred, *Alfred Roller in seiner Zeit*, Salzburg/Vienna 1996

Becker, Edwin/Grabner, Sabine, *Wien 1900. Der Blick nach Innen*, exh. cat. Van Gogh Museum, Amsterdam 1997

Das Schöne und der Alltag – Deutsches Museum für Kunst in Handel und Gewerbe 1909–1919, exh. cat. Kaiser Wilhelm Museum Krefeld and Karl Ernst Osthaus-Museum der Stadt Hagen, Gent 1997

Kapfinger, Otto/Louis, Eleonora (eds.), *Secession. Permanenz einer Idee*, Ostfildern-Ruit 1997

Patka, Erika (ed.), *Otto Prutscher 1880–1949*, exh. cat. Hochschule für angewandte Kunst, Vienna 1997

Bisanz-Prakken, Marian, *Heiliger Frühling. Gustav Klimt und die Anfänge der Wiener Secession 1895–1905*, Vienna/Munich 1999

Blau, Eve/Platzer, Monika, *Shaping the Great City: Modern Architecture in Central Europe 1890–1937*, Munich/London/New York 1999

Das ungebaute Wien. Projekte für die Metropole 1800–2000, exh. cat. Historisches Museum der Stadt Wien, Vienna 1999

Blau, Eve, *The Architecture of Red Vienna 1919–1934*, Cambridge, MA/London 1999

Fleck, Robert (ed.), *Secession: das Jahrhundert der künstlerischen Freiheit*, Munich 1998

Natter, Tobias G./Frodl, Gerbert (eds.), *Klimt und die Frauen*, Cologne 2000

Stiller, Adolph, *Oswald Haerdtl. Architekt und Designer 1899–1959*, Vienna 2000

Noever, Peter (ed.), *Ein moderner Nachmittag. Margaret Macdonald Mackintosh und der Salon Waerndorfer in Wien*, Vienna/Cologne/Weimar 2000

Patka, Erika (ed.), *Bertold Löffler. Vagant zwischen Secessionismus und Neobiedermeier*, Vienna 2000

Kristan, Markus, *Joseph Urban. Die Wiener Jahre des Jugendstilarchitekten und Illustrators 1872–1911*, Vienna/Cologne/Weimar 2000

Wien. Leben und Kunst 1873–1938, exh. cat. Fuchu Art Museum, Tokyo 2001

Brüderlin, Markus (ed.), *Ornament und Abstraktion. Kunst der Kulturen, Moderne und Gegenwart im Dialog*, exh. cat. Fondation Beyeler Basel, Ostfildern 2001

Price, Renée (ed.), *New Worlds: German and Austrian Art 1890–1940*, exh. cat. Neue Galerie, New York 2001

Noever, Peter (ed.), *Dagobert Peche and the Wiener Werkstätte*, New Haven/London 2002

Noever, Peter (ed.), *Der Preis der Schönheit. 100 Jahre Wiener Werkstätte*, Ostfildern-Ruit 2003

Huey, Michael (ed.), *Viennese Silver: Modern Design 1780–1918*, Ostfildern-Ruit 2003

Ambros, Miroslav (ed.), *Wiener Secession – die angewandte Kunst in Mähren, Schlesien und Böhmen in den Jahren 1900–1925*, Brno 2003

Neiß, Herta, *100 Jahre Wiener Werkstätte. Mythos und ökonomische Realität*, Vienna/Cologne/Weimar 2004

Klein-Primavesi, Claudia, *Die Familie Primavesi und die Künstler Hanak, Hoffmann, Klimt. 100 Jahre Wiener Werkstätte*, Vienna 2004

Klein-Primavesi, Claudia, *Die Familie Primavesi und die Künstler der Wiener Werkstätte, das Ende einer Ära*, Vienna 2005

Klein-Primavesi, Claudia, *Die Familie Primavesi. Kunst und Mode der Wiener Werkstätte*, Vienna 2006

Noever, Peter et al. (eds.), *Yearning for Beauty: The Wiener Werkstätte and the Stoclet House*, exh. cat. MAK, Ostfildern-Ruit 2006

Leopold, Rudolf/Pichler, Gerd (eds.), *Koloman Moser 1868–1918*, Munich et. al 2007

Vybíral, Jindřich, *Junge Meister. Architekten aus der Schule Otto Wagners in Mähren und Schlesien*, Vienna/Cologne/Weimar 2007

Buhrs, Michael/Lesák, Barbara/Trabitsch, Thomas (eds.), *Fledermaus Kabarett. 1907 bis 1913. Ein Gesamtkunstwerk der Wiener Werkstätte. Literatur. Musik. Tanz*, Vienna 2007

Husslein-Arco, Agnes/Weidinger, Alfred (eds.), *Gustav Klimt und die Kunstschau 1908*, exh. cat. Austrian Gallery Belvedere, Vienna 2008

Asenbaum, Paul/Kos, Wolfgang/Orosz, Eva-Maria (eds.), *Glanzstücke. Emilie Flöge und der Schmuck der Wiener Werkstätte*, Stuttgart 2008

Achleitner, Friedrich, *Österreichische Architektur im 20. Jahrhundert. Wien 19.–23. Bezirk*, vol. III/3, Salzburg/Vienna 2010

Witt-Dörring, Christian (ed.), *Vienna, Art & Design: Klimt, Schiele, Hoffmann, Loos*, exh. cat. National Gallery of Victoria, Melbourne 2011

Nierhaus, Andreas/Orosz, Eva-Maria (eds.), *Werkbundsiedlung Wien 1932. Ein Manifest des Wohnens*, Vienna 2012

Thun-Hohenstein, Karin, *Josef Hoffmann – Sanatorium Purkersdorf (1904–1905)*, thesis at the University of Vienna 2012

Thun-Hohenstein, Christoph/Murr, Beate (eds.), *Gustav Klimt. Erwartung und Erfüllung. Entwürfe zum Mosaikfries im Palais Stoclet*, Ostfildern-Ruit 2012

Ploil, Ernst, *Wiener Gläser: Österreichischer Werkbund, Köln 1914*, Vienna 2014

Franz, Rainald (ed.), *The Glass of the Architects: Vienna 1900–1937*, exh. cat. MAK and Le Stanze del Vetro, Milan 2016

Kristan, Markus, *Kunstschau Wien 1908*, Weitra 2016

Husslein-Arco, Agnes/Klee, Alexander (eds.), *Kubismus – Konstruktivismus – Formkunst*, exh. cat. Austrian Gallery Belvedere, Munich 2016

Helle-Thomas, Lil, *Stimmung in der Architektur der Wiener Moderne: Josef Hoffmann und Adolf Loos*, Vienna 2017

Kristan, Markus, *L'Autriche à Paris 1925 – Österreich auf der Kunstgewerbeausstellung 1925*, Weitra 2018

Krautgartner, Lena, *Die Inszenierung der neuen Frau. Der Modesalon "Schwestern Flöge" als architektonische und modische Darstellung von Weiblichkeit zur Jahrhundertwende in Wien*, thesis at the TU Wien, Vienna 2019

Steinhäußer, Lara, *Die Wiener Werkstätte und Paul Poiret: Kooperationen, Einflüsse und Differenzen der Wiener und Pariser Mode in ihrer medialen Präsentation zwischen 1903 und 1932*, MA thesis at the University of Vienna 2019

Thun-Hohenstein, Christoph/Rossberg, Anne-Katrin/Schmuttermeier, Elisabeth (eds.), *Women Artists of the Wiener Werkstätte*, Basel 2020. Trans. Maria Slater and Christina Anderson

JH, design for a fireplace with fauteuil and floor lamp, ca. 1934
UAA, Collection and Archive, 108

Index of Names

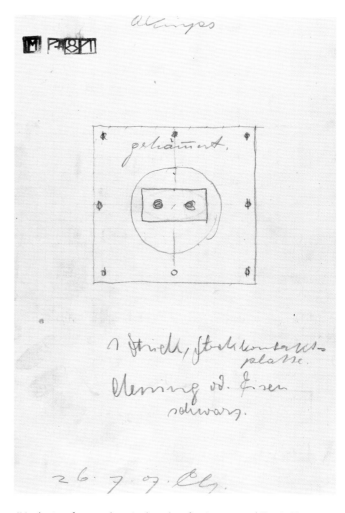

JH, design for an electrical socket for Anton and Sonja Knips's apartment, executed by the Wiener Werkstätte, 1907
MAK, KI 12170-5

Authors

Matthias Boeckl studied art history at the University of Vienna (awarded his doctorate in 1988), qualifying as a professor at the University of Innsbruck in 1999. He is professor of architectural history at the University of Applied Arts Vienna and editor in chief of the Vienna-based international and bilingual journal *architektur.aktuell.* As an author and editor he has published numerous articles and books and curated a series of exhibitions about topics of modern and contemporary art and architecture.

Elisabeth Boeckl-Klamper studied history and German philology at the University of Vienna. Since 1981 she has been an archivist and research assistant at the Documentation Centre of Austrian Resistance (DÖW). Curator and research assistant for numerous exhibitions by the City of Vienna, and at the Jewish Museum Vienna (1991–1995); also worked as a consultant at the Museum of Jewish Heritage in New York. She is the author of numerous publications on recent history, especially on the topics of "resistance and persecution in Austria 1938–1945," "Austrians in exile," and "art and culture in the Nazi regime." Most recently *Gestapo-Leitstelle Wien 1938–1945* (with Thomas Mang and Wolfgang Neugebauer).

Rainald Franz is curator of the Glass and Ceramics Collection at the MAK – Museum of Applied Arts, Vienna, and curator of the Josef Hoffmann Museum, Brtnice (CZ). He has curated numerous exhibitions and organized several symposiums, e.g., *Adolf Loos: Our Contemporary*; *THE GLASS OF THE ARCHITECTS: Vienna 1900–1937*; *300 YEARS OF THE VIENNA PORCELAIN MANUFACTORY*; and most recently *OTTO PRUTSCHER: Universal Designer of Viennese Modernism*. He is the author of a large number of publications and essays, e.g., about Gottfried Semper and Vienna around 1900. In addition to his work at the museum, he is a lecturer at the Institute of Conservation and Restoration at the University of Applied Arts Vienna.

Anette Freytag is a tenured professor of the history and theory of landscape architecture at Rutgers University in New Jersey, USA. She also researches contemporary methods of design and depiction. Her historical study and expert assessment for the protection of the garden of Stoclet House in Brussels (2005) led to the ensemble being made a UNESCO World Heritage Site. Her research and books have won several awards, including the ETH Zurich medal for excellence in scientific research, the German and European Garden Book Awards, as well as the DAM Architectural Book Award.

Sebastian Hackenschmidt is curator of the Furniture and Woodwork Collection at the MAK, where he has curated numerous exhibitions since 2005 on subjects of architecture, furniture, art, and design. He is coeditor of the *Lexikon des künstlerischen Materials* (2002/2010) and the volume *Möbel als Medien* (2011). His book *Knochen. Ein Material der zeitgenössischen Kunst* was published in 2014.

Otto Kapfinger lives in Vienna as a freelance architecture expert, author, and curator. While studying at the TU Wien (1967–1972), he founded the group "Missing Link" in 1970 together with Angela Hareiter and Adolf Krischanitz. In 1979 he was cofounder of the theoretical journal *UmBau*; between 1981 and 1990 he was an architecture critic for the daily newspaper *Die Presse*. He has curated and designed numerous exhibitions on 20th-century and contemporary architecture and published books on the subject—most recently *Architektur im Sprachraum. Essays, Reden, Kritiken zum Planen und Bauen in Österreich* (Zurich 2014) and *Fundamente der Demokratie. Architektur in Österreich – neu gesehen* (together with Adolph Stiller; Salzburg/Vienna 2018). In 2019 he was awarded an honorary doctorate by the TU Wien.

Markus Kristan started his professional career at the Federal Monuments Authority after graduating in history, art history, and archaeology from the University of Vienna. Since 1993 he has worked as curator of the architecture collection at the Albertina, where he has also been responsible for the Adolf Loos Archives. He has written numerous articles and books on 19th and 20th-century Austrian architecture, e.g., on Hubert Gessner, Carl König, Oskar Laske, Adolf Loos, Joseph Urban, the artists' colony on the Hohe Warte, the Vienna Kunstschau of 1908, and the *International Exposition of Modern Decorative and Industrial Arts* in Paris in 1925.

Christopher Long is Martin S. Kermacy Centennial Professor of Architectural and Design History at the University of Texas at Austin. His recent books include *The New Space: Movement and Experience in Viennese Modern Architecture* (New Haven/London 2016); *Adolf Loos on Trial* (Prague 2017); *The Rise of Everyday Design: The Arts and Crafts Movement in Britain and America* (coedited with Monica Penick, exh. cat., New Haven/London 2019); *Essays on Adolf Loos* (Prague 2019); and, most recently, *Adolf Loos: The Late Houses* (Prague 2020).

Klára Němečková studied art history and modern German literature at the Freie Universität and at the Humboldt-Universität zu Berlin. From 2008 to 2011 she worked as a research assistant at the Royal Porcelain Manufactory Berlin. Thereafter she was a doctorate scholar in the "art and technology" DFG research training group at the Universität Hamburg-Harburg. Her research focuses on late 19th and 20th-century design, Modernist porcelain, the Deutsche Werkstätten Hellerau, and the history of collections at arts-and-crafts museums. Since 2015 she has been a research assistant at the Kunstgewerbemuseum of the Staatliche Kunstsammlungen Dresden, where she curated e.g., the exhibition *Against Invisibility—Women Designers at the Deutsche Werkstätten Hellerau 1898 to 1938* (2018) and edited the accompanying exhibition catalog together with Tulga Beyerle.

Andreas Nierhaus worked as a research assistant at the Austrian Academy of Sciences after graduating in history and art history from the University of Vienna. Since 2008 he has been curator of architecture at the Wien Museum. In 2019 he was deputy professor of art history at the Goethe University Frankfurt. His research focuses on architecture and fine art in the 19th and 20th centuries, Historicism and Modernism, the media used in architecture, architectural drawings, and Otto Wagner and his school. In numerous exhibitions and publications he has explored e.g., the Viennese Werkbundsiedlung (Werkbund Estate), Vienna's Ringstraße, as well as Otto Wagner and Richard Neutra.

Jan Norrman is a Swedish design historian based in Vienna with the 20th century as his main field of interest. He was formerly a curator at Röhsska museet in Göteborg and most recently worked as a curator at the Nationalmuseum in Stockholm. In these roles he has published on plastic design, furniture, and ceramics. He has recently written articles for the catalog *JOSEF FRANK: Against Design* (Basel 2015) to accompany the exhibition at the MAK.

Eva-Maria Orosz studied art history, history, and archaeology in Vienna. From 2000 to 2002 she compiled the catalogue raisonné of the architect Ernst A. Plischke (1903–1992) in the context of a project by the FWF (Der Wissenschaftsfonds). Since 2004 she has been curator of applied art and furniture at the Wien Museum. She has curated numerous exhibitions, including *Ernst A. Plischke* (2003), *Glanzstücke. Emilie Flöge und der Schmuck der Wiener Werkstätte* (2008), *Werkbundsiedlung Vienna 1932* (2012), and *Otto Wagner* (2018). In her research and publications, Eva-Maria Orosz focuses primarily on "period rooms," domestic culture and the history of furniture in the 19th and 20th centuries, the history of art and culture in Vienna, and the history of museums and collections.

List of Abbreviations

Adrián Prieto is an architectural historian and writer based in Vienna. He is currently completing a PhD in architectural history at Complutense University of Madrid that is focused on Robert Mallet-Stevens's work and the Viennese context. Additionally, he was also a visiting researcher at University of Applied Arts Vienna and the Centre d'histoire of the Sciences Po, Paris. His research explores the cross-cultural relationships within modern architecture and design, particularly between the Francophone and Austrian context.

Ursula Prokop has worked as a freelance art historian and writer since studying history and art history at the University of Vienna. Her research focuses on the late 19th and early 20th-century history of architecture and culture in Austria. She has published numerous specialist articles and books, including *Margaret Wittgenstein-Stonborough* (2003) and *Zum jüdischen Erbe in der Wiener Architektur* (2016). She also contributes her expertise to diverse exhibitions and research projects, is a long-term project assistant on the Encyclopaedia of Architects by the Architekturzentrum Wien, as well as a freelancer for the *Österreichische Biographische Lexikon/ÖBL* by the Austrian Academy of Sciences and the Jewish culture magazine *David*.

Lara Steinhäußer has been curator of the MAK Textiles and Carpets Collection since 2019 and has worked at the museum since 2011. She completed her art history degree at the University of Vienna with a master's thesis on the Wiener Werkstätte and Paul Poiret. In addition to her research focus on early 20th-century Austrian textile art and fashion and their international networks, she is currently investigating contemporary approaches at the intersection of art and fashion, as well as the historical development of textile consumption up to the advent of slow fashion.

Valerio Terraroli was professor of contemporary art history and history of the decorative arts at the University of Turin between 2001 and 2012. He has taught the history of art criticism, museology, and the history of the decorative arts at the University of Verona. Since 2015 he has also led the Research Centre "Rossana Bossaglia" for the decorative arts, graphics, and arts of the 18th to 20th centuries. His focus is the evolution of style and taste between Symbolism and the 20th century, particularly the artistic phenomena known in Italy as "Liberty e Déco." His main interest is the decorative arts and the connections between architecture and decoration in the same historical period.

Wolfgang Thillmann is a collector, author, exhibition curator, and consultant for various museums. The focus of his work is furniture made of bentwood and plywood; his numerous books and articles on these topics are the result of many years of intensive research. His most recent publication is the catalog to accompany the exhibition *BENTWOOD AND BEYOND: Thonet and Modern Furniture Design* at the MAK (edited with Sebastian Hackenschmidt; Basel 2019). He is currently working on a biography of Thonet.

Christian Witt-Dörring studied art history and archaeology in Vienna. He was head of the Furniture Collection at the MAK – Austrian Museum of Applied Arts in Vienna from 1979 to 2004 and from 1999 to 2018 curator at the Neue Galerie New York. Wide-ranging exhibition, curatorial, and teaching work on subjects of art and cultural history in the field of the decorative arts, especially the history of furniture and interiors.

AdR	Archiv der Republik
ALA	Adolf Loos Archiv, Albertina Vienna
AMAI	Austrian Museum of Art and Industry (today's MAK)
ANL	Austrian National Library
ASA	Austrian State Archives
BuWK	*Bau- und Werkkunst*
DI	*Das Interieur*
DK	*Dekorative Kunst*, Munich
DKuD	*Deutsche Kunst und Dekoration*, Darmstadt
HStADD	Hauptstaatsarchiv Dresden
HW	*Hohe Warte*, Vienna
ID	*Innendekoration*, Darmstadt
JH	Josef Hoffmann
MAK	Museum of Applied Arts
MBF	*Moderne Bauformen*
MPAV	Municipal and Provincial Archives of Vienna
ÖNB	Austrian National Library, Vienna
ÖWB	Austrian Werkbund
UAA	University of Applied Arts Vienna
VS	*Ver Sacrum*, Vienna
WW	Wiener Werkstätte

JH, *Gedicht* [Poem], 1950
Pencil and ink on paper
MAK, KI 23525-069

This catalog has been published on the occasion of the exhibition
JOSEF HOFFMANN: Progress Through Beauty
MAK, Vienna
15 December 2021 – 19 June 2022

Exhibition

Guest Curators
Christian Witt-Dörring, Matthias Boeckl

MAK Curator
Rainald Franz, Curator, MAK Glass
and Ceramics Collection

Assistance
Michael Macek, MAK Glass and Ceramics
Collection

Exhibition Design
Eichinger Offices

Graphic Design
Maria Anna Friedl

Exhibition Management
Alena Volk

Catalog

Editors
Christoph Thun-Hohenstein, Matthias Boeckl,
Rainald Franz, Christian Witt-Dörring

Catalog Editing
Matthias Boeckl, Rainald Franz,
Christian Witt-Dörring

Publication Management
Astrid Böhacker

Copy Editing
Maria Slater, Cornelia Malli

Translations GER > ENG
Unless stated otherwise, all Maria Slater.
Lisa Rosenblatt pp. 93, 109, 179, 215, 263,
327, 341, 365, 431, 439

Graphic Design
Maria Anna Friedl

Reproductions
Pixelstorm, Vienna

Type
Avenir

Paper
Luxoart Samt 150 g

Printing and Binding
Holzhausen, die Buchmarke der Gerin Druck
GmbH, Wolkersdorf

Printed in line with regulation UZ24 of the Austrian Ecolabel
by Gerin Druck GmbH, license number UW 756.

Published by
Birkhäuser Verlag GmbH
P.O. Box 44, 4009 Basel, Switzerland
Part of Walter de Gruyter GmbH,
Berlin/Boston

Acquisitions Editor
David Marold, Birkhäuser Verlag, Vienna

Content & Production Editor
Bettina R. Algieri, Birkhäuser Verlag, Vienna

9 8 7 6 5 4 3 2 1 www.birkhauser.com

ISBN: 978-3-0356-2296-6

Library of Congress Control Number:
2020946673

Bibliographic information published
by the German National Library:
The German National Library lists this publication in the Deutsche Nationalbibliografie;
detailed bibliographic data are available on
the Internet at http://dnb.dnb.de.

Picture credits

Picture credits can be found next to each
illustration. Unless stated otherwise, the location
or lender of the object is simultaneously the
copyright owner.

The editors and the MAK have endeavored
to establish and identify all right holders.
In the event that any legitimate claims have
nevertheless been omitted, the MAK requests
to be notified and provided with the necessary
evidence in order to settle these claims as
per customary fee agreements.

Front cover
JH, table for the living room in
Dr. Hermann and Lyda Wittgenstein's
apartment, executed by the Wiener
Werkstätte, 1905
MAK, H 2082
© Wolfgang Woessner/MAK

Back cover
Yoichi R. Okamoto, Josef Hoffmann at
the desk in his apartment, ca. 1955
MAK, KI 13740-13

Fig. p. 2
Primavesi country house, perspectival,
colorized design drawing for a bedroom,
drawn by Karl Bräuer after a design by
Josef Hoffmann
DI (XV) 1914/15, plate 65

Endpaper (front)
JH, design for a decorative fabric for
Backhausen & Söhne (design no. 6030), 1906
Backhausen Archive, BA03920

JH, carpet for the dining room of Dr. Edmund
Bernatzik's villa, executed by the Lois Resch
carpet factory, Vienna 1930
Cotton, linen, wool
MAK, T 11644
© MAK/Katrin Wißkirchen

Endpaper (back)
Invitation by the Neue Sammlung to a
slideshow about Josef Hoffmann by Hans
Ankwicz-Kleehoven at the Bayerisches
Nationalmuseum, Munich, 1930
MAK, KI WWGG 479

JH, design for a tea set, ca. 1950
Augarten Porcelain Manufactory
© MAK/Georg Mayer

MAK
Stubenring 5, 1010 Vienna, Austria
T +43 1 711 36-0, F +43 1 713 10 26
office@MAK.at, MAK.at

MAK Center for Art and Architecture
Los Angeles at the Schindler House
835 North Kings Road, West Hollywood,
CA 90069, USA

Mackey Apartments
MAK Artists and Architects-in-Residence
Program, 1137 South Cochran Avenue, Los
Angeles, CA 90019, USA

Fitzpatrick-Leland House
Laurel Canyon Boulevard/Mulholland Drive,
Los Angeles, CA 90046, USA

T +1 323 651 1510, F +1 323 651 2340
office@MAKcenter.org, MAKcenter.org

Josef Hoffmann Museum, Brtnice
A joint branch of the Moravian Gallery in Brno
and the MAK, Vienna
náměstí Svobody 263, 588 32 Brtnice,
Czech Republic
T +43 1 711 36-220
josefhoffmannmuseum@MAK.at, MAK.at

Cooperation partner

dɪ:'ʌngewʌndtə

Universität für angewandte Kunst Wien
University of Applied Arts Vienna

For their generous support we would like to thank

Richard Grubman† and Caroline Mortimer

With cordial thanks to

Heinz Adamek
Paul Asenbaum
Stefan Asenbaum
Wolfgang Bauer
Kerstin Bauhofer
Elisabeth Boeckl-Klamper
René Edenhofer
Markus Fellinger
Irene Fuchs
Ursula Graf
Almut Grunewald
Matthias Haldemann
Silvia Herkt
Roger Howie

Michael Huey
Elke Königseder
Robert Kotasek
Patrick Kovacs
Markus Kristan
Beatrix Kroll
Ludwig Kyral
Michaela Laichmann
Araya Laimanee
Markus Langer
Claudia Lehner Jobst
Bernd Nicolai
Josef Offner
Eva Maria Orosz

Ernst Ploil
Andreas Rath
Peter Rath
Franz Rendl
Brigitte Riegele
Elisabeth Schmuttermeier
René Schober
Philip Schönthal
Katrin Schwarz
Johannes Semotan
Janis Staggs
Manfred Trummer
Angelika Tunhardt
Herbert Vopava

Roland Widder
Georg Wieser
Christopher Wilk
Blanda Winter
Gertrude Wojtczak
Anja Wolf
Katharina Zetter-Karner
Ulrike Zimmerl

and all contributing colleagues
at the MAK

as well as the following companies and collections

ALB Antiquités Gallery, Paris
Albertina, Vienna
Augarten Porcelain Manufactory
Backhausen GmbH
Canadian Centre for Architecture
Galerie bei der Albertina · Zetter
Galerie bel etage, Vienna
Galerie Yves Macaux, Brussels
Georg Kargl Fine Arts
Graphic Collection, Academy of Fine Arts Vienna
Hessisches Landesmuseum, Kassel
Hofmobiliendepot Möbelmuseum Wien
J. & L. Lobmeyr GmbH
Kunsthandel Widder, Vienna

Kunsthaus Zug
MA 37 of the City of Vienna
Moravská galerie v Brně
mumok – museum moderner kunst stiftung ludwig wien
National Gallery Prague
Österreichische Werkstätten
Picture Archives, Austrian National Library
Technisches Museum Wien
University of Applied Arts Vienna, Collection and Archive
Wien Museum
Zentralvereinigung der ArchitektInnen Österreichs

and all other lenders

DIE NEUE SAMMLUNG läd

über PROFESSOR JOSE

Herrn Dr. v. Ankwicz-Kleeh

Woche am Montag 10. NO

Berechtigt zum freien E

BAYER. NATIONALMUSE

ein zum Lichtbild-Vortrag

HOFFMANN-WIEN von

ven im Rahmen der österr.

EMBER ABENDS 8 UHR

tritt für zwei Personen

PRINZREGENTENSTR. 3

123